The Films of Alan Parker,
1976–2003

The Films of Alan Parker, 1976–2003

DAVID F. GONTHIER, JR., and
TIMOTHY M. O'BRIEN

McFarland & Company, Inc., Publishers
Jefferson, North Carolina

LIBRARY OF CONGRESS CATALOGUING-IN-PUBLICATION DATA

Gonthier, David, author.
The Films of Alan Parker, 1976–2003 / David F. Gonthier, Jr., and Timothy M. O'Brien.
    p.   cm.
Includes bibliographical references and index.

ISBN 978-0-7864-9725-6 (softcover : acid free paper) ∞
ISBN 978-1-4766-1927-9 (ebook)

1. Parker, Alan, 1944– —Criticism and interpretation. 2. Motion picture producers and directors—Great Britain. I. O'Brien, Timothy M., 1982– author. II. Title.

PN1998.3.P3587G66 2015   791.4302′33092241—dc23   2015023894

BRITISH LIBRARY CATALOGUING DATA ARE AVAILABLE

© 2015 David F. Gonthier, Jr., and Timothy M. O'Brien. All rights reserved

No part of this book may be reproduced or transmitted in any form or by any means, electronic or mechanical, including photocopying or recording, or by any information storage and retrieval system, without permission in writing from the publisher.

On the cover: Bob Geldof in the 1982 film
Pink Floyd—The Wall (MGM/Photofest)

Printed in the United States of America

*McFarland & Company, Inc., Publishers
Box 611, Jefferson, North Carolina 28640
www.mcfarlandpub.com*

To my son, Isaac, my best buddy and
fellow viewing companion…
—David F. Gonthier, Jr.

To my late grandmother, Lillian Pelletier.
And also to my mother,
whose light will always lead me home.
—Timothy M. O'Brien

Acknowledgments

Co-writing this book on the films of Alan Parker has been a completely pleasurable and rewarding experience. I want to first thank my co-author, former student and good friend Timothy O'Brien, who has proven that you *can* indeed make a long-distance professional relationship work. For a majority of this project, Tim and I corresponded back and forth via emails, text messages and phone calls from New Hampshire to New York City. When I began thinking about this project in the summer of 2009, I asked Tim if he wanted to co-write this manuscript with me and from that moment forward we juggled our busy lives and made it happen. This has by far been the best collaboration I've ever had; it was fun and seamless and we were completely compatible along the way. I am also very grateful for the generous participation of Sir Alan Parker, the subject of this book, who provided us with a plethora of information that has helped us write this first book on his films. It's been an honor to have gotten to know him over the years while studying his very impressive and ambitious canon of films. I also thank my wife, Caron, for all of her dedication, advice, help and support. Finally, I would like to thank my parents who first exposed me to a film called *Midnight Express*, which to this day remains one of my all-time favorites.

—David Gonthier

Firstly, I'd like to thank my co-author David Gonthier. I am honored and grateful that you came to me with this project (now I get to brag to my snotty academic friends that I'm getting a book published!). It was an absolute pleasure writing with you, and I look forward to doing it again in the future.

Many thanks to Pamela Bloom, and to all the librarians and archivists at the Elmer Holmes Bobst Library. Your help transformed what could have been a chaotic nightmare into a navigable research process. Thank you.

Thanks also to the extremely helpful staff at Jerry Ohlinger's Movie Materials in New York City. Because of your colossally expansive collection of stills and movie photos, you were literally the one-stop-shop for all the photographs in this book.

Appreciation is also due to the two amazing women I dedicated this book to. Without them, this book would not have been possible:

Firstly, my grandmother, Lillian Pelletier, who recently passed away, God rest her soul. Thanks, Grandma, for always doing the crossword puzzles and word searches with me when I was a kid. When most boys were out subjecting themselves to possible concussions, and contusions uncounted, you helped me realize that my fascination with letters and words was not only acceptable, but something to aspire to. It meant the world to me, and every time I struggle to write a word, sentence, or thought, I will ask myself: "What would Grandma think of this?" Love you, Grandma, wherever you are.

But no one can have a grandmother without a mother, and I also devote this book to my mother. There's an old saying: "A Mother knows." I wholeheartedly endorse this truism because my mom always knows: she knows when to coddle me, when to kick my ass, and when to remain silent because she knows I can figure it out for myself. You'll always be my candle on the water, Mom.

—Timothy M. O'Brien

Table of Contents

Acknowledgments	vii
Introduction by David Gonthier, Jr.	1
1. The Early Life and Career of Alan Parker	11
2. *Bugsy Malone*, 1976	22
3. *Midnight Express*, 1978	40
4. *Fame*, 1980	63
5. *Shoot the Moon*, 1982	83
6. *Pink Floyd—The Wall*, 1982	103
7. *Birdy*, 1984	120
8. *Angel Heart*, 1987	138
9. *Mississippi Burning*, 1988	162
10. *Come See the Paradise*, 1990	183
11. *The Commitments*, 1991	199
12. *The Road to Wellville*, 1994	215
13. *Evita*, 1996	233
14. *Angela's Ashes*, 1999	252
15. *The Life of David Gale*, 2003	269
Conclusion	290
Chapter Notes	295
Bibliography	301
Index	303

Introduction
by David F. Gonthier, Jr.

A Personal Journey Discovering the Films of Alan Parker

My earliest introduction to filmmaker Sir Alan Parker must have been sometime in the late months of 1978 when I was six years old: I remember my parents returning home from a night at the movies and they were raving about the film they had just seen—something called *Midnight Express.* I remember only two significant things about this day: First, the title, which for some reason resonated with me for years before I actually saw the film; and second, the emotional response my parents exuded when they were discussing how effective the film was. I recall my father saying something along these lines: *Now that was a movie!* I suspect that this is exactly the type of cathartic response the director was expecting. According to Parker: "I think my films often operate on an emotional or visceral level ... in *Midnight Express* I tended to grab the audience by the lapels, drag them through the movie, and chuck them out of the cinema at the end, drained and exhausted."[1]

The above quotation speaks to what I have come to surmise about the films of Alan Parker and his vision as an artist: He is a storyteller who demands that his audiences *feel* the impact of his work—not just to shock them, but to heighten their awareness of particular human conditions and ideologies like American Billy Hayes's battle with the injustice of a corrupt Turkish penal system in *Midnight Express*, the violence and racism in *Mississippi Burning* (1988) and the dehumanization of a musician battling with his internal demons in *Pink Floyd—The Wall* (1982). Parker despises intellectual approaches toward the making of (and the reading of) his films even though his films may have intellectual components to them; to him, films serve as expressions of (not necessarily documentations of) the lives we live. When *Midnight Express* was criticized for not adhering more closely to Billy Hayes's and William Hoffer's book of Hayes's experiences in Istanbul, Turkey, Parker retorted by saying that the film was *based* on a true story, which didn't mean that all the information was factual.[2] Similarly, *Mississippi Burning*, also based on a true story, elicited political controversy when Martin Luther King's widow, Coretta, claimed that "the black civil rights struggle had somehow been usurped by a bunch of white guys," and journalists had problems with the historical accuracy of the case. In response to these criticisms, Parker said, "Movies are an artistic expression, which communicate viscerally. Great cinema is as much about ideas and possibilities as it is about facts." But despite what critics, journalists and activists may have stated, a film like *Mississippi Burning* did its job—it evoked a response and affected people on many levels. Parker further stated: "Everyone was talking about the odious effects of racism in America and my film was the punch[ing] bag for people to get on the air and express their views furthering their own agendas."[3] According to Jonathan Hacker and David Price, who dedicate a chapter on Parker in their book *Take Ten: Contemporary British Film Directors*, "[Parker's] great talent has been the ability to make films which appeal to a mass audience, are emotionally compelling, and employ evocative visual imagery."[4]

In the 1980s, when I was an adolescent discovering my penchant for the cinema, I finally watched *Midnight Express*, which soon became one of my favorite films. By 1988 I was an Alan Parker aficionado and I credit this to the two films I watched repeatedly after *Midnight Express*: *Mississippi Burning* (starring Gene Hackman, one of my favorite actors), and *Pink Floyd—The Wall*, a film I watched because of my interests in Parker, not Pink Floyd (I would later become a Pink Floyd fan *because* of the film). Thus, this film triad—*Midnight Express*, *Pink Floyd—The Wall* and *Mississippi Burning*—became the foundation, I suppose, to what would eventually evolve into a lifelong relationship with a director and his canon. As an adolescent I am not sure I was completely tuned in to the significant impact surrounding the ideologies of all of these films; instead, it was a cathartic response to the visual execution of Parker's formalism that initially drew me into his idiosyncratic microcosms.

In my final year of high school, I watched the remainder of Parker's films in chronological order, beginning with *Bugsy Malone* (1976), the director's first feature film, an homage to 1930s Hollywood gangster pictures and musicals with an all-child cast. Because of my growing knowledge in film studies, I actually *got* many of the classic movie references throughout the film. In the same week, I watched *Fame* (1980), which appealed to my budding interests in drama and music. To this day I have an affinity for a number of Parker's films like *Fame*, *Pink Floyd—The Wall* and *The Commitments* (1991) because each film chronicles not just the lives of artists but also the creative process of making art. These films are additionally successful because they explore art-making in a more accessible and less esoteric fashion than some European masterworks of the previous decade, like *Contempt* (1962, Jean-Luc Godard), *8 ½* (1963, Federico Fellini), *Blow-up* (1966, Michelangelo Antonioni) and *Partner* (1968, Bernardo Bertolucci)—all great films in their own right, but each of these films, admittedly, appeal to a more selective, avant-garde audience. According to Parker:

> For me a film doesn't exist in a can or as a column in a newspaper. It lives only when an audience reacts to it. And to have as wide an audience as possible, from many different backgrounds and sensibilities, go through this experience is the very reason I make films. I feel the filmmaker has a responsibility to find a large audience, and certainly this is true in America. Maybe this means you have to change the way you make a film, but personally I don't think there's anything wrong with this, because I think that what you do is so hard and you spend so long on it that if you don't find an audience it's kind of irrelevant. Besides, there are many directors like Woody Allen and Martin Scorsese who work under that commercial umbrella and who do very individual and very good work.[5]

The next group of films I watched included *Shoot the Moon* (1982), *Birdy* (1984) and *Angel Heart* (1987). This new film triad would affect me in a number of ways. *Shoot the Moon* captured the effects of divorce on children during a time when my own parents were separated. Plus, it was intriguing to watch "Scrooge" (Albert Finney) and "Annie Hall" (Diane Keaton) as a couple on the rocks. Parker called this film his most personal one to date: "Up to now I had only made films about other people's lives—other people's predicaments and pain—a world away from my own and suddenly I was going to work every day to shoot a fiction that I was also living through."[6] *Birdy* was another "prison" story that, like *Midnight Express* and *Pink Floyd—The Wall*, created a stifling world of confinement. I was so drawn toward these films of imprisonment that eventually, many years later, I would write and publish a book about Hollywood prison films. Finally, *Angel Heart*—a film that took me time to process (due to its complex storyline)—included a number of horrific moments that have stayed with me over the years, namely the controversial, erotic sex scene between Harry Angel (Mickey Rourke) and Epiphany (Lisa Bonet) that climaxed in a surreal bloodbath montage, and the eerie final scene of the film when Angel is trapped hopelessly in an elevator descending into hell. It wouldn't be until years later that I would admire *Angel Heart* for the truly ambitious film it is: the merging of the Faustian tale within a film noir milieu makes this movie, along with *Bugsy Malone*, one of the most unique revisionist variations on a genre to ever hit the screen.

Admittedly, by 1990 when *Come See the Paradise* was released, I had moved on to other things, namely a college career studying theatre and I wouldn't see the film until nearly twenty years later. I may have lost touch with Parker's career in the 1990s but the impact of his films I had *already* seen never left me. I revisited Alan Parker during my junior year of college when I was elected to be a teaching assistant for a screenwriting course, and in my debut as a "college instructor," I presented my first lesson to the class: an analysis of the opening of *Midnight Express*. I instructed the class to watch the first ten minutes of the film up to the moment when Billy Hayes was arrested. We viewed the clip a few times then discussed how Oliver Stone's words were brought to life by Parker's directorial vision. In short, *Midnight Express* was responsible for two major events in my life: my general appreciation and understanding of film from a young age; and my eventual career teaching college film courses.

As the years passed, I finished my undergraduate degree and within the course of the next ten years—after two master's degrees and over a decade of teaching cinema—I embarked upon my second phase of Alan Parker's films, movies I had not seen until fairly recently: *Come See the Paradise* (1990), the lavish melodrama about Japanese/American life in the World War II era; *The Commitments* (1991), the charming story of an "almost famous" Irish soul band; *The Road to Wellville* (1994), the outrageous, stylized filmization of T. Coraghessen Boyle's 1993 literary novel about the eccentric early twentieth-century health enthusiast Dr. John Kellogg; *Evita* (1996), the exquisitely filmed version of the Andrew Lloyd Webber–Tim Rice opera about the life and death of María Eva Duarte de Perón, the charismatic first lady of Argentina from 1946 to 1952 (a film Leonard Maltin calls "the world's longest rock video"[7]); *Angela's Ashes*, the adaptation of Frank McCourt's internationally acclaimed Pulitzer Prize–winning memoir about the author's early life in Brooklyn and Ireland; and the thriller *The Life of David Gale* (2003), about an anti-death penalty activist on death row in Texas who tells his story to a young reporter. Watching this second round of films assured me that this project was meant to be. It would also be (surprisingly at that) the first complete book on the films of Alan Parker.

Introduction

Reconsidering the Auteur Theory

Auteur is a French word like montage, *mise-en-scène*, *cliché* and *caca*.[8]—Alan Parker

I and coauthor Tim O'Brien intend this book to be an unbiased look into Parker's films—studying his career as individual pieces of art without trying to formulate a thesis that labels his films as *this* or *that*. According to Italian filmmaker Federico Fellini, "I am not a man who approves of definitions. Labels belong on luggage as far as I am concerned; they don't mean anything in art."[9] Along these lines, I wish to veer away from the overused and not always relevant Auteur Theory used by French New Wave film critics-turned-directors like François Truffaut (*The 400 Blows*, 1959), Jean-Luc Godard (*Breathless*, 1959) and Éric Rohmer (*Claire's Knee*, 1970). This theory (which ironically is not a film theory at all, not like Eisenstein's Theory of Montage or Siegfried Kracauer's Realist Film Theory—it's more of a doctrine) creates a scientific language of nomenclature, similar to the method in which genre films are labeled according to a selected group of universal codes and conventions. The main premise of this theory can be outlined thus: it identifies a director's "signature" based on the idiosyncrasies of his/her thematic and stylistic motifs which enables a viewer to "recognize" the artist's presence on celluloid in the same way that a zoologist can classify starfish and lobsters as members of the Crustacean phylum. So by knowing a director's *oeuvre* an audience member can point out his/her traits and, in doing so, a director's work becomes its own (predictable) label or genre. The overall problem I have with the Auteur Theory nowadays (beyond the fact that it looks at a director making the same movie over and over again) can be summarized in three parts.

First, the "theory" has been recycled so often since the 1960s that it won't offer a fresh approach to Alan Parker's films, especially since his films can't be studied along with the original auteurs like Hitchcock, Hawks, Wilder, Bergman and Fellini; his films come a generation later, beginning in the mid–1970s. In *Signs and Meaning in the Cinema*, Peter Wollen dedicates one of his three chapters to the Auteur theory, a term that was coined by Andrew Sarris in 1962 in an article he wrote for *Film Culture*, which introduced *la politique des auteurs*, a style of criticism that the *Cahiers du Cinéma* writers like Truffaut were using to highlight Hollywood filmmakers, namely multi-genre director Howard Hawks (the gangster film *Scarface* [1932]; the screwball comedy *Bringing Up Baby* [1938]; the film noir *The Big Sleep* [1946] and the western *Red River* [1948]). Hawks's oeuvre became labeled because of the classical age when he was working.[10] The same can be said of John Ford (who did westerns, melodramas and war films), Alfred Hitchcock (suspense and horror films) and George Stevens (who, like Hawks, worked in a number of different genres, from screwball comedies like *The Talk of the Town* [1942] to westerns like *Shane* [1953]). Thus, directors working in an evolving "genre factory system" were perhaps in some ways emulating genre characteristics themselves, but a director like Alan Parker, whose roots stem from the influences of British filmmakers like David Lean (*Great Expectations*, 1946), Carol Reed (*The Third Man*, 1949) and Ken Loach (*Poor Cow*, 1967), needs to be studied differently.

Second, although I *do* think Sarris's auteur approach is valid for its time and is, admittedly, a decent way to introduce people into a director's works, I can also see how this theory may be detrimental to *any* artist, even the ones working in the studio system. On the Auteur theory, Alan Parker once said, "I never understood the philosophy that a director should make twenty versions of the same film throughout his career. I never look at different stories and consciously think of thematic continuity. In the end it can only be subconscious."[11]

Third, the very nature of the Auteur theory gives complete control and credit to the writer/director even at the expense of the other valuable crewmembers like editors, film composers and cinematographers, all of whom, arguably, have *their* own unique styles. The assumption that a director is a "one-person show" offers a skewed perspective to the film as a whole. In the 1946 issue of *Revue du Cinéma* American director Irving Pinchel had an article titled "La Creation doit être l'ouvrage d'un seul" ("Creation Must be the Work of One Person")—and Truffaut prefaces his own collection of writings with a line from the notorious megalomaniac Orson Welles, who said, "I believe a work is good to a degree that it expresses the man who created it." Furthermore, auteurship has been associated to the

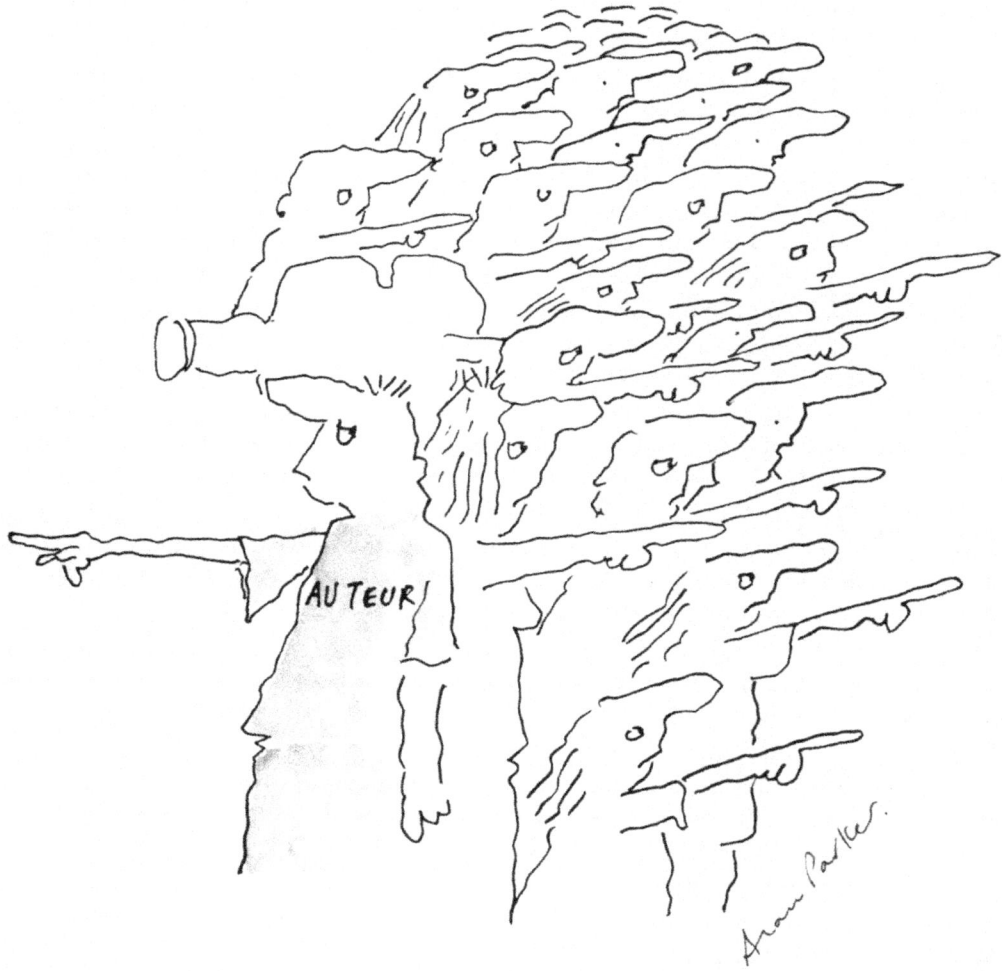

Cartoon by Alan Parker from his book, *Will Write and Direct for Food* **(London: Southbank Publishing, 2005).**

"solo" art of the painter, photographer and poet.[12] Despite the fact that Parker has admitted that "directing is a crash course in megalomania,"[13] he certainly does not take this megalomaniacal approach toward his filmmaking. In fact, his outlook is more democratic and less autonomous: "Listen to everyone. Filming is a collaborative art form. No filmmaker in history ever made a film on his or her own. Film crews are your best friends and the true heroes of the film business. Let's face it, even Leonardo needed a little help painting *The Last Supper*, but Fellini needed a hundred people to help him shoot *La Dolce Vita*."[14]

In this way, we must give credit to the other practitioners who allow the director's vision to resonate. After all, what would Alfred Hitchcock's films be like without the full-orchestrated score of Bernard Herrmann? Isn't editor Thelma Shoonmaker the major rhythmic force behind Martin Scorsese's *Taxi Driver* (1976), *Raging Bull* (1980) and *Goodfellas* (1990)? Would Ingmar Bergman's films like *Cries and Whispers* (1973) and *Fanny and Alexander* (1983) be the same without the lavish photography of cinematographer Sven Nykvist? Similarly, the films of Alan Parker have been fueled by the detail-driven cinematography of Michael Seresin and the finely tuned editing of Gerry Hambling.

Perhaps the Auteur theory and its focus on the individual can be linked to post–World War II existentialism where thinkers and writers like Jean-Paul Sartre studied the idea of "man alone in the universe," proving that an individual must use free will to come to terms with his own predestined fate of living the same life over and over again. Incidentally, when I began thinking about writing this book, I was initially drawn to the Auteur theory. The theory is so powerful that it has become an ingrained part of the cinematic language we speak. In fact, it is its own phenomenon. After all, how else *does* one approach the works of one director? On the surface, Alan Parker is a director of many musicals (*Bugsy Malone, Fame, Pink Floyd—The Wall, The Commitments, Evita*) and his films (like anyone else's) can be thematically linked, especially when one is trying hard to make such connections. Merely for the purpose of illustration, here are some examples of Parker's thematically linked films that might be considered within this auteur phenomenon: The process of making art (*Fame, The Commitments, Pink Floyd—The Wall*); ideologically conscious true stories (*Midnight Express, The Road to Wellville, Angela's Ashes, Evita*); films about the working class (*The Commitments, Evita, Angela's Ashes, Come See the Paradise*); political activism (*Mississippi Burning, Come See the Paradise, Evita, The Life of David Gale*); jail/institutionalization/imprisonment (*Midnight Express, Birdy, Pink Floyd—The Wall, The Life of David Gale*); and detective stories (*Angel Heart, Mississippi Burning, The Life of David Gale*). The so-called "neat" ways these films can be categorized show how the Auteur theory can work for *any* artist's canon; it is such a strong phenomenon that anyone looking to classify these things will more than likely be successful doing it.

It is our goal in this book to simplify the interpretation process by honoring primary sources—in this case, the words of Alan Parker. As scholars we are all obligated to interpret the meaning of a work through an "artist's statement" in the same way that it is the duty of the writer adapting a novel into a play or screenplay to remain true to the original author's vision. But, alas, scholarship itself is *already* an adaptation process and even though it *should* be the goal of the adapter to stay true to the original work, sometimes it is not possible to do so completely because we are looking at two different disciplines—in this case, a creative project versus critical analysis. In their book, *Film Adaptation*, John Desmond and Peter Hawkes write: "Take your favorite novel and imagine making it into a film....

Assume you have a fine director, talented actors, a good screenplay, cutting-edge equipment, and a production crew of thousands to make the movie. Have you succeeded in producing a *truly faithful* adaptation? Our view is that you have not and you cannot because *strict* fidelity is impossible. An adaptation is different and original because it is a work in another medium. Literature and film are apples and oranges."[15] Similarly, filmmaking and film criticism are "apples and oranges." Maybe this is the reason so many films are often misread and why there are so many clashes between artists and their critics. That said, it is my assumption that *anyone* interpreting something from an original source has an obligation to do the work justice without judging it, which is, admittedly, not an easy task in the same way that it isn't easy to adapt a novel into a film. So what interpreters have before them is quite challenging: They must find the roots of the author's voice, and then transpose that voice to adequately fit the needs of the other discipline (in this case, film criticism).

Along these lines, we are attempting to honor Alan Parker's works—and the reason I have spent so much time on the role of the Auteur theory is to get us all into a new mode of thinking, if possible, so we can understand and appreciate what it means to be an artist, not just a critic or an academic. Our goal here is to "adapt" the works of Alan Parker in a way that does justice to his creative vision (whether or not his films have been "successful" in the eyes of reviewers and/or the general public) and to discover some pertinent meaning to the films by looking at them one by one as collaborative pieces guided by Parker's personal visions as a filmmaker. As with any art, we believe that the audience has a responsibility to the artist and his/her works, meaning that in addition to experiencing the work itself, we must all be aware of the artist's reasons for producing the work in addition to any other contexts—historical and otherwise—that surround it. Then, perhaps later on, one can talk about how effectively the material was executed, but not until we have all done some work first.

The Breakdown and Genesis of This Book

This book is divided into sixteen chapters following this introduction: a chapter on Parker's early life and career in commercials and short films (including several email interviews with the director, who comments extensively on his career in commercials and the films *Melody* and *The Evacuees*); fourteen chapters studying his feature-length films—each chapter beginning with a quotation by Parker commenting on the film, a line from the film, one of the director's cartoons from his book *Will Write and Direct for Food* and one frame from the film, followed by a brief history of the production (and in some cases, a short written piece on a particular novel or topic, like the background information on *Mississippi Burning* that Parker wrote specifically for this book) and an "annotated summary" of the movie; followed by a conclusion that includes Parker's own words, based on a series of email exchanges. The annotated summary will be a chronological synopsis of the film as it unfolds scene by scene, act by act and, in some instances, details from individual moments or frames will be deconstructed with analytical commentary.

It is our intention to give the reader a deeper appreciation for a filmmaker who approaches his craft in a highly pragmatic manner, a manner that is not initially glamorous or intellectual. In short, Alan Parker is a hard worker. "A film director," Parker states, "has the sensitivity of a poet and the stamina of a construction worker ... filmmaking is rarely glamorous. Being ankle-deep in pig shit every day is the reality."[16] Additionally, Parker is a fine director because he is a decent leader, a foreman on a construction site who knows what he wants, yet he also knows how to allow others to utilize their talents and skills. In this way, the book will embrace the collaborative process of this "working-class" filmmaker. Despite the fact that Parker does not work with the same actors from film to film (a characteristic that further removes him from being an auteur like Alfred Hitchcock, who frequently worked with James Stewart, or Martin Scorsese's collaborations with Robert DeNiro and Leonardo DiCaprio), he *does* work repeatedly with producers Alan Marshall and David Puttnam, the aforementioned Gerry Hambling (editor) and Michael Seresin (cinematographer), to name a few. This book gives full credit to these individuals as well.

As stated earlier, instead of taking one specific approach to Alan Parker and his films by exploring a particular academic thesis, the book will consider each individual film as its own entity, its own unique being, and instead of relying on well-known film theories, the plan is to give a fresh look to every film by beginning the analysis with primary sources, namely Parker's words, and when applicable, secondary sources that enhance the film's universal meanings, themes and overall verisimilitude.

Like the filmmaking process, this book, too, is a collaborative effort. My co-author is Timothy O'Brien, my former film studies student at Keene State College in New Hampshire who at the time of this writing is a graduate student in the Cinema Studies program at New York University's Tisch School of the Arts. Parker once stated that no filmmaker has ever made a film alone.[17] Similarly, no effective teacher has ever taught a class without the aid and knowledge of his/her involved students. As co-authors, Timothy and I discovered how we wanted to write and structure the book and then we decided to split our duties by half: I wrote the chapter on Parker's early life and the conclusion (in which director Parker discusses what projects he been doing since 2003) as well as chapters on the films *Midnight Express*, *Shoot the Moon*, *Birdy*, *The Road to Wellville*, *Angela's Ashes* and *The Life of David Gale*; Tim wrote the chapters on *Bugsy Malone*, *Fame (1980)*, *Pink Floyd—The Wall*, *Angel Heart*, *Mississippi Burning*, *Come See the Paradise*, *The Commitments* and *Evita*.

Once the project had begun, I called the William Morris Agency in Los Angeles and a representative directed me to the Director's Guild of America, where I was put into contact with the office of Jeremy Barber. Less than two weeks later, on Thursday, October 8, 2009, Sir Alan Parker sent me an email. The subject line read: *Book*. The email read:

Dear David,
Your email has been passed along to me here in London by my agents U.J.A. I am flattered that you would want to write a book about my films, although I compliment you on your good taste. I'd be pleased to make an introduction on the phone and discuss it further....

On October 12, 2009, I called Mr. Parker at Dirty Hands Productions in London and had the pleasure of talking with him for about twenty minutes, during which we chatted about his career. Eventually I informed him that I wasn't looking for a traditional interview, asking him about the themes in his films (he seemed relieved). What I *was* looking for was a comment on each of his films that I could include with my research. Consequently he informed me of the book that he had published in Łódź, Poland (*Alan Parker*), a collection of essays on his early life and each of his feature films that he did mainly for press releases; the book also includes a number of photographs, cartoons and a personal quotation page at the end—all printed on beautiful glossy paper. To help with our research, Mr. Parker offered to mail this book to me (which he eventually plans to have published on a larger scale) as well as his book of cartoons, *Will Write and Direct for Food*. In the package he sent me, he also included a postcard featuring the "God Is Your Tongue" scene from *Angela's Ashes* and in a note, dated October 12, he wrote:

> *Dear David,*
> *Hope these are of some help to you.*
> *Best, Alan P.*

The book, *Alan Parker*, has served us in many ways, mainly as an essential primary source for this project. Our phone conversation, email exchanges, plus the gift of Mr. Parker's two books and DVD copies of his two early films *Melody* (1971) (which he wrote), and *The Evacuees* (1975) (which he directed)—has served as its own unique interview process, providing us with valuable research for this book. In addition to Parker's book, we have also referred to existing interviews in such journals as *Cineaste* and *American Film* plus material in Hacker and Price's book *Take Ten: Contemporary British Film Directors* (wherein Parker is studied along with Lindsay Anderson, Sir Richard Attenborough, Stephen Frears, Nicholas Roeg, Ken Loach and John Schlesinger).

Additionally we have used other resources, like Parker's generous DVD commentaries, passages from selected novels of which Parker based some of his films (*Midnight Express, Angel Heart, The Road to Wellville, Angela's Ashes*, etc.), in addition to other resources that have helped to contextualize the films into broader universal understandings: biographies on María Eva Duarte de Perón (*Evita*); histories of the Civil Rights Movement (*Mississippi Burning*); research on Billy Hayes (*Midnight Express*) and Dr. John Kellogg (*The Road to Wellville*); and selected writings on the Irish working class (*Angela's Ashes, The Commitments*), to list just a few examples.

1

The Early Life and Career of Alan Parker

> I grew up in a block of flats in a working class part of Islington, North London, where the German bombs had flattened many of the cinemas during the Second World War. Curiously, this devastation was quite wonderful for a small boy growing up amongst the postwar debris. The bombed buildings were our playground and although the signs very clearly said "Dangerous Building. Keep Out," we of course ignored this and after climbing a fence or two and dodging the local police, the burned out, crumbling churches, houses and factories became our own private Disneyland.[1]

The above quote gives the viewer a glimpse of how Parker's early cataclysmic life began. He was born on Valentine's Day, February 14, 1944, during the London Blitz among a war-torn working-class section of Islington, North London. This undoubtedly influenced his films about children (*Melody, The Evacuees, Bugsy Malone, Shoot the Moon, Angela's Ashes*) and the working class (*Fame, The Commitments, Angela's Ashes, Come See the Paradise*), but, more importantly, it explains how he has taken a true working-class/blue collar approach toward his career as a filmmaker. Unlike a number of his contemporary peers—Martin Scorsese, George Lucas, Francis Ford Coppola and Brian DePalma—all of whom were part of the "Film School" generation (although British, Parker has often been called an "American" filmmaker), Parker learned his craft not in a classroom but on the job, directing commercials, with *his* peers like Ridley Scott (*Alien* [1979], *Blade Runner* [1981], *Gladiator* [2000]) and Adriane Lyne (*Flashdance* [1983], *Jacob's Ladder* [1990], *Lolita* [1996]). Although filmmaking may appear to be glamorous and romanticized, Parker calls it: "rarely glamorous."[2] His pragmatism can be further defined with another quotation on the filmmaking process: "The moment you start a film you take a deep breath and leap off into the black hole of uncertainty and doubt."[3]

Parker's "working-man" philosophy helps to identify his work ethic. As part of this working-class image comes a quality that speaks to Parker's reputation as a passionate, even "angry" man, an idea that has been lifted from the "kitchen sink" realism of the Angry Young Man movement in the British films of the 1960s (In 1986, interviewer Andrew Horton from *Cineaste* referred to Parker as "Britain's Angry Young Man in Hollywood").[4] Aside from the fact that this is a somewhat esoteric connection between Parker's personality and the famed film movement, it is also an incorrect representation of Parker. He asserts: "People think I must have been [influenced by the Angry Young Man films], but it's not true. My work's much more influenced by the generation *before* them, which includes Carol Reed and David Lean. I know every shot of *The Third Man* and *Great Expectations* by heart."[5] In this way, the film-noir style of Reed's *The Third Man* (1949) and the socially conscious, class-centered nature of Lean's *Great Expectations* (1946) complements the director's frequent use of expressionistic lighting and social realism in his own films.

Perhaps Parker's so-called personal "anger" that is often addressed in interviews with him can better be translated as a *catharsis*, one that serves as a necessary catalyst for his creative process; after all, passion needs to exist to create emotional work. Parker states, "To me, arguing passionately—sometimes violently—is not such a terrible thing. That's probably why I have become so argumentative in my work. I enjoy seeing what kind of reaction I can get from someone."[6]

The remaining parts of the opening quotation speak to Parker's penchant for visual storytelling as well as his personality, that of a young troublemaker. The imagery he describes about his childhood in the aftermath of the war is literary and cinematic, replete with rich description: "This devastation was quite wonderful for a small boy growing up amongst the postwar debris. The bombed buildings were our playground and although the signs clearly said 'Dangerous Building. Keep Out,' we of course ignored this and after climbing a fence or two and dodging the local police, the burned out crumbling churches, houses and factories became our own private Disneyland." In many ways, Parker's childhood memories (like Italian director Federico Fellini) are translated into some of his films that feature the antics of young children, from *Bugsy Malone* to *Shoot the Moon* to *Angela's Ashes*. And stylistically, Parker creates in many of his films a wonderfully ironic, aesthetically pleasing world view of otherwise sordid locations, like the prison in *Midnight Express*, New York City in *Fame* (1980) and working-class Ireland in *Angela's Ashes* and *The Commitments*.

In his childhood, young Alan Parker and his friends would frequently attend a movie theater called the Blue Hall that had been bombed during the war. They would all sit in the seats and imagine they were watching movies, despite the fact that the back of the building and movie screen were no longer there. After the war, the cinema was renovated and the Blue Hall showed what Parker called "second run" movies—"those films that were not up to date, frequently awful, always terribly scratched and sometimes quite wonderful."[7] One of Parker's great passions was the "Saturday Morning Pictures" at the local odeon, designed just for children, showing old black-and-white westerns and short films. "It was absolute bedlam," Parker writes, "the noisiest audience you could imagine, with fighting everywhere. Kids piled up on top of one another with attendants rugby tackling the kids as they ran up and down the aisles."[8]

Although Parker's parents (mother Leslie and father William) weren't traditional fans of the cinema, his father was an amateur photographer whose hobby was photographic printing. William would spend many hours making images from available scraps and once he even made an enlarging machine with bits and pieces ranging from wood, bolts, lenses and a "Fox's Glacier Mint" tin can. The five-foot machine remained in the bathroom, which became its own darkroom, and Parker remembers his father sitting at the kitchen table coloring the black-and-white imagery by hand, with colored inks. There is a great story Parker tells concerning the time he was in the bathroom/darkroom brushing his teeth: he noticed two "R Whites" lemonade bottles under the sink and the young boy, excited to discover this treat in the severely rationed postwar England, drank the contents, not realizing that the "lemonade" was, in fact, his father's photographic developer chemicals! Parker, who obviously survived the poisoning, later stated, "It had been pointed out that this inadvertent chemical infusion into my blood stream might have given some cause to my future profession."[9]

When discussing his early career, Parker says this: "I never intended to direct,"[10] but when looking at his early life it may be argued that fate dictated otherwise. In addition to attending Saturday Morning Pictures, pretending to watch the films in dilapidated wartorn movie theaters and observing his father's creative outlets, he speaks of an early memory that may further add to the fate of this budding filmmaker: "My first taste of 'directing' was at my junior high school. I was aged about ten. We had been to see Jack Palance in *Sign of the Pagan* at the local odeon cinema and at playtime I divided up the whole school into Romans and Huns as the Pagans charged the outside toilets defended by the Romans. It was quite a spectacle and was repeated each playtime, until the resultant bruises and bloody knees got out of hand and I was hauled off to the headmaster as the ringleader."[11]

Before directing what would become Alan Parker's first feature film—*Bugsy Malone* (1976), which, according to the director, was "a totally pragmatic exercise to break into film"[12]—the director's apprenticeship into mainstream moviemaking can be broken up into three early phases: advertising; commercials and early short films—a real "pragmatic" evolution that plays into Parker's knowledge, experience and overall creativity.

Parker began in the mailroom for a small agency at Fleet Street and in the evenings he started writing ads and showing them to the creative department. In his humble beginnings, his supervisors would "grade" these ads, and one memorable response was labeled thus: "6 out of 10—must try harder." Through repeated hard work, he became a junior copywriter, composing hundreds of ads ("most of them not very good," he stated, "but I was prolific."). He then moved up the ladder, eventually taking his massive portfolio and years of experience to Collett, Dickenson & Pearce (CDP), the "most prestigious creative energy of the day." Over time he became a creative group head, becoming part of what would be known as the golden age of advertising.[13] By the age of twenty-two he was one of the highest paid writers in the industry and two years later he was directing commercials.[14]

While still working at the CDP, Parker took advantage of the fast-emerging business of commercials, of which he was on the ground floor. He asked his boss, John Pearce, if he could have funds to experiment on 16mm film. He admits to having no real experience or training in the technical side of things and "because of [his] ineptness," he was elected by the others to be the "director." He had no background operating cameras so, by default, he became the ringleader who got to yell "action" and "cut." Consequently, the advertising crew used vol-

Self-portrait caricature by Alan Parker from his book, *Will Write and Direct for Food* **(London: Southbank Publishing, 2005).**

unteers to make these short basement films that, over time, became better and better. One sophisticated commercial was an arty Benson & Hedges pipe tobacco advertisement depicting a Russian ball, replete with Jacques Loussier music. When Pearce discovered that Parker and the other workers were in the basement working on these commercials (instead of at their desks) he approached the novice "director," and to Parker's surprise, Pearce didn't fire him. Instead, he encouraged him to leave CDP to begin his own commercial production company—and he even gave Parker money to start the company! Thus began the genesis of the Alan Parker Film Company produced by Alan Marshall, a fellow CDP employee who would go on to be one of Parker's major feature-film producers. During these years he made a Heineken commercial that had a *Ben-Hur* theme, a Hamlet Cigars commercial set to a Napoleonic theme and even a short rendition of *Oliver Twist* (no doubt influenced by David Lean's adaptations of Dickens's *Oliver Twist* and *Great Expectations*, the latter which was mentioned earlier as being one of Parker's favorite films).[15] Incidentally, at the very end of *this* chapter following his essays on *Melody* and *The Evacuees*, the filmmaker lists a number of links to many of these commercials that can be viewed on www.youtube.com—and among them is the aforementioned Heineken and Benson & Hedges pipe tobacco commercials.

Doing commercials was very lucrative for Parker. The sophistication of these productions became yet another stepping stone to his next creative phase: writing his first feature film. While at CDP, Parker wrote the original screenplay for *Melody* (1971)—partner David Puttnam's first film as producer. The story takes place in a South London comprehensive school and focuses on a love affair between two children. *Melody* shows Parker's influences of the works of Ken Loach (whose 1966 film *Cathy Come Home* was what Parker called "the most important reason [he] wanted to become a film director),"[16] as well as Tony Garrett, who made socially conscious, working-class political films in the tradition of Loach. The film, incidentally, did very well in Japan but not in the U.K., which perhaps can be seen as a sort of foreshadowing for this director's fate—that he would be predestined to make many of his films abroad, not in England.

The next creative phase included writing and directing several short films. *Our Cissy* (1973) was a more sophisticated reality-based film about an elderly worker from Preston who comes to London to learn the reasons behind his daughter's suicide. The following film *Footsteps* (1973) combined social realism with a mystery subplot and tells the story of a lonely old woman, afraid for her safety, surrounded by an unfriendly world, a premise somewhat reminiscent of Vittorio De Sica's Italian neorealist classic *Umberto D* (1952), which concerns an old man who battles with a harsh post–World War II society. The next film was *No Hard Feelings* (1974), a World War II story set during the London Blitz.[17] On this film Parker states: "I had a particular affinity for this period as I had the dubious distinction of being born during a German air raid."[18] The film was funded by Parker's own production company and was initially meant to be part of a six-part series called *Stories of the Blitz*—but because it was independently produced it wasn't able to make it to BBC and ITV. The film, however, was shown to Mark Shivas, who was in charge of the BBC Drama Department. Impressed with what he saw, he offered Parker the chance to direct a feature-length film called *The Evacuees*, written by dramatist Jack Rosenthal, about Jewish kids being evacuated from wartime Manchester to the coastal safety of Blackpool. It won the BFTA in the U.K. and the International Emmy for Best Drama in the U.S. Parker did not write *The Evacuees*, but he did eventually write an "evacuee novel" called *Puddles in the Lane*, published by Star in 1979, which was originally going to be part of a "Blitz" series. The email interview following this chapter provides more detailed information on the making of this film and the aforementioned *Melody*.[19]

When asked by an anonymous source in *American Film* what he felt about the system of making films in America, Parker replied: "Pragmatically, if you want to reach the largest possible world audience it's the only place to work. But you do get absorbed into a system that can gobble you up if you're not careful. Because ultimately this film industry is about the pursuit of the dollar, and so a greater deal of art has been lost [sic]. A lot of people scoff if you say it's an art form; they say it hasn't been an art form for sixty years. The more asinine the bulk of films become, the more ashamed I am of being a film director. In a way I think many of my generation have sold out.... I have tried to do good work within an enormously powerful commercial movie machine ... it's great to think you can reach a large audience but it's also nice to think that you can affect people's lives in some way. So when they write the three-line biography of me in the *London Times* when I'm eighty-three, they can say I tried, even if sometimes I didn't succeed. I'd be happy with that."[20]

And with these words, let us leap into Parker's feature film career. For a filmmaker who appeared to be heading in the direction of making "kitchen sink" social-class films (in the tradition of Britain's Angry Young Man Movement) comes the voice of a director whose universally accessible films would eventually reach a global audience. Did he sell out to reach a mass audience? Or did he approach his craft in a different (more pragmatic) manner—especially since the films he *had* been making in the struggling British film industry of the 1970s (where he was trying to receive international financing) were being returned to him with these two common rejection phrases: "Too parochial" and "Too English"?[21]

Alan Parker email interview (May 19, 2012)[22]: The following information was provided by Alan Parker in an email response regarding information about two British films (*Melody* [1971], which he wrote, and *The Evacuees* [1975], which he directed) and his career directing commercials.

Melody

I hadn't really thought about writing a screenplay at the time of writing Melody. *I had yet to start directing, except for a few things in the basement of CDP—(Collett Dickenson Pearce) the advertising agency where I was working as a copywriter.*

David Puttnam was an account executive at the same agency and left the day I joined. He was going off to start a photographic agency (and eventually handled most of the stellar '60s British photographers). Charles Saatchi, was a copywriter at CDP, along with myself. We were very well paid (thanks to Charles) and it was a seminal time in British advertising—CDP was the most creative agency and responsible for the best work in the UK. We were all in our early twenties.

Eventually Charles left, originally to start a creative consultancy, and then an advertising agency. During Charles' "creative consultancy" period—and Puttnam's "photographic agency" period—they both asked me to lunch at a Greek restaurant in Soho (in 1969).

During the lunch they both leaned across, conspiratorially, and said, "Alan, we're thinking of going into film and today we are going to discover you." I said, "Why are you discovering me? Why can't I discover you?"

The plan was for me to write a script, and Charles to write a script, and Puttnam would raise the money and produce. I was still a copywriter at CDP and working quite hard and so wrote a treatment, late at night, called "Sophie Breams," based on the Beatles song "Eleanor Rigby." David and Charles were very polite about it, if not overly enthusiastic. Puttnam then told me that he had managed to secure the rights to seven Bee Gees songs (pre-falsetto Bee Gees) and suggested that I should write a script based on these songs. So I wrote Melody *based on the lyric of a Bee Gees song, "The First of May.".. The film's original title came from another song, "Melody Fair." I wrote the story based on many memories of my own childhood and school days, growing up in Islington, North London. I had never written a film script before and hardly knew even how to lay it out.*

Puttnam went to the U.S. to raise the money. It was tough and he wasn't received well (a resentment he continually harbored even when he ended up as Chairman of Columbia Pictures) but miraculously he got interest from Edgar Bronfman, the Seagram's billionaire. Apparently his 16-year-old son, Edgar Junior (who went on to become a Hollywood mogul himself and own Universal etc.) read the script and told his father to make the film.

Charles Saatchi lost interest in the film business very soon after this and, as David and I went on to make the film, he said he was going to start an advertising agency with his younger brother Maurice.

And so Puttnam and I were set on a path of film Saatchi in advertising with his own (eventually) mega agency Saatchi & Saatchi. I often wondered what would have happened if Puttnam had sold Charles' script and not mine. If he had sold the Saatchi script maybe Charles would have become a humble film director and I would be the gazillionair advertising mogul and the owner of the greatest personal collection of modern art in the world!

David Puttnam called me to say that we were going to make Melody. *I had little experience in film and so was not much use to him in the early production meetings where we were both bluffing our way. Puttnam, equally, had no experience in making a film but took to it like a duck to water. He had chosen the Indian/British director Waris Hussein to direct. Waris was one of many hot young Cambridge educated British directors who had cut their teeth with BBC drama. (Waris had got his start at the BBC because of his mother, who was famous for reading the news in Hindi for the World Service.)*

I never really worked with Waris on the screenplay. He shot it pretty well as I had originally written it, (longhand, late at night, on my kitchen table in London.) I remember having to "flesh out" certain scenes like Melody with the rag-and-bone man and the subsequent scenes with the goldfish: Waris insisted I had every shot written down for the musical montages. He wouldn't let me get away with "We cut to musical montage." I had to dot every "i" and cross every "t."

I can't say I was actively involved in the filmmaking process—any nuance regarding the acting was down to Waris, who was a very sensitive director. However, I visited the set a few times but wasn't there all the time. On one occasion, when they were filming in the old, empty St Paul's School, whilst chatting to Puttnam in his make-shift office, a young freckled boy in a baseball cap silently and obediently brought in the coffees and then left.

"That's Edgar Junior" said Puttnam. "His Dad's financing the film." It was like a scene from Great Expectations in Mr. Jaggers' office.

As, at the time, I had started directing in the basement at CDP Puttnam suggested that I take the spare, second camera and a couple of crew [members] and film some vignettes to augment the sports day scene that Waris was filming outside on the school field. I did some shots and then got a bit carried away with the long jump scene, and the focus of the day's filming shifted to my noisy endeavors. Waris promptly asked me to stop and I wasn't asked to do any more second unit! The sequence I shot is still in the film.

I am often credited with doing second unit on this film, but in truth the above few hours of filming was all I did.

A lot of the characters in the film were drawn from my own school memories: teachers (Latin master, History master), classes, etc. The character, Dadds, who made the bomb was in my class and often would show off his expertise on the long walk back from swimming lessons. I often wonder what profession Dadds eventually chose! The Jack Wilde character I suppose is close to me and the Mark Lester character is probably more like Puttnam.

The film was not a great success in the UK and U.S. In the UK the distributors renamed the film S.W.A.L.K. (from Sealed with a Loving Kiss which pubescent children traditionally wrote on envelopes). In the States the film was called To Love Somebody after one of the Bee Gees songs in the film—quite a good title. However it was a big hit in Japan under its original title Melody. The year after release, Tracey Hyde (the unknown young actress who played Melody) was the number three foreign star in Japan, after Robert Redford and Barbara [sic] Streisand.

It was a strange feeling for me being the writer on a film set. Everyone appreciates that without your script they wouldn't be there, but when it comes to filming, no one quite knows what you're actually doing, except getting in the way of the electricians. I vowed that if I ever wrote another screenplay then I would direct it. Also my days as an advertising copywriter were coming to an end.

I joined CDP around 1967 and it was the very beginnings of TV advertising in the UK. CDP had become famous for it's press advertising—often cleaning up on the annual advertising awards, year after year, but no one knew how to make commercials. I asked our boss, the creative director Colin Millward, if we could have a small budget to experiment with making rough commercials in the basement of the agency. (The basement area, curiously, was a huge empty cavernous space which should have been a car park, except someone forgot to build a ramp down to it—so it remained empty and became our own film studio.) We filmed on 16mm and had as professional a crew as we could assemble. We built sets, which were simple at first but became more ambitious the more pilot films we made. For the filming we used non-actors, just personnel from the agency: a woman from "media buying," a secretary from marketing, a man from accounts, etc. With the crew, each person had a job to do—someone operating the Nagra tape-recorder; the Spectra light-meter; the camera etc.—and the only person who didn't have any technical expertise was myself, so it was decided that as I was the writer, I would say the magic word "Action!" After a few seconds I yelled "Cut," walked forwards and gave the actors instructions and everyone looked at one another at my presumption, "Oooo, a film director," said the man from accounts, rather sarcastically. But a film director I suddenly was. Up to that point I had no such ambitions.

Our pilot basement commercials became more and more elaborate as they became a great tool to get new business. On one occasion, when the boss, John Pearce, was showing a prospective client around, he observed that there was no one in the accounts department, or the media department, or indeed any *department. "Where is everybody?" he said, somewhat perplexed. "They're all in the basement making a commercial with Alan," came the reply. I was in the middle of my most ambitious production: a pre-revolutionary, Russian ball, involving most of the agency personnel in full period costume—a glittering array of medals and tiaras.*

The next day I was called into the boardroom and confronted by the agency bosses. They wanted me to leave. Crestfallen, I thought I was being fired. But they wanted me to leave to start a production company so that I could direct their commercials full time. They would give me an interest free loan to get us set up and on our feet, and "probably they would give me a lot of work." The agency TV producer, Alan Marshall, left with me to start the new endeavor and produced all of my commercials and many of my films.

Addendum: Melody

(a). Often, when talking to film students, etc., about film construction, I use the example of Melody. *The film starts quite slowly—too slowly—but when it gets to the rag-and-bone sequence, where Melody swaps her parents clothes for a goldfish, the film kicks up a gear and takes off. When I started my next screenplay, David Puttnam said to me, "This time can you get to the goldfish a bit quicker—earlier—preferably in the opening scenes?"*

Consequently in all my scripts I have endeavored to "get to the goldfish" as quickly as possible. I've always thought that you present your credentials for the film that follows in the opening scenes and so great care should be taken with them.

(b). Curiously, Wes Anderson mentions Melody *as an influence on his film* Moonrise Kingdom: *http://blogs.indiewire.com/theplaylist/wes-anderson-says-françois-truffauts-small-change-ken-loachs-black-jack-alan-parkers-melody-are-influences-on-moonrise-kingdom-20120410. His film has not been released here yet. It opened the Cannes Film Festival.*

I'd be interested to know if there are any similarities with Melody. *It's written by Roman Coppola. Roman and Sofia Coppola have always liked* Melody *and* Bugsy Malone *since childhood. Sofia's representatives recently enquired as to putting Bugsy Malone on stage. (I said no.) I am also told that Roman is now working on a "Bugsy Malone type film" with pirates.*

The Evacuees

I e-mailed you previously about writing a series called "Stories of the Blitz." I had originally thought of six films but we trimmed it to three, but still couldn't get any interest because, at the time, almost no work was bought or commissioned outside of the "in-house production" system at the BBC. I made one film, for this "Blitz" series, financed by our commercials work, called "No Hard Feelings" (52 mins), which was a dramatic love story set against the background of the wartime bombing on London. This film was seen by

Mark Shivas, the BBC's senior drama producer, who then offered me a script called The Evacuees *written by Jack Rosenthal. He also arranged to get "No Hard Feelings" bought by the mysterious BBC acquisitions department and it subsequently had two showings on the BBC.*

Jack Rosenthall was a well known television playwright with many notches to his belt. The most difficult thing for me in making The Evacuees *was that I would lose the comfort zone of my own production company which, by then, had many dozens of commercials. Most specifically, I wouldn't have my usual producer, Alan Marshall, or editor, Gerry Hambling (who went on to cut all my subsequent films). Also, the BBC system and unions decreed that all crew [members] were on staff and so you had to have whoever came up on the roster. I asked Mark Shivas if I could have Brian Tufano as cameraman as I had admired his work with directors like Ken Loach, Alan Clarke and Jack Gold. With a great deal of shenanigans and in-house politics we secured Tufano's services.*

The (75 min) film was shot in six weeks all on location in Manchester, Salford, Lytham St Anne's and Blackpool. To the consternation of the BBC casting people, I spent an inordinate amount of time trawling through the Manchester school to find our young actors. I've always been of the opinion that if you get the casting right, you get the film right. Also, when shooting started it was evident that the young actor playing Zuckerman was awkward in front of camera and I promptly swapped him with Paul Besterman who proved to fit the part perfectly and delivered an outstanding performance. As Maureen remarked, "Paul looks like he's eaten nothing but gefilte fish and salt beef all his life."

It was very hard for me as I gradually tried to impose my way of filming on the BBC crew and they initiated me in their process. I admired Tufano immensely, but he was a hard task-master and pushed me considerably, which he always did with his directors. We had to shoot fast, often with available light and I was forever pushing the process to be more cinematic and Tufano was forever finessing my instructions with the limitations (and freedom) of the 16mm film camera. (For example, we had no dolly and I wanted to track across the faces of the boys in the Salford classroom as they heard news of their evacuation. Tufano put the camera on a carpet and the camera assistant dragged it slowly across the wooden floor.) Tufano had graduated at the BBC from documentary to film drama and had cut his teeth in black and white film, as had I with my commercials. I think we had a similar penchant for single source, dramatic light: a sensibility where shadows are as important as the lit areas. (Not that we had much choice as we didn't have many lights anyway.) The tastes of the time were to over-light everything, especially in color, and our work opposed that trend—and harkened back to more expressionistic lighting of the thirties and forties.

I got on well with Jack who was a much-respected figure [in] British television. He wasn't there all the time but visited often, Jack was often pacing and chain smoking as we bumbled through but only offered encouragement and rarely interfered. Also his wife, Maureen Lipman, was playing the evacuated boys' mother. If ever I improvised on her lines, she would politely guide me back to the words in the script that Jack had originally written.

The pace of filming was arduous compared to the more leisurely pace of TV commercials that I was used to. It was shot in thirty days. We were forever improvising with our shots to push it beyond the normal BBC drama production and to add cinematic width to Jack's

TV script. On one shot I wanted to get the school teacher and the lonely Zuckerman trudging along the seafront, silhouetted, against the falling sunlight. Tufano and I ignored the rest of the crew, roared off in the station wagon and grabbed the shot with me yelling into the sunset, the camera cradled in Brian's arms. We improvised many shots like this, chasing the light and so Tufano and I forged a fruitful relationship. After the film, I even convinced him to leave the cozy roster of the BBC and go freelance. This he did and went on to [do] some stellar work (Trainspotting, Billy Elliot, etc.). He is presently running the cinematography department at the UK National Film School.

Directing the mainly Jewish cast, as a non Jew, had its interesting moments for me. There is a scene where the two evacuated boys had to eat a pork sausage for the first time in their lives. I had asked their Rabbi if we could have special dispensation for the film. This was refused. I told the two boys that we were going to use good old fashioned pork from the local butcher. The authentic reactions on their two faces on film are testament to their repulsion at eating pork for the first time. At the end of the shot the younger boy, Gary, went into the street and threw up on the cobbles. I went out to comfort him. I put my arm around him and said, "Don't worry, they weren't pork, they were kosher sausages." He suddenly stopped throwing up and said, "I thought they tasted OK."

I had developed a way of shooting children with my commercials. Rather than cutting the camera after each take, I would keep the camera rolling and talk over the take—instructing the young actors to repeat over and over a phrase or line to get the correct reading. Sometimes I would isolate a single word and do a dozen different intonations for emphasis and subtlety. I knew that I could cut out my voice later and judiciously snip out the preferred take in editing.

I remember that the final sound mix of the film was not liked by the BBC head of drama. He didn't like the use of music as BBC drama at the time was very purist and the use of music on the soundtrack was frowned upon as being too manipulative.

As I said before, the film was well received winning a BAFTA for best TV drama and also an Emmy for best International Drama. The Evacuees probably made it easier persuading the financiers that I could direct children in Bugsy Malone—which had a cast of nothing but!

Parker also mentioned that many of his commercials have been posted on YouTube and provided a list:

Birds Eye Dinner For One Brief Encounter: http://www.youtube.com/watch?v=fABzM0lPhsM
Cockburns Shipwreck: http://www.youtube.com/watch?NR=1&feature=endscreen&v=wRL9P99EOBs
Supersoft Shampoo—Coming Attractions: http://www.youtube.com/watch?v=q_u_XExwDRM
Parker Pens Finishing School: http://www.youtube.com/watch?v=sYH2WMGq8c0&feature=relmfu
Hamlet Cigars—Tennis: http://www.youtube.com/watch?v=qg6RzvZBsp8&feature=relmfu
Heineken—Galley: http://www.youtube.com/watch?v=8g—qAt5Ibc
Silk Cut Cigarettes—Zulu: http://www.youtube.com/watch?v=ncfLTD34CiA
Daily Express—Howard Hughes—Tissue Trail: http://www.youtube.com/watch?v=P_pVIrfGIiU
Cinzano: http://www.youtube.com/watch?v=PirMZGL-0mQ&feature=related
Birds Eye Beefburgers—Gangster: http://www.youtube.com/watch?v=7mvuE821_MM&feature=relmfu

Olympus Cameras—David Bailey: http://www.youtube.com/watch?v=Uhfz3eZ51Xc&feature=relmfu

Birds Eye Supermousse—Oliver Twist—More: http://www.youtube.com/watch?v=2zgKQkstEFo

Nescafe Coffee—Married Couple: http://www.youtube.com/watch?v=_uRE9YlofEE&feature=relmfu

Benson and Hedges Pipe Tobacco—Bridge: http://www.youtube.com/watch?v=gVg9rcarI3M

Birds Eye Beefburgers—Dan and Ben—Starving Artist: http://www.youtube.com/watch?v=Zdylqnz-4uQ

Benson & Hedges Cigars—Hat: http://www.youtube.com/watch?v=1KqHaA-np9Q

Hamlet Cigars—King Canute: http://www.youtube.com/watch?v=4unl87oUWjY

Texaco—Morcambe and Wise and James Hunt: http://www.youtube.com/watch?v=LDG2A8jX6Ds&feature=related

Benson and Hedges Pipe Tobacco—Boyfriend: http://www.youtube.com/watch?v=Tk8PZ93Zqrk

2

Bugsy Malone, 1976

November 4; 93 minutes/Color
Production Company: Paramount Pictures (U.S.) & Fox-Rank (U.K.)
Director: Alan Parker
Screenwriter: Alan Parker
Producer: David Puttnam (Executive Producer), Alan Marshall
Production Designer: Geoffrey Kirkland
Cinematography: Peter Biziou & Michael Seresin
Editor: Gerry Hambling
Original Music: Paul Williams
Cast: Scott Baio (Bugsy); Florrie Dugger (Blousey Brown); John Cassisi (Fat Sam); Jodie Foster (Tallulah); Martin Lev (Dandy Dan); Paul Murphy (Leroy Smith); Albin Humpty Jenkins (Fizzy); Sheridan Russell (Knuckles)

> Frankly, the film was a lunatic idea that would only be attempted at the beginning of a career.—Alan Parker, The Making of *Bugsy Malone*, pg. 28

> Okay fellas, this is our moment. Keep a cool head and keep those fingers pumpin', 'cause remember, it's history you'll be writin'.—Fat Sam to his crew in *Bugsy Malone*

Notes on the Production

Parker credits the inception of *Bugsy Malone*, the story that would eventually become his first feature film, to his four children. During their many long drives to the country, Parker would tell his children stories to abate their restlessness and boredom. He would try to

> alleviate their considerable car-sick boredom by inventing and improvising a gangster story which, on my eldest son Alex's insistence, was peopled with kids, just like the four of them sitting in the back of the car.[1]

Parker transformed this unique gangster story into a screenplay, which was, according to Parker, not so much about "America" as it was about "American movies." Parker states: "My script was a cinematic pastiche, after all, with echoes and references to Astaire, Raft, Kelly, Cagney, Brando, and Welles."[2] He crafted a gangster story that was "to be taken completely seriously … except the guns will fire custard pies and it will have a cast entirely of kids aged about twelve."[3]

Once it was finished, he began touting it around the British film industry, mostly to no avail. His sales pitch was not met with much alacrity, as producers did not seem to grasp the novel concept of the fusion of two genres—the Hollywood musical and the gangster

Leroy Smith (Paul Murphy, left) looks on as child gangster Bugsy Malone (Scott Baio, center) wields his "splurge" machine gun, which, instead of shooting bullets, "splats" its victims with whipped cream. *Bugsy Malone* (1976), Paramount Pictures (U.S.) & Fox-Rank (U.K.).

film. Not to be deterred, Parker, along with David Puttnam and Alan Marshall, managed to stitch together the financing for the film in both the U.K. and the U.S. It was then that the interesting task of casting began.

Since the film was to consist of a cast made up almost entirely of child actors, the conventional audition process did not seem appropriate. Parker visited U.S. Air Force bases, Brooklyn schools and Harlem dance classes to find his "gangsters." He cast Scott Baio out of Manhattan. Parker says that he "loved his gravely voice—still a child's voice, but with that wonderful New York timbre of scraped tonsils that we needed to make our dialogue believable."[4] He found Johnny Cassisi (Fat Sam) at a school in Brooklyn and cast him based on his reputation as the "troublemaker." He found Florrie Dugger (Blousey) at an American Air Force base in England, and was blessed to find Jodie Foster who, at fourteen, was already an accomplished actress, having been in myriad films and television spots. "Jodie was impeccable as an actress," states Parker—"at age twelve, she had made more films than the rest of us and I joked that if I got sick she could easily have taken over."[5]

With his intrepid cast in tow, and with principal photography set to take place at Pinewood Studios in London, there was one more piece of the puzzle to go—Parker needed a composer to write the musical numbers; someone who could write songs and melodies that were contemporary sounding, yet at the same time redolent of the glitzy, nightclub-infused Jazz Age that the film was to so strongly recall. After much deliberation, Parker settled on veteran composer/songwriter Paul Williams.

By March 1975, the finished draft of the script was ready, and Parker, at first, was frustrated with the apparent dearth of composers who seemed the right fit for his admittedly unique film. He states, "We thought film musicals had moved on a bit since the hands-across-the-table, bursting-into-song days and no composer suggested seemed quite right."[6] Of the composers suggested, however, Parker admitted that Paul Williams was his favorite. Not only was Williams already an accomplished songwriter (having written the hit songs "An Old Fashioned Love Song" for Three Dog Night and "We've Only Just Begun" for the Carpenters, among others), but he had written songs for and performed in Brian De Palma's 1974 film *Phantom of the Paradise*, which earned him an Oscar nomination for his music. De Palma's film was an eclectic fusion of genres, incorporating elements from *The Phantom of the Opera*, *Faust*, *Psycho*, and *The Cabinet of Dr. Caligari* into a musical. The experience of working on such a unique hybridization of genres is that which made Williams the optimal choice for Parker's cross-pollinated gangster/musical. Knowing this, Parker traveled to Las Vegas to meet with Williams, who was performing in cabaret at the Sands. Over a meal at Fox's Deli, the two men went through the script line by line, song by song. According to Parker: "Paul has a remarkable facility for humming a melody the moment you mention a phrase or situation. Each tune seemed marvelous and I was terrified he would forget them, but he seems blessed with a tape recorder locked away up inside his head somewhere."

With his team assembled, Parker began principal photography at Pinewood Studios' "H" stage, and the making of a very unique and interesting film was underway.

Summary

The opening shot of the film invites us into a shadowy, seedy world of urban decadence. It is an aerial shot of a desolate big city street at night, with what is ostensibly a 1930s Ford or Oldsmobile parked by the curb, signifying the film's time period. There is a squalid, fetid texture to the shot, which is augmented by the steam rising up off a grate in the middle of the street, the sound of an alley cat screeching, and the implacable *drip* of water, which is conceivably coming from a water pipe offscreen. In the next shot, the source of the sound is revealed as we cut to a close-up of water cascading down a leaky water pipe. This second shot has a haunting, eerie quality, and the falling water seems to serve as some kind of harbinger, but of what, we are unsure (of death? of the inexorable march of time? of existential despair?).

With these ominous opening two-shots, Parker seems to be calling us to brace ourselves, to beware the double and triple crosses that are to unfold, to warn us that we will be cavorting with an unsavory cast of characters. At first, it feels like the kind of steamy, sultry opening which populated the noirs of the 1940s and 1950s. We almost expect Humphrey Bogart to come traipsing around the dark street corner puffing a cigarette, wearing his signature fedora and trench coat. However, the lighting and obtrusive sound effects take the noirish flavor of the opening into darker territory; it actually feels like the opening to a horror film. When the film cuts to the dark alley, the leaky water pipe feels like the

Sword of Damocles—a herald of impending doom. The arrival of a lurking, menacing predator who wishes to inflict harm feels imminent.

It is at this moment that the voice-over is introduced. On the soundtrack, Fat Sam (played by John Cassisi) says: "Someone once said, 'If it was raining brains, Roxy Robinson wouldn't even get wet.'" This moment is a bit jarring, and the audience is still not sure what or how to feel. The voice-over is an archetypal narrative trope of the noir genre, and it has been utilized in the most canonical works of the genre, from Jacques Tourneur's *Out of the Past*, to Billy Wilder's *Sunset Boulevard*, to the majority of the Humphrey Bogart detective films. So, with its implementation, Parker seems to be coaxing us back into crime/noir territory and away from that of horror. However, that which makes this moment jarring is the fact that it is a child's voice we are hearing—it is not the coarse baritone of Robert Mitchum or the nasally glib recitation of Humphrey Bogart. Although it is clearly a child we are listening to, however, it is not a pure, innocent, cherubic voice, but rather a gruff, gravelly voice infused with a scratchy timbre and dripping with a rough Brooklyn accent. It is at this moment that we realize that we are experiencing some sort of hybridization—a reinvention of tried-and-true genre tropes. This realization is augmented in the ensuing action in which Roxy Robinson flees from his pursuers. When he comes frantically running around the corner into the alley, we see that Roxy is, himself, a child. His pursuers (a gang of children sporting fedoras and tommy guns) then come into the frame and we are, again, unsure how to feel. Are these young children going to murder Roxy? They chase him into the alley (which is a dead end, trapping Roxy, forcing him to face his assailants), raise their weapons and fire. At this point, we cringe with anxiety, preparing for the blood to start flying as a result of this heinous, senseless act of violence. Children using guns is a disturbing (and very real) phenomenon (the harsh tragedy of which was expertly conveyed by Fernando Meirelles in his powerful film *City of God*), and we as the audience, at this moment in *Bugsy Malone*, are not sure we are prepared to witness such a gruesome incident. Parker, however, expertly attenuates this tension by revealing that the guns do not fire bullets but, rather, custard pies. Roxy is inundated with a barrage of white slop, informing us of just how revisionist this experience is going to be. Whimsical, Three Stooges–style lunacy has supplanted tension and anxiety. Parker places us on the highest branch on the tree of anxiety, then quickly (and without announcement) gets us down. (This technique—the sharp contrasting of tension and relief—would be perfected by Parker two years later in his film *Midnight Express*, which is a sonata of anxiety interspersed with moments of levity.)

The "massacre" of Roxy displays another interesting technical choice made by Parker, which is the implementation of the freeze frame. When a large chunk of white sludge smacks Roxy in the face, the frame is frozen in place, the audience now looking at a still photo as opposed to a moving picture. Over this one frozen frame, Fat Sam's voice-over starts up again. This technique—of freezing on one frame over which the narrator speaks—would later be used to great effect by Martin Scorsese in his gangster film *Goodfellas*. However, whereas Scorsese implemented this technique to accentuate a pivotal change in Henry Hill's (the main character) life, Parker uses this Brechtian device to heighten both the whimsicality and the artifice of his highly unique hybridization. The freeze frames in *Goodfellas* all occur at moments of startling and brutal violence, bolstering the narrative concept of Henry's life being shaped and defined by his experiences with such. However, in *Bugsy*

Malone, Parker freezes on a close-up of Roxy's face being splattered with white custard, inviting us to relax in our seats; while the cinematography and overall visual aesthetic may be redolent of seething dread, this moment signifies that the film will never devolve too deeply into such depths of dire gravity—it's all in good fun.

After the opening shootout, the film cuts to the title sequence. Over a montage of shots from the ensuing film, Paul Williams sings a jazzy, Cole Porteresque tune, which both introduces us to the main character, and reaffirms the film's whimsical, breezy tone. There's an "aw, shucks" quality to the song, and when Williams sings the chorus ("Everybody loves that man—Bugsy Malone"), we are invited to endear ourselves to Bugsy (played by Scott Baio). The spectators' response to the character of Bugsy—that is, the fact that we are invited by Williams's whimsical introduction to endear ourselves to him—is where Parker's film departs from the classic 1930s gangster films to which *Bugsy Malone* is clearly paying homage. In those films, we revel in our perverse attraction to the menacing charms of the volatile protagonists (e.g., James Cagney in *Public Enemy*, Edward G. Robinson in *Little Caesar*, Paul Muni in *Scarface*, et al). As Robert Warshow states in his essay *The Gangster as Tragic Hero*:

> [The gangster] is what we want to be and what we are afraid we may become ... we gain the double satisfaction of participating vicariously in the gangster's sadism and then seeing it turned against the gangster himself.[7]

In other words, the spectator of the gangster film traditionally has the luxury of reviling the criminal behavior of the protagonist, while at the same time taking a perverse pleasure in his iconoclastic, rebellious behavior. With the lighthearted title sequence of *Bugsy Malone*, however, Parker is disavowing the possibility of such a layered, complex psychological response. He is reaffirming that this film is an homage to American gangster films, not an American gangster film.

After the title sequence, we follow Bugsy as he walks into a bookstore. He removes a group of books from one of the shelves to reveal a window. The boy (man) on the other side of the window pulls back the entire bookshelf to reveal a speakeasy. Bugsy walks into a bustling, raucous Prohibition-style nightclub replete with live music, female dancers, waiters, and a horde of rambunctious, boisterous patrons whistling at the women (girls) and demanding drinks. This is Fat Sam's Grand Slam Speakeasy. We then cut to Fat Sam's office, where Sam is berating his bumbling, incompetent henchmen for allowing Roxy Robinson to be killed. This scene takes the comedy to new levels of silliness, as it is fraught with slapstick Three Stooges–style gags. The first shot is of one of Sam's henchmen lining up a pool shot. He hits the cue ball, it goes flying off the table, and, offscreen, we hear the sound of a glass window being broken. This use of offscreen sound to signify some sort of comedic outbreak of chaos recalls the screwball antics of Abbott and Costello. This is Parker's version of the inept wanderer opening a door, hearing a woman scream with embarrassment, apologizing, and then shutting the door. Sam then begins his verbal lashing. In mid-rant, he leans back too far in his chair and topples over. Then he lines up his bumbling henchmen, who are all, off course, taller than he is, and, à la Moe Howard from the Three Stooges, sprays water in each of their faces. (With this scene, Parker is not so much paying homage to American gangster films as he is to American comedies. The dimwitted henchman apologizing to his exasperated, more competent boss is a classic trope of American comedy. It could be seen as a comedic permutation of the relationship between George and Lenny in John Steinbeck's *Of Mice and Men*, and it is a device that has been implemented in such diverse projects as the cartoon *Pinky and the Brain* and Harold Ramis's gangster/comedy *Analyze This*.)

We then cut back to Fat Sam's Grand Slam for the first real musical number of the film, notwithstanding the title sequence. It is an upbeat, vaudeville-style song called "Fat Sam's Grand Slam," and it marks the first time the audience witnesses that, while the children who populate the film are doing the dancing and mouthing of the words, their voices have been supplanted by those of adults. The piano player, Razamataz (played by Michael Jackson), sings the verse but it is clearly not his own voice; it belongs to that of an adult baritone. This Brechtian device of replacing the children's singing voices with those of adults has been one of the most oft-debated topics of the film. Some find it charming and cute, in a cheeky sort of way, others find it jarring, distracting, and unnecessary. For instance, both Paul Williams and Alan Parker admit to their dissatisfaction with the results. Williams states, "The only thing I've ever doubted is the choice of using adult voices. Perhaps I should have given the kids a chance to sing the songs."[8] With a similar sentiment, Parker states:

> Watching the film after all these years, this is one aspect that I find the most bizarre. Adult voices coming out of these kids' mouths? I had told Paul that I didn't want squeaky kids voices and he interpreted this in his own way. Anyway, as the tapes arrived, scarcely weeks away from filming, we had no choice but to go along with it![9]

However, despite Williams's and Parker's misgivings, some critics felt that dubbing adult singing voices over those of children was entirely appropriate. In their review, *The Sounds of Silence: Songs in Hollywood Films since the 1960s*, Todd Berliner and Philip Furia state:

> [*Bugsy Malone*] calls attention to the lip-synching, rather than trying to conceal it as earlier musicals had done. The effect is jarring and the kids look somewhat ridiculous as they impersonate gangsters and lip-synch the voices of grown-ups, but it all seems somehow appropriate for a revisionist gangster movie, since the genre often portrayed characters who posture and perform. The film also plays on our impression that old gangster films now seem quaintly contrived. Hence, when the characters break into song, the film associates musical outburst with the artifice of film itself.[10]

Berliner and Furia's review invites a more reasonable reading of this aesthetic audio choice. From the outset, Parker intimated that *Bugsy Malone* was not intended to be about "America," but about "American movies." It was always intended to be a self-aware, generic pastiche, so it is both fitting and appropriate that the film would accentuate the artifice of performance. Performance and all its stages (auditioning, rejection, rehearsal, etc.) is a topic which is clearly of great interest to Parker (as many of his later films would reveal), and *Bugsy Malone* offers an interesting treatment of the concept of performance. Not only does the narrative itself contain aspiring performers (Blousey, Fizzy, the janitor, etc.), but the performances in the film are, themselves, being given a revisionist, post-modern spin. The actors perform in that they gesticulate, dance, and lip-synch, but they are simultaneously *not* performing—they are not, in fact, singing. This paradoxical concept augments the film's self-aware, revisionist status. In other words, as Berliner and Furia state, Parker is accentuating the artifice of filmmaking and performance itself.

The musical number "Fat Sam's Grand Slam" continues and progresses into a Busby

Berkeley-inspired dance number, featuring glitzy girl dancers singing the chorus. Although there is an entire chorus line of sultry performers, Parker's camerawork cues us to focus primarily on one of the singers/dancers in particular—a platinum blonde with confidence and spunk, whom we later discover is Fat Sam's gal, Tallulah (played by Jodie Foster). By frequently cutting to close-ups of her throughout the chorus line dance number, Parker alerts us that Tallulah will have narrative agency later on in the story.

After "Fat Sam's Grand Slam," Bugsy literally bumps into a girl (woman) named Blousey Brown (played by Florrie Dugger, who originally had a much smaller part in the film, but, due to the fact that the actress who was originally hired to play Blousey grew taller than Scott Baio, was upgraded to the role of Blousey). Their rapport is scintillating and they engage in a vibrant, rapid-fire verbal *pas de deux*, replete with one-liners and double entendres. With their lightning-fast repartee, Parker is again reaffirming that this film is a tribute to American movies. The quick-witted put-downs are reminiscent of Cary Grant and Rosalind Russell in Howard Hawks's screwball comedy *His Girl Friday*. When Bugsy introduces himself to Blousey, she simply glowers at him derisively and says: "Don't call us—we'll call you," which strongly recalls the caustic yet innocuous insults Hildy Johnson and Walter Burns hurl at each other in Hawks's film. The wordplay between Blousey and Bugsy also has roots in the gangster genre, particularly in that it strongly recalls the banter between Humphrey Bogart and Lauren Bacall in the noir and crime films of the 1940s. When Bugsy says that Blousey's name reminds him of a stale loaf of bread, one is fondly reminded of the scene in *To Have and Have Not* in which Bacall tells Bogey that all he has to do is whistle. She then says, "You know how to whistle, don't you, Steve?" Of course, since Bogey and Bacall were adults at the time of filming, there is a more erotically charged sexual tension buried beneath the banter. There is still a romantic tension between Blousey and Bugsy, but, at the risk of being inappropriately salacious, Parker keeps it lighthearted and it is more indicative of puppy love than of steamy sexual attraction.

The following two segments of the film are interesting in that they both deal with similar subject matter (i.e., "violence"), but the directorial treatment of each respective scene marks a sharp contrast between the two. The first is the gangland raid of Fat Sam's. During Blousey and Bugsy's conversation, a rival gang bursts into the nightclub armed with their "splurge guns" and they proceed to shoot up the place, bombarding the speakeasy with a hail of bullets (custard). The tone of the scene is quite comedic, however, and Parker, again, displays his aptitude for comedic timing. As the gang shoots up the joint, Parker rapidly cuts back and forth between the gunmen and Fat Sam and his cronies. Each time a "bullet" hits its mark, Parker cuts to Fat Sam and friends reacting. In true slapstick fashion, their expressions are exaggeratedly wide-eyed, and each time the "bullets" are aimed at a different section of the room, Fat Sam and his gang swivel their heads in unison to follow their trajectory. Finally, the gunmen fire at Fat Sam and his gang, and they all duck in unison as custard splatters the wall behind them. Again, Parker is implementing Three Stooges–style comedy.

We then cut to another act of gangland violence, but Parker handles this scene quite differently. The scene follows a lone gunman, stealthily crawling down a fire escape. He then stands outside a barbershop, in which a lone customer is getting a haircut. This scene is directed with stark conviction and is actually quite suspenseful; there are no gags, pratfalls, or one-liners. Parker masterfully cuts back and forth between the intended target, insouciantly enjoying his haircut, and the would-be assassin, assembling his "splurge gun." The gunman then gives the barber a knowing nod, and the barber runs away, leaving the customer to meet his "doom." The gunman bursts in, fires his gun, and a glob of custard smacks the customer in the face. Outside of the fact that the assassin, victim, and barber are all children, and that the gun shoots custard and not bullets, there is nothing about the direction of this scene which suggests levity, or that the material is not to be taken seriously. Whereas, in the previous scene, Parker directed the "violence" with a strong sense of whimsicality, this scene is directed as though it were in an actual suspense/crime/gangster film. Parker ratchets up the tension as the gunman slowly prepares and then implements rapid cutting to amplify the spectator's sense of anxiety as we anticipate the customer's demise. Stylistically, it is strongly reminiscent of Francis Ford Coppola's *The Godfather*, in particular, the scene in which Moe Greene is shot in the eye by an assassin in the middle of his massage.

By juxtaposing these two scenes, Parker is displaying an aptitude for and understanding of multiple genres and how to effectively depict them cinematically. Whereas the first scene depicts his affinity for comic timing, the second is testament to his ability to effectively build suspense, a talent which he would expertly implement in his next film, *Midnight Express*. It also augments the notion that this film is a pastiche, a generic stew to which Parker is adding myriad spices and ingredients. He did not intend to tether himself to one singular tone which allows him to weave seamlessly in an out of genre moments. In other words, Parker is emulating the filmmaking expertise of directors such as Robert Wise and Howard Hawks, who were able to expertly and effectively make films in a diverse set of genres.

After the stark direction of the barbershop hit, Parker shifts back to Bogey and Bacall territory as Bugsy walks with Blousey down the street. There is some beautifully insolent dialogue between the two. In one memorable exchange, Blousey tells Bugsy that she's watching her weight, to which Bugsy replies, "Yeah, I do that when I'm broke, too." The two of them then head into a diner and share a drink. Bugsy tells Blousey that he wants to be a fight promoter and that he was once a boxer himself. When Blousey asks him if he was any good, he replies, "I could have been a contender, Charley," which is clearly a reference to Elia Kazan's film *On the Waterfront*. Bugsy's reference is anachronistic, as Kazan's film wasn't released until 1954, and the diegesis of *Bugsy Malone* ostensibly takes place in the '30s. In any other film, such a chronological oversight would surely be construed as a mistake. However, in this film, it only serves to augment the notion that Parker's film is a cinematic grab bag, a potpourri of genre moments and conventions. Bugsy's anachronistic quote serves to wink at the audience, reminding them that this film is a cinematic stitching together of American movies and their paradigmatic properties.

The next scene introduces us to Tallulah, Fat Sam's moll. Fat Sam's Grand Slam is closing up for the night and only a few scattered people are left, including Fat Sam, Fizzy, the African American janitor, and Tallulah. Fat Sam is hurriedly trying to get out the door and he is rushing Tallulah. He says to her, "You spend more time prettying yourself up than there is time in the day." With a sultry, feline derision, Tallulah responds, "Listen, honey, if I didn't look this good, you wouldn't *give* me the time of day." Tallulah evokes the torrid, resigned world weariness yet confidence and strength exemplified by the consummate gangster molls who populated the gangster films of the 1930s, such as Mae West and Jean Harlow.

From left to right: Speakeasy-owner "Fat Sam" (John Cassisi) converses with nightclub singer Tallulah (Jodie Foster) and womanizing ex-boxer Bugsy Malone (Scott Baio). *Bugsy Malone* (1976), Paramount Pictures (U.S.) & Fox-Rank (U.K.).

To a certain degree, she is a doormat, like Mae Clarke in *Public Enemy*. She admits that she only attempts to look good for "her man" and not for herself. However, her tone is suggestive of a tough, self-sufficient street girl, which is reminiscent of Greta Garbo in *Anna Christie* ("Give me a whiskey, ginger ale on the side—and don't be stingy, baby.").

The next moment shifts gears and becomes introspective and despondent. After trying to get an audition with Fat Sam, Fizzy (played by "Humpty" Albin Jenkins) is crestfallen when Fat Sam blows him off. Left by himself in the Grand Slam to sweep the floor, Fizzy morosely sings the tune "Tomorrow," in which he dejectedly expresses his frustration with always being told that he'll get his chance "tomorrow," only, according to the lyrics, tomorrow never comes. This scene is fraught with pathos and Parker stays with Fizzy as he sings his tune, as opposed to cutting away to the main characters to "move the plot along." This narrative choice, to represent the suffering and turmoil of his characters in intimate, private moments that the characters themselves would most likely not want anyone to see, would become a trademark of Parker's style. In his later films (most notably *Shoot the Moon*, *Midnight Express*, and *The Life of David Gale*), Parker would demonstrate great skill in diverting the narrative thrust from the "plot" to intimately (and almost obtrusively) show us the turmoil and spiritual, emotional strife that his characters are going through. In this case, Fizzy is not even a main character *and* he is African American, which bolsters the emotional impact of the scene. We feel for Fizzy, as he is summarily dismissed and ignored, relegated to his menial task. In this regard, Parker is displaying a Robert Altmanesque interest in spending time with "the help" as opposed to the financially stable bourgeoisie (which Altman effectively utilized in films such as *Kansas City* and *Gosford Park*).

This moment employs another narrative device that would eventually become a hallmark of Parker's style: the depiction of the struggle and anguish that performers must endure to hone their craft and achieve appreciation for their abilities. Not only would this theme permeate the remaining narrative of *Bugsy Malone*, but Parker would revisit this theme in *Fame* and *The Commitments*. The impatience and frustration that performers feel in the face of an obstinate, grueling, and unforgiving audition process is clearly of great interest to Parker, and he showcases this interest to great effect in this film (which I will delineate further later in this chapter).

Following this somber, introspective musical number, Parker shifts again to comedy territory, as we cut back to the diner with Blousey and Bugsy. The diner is closing, and the waitress asks Bugsy to settle the bill. To unctuously weasel out of paying, Bugsy concocts an elaborate scheme. He enters the phone booth, calls the operator, and tells her to call back to check the phone line. Bugsy then exits the booth, the phone rings, and the waitress enters the booth to answer it. Bugsy then slides a broom into the door handle, trapping the waitress within the phone booth, which allows Bugsy and Blousey to skip out on the bill. By presenting this scene immediately after the downtrodden, morose performance of "Tomorrow," Parker is again demonstrating the delicate juggling act he is employing with this film. The tone is light, but Parker never allows the goofiness to completely subsume the narrative, still paying close attention to his characters, their struggles, and their humanity.

The next scene is a clear-cut homage to one gangster film convention in particular, the spinning newspaper montage. This trope was implemented in many Prohibition-era gangster films and serials, and was used to great effect in *Citizen Kane*. The idea is to transition between scenes by implementing a montage in which a newspaper spins at the screen then stops, displaying a pertinent headline that has ostensibly happened after the previous scene and before the upcoming scene. Parker is clearly paying homage to old Hollywood here, right down to the offscreen utterance of the now-clichéd phrase "Extra! Extra! Read all about it!" The featured headlines in this montage are "New Gang War Flares," and "New Weapon for Mobsters," alerting the public to the arrival of the new "splurge gun." Parker keeps this scene light and whimsical, drawing attention to the homage itself. It does not possess the stark, documentary feel of the headline sequence in *The Godfather*, in which Coppola used actual photographs of 1940s crime scenes to augment the hard-hitting brutality of gangland violence.

We then cut to Dandy Dan's palatial estate. Dan is outside, riding on horseback, and there is a stringed orchestra playing a classical piece in his massive yard. The set design is fraught with a sense of snotty, uppity excess, and Dandy Dan is portrayed as complete snob. The absurd excess of Dan's wealth serves to make him all the more unlikable, inviting us to root *for* Fat Sam and his likable gang of hoodlums, and *against* Dandy Dan and his elitist, bourgeois clan.

Parker then cuts to the audition sequence, in which Blousey is preparing to perform in front of two impatient, hard-boiled judges. This scene, again, displays Parker's interest in the process of performance. He implements a tracking shot, which slowly reveals an eclectic rogue's gallery of performers who are all waiting in line, waiting for their turn to perform onstage. This shot strongly reflects a guerrilla, "in the trenches" feel to it, as Parker seems to be not only concerned with displaying the performance itself, but the intense, anxiety-inducing preparation of performance (i.e., the *process* that performers go through). We then see myriad, vaudeville-style performances, from singing to dancing to ventriloquism, giving us a true fly-on-the-wall perspective of just what it is like to stand up in front of people and audition.

This scene also demonstrates Parker's affinity for juxtaposing (or contrasting, if you like) levity and gravity, whimsicality and seriousness. The performance sequence itself is hilarious—the judges' brusque dismissal of the over-the-top performances is a sendup of the gruff Hollywood producer cliché. There is one particularly funny moment in which a harp player starts schlepping her giant harp onto the stage, but before she even arrives at center stage—that is, before she even gets to perform—the male judge screams from off-screen, "NEXT!!"

This madcap sequence is undercut with sincerity, however, when Blousey takes the stage. Just as she is about to sing, a screeching, obnoxious girl bursts into the auditorium, screaming at the male judge. The fracas completely disrupts Blousey's audition, and she never gets to perform. Disheartened, she storms off, professing to Bugsy her frustration, stating that she'll never get her chance, to which Bugsy replies, "So, you'll come back tomorrow." Blousey then angrily replies, "Come back tomorrow, come back tomorrow.... I've spent my whole life coming back tomorrow!" Once again, Parker has infused an otherwise silly scene with heart-wrenching sincerity. Even if we have never, ourselves, been on an actual audition, we can identify with Blousey's impatience and abject frustration. With this powerful moment, Parker again shows us that, not only is he interested in displaying the disheartening, arduous journey performers must embark on, but he possesses an affinity for infusing his characters with identifiable and credible humanity.

Back at Dandy Dan's palatial estate, Dan is further vilified when he executes one of his henchmen. In true gangster film villain fashion, Dan targets one of his cronies, who apparently made a mistake, and says that he doesn't tolerate mistakes. Instead of "killing" him with guns, however, Dan and the rest of his crew throw actual pies at him. This is a clever and interesting manner to depict that, in keeping with the sadistic, sociopathic behavior of gangster film bad guys, simply shooting someone who makes a mistake is letting them off too easy. Throwing full pies at the transgressor is Parker's wacky way of suggesting that, as opposed to shooting him, Dan subjected him to torture with some kind of blunt instrument, which was most definitely not a gun.

We then cut to another memorable Paul Williams song and dance number. In the middle of the street, a gang of four thugs sing "Bad Guys." Not only is the melody and song itself memorable, but the lyrics represent an interesting diametrical opposition to another popular musical about juvenile delinquency, *West Side Story*. In that musical, the equivalent of "Bad Guys" would probably be "Gee, Officer Krupke," in that, in each of these numbers, the lyrics delineate the explanation for the criminal behavior of the juveniles. In the *West Side Story* song, the lyrics favor a nurture-over-nature explanation for juvenile delinquency.

The blame is not placed on the boys themselves, but on their poor upbringing. This leftist sociological explanation suggests that bad people are not born bad, but are made that way through years of systematic negligence and abuse.

The lyrics of "Bad Guys," however, offer quite a different explanation for why bad kids are bad. In this song, the hoodlums sing about how much opportunity they had, and how they could have chosen to be anything they wanted to be; they simply discovered that they possess an aptitude for being bad. In other words, the kids have no one to blame but themselves, and they know it. There is no "my daddy didn't love me" rationalization for the fact that they do what they do—they are simply bad kids and they were born that way. The number itself is whimsical and lighthearted, but Parker underpins the lightheartedness with a hint of gravity by overturning the *West Side Story* paradigm of blaming a bad upbringing for juvenile delinquency in favor of a more right-wing, "everyone-is-responsible-for-their-own-actions" explanation. The fact that the hoodlums acknowledge that they had talent and opportunities, and simply chose to be hoodlums, also serves to starkly contrast Robert Warshow's assertion concerning a particularly salient paradigmatic gangster convention. Warshow states:

> Usually when we come upon [the gangster], he has already made his choice or the choice has already been made for him, it doesn't matter which: we are not permitted to ask whether at some point he could have chosen to be something else than what he is.[11]

Warshow, here, is delineating a component of the gangster, which has occurred with such generic frequency that it has become an established convention of the character of the gangster. With this song-and-dance sequence, Parker has implemented a very interesting way to subvert an established convention of the character of the gangster. Counter to what Warshow asserts, Parker does, indeed, permit us to ask whether his hoodlums could have chosen to be something other than what they are—they very explicitly explain to us that they "could have been anything they wanted to be." Parker very subtly informs us here that he is not simply cinematically regurgitating American gangster conventions and surrounding them with song-and-dance numbers; he is taking advantage of the film's revisionist aesthetic to manipulate and even overturn those very conventions.

With the next pairing of scenes, Parker again implements the technique of starkly contrasting levity with gravity. First, we're back at Fat Sam's, where Sam is again castigating his bumbling, inept group of thugs. He tells them that their guns and "hardware" are outdated and they need to get their hands on the new "splurge gun." The scene has the frenetic, fast pace of a screwball comedy, with Sam screaming and yelling comedically, yelling at "Knuckles" for cracking his knuckles, and throwing pies at his dimwitted cohorts. He then gets a phone call, alerting him to the fact that Dandy Dan is hiding his guns at the Hung Fu Shin Laundromat. He sends his boys to the laundromat, which, as it happens, turns out to be a setup, and an ambush ensues. Dandy Dan's men burst out of laundry baskets and massacre Fat Sam's boys, spraying them with a barrage of gunfire. Much like the hit in the barbershop, Parker directs this scene with stark honesty, as if we are watching an actual gangland act of violence. There is no slapstick or comedy whatsoever. Again, if the guns were firing real bullets as opposed to custard, this scene would be reminiscent of a hit from *The Godfather*. The rapid-fire editing, lack of music, and the amplified sound of gunfire are all technical devices which recall Coppola's hard-hitting, powerful scenes of violence. Once again, Parker gives us a light scene that we can laugh at, then almost immediately negates it by changing the directorial style, only to return again to levity by cutting back to Fat Sam, who has just found out about the ambush, and is venting to "Knuckles." He is flustered, animatedly thinking about what to do. He then utters a phrase in Italian, and "Knuckles" admits to not being able to understand him. Fat Sam is outraged and yells, "You don't know how to speak Italian!" "Knuckles" says that he doesn't because he is Jewish, to which Fat Sam replies, "Then read the translations!" We then cut back to "Knuckles," who looks down and sees the subtitle, which reads "Everything's Hunky Dory." With this moment of sheer lunacy, Parker takes the comedy into Mel Brooks territory, once again reminding us that, with this film, Parker is grocery shopping through the aisles of Hollywood movies, selecting whichever genre moments and conventions he deems fit.

The next scene features an interaction between Tallulah and Bugsy, but Parker implements a very interesting transition to this scene. He cuts from the Mel Brooks bit in Fat Sam's office to Fizzy despondently playing the piano. He is standing up, dejectedly hitting a few choice notes, then he picks up his broom and continues sweeping. Parker again gives us a moment in which to savor and appreciate the sometimes unfulfilling life of a performer. Fizzy *is* a performer and he can't help but be drawn to the piano during his down time. There is no dialogue, but we feel for Fizzy, and we want to see him shine. This is, yet again, a moment in which Parker takes time away from the "plot" to give us an intimate moment of introspection.

Tallulah then comes down the stairs and sits with Bugsy over a drink. The conversation that follows is an overt tribute to the steamy, torrid dialogue which populated the film noirs of the 1940s and '50s, with Tallulah fulfilling the role of the sultry, mysterious, and alluring femme fatale. She is Fat Sam's gal, but she is quite obviously flirting with Bugsy, saying things like, "I always thought you were kind of special; you're aces," and "Give a girl a break!" Like Jane Greer in *Out of the Past*, she is treading on dangerous water by flirting with a member of her own boyfriend's gang. Blousey then comes walking in and witnesses Tallulah kissing Bugsy on the forehead. She is jealous and hurt, and storms off. This moment clearly differentiates Blousey from Tallulah, assigning the dangerous yet alluring qualities to Tallulah and the wholesome qualities to Blousey. In other words, if they were characters from *Public Enemy*, Tallulah would be Joan Blondell (the confident, dangerously feline tomcat), and Blousey would be Mae Clarke (the subservient, mousey doormat).

We then cut to Blousey's audition for Fat Sam as she finally gets the opportunity to perform for him. It is of particular note, however, that Parker chooses to present this scene immediately following the moment in which Blousey catches Tallulah kissing Bugsy. She sings a heartfelt, down-tempo number called "I'm Feeling Fine." The lyrics are a forthright confession of love, and were clearly written by a timid, reserved girl who has just discovered these feelings and is earnestly hoping that the object of her affection feels the same way. However, when sung by Blousey (after having just witnessed Bugsy being kissed by another girl) the song becomes a somewhat angry, accusatory song in which the singer regrets that she ever fell in love. As she sings the song, she glowers at Bugsy, who is sitting in the front row, watching the performance; the song is her way of telling him how she feels. This is a particularly unique, effective moment. If Blousey had not seen Tallulah kissing Bugsy immediately before her performance, the song most likely would have remained an innocent disclosure of puppy love. However, having seen that heartbreaking display, Blousey cannot help but incorporate her pain into the lyrics. Parker, here, is making a very interesting comment on the nature of performance. First off, Blousey sings her confession of disappointment to Bugsy rather than speaks it. This suggests that, to Parker, although the act of singing in musicals is inherently artificial, it can somehow transcend that artifice to become an honest form of communication. Secondly, this is Parker's way of saying that the true meaning behind a performance is not that which is written on the page, but what the performer *brings* to material.

Back in Fat Sam's office, Sam is mulling over a plan to get back at Dandy Dan—payback for the laundromat massacre. He tells "Knuckles" that they are going to enlist the help of a mercenary—a hired gun named Looney Bergonzi, who is allegedly a volatile, erratic loose cannon. Cut to Bugsy fruitlessly trying to make amends with Blousey, still crestfallen at the sight of his flirtatious encounter with Tallulah. Bugsy tells her that he is trying to land himself a legit job to gather up some money so that he and Blousey can run away together, to Hollywood. Blousey is dubious of Bugsy's sincerity, and the viewer is as well. The gangster trying to go straight after pulling off "one last job" before he does so is a recurring theme, which (as fans of the genre well know) usually ends badly, with the gangster either being caught or killed. *Rififi* (1955), *Kiss of Death* (1947), and *Carlito's Way* (1993), to name a few, are all gangster films which feature this very element. However, since Parker's film is not a straight gangster story and possesses a whimsical, silly quality, the film could very well eschew this convention and supplant it with a much more innocuous, upbeat ending. Since Parker has been straddling the line between levity and gravity throughout the entire film, the audience is left wondering.

Since Sam doesn't know anyone else who drives, he offers Bugsy some money to drive him to his meeting with Dandy Dan. Bugsy agrees, and Sam then calls Dandy Dan to set up the meeting. They agree to meet out of town, and to come alone. At this point, Parker infuses an established genre convention with comedy. As *The Godfather* (which had been released just four years before *Bugsy Malone*) taught audiences, whenever two rival gangs agree to have a "civil" meeting with each other, bad things happen. Someone reneges on the truce and violence ensues. Hence, if *Bugsy Malone* were a traditional gangster film, we would fear for someone's life after each respective gangster hung up the phone. However, Parker defuses any anxiety by adding a joke. When Dandy Dan hangs up, he says, "Got 'im, the knucklehead." We then cut to Fat Sam hanging up, saying, "Got 'im, the salami."

We then cut back to the nightclub, where Tallulah is onstage, performing "My Name is Tallulah." Here, Parker demonstrates his aptitude for deftly handling difficult material. The song is a sensual, slinky nightclub number, and as she sings, Tallulah mingles with the crowd, caressing the "men's" faces. Tallulah then seductively leans against the wall with one arm in the air, in what could be construed as a sexually inviting gesture. After having watched this scene, one is reminded of Rita Hayworth singing "Put the Blame on Mame" in *Gilda* to a crowd of lecherous nightclub patrons. Having Tallulah (being played by a twelve-year-old Jodie Foster) perform such a borderline lusty number could easily be deemed as unsavory and completely inappropriate. However, Parker deftly handles the material, knowing just how to walk the line between cute and prurient, acceptable and unacceptable. Tallulah engages in just the right amount of touching and swaying so as to suggest adult-themed subject matter without crossing the line into gratuitous sexualization. The scene actually feels more akin to a nightclub scene in a Tex Avery cartoon, in which the wolf's eyes bug out of his head and his tongue rolls out of his mouth like a carpet as he swoons over a sexy nightclub performer.

Next, we cut to the meeting of Dandy Dan and Fat Sam. It is in the country somewhere, and as we see Dandy Dan's car pulling up, we see that the driver is powering the vehicle by pedaling, like a bicycle. Dan tentatively gets out of his car, and he and Fat Sam have an uneasy, tension-filled discussion. At one point, Sam wags a finger at Dan and says, "You're a dirty rat, Dan," to which Dan replies, "You've been watching too many movies, Sam." Like the *On the Waterfront* quote that came before it, this moment serves to remind us that we are in a post-modern, revisionist narrative. In the cultural lexicon, "You dirty rat" is the signature catch phrase of James Cagney (although, ironically, he never actually said the phrase in any of his films). This exchange is yet another wry wink at the audience, reaffirming that the film is an amalgamation of conventional genre moments.

At the end of the discussion, Sam signals to Looney, who emerges from behind the car, armed with a green-colored pie in each hand (the green color ostensibly signifies that Looney, who has been set up as violent, erratic, and mad, kills his victims in a more exotic, "colorful" manner than Sam). However, Dan, prepared for the double-cross, summons his backup, and a horde of hoodlums descend upon Sam's car, spraying Looney, "killing" him. Bugsy thinks fast, helms the wheel, and drives Fat Sam away to safety, but not before a comedic car-chase sequence occurs. Again, the scene is handled in such a way as to suggest that, if this were a traditional gangster film, Parker would have no problem directing this particular genre moment with aptitude. He builds the tension by cutting back and forth between Bugsy and Sam and Dandy Dan's vehicle, implementing quick cuts and a shaky-cam shot from Bugsy's point of view just as he is about to crash into another car. In other words, if this scene needed to be hard-hitting, exciting, or brutal (in keeping with the ethos of most traditional gangster film chases), Parker would have had no problem. However, since we are in a cross-genre, revisionist film with a whimsical edge, Parker effectively infuses the scene with comedy. As Bugsy is fleeing his pursuers, he drives the car through an open barn. The audience sees the car enter the barn from one side, then re-emerge on the other side, covered in chicken feathers and sawdust. This screwball moment of slapstick is strongly reminiscent of the zaniness of the car chase in *The Bank Dick*. As we watch Bugsy's car emerge from the barn, covered in chicken feathers, we can almost hear W. C. Fields uttering a snide one-liner.

Infinitely grateful for having rescued him from certain doom, Fat Sam endows Bugsy with money, and tells him to get a nice suit. We then cut to a very pensive Blousey, sitting and staring off into space in the dressing room of Fat Sam's. Parker then cuts to Blousey's dream sequence, in which she envisions herself in Hollywood, performing in a silent film. This scene's effectiveness is twofold. First, it reaffirms Parker's penchant for depicting the performance process. Again, he is giving us a glimpse into the desires and struggles of someone yearning to perform and be appreciated for it. Secondly, it demonstrates a nostalgic tribute to American movies, augmenting the idea that this film is not so much concerned with commenting on American mores or ideologies as it is with commenting on American movies themselves. However, by doing so within the framework of a dream sequence, in which a character is experiencing a deep desire and yearning, Parker again demonstrates that, irrespective of the film's postmodernist, self-aware revisionism, devotion to character and the struggles they face is of the utmost importance to him.

Next is a sweet, playful montage of Bugsy and Blousey driving through the country, having fun and enjoying each other's company. The montage is set to the title song "Bugsy Malone," and it is redolent of the "Raindrops Keep Fallin' On My Head" sequence in *Butch Cassidy and the Sundance Kid*, in which Paul Newman gives Katharine Ross a ride on his bicycle. That scene possesses a sweet, carefree innocence and romance, and Parker implements a similar style to visually depict Bugsy and Blousey frolicking in the meadow of puppy love. Bugsy then reassures Blousey that he is going to use the money Fat Sam gave him to buy two tickets to Hollywood. Blousey is, of course, ecstatic, but in the next scene, Bugsy is mugged in a back alley and his money is stolen. A stalwart boy named Leroy Smith (played by Paul Murphy) comes to Bugsy's rescue and roughs up the attackers. Impressed by Leroy's fighting ability, Bugsy, now broke, agrees to train Leroy to be a boxer and become his manager. This moment shifts us back into noir territory, and Bugsy's smooth talking as he convinces Leroy to become a fighter is reminiscent of Richard Widmark's character Harry Fabian from Jules Dassin's *Night and the City*. In Dassin's film, Fabian is a two-bit hustler who attempts to take control of the professional wrestling game. However, as Fabian's plans go wrong, he manages to burn every bridge and effectively irritate the wrong people. The film is gritty, dark, and tension-filled, and by echoing Fabian's character in this manner with Bugsy, Parker is again reminding us of the possibility that, although this is a comedy, things may not work out for Bugsy and Blousey.

After a montage of newspaper headlines proclaiming that the gang war is still raging, we cut to Bugsy showing Leroy around a gym, fraught with would-be boxers working out and training. Parker again displays his affinity for spending time with characters as they train or prepare for an audition. Leroy must "audition" for the fight promoter to prove that he has what it takes, and Leroy's audition is set to an upbeat musical number called "So You Want to Be a Boxer?" Leroy, of course, demolishes his sparring partner and Bugsy and the promoter both believe they have discovered a potentially valuable contender.

Fat Sam sends Tallulah to retrieve Bugsy, as Sam has a proposition for him. While Sam waits for Bugsy to arrive, Parker brings us squarely back into comedy territory. First, Sam throws water in the bartender's face after having been insulted by him, then, in a moment of sheer slapstick, Sam slips and falls on the floor, which is wet due to Fizzy's mop job. Sam then chases Fizzy around the dance floor, like Elmer Fudd chasing Bugs Bunny.

When Bugsy arrives, Sam asks Bugsy to help him fight his battle against Dandy Dan. Bugsy is hesitant at first, but Sam offers him a substantial amount of money, which ultimately convinces him. Blousey then calls him and asks if they're still leaving for Hollywood. In keeping with the gangster in the heist film who wants to pull off "one last job" before he escapes with his girl to paradise, Bugsy tells her that there's one more thing he has to take care of before they leave. Blousey is heartbroken and disappointed, which segues into her somber, downtrodden solo number "Ordinary Fool," in which she sings about her unfortunate predilection for always thinking with her heart and paying the price for it. While she sings this heart-wrenching song, Blousey flashes back to the carefree montage of she and Bugsy having fun, only this time the montage is bittersweet, as Blousey is heartbroken, regretting that she ever fell for him. Once again, Parker inserts an emotionally powerful scene fraught with pathos into an otherwise lighthearted, whimsical narrative, a testament to his ability to expertly straddle the line between sincerity and silliness.

After doing some reconnaissance with Leroy at Dandy Dan's splurge gun factory, Bugsy sees that the factory is heavily guarded. In order to infiltrate it, they are going to have to recruit some help, which they decide to do at a soup kitchen. In a rousing, galvanizing number—sung by Bugsy—called "Down and Out," Bugsy convinces the impoverished, starving men at the kitchen, who were clearly ravaged by the economic strain of the Great Depression, to help him and Leroy infiltrate the splurge gun factory.

The "Down and Out" scene is of particular interest in that it, once again, displays Parker's ability to infuse a lighthearted narrative with moments of hard-hitting gravity. The film takes place during the Great Depression, which forced millions of Americans out of their jobs and into soup kitchens. Not wanting to simply gloss over this catastrophic piece of history, Parker allows the audience to see the harsh reality of the Depression. Although the film is, overall, a musical-comedy (and the soup kitchen sequence itself is a musical number), Parker again demonstrates his ability to juggle levity and gravity.

Also of note in the "Down and Out" sequence is that the lyrics to the song are surprisingly conservative. Bugsy sings about not wallowing in misfortune, and mustering the temerity to get back out in the workforce. There's a pick-yourself-up-by-your-bootstraps air to the lyrics, which in some ways, mirrors the sentiment put forth by the lyrics to "Bad Guys." *Bugsy Malone* could hardly be described as a political film, but it is noteworthy that, at least as it pertains to the issues of poverty and juvenile delinquency, the lyrics in the musical numbers seem to veer strongly to the right on the political spectrum, championing the notion of self-sufficiency.

Cut to the heist, in which Babyface (one of the indigents from the soup kitchen, played by Dexter Fletcher) creates a diversion, allowing Bugsy and crew to steal the splurge guns, which they transport back to Fat Sam's, where they anxiously await the arrival of Dandy Dan's gang. This leads us to the film's finale, in which Dandy Dan's gang bursts into Fat Sam's, precipitating a cataclysmic firefight. *Every* person in Fat Sam's, at some point, is walloped by flying custard as "bullets" and pies fly all over the place. The scene plays like the climactic shootout of *The Wild Bunch*, if that film featured custard instead of bullets. At one point during the fracas, Fat Sam, covered from head to toe in white sludge, states, "This is getting ridiculous." In a way, this line serves, in a Brechtian way, to remind us of the overt accentuation of artifice which has permeated the entire film. For the first time in the film, the characters themselves seem to step out of their respective narrative functions to objectively examine the silliness in which they have been partaking for the last hour and a half. Then, suddenly, everyone simply stops dead in their tracks as Razamataz starts playing the piano and singing "You Give a Little Love." The song is a reprise of "Bad Guys" with revised lyrics, this time suggesting that the two gangs stop fighting and forge a friendship. During this boisterous musical number, the rival gangs make amends and shake one another's hands. It culminates with everyone in Fat Sam's singing in unison, joining together in harmony to celebrate that they are ending their reactionary war in favor of camaraderie and friendship. This finale feels, in a way, as though this is Parker's goofy way of having the actors do a curtain call following the play so that they can be recognized for their performances.

This ending seems a bit abrupt and startling at first. There is nothing to foreshadow its arrival, and it seems antithetical to both Dandy Dan's and Fat Sam's obdurate vendetta against one another. However, although it may be unprecedented narratively, tonally it makes sense. From the outset, Parker invited us into a world of artifice and Brechtian postmodernism. Although the film is interspersed with moments of gravity and, at times, hard-hitting realism (which would become a hallmark of Parker's style), the whimsicality of the material prevailed.

3

Midnight Express, 1978

October 6; 121 minutes/Color
Production Company: Columbia & Casablanca Filmworks
Director: Alan Parker
Screenwriter: Oliver Stone, based on the book by Billy Hayes (with William Hoffer)
Producers: Peter Guber (Executive Producer), Alan Marshall, David Putnam
Production Designer: Geoffrey Kirkland
Cinematographer: Michael Seresin
Editor: Gerry Hambling
Original Music: Giorgio Morodor
Cast: Brad Davis (Billy Hayes); Irene Miracle (Susan), Bo Hopkins ("Tex"); Paolo Bonicelli (Rifki); Paul L. Smith (Hamidou); Randy Quaid (Jimmy Booth); John Hurt (Max); Mike Kellin (Mr. Hayes); Norbert Weisser (Erich)

> The raw energy and voice of the film, its uncompromising visceral power, still remains as fresh and modern as a piece of filmmaking today.[1]—Alan Parker

> I already know that you are a bad machine. That's why the factory keeps you here. You know how I know? I know because I'm *from* the factory. I make the machines!—Billy Hayes to Ahmet in Section 13 for the Criminally Insane

Notes on the Production

According to Alan Parker, his second feature film *Midnight Express*, was "a reaction against making the more pragmatic *Bugsy Malone*."[2] It became the type of film he was destined to create—an emotionally charged prison drama that more closely resembled the types of films he had written and directed in Great Britain.

After the success of the Hollywood genre parody *Bugsy Malone*, Parker met with Universal Studio executives who wanted him to direct a film version of the musical *The Wiz* (a project that would later be given to Sidney Lumet). After "politely [passing] on the project," Parker soon afterwards came into contact with producer Peter Guber on the sidewalk of Fifth Avenue just as he was exiting the Columbia building. He told Parker that he was involved in the beginning stages of a film project about the Billy Hayes story, the American who had spent five years in a Turkish prison for attempting to smuggle hashish out of Istanbul back to the United States. Hayes (along with William Hoffer) had written a book about his experiences, published by Popular Library (a unit of CBS Publications) in 1977, and was dedicated to Hayes's father. It became a best seller, and since its publication, the story has gone through a number of permutations—including Oliver Stone's adaptation, Parker's

3. Midnight Express, *1978* 41

Billy Hayes (Brad Davis), in a rage, gets ready to ambush a fellow prisoner who framed another prisoner for the possession of hashish. *Midnight Express* **(1978), Columbia and Casablanca Filmworks.**

direction and recently the real Billy Hayes's version of the story on the cable series *Locked-Up Abroad: The Real Midnight Express* (also note that Parker did not choose to cast a Billy Hayes look-alike; Brad Davis had dark features whereas Hayes has blond, curly hair and blue eyes). The following quote from Alan Parker addresses a few of these inevitable changes, which we will address in detail later.

> The caption "Based on a True Story" [was] misleading. Certainly it is *based* on a true story. But that didn't mean it was true. It had gone through too many hands and minds with too many agendas for it to be really true. What is *truth* anyway, with such a project? Billy Hayes was caught smuggling drugs and was convicted. Unreliable memory (which we all have) is probably responsible for moving away from the truth—as was his own hubris. He escaped with some notoriety and sat down with a ghostwriter, William Hoffer, who added his literary slant to the story to satisfy the publishing needs. Oliver Stone wrote his screenplay and undoubtedly moved further away from the original truth adding his own unique slant to the proceedings. Then there were the exigencies of the studio and the producers' own agenda.... I then did my version of the story when I made the film and I moved it even further away creating the world of as mythical Billy Hayes as I had imagined it and considerably changing the ending.... The beauty of film is that it is a totally organic process.[3]

Peter Guber had been discussing a partnership with David Puttnam (coincidentally Alan Parker's partner in the commercial business and the executive producer of *Bugsy Mal-*

one) in his new company, Casablanca Filmworks, which, along with Columbia Pictures, would become the production companies for *Midnight Express*. Eventually, Parker agreed to the project and, before long, he was once again working with Alan Marshall, who, from this moment forward, became his collaborator.[4]

Parker first met Oliver Stone in Los Angeles (at the time Stone was a novice screenwriter who had been hired to adapt Hayes's book into a film). Although Stone had no screen credits, he showed immense promise, having written a number of impressive unproduced screenplays, one of these a Vietnam drama that would, in less than a decade, become the Oscar-winning *Platoon* (1986). Stone's first draft of *Midnight Express*, which he wrote in London in April 1977, was, according to Parker: "edgy, uncompromising, succinct, full of rage and with a cinematic energy that tore through the pages like an express train from hell. None of us had ever read a screenplay like it."[5] According to Oliver Stone, "I think that Billy Hayes is a sympathetic character, a hero even. It's the story of how he overcomes his victimization ... it's based on the classic underdog theme."[6] All in all, the project certainly adhered to Parker's vision and philosophy that films must be emotional, organic experiences—and it was a much more mature project, a very different turn from the Hollywood genre parody he had just directed.

In the spring of 1977, Parker, along with casting director Penny Perry, began searching for an actor to play Billy Hayes. Initially the studio favored Richard Gere, who was hot at the box office after starring in *Looking for Mr. Goodbar* (1977, Richard Brooks) and *Days of Heaven* (1978, Terrence Malick). What Parker found with Gere, however, was something less impressive: the actor refused to read for the part of Billy Hayes; he told the director that he did not like cold reading auditions. Eventually, Brad Davis (who acted in the very successful and critically acclaimed 1970s TV miniseries *Sybil* and *Roots*) became a contender and consequently would be the one to win the part. According to Davis's wife, Susan Bluestein Davis, who wrote *After Midnight: The Life and Death of Brad Davis* (Davis died of complications leading to AIDS in 1991 at the untimely age of forty-one), *Midnight Express* was "the kind of success that launched several Hollywood careers," her husband's included. "[It] turned newcomer Alan Parker into a bankable director, gave a little-known screenwriter named Oliver Stone credibility and elevated the career of British character actor John Hurt."[7] For the part of Billy Hayes, Parker envisioned "a non-familiar face with plenty of raw energy," so despite the studio's interest in the seemingly disinterested Richard Gere, Davis, who would land the part, appeared to have Parker's vote early on in the casting process.[8]

On September 12, 1977, the fifty-three-day shooting schedule for *Midnight Express* began in the south European country Malta in the Mediterranean—a substitute for Istanbul. Parker considered himself fortunate to be working with experienced crew members who had worked with him in commercials in London.[9]

In post-production, Parker's friend Hugh Hudson (one of his former commercial-making partners) had suggested to him composer Vangelis Papathanassiou, with whom Parker and the crew were extremely pleased. When Parker wanted to further experiment with other musicians, the head of Casablanca Filmworks, Neil Bogart, suggested Giorgio Morodor, who produced disco queen Donna Summer records (Casablanca was originally a studio that produced music). Morodor came aboard and experimented with electronic sounds, quite a shift from the traditional orchestrated scores that had defined many Hollywood movies of that time, especially in the era of John Williams (*Jaws, Close Encounters of the Third Kind*, et al). Parker liked what Morodor was doing and consequently the composer was hired—and his now-signature soundtrack for *Midnight Express* went on to win an Oscar.[10]

Midnight Express was screened at the Cannes Film Festival in May 1978, to mixed reviews, especially from the British and French press (the French would later warm up to it): the film was seen as a "masterpiece" by some and by others, a "CIA-backed U.S. fascist scandal of the festival."[11] In addition to Morodor's score, Stone's screenplay won an Oscar. Alan Parker notes: "To this day the Turkish government is still irked by the film. After all these years you'd think they'd have got used to it."[12]

Summary

Anxiety and distress begin immediately following the appearance of the production company logo. The sound of a machine gun firing and what sounds like a woman muttering something horrific in Turkish, juxtaposed with Giorgio Morodor's piercing electronic score, the sound and image of hovering seagulls (like birds circling a carcass) and the image of Istanbul, Turkey, in the background, all indicate that even before any of the action begins, the viewer has entered a surreal nightmare. In fact, even the title *Midnight Express* (which is later revealed to be the prison term for escape) suggests a horror movie, and as the film unfolds, the viewer will realize that although the film claims to be "based on a true story," it is, in fact, a highly stylized, expressionistic, Kafkaesque descent into madness, replete with Gothic, grotesque characters who resemble the likes of Quasimodo and Dracula. In addition to the characteristics of this dystopian milieu, a quick glimpse of Istanbul from afar reveals the country as an industrial wasteland—a real factory (a theme that will become prominent as the movie progresses). Following this image is a brief montage of the sordid country—a dilapidated world infested by the expressionless zombie-like inhabitants who are seen smoking, sleeping and mindlessly existing. They are all human machines, products of the factory ... and of industrialization.

A quick cut reveals an unseen person with cloth bandages, wrapping something around his body. Then a closer shot shows a series of square objects encased in a tinfoil material as well as an open suitcase with a Frisbee sticking out of it. Rapid heartbeats commence (according to the DVD film commentary, Parker says that this was the first time that heartbeats as sound effects were successfully used as means of creating suspense).[13] A blurred image comes into focus: It is a close-up of Billy Hayes (Brad Davis), looking at himself in a bathroom mirror while contemplating his next move, which is to exit the bathroom and re-enter the airport terminal.

The next shot reveals Yesilkoy International Airport (the viewer sees the sign on which is printed TURK HAVA YOLLARI) and another mini-montage of the people and the surroundings begins (if you look closely, you can spot Alan Parker in one of these shots). As mentioned earlier, this is not Turkey at all; it's Malta—and in the scene (and throughout the film) the "Turkish" language that we are hearing is actually a hybrid of several languages, ranging from Turkish to Maltese to Italian.[14] Although many critics might impugn the authenticity of the film because Turkish is not the primary language, the point wasn't necessarily to be truly authentic; the real purpose was to single out an American in a foreign environment. The absence of subtitles in the film helps the English-speaking viewers sympathize with Billy's xenophobia.

Next, Billy is observed smoking a cigarette as he nervously looks around the airport, giving way to another mini-montage, making a transition to Billy's girlfriend Susan (Irene Miracle, who, along with Paul Smith, were not actors with whom Davis enjoyed working).[15] One of the major differences between the book and the film was that in the book there is no girlfriend, Susan; instead, in the opening of the story, Hayes was alone, "stood up" by a belly-dancing English girl whom he met in Turkey.[16]

When we first see Susan, she is looking into a bird cage. Is this visual foreshadowing, something that will soon become Billy's fate? The caged bird motif is ever-present in many prison films, ranging from *Birdman of Alcatraz* (1962, John Frankenheimer) to *Escape from Alcatraz* (1979, Donald Siegel). Later on in the film, when he is being chased at the bazaar, he knocks over a chicken in a cage, which further maps out his fate of ending up behind bars.

When Billy and Susan meet up, she is immediately aware of his disposition. "Nervous?" she asks him. He responds by telling her his stomach hurts, that he thinks he has been "poisoned" by the *baklavas* he ate earlier (this line becomes one of many critiques against Turkey). He tells her he needs to use the bathroom and asks her if she'll wait for him, assuring her that he will be back soon. "Okay? Okay?" he thunders at her, anxiety-driven. She nods and replies, "Okay." She knows something is not right.

Back in the bathroom Billy revisits his reflection in the mirror. The heartbeats continue and intensify. He breathes deeply a number of times, checks the position of the hashish, making sure it is secure, and returns to the airport terminal where security officers check his bags—a scene of unrelenting suspense built through abrupt shot juxtapositions, intensified by the heartbeats and shots of Billy anxiously attempting to move onward to meet up with Susan. The security officer takes out the Frisbee and asks Billy (in Turkish) what it is. When Billy answers, the officer doesn't understand him; Billy tries to explain to him that Frisbee is a throw-catch game. Another officer informs him (in their native language) that Frisbee is an "American game." The officer smirks and smacks the Frisbee against the bag, then places it back in, as if critiquing the stupidity of America. This scenario, plus the ongoing language barrier from Billy's perspective (words like "Chantra" that have no meaning to the protagonist are spoken repeatedly) continue to heighten Billy's xenophobia. The officer then motions for Billy to remove his sunglasses and, when Billy does so, he sees and studies the sweat collecting around the American's eyes. He feels Billy's rapid heartbeat, which the viewer hears clearly. Abruptly, the officer lets him go, which provides the film with its first major cathartic release (from this moment forward, the film is a series of these types of captured/release actions, another example of how Alan Parker successfully manipulates his viewers' visceral expectations). Billy runs toward the bus and just as the door is about to close, he slips in just in time, making his way toward Susan.

Susan is reading the *Herald Tribune*, dated October 6, 1970, and the headline reads: "NIXON OUTRAGED AT PALESTINIAN HIAJCKERS: CALLS FOR CAPITAL PUNISHMENT." Screenwriter Oliver Stone does two things with this detail: first, he provides exposition for international terrorism and, second, he paints Nixon as a mythical villain in the film, the main culprit who eventually causes Billy to get life in prison. In a later scene, Mr.

Hayes tells his son that "Nixon has upset the hell out of [the Turks]." The Nixon administration made foreign aid dependent on a ban on opium poppy growing, which, naturally, outraged Turkish farmers; consequently, the Turks wanted pressure applied to the U.S. and, according to the Turkish Ankara Court, penalties from drug offenders would be enforced, especially to Americans found with drugs.[17] In a way, this moment serves as historical context and a foreshadowing, linking terrorism with the International Drug Trade Wars. And in less than a year after Billy's arrest, Nixon officially declared *his* war on drugs, which he referred to as "our number one enemy."[18] Although this film has been controversial because of how it represented the Turks, it is also curious that President Richard Nixon was portrayed to be just as evil as the Turks who were abusing Billy. But, by 1978, Nixon was already deemed a "crook" and the first U.S president ever forced to resign from office because of foul play, so perhaps he was seen as a threat to the United States and therefore re-examining his crooked politics only reminded the world of how "un–American" he was. Incidentally, several days after Stone returned from Vietnam he was busted for marijuana in Nixon's border war in Mexico. As Stone recalls, "I was thrown back in the tank in San Diego. Federal charge, smuggling, five to twenty years. And I was just back from Vietnam, right? I was really pissed off. That's the way they treat the vets?"[19]

The political news, however, is overridden by the latest popular culture flash: Janice Joplin's death, which Billy trivializes as he fondles Susan. "You never take anything seriously, do you?" she asks. Billy, smiling, says, "Nothing," but is then immediately startled by what he sees outside as the bus slows down: a large swarm of officers … the lighting in the scene switches from moderately high-key to an expressionistic nightmarish low-key and high-contrast tone. Another short montage follows, including a shot of an officer aggressively and rapidly approaching the screen, captured in an extreme low-angle perspective, emphasizing his looming prominence. In this moment, Susan becomes a critic of the country by asking, "Is everything always *ass-backward* in Turkey?"

The officers order everyone off the bus—and Billy, whose mood has drastically shifted again, demands that Susan get on the plane. He is left alone on the bus frantically trying to discard the hashish, but when he is approached by a guard (whose stoic disposition emulates that of an SS officer) points a gun at his head, Billy makes it look as though he has been searching for his passport all along. In the background, we hear another "ugly American" response as the voice of a woman facetiously says: "Harry, you better get rid of those grenades."

As Susan heads toward the plane, Billy, amidst the chaos, slips past the officers, taking the contents out of his bag, then puts them back in to make it look as though he has already been searched. He walks toward the plane rapidly, not making eye contact with anyone, and just as he is about to step foot on the plane—a hand grabs his shoulder, stopping him in his tracks. This moment is juxtaposed with Morodor's piercing electronic score, indicating Billy's doom. An officer searches him, discovering that there is something under his clothes. *Is it a bomb?* The officers aim their guns at Billy, who has no other choice but to raise his hands (this is the image that is most associated with the film). This scene, more or less, happened the way it happened in reality. According to Hayes, "I had my foot in the air, ready to step onto the plane."

As the officer inches his way back to the distressed Billy, he discovers that they are all safe. Then he laughs and in a foreign tongue says something that might translate thus: "He's not a terrorist; it's only hashish!" Morodor's haunting and memorable electronic piano theme commences—a series of individual notes in various minor key variations, a *leitmotif* that throughout the film signals the harrowing fate of Billy Hayes. Meanwhile, Susan, pathetically helpless, looks down on Billy as she boards the plane with tears in her eyes. Billy looks at her and shakes his head, indicating that there is nothing she can do but get on the plane and go home. He is taken away.

The next scene begins the investigation following Billy's arrest: a short montage of Turkish officers scrutinizing Billy's belongings (one of Billy's pieces of luggage is a product-placement Marlboro bag). In these few minutes a good deal occurs: The Turks are immediately portrayed as buffoons, clowns and trickster authority figures (not unlike Billy Wilder's depiction of the Nazis in the 1953 POW film *Stalag 17*): They argue with one another and speak rapidly and neurotically, all of which is highlighted by the use of a handheld camera, which gives this section of the film a more authentic documentary-style feel—and when Billy reveals the last of the hashish in the bottom of his boot that the Turkish officials failed to confiscate, the lead officer slaps the others in the face as if he were Moe Howard of the Three Stooges. Also, when Billy is strip-searched, standing there naked, two officers "make eyes" at him, indicating they like what they see. The low-key lighting, which reveals a peculiar mix of green, blue and dark-gray hues in the background of this unappealing place, suggests a dirty, cold dampness.

The horrors of this foreign world are temporarily relieved by the abrupt introduction to a new character who greets the prisoner: "Howdy, Billy," he says gracefully. This is Tex (Bo Hopkins), a tall "Texas cowboy" type who, at this stage, serves as a sort of symbol for America. At first, Tex is soothing, even nurturing, as he places his hand on Billy's shoulder and tells him that "the officers are finished for the time being."

In the next scene, beginning with an extreme close-up of an obese Turkish man, another grotesque being (this becomes a common representation of Turkish authority figures throughout the film) putting sugar cubes in a cup of tea. This is a chief officer, explaining what the next step will be; Tex serves as the translator. The officer wants to know where Billy obtained the hashish. Billy informs them that it was from a cab driver at the bazaar. When asked if he would recognize the driver again, Billy says, "I think so." In this moment, yet another vision of hope prevails, a hope that will eventually be shattered because of other circumstances.

During the car ride to the bazaar, Tex talks to Billy. During this exchange, his character serves as an archetypal guide, like the poet Virgil who leads Dante through the depths of purgatory in *The Divine Comedy*. He informs him that he has chosen a bad time to travel on Turkish airlines, that there are guerrillas all over the place, blowing places up... This broken conversation is juxtaposed with images of the sordid country as they drive down narrow streets, overpopulated by masses of people. The tight closed-framing composition of the *mise-en-scène* suggests to the viewer that Billy is already in a prison. Moreover, Tex further explains to Billy about how Turks love catching foreigners with drugs: "It shows the world they're fighting a drug trade." When Billy asks him if he is with the consulate, Tex, looking away from him, responds ambiguously, practically cryptically: "Something like that." What does that mean? The American "cowboy" appears to be just another character in his nightmare, someone who may symbolize aspects of America, but someone who is certainly not on his side. He's a symbol, perhaps of temptation—someone charming and dangerous. And in the back seat, an unnamed man sits reading a newspaper. *Who is he? An officer?*

At the bazaar, the Turkish world is again revealed and it's not in the least bit appealing. The low-key, foggy lighting highlights this expressionistic-like nightmare through the underworld. Cut to shots of remote, zombie-like people within this industrial wasteland, many of them smoking cigarettes and appearing to be disconnected from their environs; they are mindless machines within the factory of industrial Istanbul (again, a theme that is explored throughout the film). As Billy sits in the bazaar (it's curious that Tex and the other officers let him sit at a table alone, as if they are testing him). A number of shots, in montage fashion, build rapidly as Billy bites his nails and looks around, realizing there might be a possibility to escape. Alas, the decision has been made, for better or for worse; he is going to flee the scene—and thus begins his first escape attempt through the harried streets of the bazaar.

As Billy runs from the Turkish officers who are almost immediately on his trail, he is led to a chicken slaughterhouse where he momentarily hides; he watches a butcher decapitating a chicken and in a panic he tips over one of the cages, revealing his location (more foreshadowing, indicating that he, too, will soon be a caged bird): Giorgio Morodor's exciting disco soundtrack begins (the piece is called "The Chase," which went on to become a popular 1970s single) and this segment unfolds like a music video, a style that Parker would perfect throughout his canon with films like *Fame, Pink Floyd—The Wall* and *Evita*.

Billy continues to run up a spiral staircase that surrounds what looks like a low-income housing project. Despite the location, the scene is exquisitely shot, using extreme high and low angles as well as high-contrast lighting. The scene slows down dramatically here: Billy appears to have lost his chasers; the music fades to ambient sounds of melting water that may be falling from gutters, and a poor-looking old woman opens her window from the inside. He is officially removed from the mayhem of the bazaar. As he ascends farther, he stops his pursuit and smiles (*I've made it*, he thinks). There is a cathartic release for a short beat ... until he turns into a gun pointing at his head. It is Tex, an ironic symbol of the western American hero, who almost mythically appears there, yet he is anything but a reassuring presence of home; he is the antithesis of Americana—again a sort of devil figure tempting his prey. Tex speaks: "You seem like a nice enough kid, Billy, but try it, and I'll blow your fucking brains out!" Billy's stupidity dooms him again (and it won't be the last time).

Abruptly, Billy is brought into his new world—the Sagmalicar prison. Note how frequently Parker creates these abrupt transitions; already in less than a half hour, the viewer has been dragged along with Billy in a series of false starts and sudden twists of fate. At this point, the viewer has experienced a highly stylized self-contained film, replete with a beginning, a middle and an end. According to Parker, "It's very fashionable to talk about visual style, but I really do care how my films look. Technically [with *Midnight Express*] I don't think I could do better."[20] Furthermore, in the words of Hacker and Price: "[Parker] places a strong emphasis on lighting to help create the desired mood. His Gothic imagination often manifests itself in his strong use of beams of light which fall through windows, often at acute angles, diffused by bars and grills."[21] This is true not only in *Midnight Express* (which lends itself to this type of expressionism), but in a number of other films like *Birdy, Angel Heart* and *Angela's Ashes*, all films where lighting is, undoubtedly, its own idiosyncratic character.

Once Billy is imprisoned, the film's narrative moves in many different directions. As the camera captures the Turkish architecture of the prison (it is both sordid and [somehow] aesthetically pleasing), Billy's voice-over is heard as he narrates a letter to his parents: "Dear Mom and Dad: This is hardest letter I've had to write.... But what can I say? Will 'I'm sorry' ease the pain you must be feeling?" The rapid pace has slowed down and for the first time in the film the viewer is able to identify and sympathize with Billy's personal plight.

When Billy is finally put into his cell (his buzz-cut haircut has drastically changed his identity) he encounters Rifki (Italian actor Paolo Bonicelli, who a few years earlier starred in the harrowing fascist torture film *Salo* [1975, Paolo Pier Pasolini]), a grotesque prisoner who is later revealed as one of the informers who works closely with the prison authorities. Rifki is certainly a monster in his own right, a sort of Quasimodo. When Billy asks him for a blanket because he is cold, the camera moves to a close-up on the glass-eyed Rifki (Bonicelli actually has a glass eye), who tells him he can't have one tonight ... but tomorrow. He sadistically adds: "You will be here tomorrow, I think."

Billy, alone in his cell, hears another prisoner in the next cell who informs him that his cell door is unlocked and that there are extra blankets in one of the adjacent cells. Consequently, Billy gets a blanket for himself and the other prisoner. The scene is shot in an eerie, low-key lighting style that resembles the type of film stock someone would see in a low-budget independent film of the era (incidentally, the film's budget was an astonishingly low $2.7 million).[22]

Another abrupt shift: Billy is awakened suddenly by Rifki punching him. The disoriented Hayes is blindfolded and taken below, the "underworld" of Sagmalicar, where he meets his shadow archetype, the brutish chief guard/warden Hamidou (Paul Smith). He speaks to Billy in Turkish, then touching his own cheek almost erotically with the back of his hand, extends his hand to Billy's face, knocking the naïve prisoner to the floor. The character of Hamidou is actually a composite of the characters of Hamid (the chief guard known as "The Bear," who carries a gun) and Mamur (the second director of the prison).

In another abrupt cut we are watching Billy being pulled up from his feet by some kind of a pulley torture device and Hamidou beats his feet with a club. The real Billy Hayes said that this pain was so horrific that he really thought he was being killed.[23] Parker met Israeli-American actor Smith in New York during casting calls; apparently Smith was very aggressive during the filming; he took his performance so seriously that at times he even inflicted pain on the actors. For example, he broke Bonicelli's false teeth and ripped facial hair out of John Hurt's chin.[24] Several times throughout the film, the fierce Hamidou is seen sweating, which, according to Parker, was real.

Next, an extreme low-angle shot looks up at the empowered Hamidou who, after beating the prisoner, stands with his legs spread wide and looks down at him. The viewer knows that Billy has encountered a dangerous, sexually aggressive character.

The following day, broken light filters through the dark prison (a good example of chiaroscuro that complements the aforementioned quotation by Hacker and Price regarding Parker's use of lighting). The camera pans and reveals Jimmy (Randy Quaid) and Erich (Norbert Weisser), who help Billy to his feet. "You must stand," Erich says. Jimmy informs him that he had been out for days "talking all kinds of shit." During this exchange, Billy hears the Turkish phrase *getchmis olsun*, which means "may it pass quickly." (This is another foreshadowing device that is mentioned again later in reference to Billy's final thirty-year sentence.)

Outside in the *kogus:* This sequence serves as exposition for the viewer as Billy is being led through the area by these two men who may be viewed as his alter-egos. Billy, the protagonist is the *ego;* the sporadic Jimmy Booth (whom Erich has characterized as having "more balls than brains") is the *id;* and the gentle-minded, optimistic, hopeful Scandinavian Erich is Billy's nurturing conscience, his *superego*. During this time, Billy witnesses the new world and the viewer learns quite a bit in just a few moments. He watches prisoners play volleyball, wrestle, drink tea, etc. In the background, the enigmatic piercing screeches of peacocks are audible (peacocks were used in place of watchdogs because, according to Jimmy, "They scream like mad and don't give rabies"). Here, he learns about Rifki, "the squealer" who "will do anything for a buck." Additionally, Billy's alter-egos give him their philosophies on life on the inside. Erich says that sometimes the law is wrong. Angrily, Jimmy responds to Erich's optimism: "The law is never wrong, asshole! The fucking law *is*!" Perhaps this statement can speak to the unjust legal system. After all, Jimmy was only a petty thief who stole two candlesticks at a Mosque; he is not a killer, but maybe it was the penal system itself that brought out his worst qualities. The dichotomy of hope and doom tug at Billy as if he were communicating with his own personal angel and devil. In the 1930 George Hill prison film *The Big House*, the warden tells the incoming prisoners: "Prison does not give a man a yellow streak, but if he has one, it can bring it out." Jimmy's stupidity is a reminder that Billy's own stupidity must be kept in check. And Erich is a symbol of hope, a "Pandora" motif that would be utilized in later prison films, including *The Shawshank Redemption* (1994, Frank Darabont). Erich is also a *herald* archetype who leads Billy to the next phase of his journey, to the *mentor* Max, the veteran prisoner of seven years, a character who, according to Erich, can provide the newcomer with some "prison wisdom."

This portion ends the first act of the film. Billy has officially entered his descent into hell, à la Dante's *Inferno*, and the rest of the film will reflect this journey through the next several stages of hell, beginning with the upcoming scene where the prisoner learns about Turkish lawyers and corruption as well as the meaning of title of the film, *Midnight Express*.

The second act opens on a shot of Max (John Hurt) with a syringe, shooting drugs into his arm. In a series of shots, the camera focuses on other paraphernalia as seen from Billy's point of view. Max is smoking hashish as well. The medication in the needle is for his stomach pain. In a mumbling British accent, Max explains: "Gastro ... it's the best I can do around here." Erich, the herald, "interviews" Max for Billy's sake. "Lawyers?" the Swedish man inquires in hopes that the prisoner can invoke some wisdom on the Turkish legal system—and Max is certainly a scathing critic, saying things like, "There are no straight lawyers in Turkey"; "[Lawyers] take special classes in corruption"; and "If [the lawyers] are suspected of honesty, they get disbarred." In this moment, the viewer gets the first glimpse of the trickster side of Max, which plays itself out as the film unfolds. Max is a multi-layered character who shares the archetypes of mentor, trickster and flawed antihero. Through the discussion, Max mentions a lawyer named Yesil who, in the past, helped to free a French man who had been caught with two hundred kilos of hashish. The intoxicated "sage" mutters: "Best thing you can do is get your ass out of here—the best way you can ... catch the 'mid-

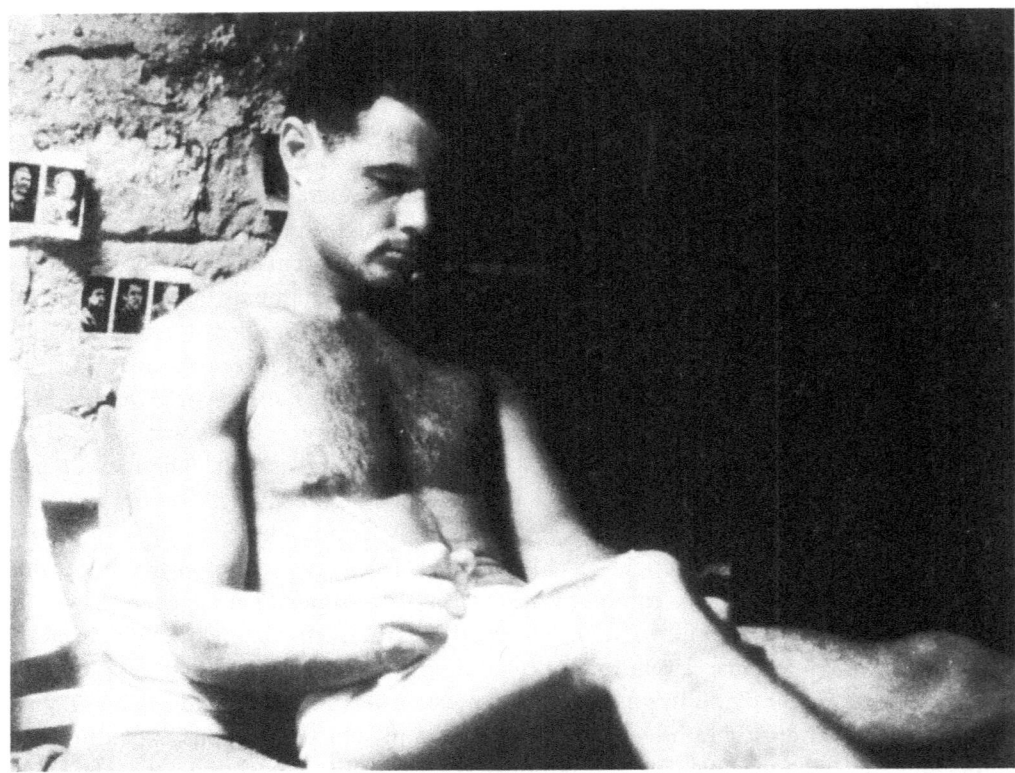

Billy Hayes (Brad Davis) writes a letter to his girlfriend, Susan, from inside the Sagmalcilar prison in Istanbul, Turkey, in 1970. *Midnight Express* **(1978), Columbia and Casablanca Filmworks.**

night express' … it's not a train; it's a prison word for … *escape*. And then, contradicting himself, he nods off to sleep after mumbling, "But it [the train] doesn't stop around here." In the same tradition of Erich and Jimmy, a dichotomy is once again presented—hope and doom. The literal quality of this "midnight express" indicates, through metaphor, that escape is always an option when one is locked up; it also conjures up an image of horror: "Midnight" is associated with the witching hour—and we've already established that this film is an expressionistic nightmare. Billy Hayes is similar to Joseph K in Franz Kafka's *The Trial*, the character who wakes up one morning and finds himself being arrested and indicted for a crime that is never revealed to him. Although Billy may know what his crime is, the means and methods of *why* he is being punished mirrors the corruption and injustice of K's ongoing nightmare.

Moreover, as a simple side note: the actual term "midnight express" (which is never explained beyond the fact that it is a prison word for escape) is curiously similar to the ideas presented in the prison-blues standard "Midnight Special," which is a hopeful song about a metaphorical train that will arrive to the Sugarland prison to free its prisoners. The lyrics "let the Midnight Special shine a light on me" seems to have the same meaning as Max's explanation of the term, which he specifically (and ironically at that) says "is not a train."

The following scene introduces Billy's father (Mike Kellin), accompanied by Turkish lawyer Yesil (Franco Diogene) and Stanley Daniels (Michael Ensign, who has a walk-on role in *Pink Floyd—The Wall*), the American consulate (note how often there are scenes in the film with a triumvirate of characters). The reunion of father and son (a common theme dating back to Homer's *Odyssey*) is emotional and poignant. In the book, the reunion is described thus:

> His face filled my eyes. We moved toward each other. Our hands locked. His left hand had grabbed my arm as though it would never let go. We stared into each other's moistening eyes. He looked so tired. Pain was all over his face. Never before did I realize how much I loved my very own father.[25]

These words are captured effectively in the beginning of the scene. After a beat, Billy apologizes to his father, and Mr. Hayes replies: "I'll punch you in the nose later. Right now we've got to get you out of here." An empathetic shot of Daniels shows him to be kind, gentle and even timid compared to the obese, grotesque Yesil. The low-angle shot highlights this lawyer's prominence. Mr. Hayes reports to his son that relations with the Turks are not good, that "Nixon has upset the hell out of them." (As mentioned earlier, Nixon's ban on opium poppy growing outraged Turkish farmers). Also, Turkish history itself undoubtedly contributed to Billy's turmoil. By late 1967, demonstrations from leftist and rightist groups became very violent: "On the left, America and American interests represented Turkish subservience to international capitalism and militarism in Turkish society."[26] In January 1966, the letter between Lyndon B. Johnson and then–Prime Minister Inönü addressed the Cypress Crisis in 1964, during which Johnson threatened not to support Turkey in the event of a Soviet attack. Consequently, public opinion now turned against the U.S. to the Turkish leftists, Johnson's letter "confirmed that the United States had no real interest in Turkey outside a cold calculation and its place in the international power matrix."[27] In 1966 and 1967, various anti–American violent acts broke out: in November of 1966, for instance, the U.S. consulate, the office of the U.S. Information Agency and the Red Cross in Adana were stoned and attacked by rioters; and, in October 1967, the reading room of the United States Information Agency in Ankara was bombed."[28]

This real "backstory"—which is not mentioned in the book or film—certainly helps explain why Billy Hayes was such a target. But in other ways—Oliver Stone's politics aside—the film is not just an overt political treatise or doctrine; when all is said and done, in its simplest terms, it's about an American in a foreign world, trying to return home.

The rest of the scene continues with the father/son exchange. As an extra attack against the country, Mr. Hayes asserts his hatred for Turkey when he comments on the "crap" that is served in the little restaurants—and if he had his druthers he'd eat at the Hilton every night with steak, French fries, and lots of ketchup—the ultimate American "comfort food."

When Mr. Hayes asks his son why he did what he did, Billy answers: "Money." Ideologically this "root of all evil" can be seen as major culprit for Billy's turmoil—perhaps this is a left-winged critique against capitalism.

The courtroom scene follows. Billy and Mr. Hayes (who experience this horror together; this is seen through a series of parallel juxtapositions as if they are the same character) are overcome by the Turkish language as well as the Gothic-looking district attorney whose prominent features and dark cape make him a quintessential shadow archetype—the one who wants to destroy Billy. He resembles a blood-sucking vampire like Count Dracula, as well as a Hades figure who is attempting to lure Billy deeper and deeper into the realms of the Turkish underworld. His voice is loud, angry and menacing and in a violating Turkish tongue he points at the prisoner and yells, "Bu!" This startles Billy as well as the viewer. (Incidentally, in Turkish the word *bu*—which to foreigner Billy Hayes has no meaning except it sounds like another version of the word *you* or even the exclamatory word *boo!* associated with scaring people—translates simply as "this." I received this information after interviewing a Turkish food server who wishes to remain anonymous). Meanwhile, the equally evil and deceptive Yesil tricks Billy and Mr. Hayes into thinking that everything will be okay, downplaying the severity of the situation (in an earlier scene, he even downplays the capitalistic part: "Money is not important—not at this stage anyway."). When Billy and Mr. Hayes grimace at the prosecutor's speech, Yesil nonchalantly waves his hand, indicating that this is nothing to worry about. Even at the end of the scene, when Billy is sentenced to four years and two months (this electrifies Mr. Hayes who repeats the words "four years?" in disbelief), Yesil tells them that this is a "good" sentence, that the prosecutor wanted a life sentence for smuggling. When Billy exits the courtroom, he makes eye contact with the prosecutor, who peers through him like a demon or warlock casting a spell.

One of the major criticisms of the film was that there were no redeeming Turks. Years later Parker admits: "Perhaps in our zeal to tell our story and make our points, some light and shade were lost. The 'good guy' Turks got left out. This is easy to say in hindsight with the intellectual and political maturity that comes with the passing years ... but the raw energy of the film still remains as fresh and modern a piece of filmmaking today."[29] Furthermore, Oliver Stone stated: "I saw *Midnight Express* as a story about justice, really. He could have been busted for carrying a pistol. The charge really didn't interest me; it was the sentence."[30]

On another level, however, one can indeed see that the adapted screenplay may have, in fact, tapped into the screenwriter's personal life. As briefly mentioned earlier, Oliver Stone has spoken about the time he was busted for marijuana possession in "Nixon's border war" in Mexico and jailed in San Diego. A Vietnam veteran, he was outraged at the way he was treated. When he contacted his father he told him he was out of Vietnam, but in jail. He called an attorney and offered him twenty-five hundred dollars. "This guy showed up that afternoon, beaming ... [it was like] a scene right out of *Midnight Express*."[31]

The following scene with Billy and Mr. Hayes sets up a new and abrupt chain of events. Billy must serve his sentence while his father fights for his freedom. He stares at and touches Susan's picture as his father (again the herald of historical exposition) tells his son that the consulate Daniels "thinks that there will be a political amnesty any month now." Hayes explains this in the book: "Everyone believed there would be a general amnesty in 1973, to celebrate the fiftieth anniversary of the glorious Turkish republic."[32] As the scene progresses, the viewer catches a glimpse of what Hayes refers to as his father's "Irish temper."[33] After years of working he has to watch his son be imprisoned! Where is the justice in that? He yells, "Jesus!" twice as if to curse his fate, then turns his emotions in toward his son—a tender two-shot scene where the men hold on to each other's hands, not wanting to let go. Hamidou—the sadistic shadow figure who looms by the doorway—becomes the one who disrupts this father-and-son bond. As Billy is taken away, the distraught Mr. Hayes curses Hamidou, which undoubtedly makes Billy's future life in Sagmalicar even harder: "You take good care of my boy, you hear? Or I'll have your *fucking head*, you *Turkish bastard*!"

Mr. Hayes is part grieving father and part ugly American, a tough dichotomy that creates another level of this ongoing catharsis. The irony here is that earlier in the scene, Mr. Hayes tells Billy not do anything "stupid" so that the authorities don't "play" with his sentence. Like father, like son.

Giorgio Morodor's melodramatic keyboard score bridges into the next scene, a mini-montage with high-contrast lighting that serves as yet another abrupt perception shift in the story—another descent into the depths of this hell. Or is this purgatory—that existential limbo where Billy Hayes waits for what seems like eternity to find out what his ultimate fate will be? Billy looks upward. Is he searching for answers in this shot? Is he looking to God?

In the next scene, Billy's voice-over narrates a letter to Susan. "Nineteen-seventy has passed into nineteen seventy-one," and for him "loneliness is the physical pain that hurts all over." Billy Hayes has become an antihero caught in the clutches of this perpetual isolation, like a character in a Sartre play. For the time being, there is "no exit" for him. The story is juxtaposed over the reading of the letter while Billy is in the *kogus*. The following details are revealed to Susan: To the Turks everything is *sula bula* (pronounced "shirla birla"), which means *like this, like that*; *ayip* means dirty—foreigners and homosexuals are *ayip*; and *Turkish Revenge* is when people go around stabbing people below the waste ("in the ass") since stabbing above the waste was not allowed because that was an "intent to kill." He tells her about the time a young boy was raped in the children's *kogus* and since no one knew who did it, Hamidou beats the feet of four of the worst-behaved kids. The eerie sound of the peacock in the background adds to the anxiety. Hamidou has his own two sons with him (young obese versions of himself) who watch as their father punishes the boys. After the deed is done, he takes his sons by the hand and speaks to them in Turkish—most likely telling them that if they don't behave they, too, will be beaten in this manner. This moment is quite ironic because Hamidou is a rapist!

The following sequence features Rifki—the informer—who tells Max and Billy that "it's a dog eat dog world" and that "we all must fuck lust." The two prisoners laugh at his absurd "philosophy" and Billy yells at him for giving them "crummy tea" and "ripping him off on the hash." The ugly American is still doing drugs despite his sentence! Perhaps this is the first time the viewer loses sympathy for Hayes, who really *is* stupid. Furthermore, Max calls Rifki a *pig* and this begins the malevolent relationship between the two men that will eventually, in different ways, doom them both. Rifki retaliates by swatting Max's cat, Egbert, who runs and hides in the rafters. Moments later there is a cut to a visually stunning blue-lit shot (emphasizing the cold) of Max calling for Egbert, who refuses to descend. Max, giving up on Egbert, calls him a "stupid cat," then leaves.

A quick cut, indicating that many hours have passed, reveals a panning shot of the façade of Sagmalicar as the sound of an oncoming train gets louder and louder. The sound, juxtaposed with the beaming blue lights given off by the locomotive is abruptly intensified by a screeching sound that jumps to a shot of Billy waking up, startled. Has he had a nightmare?

The next morning: The background sound of a Turkish chant, perhaps a Muslim prayer to Allah, as Billy and the other prisoners look at something in the distance. Max is the last to get up and, before long, discovers that Egbert has been hanged. A shot of Rifki shows him smirking with a vengeful delight. Max takes the cat out of the noose and holds him, crying. The chanting is all the audience hears as the scene fades.

April 1972. Yesil, whom Billy now knows is nothing more than a money-hungry shyster lawyer, meets with the prisoner and talks to him about some "clerical error" that has interfered with his attempt to get Billy out of jail (knowing the nature of the lawyer's motivations, this is probably not true) and he uses another corrupt approach where he says he can convince certain officials to lose track of his paperwork (for the proper fee, of course) and before long he could be in Greece. Billy, watching Yesil behind bars, elicits a look of distrust and disgust, rolling his eyes to this seemingly absurd and potentially very expensive proposition. Hope has been lost.

Inevitably, the conventions of the prison film genre deal with the possibility and usually the attempt at escape. In the next few sequences, *Midnight Express* switches its tone and becomes a prison-break film. Often, this escape convention serves as a metaphor for escaping the hierarchy and inevitable rules and regulations of institutionalism as a whole. Although the film has many unique aspects, it still does adhere to the universalities associated with the genre in the tradition of such films as *Stalag 17* (1953, Billy Wilder), *The Great Escape* (1963, John Sturges) and *Cool Hand Luke* (1967, Stuart Rosenberg). This concept is addressed in the book *Seventy Years of the American Prison Movie:*

> The prison movie is by nature a socially-conscious film which explores the inner struggles of life (the ideologies) beyond physical imprisonment.... Thus the prison film is as much about the hierarchal structure of institutions as it is about contemporary culture, politics and society.[34]

Incidentally, *Midnight Express* even has its own self-reflexive reference to the genre, a postmodern technique that is evident in other films like *The Longest Yard* (1974, Robert Aldrich) and *The Shawshank Redemption* (1994, Frank Darabont), to name just a couple. When Jimmy pitches his far-fetched prison escape plan to Billy and Max, Max retorts in his typically droll manner: "This is Sagmalicar prison—not Stalag 17," to which Jimmy replies, "That's where you're wrong, fuck-face!" Jimmy, still the "id" identity, angrily announces: "I'll go myself," again not thinking about the consequences of his actions.

The next transition is a jump-cut to a hallway where the camera slowly zooms toward a door. Meanwhile, the viewer hears the piercing juxtaposition of two sounds (a technique that may have been seen in a Roman Polanski film)—a haunting Turkish song with stringed accompaniment along with Jimmy's horrific screaming. The camera continues to zoom in on the screaming and in moments the door opens, revealing Jimmy being dragged by Turkish officers; he has been severely beaten: In addition to being unable to walk (undoubtedly, Hamidou beat his feet), he is bleeding and, upon quick glance, his eye appears to be out of its socket.

Another abrupt perception shift, serving as the passing of time: A cut to Billy pacing in the *kogus* as his voice-over is heard narrating a letter to Susan, accented by another haunting Turkish song with chanting female voices. Billy explains to Susan (which serves as exposition to the viewer as well) that Jimmy had lost a testicle and how, after two and a half years of being in jail, "The Turks were slowly draining his [own] life away."

The following scene (one that infuriated the studio executives) shows Billy and Erich in an intimate moment—first bathing one another, then practicing yoga with the mantra: "Prison, Monastery, Cloister, Cave (in the book, it's "cage").[35] The camera observes them in a quasi-voyeuristic manner and the men move their bodies to fit the different parts of the mantra. In the book, this encounter was described thus:

3. Midnight Express, 1978

Arne's long fingers felt good kneading the tired muscles of my back and shoulders. I liked the human warmth of his hands on my back. He was Swedish, and he knew how to give a massage. He handled my body like he handled his guitar. Gentle strength. Easy rhythm....

I opened my eyes. A long erection stood up out of his shorts.

I rolled over on my back. He held me in his hands and lowered himself onto the bed.

"It's all right, Willie. It's only love," he said.[36]

The film—as homoerotic as it may have appeared, especially to the studio bosses—subverts the actual truth presented in this passage. At the end of the mantra, Billy discouragingly mutters, "Prison." (This is a reminder of his fate. In the book, Hayes explains the meaning of the words *prison, monastery, cloister* and *cage*: "Prison can be any one of those things. Perspective. Everything depended on that.")[37] Erich embraces him and the two kiss for a moment until Billy, rather affectionately, pulls back and shakes his head "no." The scene is lit in an extremely low-key manner and the saturated steam of the bath waters, along with Morodor's romantic piano score, places this arguably important scene in a different league than the rest of the film—a scene with its own style, mood and agenda. Despite the distortions of the actual reality (remember that Alan Parker has explained that films are "reflections" of reality), the scene is tastefully done—it doesn't resort to the extremes—*homophobia* or *homoeroticism*—and it doesn't hold back on the poignancy of the warmth between the two men. As Arne (Erich) states in the book: "It's only love." Perhaps Billy's choice to reject Erich's further advances was altered to satisfy the nervous producers and a potentially uncomfortable audience who may not be used to seeing mainstream films with such intense love scenes between two men. Nevertheless, it addresses the reality of the moment—and even later on, when Erich leaves Sagmalicar, he and Billy hold each other's hands tightly, reiterating their special bond. Luckily, Parker was able to stand his ground and convince the producers to keep the scene in, which undeniably added another significant layer to the film's rich characterization.

The following scene begins with Billy washing Jimmy and, while doing so, Jimmy discusses yet another prison break plan (Erich must have been right when he said, "Jimmy [had] more balls than brains"). In the midst of conversation, Billy receives a message that Daniels has arrived, and he jumps up, ecstatic, thinking that he is going to be released *before* his final fifty-three day sentence. He yells in elation: "*Sula bula*—Turkish justice has done it again!" In other words: Turkish justice is unpredictable, *like this, like that…*

Billy's hope is shattered immediately when he looks at Daniels's defeated expression. The consulate is a herald, the bearer of bad news, as he explains to Billy that the judge did not like the fact that he would be getting released with a mere possession charge; consequently, a new court was assigned to his case. When Billy hears this, he grimaces (a trait he does several times throughout the film), accompanied by Morodor's dissonant music. *Sula bula*! Daniels continues, informing Billy that out of thirty-five judges, twenty-eight voted for a life sentence. Billy is now a juggernaut—a mad, caged creature. "Life?!" he yells. "For what?! *For what*?!" He reaches through the bars to "kill the messenger" and grabs a hold of Daniels's shirt: "I had fifty-three days left! I had *fifty-three* days left!" (Incidentally, the film was shot on a fifty-three day schedule).[38] Hamidou, the shadow archetype, comes to take him away. What is additionally emotional about this scene is that Daniels— although we don't know too much about him—is also greatly affected. The viewer senses that he is a gentle soul, a decent man, and when Billy leaves, Daniels is clearly horrified and disappointed. The sound of a slamming door further reinforces this new reality for Billy's fate.

The expressionistic nightmare continues in the very next shot following the slamming door: Billy's shadow is projected on the wall of the courtroom. This highly charged, provocative scene features Billy on the stand, offering his final words before receiving his sentence. The speech is raw and unrelenting. For the first time in the story, Billy Hayes—albeit ironically—is in charge. Various low-angle shots and close-ups accent this short-lived power. High-angle shots look down on both Daniels and Yesil, who sit next to each other shamefully; they can't even face him. The following monologue is delivered flawlessly by Brad Davis in *the* performance of his short life—and one of the most viscerally charged moments in any Alan Parker film. When he speaks he captures the rage, vulnerability and even wisdom of Billy's inner turmoil:

> So now it's time for me to speak. What is there for me to say? When I finish, you will sentence me for my crime. So let me ask you: What is a crime? What is punishment? It seems to vary from time to time—place to place. What's legal today is suddenly illegal tomorrow because some society says it's so. And what's illegal yesterday is suddenly legal because everyone is doing it. And you can't put everyone in jail. I'm not saying this is right or wrong; I'm just saying that's the way it is. But I've spent three-and-a-half years of my *life* in *your* prison and I think that I've paid for my error. And if it's your decision today to sentence me to more years, then I ... [pause]. My lawyer—*my lawyer*, that's a good one. He says, "Be cool, Billy. Don't get angry, don't get upset. Be good and I'll get you a pardon, amnesty, an appeal"—a this, a that, the other thing. Well this has been going on now for three-and-a-half years, and I've *been* playing it cool. I've *been* good. And now I'm damn tired of being good. Because you people gave me the belief that I had fifty-three days left. You HUNG fifty-three days in front of my face and then you just took those fifty-three days away. *And you!* [To the prosecutor, using the next Turkish word out of context.] *Bu!* [translated as *this!*] I just wish you could be standing here and feel what it feels like because then you would know something, Mr. Prosecutor. *Mercy!* You would know that the *concept* of a society is based on the *quality* of that mercy, its sense of *fair play*, its sense of *justice*. But I suppose that's like asking a bear to shit in the toilet! [Beat] For a nation of pigs it sure is funny—you don't eat them. [Beat] Jesus Christ forgave the bastards, but I cannot. I hate you—I hate your nation—and I hate your people. And I'd fuck your sons and daughters because they're pigs. [To prosecutor] *You're* a pig! You're all pigs!"

As the authorities speak, the doomed Hayes hunches down in his chair, defeated, hands locked over his head as he receives his sentence: "A term no less than thirty years." This is followed by the now-familiar phrase *getchmis olsun*—"may it pass quickly."

The scene bridges back into prison: Jimmy, on guitar, along with Max and other prisoners sing the cryptic "Istanbul Blues" and when Jimmy sings the lyrics "And they gave me thirty years," Billy shuts his eyes and grimaces, the words of reality resonating through him. In the book, Billy picks up Arne's guitar and he and another inmate begin to sing some old Alabama blues tunes. After some time improvising, Hayes says that "('The Istanbul Blues') just sort of wrote itself."[39]

During the blues, Billy lies on his bed and listens to two prominent voices in his head: his father reminding him not to do anything stupid because they (the Turks) could play with his sentence; and Max telling him about the "midnight express." The film then makes a transition to Jimmy, Max and Billy chipping away at a corroded wall that they hope will lead to a tunnel like Jimmy had mentioned earlier—all this occurs while Rifki, the "guard dog," sleeps before them. There is really nothing for Billy to lose now; all hope has otherwise been lost. Why *not* plot an escape?

Once in the tunnel, the three prisoners move hopefully through the sewerage in shadowy low-key lighting only to discover that the entrance had been blocked. They decide to go back to the prison and come back out each night until they can get through.

This goal, however, is never accomplished. The next shot shows Rifki's hand clawing through the clay-like remnants of the wall as if he were a creature who discovered something magical. This leads to the arrival of Hamidou, who immediately approaches the "escape artist" Jimmy and says, "*Noldu, noldu*." (In the book this is how the Turkish expression is phonetically spelled for American eyes and ears; the Turkish phrase *Ne oldu*, however, means *what happened?* and is used a few times throughout the book and film). Jimmy takes the stick that he has been known to carry on him and breaks it over the hulking man and yells, *No!* repeatedly and then is taken away; we never see him again. Meanwhile, Billy threatens to fight Rifki and the monster retorts by accepting this offer (he will fight him "man to man") and finishes with the threat of bringing Hamidou along to "kick his fucking ass." This scene serves as foreshadowing for what will become both Billy's and Rifki's eventual fates.

The following scene features an angry Max talking to Billy about his enemy Rifki. "I want to cut his fucking throat," he tells Billy rhythmically, almost poetically, focusing on each of the eight syllables for emphasis. And when Billy says that "it has already been cut" (a line that is meant to divert Max's anger but also serves as another foreshadowing—*Billy* will be the one to do the killing!), Max, always a trickster, comically mumbles: "Well, then I'll cut off his balls." The conversation further leads to Max's revelation that Rifki hides his money in his radio. Max laughs and says that sometimes he even catches him talking to the money. Billy, delighted, knows that taking Rifki's money will serve as sweet revenge. A jump-cut shows Rifki frantically searching his radio for the money. Another jump-cut shows Turkish officers searching for Rifki's money. Eventually the money is discovered scattered about in little pieces. Moments later, when Rifki appears dressed up in a suit, Max jokes to Billy: "Maybe he got a new job."

Rifki hears this joke and this leads to yet another abrupt jump-cut. A stampede of Turkish officers enters the prison, led by Hamidou, while prisoners stand in a lineup. Hamidou finds hashish on Rifki and the informer looks toward Max, who is surprised by the accusation. Hamidou motions with his finger for Max to "come here" and consequently rips off his the eyeglasses and crushes them. Rifki has retaliated. This injustice serves as the final catalyst for Billy's rage. He turns to defend his friend—this time speaking in a fluent Turkish tongue, but is only pushed away. Morodor's minimal score resonates while Billy Hayes transforms into something subhuman; he has become mentally and physically dehumanized. After Max is taken away (and the rest of the officers leave) a prisoner closes the door, as if to predict what is about to happen. Hayes screams Rifki's name and moves violently through the room, eventually jumping on him like a bird on its prey, following him up a staircase, dragging him down again and pounding his face into the stairs repeatedly ... until his death! (There is no evidence in the book or documentary that this murder ever occurred.)

As Rifki's lifeless face turns to one side, a puddle of blood gushing from his mouth, Billy finishes the job by ripping out Rifki's tongue and spitting it out; the image is seen in slow motion. An extreme low-angle shot captures the short-lived power of Billy Hayes, who, over Morodor's unbearably loud and invasive electronic score, smiles sadistically, his face covered in blood like a wolf who just devoured his worst enemy in the woods, until his eyes shift into an image of pure madness. Over this horrific close-up, we hear Turkish music while high-contrast lighting emulates a raw, almost vanguard cinematic experience; it is both highly stylized and realistic—a combination that Parker continues to employ effectively.

An immediate cut shows a group of Turkish officers dragging Billy away (his feet have been beaten again) set to a signature Alan Parker visual aesthetic: the shot is equivalent to a beautiful photograph saturated with blue lighting and fog that ironically mirrors the horror of the nightmare.

In a standard screenplay, the third act begins around ninety minutes into the film and such is the case with *Midnight Express*. The final half hour tells the story of Billy Hayes in "Section 13 for the Criminally Insane" through his eventual escape, a sort of self-contained short film unto itself with its own beginning, middle and end. This new milieu is undeniably the ultimate and final descent into hell, the climax of this nightmare. Set once again to a contradictory visual aesthetic (the *mise-en-scène* is carefully crafted with rich compositions and detailed lighting and color layering). The scene reads: "January 1975, 7 Months Later." The viewer is brought into a montage of the goings-on at Section 13, replete with chaotic sounds of people singing out of key, musical instruments being played haphazardly and various mumbling and other human noises all play out like dissonant notes in a musical composition. Apparently several of the people we see were actual asylum patients. In his DVD commentary, Parker looks back and questions whether it was a good idea to use actual mentally ill people: "How much real life should you interject into a movie?"[40] After a number of shots, Billy is revealed sitting among the ruins; he is a zombie among the living dead. Another "zombie" passes by him and repeats: "Cigars? Cigarettes? *Si vous Plais*?" This individual is based on one of the characters in the book.[41] Then we see a shot of Max sleeping; he has blood on his forehead (Is this the mark of Hamidou who, in an earlier shot, was seen chasing him?) and he is moaning in pure horror.

In reality, Hayes's only connection to Section 13 was when he pleaded insanity and consequently spent a short time in the sanitarium. This insanity act did not last, however, and soon afterwards he was sent back to Sagmalicar, where he received his life sentence. Later he was transferred to Imal, which according to Hayes, was "heaven compared to the prison." It was a work island, seventeen miles off the coast that had natural surroundings, where prisoners worked as laborers canning produce.

The next major sequence begins with Billy descending the stairway (yet another level of hell): The lighting at the top of the stairs is pure white, juxtaposed with the empty black light from below. Symbolically this becomes the traditional dichotomy of good versus evil. Billy is moving away from the hopeful "heavenly" light and into a new phase of hell. Men dressed in white chant Muslim prayers while walking around a partition: They are zombies, victims of institutional conformity. Billy mindlessly joins them.

While the men "walk the wheel," a tall figure approaches the newcomer. He introduces himself as Ahmet (Negdir), a cryptic character who speaks in a King's English dialect. He tells Billy that he once studied philosophy in Oxford, Harvard and Vienna. He further states: "Now I study here." He explains to Billy that *they* (which means "the institution") say he raped a small child and consequently *they* will never let him go. This dialogue is the first indication that Ahmet represents the ideology of institutional conformity: he neither denies nor admits to this heinous crime; his response is neutral. The truth lies in the hands of "them." Ahmet becomes a mentor archetype to Billy's naïveté; he is also a herald who serves as a messenger and as an informer to the newcomer. "You will never go from here," he insists. He explains to Billy that everyone in Section 13 comes from a factory ... and sometimes the factory makes "bad machines" that don't work and that's why these damaged goods get sent to Section 13. "The bad machines don't know that they are bad machines, but the factory knows," he adds. Quite simply: part of Billy's nightmare is linked to the predestined fate of many people—succumbing to the capitalistic, corporate reigns of authorities whose sole purpose beyond making money is that of *absolute autonomy*. The opening shots of the film, showing the industrialized Istanbul, served as visual foreshadowing for one of the film's most significant thematic messages. The prison can be seen as a metaphor for *all* factories—industrialized factories, corporations, other prisons and even schools and universities ... all of these are "factories," products of the age of modernism, that in one way or the other make and control the human "machines" who eventually devolve into mindless entities. This universal George Orwell/Aldous Huxley/Kurt Vonnegut *dystopia* becomes a prominent theme in the post–World War II era, especially in the light of fascism, xenophobia and existentialism.

Time progresses. The camera pans (voyeuristically, like a panopticon) through Section 13, capturing prisoners praying to Allah. The next shot shows Billy sleeping. He is awakened suddenly by an orderly who strikes him on the stomach with a club. He jumps up, startled, and lets out a shriek. He has been awakened by another "nightmare."

Billy is next led to the visitor's station. A high-angle shot looks down at the vulnerable prisoner who is blinded by the sudden bright sunlight that reminds the viewer that he has been in darkness for a long time. He sits and waits until Susan enters. She is a gracious and beautiful muse, an angel dressed in white, who comes to symbolize a kind of hope from the outside. Billy sees her and moans like a caged animal. From his point of view, he stares at her cleavage. She tells him that the senator has a plea for him regarding Nixon's status with the Turks. "Letters are coming in—people *do* care," she adds. Billy, however, is only driven by his id; all he wants to do is meet his sexual needs and desires. He tells her to take off her blouse. She reluctantly obliges and she weeps for her disheveled boyfriend, who proceeds to masturbate while her breasts remain pressed against the window. In this scene, she unwittingly also becomes a temptress, the female archetype that seduces him ("I wish I could make it better for you," she tells him). He reaches out, fingering the contours of her body behind the glass—but he *can't* have her, so he settles for pleasing himself. When he ejaculates, however, this "release" is not satisfying; it is almost painful. He yells and cries: "Susan!" And Susan's now-famous "Oh, Billy!" response creates a haunting tension between the two tortured souls who can't be with each other.

Susan gives Billy a family photo album and informs him by patting her hand on the album that "in the back there is a picture of [his] 'old friend' Mr. Franklin from the bank. He's over in Greece now. He bought a ticket...." Billy eventually figures out that he has been given money to escape. And Benjamin Franklin, his "old friend" pictured on the greenback, is a symbol of American hope. In prison films the outside world for the prisoner is a *utopia-of-promise*, the opposite of the dystopian prison milieu, and in *Midnight Express* that utopia is the safety of his own home in the U.S.[42] Similarly, in *Stalag 17*, the prisoners of war's utopia-of-promise is also back in the U.S. Even at the end of the film when Sefton and Dunbar break out of the German prison camp, the film concludes with the patriotic American song "When Johnny Comes Marching Home." Billy Hayes, similarly, is a P.O.W. within the realm of the International Drug Trade War. Furthermore, Hayes and Sefton are updated versions of Odysseus, both trying to find their way home at the end of their respective "Trojan Wars."

A new and final perception shift: Billy has been enlightened by Susan's visit, which drives him to the end of the film. He has been saved. He returns to the wheel and deliberately walks in the opposite direction and this creates controversy with the other wheel walkers. Ahmet returns—once again, like some kind of a mythical figure—and warns his "American friend": "There will be trouble if you go this way. A good Turk always walks to the right … left is communist, right is good." Billy realizes that for months he has been conforming to the Turkish way of life; he has lost his American identity and he has inadvertently become a "good Turk." Perhaps this moment critiques political and religious ideologies—the *left* versus the *right*. In other words, a "good Turk" (who is also often a good Muslim) walks to the "conservative" right.

Billy walks up the stairway, followed by Ahmet, who continues his earlier conversation about the factory. The English prophet didactically states: "A bad machine doesn't know he's a bad machine? *Tsk, tsk, tsk.* To know yourself is to know God, my friend." Billy retorts, soaked in a brooding white light leading up the stairs that undeniably exudes heavenly hope: "I know that you are a bad machine—that's why the factory keeps you here. You want to know *how* I know you're a bad machine?" Ahmet shakes his head, unprepared for this exchange. "I know because I'm *from* the factory. *I make the machines!*" He pushes Ahmet on the arm and the frightened soul leaves hurriedly. Billy Hayes's free will has prevailed; like Winston in *1984* and Guy Montag *in Fahrenheit 451*, he learns to break free from the totalitarian rule. He is now, for the first time in the film, in control of his existential nightmare.

In a bathroom stall, Billy opens the photo album, his "Pandora's box" (a similar box appears in *The Shawshank Redemption*). An extreme low-angle shot accentuates this newfound power. He finds Max, whose body and soul are really already dead as he lies comatose, and tries to instill hope into him, telling him to hang on, that if he doesn't, then he will surely die. Billy temporarily becomes his mentor. Unfortunately, this burst of hope will only render itself hopeless. Max will never leave from there. He is destined to die in the same way that Billy is destined for freedom.

In the next scene, Billy tracks down Hamidou, calling after him: "Luthtan! Luthtan!" He holds up a "Mr. Franklin" and (in Turkish) he bribes him—money for freedom. The brutish officer extends his hand the way he does with others and Billy takes it. (Hamidou is both a patriarch and a sexual sadist. Earlier in the film he reveals his power when he beats the four boys in the children's *kogus*. Immediately following the beating [he shakes the sweat off his forehead as if he has just had sex] he takes his two sons' hands and gives them his "fatherly" advice as they walk away.) Hamidou takes Billy to the sanitarium and the prisoner resists, trying to break free from his captor, heightened by the Morodor's birdlike electronic score.

Inside a cloak room, Hamidou pulls Billy into him and violently dry-humps him several times before hitting him in the face and knocking him to the floor. In the next beat, Hamidou unbuckles his pants, indicating that he intends to rape Billy. Instinctively, like a football player blocking the offense, Billy charges Hamidou and instantly this force overtakes the hulking man who is fatally wounded when the back of his head penetrates a spike on the wall. This moment, replete with an unsatisfying crunching sound (similar to the horrific moment in *American History X* when Derek stomps on and crushes the car thief's head into the pavement) has many times made audiences shriek—a response that is, once again, part of Alan Parker's mission as a filmmaker ... to affect his audience in the most visceral way possible.

White light surrounds Billy as he aims the dead man's gun at him. A number of quick juxtapositions builds the anticipation that Billy, feeling violated, may shoot the rapist. Vehemently, he shakes his head "no" and puts the gun down.

Next transition: Over black, we hear the prominent sound of footsteps, which reveals Billy in a low-key lit frame. He is wearing a police uniform. Is it Hamidou's uniform (the uniform, curiously, fits him very well) or does he locate another one in the cloak room? Nevertheless, the prisoner is on his way to freedom. The sound of the rapid heartbeats begins—a full circle from the beginning of the film. In the background, we hear the distant sounds of machine guns and a screaming woman coming from a television set (another circle; the film opens with these sounds). As Billy descends the stairs, a Turkish guard, thinking he is an officer, offers him the keys to unlock the outside door. This seems all too easy! The moment begins the final mythical journey for Billy, the "Return with the Elixir," which according to Stuart Voytilla, is the final stage in the Hero's Journey. As he states in his book *Myth and the Movies*:

> The Elixir is the final Reward earned on the Hero's Journey. The Hero has been resurrected, purified and has earned the right to be accepted back into the Ordinary World and share the Elixir of the Journey. The true Hero returns with an Elixir to share with others or heal a wounded land. The Elixir can be a great treasure or magic potion. It could be love, wisdom, or simply the experience of surviving the Special World. Even the tragic end of a Hero's Journey can yield the best Elixir of all, granting the audience greater awareness of us and our world. The Hero may show the benefit of the Elixir, using it to heal a physical or emotional wound, or accomplish tasks that had been feared in the Ordinary World. The Return signals a time when we distribute rewards and punishments, or celebrate the Journey's end with revelry or marriage.[43]

This escape sequence is yet another substantial departure from the way it happened in reality. In the real story, Billy seized an opportunity one night, during a brooding storm on Imal. A cargo boat remained anchored at the dock, and Hayes said his "escape button" was pushed and he took advantage of this opportunity to attempt a prison break. Eventually, he successfully cut the rope to a dingy attached to the cargo boat and rowed to his freedom in Greece. As he rowed, he muttered the following mantras that served as his incentive and hope: "If I die I am free; if I escape I am free" and "If they catch me they'll beat me; if I make it I'm free...."[44]

Morodor's haunting electronic score—the leitmotif that formerly symbolized Billy's nightmare of imprisonment—commences at this instant and it takes on a new meaning: *freedom*. On the outside, Billy Hayes walks, heartbeats intensifying, and then he slows down when he sees an oncoming vehicle (Is this the arrival of a new prisoner?). He stands, frozen, the suspense building to a visual and aural crescendo. As the truck passes by, Billy slowly watches it drive off and looks toward his freedom. When he realizes that he is now truly free, he runs off and jumps in the air: *Freeze frame. Insert:* "On the Night of October 4, 1975, Billy Hayes successfully crossed the border to Greece." Then: "He arrived home at Kennedy Airport 3 weeks later."

Although this appears to be an adequate place to end the film, the studio originally wanted there to be another act, a coda that showed Billy going to Greece and reuniting with his family, and the executives even threatened to sue Parker and others if this was not in the film.[45] The epilogue tells the story in a series of black-and-white photographs, a short still-frame gallery that captures Billy's reunion with Susan and his family. In addition to the photographs of him and Susan and his father there is one prominent close-up that shows the teary-eyed Mrs. Hayes, Billy's mother, whom we see for the first time. The "prisoner of war" has finally returned home.

4

Fame, 1980

May 16; 134 minutes/Color
Production Company: United Artists
Distributor: MGM
Director: Alan Parker
Screenwriter: Christopher Gore
Producers: David De Silva, Alan Marshall
Production Designer: Geoffrey Kirkland
Cinematography: Michael Seresin
Editor: Gerry Hambling
Original Music: Michael Gore
Cast: Eddie Barth (Angelo); Irene Cara (Coco Hernandez); Lee Curreri (Bruno Martelli); Laura Dean (Lisa Monroe); Antonia Franceschi (Hillary van Doren); Boyd Gaines (Michael); Albert Hague (Mr. Shorofsky); Tresa Hughes (Mrs. Finsecker); Steve Inwood (François Lafete); Paul McCrane (Montgomery MacNeil); Anne Meara (Mrs. Sherwood)

> Don't you kids ever think of anyone but yourselves?—Mrs. Sherwood to Leroy in *Fame*

> I went through a stage where I had so many things to consider, I got a little punch-drunk.—Alan Parker, Interview with Bobbi Leigh Zito in *Focus on Film*, pg. 5

Notes on the Production

Parker's powerful, hard-hitting prison drama *Midnight Express* was an enormous success, garnering six Golden Globes (one for Best Picture), as well as an Oscar from the British Academy for Best Director. It was also nominated for six American Academy Awards, including Best Picture and Best Director, being ultimately overshadowed, however, by Michael Cimino's *The Deer Hunter*. Parker jokes, "When I accepted my award for Best Director in Britain, I should have thanked Columbia Pictures for producing *Midnight Express*, and EMI for not yet releasing *The Deer Hunter* in Britain."[1] Off the coattails of this tremendous success, Parker was in a position to do almost any film he wanted, but he was admittedly indecisive as to a new project. He states:

> I went through a stage where I had so many things to consider I got a little punch-drunk. You get so fussy you end up doing nothing. I couldn't afford for that to happen. I think the important thing about directing is that you direct. When John Ford was making movies, he made three films a year, and one of them was *The Grapes of Wrath* and one of them might have been terrible. But he did get on and do it, and so I thought I ought to get on and do it.[2]

Director Alan Parker (front, center), with Robert Colesberry, Sal Piro and Rennee Bodner, on the set of *Fame* (1980), United Artists.

He was able to "get on and do it" courtesy of a script called *Hot Lunch*, which was sent to him by MGM shortly after the release of *Midnight Express*. It was a story about the trials and tribulations of young students matriculated at the School for the Performing Arts in New York City (or "PA," as it is colloquially known), which was an actual New York City high school for the performing arts, founded in 1947 by educator Franklin J. Keller. Parker intimates his attraction to the story as it represented the "flip side of the American Dream."[3] As he explains: "*Fame* is about seven kids at the High School of Performing Arts in New York ... music and dance figure very much in it because they are part and parcel of the school—but it's not a musical as such. It's a dramatic piece that happens to have music and dance at its center."[4] Parker wanted all of the musical numbers to feel organic, evolving from real situations and not, as he notes, "suspending belief as in a traditional Hollywood musical, like 'Hey, let's stop the story while we put on a show.'"[5] Another aspect of the story which appealed to Parker was the script's unabashed, candid examination of the plight of a performer. He states:

> The essence of what *Fame* is about is: it's a very strange thing to grow up to be a performer, to expose yourself at a time when growing up is difficult enough anyway. It involves a great deal of courage and the risk of enormous pain. *Fame* is a film which shows how kids prepare themselves for failure as well as success.[6]

Having grown up watching and extolling American movies, Parker was also excited about the prospect of shooting his first film in America, particularly New York City. He spent six months preparing for the film, visiting the school (as well as the sister school, Music & Art, in Harlem) and conversing with the kids there, gradually incorporating many of their real-life stories into his screenplay (which would ultimately augment the film's "realist" aesthetic). The lunchroom was his favorite place to hang out and listen to the kids—their humiliation and rejection at cattle calls. He recalls, "It was common to sit opposite a kid playing a cello, next to a dancer with her leg behind her ear, while half a dozen Stanley Kowalski's belted out their lines!"[7]

To assemble his cast, Parker held an "open call" for actors, singers, and dancers, which opened the floodgates for, as Parker puts it, "half of New York to show up"[8] (legend has it that Madonna, a then-twenty-one-year-old New York showbiz wannabe, showed up, although Parker does not recall seeing her there).

Parker had originally intended to shoot the film on location, at the actual High School for the Performing Arts, located on Forty-sixth Street in New York City. However, this plan was resoundingly rejected by the New York Board of Education, who did not want Parker (whose allegedly insensitive and racist treatment of the Turks in *Midnight Express* had garnered some incendiary criticism) sullying the good name of a prestigious school. Parker recalls one of the members of the board asking him if there had to be so much profanity. Another board member had told him that "no one in our school talks that way," to which Parker's partner, Alan Marshall, responded, "Like fuck they don't."[9] The problem was solved when Parker's crew discovered two empty schools where they could rebuild, paint, and dress their sets, one of which was Haaren High on Fifty-ninth and Tenth. Parker was faced with yet another obstacle, however, when he was in a taxi going down Eighth Avenue. He looked out the window and saw a marquee for a porno film called *Hot Lunch*, which was still the working title of his screenplay. After finishing his version of the screenplay in Connecticut, he simply crossed out "Hot Lunch" on the front page, and wrote in "Fame."[10]

Filming began on July 9, 1979, for a scheduled eighteen-week shoot, and Parker and his crew certainly faced their share of adversity. Cinematographer Michael Seresin and operator John Stanier were the camera team keys, and their European style of single-source, diffused lighting was not immediately met with approval from the American crew.[11] Parker adds, "We had always used smoke in scenes to diffuse the light. [These were] incense burners to catch the shafts of light, which posed a problem for the New York crew." The unions stepped in and forbade Parker to continue using smoke due to the noxious atmosphere it created.[12] The unions further complicated the shoot when, in order to gain work permits for the British crewmembers, the British crew had to pay the price by doubling up with New York union people, which led to the crew's becoming grossly overstaffed. It was also one of the hottest summers on record (which consequently made the shooting conditions extremely uncomfortable), and Parker openly admitted that he did not care that much for his young cast.

The film's most logistical problem, according to Parker, was the sequence outside the school where the kids flood into the Forty-sixth Street traffic, erupting into a grand-scale, choreographed expression of chaos. Parker had procured three days to shoot the whole sequence, and the NYPD had evidently been exceedingly cooperative. On the second day, however, they said that the crew had caused such traffic jams that they would refuse to offer any security or traffic control after four p.m. (To add insult to injury, the dancers went on strike and their union representatives demanded "stunt" money for dancing on top of the taxicabs, to be added to their hundred-dollars-a-day dance pay. Parker recalls that, at this point, his stress level had reached its apogee. He recalls, "I have a sad memory of sitting on a grip box on the Forty-sixth Street sidewalk, full of fear, looking at the traffic jam we had caused as far as the Hudson River, wondering how I was ever going to complete the number, let alone the film."[13]

Not only did he finish the film, but it was a film that won two Oscars (one for Best Original Music and one for Best Song ("Fame"), spawned both a successful television spinoff and many theatrical versions, inspired the creation of many similar performing arts schools around the world (including LIPA, in Liverpool), and, most recently, in 2009, inspired a Hollywood remake. Not bad for a film whose shoot was fraught with so much disaster.

Summary

While the opening credits appear over a black screen, a muted, subtle cacophony plays on the soundtrack: a piano plays faintly in the background, people are heard gathering, chairs and tables are being moved around. It sounds like the preparation for a concert of some sort, like the intro to the Beatles' *Sergeant Pepper's Lonely Hearts Club Band* album—a performance is about to take place.

The first shot is a close-up of a large poster of Laurence Olivier as Othello. His face is frozen in an expression of motivated ire, and he is poised in an aggressive pose, with his right arm raised above his head as if he is about to attack the photographer. It is an aggressive, antagonistic image, and it tersely exemplifies one of Parker's narrative hallmarks: the petulant, angry desire to fight back and break through constrictions and shackles. Parker acknowledges this permeating anger in his work, stating, "I think that anger never leaves you, and is in all my films. Sometimes I look at them and think they're *too* angry."[14]

The camera pulls back from the angry poster to reveal a young white boy named Montgomery MacNeil (played by Paul McCrane) giving a confessional interview, ostensibly to the camera itself (although he is looking slightly screen-left). Michael Seresin's stark cinematography deftly establishes that this boy is being looked at and examined, that he is in a lab-like microcosm. The background is entirely black, and the boy is the only thing which is visually decipherable in the frame. He is discussing the insecurity and self-deprecation he feels when he attends parties—he desperately wants people to like him. He tells a story about his mother and how lovely she is. He regales us with the anxiety he felt whenever he walked into the military barracks where he was stationed. The audience immediately begins investing in this boy; we find his candor and vulnerability compelling and we are interested to see how he develops. Parker then cuts, however, to a man listening intently to the boy's speech, and the boy flubs a line, apologizes, and consults the script he is reading from—the boy is an actor auditioning in an auditorium, and Parker has tricked us with a snarky visual ruse. The tone then shifts from sympathetic emotional investment to awkward anxiety as the boy apologizes to the stone-faced observers for flubbing the line. Parker effectively captures the awkwardness of performance and preparation for such (which, again, is one of Parker's staples). This opening scene succinctly captures Parker's mission statement (of sorts) of what the film is about:

> The essence of what *Fame* is about is: it's a very strange thing to grow up to be a performer, to expose yourself at a time when growing up is difficult enough anyway. It involves a great deal of courage and the risk of enormous pain. *Fame* is a film which shows how kids prepare themselves for failure as well as success.[15]

By opening the film with this candid confessional (which would become a cliché in the Generation X films of the early '90s), Parker is also establishing the tonal ethos of the film (an ethos which he would later apply to *Evita*), which is, "Music and dance figure very much in it because they are part and parcel of the school—but it's not a musical as such. It's a dramatic piece that happens to have music and dance at its center."[16]

Parker then cuts to a frenzied, frenetic montage which comprises inserts of instruments being played emphatically: first, a kinetic drum solo, then a piano, then bagpipes, etc. The editing of the montage establishes the visceral, raw power with which Parker will be approaching the material. A title card reading "The Auditions" then appears on the screen. The film, at this point, seems to be echoing the stage musical *A Chorus Line* (the film version of which would not be made until 1985), in which auditioning performers delve into themselves, their personalities and their struggles. Parker then furthers the concept of auditioning being a grueling process when a young Asian boy is playing the violin for a judging magistrate. The magistrate then tells the boy to sing the notes that the pianist plays, which clearly catches the boy off-guard—he did not expect to sing, but the magistrate forces him to anyway. Again, Parker is espousing a sort of anger, subtly impugning the despotic rule of the powers that be.

Next is another montage which painstakingly illustrates the tedious process through which these students are being put. This montage, however, is more subdued than the previous one, and it actually has a feeling of lethargy or boredom. With these contrasting montages, Parker is visually able to capture the psychological rollercoaster these students are on: excitement at the prospect of performing to the apathy brought on by the tedious repetition.

As a group of young female dancers anxiously anticipate the possibility of having to sing, dance, *and* act, Parker displays his affinity for comedy when one of the white girls admires one of the black girl's nose ring. The white girl says, "Now, does that hurt, or is it ethnic?"

The next shot displays yet another Parker hallmark: locational authenticity. It is a shot of a crowded New York City street, cluttered with honking cars, cabs, and indignant pedestrians. The anger that Parker discussed resurfaces in the next shot, which is a close-up of a young Asian girl, screaming into the camera, "You swine, you coward, you cad!" The girl is, of course, only reading from a script, but Parker's framing elicits a visceral response, and we are, again, invited to allow ourselves to engage with the indignation and frustration these young performers feel.

The frenzied montage of the auditioning process continues, replete with actors silently rehearsing their lines, musicians boning up on their Bach, and impatient judges screaming "Next!" The montage, which is bolstered by Gerry Hambling's kinetic editing, creates an atmosphere of complete and utter chaos; there appears to be no order whatsoever to this process, and Parker nicely captures the insanity and chaos, and the film already possesses an exciting, powerful feel. As film critic Al Auster describes the film's opening, "These kids and others provide so much energy and excitement that they make the first forty-five minutes of the movie an absolute joy."[17]

We then cut to a young black girl, Shirley (played by Carol Massenburg), who is being asked for her name at a check-in desk. She is accompanied by a young black boy, who also must give his name to the woman at the desk. Shirley informs the woman at the desk that he does not need to give his name as he is merely her partner. The woman insists, however, that the boy, Leroy Johnson (played by Gene Anthony Ray), not only check in and give his name, but that he also relinquish the knife he is carrying. The fact that Leroy is carrying a knife subtly suggests the beleaguered plight of inner-city schools in New York City at that time. According to critic Stanley Kauffmann, this moment in the film also signals the viewer about the film's narrative development. He states, "When a girl applies as a dancer and says that the fellow with her is not applying, that he's just partnering her for the audition, we know he's the one who's going to be accepted."[18] Perhaps this is evident because the deliberate diversion of attention, from the silent, insouciant partner to the strident, loud applicant, has since become a cliché—we are now aware that it is the character from whom attention is being diverted who will have the most agency.

We then cut to Doris Finsecker (played by Maureen Teefy), a mousy, demure actress auditioning onstage. She is told by the teacher for whom she is auditioning that she needn't sing for her audition, despite her desire to do so. Doris's overbearing mother intrudes, assuring the teacher that Doris can sing very well. When the teacher asks for Doris's name, she is not able to answer, as her doting mother does so for her. With this moment, Parker is espousing a theme which would later be explored by Peter Weir in *Dead Poet's Society*: the pressure teens face at the hands of their domineering, overbearing parents. We then cut to the introduction of Ralph Garci (played by Barry Miller), who is clearly coded as the rebellious, iconoclastic ruffian who is going to give the teachers problems. His appearance is indicative of a gang member, as he is wearing a headband and a long black trench coat. He is brash and strident, and clearly rubs the uptight teachers the wrong way. He is the antithesis of the meek, mild Doris Finsecker, whom we cut back to as she explains to her teacher that she applied to this particular school because her family could not afford a "regular" school. Parker then implements cross-cutting to, again, illustrate the myriad emotions these kids undergo during the grueling audition process. He cross-cuts Doris singing "The Way We Were" with shots of a heavyset black girl doing a scene as O.J. Simpson from "The Towering Inferno." Doris is clearly wracked with anxiety and nervousness, and she starts to sing the song, albeit badly. Although she is not performing well, she still puts forth a valiant effort, until halfway through the song. She essentially gives up, and begins insouciantly speaking the words, almost conversationally, as if she has resigned and is not even trying anymore. The pressure is too much for her, and the viewer suspects that Doris may not last long at this demanding academy.

The shots of the black girl are strictly played for laughs, however, to counterbalance the heart-wrenching poignancy of Doris folding under pressure. She annoys the teachers by using up half her audition waiting for an invisible elevator, and one of the teachers removes his glasses and wipes his face, exasperated. This scene of levity contrasts with Doris's resignation to create an eclectic emotional atmosphere; there are all kinds of students at this school, with all kinds of attitudes and approaches.

Parker then cuts to Ralph preparing to dance to "Swanee River" for an audition. He is wearing a placard around his neck with the number "73" etched on it. This prop could be seen as Parker's subtle insinuation that the audition process can be dehumanizing, as Ralph seems to have been reduced to merely a number. The obdurate, stuffy judges augment this assertion when they emotionlessly tell him to try the drama department after he is done dancing.

We then cut to an intimate conversation between Ralph and a young, seemingly street-smart girl of mixed ethnicity. This is Coco Hernandez (played by Irene Cara). Coco tells Ralph that there is a quota system at the school, so "your chances are better if you're black, or Puerto Rican, or everything, like me." Already, the viewer is informed that Coco is the precocious girl who is wise beyond her years.

The next shot is of a room into which two men are wheeling bulky, cumbersome musical equipment (amplifiers, synthesizers, etc.), which clearly catches the judges off-guard. After the boy to whom the equipment belongs identifies himself as Bruno Martelli (played by Lee Curreri), Parker cuts back to Ralph, who is now auditioning in front of the drama judges. At this point, Parker has adumbrated Ralph as the one with the most prominent identity crisis—he has now auditioned (or attempted to) in the music, dance, and now the drama department. His story concerning the whereabouts of his father seems to be constantly changing as well: in one version, he is doing work for the government, but in this scene, he tells the judges that he is in Spain making Spaghetti Westerns. He is searching for himself, which is reinforced when he begins to perform for the judges. He starts off with, "Judy, Judy, Judy!" which is one of the most identifiable Cary Grant quotations (although, interestingly enough, Grant never actually uttered the name Judy in this manner in any of his films, although Rita Hayworth's character in *Only Angels Have Wings* was named Judy), after which, he jumps into "Top of the world, Ma!" which is a reference to a famous James Cagney line in *White Heat* (which, again, is technically a misquote; the actual line is "Made it, Ma! Top of the world!"). Even in the realm of performance, Ralph isn't sure who he wants to be. One of the judges preemptively cuts Ralph off and tells him to be himself. With this moment, Parker informs us that the teachers and judges at the school will not be treated as two-dimensional, despotic villains who are purely out to make things hard on the kids. The teacher telling Ralph to be himself suggests that perhaps these teachers are here to help, and they will not simply be the film's "villains."

We then cut to Bruno Martelli's audition. He has set up his elaborate instruments, creating a wall of sorts, behind which he is sitting, ready to play. He begins, and by implementing synthesizers and other sophisticated "futuristic" equipment, he emulates a full-symphony orchestra. Of course, the obdurate, haughty music teacher, Mr. Shorofsky (played by Albert Hague) stops him and tells him that one instrument will be sufficient. Here, the depiction of the teachers reverts to that of reactionary, stuffy curmudgeons. Bruno's audition also perpetuates another Alan Parker theme, which is the encroachment of modernity and industry on underdevelopment. The conflict and tension that exists between the old guard (underdevelopment, agrarianism, etc.) and the new guard (modernity, technology, etc.) is a topic that surfaces in a number of Parker's works, particularly in *Evita* and *The Road to Wellville*, and the technological advancement in these films (as well as in *Fame*) are almost always instruments which allow one of the characters to vanquish oppression and break free from shackles—Eva uses the train (modernity) to break free from her impoverished life (underdevelopment), and Bruno uses his sophisticated instruments to break free from his low-class background.

We then cut to another dance audition, in which Leroy and Shirley dance suggestively (to the point of downright vulgarity) to Linda Clifford's "Red Light," an up-tempo, Sister Sledge–type disco song. The dancing is explicitly sexual in nature, which, of course, elicits disdain from the uptight judges. Parker inserts a brief shot of the sexless, schoolmarm piano player reading the paper, paying no attention to the raucous dance number, which suggests that there is a new vanguard of youth sweeping the music world, one which the old guard is not ready to accept.

After a brief and hilarious scene in which an overtly Italian boy inadvertently reads Juliet's part in *Romeo and Juliet*, we cut to Shirley and Leroy having an argument in the hallway—Leroy was accepted and Shirley was not, and she is traumatized. Shirley throws a fit after being rejected, shouting obscenities as she walks down the stairs, loudly proclaiming that she did not want to go this school anyway. Once again, Parker demonstrates his affinity for presenting the entirety of the performance process, warts and all, and he is not content with simply focusing on the successful students, as he casts a light on the ugly, unfortunate repercussions of rejection.

In the interest of dramatic complexity, Parker contrasts Shirley's vitriolic rejection with shots of Ralph and Doris's mother celebrating—both Ralph and Doris have been accepted. Again, we see both sides of the coin: the brutality of rejection and the transcendent joy of approval and acceptance. Parker also shades in Ralph's character a bit more by depicting the abject poverty of his apparent hangouts. He runs through the rubble of demolished buildings to gloat to some friends that he got into the school, and we suspect that Ralph had a troubled childhood.

Acting student Ralph Garci (Barry Miller), dressed in a *Rocky Horror Picture Show* outfit, tries to woo his love interest, the introverted acting major Doris Finsecker (Maureen Teefy). *Fame* (1980), United Artists.

We then cut to shots of Montgomery, Ralph, Coco, Leroy, and Doris all walking through the streets of New York City, all ostensibly on their respective routes to the school as the title card "Freshman Year" appears on the screen. Next is what can only be described as a "Montage of Admonitions." It is a series of vignettes featuring the hardened, oppressive teachers instilling fear and anxiety into the students by warning them how difficult the curriculum is and how much they are going to suffer.

The first vignette features roll call in English class. When the teacher, Mrs. Sherwood (played with stern conviction by Anne Meara), calls Leroy's name, he does not respond, as he is listening to music through headphones. Once he removes the headphones, he and Mrs. Sherwood get into an altercation, pitting the rebel against the institution. One is reminded of Jack Nicholson constantly butting heads with Louise Fletcher in *One Flew Over the Cuckoo's Nest*, and Mrs. Sherwood assures Leroy that he will do things her way or no way at all.

The ensuing vignettes are all similar, as they all feature stringent authority figures demarcating the parameters of their institution, the breaching of which is expressly forbidden. This touches upon the perennial Parker theme of breaking through constraints and boundaries (usually put up and withheld by obdurate authority figures) and the intrinsic anger that comes with the struggle of breaking boundaries.

The "Montage of Admonitions" culminates with the dance teacher, the drama teacher, and the music teacher all claiming that theirs is "the hardest profession of them all," which has a comedic effect, superficially, but it can also be seen as a snarky, subtle attempt by Parker to undermine the establishment by pointing out its inherent hypocrisies and delusions. We then cut to the cafeteria, which is simmering with excitement and activity, as the fast-paced editing and cacophony of sound combine to create a frenzied atmosphere of energy. The energy in the room cannot contain itself, and eventually erupts into a full-on song-and-dance number, with everyone (including the lunch ladies) joining in, dancing and singing. Irene Cara takes the lead vocal as she sings "Hot Lunch," a rousing song which is not only indicative of the students' energy and drive, but it becomes a sort of rebellious ritual, sticking it to the oppressive, tyrannical teachers who are trying to control and restrict their energies and talents. The entire cafeteria is dancing, save for Doris; the excitement is too much for her and she meekly slinks out the door to find Montgomery. Sitting together on the stairs, the two outcasts share a moment. We discover that Montgomery's mother is Marcia MacNeil, a famous actress. Montgomery then tells Doris about his analyst, and the seeds of his Oedipal issues are planted, culminating with Montgomery telling Doris that he has "issues with women." Immediately after Montgomery utters the word "women," there is a jarring, startling cut to a close-up of Doris, screaming at the top of her lungs. We eventually see that it is part of a warm-up exercise for her drama class, but the effect is interesting. Not only is it abrupt and startling, but it suggests that, deep down, Doris is not as mousy as she appears; perhaps she longs to come out of her shell sexually, and is disappointed to hear that she may not get to do so with Montgomery, as he has "issues with women."

The warm-up exercise in the drama class devolves into a demeaning display, the students becoming like trained dogs, as the teacher, Mr. Farrell (played by Jim Moody) barks commands at them, augmenting the opposition between the oppressed and the institution. Parker then maintains the energy level of the film with another montage of practices, rehearsals, false starts, etc. We then cut to a beautifully photographed shot of a large window pouring light into a hallway as Coco walks down the hall, ostensibly looking for someone. Michael Seresin's cinematography is breathtaking, as the shot possesses a golden-hued sumptuousness, giving the shot a sacramental, angelic look. Coco eventually finds the object of her search—Bruno Martelli. She suggests that the two of them join forces to play some "real music" and earn some money, playing at weddings and such. Coco is furthering her depiction as the street-smart, Artful Dodger–type. Bruno, of course, declines, telling her that he feels more comfortable playing alone in his basement. Compounded with Doris and Montgomery's budding friendship, this scene illustrates that the students are beginning to come out of their respective shells, reaching out to other classmates and forming relationships.

This bonding between the students is furthered in the next scene. Doris and Montgomery are reciting dialogue which requires Doris to be crying hysterically. Montgomery stops her and says the scene feels phony, causing Doris to vent her frustrations in a self-deprecating diatribe about how "ordinary" she feels. An older male student then walks by and smiles at Doris, and she is clearly attracted to him—the seeds of a possible romance are planted. Ralph then walks over to them and retrieves some pills from Montgomery, which he has procured from his analyst. Before walking away, Ralph makes a crack about Montgomery not liking girls, and we see an expression of genuine hurt on Montgomery's face. Although it has not yet been made explicit, we now suspect that he is gay.

We then cut to English class, and Mrs. Sherwood and Leroy are once again at odds. She is castigating him for not turning in his homework, and he recalcitrantly defies her. She submits that Leroy can't read, and challenges him to read a passage from a book, which arouses his aggressive ire, as he curses her and leaves the room. This moment has a stark, visceral power, an Alan Parker hallmark, and we are conflicted, feeling for both Leroy, who most likely had a troubled childhood, and Mrs. Sherwood, who, while she is strict and, at times, harsh, presents herself as a dedicated teacher who demands good work from her students. This battle of wills between Leroy and Mrs. Sherwood will form one of the most prominent dramatic conflicts of the film, and, according to *Variety*'s review of the film, "His [Leroy's] continuing fight with Mrs. Sherwood (Anne Meara) is the most believable plotline in the entire film."[19]

While the school chorus sings a haunting, operatic melody on the soundtrack, Leroy bursts into a violent fit of rage in the hallway, throwing things at the walls, breaking glass. Mrs. Sherwood relents, opting not to persist with her scolding, and she simply shuts the door. According to Parker, the contrast between the classical, choral music and the guttural, violent outburst, was intentional. He states:

> I wanted to counterpoint the raw black anger of the kid. So against that scene we had a piece of choral music by Rossini, "Stabat Mater"—very white classical music which is absolutely the opposite of what you would expect to hear in that situation. But immediately after we finish the scene, we cut to the voices who are singing it, and they are not white, but black faces.[20]

We then cut to Bruno, sitting in the back of a taxicab, being driven by his gruff, proletariat father, who tells Bruno that it is unnatural that he doesn't have any friends or girlfriends. Not only does this scene explore the generational conflict between kids and parents, but it showcases a perennial Parker theme which crops up in most of his work—the exploration of working-class mores. As Hacker and Price put it, "Few of the central characters in Parker's films are middle or upper class; and *Birdy* and *Fame* have strong working class themes—*Fame* is about predominantly working class youths with burning aspirations, tremendous energy, and varying degrees of confidence."[21] Although the viewer has surmised at this point that most of these students come from meager, working-class upbringings (this is certainly the case with Ralph, which is parlayed through his ramshackle, decrepit hangouts, and Doris, who claims that her family can't afford a "normal" school), this scene drives the point home. Bruno's father is a hard-working cab driver, the epitome of working class, and we understand his anxiety about his son performing well and achieving success. Parker illustrates that, like Robert Altman (particularly in his films *Kansas City* and *Gosford Park*), he is much more interested in spending time with the servants than with the stuffy bourgeoisie.

The next scene finds Leroy traversing a rundown, ramshackle area full of rubble, detritus, and homeless people gathered around a fire—he is clearly in a bad part of town. Michael Seresin's haunting cinematography augments the mood, using stark, high-contrast lighting with harsh shadows. The setting takes on a noirish, even nightmarish, feel, as Seresin shrouds the entire frame with tendrils of smoke and steam, which feel like portents (Seresin would create a similar atmosphere in the opening shot of Parker's later film *Angel Heart*). Leroy sits down amid the rubble, grabs a random piece of paper and attempts to read the inscription on it. He struggles, sounding out the words, and we see that Mrs. Sherwood was correct: Leroy cannot read. He does eventually sound out the words on the paper, however, which are, interestingly: "Welcome to the wonderful world of the machine" (an offshoot of "Welcome to the Machine," a song off the album *Wish You Were Here* by Pink Floyd, the band that would go on to serve as source material for Parker's film *The Wall*). Parker lends this moment additional gravity by implementing another haunting song sung by the school chorus on the soundtrack while Leroy buries his face in his hands in frustration.

Parker then implements another sound cue over a shot, but this time, purely for comedic effect. He cuts to a group of boys in the men's room, standing on the stall, looking through a peephole to spy on the naked girls in the girl's room. Over this visual, we hear Mr. Farrell say, "I want you to observe yourself doing ordinary, everyday things." On the surface, this juxtaposition of sound and image is humorous, but it also bolsters the notion that there is a disconnect between generations (and between the institution and the students). The surreptitious act of spying on the girls juxtaposed with Mr. Farrell discussing "everyday" things suggests that the teachers will never understand just what it is the students are up to. The "anger" that Parker discusses surfaces in the culmination of Mr. Farrell's suggestion that the students observe themselves doing "everyday" things. As if to mock Mr. Farrell's suggestion, Ralph simulates a bowel movement, as he sits on a chair with his pants around his ankles, panting heavily and shouting, as if it is a painful experience. The students all laugh, but Mr. Farrell is disgusted and frustrated—Ralph has taken his serious suggestion and made a mockery of it, again reinstating the divide between institution and subjects, subjects whose unbridled enthusiasm and energy cannot be shackled by the restrictive prescriptions of the powers that be.

This is further augmented with the next two vignettes, the first of which finds Mr. Shorofsky scolding Bruno for holding his violin bow improperly. He screams at Bruno, saying, "It's not your dick you're holding! Show it some respect, like ..." he trails off and Bruno finishes his sentence for him by saying, "Your dick?" Again, the students laugh, while Mr. Shorofsky becomes angry and indignant. We then cut to the dance teacher, Miss Berg (played by Joanna Merlin) scolding Lisa (played by Laura Dean) for not trying hard enough. Again, there is a contrast, however, as Lisa does not rebelliously fight back, like Ralph and Bruno did. She, like Doris, internalizes the criticism and it appears to hurt her deeply. Once again, Parker deftly weaves back and forth between the myriad personalities (and, therefore, reactions) of these students.

We then cut to Doris walking up the stairs as she notices Michael (played by Boyd Gaines), the boy on whom she has a crush. She stops him and congratulates him on the scholarship and award he has received. She awkwardly flirts with him, and he tells her that he is not going to college, that he has connections at the William Morris agency and he is going to Hollywood to hit the big time. Doris's complex emotional reaction to this news is wonderfully captured in Maureen Teefy's performance. She exudes both pride and excitement as well as hurt and disappointment, as she realizes that this news means she will not be seeing a lot of him.

Over a striking shot of a staircase (which, once again, is expertly lit and photographed by Michael Seresin—the lighting and shadows suggest a welcoming vibe and one of haunting admonition simultaneously, which visually conveys the unwritten fate of these students), a title card reading "Sophomore Year" appears. Parker then cuts to another comedic scene of the hormone-driven, lecherous boys spying on the girls undressing. As they argue over who gets to look through the peephole, the girls are alerted to their spies, and they shriek and scream, causing the boys to tumble and nearly fall off the stall, which they prevent by grabbing the overhead pipes. The stall splits in two, revealing a boy, sitting on the toilet, in the middle of a bowel movement, playing a French horn. The scene is humorous in a vulgar, raunchy sort of way, and it foreshadows the type of humor Bob Clark would implement in his teen comedy *Porky's*.

We then cut to Mr. Farrell informing his drama students that whereas the previous year he asked them to engage in simple observation, this year he wants them to dig more deeply and look inside themselves to find their essence. He gives them an assignment: to revisit a painful memory in order to get in touch with their emotions. In this scene, Mr. Farrell is clearly veering the students towards the Stanislavsky, Lee Strasberg approach to method acting, the acting style employed by the likes of James Dean, Montgomery Clift, Marlon Brando, and Robert De Niro, et al. This is actually a clever narrative device which informs the audience that, while the students plumb the depths of their souls, we will be doing it with them—ergo, the audience is going to get to know the characters more intimately.

We then cut to the dance class engaging in stretching exercises. Lisa introduces herself to the new girl, Hilary van Doren (played by Antonia Franceschi). There is a clear socioeconomic class divide between Lisa, the working-class girl, and Hilary, the WASPY, affluent type, who ostensibly comes from money. Miss Berg, again, singles Lisa out and tells her to work harder. Parker, again, accentuates his predilection towards focusing on the working class and their struggles, as the attention shifts away from Hilary and back onto Lisa. Miss Berg's singling out Lisa is mirrored in the next scene, in which Mr. Shorofsky picks on Bruno, again impugning his bow-holding technique while he and the rest of the class perform Mozart's "Eine Kleine Nachtmusik." Unlike the meek Lisa, however, Bruno argues back, telling Mr. Shorofsky that Mozart wouldn't even use a bow nowadays, what with all the technical advancements in musical equipment. According to Bruno, Mozart would simply "plug his keyboard into an amp." Again, we see the perennial Parker theme of modernity and technology plowing through an obdurate, reactionary landscape. Parker also sheds more light on Bruno's character. He is a lonely young man, and feels that one can play music alone, without collaboration or assistance.

We then cut back to Miss Berg's dance class and Parker plants the seeds of a rivalry developing between Hilary and Coco. Hilary lustfully gazes at Leroy, and tells Lisa that "she digs his black ass." Coco overhears, and warns Hilary to stay away because Leroy's taken. Hilary says, "Don't count on it," and the viewer is aware of a nascent tension between these two girls.

In the next scene, Doris and Montgomery are walking down a New York street together. Doris is pretending to be blind, wearing dark sunglasses and carrying a walking stick. Doris expresses her difficulty in locating a painful memory for her acting class, and Montgomery says he has lots of them. His Oedipal issues are furthered when he says that one of his most painful memories was when his mother flew to L.A. and didn't return for six weeks. He clearly has attachment issues with his mother, and the viewer is interested to see how his emotional problems contribute to the drama.

Back in the dance classroom all of the students (as well as Miss Berg) are gone, save for Hilary, who is dancing alone to a classical piano piece. Michael Seresin's cinematography bathes the scene in a contrast between luscious, golden-hued lighting and harsh shadows, which strike Hilary's face as she elegantly dances, giving the tableau a romantic, operatic look. Leroy then walks in and watches her, his emotional reaction being an amalgamation of respect, admiration, and lust. Parker then reaffirms his mastery of the cinematic language by parlaying, without the use of dialogue, that Hilary and Leroy have sex. Hilary walks over to Leroy, looks at him seductively, and gestures her head towards the door marked "Boys' Locker Room." She walks into the locker room as Leroy absorbs the information, smiles exuberantly, walks in after her, and shuts the door. Had either one of the characters discussed their intentions verbally, it would have seemed crass and unnecessary and would certainly have cheapened the scene.

In the next scene, Montgomery's homosexuality is made explicit when he tells Doris that he has fallen in love with his analyst. Doris says that everyone falls in love with their analysts, and then says, "There's a word for that, isn't there?" to which Montgomery replies, "Homosexual." Parker then cuts to a close-up of Doris and stays on her while she absorbs the information, which heightens the dramatic impact of Montgomery's disclosure.

The next scene is one of the most (if not the most) notorious scene in the film. Bruno's father pulls his cab over to the side of the street, puts a cassette in the tape player, and blasts the film's title song over his loudspeaker. What follows, as Parker refers to it, is "choreographed bedlam"[22] as a horde of young students riotously dance in the street, jumping on top of cars, doing backflips, etc. It is a triumphant sequence of youthful celebration, which would eventually become a staple of 1980s teen films (*Footloose*, *Flashdance*, etc.). There is an interesting moment amidst the raucous dancing which further augments the theme of youth celebrating in opposition to the old, reactionary vanguard. A disgruntled truck driver, fed up with the antics in the street, gets out of his truck, and vandalizes Bruno's father's cab, ripping one of the speakers off the roof. Bruno's father retaliates, punching the truck driver; a tussle ensues, with the two men fighting, dwarfed by the exuberant dancing which encircles them. This further substantiates that this film is about youth, about their ambitions, their energy, their drive, and the adults (who clearly don't understand) are drowned out by the exuberance of their sons and daughters.

Parker then cuts to a shot of a row of empty seats in an empty, dark auditorium. Michael Seresin's cinematography infuses the scene with a sense of intense gravity, as the seats are all apparently being slashed by the harsh shadows. The camera then pulls up to reveal Montgomery, sitting by himself, confessing his homosexuality to the other students (who are offscreen). The scene has an intense seriousness to it, and the trope of the gay character confessing to his friends would go on to become somewhat of a cliché in the early to mid-'90s. The Generation X movies and television shows of this decade, from MTV's *The Real World*, to *My So-Called Life* to *Reality Bites*, all invariably featured the gay character (some of whom confessed to having AIDS on top of being homosexual) "coming out" in a scene of gut-wrenching candor.

We then cut to the dressing room, in which Montgomery, Doris, and a slew of other students are getting into costumes and putting on makeup. Ralph brazenly walks in, in full drag, and makes an uncouth joke about Montgomery being gay. He then tells Doris that she would be perfect for a role being cast for a movie in the city because the role calls for just her type—a "fag hag." Doris becomes livid, and chases Ralph out of the room, but Parker stays on a close-up of Montgomery, concentrating on his shame and hurt. This scene further exacerbates the viewer's already palpable dislike for the character of Ralph. He is the only character whose backstory is still unknown, and at this point in the story, he is nothing more than a strident, obnoxious troublemaker.

Back at the Finsecker residence, Doris and her mother get into a heated argument. Doris's mother wants her to go to catered affair to perform, but Doris adamantly expresses her disinterest in going. The divide between the unbridled enthusiasm of youth and the oppressive tyranny of overbearing parents is being widened. Doris, however, acquiesces and we cut to the catered affair, which is revealed to be a child's birthday party, replete with obstreperous, whiny brats who are all shrilly crying as Doris sings "Happy Birthday." The scene is mostly played for laughs, and we sympathize with Doris, who clearly feels ridiculous, as her voice is drowned out by the cacophony of crying children. The *mise-en-scène* is quite interesting, however. As Doris sings unhappily, a painting of some sort of tropical paradise (replete with palm trees, a white sandy beach, and an ocean) can be seen in the background although it is somewhat blurred. This visually suggests that Doris is extremely unhappy, and her happiness (her "paradise") is blurred and out of her purview.

Mr. Farrell's soul-probing continues in his drama class, and, after a brief snippet of Doris proclaiming that she yearns to assert herself, Parker cuts to another stark, funereal confession scene, this time with Ralph sitting in the hot seat, as Parker frames him in front of an all-black background (much as he did with Montgomery in the film's opening scene). Ralph begins telling a story about how he came home from school one day, and Eddie Barth's deliberately paced delivery of the lines suggests that he is going to recount a tragedy that happened in his life. While the story does end up recounting a tragedy, it is not necessarily one that involved Ralph personally. He breaks down as he tells the class about the day he heard that Freddie Prinze (Ralph's idol) shot himself. Eddie Barth's performance in this scene is sensational, as his frenzied grief completely subsumes him. His grief quickly turns into vitriolic indignation and he blames Freddie's death on society's callousness, claiming that the world wants its inhabitants to be unhappy. Ralph's angry tirade finally gives the viewer a window into his character—he is an angry, misguided boy who doesn't know who he wants to be, his only identity being an idolizer of Freddie Prinze. Perhaps Ralph sees that his life is heading in the same direction as Prinze's (i.e., a comedian who kills himself due to clinical depression), and it makes him angry. Whatever the reason for his obsession with Prinze (and for his anger), we at least see Ralph as a person, as opposed to just an obnoxious blowhard.

Parker then cuts back to what is perhaps the most compelling subplot in the entire film: the conflict between Leroy and Mrs. Sherwood. While shelving books, Mrs. Sherwood sees Leroy whisk by her door on roller skates. After scolding him for his footwear, she tells him she wants his book report. He says that reading "ain't his style," to which Mrs. Sherwood says delicately, "If you don't read, you're missing so much." Anne Meara's performance gives depth and shading to Mrs. Sherwood's character as she utters the line; we see in her genuinely fostering eyes that she does truly care about the welfare of her students. She wants to see Leroy succeed and is not simply a despicable constituent of the tyrannical old guard, inexplicably being harsh and tough on young people.

In the next scene, Miss Berg calls Lisa into her office and tells her that she is a subpar dancer and there is no room in her class for someone with her unimpressive talent, effectively expelling her. She delivers the information emotionlessly and callously, as though she does not care that she just shattered the dreams of a young girl. Lisa is, of course, traumatized and she leaves, dejected. Parker, however, stays in the room with Miss Berg after Lisa leaves, and, as she leans on the door, her unfeeling veneer melts into empathy and self-loathing as she whispers "Shit" to herself. Expelling Lisa was difficult for her, but she did not want Lisa to see her vulnerability. Once again, Parker displays his aptitude with creating balanced narratives, never devolving into two-dimensional caricatures—each character is a human being with emotions and Parker is always willing to linger on shots of characters dealing with those emotions.

We then cut to a subway station where Coco, Leroy, and Lisa are waiting for a train. Coco and Leroy, true performers through and through, dance exuberantly while Coco croons "Singin' in the Rain." Lisa, of course, sits despondently. As the train pulls into the station, Lisa slowly walks towards the platform as if in a trance, as she is ostensibly going to throw herself in front of the train and kill herself. This sequence is extraordinarily anxiety-inducing as Parker implements sound and editing effects to generate nail-biting suspense. As Auster puts it, "Not content merely to pull at the viewer's heart strings, Parker also wants to take one's breath away,"[23] which he does in this scene, to an alarming degree. He intercuts Lisa walking to the train with a series of quick shots of close-ups of Coco's and Leroy's feet as they dance, creating a frenzied, unnerving sense of apprehension, and Parker displays (as he did marvelously with *Midnight Express* and would later do with *Angel Heart* and *Mississippi Burning*) his ability to effectively build tension and suspense.

The tension is relieved when Doris decides against taking her own life, glibly stating, "Fuck it. If I can't dance, I'll switch to the drama department." We then cut to another golden-hued, romantic (and dreamlike) shot of the dancers practicing and Coco and Hilary engage in another heated *pas de deux* over the affections of Leroy. Coco says (of Leroy),

"He's not into vanilla," to which Hilary replies, "It might be a nice change from black cherry." Coco then says, "The darker the berry, the sweeter the juice," to which Hilary says, "Yes, but who wants diabetes?" Their steamy, sultry rivalry is indicative of the film noirs of the '40s and '50s, and Hilary is coded as the femme fatale—the exotic, mysterious, sexually aggressive foil to the "good girl."

Ralph is given a bit more shading in the next scene, in which he is interrupted by Mr. Farrell in the middle of performing in front of the class. Mr. Farrell says that Ralph needs to enunciate, and Ralph responds by saying that the greatest actors (James Dean, Marlon Brando, Montgomery Clift—the rogue's gallery of method actors) slurred their words. The class laughs and Ralph doesn't understand why, asking frustratedly, "What's so funny?" Whereas, in previous scenes, Ralph was always willing to present himself as the clown, engaging in silly and ridiculous set pieces to get a laugh, he now wants to be taken seriously, but can't, which frustrates him. Perhaps he does not want to be the clown anymore.

The perennial Parker theme of the struggle to break through barriers resurfaces in the next brief scene, in which Leroy is harassed by a car full of hooligans as he walks down the street. In an act of defiance, Leroy picks up a trash can, pours the trash into the convertible, and gives the hooligans the finger. The "anger" that, by his own admission, permeates his work, shows its face again, as Leroy must fight for the right to be himself and break through the boundaries of harassment.

In the next scene, Parker cross-cuts shots of Mr. Shorofsky conducting his orchestra of students with shots of Bruno, plugging in and setting up his sophisticated equipment. He blows a fuse and the power goes out, inciting the ire of Mr. Shorofsky (which, of course, is played for laughs). With this moment, Parker seems to be equivocating his thoughts on the role of technological advancement in the development and advancement of individuals. Here, Bruno's provincial dedication to being alone and utilizing sophisticated equipment has become a hindrance, an obstacle—he has eradicated the very power he relies on to use his electronics.

We then cut to a shot of the interior of Montgomery's apartment, and a title card reading "Junior Year" appears on the screen. Ralph, Doris, and Montgomery enter, and prepare to read a scene together, at which point Parker cuts to a close-up of a statue of the Virgin Mary and other Catholic iconography mounted on a mantelpiece (Parker would go on to implement religious imagery to great effect in both *Angel Heart* and *Evita*). We see that it is Ralph's apartment, although Ralph is not home. In a haunting, ominous sequence, one of Ralph's little sisters walks out into the dark, unwelcoming hallway of their tenement building to investigate a sound. It is an eerie scene (a mood which is, again, augmented by Michael Seresin's dark, noirish lighting), and it feels almost like a horror film scene. Parker then cuts back to Montgomery's apartment, where Ralph and Doris are dancing, as they are performing a scene for Montgomery. They exchange compliments, and the scene ends with the two of them kissing. Montgomery tries to stop the scene, saying that they went into the kiss too early. We see, however, that the two of them are kissing for real. Once again, we are given a trope that would go on to become clichéd (most specifically in *the Breakfast Club*, in which Molly Ringwald falls for Judd Nelson): the two teenagers from opposite sides of the tracks, who mutually hate each other at first, fall for each other.

In the next scene, Hilary is talking to Leroy about her family as they take the elevator up to her opulent apartment, kissing intermittently. She says that her stepmom's credit card was stolen, but her father didn't report it because "the thief is spending less than she did." When the two of them walk into Hilary's apartment, they are completely ignored by Hilary's stuffy, elitist parents. Parker then cuts to Bruno and Coco (who is sitting behind a piano) in an empty auditorium. Coco then begins playing and singing the Oscar-nominated song "Out Here On My Own." Although the song does not necessarily possess any narrative significance, it is a beautifully soulful song, and this moment in the film is essentially an excuse to showcase the immense singing talent of Irene Cara. According to Auster, this inability of Parker to infuse the songs with any narrative significance is a weakness in the film. He states, "Parker also misses the opportunity to connect the story to the songs and dances in some original way. We get Hollywood High instead of Big Apple Angst."[24]

After the song, Bruno's father, who sneaked in to watch, gives Coco a ride home and he is surprised and impressed when he drops her in front of a palatial apartment building. Before she gets out, Bruno's father tells Coco that she makes Bruno happy, which lays bare Bruno's shyness (he cannot tell her himself) and plants yet another seed of possible romance. When the cab pulls away, we see that Coco lied about living in such a nice neighborhood as she waits until the cab is out of sight, and walks to the train stop. Again, Parker does not shy away from the perennial theme of struggle, both personal and socio-economic.

We then cut to a funereal, stark tableau in a church. Ralph's mother is crying in one of the pews, holding her young daughter (Ralph's sister) in her arms. Ralph bursts in and consoles his sister, who was apparently attacked in the hallway of their building by a junkie. Ralph asks if they took her to a hospital, but his mother insists that all she needs is the comfort and grace of God. Ralph erupts in a fit of rage, saying she needs a doctor, verbally eviscerating the priest, accusing him of "living in the fucking Dark Ages." This scene furthers two of Parker's perennial themes: the angry, indignant struggle on the part of his characters to break through barriers, and the idea of technological advancement and modernity eradicating outdated ideas. Ralph's angry desire to break through not only his socio-economic barriers but his emotional ones shines through, and Eddie Barth's performance makes Ralph's character a bit more sympathetic. The struggle for modernity to break through is also evident in the form of the age-old science and medicine-versus-religion debate. Ralph, the representative of the ambitious, angry young vanguard, wants to see (much like Bruno does) technology and modernity depose the reactionary prescriptions of a fading generation.

Ralph then returns to Montgomery's apartment, where he and Doris are pensively waiting for him. Ralph walks in and regales the two of them with the details of his sordid past. His mother ran a boarding house of sorts, with all kinds of strange men coming and going, and Ralph was constantly faced with a revolving door of father figures. Ralph's plaguing sense of guilt and his complicated relationship with comedy is revealed in a story which Ralph tells about how, one night, he was making his five-year-old sister laugh, which aroused the ire of his alcoholic father, who inadvertently hit Ralph's sister and put her head through the wall. She was then taken to a hospital, where she was diagnosed with permanent brain damage. Ralph's anger becomes more and more understandable as he is left with both debilitating guilt, and a built-in hatred of his talent for making people laugh.

The lighting and framing of this scene are quite remarkable. As Ralph tells the story, he walks over to the windows and sits on the sill. Just outside the windows is an enormous, red, flashing neon sign, which intermittently bathes the entire room with haunting red light. The sign becomes a grotesque mockery of the "flashing lights of Broadway," and serves as a haunting portent, reminding these students that the road to the lights of Broadway is paved with strife and difficulty.

In the next scene, Doris and her mother are walking home from the store, with Doris carrying two bags of groceries. She tells her mother that she wants to change her name to Dominique DuPont, because she cannot relate to a boring, middle-aged–sounding name like Doris. She seems to be slowly coming out of her shell and asserting herself. Her mother, of course, vehemently disagrees and tells her that "Dominique" is the kind of girl who would get pregnant and have an abortion, and she refers to the one night that Doris stayed out late with Ralph. Doris says, "It was just one night," and her mother becomes silent and pensive and says, "That's all it takes." This subtly impactful moment suggests that Doris had become pregnant, the result of "just one night." Once again, Parker does not shy away from granting the adults in the story with subtle humanity.

We then cut to a raucous, wild screening of *The Rocky Horror Picture Show*, with Ralph and Doris in the audience. Ralph lights up a joint, and Doris, hesitant at first, lets loose and smokes it with him. Doris's transformation is almost complete—she is jettisoning her meek, mousy insecurity and allowing herself to live and have fun. As the rowdy, loyal *Rocky Horror* fans clamor for the film to start, Parker seems to be reminding the viewer of the unifying power of cinema. The emcee of the screening announces that one girl in particular is attending the screening for the 150th time. Sometimes films transcend their status as simple entertainment and become worldwide phenomena, bringing together passionate, dedicated people, all with a common interest. Such is the power of cinema.

The next scene is of Montgomery, alone in his apartment, strumming an acoustic guitar, singing a somber lament: "Is it okay if I call you mine?" Once again, the lighting and framing are striking as Parker zooms in from the dark, shadowy streets to Montgomery's window, which is emitting a fiery, golden-hued but melancholic shade of light. If the lighting were brighter in tone and saturation, Montgomery's window would appear as a beacon of joy and hope in an otherwise dark city, but the dimness and low-key quality to the light shrouds him in sadness, as he sings the song with a heart-wrenching sense of *ennui*.

Parker then cuts back to the *Rocky Horror Picture Show* screening, and again reminds us of the wonderfully unifying power of cinema, as the entire crowd is actively engaging with the film, quoting the lines in unison. Parker lingers on this scene for almost three minutes, showing clips of the film, focusing on the crowd's reaction. He does not want to rush through this moment, as he, a cinephile himself, seems to want to revel in the enjoyment an audience can glean from a cinematic experience. Doris then really lets loose, removing her shirt and running up to the front of the theater to join in on the crowd's dance rendition to the song "Time Warp." Her evolution seems to be complete.

We then cut to a diner in which Doris is jubilantly telling Montgomery about her experience. She says, "If I don't have a personality of my own, so what! I'm an actress; I can put on as many personalities as I want." Although this declaration does seem to be Doris's resolution of her inner conflict, it feels, dramatically, somewhat rushed and forced. As Hacker and Price put it, "The problem is that these characters do not evolve, they suddenly burst forth. It is a little too crude."[25]

As the waiter comes to their table to get their order, Doris, Montgomery, and Ralph look up to see that it is Michael, the actor on whom Doris had a crush and who moved to

L.A. to make it big as an actor. He tells them that L.A. was not all it's cracked up to be, and that becoming a movie star is extremely difficult. This moment furthers one of Parker's most prominent assertions in this film, which is that hardships and humiliations one must endure to achieve success, particularly in the entertainment industry, are a prerequisite.

As a title card reading "Senior Year" appears over a black screen, we hear the voice of comedian Richard Belzer, who, it is revealed, is emceeing for "Catch a Rising Star." He introduces Ralph, who comes out and performs some stand-up comedy. He tells numerous jokes about his impoverished socio-economic status and how hard it is living in the South Bronx. He performs quite well, the audience responding with laughter. Afterwards, he and Doris walk into a train station, Ralph still giddy with excitement. He delves into an excitable litany of things he wants (his face on the cover of *TV Guide*, a hit TV series, a twenty-thousand-dollar-a-week salary, etc.) which all seems completely unrealistic. We want to celebrate with Ralph, but we can't help but feel that he may go the way of Michael—i.e., he seems to be reductively oversimplifying the work that it takes to become extremely successful.

Parker contrasts Ralph's jubilant, hopeful look toward the future with a shot of Hilary, sitting alone in a lobby, sobbing and confessing aloud (ostensibly to no one) that she is going to move to the West Coast and try to make it out there. She still has hopes of success, but hers is a far more defeatist outlook than Ralph's. Parker then cuts to an insert of a nurse, sitting behind a desk doing paperwork, not at all listening to Hilary as she bares her soul. Hilary then says, still sobbing, "There's no room for a baby." It is now evident that she is at an abortion clinic. After her candid unburdening of her fears and insecurity, the nurse callously and apathetically says, "Will that be Master charge or American Express?" Her lack of concern is quite disturbing, and Parker seems to be underscoring one of the film's latent messages, which is that the world is a cold, unforgiving place, not just for performers, but for everyone.

We then cut to Coco, eating in a diner, minding her own business. A strange, mysterious man approaches her and compliments her, telling her that she has all the traits necessary to be a star. He introduces himself as François Lafete (played by Steve Inwood). François says that he is casting for a film, and he wants Coco to do a screen test for him. Coco is thrilled, and the excitement in Irene Cara's eyes conveys her wide-eyed innocence, and desire to hit the big time. The audience, however, knows better. François is coded (in both his attire and his appearance) as a sleazy, underhanded letch.

After hearing from a fellow student that Mrs. Sherwood's husband is in the hospital, we cut to Leroy, walking down a hospital hallway, eventually finding Mrs. Sherwood, sitting alone on a bench, clearly grieving. Leroy launches into a heated tirade, begging her not to flunk him so he can pursue a dancing opportunity. Mrs. Sherwood politely tells Leroy that his timing for such a discussion is inappropriate, but Leroy persists, shouting at her, essentially calling her a racist. Mrs. Sherwood then erupts, shouting over Leroy, "Don't you kids ever think of anybody but *yourselves*?" Again, Parker sheds light on the ugly reality of the necessary steps one must take to achieve stardom. As Hacker and Price put it, "The film also says something about the nature of success, of single-mindedness, which all too often becomes selfishness."[26] Parker, however, is not content with merely showcasing the harsh, selfish reality of the climb to the top. In this scene, he offers the possibility of redemption. Realizing his callousness, Leroy sits down next to Mrs. Sherwood and consoles her, offering her a tissue. With this scene, Parker seems to be suggesting that the possibility of these two aggressively opposed camps (the ambitious youth and the reactionary old guard) reconciling does, in fact, exist.

We then cut to Coco ascending the staircase of François's seedy apartment building. She enters, and when she asks him where the crew is, he says that he it comprises him and him alone, as he needs to have complete control of the process (he even uses the word *auteur*). Here, Parker seems to be poking fun at the ego of directors, and, in particular, of directors who put stock in the "auteur theory," which Parker describes as "pure nonsense."[27] As Coco sits down in front of the camera, the scene devolves into a disturbing, creepy and unsettling casting session. François asks Coco to take her top off. Parker infuses the scene with his signature uncompromising, raw power as Coco cries and removes her top against her will, as François lecherously watches. It is an extraordinarily difficult moment to watch, and it displays Parker's ability to arouse guttural, primal emotions in his audience. Like the preceding exchange between Leroy and Mrs. Sherwood, this scene also furthers the assertion that the road to success is paved with hardship, and it has the potential to destroy heretofore-decent people.

The next scene takes place in another comedy club, and Ralph is extremely strung out as he prepares for another set. Doris and Montgomery tell him that he needs sleep, and he violently tells them to "get off his case." Montgomery says, "I'm your friend," to which Ralph replies, "You're my friend? I know what you've been after, you fucking faggot." We are witnessing the decomposition of Ralph's sanity—the demands of making it as a comedian are taking their toll on him. Doris tells him that he is an original person with a unique personality (full of rage and pain and love) and that he does not need to pretend to be somebody else. This speech would have had more of a dramatic impact if it were not completely antithetical to Doris's own admission in a previous scene about how it is not important to have a unique personality. Ralph then gets up on stage and bombs—the audience is far less receptive to his jokes than the previous one. He completely blows it and walks backstage, defeated. Montgomery walks in to console him, reassuring him that having a bad night is part and parcel of the entertainment business. Ralph then brings up Freddie Prinze again, as he finally seems to realize that he (Ralph) is not Freddie—he is his own person, and Montgomery, in a quiet, touching scene, reassures him of that.

At this point we see a montage of the kids preparing for graduation. Parker then cuts to the grand finale, which starts with Lisa, Coco, and Montgomery trading verses of "I Sing the Body Electric," a hopeful, ambitious song about the future. It then segues into an up-tempo, rocking musical interlude, featuring a guitar solo and Bruno banging away on the piano keys.

The performance continues to build to a fever-pitched crescendo, a mad painting of catharsis, hope, and energy. The dancers perform a choreographed ballet while the symphony plays, and the audience members watching the performance (adults and students alike) stand up and join in on the harmonious, operatic celebration of life and of the pursuit of artistic dreams.

In this way, the operatic musical ending of *Fame* echoes the ending of Parker's previous musical, *Bugsy Malone*. The ending of both films finds the heretofore-bickering opponents coming together harmoniously to celebrate the fact that, although there may be differences and divisive forces which incite sometimes violent opposition, the opportunity for two warring factions to reconcile does exist.

5

Shoot the Moon, 1982

February 19; 124 minutes/Color
Production Company: Metro-Goldwyn-Mayer
Director: Alan Parker
Screenwriter: Bo Goldman
Producers: Stuart Millar (Executive Producer), Edgar J. Scherick (Executive Producer), Alan Marshall (Producer)
Production Designer: Geoffrey Kirkland
Cinematographer: Michael Seresin
Editor: Gerry Hambling
Cast: Diane Keaton (Faith Dunlap); Albert Finney (George Dunlap), Karen Allen (Sandy); Peter Weller (Frank Henderson); Dana Hill (Sherry Dunlap); Viveka Davis (Jill Dunlap); Tracey Gold (Marianne Dunlap), Tina Yothers (Molly Dunlap)[1]

> Undoubtedly there were aspects of the marriage in the film which closely reflected my own. [Albert] Finney plays a writer in the story not to [sic] dissimilar to me and the intimate exploration into the fragile and delicate state of marriage I found to be uncomfortably close to home ... probably the most personal of all my films.[2]—Alan Parker

> This city could die of quaint.—George Dunlap to his wife, Faith, regarding San Francisco

Notes on the Production

While Parker was developing *Fame*, he received a script entitled "Switching" from 20th Century–Fox, the story of a marriage on the rocks, written by Oscar-winning screenwriter Bo Goldman (*One Flew Over the Cuckoo's Nest* and *Melvin and Howard*). Eventually Parker ended up working with Goldman in what he called "one of his happiest collaborations ... my sessions with Bo were a delight. Both married with ten kids between us, we poured our hearts out to one another like a couple of shrinks lying on couches at opposite ends of the room."[3] "Switching" eventually became *Shoot the Moon*, a metaphoric title that reflected the film's reference to the risky move of "shooting the moon" in the game of Hearts.

When Parker finished *Fame*, he and Alan Marshall purchased a one-hundred-year-old clapboard ranch house on the edge of a golf course and transported it to Northern San Francisco, where the film was to take place. Parker met with MGM head David Begelman (who produced *Fame*) and after a drink at the Russian Tea Room in New York, Begelman agreed to make the film on two conditions: First, Parker needed to stay on budget; and second, Diane Keaton (who won the Best Actress Oscar for *Annie Hall* [1977, Woody Allen]) was to play Faith Dunlap.

Additionally, Parker cast versatile British actor Albert Finney (*Tom Jones, Saturday Night/Sunday Morning, Scrooge*) whom he had admired since his teenage years. Finney—a serious actor who had played a number of comedic, dramatic and musical film roles including Luther on the stage—had a curious resemblance to Parker, which certainly added to the personal nature of the film.[4] "It was the first time I ever did a film that was close to my own life," Parker told *Cineaste* in 1986.[5]

Despite the certainty of the lead roles, the casting for the four Dunlap daughters—a process that spanned New York, Los Angeles and San Francisco—was more challenging. Luckily, however, Parker was able to get British actress Karen Allen (*Raiders of the Lost Ark* [1981, Steven Spielberg]) and successful Broadway actor Peter Weller, who later starred in *Robocop* (1987, Paul Verhoeven). Three of the young actresses who were eventually cast went on to have very successful careers in film and/or television (the late Dana Hill played the daughter in *National Lampoon's European Vacation* [1986, Amy Heckerling], Tracy Gold played the daughter in the television series *Growing Pains*, and Tina Yothers was the young daughter in the sitcom *Family Ties*).

Director Alan Parker on the set with lead actress Diane Keaton. *Shoot the Moon* (1982), Metro-Goldwyn-Mayer.

Part of the great success of *Shoot the Moon* was the fact that Parker had such skilled performers: Keaton, "The consummate film actress" had "a built-in bullshit detector which makes it impossible for her to do a phony performance,"[6] and Finney, "The lion of the London stage" would repeat his performances over and over again until he was happy with it."[7]

Filming was completed on April 9, 1981, after sixty-two days of shooting and released in theaters in February of 1982 (the same year *Pink Floyd—The Wall* was released). Although the film was not popular at the Box Office, it *was* critically acclaimed. Scathing film critic Pauline Kael, who had not liked Parker's previous films, wrote that *Shoot the Moon* "is perhaps the most revealing American movie of the era."[8] The film exudes a quiet intensity regarding the complex dynamics of family relationships. In many ways, the film may have been his most "bare bones" project to date: There is no social commentary, no theological imagery, no themes of corruption, no rebellion against oppressive authority ... it is just an effective family drama (exquisitely photographed by Michael Seresin) about the adverse effects of divorce.

Summary

Leo the Lion roars, beginning Alan Parker's second feature film with David Begelman and MGM. The film opens with David Serensin's captivating cinematography, revealing a picturesque establishing shot of mountains, soaked in a layered cold blue hue on a very hazy day in Northern San Francisco, which helps set the somber, melancholy tone for the entire film. Juxtaposed over this imagery is the title accompanied by a minimalist piano score—a piece called "Don't Blame Me" that was retrieved from a catalogue of MGM-owned songs. Parker said, "I had it played on a piano with one finger—like a child would play, with innocent simplicity."[9] The music serves as a leitmotif that appears throughout the film to accent the Dunlaps' brooding moments of intensity. As the music plays, an opening montage begins—the layering of images moves effectively as if the viewer were experiencing still-frame photography in an art gallery, zooming slowly into a long shot of the façade of a house located within a valley, surrounded by the beautiful mountains looming overhead as if they were visual characters unto themselves. This is followed by a series of shots, each one displaying themes of abandonment: a low angle of an automobile in a blue night light; a bicycle in a black/gray silhouette (there are many silhouettes throughout the film that add to the film's ambiguity); an obscure shot of a bed, surrounded by beams of light (the claustrophobic closed-form composition and high-contrast lighting suggests an expressionistic nightmare); dolls; a swing, swaying back and forth; and a stuffed animal on the front porch. Activity has recently taken place here, but whoever was riding the bike or swinging in the swing or playing with the dolls and stuffed animal have now disappeared, suggesting loneliness and, thus, foreshadowing the doomed fate of this family.

The camera transitions into an empty hallway in the home, and, after a long beat, George Dunlap (Albert Finney) enters into the right side of the frame. He is distressed, cupping his hands over his eyes. He descends the stairs slowly and methodically, pauses, anxiously looks upstairs (where his family is), and after another long beat he nervously enters his study. Inside the study he cries, the camera abruptly switching from a long-shot to a close-up. The shot—like many throughout the film—lingers as the camera stays with him for a few more uncomfortable beats. Parker is not afraid to hold the shots on his characters. Although this is a Hollywood film, *Shoot the Moon* is paced like a character-driven European film or a John Cassavetes film that oftentimes captures intimate and candid moments of male and female relationships, like in the independent family dramas *Faces* (1968), *Husbands* (1970) and *A Woman Under the Influence* (1974).

The silence gives way to a noisy transition: Four young girls—Sherry (Dana Hill), Jill (Viveka Davis), Marianne (Tracey Gold) and Molly (Tina Yothers)—are "helping" their mother, Faith Dunlap (Diane Keaton), as she sits in front of her bedroom mirror, preparing for what will be a night out with her husband. Immediately—even in chaotic overlapping dialogue (a technique used throughout the film to add to the more realistic, less scripted world of family conversation—a technique that Robert Altman used in *Nashville* [1975] and *M*A*S*H* [1970])—the girls' personalities begin to take shape, especially Sherry, who unlike her sisters, sits in a chair, scolding her siblings and telling them to leave their mother alone so she can get ready. As the oldest of the four, she is the "matriarch" of her sisters—and as the narrative progresses, the film becomes not just a story about a marriage on the rocks; it is also a rites-of-passage story for this troubled adolescent who is coming to terms with her own maturity while enduring her parents' dissolving relationship.

Cross-cut to George, crying. Then after some contemplation, he picks up the phone and the scene quickly cuts back to Faith and her daughters. Faith playfully puts lipstick on Molly, which may suggest that she, like Sherry, is growing up faster than she may want to. She is a dedicated, nurturing mother (which most likely helps to explain Sherry's knack for "mothering"). Another cut to George shows him on the phone talking with a woman; this is later revealed to be his mistress, Sandy. He tells her, "It won't be easy in the middle of all these people, where all I will be doing is thinking of you." An abrupt cut to Sherry, who almost instinctively picks up the telephone in the bedroom to discover her father's secret conversation downstairs; she is his superego, a critic of his adultery and, undeniably, she appears to be prophetic. It may be argued that she is the main character of the film. Back in the study, the conversation continues. Sandy calls him a winner (the first reference to the film's major theme of game-playing) and he responds: "Even if I win—I lose. You know what I mean?" Then a high-angle shot looks down on him, complementing his vulnerability. He continues: "It's been so long since I've had a good time; I wonder if I still know how." The quick parallel edits back and forth serve as two critical narrative devices; first, to build suspense like watching two tennis players competing in a match (later on, it will be discussed how tennis is used as a metaphor throughout the film); and second, to serve as exposition: In the first few minutes of the film the viewer knows that the story involves an already-troubled marriage, and that there is some major awards event that is about to take place.

Additionally, the opening of the film speaks to family and society, specifically the role of gender, which may help give meaning as to *why* the Dunlaps are a troubled institution. The film never overtly specifies (refreshingly so) why the Dunlaps are unhappy; we just know that they are. All we know is that George is carrying on an extramarital affair—and, in the next scene, when the married couple is together, we observe how unhappy they actually are. Let's begin by looking at George as being the only male in a household of five females. How does that dynamic alone affect both partners in the film and in real life? (This will be addressed in more detail later on in the summary.)

After George gets off the phone with Sandy, he meets Sherry on the stairway. (Sherry seems to be George's favorite child and, during the course of the film, the one with whom he has the most conflict.) She corners him by asking directly who he was talking to on the phone. He lies and says it was "Jim," and she responds, "Is that why you were whispering?" Defensively he says, "Yes, that's why I was whispering." Judgmentally (and prophetically), she retorts: "Better hurry, Mom looks terrific." George understands this subtext and, although he knows that she suspects he is having an affair, he still chooses to be in denial.

In the bedroom, Faith continues to dress for the event and puts on a pair of red gloves, symbolizing the duality of love and danger. George enters the room and tells her she looks pretty. She replies: "You seem surprised." Furthermore, she brings up a past event, when he spilled wine on her dress. A low-angle shot looks up at him, almost ironically, giving him a sort of false sense of masculinity. "You always remember the wrong things," he says and storms off. Faith is, conversely, captured in a low-angle shot that momentarily gives her the upper hand.

As the sequence comes to a close, the girls circle Faith outside by the car, and George is left out of this bond, yet he shares a moment with one of his daughters as they briefly discuss the bow tie he is wearing which once belonged to his father (another absent male figure). Part of the film's real charm and success is in its realistic portrayal of the mundane. A number of times throughout the film a catharsis is captured by the frequent shifting of moods and character emotions ... an inconsistency that truly gives depth and substance to these people; they aren't just stock characters. The car drives off and the camera lingers on Sherry as she stands apart from her more rambunctious and naïve sisters, who don't quite understand the nature of their parents' turmoil.

Furthermore, as briefly touched upon earlier, *Shoot the Moon* is a simple tale that explores the complex nature of the nuclear family. In the 1980s, when the feminist movement was reaching new heights, the Dunlaps are still trapped in their traditional gender roles: Faith has chosen to be a stay-at-home mother of four daughters, and George, the consummate breadwinner and victim of the status quo who, being the only male in a house of females, seeks solace and even a newfound masculinity by having an affair (and even forming a surrogate family, replete with a "son," which will be explored later in this study). According to sociologist Scott Coltrane: "When fathers are intimately involved in the lives of young children, men are unlikely to celebrate their manhood through combative contests, vociferous oratory and violent rituals."[10] Clearly George, despite a gentle side that he keeps well-hidden (yet at the appropriate times in the film he allows it to emerge), does have anger issues and is also violent, as we see in the scene when he breaks into the house. Could this possibly be because there is a real desire for him to be nurturing (to his wife and daughters) but the gender dynamics forbid him from becoming involved in this web of females? Moreover, is his own wife, in her choice *not* to be part of the rise of working mothers, such a strong nurturer that she, inadvertently even, emasculates him—forcing *him* to search elsewhere to fulfill his needs as a father and husband? Coltrane says, "Women are seen as naturally self-sacrificing and emotionally sensitive, rendering them perfectly suited to care for children, serve husbands and keep house. Fathers, in contrast, are seen as competitive protectors and providers, enabling them to assume their 'rightful' position as head and master of the family."[11]

In an interview with *Cinesaste*, Parker said, "The film was an homage to the housewife of today. It's about what happens when a woman today chooses not to have a career but to raise a family instead.... *Shoot the Moon* was a personal thing for me in that it was about my views of my marriage ... of course, the feminist backlash was that the film portrayed the wife as inferior. A lot of women really loathed the film."[12] Despite the obvious ideological controversy, let's consider this family situation: Faith Dunlap *was* evolving beyond the "soccer mom" mentality, and this is part of the crisis. The Dunlaps became stagnant; their inability to adapt to moderation *is* arguably a major reason the family unit disintegrates.

After the initial exposition of the congested family life, the film literally begins its journey with George and Faith driving through the streets of San Francisco (a saturated blue hue accents the couple's anxieties) en route to the awards ceremony. While driving, George's high-strung temperament is exposed as he curses a moving streetcar he comes close to hitting ("Goddamned things," he thunders) while Faith sits quietly and broods in her misery. George cracks a cynical joke about San Francisco: "This city could die from quaint"—and Faith does not respond. With these two lines, is he critiquing urban modernism? He makes a further comment about how she no longer laughs (later in the film, when the couple reconciles after a night of drinking, Faith tells George that once upon a time he used to make her laugh).

The following scene is packed with emotional energy. The Dunlaps arrive to the awards banquet as they begin their charade. When George asks his wife if she is with him, she responds in a neutral, cold tone, but in a manner that still somehow shows that, beyond their problems, she is a dedicated spouse: "It's your night, George." The only redeeming aspect of this scene is the ironic juxtaposition of the girls watching their parents on television. A dichotomy of happiness and tragedy is constantly being portrayed throughout the film, which continues to build tension and create suspense.

While Faith sits at the V.I.P. table, very out of place, she is approached by a catty NYC society woman who asks her about the children, but when Faith proceeds to show her a picture of them, the hypocritical woman flamboyantly says, "Don't bother, darling. I can just imagine how fabulous they are." Does this sort of social role-playing—a world that George has obviously been a part of for many years as a respected writer—also contributed to the couple's tension? Does Faith feel inferior as a housewife in this much bigger world of culture and high society? Does she have her own dreams and aspirations that have been suppressed because she chose to take care of her four daughters? What initially attracted George and Faith to each other?

When George *does*, in fact, win the writing award (and it's not a menial award either—it's the 25th Annual International Book Award Ceremony), he continues playing his game and, in his acceptance speech, he says, "I never thought *The Court Game* would be so good to me and my family." He then praises Faith, and kisses her. Despite their current state of affairs, his words *are* genuine. The film, interestingly enough, downplays George's talents and fame; beyond this scene, there is no other focus on his accomplishments, which teaches a valuable humanistic lesson: celebrities and artists are people, too. In the film, George is "nobody special," let alone an acclaimed international author. He is a flawed man trapped in a world of mediocrity where he needs to play the role of a family man—even if it's not in his nature. *What price, fame?* (Additionally, films like *Fame*, *Evita* and *The Commitments* critique the outcomes and circumstances of "making it big"—often looking negatively at the social repercussions of what it means to be well known).

Incidentally, nothing more is ever mentioned about *The Court Game*. Why? What is the book about? Does it concern relationships—a "courting game," maybe? Notice that it has the word *game* in the title (in fact, I argue that *The Court Game* would have been an even more appropriate title of the film itself since it clearly has more connection to the film than the game of Hearts does). As the film unfolds, it becomes obvious that the tennis court becomes a very clear metaphor for two people competing with each other in their own type of tennis match.

The next sequence involves the journey back home. George has "won" the writing game, so to speak, but is losing badly at the game of marriage. The low-key lighting in the car, replete with an image of the award and the pounding rhythm and dissonance of "Don't Blame Me" accents the already sullen atmosphere. Faith is beyond unhappy—she looks at George with sour hatred. No words are needed to capture this subtext.

George and Faith arrive home and immediately they separate from each other by going off into different rooms. George goes into his daughters' room and places a pillow under Molly's head, which shows two things: First, he desires to be a father; and second, to foreshadow his eventual departure from his home. He is then greeted by Sherry (who seems to appear as his conscience during the times when he is at his lowest), who asks him if he and her mother have been fighting again. Clearly she knows the answer is *yes* in the same way that she *knew* he was not talking on the phone with "Jim."

"Aren't you going to congratulate me?" he asks her. She retorts: "Congratulations," and slams the door, a subtext that may be translated as *congratulations for being a poor family man. Your successes mean nothing now.*

Faith is in the bedroom, taking off her red gloves (removing the passion from her relationship) and the camera pans, eventually lingering on her looking hopelessly out the window, crying. This long-shot switches (abruptly again, like many of the film's transitions between long-shots, medium-shots and close-ups) to a medium-shot in which the viewer sees Faith surrounded by the dichotomy of dark and white light—a clashing of good and evil—of conflicting emotions about her life and marriage. This scene allows the viewer to become an intimate voyeur into this woman's private world.

The next morning: the somber low-key lighting gives way to a breathtaking green landscape with rolling hills as the girls leave for school. The film is filled with these visual transitions that represent the story's ever-changing moods. These transitions serve as subconscious parallels to the characters' inconsistent emotional states. George and Faith—even in some of their most uncomfortable moments—show signs that there is still love in the relationship, that despite their dysfunction, a little bit of hope and "faith" continue to linger.

The following scene captures a private moment with Faith and George in the kitchen: George, harried and anxiety-driven searches frantically for his eye glasses while complaining about certain seemingly mundane hassles like missing pencil points and an empty orange juice container. Although this may appear to be trivial, it is very authentic to real life, captured stylistically by a disoriented hand-held camera. George's idiosyncrasies are further defined here: He purposely instigates trouble with Faith; in fact, he is frequently "pushing her buttons" throughout the film (not unlike the scene en route to the awards ceremony, when he reminds her that she has forgotten how to laugh). The tension builds to a crescendo when Faith, for the first time, makes reference to her husband's affair—calling Sandy his "lady friend." Defensively, he asks her, "What kind of a word is that?" The brooding Faith, who up to this moment has controlled her anger and betrayal, explodes: "It's like *fucking*, only you don't tell anyone about it. That's what it is!" George's response: a look of rage that is intimidating and potentially dangerous.

The camera and the characters take their time with this scene—this hyper-realism creates discomfort for the viewer. George and Faith break several dishes and have a yelling match. Then, a low-angle shot looks up at George, whose rage continues. An over-the-shoulder high-angle shot looks down on Faith, accentuating her vulnerability. The tension breaks when George announces that he's leaving, and that he is packing his bags. Faith replies, "They're packed. I packed last night." This is followed by another shot of George with that same rage in his eyes. What cataclysmic emotion could now prevail—violence or tears? Or both? Finney plays these emotions so closely to one another that viewers simply don't know which way to release their own tense energy. Eventually he leaves, takes his bags and heads for the front door.

Next, a close-up of George's hand gripping the doorknob; he hesitates (adding more tension to the scene) then, after a beat, he makes the final decision to turn the knob and exit. Despite what the viewer knows at this point—that George is having an affair and Faith is unhappy—it is still not clear who is to blame for this (again, the film's piano score is called "Don't Blame Me"—maybe it's nobody's fault); we don't know the events that have led up to the opening of the film. Did one of them inadvertently choose to end things, or was this just gradual erosion? Part of the success of this very suspenseful scene is in the abrupt parallel editing and montage—a disjointed rhythm that further subverts the expectations of where the scene may be heading. The scene ends, poignantly, with Faith's muffled whispers and George's exit and a sustained shot of the back side of Faith as she looks hopelessly out the window. Life moves on, even at this moment. Again, the camera captures this realism by refusing to cut away immediately. Perhaps the viewer is ready to turn away and move on to the next scene before the camera allows for this freedom. The scene then fades out, and this ends the first act of the film.

The next scene opens with Sherry multi-tasking in the kitchen; she is playing mother. She balances the telephone to her ear while cooking breakfast for her siblings as she attempts to schedule an appointment for her sister Jill, who hurt her foot in ballet class. Meanwhile (through parallel editing), the other siblings continue to banter with one another while getting ready for school. Faith is still in bed, which is very uncharacteristic of her, and when she tells her children she's tired, Molly says, "You're never tired." Faith has slipped into a state of depression. Nevertheless, Sherry is taking care of business—a maternal trait that she has taken on long before the story began. According to University of Akron professor, Susan D. Witt:

> Children learn at a very early age what it means to be a boy or a girl in our society. Through myriad activities, opportunities, encouragements, discouragements, overt behaviors, covert suggestions, and various forms of guidance, children experience the process of gender role socialization. It is difficult for a child to grow to adulthood without experiencing some form of gender bias or stereotyping, whether it be the expectation that boys are better than girls at math or the idea that only females can nurture children. As children grow and develop, the gender stereotypes they are exposed to at home are reinforced by other elements in their environment and are thus perpetrated throughout childhood and on into adolescence.... A Child's earliest exposure to what it means to be male or female comes from the parents.[13]

In fact, Sherry even takes on the role of the "under-appreciated mother," one who slaved all day long in the kitchen, preparing food, when her siblings tell her they don't want any breakfast. She yells, "I fix the goddam breakfast and no one wants to eat it. I'm tired of this shit!" This line implies that this is an ongoing ritual, a curious fact that alludes to the unknown backstory. Has Faith been further removing herself from the duties of parenthood, forcing her oldest daughter to take her place? In the following scene, when George sees Sherry and wishes his "princess" a good morning, she storms past him, shunning him and heads to the bus. Moments later, there is a shot of her on the bus; she sits plaintively and cries ... this young girl is already years ahead of her age. Is she crying for herself, her mother or her father? *Shoot the Moon* uses the vehicle of divorce to capture its real central theme—the rites-of-passage for both Sherry (adolescence into womanhood) and her parents (mid-life crises).

Meanwhile, George drives his other three daughters—Marianne, Jill and Molly—to school while they all whimsically sing the theme to *Fame*, an obvious tongue-in-cheek homage to Parker's previous film, also produced by MGM. This segment shows George in father mode: He continues to sing songs with them in the car as time passes through a series of dissolves, then he takes his boisterous girls out to breakfast. In the restaurant one of his daughters spills a cup of hot chocolate and the waitress behind the counters states the obvious, saying that his daughters are a real handful, leading to the next scene where George, exhausted after dropping the girls off to school, pauses and mutters: "How does she [Faith] do it?"

The next scene shows George at his beach house—his much-needed refuge—his home away from home—where he sits pensively at his typewriter in a state of cerebral contemplation. There is no dialogue, only the minimal piano score ("Don't Blame Me") and a picturesque shot of the ocean behind him, the waves crashing forcefully, undoubtedly reflecting his tumultuous being and the continuation of life. In the next scene, represented by a dissolve, he is walking on the beach, his image captured in silhouette, and this creates a rich chiaroscuro, giving the image a strangely beautiful and frightening vision of George's conflicting subconscious states of mind. He sits on a dock and thinks; this is his "man cave"— an escape from the females in his life.

Back at the Dunlap house. Faith and her daughters are once again in her bedroom (more or less *their* refuge together), playing the board game *Sorry* while *The Wizard of Oz* plays on television. It's the scene when Dorothy is locked in the wicked witch's castle and she tells the witch that it is okay to take the ruby slippers so long as she can have her dog, Toto, back—but the witch tries to take the slippers, their magical powers overcome her with a cataclysmic zap similar to an electrical shock, and consequently Dorothy is given only an hour to live. In this brief moment, lasting only seconds, there are many things occurring. First off, Faith and two of her daughters (Marianne and Molly) are playing a game in which the object is to be the first player to get all four color pawns from the start location to the home space. Like Hearts, although not nearly as complicated, it is a card game, yet in this game the "winner" gets to go home.

Similarly, *The Wizard of Oz* (Jill watches the film intently as she "plays the roles" of Dorothy and the wicked witch, mouthing the dialogue in perfect unison) is an archetypal story (like the *Odyssey*, and even the game of baseball) in which the "players," in their own ways, journey away from the home and encounter many obstacles in their paths that prevent them from returning. Not only does this scene mirror the quest for the home theme; it also comments on the family's own "search" for an ideal home life (which, by the end of the film, even becomes George's goal); it also critiques the role and effects of popular culture—from *Sorry* to *The Wizard of Oz* to the *Fame* theme song to the significance that author Jack London plays in an upcoming scene. Without going into the detailed research of the effects of media and culture on the American family, the film *does* propose a curious question: In what ways have the influences of movies, books, sports and games affected the long-term behaviors of these family members (and families in general) who have been inundated with these false realities? Jill has obviously seen *The Wizard of Oz* so many times that she can recite the film, line by line. George is enamored by the life and works of talented yet troubled writer Jack London, and he himself writes books for a living. Other characters—including Sandy and her son—pass the time by playing cards and other games. Is life itself a game? Or a movie?

Jill is interrupted when she hears something outside the window—and, moments later, George appears with a police officer; he has returned home to retrieve his belongings—mostly his books. While Faith is in the other room, talking and making coffee for the officer (who appears more uncomfortable than George and Faith), a shot of George adds tension to the moment. Is he suddenly angry? Regretful? Both? Is he going to *do* something?

Moments later, George and Faith are together by the bookshelf while George continues to pack. The conversation leads to a memory they had when they recalled watching a terrible piano player singing The Beatles' "If I fell" in French. They use popular culture as a vehicle to have their exchange. At this time, George compliments Faith on her smile but the tender moment switches abruptly when he finds out that she has gone out on a "date" with their insurance man. The tennis match continues. Despite the couple's disdain for each other, they are both trying hard to hold onto the good memories.

A new plot point takes *Shoot the Moon* into another chapter: first with the introduction of George's mistress, Sandy (Karen Allen), and, soon afterwards, with Faith's love interest, the carpenter Frank Henderson (Peter Weller). Time has passed, and George takes his daughters (minus Sherry) to meet Sandy. Reluctantly, the girls enter the strange woman's home. George kisses her and the girls exchange looks of disapproval with one another. The scene cuts to Faith in the bathtub. The camera zooms very closely in on her—we have encountered a very private and vulnerable moment in Faith's life: she is naked in her bathroom and smoking marijuana; this is a place the viewer really doesn't belong. As the camera invades her space in a suffocating closed-form composition, she begins singing the Beatles love song "If I Fell," which brings her to tears. The intimate moment is interrupted by a phone ringing—Faith's mother—and although we don't hear her dialogue, her presence is very prominent. Based on Faith's responses, her mother is very aware of the divorce proceedings—perhaps knows more than she should. When Faith attempts to give her mother health advice (she mentions something about a holistic health spa) she is criticized on the other end, leaving Faith with the words: "I wouldn't dream of interfering." The scene adds more character depth to Faith and may help explain her own complexities that may be to blame for the marriage going sour. Although we learn very little about her mother (except that she is bossy, and according to George "a lousy mother and a lousy wife"), it *does* present some dynamics that speaks to Faith's character. In this way, does Faith overcompensate her own mothering skills because she—apparently—was never close to her own mother? After all, on the surface anyway, they *are* very different women. Or are they really the same at the core? Maybe George has always had trouble with his mother-in-law—another female adding a burden to his already-bruised masculinity.

In the next scene, Faith meets Frank Henderson, a boyish contractor initially hired to build the Dunlaps' tennis court (a detail that had been forgotten because of the recent goings-on) when he comes to the door asking for a check for their previous contractual agreement. During this meeting (the two of them are mutually attracted), Keaton's performance is multi-layered, as she skillfully combines a disposition that reflects her no-nonsense honesty, her sincerity and her awkward vulnerability. She finally decides to hire Frank. The construction of the tennis court has obvious symbolic significance: Ultimately it represents an aspect of George's and Faith's marriage (the court game) that needs to be "rebuilt."

Shoot the Moon overtly reflects *homo ludens*, a study of the element of play in society and culture, literally translated as "Man the Player." Arguably, the characters reflect the ideas of *homo ludens* to live their lives. According to Northrop Frye, a sociologist who has written extensively on this topic, there is a need for humans to "emerge from *homo sapiens* into *homo ludens*—from 'man the knower' into 'man the player' ... only when playfully detached are humans able to stand at arm's length from a subject and see it holistically see the relation of whole to part, subject to object, present to past." According to Frye, "Literature is the quintessential playful medium because it is detached from immediate action."[14] Similarly, Stanley Kubrick's 1980 horror film *The Shining* utilizes *Homo Ludens* as way to interpret the American family through the direct intertextual references to *Alice in Wonderland*, darts, balls, *The Three Little Pigs*, even card playing, as represented through the design and execution of the green labyrinth.

The next major link to literature is introduced through a brief but significant history of San Francisco–born author Jack London (*The Call of the Wild*, *White Fang*, *The Sea Wolf* and the short story "To Build a Fire"), whom George redeems as "a wonderful man" as he, three of his daughters and Sandy stroll through London's former property, which has become an historic park. The scene becomes not just an homage to the famous, controversial, prolific writer (who was a celebrity in his day)—it becomes much more (which may also, on another note, reflect screenwriter Bo Goldman's admiration for the writer, who, like London, had four daughters).[15] George is the historical tour guide who professes his knowledge of the author's biography that undoubtedly parallels his own life, including the fact that London was divorced from his first wife. After one learns a little more about London's personal life, it may be safe to surmise two major possibilities regarding *Shoot the Moon*: First, that George Dunlap is figuratively a "ghost" of the writer (the film mentions that, in 1913, London's Sonoma Valley home—Wolf House—mysteriously caught fire and was burned to the ground. Additionally, some legends say that he left his spirit behind)[16]; secondly, George may be living in the shadow of his favorite author and may even inadvertently be taking on his persona (Is the title *The Court Game* influenced by London's own boxing novel *The Game*? Also, coincidentally or not, London published a novel called *Valley of the Moon:* The film takes place in a San Francisco *valley* and has *moon* in its title). Thus, *Shoot the Moon* may be about a writer whose personal obsession with "being" Jack London drives him away from his own family.[17]

Jack London was born in 1876 and died of kidney disease at age forty, on November

22, 1916. In addition to being perhaps the first real celebrity author, he had been a journalist, an avid boxing fan, an endorser of socialism, a supporter of women's suffrage and prohibition, an agriculturist, a gold prospector in the Yukon, not to mention a notorious hedonist who drank incessantly. He was born the only (bastard) son of five children (leaving four females, the same number of daughters George has) and, in two marriages, he fathered three daughters. The absence of male figures may have greatly defined him as it may have George Dunlap. In a way, Jack London is George Dunlap's contemporary doppelgänger and although by default they have a connection to the females in their lives, maybe they both need to remind themselves (belligerently, even) that they are still men.

Back at Sandy's house: The Dunlap girls are realizing that their father and Sandy have replaced their own parents. During bedtime, it is obvious that Sandy (a divorced woman with only one child—a son—who appears to have little patience and connection with the girls) lets it be known that she wants the girls to go to sleep so she can be with their father. She reminds the girls, quite bluntly at that, that she does things differently than their mother does—a subtext indicating that she has no real intention of being a mother figure to them. When Marianne says to her, "I bet you want to make love with Daddy," she frankly retorts: "Yes, I do. What's wrong with that?" Jill then asks, "What's it like making love to Daddy?" Sandy replies: "It's like eating ice cream," a comment that eventually gets a laugh from the girls after Sandy leaves. Sandy's strange response to the question (she tries to equate love-making to something that would typically appeal to children, not realizing perhaps that this ridiculous response is also absurdly Freudian!) insults the intelligent girl's question, which further accentuates her lack of perception and connection to George's daughters—and maybe motherhood in general.

The next scene transitions to George and his three daughters singing "Row, Row, Row Your Boat" while driving through the pouring rain. This singing ritual is the one real moment in the film when George gets to be a daddy. Marianne, however, sits in the back seat, brooding. It can be deduced that she is depressed about her parents, yet it is never mentioned: The film does not rely on exposition, which adds refreshingly to the story's realism. She, like her big sister Sherry, is living inside her head and is, in her own way, experiencing her own rites of passage.

When George returns home, he finds things to be quite different. He attempts to give Sherry her birthday present—a typewriter. Although never directly addressed, this gift suggests that Sherry is a budding writer herself; maybe she acquired these creative interests from her father. Furthermore, the viewer can deduce that George and Sherry have a special bond, that they are even each other's alter-egos to a degree. As the film progresses, the audience discovers that this relationship may, in fact, be the glue that adheres the entire story together (even the film's title is mentioned in an upcoming scene when they converse on the beach). Furthermore, the tennis court is being built and George sees his wife in an intimate pose with Frank. Outraged, George's temper flares. When Faith approaches him, the two argue about their relationship and, in one of her stronger moments, Faith "wins" the fight. George, defeated, is left out in the rain and becomes a bigger "loser" when he waves at Sherry from the window; instead of waving back, his daughter shuns him and disappears from sight. He has truly lost everything.

Following a transition into an image of the mountain—indicating a passage of time—the camera brings the viewer to yet another perception shift: the development of Faith and

The troubled married couple from California, Faith and George Dunlap (Diane Keaton and Albert Finney). *Shoot the Moon* **(1982), Metro-Goldwyn-Mayer.**

Frank's romance (the names are curious, too—"faith" has to do with hope, and "frank" is about being honest and truthful). They sit together in the construction site—"the court game" in session. They chat rather awkwardly and Faith asks Frank if *the court* (a metaphor for their relationship) will be beautiful. He says *it* will be, but there is a trace of uncertainty in his response.

The next sequence focuses on their ongoing courtship. Frank is a guest for dinner, and Faith, like a nervous school girl, makes him feel at home. In fact, she waits on him as he sits at the table; he has inadvertently become a household patriarch, even if for only a moment. Faith is still caught up in a rather old-fashioned, somewhat submissive role in this new courtship. Sherry, always a critic of her parents' actions, responds angrily when Faith keeps calling her "honey." Sherry yells, "What's with this honey shit all about, anyway?" Obviously this is all so new for Faith and she doesn't know how to act naturally; this is not a game she knows or plays well, but under the circumstances, she is trying to make it work.

Faith and Frank's date officially begins when they move into the study. She offers him a cigar and brandy as he sits on the couch next to her in a tense, rigid manner; both are equally nervous. Faith appropriately plays the plaintive Rolling Stones song "Play with Fire," which serves as a narrative for the scene, as Mick Jagger staunchly admonishes the listener to take extreme caution. During the song, Frank asks Faith if she wants to dance, and she admits to being nervous and scared, that it had been a long time since she'd been with anyone besides George. Frank asks her to kiss him—and instinctively she says, "No, I don't think so," but after a long awkward beat of several two-shots, she says, "I mean, yes." And they kiss—which plays out as awkwardly as the lead-up.

The song may serve as a type of foreshadowing: From the word *go*, the relationship appears to be doomed. Faith is working on a rebound, and Frank (who has no known background) is an enigmatic "stranger" archetype who appears to just want her sexually. Are both of them "playing with fire" by becoming involved, even if, for the time being, they seem to fulfill a certain symbiotic need?

A parallel edit to the parallel couple: George and Sandy in the bedroom. Sandy's son, Timmy, is coughing in the bathroom and in this segment, George becomes the temporary surrogate "father" for the little boy. Sandy is not a nurturing, maternal character (she doesn't get up to comfort her son) but, conversely, George takes a nurturing approach toward the young boy, which leads to a short but profound scene in the bathroom, during which a candid conversation occurs. Timmy asks George where his own father is and George reminds him that he's in Los Angeles, further reminding him that he "already knew this." Does Timmy feel awkward with George by his side? George doesn't appear to be fazed; in fact, there is something oddly natural about the way he converses with Timmy—"the son he never had." Timmy is missing his absent father, who, according to Sandy, was never a good family man. Timmy asks George, "Don't you want to go home and be with your own children?" Like his own daughter Sherry the child here serves as a type of superego that causes him to have a reality check. George is certainly searching for the ideal family (acting as a "husband" to a lonely, needy woman who, in a previous scene, tells him that she loves him, but in the same breath she pragmatically informs him that "if [he doesn't] come through, [she'll] find somebody else"). Thus, both Faith's and George's respective significant others seem to be right for one another only in the moment, but certainly not for the long-term. George had mentioned that he *does* enjoy being with her, but as the film unfolds we realize that he and Faith are really destined to remain together. In a way, *Shoot the Moon* (like Michelangelo Antonioni's *Eclipse*) is a story about a troubled couple who finds solace in the arms of other people only to discover that they are still destined to be together.

The next scene focuses on the mother/daughter relationship between Sherry and Faith, another raw, truthful slice of life that looks more closely at Faith's mothering skills. At this pivotal moment, the *mise-en-scène* becomes its own character: the framing and the composition reflect the characters' intimate moment. In a picture-perfect view, they stand at opposite ends of the window frame (which is its own frame within the frame) exposing the aesthetically pleasing green background of the San Francisco landscape outside. Sherry reports that she hates her father and that she is never getting married. Faith unselfishly tells her daughter that, despite the fact that marriage is indeed a troubled institution, it can *still* be a positive experience despite the problems that often prevail. Faith uses the metaphor that a married couple "walks through doors" with one another—at first they walk together, and then what sometimes happens is that one partner eventually gets a head of the other and then they are no longer together. Sherry asks, "If they love one another why don't they wait for each other?" Interestingly enough, Faith answers her with a quote from George (another clue that their love remains strong) regarding the need to remain hopeful. "Wishes are sometimes all we have." Sherry wants immediate answers (part of her naïveté) but Faith, more weathered in relationships and life in general speaks words of wisdom: "When you get older, you'll learn to take things as they come." She defends George in front of Sherry for at least two reasons: First, and most simply, because she still loves him; second, it is her duty as a parent to look objectively at the situation so that she can accurately teach her child how to live in the moment, indicating that sometimes in life there are "no rules." Faith continues to live up to her name. The scene ends when the two of them hug, both a bit more grounded and a bit wiser in this ongoing game.

In the following scene, Faith, Jill, Marianne and Molly experience a very awkward chance encounter with Sandy on a sidewalk. The children recognize her, call her by name, and Sandy stops and acknowledges them. This obviously takes Faith by surprise, breaking her continuity and changing her mood. When Sandy walks away, the girls, in their typically sporadic, overlapping dialogue makes comments like "She's not pretty" and "She looks like a ghost.." undoubtedly said more for the sake of their mother. Faith—who is typically even-tempered—yells at her girls: "Shut up and get in [the car]!" They drive home, the beautiful green valley surrounding them.

Meanwhile, George has arrived and aggressively requests to see Sherry to give her a typewriter for her birthday. In the kitchen, he smells something cooking and when Faith tells him that she is making Syrian bread for Frank, he retorts condescendingly: "What is he, an Arab?" This scene serves as the foundation for the following scene, which is arguably the most intense moment in the entire film; this present scene is synonymous to a volcano on the verge of erupting. In fact, when George leaves he yells as Frank: "It [the tennis court] looks like shit. You couldn't put horseshoes on that volcano!" Because of the noise and the distance, Frank can't hear him, prompting George to shout his next line: "I said, 'Fuck you!'" Frank's feelings are hurt. "What's *that* for?" he asks Faith, who walks away in embarrassment.

Nighttime has arrived and the camera takes its time capturing the details of the outside landscape: a stunning blue sky at dusk and a zoom-in on a family of ducks swimming in a pond. The film spends time showing the juxtaposition of the picturesque *outdoor* landscape with the frequently claustrophobic, tightly framed anxiety-driven *indoor* shots, a dichotomy that implies freedom versus imprisonment.

George's arrival at the house immediately begins in a traditionally suspenseful manner. He exits from the car but all we see at first is a close-up of his legs walking through the muddy clay dirt; undoubtedly he is an invader on his own turf. He uses Sherry's gift as a way to re-enter his home. He yells at Faith, telling her he wants to "give [his] kid her birthday present," and from upstairs Sherry yells back: "Your kid doesn't *want* her birthday present!" This heated exchange sets the following events in order:

George violently approaches the inside of the house, grabbing Faith and pushing her outside—literally locking her out of her home by blocking the door with a chair. The husband/father character has now crossed the line into domestic abuse. He moves upstairs while the scene cross-cuts furiously to George, Sherry and Faith as if we were now watching a horror/suspense film. George is being emasculated on both sides and the only tool he now has is his own vulnerable, rage-filled ego as he invades his daughter's room. Sherry hatefully curses him: "Get out of my room, you fucker!" This pushes George to the extreme. He forces himself toward her, takes hold of her and spanks her repeatedly, and moments later he immediately regrets his actions. Sherry takes a pair of scissors and waves them menacingly in front of herself for protection. And this brings up some significant questions: Has this type of force occurred before? Is George an abusive father and husband, or has the intensity of this moment brought out the worst in him? Immediately after this cataclysmic exchange, Sherry lies on her bed, crying, and George rubs her head, then says to her: "Talk to me." In this way, can it be said that the lack of communication is to blame for these actions? He and Sherry are obvious soulmates as well as each other's worst enemy. "Forgive me," he says and by this time his other daughters have entered the room. When he exits the bedroom, Marianne compassionately asks him if she can make him a hamburger with onions (obviously a meal George enjoys). This is the calm after the storm, so to speak, and in some ways the most effective, cathartic moment in the entire scene: Despite the family quarreling, Marianne feels the need to nurture her father (earlier in the film, she is in the car, sulking). Could she be seeking the affection of her father, an affection she knows is first reserved for Sherry, who might be "his favorite" child?

George is spent, tired and defeated as he descends the stairway; by this time, Faith has re-entered the house. The camera goes in for a close-up of Sherry and Faith at the top of the stairs, hugging. George stands at the bottom of the stairs; he has lost the game. Faith tells him to get out—and the camera follows him down the remaining steps of the staircase—a high-angle shot accentuating his vulnerability. Young Molly is at the bottom, standing there as if waiting for him to say something, and he affectionately touches her before leaving. "Don't Blame Me" plays, the simple melody serving as George's apology, of sorts. Another look upstairs and, from his point of view, we see a distressed closed-form composition: the typewriter and Jill are on the left side of the frame and Faith and Sherry are in the middle while Marianne is looking away on the right side, crying. George pushes aside the chair he used to block the door and exits. The broken glass on the door adds to the theme of fragmentation.

George's "court game" continues into the next scene: He and Faith are in court, beginning the first stages of their divorce proceedings. The judge sternly informs them of the new custody deal, asks if what she has said is agreeable, and further tells them she doesn't want to see them there again. Faith's lawyer, Howard Katz (Irving Metzman), assures her that they can "play hardball" (more games) to ensure that she gets full custody of the kids; Faith says she does not want to go that route—she's not interested in this game, and this baffles Katz. The custody battle and divorce proceedings take a back seat, however, when Faith tells George that her father is in the hospital. George is immediately concerned about the well-being of his father-in-law and, with both lawyers standing between him as if they were referees to Faith's and George's conversation match, he tells Faith he is willing to take the kids to her parents. Furthermore, George tells Faith: "Well, give Dad my love, and tell him I am going to come up and see him." Once again, the upheaval and unpredictability of these characters' emotions bring the film into yet another realm of visceral realism.

In the next beat, Faith sits quietly, in distress, with her father in the hospital room. Cut to George walking through the hospital hallway. He makes eye contact with his mother-in-law, who sits outside the room. She shuns him. It is never explained why Faith's mother doesn't like her son-in-law. George does, however, have a rapport with his father-in-law, the only other male figure to whom he relates; the two men appear to have a long-standing admiration for each other. Inside the hospital room, George and Faith downplay the disintegration of their marriage, but Faith's father, even in his ill state, knows the score. When he asks if they are currently together, George answers with an unconvincing, "Sure." He then responds: "You wouldn't shit me, would you George?" Then he asks about the condition of their home and, in overlapping answers, they answer differently: Faith says, "Terrific," and George replies, "It needs work" to which Faith's father says, "You are both a couple of liars." When Faith asks him if he will forgive her, his immediate reply of "Not a chance" indicates his affection for George. Curiously, nothing is ever mentioned about George's parents. As far as the film is concerned, this *is* his father. When Faith leaves the room, George remains there, hopelessly and aggressively demanding that his father-in-law fight the sickness. When Faith's father dies, George, too, has lost a father, and another chapter in the Dunlaps' life has ended.

The second act ends with the funeral. In addition to the loss, George is shunned by Sherry (who refuses to walk with him to get a flower for the coffin) as well as his mother-in-law (who admits that there is "no place" for him to ride with the family in the limousine en route to the grave site).

Next, George's silhouette is captured in an extreme long-shot on his boat at his beach home, followed by a shot of him sitting at his desk, a pensive and morose figure. Does the loss of his "father" make him reconsider his marriage with Faith? The camera holds on him as he cups his hands over his head: He is overwhelmed with emotional loss. The haunting high-contrast expressionistic lighting—replete with blue hues and dark shadows—continues to reveal, in a stylized manner, a clashing between George's states of mind. Furthermore, this is not just an ordinary man's human tragedy; it is the drama of an artist, a writer who lives his life within the realm of his own imagination, replete with literary archetypes (like the absent father), and even the worlds and words of other writers, particularly Jack London.

Time has passed since the funeral. The following scene lands George at a restaurant, a place he and Faith have evidently gone before. Faith enters the restaurant, only to find George eating. (Is this a fate encounter?) Faith tells the host—who assumes she wants to sit with her husband—that she wants her own table, and she is seated. Without skipping a beat, George picks up his meal and joins her. The conversation that follows is filled with backstory, anger and passion—another manic, whirlwind of emotions that Alan Parker presents to his audience. Again, the director never makes it easy for the viewers to settle with just one emotion ... and this creates even more visceral realism. George tells his wife that he had been spending time at the lake. "I like the lake," he reminds her. Faith tells him that she has had enough of her mother's company and this moment breaks the ice for an intimate, even comical, exchange that is paced quickly and deliberately along the lines of a Howard Hawks screwball comedy. In the midst of conversation, George cuts her food and even feeds her as if he were her father—a critical moment that shows his nurturing side, perhaps one of the traits that initially attracted Faith. Before long, the conversation switches to a heated, passionate exchange; they become exhibitionists, arguing about their relationship. Faith mentions Sandy and, in a strangely nonchalant manner, he trivializes his infidelity and reminds her that over the years he has worked hard to support her and the children. In the next breath, however, before she can really respond to this ridiculous line of logic, he praises her mothering skills, while he admits to being a poor husband and father. He admits that he "had [his] thumb up [his] ass, sharpening pencils while [she was] changing diapers and scraping shit off the walls."

Furthermore, he tells her that he "worshipped her." When she asks why he didn't treat her that way, and why he was always losing his temper, he responds, "You know I didn't mean it."

"Tell that to the children," she says tersely.

When Frank's name comes up in the conversation, Faith tells her husband, "That was *you*, fifteen years ago." Does this mean that Faith, even in the midst of an affair with another man, still desires a man like her husband?

The scene ends with another cathartic release. When George insecurely says that everyone else "loves" him (so why can't she?)—Faith gets angry and says, "Just like eating ice cream, isn't it? Just like eating ice cream!"—a line that is tragically funny. It is obvious that Faith's daughters told her about Sandy's simile for making love with George. The comedy evolves even further when their argument affects the couple dining next to them. Already offended at the level of their conversation, the man says to George, "She [Faith] would rather fuck Frank, buddy!" George shoves him and in this slapstick routine even the two women exchange words with one another. Another beat shift—George and Faith sit back down at the table and quietly George says to his wife, "I think we won." George, it seems, is forever playing games.

A new, ironic perception shift: George and Faith get drunk and carry on with each other as if *they* are now having an affair. For the first time in the film, the viewer sees the couple the way they may have been years earlier, before things turned sour. Eventually they kiss and the inevitable occurs: they end up having sex, leading to another level of conversation in the bedroom: "I was never right for you," George tells her. He left her not because he wanted to, but because he felt he was not worthy of her; in fact, he calls her a saint. She admits to him that she had forgotten how to be a good wife. Was this disintegration a direct result of having four children? George says, "Jesus, I loved you." Similarly, Faith reflects on how he used to make her laugh and how kind he once was. They admit to each other that they are no longer kind like they were and that being with their respective partners ("strangers") is easier than being with one another. Do they both need to carry on with these strangers in order to refuel their own relationship, or is it really over?

When Sherry enters the bedroom to report that Molly had just thrown up, she sees her parents back together. She is pictured in a menacing low-key lighting as she leaves the room. Faith says, "You better go, George." The scene ends with a close-up on the couple, an intimate shot that suggests their intimacy on two levels: First, they are still a married couple; second, the closed-form of the *mise-en-scène* places them in a tight composition, showing the inevitability of their own confinement—even imprisonment. Do they, in fact, have a symbiotic relationship that renders them inseparable?

The final sequence of the film has begun and the narrative shifts to Sherry's point of view. Soft rock music sets the scene for an outdoor party, a celebration of the completion of the tennis court, a symbolic foreshadowing for a new beginning—a new "game." As the other girls play tennis in a carefree manner (showing their naïveté), Sherry is at the grill with the adults; she asks Frank to dance with her. He playfully responds, "I'm too *young* for you." On one level, she appears to have a crush on Frank; on another level, she turns her emotions toward a school-girl jealousy of this appealing older man when Frank begins to dance with Faith.

Frank asks Sherry to join him and her mother in their dance and she humbly accepts, but within moments the emotions shift when Sherry suggests that Frank might be moving in with them (he clearly states that this is *not* his plan). Sherry yells at Faith: "You fucked Daddy last week—you fucked Frank this week—who you going to fuck next week?" Sherry gets the inevitable slap in the face and when Frank tries to interject, she yells at him: "You're not my father!" Then she runs away to find her father, who is at Sandy's house. Sherry misses her father and Frank is certainly no replacement for him; furthermore, she is a maturing young woman who has an awkward crush on her mother's boyfriend.

In the next shot, Sandy, George and Sandy's son, Timmy, are playing the game of Hearts. The scene is cross-cut with Sherry walking on the beach in front of the house. George is interrupted by a sound he hears outside and instinctively he gets up and looks out the window to see his daughter in the distance (it's as if time momentarily stands still: the camera focuses solely on George and his connection to Sherry; Sandy and Timmy are removed from this moment, unaware that anything has happened). Without skipping a beat, he takes the typewriter and a blanket and walks down to the dock and the next several minutes the audience becomes engaged in an intense, sorely needed father/daughter exchange, arguably the *soul* of the entire film. George begins by giving Sherry the gift, which pleases her. As the moment turns tender it abruptly shifts when Sherry reminds her father: "You fucked Sandy, then you fucked Mommy." George tells her, "I don't have to take that from you," and proceeds to leave but, after a beat, he returns and apologizes to her. "You're always sorry," she says. He wraps the blanket around both of them and what follows is a poignant conversation:

Sherry begins by asking her father why he left and he simply informs her, "Something happened between me and Mom." He doesn't know the answers, but he needs to figure them out. Meanwhile, he has found solace with Sandy and her son, Timmy. Sherry's jealousy ensues: She asks George if he loves Timmy more than her and he assure her he does not. The conversation shifts to the game of Hearts. Sherry asks if Timmy is good at cards and George tells her that the young boy "shot the moon," which is quite the feat to accomplish even once. In the game of Hearts, a person who "shoots the moon" is able to capture all the high cards, which ultimately leaves this player with an ideal score of zero and, ultimately, the winner. As a risk taker himself, George, a confirmed game player, is "shooting the moon" in his own personal game of Hearts—yet, ironically, this "winner" ends up with nothing—so what does this ultimately mean? Earlier in the film George talks about Jack London—certainly a risk taker in his own life—who had "[lost] everything." He tells his daughter that once the divorce is finalized he will have more time for her. Sherry, however, does not believe this, and she says, "I think you'll be closer to Timmy." Is her intuition so sharp that she can predict such things? Does George know this himself? Is this why the scene ends before he can respond to this very important statement? Is it "in the cards" that George will lose a daughter and gain a "son"?

Next, George drives Sherry back home to the party. Bob Seger's card-playing love song "Still the Same" sets the mood and tone of this scene. Although not executed in a typical rock montage style, the ambient song seems to *serve* as a metaphor for George Dunlap's life, despite the fact that in the film's DVD commentary track, Parker downplays the choice of the song, implying that it has no narrative significance.[18] The narrator in the song tells the story of a true game player—someone who constantly "shoots the moon"—but the narrator also has this player's number, so to speak. Despite the player's ability to "turn on the charm," to "[move from] game to game," and "[always winning] every time a bet was played"—the player does not evolve or change. The song, setting the mood for the party, becomes George's theme akin to the leitmotif "Don't Blame Me." Despite the fact that he becomes an archetypal searcher character—someone looking for a life beyond his own home—he proves that, in his soul, he is "still the same"—a player who *still* needs his family. As the scene unfolds, the song even serves as a form of foreshadowing: George drives to the house, bringing both himself and his daughter back where they belong. Sherry kisses her father as she exits the car; for the first time in the film, George and Sherry have bonded.

George encounters Faith, who welcomes him calmly, even warmly. He tells her, "You did it. You really did it … the tennis court." Even when Frank enters the picture, he tells him, "The court looks good…. I like it very much," which means a lot to the carpenter. On one level, the conversation has a maturity about it—Faith even suggests that in the future he can bring Sandy over! To allude to an earlier scene when George and Faith discuss their relationship, they are "acting like grown-ups." The viewer, however, is not truly convinced that the situation is as it appears on the surface. George is obviously not happy, and it reads on his face; Faith, naïvely perhaps, feels comfortable enough to ask George if he wants to meet Frank's friends and, jokingly, she offers him some tequila that will "put hair on [his] chest." She laughs. Does this line make reference to a comical moment in their past (similar to the aforementioned memory of the Beatles' song "If I Fell," sung in French)? George continues to brood, then says, "I really got to go" (subtext: *This is all too much for me to handle*), and this leads to the film's cataclysmic climax.

In a finely paced montage, George gets into his car and immediately becomes a juggernaut—driving and crashing into the new tennis court repeatedly until it is completely demolished. This obliteration represents the emotional game he and Faith have been playing. George is not happy with the decision to leave Faith, and destroying this court may be looked at as a form of creation and reinvention. Destruction is a form of creation and, in this way, he is destroying so he can "rebuild" his life from scratch.

This action, however, yields another cataclysmic catharsis—Frank's rage. After all, George has destroyed *his* creation. Frank attacks him relentlessly, leaving George helpless on the ground. Frank has won the match, and to add insult to injury, he kicks Sherry's typewriter, a gesture that may indicate he wants no future with Faith *or* her children. Like George, however, he, too, has a frightening rage. Is it safe to take a psychoanalytical route here and say that George encounters a symbolic battle with his younger alter-ego (earlier in the film, after all, Faith told George that Frank was a younger version of himself)? A low-angle shot looks up at Frank, covered in blue lighting and fog accentuated by the car's headlights: He is a "raging bull," a fighter who has beaten his opponent in the ring. Frank walks away from George and possibly from Faith as well. He simply does not belong in this world. George is psychologically and physically defeated. His daughters kneel down next him, and try to comfort him. A high-angle shot looks down on Faith—she is certainly vulnerable but the "ball is now in her court," yet her expression is difficult to read: it is neutral, but it also suggests a hint of compassion. George has part of his family back. The high-contrast lighting helps to sustain this expressionistic ambiguity. (Is this moment in favor of the dark or the light?) George reaches out his hand and calls his wife's name: "Faith." Before Faith has time to respond, the image freezes, and "Don't Blame Me" plays. Although what happens after this shot does not indicate any sort of clean resolution or easy healing, it *does* leave the viewer with a certain sense of "faith." Life will certainly not be easy from this moment forward, but change *has* occurred … and for now, at least, the games have ceased.

6

Pink Floyd—The Wall, 1982

May 23 (Cannes); July 14 (UK); 95 minutes/Color
Production Company: Goldcrest Films International; Tin Blue
Distributor: Metro-Goldwyn-Mayer
Director: Alan Parker
Screenwriter: Roger Waters; Alan Parker
Producer: Alan Marshall
Production Designer: Brian Morris
Cinematography: Peter Biziou
Editor: Gerry Hambling
Original Music: Roger Waters
Cast: Bob Geldof (Pink); Christine Hargreaves (Pink's Mother); James Laurenson (J.A. Pinkerton, Pink's Father); Eleanor David (Pink's Wife); Kevin McKeon (Young Pink); Bob Hoskins (Rock and Roll Manager); David Bingham (Little Pink); Jenny Wright (American Groupie); Alex McAvoy (Teacher); Ellis Dale (English Doctor); James Hazeldine (Lover); Ray Mort (Playground Father)

> Tear down the wall!—The judge, to Pink, in *Pink Floyd—The Wall*

> It was clear that it had dramatic possibilities further than the polemic of "We don't need no education."—Alan Parker, the Making of *Pink Floyd—The Wall*, pg. 69

Notes on the Production

Alan Parker first came to Pink Floyd's album *The Wall* as a fan. It was clear to him that it had a narrative sense and had something intrinsically cinematic about it. As he puts it, "It was clear that it had dramatic possibilities further than the polemic of 'We don't need no education.'"[1] After returning to England after *Fame*, he had a phone conversation with Bob Mercer at EMI, a conversation which started innocuously, the two of them bemoaning the British Film Industry's lack of imagination. Parker said to Mercer, "Look at *The Wall*, a number-one album in goodness knows how many countries, an obvious narrative line; where is the film?" Mercer informed Parker that Roger Waters had indeed expressed interest in making it into a film, but no one could quite figure out how to do it.[2]

Mercer called Parker back shortly thereafter and informed him that Roger Waters was interested in speaking with him about the project. Parker then met with Waters, and the two of them sat in Waters's kitchen, discussing the history and the ethos of the piece. Waters was playing some of the original demo tapes for Parker, who was floored by the raw, angry, primal power at the heart of the piece. Waters then suggested that Parker meet with cartoonist Gerald Scarfe, who had collaborated with him on the design of the live show, which

Director Alan Parker guides actor Alex McAvoy (The Teacher). *Pink Floyd—The Wall* **(1982), Metro-Goldwyn-Mayer.**

Pink Floyd had been performing for over a year at that point. Parker agreed, but informed Waters that he could not commit to actually directing the film, as he was leaving imminently to go to San Francisco to film *Shoot the Moon*.[3]

While in San Francisco, Parker received a call from Waters, who suggested that they both produce the film, while Michael Seresin (Parker's longtime cinematographer) and Gerald Scarfe direct. Once *Shoot the Moon* was finished, Parker's next line of business was to work more exhaustively on Waters's script, as Waters, by his own admission, is not a writer in the traditional sense. Waters, Parker, and Gerald Scarfe then met a number of times at Scarfe's house in Chelsea. Scarfe would monitor the often tumultuous exchanges between Parker and Waters (Parker admits that he and Waters reaching a détente proved to be impossible, stating, "Roger was a formidable challenge for anyone used to getting their own way, as I am."[4]) Scarfe would silently monitor these meetings and draw up the day's thoughts into a visual patchwork of artwork that eventually spread all over the walls of his studio.

With the band's manager, Steve O'Rourke, Parker returned to Los Angeles to shop the "script" around to the studios, none of whom could understand that the intention was not to make a straightforward concert film. As Parker puts it:

It was our intention, absolutely, not to make a concert movie. I mean, I could have put six cameras on the concert and ended up with an acceptable film, but we wanted it to be totally cinematic—a film in its own right.[5]

Eventually, David Begelman at MGM agreed to take a chance on the project, albeit uneasily, saying to Parker, "Alan, I don't understand this movie. No one in this company understands this movie. Even my nineteen-year-old son doesn't understand this movie and he's a big Pink Floyd fan. Are you sure you can pull this off?" to which Parker replied, "Quite sure."[6]

Pink Floyd performed *The Wall* concert in Earls Court in England for five nights in June of 1981, and Parker and crew decided to film these shows, ostensibly to gather footage that they would end up using in the film. The filming was a disaster, however, as Michael Seresin and Gerald Scarfe did not display a modicum of directing ability. Parker knew that he would either have to abandon the project, or sit in the director's chair, which he ultimately did. It was agreed not to include any actual concert footage in the film, and Roger Waters also agreed to step back and stay out of Parker's hair while he filmed. A détente was finally reached.

Next came the task of casting. After seeing the video for a song called "I Don't Like Mondays," by an Irish punk band called the Boomtown Rats, Parker was struck by the presence of the lead singer, Bob Geldof. Parker met with Geldof, who was unsure whether he wanted to do the project, as he was not a staunch Pink Floyd fan. He eventually agreed, however, as the Boomtown Rats' schedule was experiencing a bit of a lull.[7] To cast Young Pink (aged 11) and Little Pink (aged 6), Parker organized an open call on local radio stations in London, Manchester, Leeds, and Glasgow. A couple of thousand kids showed up, and Parker narrowed the selection down to the Bob Geldof lookalikes, Kevin McKeon and David Bingham, neither of whom had any acting experience. Parker was particularly pleased to be able to work with Bob Hoskins, who apparently was the only cast member able to elicit laughs from the miserable crew.[8]

Filming began on September 7, 1981, in East Molesey. There, Parker filmed the scenes of Young Pink's house. The crew then traveled to Bermondsey, Epsom Downs, and Hammersmith to get location footage of the playground, the rugby field, and the asylum, respectively. The Anzio sequences were filmed after the crew transformed Burnham Beaches at Barnstaple into a beachhead after an extensive amount of digging. After getting his location shots, Parker took the crew back to the "D" stage at Pinewood Studios to film the interiors of Pink's hotel room.

The shoot was certainly not without its share of headaches, and according to Parker, "It was quite the most miserable time I ever had making a film. It's a scream of pain from beginning to end."[9] Among the many problems onset included a rat wrangler who let loose wild rats on the set, causing complete chaos; Bob Geldof rebelling against the extreme abuse he was being put through (including nearly being asphyxiated with toxic smoke, having his eyebrows shaved off with a broken razorblade, almost drowning in a swimming pool of blood, and cutting his hands to shreds while destroying the hotel room); and recalcitrant doves (fifty of which were lost), which gave Parker a hard time getting even a single shot, one which lasted only a few seconds. The biggest problem, however, was the group of skinhead extras known as the "Tilbury Skins," who played Pink's "hammer guard." Parker states of this motley crew:

I really loved them because they were *my people.* In between shots they used to make me laugh. Until they started to laugh about how they'd seen this Pakistani kid and had tried to throw him off a moving train. I thought, "How can people whose sense of humor is exactly the same as mine on every level, suddenly hit something which isn't?" I found that very disturbing.[10]

Despite these problems, principal photography was completed after sixty-one consecutive fourteen-hour days consisting of 977 shots, 4,885 takes, and 350,000 feet of film.[11] Roger Waters then returned to supervise the music mix, and after eight months of editing, a final cut was achieved. The film, which Parker refers to as "probably my student film—perhaps the most expensive student film in history,"[12] went on to become a cult hit of the genre, and, after its release, *The Wall* album went on to double its sales—23 million copies (and counting), becoming the third biggest-selling album in history.[13]

Summary

Immediately following the roar of the MGM lion, the film gradually fades from black into an extremely low-angle shot of a hotel hallway as the camera is slowly moving down the hall in what appears to be a Steadicam shot. The slow, methodical rate at which the camera is moving forward (coupled with the fact that it is extremely low to the ground, almost on the floor, which gives the hallway a cavernous, frightening feel) suggests an overwhelming, childlike trepidation, as if a small child, completely dwarfed by his/her looming surroundings, is walking slowly, reluctant to go any faster for fear of being gobbled up by the monsters behind the door. The Vera Lynn rendition of "The Little Boy That Santa Claus Forgot" plays on the soundtrack, which augments the shot's suggestion of a particular type of childhood fear: that of abandonment and complete isolation.

After a cleaning lady exits one of the rooms, walks into the hallway, and turns a vacuum on, the film cuts back to black, and the opening titles are smeared across the screen in a blood-red, maniacally scribbled font—it is already evident that this film will be a walk down a dark corridor. We then hear the sound of a match being struck, and the fiery glow of the lit match appears in the center of the still black frame, shedding a minimal amount of golden-hued light into a stark, darkly lit background. We then see the man who lit the match, in a close-up, light a lantern, then a cigarette, and he proceeds to sit and smoke while the sound of bombs and explosions rings out in the background. As the man begins to clean the pistol lying on the desk in front of him (he is ostensibly a soldier), the Pink Floyd song "When The Tigers Broke Free" plays on the soundtrack (this song is not on *The Wall* album, but appeared on the 2004 re-release of the album *The Final Cut*, which was originally intended to be the soundtrack album to the film, until Waters changed it to be a reflection of war after the onset of the conflict in the Falklands[14]). The lyrics recount the events of Operation Shingle, in which Allied forces landed on a beachhead at Anzio with the intention of liberating Rome from the German forces. Roger Waters's father was killed at Anzio, and the lyrics reflect this loss, furthering the theme of a lost, petulant child without a father figure.

The camera then zooms in on the orange flame inside the lantern, which eventually dissolves into a bright sun, and we now see a wide-shot of a lone figure (ostensibly Pink) running across an empty rugby field. These rugby field scenes (which become a recurring motif throughout the film) were shot on Epsom Downs, which, according to Parker, was the only location he could find that would lend the scenes the "eerie, dream quality that we were after."[15] This scene then transitions into a close-up of a Mickey Mouse watch, which enhances the film's theme of a childhood conflict from the past resurfacing in the form of psychological trauma in the present. According to Jorge Sacido Romero and Luis Miguel Varela Cabo:

> On his bare wrist he wears a Mickey Mouse watch, a time image representing some unresolved childhood conflict that has a bearing on the present situation.[16]

In one shot, the camera pans from the watch across Pink's (played by Bob Geldof) hand, across the mountainous ash of a burned-out cigarette, and then slowly zooms in on Pink's eye. Pink's expression suggests a deep, pensive rumination—he is caught in some kind of psychological flux, and there is an exhausted, defeated look on his face. With Pink's eye still in close-up, he blinks, which serves as a transition for the cut back to the hotel hallway from the beginning of the film. Parker then implements a cross-cut involving the cleaning lady, Pink, and Pink's thoughts. First, the cleaning lady takes out her keys and goes to open Pink's door. We then cut to Pink, sitting in the dark, his eyes registering exhaustion, as they stare blankly at a television set. As the cleaning lady turns the key inside the lock and pushes on the door, Parker cuts from a close-up of the door being obstructed by the chain lock to a close-up of two heavy doors, held in place by iron chains, being plowed through by an angry mob of young people. The Pink Floyd song "In the Flesh" then kicks in, as a frenetic montage ensues. Parker cuts between shots of the angry young mob wildly running through a hallway, close-ups of Pink's insane eyes as he experiences these thoughts and hallucinations, and shots of the Anzio beachhead battle in World War II. Pink's hallucinations culminate in his imagining that he is a fascist, Hitler-like demagogue speaking on a balcony to a young, obedient audience. Pink's feelings of alienation and isolation are evident when he sings to the crowd that to see "behind [his] cold eyes," one would have to "claw ... through [his] disguise."

According to Jorge Sacido Romero and Luis Miguel Varela Cabo, in their essay, "Roger Waters's Poetry of the Absent Father: British Identity in Pink Floyd's *The Wall*," this imagery (and all the film's ensuing imagery of alienation) not only reflects Roger Waters's personal feelings of isolation and disenfranchisement, but also England's postwar disappointment with the shattering of the unfulfilled promises of egalitarianism and idealism. They state:

> In *The Wall*, the protagonist's father, a war hero who was killed in the battle of Anzio in 1944, incarnates the "national ideal" passed on as a legacy to the postwar generations (with a traditional element attached to it symbolized in his elegant uniform and gentlemanly demeanor). By interweaving the individual with the collective history, the film records how this legacy soon started to undergo a fatal process of erosion and was brought to an end in the present dimension from which the story is told.[17]

The shots of Pink addressing the crowd as a fascist demagogue segue into shots of the Battle of Anzio, replete with explosions, fleeing soldiers, and overhead planes dropping bombs. The scene strongly echoes the imagery of the Battle of Normandy, as newly arrived soldiers on a beach are bombarded with an aggressive attack. The destruction is both visually and sonically explosive, and it ends with a disturbing close-up of Pink's father's corpse in a bunker, his face smeared with blood.

We then cut to a shot of Pink's mother (played by Christine Hargreaves), reclining in an English garden, asleep. In the distance, a baby carriage is seen, and Parker slowly diverts attention from the woman to the carriage by slowly zooming in on the latter. Again, the theme of childhood abandonment is accentuated, as what is ostensibly Pink's baby carriage is separated from his mother. Parker then cuts back to shots of the bloody aftermath of the Battle of Anzio, and as the camera surveys the dead bodies and rubble, the song "Thin Ice" plays over the soundtrack. The song begins with a somber piano and lyrics about parents loving their baby.

The song is appropriately more melancholic and elegiac than "In the Flesh," and it invites the audience to ponder the emotional ramifications of war, as we see firsthand the horrors men are put through. There is one particularly effective shot in which a group of soldiers march through the sand from screen right to screen left, single file. The diffuse light of the sun shrouds each soldier in silhouette; it is a striking shot, one which suggests conformity and the dehumanizing loss of identity.

The camera then pans through Pink's demolished hotel room, objects and detritus strewn about, to find Pink, floating serenely in the pool (apparently, Geldof was not much of a swimmer, and was anxious about shooting these scenes, so Parker set him up with two weeks at Clapham Baths so he could develop a passable doggy paddle[18]). Pink's serenity soon devolves into a complete panic, however, which is stunningly depicted by Parker, with frenetic editing, dark lighting, and quick inserts of Gerald Scarfe's artwork. First, Pink begins to writhe and squirm in the water, as the camera spins on its axis vertically, creating a nausea-inducing sense of disorientation. The blue water, in a quick flash of editing, turns to blood, and Pink undulates in the pool of blood in a panic, gripping his head. To achieve this dizzying effect, Parker states, "I borrowed again from Abel Gance and suspended the camera on a pendulum to film Pink thrashing around in his own imaginary pool of blood as he recalls his father's death."[19] Parker employs lightning-fast inserts of the fiery glow of an explosion, a close-up of Pink's father's wide-eyed, screaming face, and a close-up of Gerald Scarfe's creepy, cartoonish rendering of a soldier's screaming face. It is a nightmarish scene, and Pink's tormenting internal demons are vividly realized by Parker's visuals, Scarfe's artwork, and Pink Floyd's haunting rock music.

We then cut to the interior of a church as "Another Brick in the Wall, Part 1" kicks in. Pink's mother is kneeling, devoutly praying, and Little Pink (played by David Bingham) is distractedly walking around the church, playing with a toy airplane. Again, the theme of isolation is reaffirmed, as Little Pink is left to his own devices, being completely ignored by his mother.

After she is finished praying, Pink's mother takes him to the playground, only to leave him alone there while she goes to the shops. Pink is left to ask a strange man if he will assist him by placing him on the merry-go-round. These shots were filmed in Bermondsey, and Parker and crew had to paint the playground a dirty 1940s green, and dress it with period swings and slides.[20] Abandonment and isolation are, again, depicted when Little Pink attempts to hold the strange man's hand, and the man tells him to get away. Little Pink is, again, left to his own devices and the seeds of his isolation and alienation have been planted.

We then cut to Young Pink (played by Kevin McKeon), now a bit older and once again, alone, walking through his empty house. He walks into his mother's empty room and opens one of her dresser drawers, stumbling upon some of his father's war memorabilia while the somber lament "When The Tigers Broke Free, Part 2" plays over the soundtrack. This song is, thus far, the most personal lament over the loss of Pink's (Roger Waters's) father. The obliqueness of playing with verb tenses, which made the previous songs more allegorical and metonymic, is jettisoned as Waters sings, "it was, *I* recall." Young Pink then adorns his father's military uniform and looks in the mirror, and Parker cross-cuts these shots with shots of Pink's father putting the same uniform on during the war. It is a touching scene, which invites us to empathize with Pink's loss, making his hallucinations and mental breakdown more understandable and (scarily) identifiable.

We then cut to one of Gerald Scarfe's nightmarish animation sequences. It starts with a shot of a dove flying through the sky. The live action dove morphs into a cartoon dove, which eventually explodes bloodily into the Germanic Eagle of War, which flies over postwar London, as "Goodbye Blue Sky" plays. Scarfe's animation sequence goes on to include hellish, disturbing shots, indicative of an H.P. Lovecraft story (ghostly skeletons wearing uniforms, giant monolithic demons, crawling demons with elongated, gas-mask faces, etc.). According to Parker, the animation sequence was simply intended to be a "piece on the waste of war."[21] According to Romero and Varela Cabo, however, the scene has more complex implications. They state:

> All the torment expressed in the film's opening is expanded in the first animation scene, in which the plump and lovely White Dove of Peace mutates into a sharp, metallic and menacing Eagle that flies around postwar London. The ominous Eagle represents, of course, the nuclear threat of the Cold War period, which had another main protagonist: the Soviet Union. But the Eagle is and has always been the symbol of the Empire. In this context, the Eagle is also the Bald Eagle of the Seal of the United States of America. The damaging effect that the postwar period had on British identity is symbolized in this animation scene in the rapid disintegration of the Union Jack that ends up with St. George's Cross (England's emblem) shedding its blood, incapable of fertilizing the devastated field of the Nation.[22]

Whether it was intentional or not, Romero and Varela Cabo are, once again, suggesting that the nightmarish imagery in *The Wall* is not exclusively a reification of Pink's (Waters's) internal demons; it is a representation of England's postwar angst and discontent.

We then cut to Young Pink, running through fields, playing with two of his friends. They follow a set of train tracks into a tunnel, and Parker cuts to reveal that a train is close by, about to pass the boys. Pink takes one of the bullets he found in his mother's drawer, and attempts to place it on the tracks, so the train will run over it and ignite it like a firework. Parker implements fast-pasted, frenetic editing, which, when coupled with the extremely noisy sound of the train approaching, reaffirms his ability to implement sound and editing to elevate the audience's heart-rate with tension and anxiety. At the last minute, Pink runs off the track, and the train runs over the bullet, effectively setting it off. As Pink watches the train roll by, he sees innumerable children's arms, reaching out from the train cars, as if they are captives being held against their will by the train. When the children's faces are revealed, they appear in the form of grotesque, deformed masks, which has a chilling effect akin to the climax of *The Day of the Locust*. Temporarily, Pink's face transforms into one of the grotesque masks until the apparition of a teacher (played by Alex McAvoy) appears on the tracks, pointing admonishingly at Pink, as "Another Brick in the Wall, Part 2" begins playing.

Parker then cuts to a shot of a vanguard of teachers assertively marching down a school hallway towards the camera, like soldiers. In the classroom, Young Pink's teacher scolds him for writing poetry, which the teacher reads aloud, and we discover that the lines to the poetry are the lyrics from the Pink Floyd song "Money." Parker then cuts to a shot of the teacher, eating at home with what is ostensibly his wife, in a stuffy rigid tableau of boredom and haughtiness. The lighting in this scene in striking, and it was achieved, according to Parker, when "Peter Biziou lit the interior with one enormous 'brute' light at floor level minus its glass front Fresnel."[23] He intersperses this shot with quick inserts of the teacher engaging in corporal punishment, bending students over and striking them in the rear. The lyrics of the song then kick into gear.

As the song plays on the soundtrack, Parker implements an eerie montage to highlight the theme of mindless conformity at the hands of despotic oppression. The first shot depicts a line of students, lethargically marching up a set of stairs, single file. Parker sustains the shot in one take, pulling the camera back to reveal that the students are walking into an industrial assembly line of sorts, which spits them out the other end, sitting individually and obediently at school desks, their faces now frozen in the grotesque, deformed masks. He then cuts to an aerial shot of the students marching through an elaborate hallway, which, as seen from above, makes the students appear as rats, trapped in some experiment. The next nightmarish shot is of the masked children walking off an assembly line belt and falling into a pit of some sort—they are depicted as mass-produced products, being packaged and sold. Parker also infuses the montage with shots of the wheels and gears of the machinery casting harsh, looming shadows on the wall, an image which could be seen as reflecting the postwar English angst over the rise of Soviet (and American) industry.

After the shot of the machinery's shadow, Parker reveals that it is, in fact, a meat grinder the children have been falling into—they are no longer just dehumanized products; they are being literally devoured by the machinery of tyrannical oppression.

The montage ends with an angry, rebellious uprising. The children have evidently had enough, and they burst forth from the restraints of their school desks and proceed to destroy the classroom, breaking glass, capsizing desks, etc. There are also shots of the students breaking through a brick wall (the overarching symbol of isolation and oppression) with sledgehammers. With the school ablaze in the background, the students then drag their teacher out into the open and ostensibly throw him into a blazing bonfire, which symbolizes the students' anger. It is an intense, aggressively angry scene, which (depending on your point of view) could be seen as possessing a glint of hope. Although violent recourse may be the only type of recourse, it demonstrates that breaking through barriers and oppression is, indeed, possible.

We then cut to a close-up of a polaroid of Pink (who actually appears happy, as he is smiling) standing next to a woman (a girlfriend? Wife?) gazing up at him. The shrill ring of a phone cuts through the soundtrack, and Pink, sitting on the bed in his squalid hotel room, answers the phone, although we do not hear to whom he is speaking. Parker then implements a brief insert of Pink kissing a redheaded woman. He cuts back to Pink, lying on his bed lugubriously. As Pink curls up with his pillow in the fetal position, Parker cuts to a flashback in which Little Pink is cuddling up in bed next to his mother. Again, Pink's demons are elucidated, as he struggles with the relationship he had with his mother, by juxtaposing the shots of Little Pink and his mother with those of Pink engaging in romantic/sexual relations, the film is positing that Pink is dealing with an Oedipal torture, which, according to Romero and Valera Cabo, not only problematize his sexual interactions, but force him into the arms of the oppression of industrialization and machinery, which have supplanted the "normal" father figure. They state:

> Pink confronts two modes of oppressive authority, the second being subsidiary to the first, which is the dominant one: the maddening, uncontrollable and relentless movement of capitalism and the possessive and castrating mother figure who contributes to her son's subjugation to the incessant dance of capitalism.[24]

Pink's sexual problems are further visualized in the next scene, in which Parker again implements cross-cutting to create meaning. He cuts back and forth between Young Pink staring through his window at night, watching a girl across the street get undressed through her window, and Pink in the present, displaying complete apathy and disinterest in sex as a woman undresses right in front of him in his hotel room. The song "Mother" plays over this sequence, further suggesting that Pink's overbearing mother instilled psychosexual demons in him. When Parker cuts back to Young Pink looking at the naked girl through his window, we see his mother enter from behind him. We then cut to Young Pink lying in his bed, being aggressively groped and inspected by a doctor and his mother. Parker has visually told us that Young Pink's mother caught him in a sexual act, scolded him for it, told him there was something wrong with him, and called in the doctor. This is pure Freudian imagery—the castrating mother instilling the boy with a fear and shame of his sexuality.

Parker continues his disturbing examination of Pink's Freudian, Oedipal issues with more cross-cutting. After having been examined by the doctor, Young Pink tries to go to sleep, only to be terrified and kept awake by the shadows on his wall, which appear as demonic faces. In an attempt to find solace and comfort, he enters his sleeping mother's room, and cuddles up next to her. Parker contrasts this shot with the next, which is of Pink making a sexual advance to the redheaded woman in his hotel room, who is now asleep and disinterested—she rolls over and dismisses his advances, leaving Pink to deal with his frustration. Pink is an orphan, lost without the overbearing presence of his domineering mother, and ensnared by the forces of modernity and industrialization.

With a flashback to Pink's wedding, we see that the red-

Boomtown Rats front man and "Live Aid" coordinator, Bob Geldoff, as the mad, suicidal rock musician "Pink." *Pink Floyd—The Wall* (1982), Metro-Goldwyn-Mayer.

headed woman is, indeed, Pink's wife (played by Eleanor David), and one flashback scene in particular augments Pink's sense of alienation and being closed off from the world. Pink is torpidly playing the piano, as if in an exhausted, sleep-deprived trance. His wife enters, waves a hand in front of his unresponsive face, and says, "Hello. Is there anybody in there?" (a lyric from the song "Comfortably Numb"). She then walks away, unfulfilled and disappointed.

The "Mother" sequence ends with Parker visually suggesting that Pink's wife is being unfaithful. He shows her marching at a peace rally, a rally for disarmament, and he zooms in on her face as she lustfully gazes at one of the speakers at the rally (played by James Hazeldine). He then cuts back to Young Pink, sitting idly as his mother dances with a gentleman, and Young Pink eventually spots a large girl on the opposite side of the room (a girl almost twice his size, who most likely reminds him of his mother, who is also a large girl) and dances with her, again reaffirming Pink's myriad mother issues.

Parker's implicit suggestion regarding Pink's wife's infidelity is then made explicit in the next scene, in which we see Pink's wife in bed with the man from the rally. Pink then makes a collect call to his wife, and is devastated when the man answers. The camera then slowly pulls away from Pink at the phone booth as he sinks to the ground, and Peter Biziou's stark, shadowy and smoky lighting again suggests abject and nightmarish isolation—Pink is absolutely alone to deal with his grief.

His complete isolation in this shot segues into another Gerald Scarfe animation sequence, as the extended version of the song "Empty Spaces" plays on the soundtrack. The sequence begins with two flowers against a black backdrop, coyly caressing and petting each other. The flower on the left has an elongated proboscis, coding it as the "male" flower, while the flower to the right is explicitly vaginal, as it opens (at first) welcomingly. This tableau is clearly a visual metaphor for sexual intercourse, but it quickly turns nightmarish. The (at first) welcoming vaginal flower mutates into a Venus Flytrap, aggressively devouring the "male" flower, then morphing into a menacing black bird of some sort and flying away. This flower sequence clearly mirrors Pink's deranged, warped view of sexuality, and is a hallucinatory representation of his anger towards his wife for having cheated on him.

The animation sequence continues with a grand-scale panning shot of a vast landscape, which is being encroached upon by looming skyscrapers, which reaffirms the film's theme of the oppressive onslaught of industry and capitalism. The buildings, as they pile up in a row like dominoes across the landscape, morph into a wall, which slices and razes its way through the land, turning a flower into barbed wire. Scarfe then implements more of his Lovecraftian, hellish mutations as a cherubic child sitting in the field morphs first into a long-snouted demon, then into a Gestapo-type officer who wields a baton and smashes a sitting victim on the skull, smattering blood all over the wall. The mobile wall continues its reign of terror as it crashes through a church, demolishing it, and a close-up of a decomposed face, screaming up at the sky, mutates into a snake-like entity with a grotesque parody of the female form flailing at the end of it. Parker intercuts this entire mad painting of an animation sequence with quick inserts of the iconic image of the wide-mouthed screaming face coming out of the wall, which bears a striking resemblance to Rob Bottin's designs for the grotesquely beautiful alien in John Carpenter's *The Thing*. It is a chillingly beautiful sequence, which visually allows us to enter the dark, disturbed mind of a man descending further and further into alienation and madness.

The animation sequence comes crashing back into live-action (literally) with a shot of a looter breaking through the glass display of a storefront with a hammer. The police quickly quell this criminal act, and arrest all the looters. It is hard to tell what the purpose of this quick scene is, as it appears disjointed and out of place. Are the looters representing Pink's anger in the form of a misguided Marxist uprising? Is the scene intended to further the theme of oppression and tyranny by displaying the policemen as corrupt and abusive? If the latter was intended, it is unconvincing, as they appear to be simply responding to a crime situation, simply doing their jobs.

Next comes a montage depicting the excess of "sex, drugs, and rock 'n' roll." This montage of debauchery (replete with flowing champagne, parties, and girls performing fellatio on security guards in order to procure VIP passes) is set to the song "Young Lust," the lyrics of which include "dirty" girls and women.

Although the scene is not "ahead of its time," per se (as the Rolling Stones and Aerosmith were known for their excessive drug use, drinking and partying), the scene foreshadows the glitzy (and shamelessly overt) "sex, drugs, and rock 'n' roll" of the likes of Van Halen, Guns 'n' Roses, Motley Crue, et al. Parker's montage maintains a certain neutrality, however; he neither lionizes nor denigrates this lifestyle—he simply records it.

A sexy young groupie (played by Jenny Wright), who was previously partying in another trailer, topless, approaches Pink outside his trailer with an album for him to sign. She then follows him into his trailer, another den of inequity and despair, a foil for his squalid hotel room. She attempts to engage to a catatonic Pink, who is watching *The Dam Busters*, a 1955 film about war hero Guy Gibson, on the television. This suggests that Pink is arrested in an unhealthy obsession with his father, who was also a soldier, and also that his isolation and sense of detachment is reaching a fever pitch. She attempts to get Pink's attention, to no avail, and then, after Pink rubs his temples in frustration, she very tenderly kisses his fingers while the song "One of My Turns" plays. Not only is the scene one of the very few conventional dialogue scenes in the film, but, according to Parker, "The kissing of the fingers was a spur of the moment suggestion to inject a needed amount of tenderness; a little island of normality amongst the music."[25]

Her tenderness proves futile, however, as Pink explodes in a whirlwind of anger and violence, completely destroying everything in sight, à la Charles Foster Kane. This scene of violent, cathartic release culminates with Pink throwing his television out the window. As he angrily yells out the window, ostensibly to the entire city (or, if we take it further, to the entire world), "Next time, fuckers!" he places his right hand on the wall, seemingly not noticing that broken shards of glass are slicing into his hand. Apparently, Bob Geldof actually cut his hands quite badly during each take, but, according to Parker, he still launched into each take with equal amounts of ferocity.[26]

After a brief shot surveying the wreckage of Pink's outburst, Parker fades into a close-up of Pink's right hand bleeding into a pool, as he floats in a Jesus-like pose. This shot of Pink, floating in a pool, frozen in a martyred position, is juxtaposed with shots of Pink's wife and her lover having sex while the song "Don't Leave Me Now" plays on the soundtrack. We then cut to another shot of Pink, staring vapidly at a television set, but as the camera pulls back, we see that he is neither in a hotel room nor a trailer, but in a cartoonishly large room with a green floor and a giant blue wall, which dwarfs him. A woman's shadow appears on the blue wall, and the shadow morphs into what is, at first, a snake-like creature that comes out of the wall, ostensibly to attack Pink. The snake-thing ultimately morphs into the carnivorous, vaginal flower from the earlier animation sequence, and Parker again intercuts this moment with shots of Pink's wife and her lover having sex. Once again, the editing (as well as the music, the lyrics of which, like John Lennon's "Mother," profess an infantile fear of abandonment) augments the film's visual motif of Pink's internal, sexual (and Oedipal) demons materializing in a nightmarish outpouring of his now-warped view of an alien and strange world, from which he has removed himself.

Parker then cuts to Pink, smashing his television set with his guitar. The program that is on the television while Pink does this is significant. It is a color program, whereas the film he was watching in the previous scene was a black-and-white war film. This visually reaffirms Romero and Valera Cabo's assertion that Pink represents England's disenfranchisement in the postwar landscape, and that Pink represents how all of England is composed of orphans, figuratively speaking. The black-and-white film represents an idealized time while the color program represents the encroachment of modernity and capitalism, and Pink's smashing of the television (while the color program is playing) represents the vitriolic aversion his generation possessed towards the onslaught of industrialization and modernity.

We then cut to "Another Brick In The Wall, Part III," over which Parker implements another explosive, frenetic montage of anger, fear, and alienation. Most of the shots in the montage are flashbacks, and the first one is that of Pink leaning in to kiss his wife, followed by lightning-fast inserts of Pink as the fascist demagogue and the bombs and fleeing soldiers at the battle of Anzio. The shots become even more nightmarish, however, as we see a shot of Pink's wife screaming, with an extreme close-up of crawling maggots superimposed over it. Then, there are shots of teacher screaming at Pink on the train tracks, and the strange man on the playground pushing Little Pink away. All of Pink's flashbacks are interspersed with shots of a riot—of a violent uprising, replete with Molotov cocktails being thrown at police cars and an army of police.

The lyrics of "Another Brick In The Wall, Part III" are what is significant about this montage. The lyrics are those of resignation, and the anger present in the montage perhaps reflects Pink's having given up. He is tired of fighting his demons, tired of attempting to integrate himself into a callous, misunderstanding world, etc. Pink's refusal to continue to attempt to integrate himself into the world is made clear with the next musical number, "Goodbye Cruel World." Although, on the surface, the lyrics of this song suggest that Pink is going to commit suicide, the song is more about metaphoric, rather than physical, death. Pink flashes back to being a child and running free in the rugby field. Parker then cuts to Pink placing the final bricks of his wall (the metaphor for Pink's isolation from the world) in place. He is securing his perimeter, ensuring that the world cannot penetrate his wall. The lyrics "Goodbye cruel world" are not about Pink committing suicide, but rather, about his decision to stop attempting to integrate himself into society. He is saying goodbye to the outside world because he wants his wall to stay up and remain separated and cordoned off from the world at large.

After Pink is finished building his wall, we segue into "Is There Anybody Out There?" which makes clear Pink's madness. He puts his ear to the wall, listening for potential intruders. Once again, Peter Biziou's lighting creates the perfect atmosphere of isolated madness, as Pink is lit in silhouette, with smoke swirling around him in the background, creating a nightmarish spectacle. The song (and this moment in the film) is interesting, however, in the sense that it reflects not only Pink's paranoia (he wants to know just who it is encircling his wall), but his realization of the gravity of what he has done. He has slipped into madness, and has decided to cordon himself off from the world, and this moment in the film illustrates that Pink is acknowledging the gravity of that decision.

Parker then cuts to a tableau, which explicitly illustrates Pink's madness. Pink is on all fours in his room, constructing, as would a child, a puzzle of sorts with the debris and wreckage of his meltdown. The expression on his face as he builds his makeshift city of rubble, suggests someone who has resolutely disavowed sanity or any sort of connection to the outside world—he is in a microcosm of madness. The acoustic guitar piece accompanying this scene adds a component of sadness, of funereal grief. We sense that Pink has left the world of the sane for good, which gives this moment a hint of elegiac melancholy.

We then cut to Pink in the bathroom, shaving. What starts off as a typical, normal male act devolves into a perverse act of self-mutilation. Pink smears shaving cream all over his chest, which he then proceeds to shave, ignoring the nicks and cuts and blood. Pink then removes the blade from his razor and breaks it in half. He picks at his eyebrows, and Parker then cuts to the murky suds in the sink, into which droplets of blood begin to fall. This visual allusion suggests something horribly violent without explicitly visualizing it (which Quentin Tarantino would later do in the ear-cutting scene of his film *Reservoir Dogs*). We then cut to outside the bathroom, and as the camera zooms in on the closed bathroom door, Pink opens it, revealing that he has shaved off both his eyebrows (in a botched, not-entirely-successful procedure, as there are myriad nicks and cuts) and cut his hair. Initially, Parker filmed close-ups of Pink actually cutting his eyebrows off, but decided that the dailies were too gruesome, so he decided to focus on implementing visual allusion instead.[27]

Pink's cutting off his hair takes on a particular symbolic meaning in this film, a symbolic meaning, which Martin Scorsese employed in his film *Taxi Driver*. In that film, the length of Travis Bickle's hair is directly proportional to his sanity. At the beginning of the film, he has a full head of hair. As Travis sinks deeper and deeper into a self-contained world of isolation and dementia, however, his hair gets shorter and shorter, until, when he has reached the apogee (or nadir, depending on your point of view) of his madness, he is left with nothing but a Mohawk. Parker, himself, had also implemented this motif in his film *Midnight Express*. In that film, Billy Hayes starts off with a long, full head of hair. When he is sentenced to prison, however, the experience that will savagely chip away at his sanity, his hair is shaved off. It is only when he regrows his hair that he is able to recapture his sanity.

In this scene, when Pink reveals that he has not only cut his hair, but his eyebrows as well (displaying a desire to become almost completely hairless) he is making a statement that his desire to be "normal" and integrate himself into society has dissipated—he is now fully committed to isolation and madness, and he demonstrates this by removing his hair; he is summarily rejecting normality.

The next song is "Nobody Home," in which Pink, now realizing that his wife and a normal life are out of his grasp, makes a list of the safe, mundane things he still has. His beleaguered mental health and fragile state are now laid bare, and Parker visually captures this by depicting Pink, once again glued to the TV set as he channel surfs mindlessly. He flips past commercials, cartoons, and even a speech being given by Ronald Reagan, reaffirming Romero and Valera Cabo's assertion that one component of Pink's alienation is England's acquiescence to the onslaught of industry and capitalism. Pink apathetically flips through the channels like a dehumanized, mindless consumer in a capitalist landscape, a man without a father (literally and figuratively), and a man without direction.

While maintaining the image of Pink, vapidly glued to the TV set, Parker shifts the location, and rather than watching in his hotel room, he watches the TV outdoors, in a wide-open landscape, with the tangled, snarling branches of dead trees swirling behind him. This suggests that Pink is so out of touch mentally that he is unaware of his surroundings. The decomposition of his sanity is furthered by Bob Geldof's performance, as he manically rocks back and forth in his chair, like a mental patient in an institution. As he spastically rocks back and forth, Pink morphs into Young Pink, who is also rocking back and forth. This suggests that, perhaps, Pink was destined for madness. Perhaps his surroundings, his upbringing, and forces beyond his control predetermined his insanity.

Parker then cuts to Young Pink walking through the Anzio beachhead, surveying the corpses, nonchalantly strolling through the wind, as if through the park. The scene is redolent of nostalgic reflection, and Peter Biziou's smoky and golden-hued cinematography in this scene highlights, as Parker puts it, the "yellow colors of autumn that memories always seem to be made of."[28] Young Pink then walks into a cave-like opening and down a rickety staircase, into a cobwebbed, dark hallway, which is a visual metaphor for Pink's journey through the deep, dark recesses of his psyche. This metaphor is made explicit as the dark hallway turns into a clinical, dimly lit hallway, reminiscent of a hospital corridor. Young Pink slides open the door at the end of the hallway to reveal a room full of empty infirmary beds—a creepy, nightmarish image shot with the shadowy starkness of Peter Biziou's lighting. Young Pink then ventures into a side room to find Adult Pink crouched in the corner. As Young Pink places his hand on Adult Pink's shoulder, he is startled by the demented, insane grin on Adult Pink's face and runs out of the room. Pink is facing parts of his damaged subconscious for the first time, and the effects are startling.

As Young Pink runs out of the infirmary, we cut back to the image of him running through the rugby field as the golden sun bathes the entire frame with light. It is a liberating image, akin to the final shot of *The 400 Blows*, which almost immediately turns to horror, as the rugby field turns to a muddy trench through which Young Pink is now walking. He turns a corner to see a pile of dead soldiers' corpses. The shocking brutality and horror of this image could be seen as representing that Pink is facing the ugly, horrific components of his psyche for the first time.

Next is the song "Vera," which is an ode to the World War II–era singer Vera Lynn. The song represents that Pink is drifting further and further away from reality, as he is yearning for a simpler, more idealistic time; i.e., things that remind him of home. In other words, Pink is not necessarily speaking to Vera Lynn, the person, but the idea—the nostalgic attachment to a time when such an idea was pregnant with hope and idealism.

Parker then cuts to "Bring the Boys Back Home," which plays over a parade sequence, replete with drummer boys marching and bystanders cheering for their "boys to be brought back home." It is a rousing sequence whose message is clear: that war has permanent effects and forfeiting the lives of young, innocent men to fight for irresolvable conflicts is a dangerous game (the scene takes on particular current significance in the wake of the war in

Iraq). Pink's sense of isolation is again reaffirmed when Parker cuts to a shot of Pink alone at the train station, which was heretofore teeming with hordes of people. He sits back down in his chair and watches TV, the only reality he can relate to now, and he, again, morphs back into Adult Pink, who is now unconscious in his hotel room. The door bursts open and Pink's manager (played by Bob Hoskins) and a team of paramedics come flooding in, trying to wake up Pink, carrying him out of the room while "Comfortably Numb" plays. The sequence is, by turns, haunting and beautiful and nightmarish at the same time. Pink flashes back to his childhood, and we see, in one particular flashback, Pink attempting to make contact with the outside world, with the living things that are around him outside the vacuum-sealed microcosm of his overbearing home life. He brings a rat into his home, which, of course, arouses the disgust and horror of his mother, so he is forced to take it to a private, isolated place, planting the seeds of Pink's inability to connect with reality and the outside world.

Then comes the line in the song about "just a little pin prick," which refers to the doctor's attempt to bring Pink out of his comatose state and back to reality by injecting him with some unnamed medication. As the needle enters his vein and the shot is administered, the ethereal, spectral scream of the song is mirrored by Pink's anguished scream. This suggests that Pink has now set up camp in a place that is not reality, and any attempt to bring him back into the world will result in pain.

The guitar solo is accompanied by a hallucinatory music video. Pink, being dragged down the hall and out the door into an ambulance, is decomposing. Parker implements quick inserts of extreme close-ups of maggots, and Pink's flesh is becoming gamey and ghoulish, culminating in a shot in which he, alone in the back of the ambulance, is frantically peeling away his slimy, decomposed flesh, as he is now an inhuman, disgusting zombie. This represents both Pink's psychological decay as well as his anxiety over performing at the upcoming concert. According to Parker, this grotesque makeup was a problem for Bob Geldof. He states, "The application of the vicious pink makeup was dreadfully uncomfortable for Bob and he complained, shouting in angry Dunleary: 'He's gone too far, I will not be physically abused.'"[29]

When Pink completes the shedding of his disgusting zombie-flesh, he becomes the fascist dictator once again. The paramedics have revived him so that he can perform at the concert, and the fascist dictator has supplanted Pink's rock star persona. The concert itself is a disturbing Hitler-esque Nazi rally, replete with skinhead security guards and guard dogs. As the song "In The Flesh" plays, the concert devolves into a disturbing Nazi rally akin to Nuremberg, conjuring up all of the most deplorable, despicable behaviors associated with such. Pink demands that "queers " and "Jews" be thrown against the wall, doing so in order to test the loyalty of his audience, whom he now despises, due to his alienation and isolation. One of the lyrics speaks to Pink not being "well, he's back at the hotel," which solidifies Pink's psychological detachment from reality.

After galvanizing the audience with his cross-arm salute (which mirrors his band's emblem, the criss-crossed hammers), "Run Like Hell" plays on the soundtrack over a sequence in which Pink admonishes his audience not to disobey his orders. Parker inserts a particularly stark, disturbing shot of three corpses, hanging from the gallows, up on a hill, a shot which is covered in Peter Biziou's diffuse, smoky yet golden-hued lighting. In this sequence, the violence and hysteria of the Nuremberg rally spill into the everyday reality of the streets, as the skinhead security guards terrorize unsuspecting people, people who are not following Pink's oppressive orders. According to Romero and Valeria Cabo, this sequence possesses a particular significance. They state:

> "Run Like Hell" is a potential ideological drift towards an ultranationalist, imperialist and racist stand that calls for the resurrection of a Britannia that is both pure and almighty.[30]

The fascist, despotic reign of terror continues with "Waiting for the Worms," which finds Pink overseeing a sort of ethnic cleansing. Pink now realizes that he is becoming the very forces that killed his father, and there is an internal struggle going on between the rational, idealistic Pink and the fascist dictator that has taken over. The conflict is evident when he sings the lyric, "goodbye, cruel world" again, only this time, the farewell seems to be spoken more out of remorse over what he's done. He has achieved that which he set out to, complete and utter isolation and alienation, and, like Henry V, he is examining his victory and realizing that it is not fraught with the sense of satisfaction he had hoped.

Once again, Gerald Scarfe's vividly haunting animation highlights this scene, the most indelible image being a giant army of hammers marching synchronously through the streets, demanding order and submission, while a rabid crowd chants, "Hammer! Hammer!" This sequence could be seen as a swirling mad painting, which incorporates all of the negativity associated with the wall and its construction. Hatred, fear, insecurity, rage, etc., and Pink is, even in his warped mental state, able to recognize that which he has wrought.

Pink's realization of the terror he has unleashed culminates with a close-up of his face as he screams, "Stop!" We then cut back to "reality" to find Pink in the sanitarium, which reaffirms that the Nuremberg rally of cleansing and terror all existed in his fractured psyche—he realizes the awful ramifications of having built his wall of isolation (and sees that it has turned him into the very things he has hated his entire life).

Pink then psychologically puts himself on trial, in an extended Gerald Scarfe animation "Trial" sequence that is both the narrative and musical climax of the film, and Scarfe's mad imagination swirls across every frame. It starts with the prosecutor addressing the judge as "Worm, Your Honor," which accentuates the film's theme of decay. The animation has an exaggerated, silly, circus feel to it, which is in stark contrast to the haunting, nightmarish visuals preceding it, which suggests that some type of transition (most likely in Pink's mind) has taken place. The teacher is called to the stand to testify, and he appears as a marionette, being controlled by strings. This suggests that the teacher, unlike Pink, has resigned and accepted his lack of identity. The sequence then plunges deeper into Pink's memories and psychology as he remembers his mother, who appears exaggerated and warped in shape. She is cradling baby Pink in her arms, which morph into a giant brick wall, barricading baby Pink in her grasp, cordoning him off from the world. We then cut to an animated rendition of Pink, pensively floating and spinning through the air. This imagery suggests that Pink is now recognizing and attempting to deal with the tethering psychological conditions that have forced him into constructing the wall—he now sees his mother as warped and misshapen, as opposed to the perfect, angelic caretaker; he is now questioning his relationship to her. He is no longer going to passively accept his constraints and voluntarily sink deeper into isolation. Although this film certainly does not adhere to the concept of a traditional Hollywood narrative, this dramatic development (that of the protagonist going through hell and deciding of his own volition to seek redemption) is one of the most perennial themes in Hollywood cinema.

The judge then appears, a giant, menacing (although silly at the same time) figure, who finds Pink guilty. His punishment is to "tear down the wall!" After shouting this command, the judge vomits, the contents of which are all of Pink's memories and reflections, and as the rabid crowd perpetually chants, "tear down the wall," Parker introduces yet another frenetic montage of clips and shots from Pink's past (his marriage, his wife and lover having sex, the skinheads terrorizing the public, a cartoon teacher shoving students into the meat grinder, etc.). This is Pink's introspection coming to a head. He is replaying his descent into madness in his mind one last time so that he may cathartically purge his demons and reconnect with society.

Cartoon by Alan Parker, drawn from his iPad, and part of a future collection of cartoons called *INT. ROOM.NIGHT*.

Parker visualizes Pink's ultimate victory over his demons with the monolithic, indelible metaphoric image of the giant, gray brick wall, which fills the entire frame. The camera stays fixed on the wall for a seemingly interminable amount of time—Parker wants us to savor the anxiety and anticipation. In a slow-motion shot, the wall explodes, symbolically representing that Pink has reintegrated himself into the land of the living, the land of the sane. He has broken through his constrictive barriers (a perennial Alan Parker theme) to emerge victorious.

The film's final scene finds children amid the rubble of Pink's now-obliterated wall. They are industriously marching through the detritus, picking up the bricks, and placing them in little toy trucks. The moral of the scene remains somewhat ambiguous. Are the children gathering the bricks to rebuild the wall that Pink worked so hard to demolish? Are they gathering the bricks to make sure future generations do not rebuild the wall? Either way, it is clear that the wall is an indelible metaphor for isolation and separation. For Pink, his isolation stemmed from his inability to connect with his fans, which caused him to sink into madness. The world is rife with barriers: social, economic, religious, racial, etc. The last scene, with its elegiac, quiet intensity, reminds us of the barriers that separate us from the rest of the world. Although, in an ideal world, these barriers would not exist, Parker is reminding us that they do, and it is up to us to either build and maintain them, or see to their destruction.

7

Birdy (1984)

December 24; 120 minutes/Color
Production Company: Tri-Star and A&M Films
Director: Alan Parker
Screenwriters: Sandy Kroopf and Jack Behr (based on the novel *Birdy* by William Wharton)
Producers: David Manson (Executive Producer); Ned Kopp (Associative Producer); Alan Marshall (Producer)
Production Designer: Geoffrey Kirkland
Cinematographer/Director of Photography: Michael Seresin
Editor: Gerry Hambling
Canary Trainer: Gary Gero
Cast: Matthew Modine (Birdy); Nicolas Cage (Al Columbato); John Harkins (Dr. Weiss); Sandy Baron (Mr. Columbato); Karen Young (Hannah Rourke); Bruno Kirby (Renaldi)

> Al, sometimes you're so full of shit.—Birdy

> *Birdy* was as pleasurable a film to make as *Pink Floyd—The Wall* had been miserable.... I had begun to wonder if film directing was the sort of thing a sane person should pursue. After Birdy, I [felt] my appetite for film [had been] been renewed.[1]
> —Alan Parker

Notes on the Production

After an intense run of directing *Fame* (1980), *Pink Floyd—The Wall* (1982) and *Shoot the Moon* (1982), averaging about a film a year, Alan Parker took a well-deserved one-year sabbatical before he set out to work on his next project, another ambitious undertaking: the adaption of the bizarre and very successful novel, *Birdy*. According to Parker, *Birdy* was "the hot novel of 1978,"[2] William Wharton's first novel, which went on to receive critical acclaim from an array of popular printed sources, including *People*, *Time*, the *Los Angeles Times*, the *Washington Post*, the *Atlantic Monthly* and the *New York Post*, to name a few. The *Kansas City Star* called it an "astonishing achievement ... so original you are left with a whole new concept of what a novel can do,"[3] and the *Philadelphia Enquirer* (Wharton was born in Philadelphia in 1926 and the novel takes place there) stated: "If imagination is the triumph of art over life, Wharton extends the issue until art triumphs over imagination."[4]

Wharton fought in World War II and was part of the Army Specialized Training Program and *Birdy* combines the author's Philadelphia roots with the horrors of war, and what results is a literary tour-de-force, one that is difficult to categorize.[5] Is it a coming-of-age story about fraternity? A Kafkaesque novel of psychosis, transformation and "metamor-

Matthew Modine as the eccentric ornithology aficionado. *Birdy* **(1984), Tri-Star and A & M Films.**

phosis"? An homage to ornithology? A metaphor for PTSD? Or was Wharton, a fine artist whose background is in painting, attempting to reinvent the way a story is told—more of a "painterly" than "literary" style—similar to how painter/filmmakers Michelangelo Antonioni (*Red Desert*, 1964), Akira Kurosawa (*Rashomon*, 1950) and David Lynch (*Eraserhead*, 1978) transcended the art of merging painting and filmmaking to meet the needs of their own movies?

Early in 1983, Parker had been sent an adapted screenplay written by Los Angeles writers Sandy Kroopf and Jack Behr, who had switched the narrative from the World War II era to Vietnam. Parker went to Los Angeles to work with Kroopf and Behr on a rewrite. Regarding this collaboration, Parker said, "Writers are always suspicious of directors who also write, but the collaboration was friendly and fruitful as we tugged, stretched and juggled the script into the film I wanted to make."[6]

Parker intended to film *Birdy* in the familiar territory of Northern California (Oakland) but "one visit to the Philadelphia of the book convinced [him] that it had a unique identity and would be more truthful to Wharton's story."[7] After all, the film is a "brotherly love" story about two war veterans traumatized by combat, who have now been reunited under peculiar circumstances. Although Parker and his crew shot part of the film in Philadelphia, the remaining half of the movie was shot at Agnew's Mental Hospital in San Jose (*Shoot *the Moon* was filmed in Northern California in the region he called "his home away from home").⁸

Birdy stood out as a cinematic achievement: Philadelphian Garrett Brown (inventor of the Steadicam) had a new invention called the "SkyCam" that had yet to be used for a film and it was going to make its debut in Parker's new film. The system had one-hundred-foot-high posts with four hanging wires controlled by a computer, and, at the center of these wires, a light Panavision camera was hung. It was as if the camera were invented specifically for the film. Incidentally, however, during a shoot, the "SkyCam" crashed and malfunctioned and, consequently, it wasn't used. In order to solve this problem, the camera operators ended up using a Steadicam and according to Parker, "[We] frantically began running down alleyways, across rubble, down streets—in a golf cart atop a bicycle dolly, with me charging behind on a bike. We quickly built a ramp twenty-feet high and thirty-feet long to get the POV of the canary smashing into the window. Necessity is the mother invention and the results are there on the screen—skillfully aided by Gerry Hambling's editing and Peter Gabriel's score."⁹

Nicolas Cage was considered for the role of Al early on in the process, and after extensive casting calls in New York, San Francisco, Los Angeles, San Jose and Philadelphia, Parker chose Matthew Modine for the part of Birdy. According to the director, Modine possessed a "simple honesty" that was refreshing. Parker had "become tired of 'Method acting weirdos' bringing in stuffed pigeons and photos of dead relatives for motivation."¹⁰ After a rough start (in addition to the problems with the SkyCam, the cast and crew needed to work around the challenge of filming nervous canaries, not to mention producer Alan Marshall's dealings with a member of the Teamsters union who kept tabs on all of their moving objects), the final part of the shoot at Agnew's State Hospital in Santa Clara went more smoothly. This was mostly because Nicolas Cage was always prepared for his monologues and stuck very closely to the words in the script.¹¹

Another prominent part of the production involved musician Peter Gabriel (who, after his stint with Genesis, had a successful career as a pop artist and a film composer; a few years later, he would score Martin Scorsese's 1988 film *The Last Temptation of Christ*). Parker was impressed with Gabriel's unique-sounding percussive rhythms. According to the director, the musician's tracks were highly textured pieces that had been intended for previous albums. In short, the score had already been written; it was just a matter of "finding" what original sounds would fit the mood and tone of the film.¹²

Birdy won the Grand Prix du Jury Prize at the Cannes Film Festival. During the screening of the film Parker sat next to author William Wharton. After the audience's long standing ovation, the director asked him what he thought of the film. Wharton said he liked it, but asked him, "Why did you make it *two* guys?"¹³

Summary

Over the opening credits—following the Tri-Star and A&M Films production logos—we hear the faint echo of birds chirping in fragmented sound bites over Peter Gabriel's plaintive, percussion-based musical score; this effectively draws the viewer into the cerebral world of *Birdy*. The camera captures a close-up of a storm-cloud-laden sky, then pulls back and down in a quick tilt, cutting to an extreme close-up of fence wires with a deep-blue sky in the background. Voices overlap with one another—"Dinner's ready!" "Hey, you—Bird Boy!"—as the music and bird chirping become more pronounced. The camera descends from above, bringing us to the next shot, the source of this colliding visual and aural montage. Revealed in a picture-perfect, well-balanced low-angle shot is the following image: Birdy (Matthew Modine) sitting on the floor in a cell to the right of a bed placed in the center of the frame. A large window with bright white light casts shadows on the wall. The *mise-en-scène* captures the three subjects in a rich rule-of-thirds composition, creating a clear depth-of-field and an aesthetically pleasing form of expressionism (in many of his films, Parker creates his own expressionism but not in the dark, hopeless German expressionistic/film noir manner; the use of blue hues and dark and white shading is psychologically haunting, but still, because of its peculiar beauty, renders a world of hope). In this scene within a scene, Parker's credit appears, and this visual prologue marks the transition into the opening of the film.

The next series of shots—a classic montage replete with heartbeats (like in the opening segment of *Midnight Express*)—shows a tilted camera behind bars as if we, the viewers, are in this cage. Revealed: Doctors and nurses rapidly wheeling a bed-ridden patient, whose face is covered with bandages. In the next scene, which takes place in a hospital ward, the patient, still confined to a bed, looks over to the next bed and sees a man who is badly wounded; the veins in this man's face are sticking out and it is obvious he has been severely injured. (This moment serves as exposition which is explained in the next shot.) This other patient is Alfonso Columbato (Nicolas Cage), who, represented through somber low-key lighting, is conversing with a doctor. Al jokingly says he feels like the invisible man (which comments on one of the film's major themes: the lack of identity; the doctor, providing hope, tells him not to worry. The camera then cuts to Al and lingers on his expression of deep concern.

The following scene shows Al on a train, traveling to the hospital where his friend Birdy is a patient. He sits down and faces a little girl, who can't help but stare at him and his bandaged face. Lightheartedly Al smiles then says, "Boo!" which makes the girl smile, effectively breaking the awkward tension between them. The girl's mother, changing the tone of the moment, tells her daughter not to stare, and the reality of this seemingly harmless comment changes Al's expression: he is the war veteran already getting a taste of civilian life, not to mention the prejudice and xenophobia that goes a long with it. This unfortunate reality only exacerbates the symptoms of post-traumatic stress disorder (PTSD).

According to Ghislaine Boulanger (PhD)'s article "Post-Traumatic Stress Disorder: An Old Problem with a New Name,"

> The patterns of (PTSD) symptoms which seemed to occur independent of personality type, included intrusive recollections of traumatic events in the form of dreams, nightmares and—occasionally—flashbacks, which are dissociative states during which the individual behaves as if he or she were re-experiencing the traumatic event.... The veteran felt detached from others, had difficulty maintaining close interpersonal relationships, lost interest in normal activities, and felt that life has lost its meaning. Often the veteran was quite unaware of the syndrome to which he or she had fallen prey and unaware of its origin in the traumatic experience of combat.[14]

Moreover, the formation of "rap groups" had been formed to help PTSD patients. A rap group is a tool to help veterans cope with their disorders. This symbiotic relationship provides a forum "in which the veterans value system and sense of meaning can be refashioned. A new sense of self can develop and symptoms wane."[15] In a unique way, the narrative structure of the entire film can be viewed as a type of "rap group" story, even if the only real participant is Al. Furthermore, it may be argued that PTSD can be linked to other experiences besides those associated with war. According to John Russell Smith, M.A., "All current problems in Viet Nam veterans are not the result of the Viet Nam War. But the stress recovery process shows that obsession with the past, insistence of personal responsibility or non-culpability and bizarre and unexplained current behavior are often connected to unresolved trauma."[16] If this is indeed true, then this statement can be explored further with Birdy's character—his obsession with the past, his antisocial behavior and obsession. In this case, Birdy's obsession with wanting to fly and becoming a bird may have been sparked by the war experience, and now he is locked in that unresolved past ... as a bird.

The following sequence is a flashback, which, unlike other flashbacks throughout the film, is executed in a third-person omniscient point of view, existing solely for the sake of exposition: Birdy and his parents live next to a baseball field—separated by a fence—and over the years boys would play in this field. When home-runs were hit, the baseballs would invariably end up in this yard, enraging Birdy's unreasonable mother (Dolores Sage). "This ain't no ballpark!" Birdy's mother would yell, to which her husband (George Buck) gently countered, "Kids gotta play, honey."

In the next beat, Al and his little brother, Mario (James Santini), confront Birdy, who had somehow obtained Mario's knife. Mario tells his older brother that Birdy stole the knife (which turns out to be untrue) and, consequently, Al confronts the eccentric teenager who is tending to birds in a cage; he refers to him as "Bird Boy." Eventually, through a montage, Al and Birdy end up wrestling (in a surprisingly fair fight) and, within moments, Al discovers that Birdy just *had* the knife; he didn't steal it. Al then proceeds to give the knife back to Birdy. And from this moment forward, as if destined by fate, hot-tempered Al and quiet, reserved Birdy form a unique, symbiotic relationship. Al, impressed with Birdy's wrestling "moves," encourages him to try out for the sport, but, instead, Birdy redirects his attention to his birds and their ability to fly.

The following sequence, a story-within-a-story montage, represented through quick editing and transitional dissolves, highlights the beginnings of this peculiar but genuine friendship (the montage serves as a way to condense the more lengthy descriptions in the novel): The boys go to a construction site to catch pigeons; they both ride bikes; they build a bird house; and Birdy surprises Al when he comes toward him dressed in a home-made pigeon suit made of real feathers (comically, Birdy tells his friend: "It's a pigeon suit I made for you, Al."). Birdy explains to Al (in his typical no-nonsense manner) that in this suit, the pigeons will think that he is one of them. Al, who can't comprehend this logic, says, "I don't want the pigeons to think I'm one of them.... No way I'd be caught dead in that." And, in a humorous jump-cut, Al is seen wearing his own pigeon suit—albeit reluctantly. In the next shot, a police car follows them and this causes the boys to run back to the construction site. (The images of the industrial landscape in the background provide a dichotomy: man-made machinery versus the simplicity of nature.) When Birdy and Al get to the top of the site (in beautiful low-key lighting, soaked in a blue hue that accentuates the approaching cooling nightfall, underscored by Peter Gabriel's rhythmic music), Birdy announces his need to fly, which scares Al. At this time, Birdy slips and is left hanging off the edge of the site, inexplicably calm and smiling, while Al panics. This two-shot juxtaposition (seen in alternating high- and low-angle POV shots from the respective characters), gives way to Birdy's fall. As he lets go, he "flies." Peter Gabriel's music builds to a melodramatic crescendo and the quick succession of the shots, creatively paced by Gerry Hambling's discontinuous editing (similar to that of a Sam Peckinpah or Sergio Leone western) gives the stylized illusion of Birdy in flight. The frames are captured in slow-motion and the rapid juxtaposition of the images moves forward to capture Birdy's descent ... then the segment returns to the beginning of the fall and once again moves forward a few frames two more times. Time stands still during this moment. Does Birdy actually fly in this short time period? After the "third descent" Birdy falls and hits the ground, hard. Al rushes toward him, anxiety-driven, as Birdy lies there, blood dripping from his mouth, at peace with himself: "It was beautiful," he tells Al. Holding his injured friend, Al says, "God, Birdy. Don't do anything like that again."

The next perception shift returns to the present: Birdy is in the army hospital, hopelessly looking out the window. Al has arrived and he looks in the window frame of the door and taps on the glass to say "hello" to his friend: this is the first time he has seen Birdy since the war. An offscreen voice is heard: "What do you think, Sergeant?" The voice is revealed: It is Doctor/Major Weiss (John Harkins), the ward psychiatrist, who, in some ways, serves as the villain in the story. He comes to represent the symbol of institutional authority (like Nurse Ratched in *One Flew Over the Cuckoo's Nest* [1975, Milos Forman] or Hamidou in *Midnight Express*) who doesn't appear to have a true vested interest in Birdy's reform. Al asks him if Birdy was wounded in the war. Weiss replies: "Yeah, but his wounds were relatively minor," further explaining that what Birdy is experiencing is not a physical condition; all they know is that he was missing in action for a month before he was found. So what actually happened to Birdy exists in this theoretical month after combat, a time period not explored in the film. Might it be safe to say that in this time Birdy experienced his "transformation" from man to bird? While the discussion with Weiss continues, an image of Birdy is captured on the floor, crouching in his birdlike pose. Is Birdy *actually* a bird? Is he suffering from symptoms of PTSD? Have both things occurred? Incidentally (and quite ironically) it was Birdy's mother who told the hospital staff that Al may be a key component in her son's rehabilitation, and this explains why he is there. Weiss, consequently, believed that this experiment would be "an interesting therapy for both of [them]." He may represent the ignorance that surrounds PTSD. It is curious (refreshingly so) that PTSD is not explicitly mentioned in the film.

In the following scene, Weiss shows Al a series of photographs. An extreme low-angle shot, the camera slightly tilted, looks up at the two characters, who sit at a table studying the pictures. Behind them, a grid-wire background reminds the viewer that we, too, are imprisoned in a cage. One of the photographs shows Birdy in his recognizable crouched position: Weiss interprets this as Birdy trying to escape, but he is baffled as to why he remains in this position. (Weiss is never informed, incidentally, that Birdy has become the bird he always wanted to be; Al knows that if Weiss ever finds this out, his friend would surely be treated for schizophrenia/psychosis and possibly *never* leave the hospital.) Weiss becomes increasingly more authoritative as the scene unfolds. He insists that Al refer to him as "Major"; insensitively asks him what happened to his face; he even brings up the fact that Al had been brought up on charges of insubordination toward an officer. He makes it known that he won't put up with similar behavior from him.

In many ways, *Birdy* is a critique on the institution (not unlike *Midnight Express* and *Pink Floyd—The Wall*) and an anti-war film (in the tradition of *All Quiet on the Western Front* [1930, Lewis Milestone], *Stalag 17* [1953, Billy Wilder], *Paths of Glory* [1957, Stanley Kubrick] and *Catch-22* [1970, Mike Nichols]). The film next introduces the character Rinaldi (Bruno Kirby), a "conscientious objector," who is now reduced to taking patients for walks, reading them the funny papers and changing their bed pans. Although his character is not very developed (at least not as much as it is in Wharton's novel), he *does* come to represent another companion for Al. Rinaldi and Al are both Italians, not to mention military mavericks (conveying an anti-war message), which may suggest that they are one and the same (another duality).

The following scene begins Birdy's and Al's "conversations." Al enters Birdy's room, only to find his friend is in his bird pose. Al, concerned and frightened, says, "If this is an act to get out of Nam—it worked. You can stop now." He walks over to Birdy, leading to another elegantly composed shot: Birdy is on the extreme left of the frame and Al is on the extreme right next to the centered bed emulating an impeccable depth-of-field, which brings all objects on all planes into a deep focus. Framed by a series of these richly textured shots, Al speaks about his stay at the hospital at Dix in New Jersey, which leads to a very tightly framed shot of Al kneeling next to Birdy, poignantly asking his friend what happened to him. He then explains that he is there to help him. The closed form of the *mise-en-scène* and cinematography captures two significant things: the tightness of this symbiotic friendship, and their inevitable imprisonment.

While Al reflects upon a sexually related memory, Hannah York (Karen Young), the nurse, enters. At first this young woman appears rigid, a product of institutional micromanagement, until Al puts her at ease by asking her to call him by his first name. Although not a major character, Hannah *does* come to represent something mythical, even angelic. She is the only one Birdy allows to feed him, which is indicative of her nurturing quality. At this time, however, Al is overwhelmed with everything and proceeds to leave. Time passes. Peter Gabriel's otherworldly music sets the tone of the scene as the camera captures Birdy staring out the window. Offscreen we hear a voice saying, "Hi, there." Birdy is in flight again. Throughout the film the window serves as his portal into the past, and this leads to another flashback, which is a continuation of the previous flashback.

A doctor is feeding the injured Birdy in a hospital bed. In the waiting room, Al, dressed in the pigeon suit, sits next to a humorless woman and comically tells her about Birdy, his friend who *thinks* he can fly, who *thinks* he's a bird. With this exchange, she looks at him and nothing more needs to be said; the punch line, so to speak, is captured through her dry, expressionless look alone.

Another flashback: Birdy's mother is violently kicking her son's aviary while her husband works outside, burning wood. Oddly, Al is there—sitting in a chair, reading a newspaper, which features the story concerning Birdy falling off the gas tank while trying to "fly." Birdy's mother says she doesn't want to hear any more about birds—all she wants is to get the "pigeon shit" off her porch. She is the archetypal "henpecking" matriarch. Her character can serve as an interesting Freudian study regarding Birdy's overall character.

She is an unreasonable mother and Birdy's father is a more passive figure. How has this parental dynamic shaped Birdy's personality? On the flip-side, Al's father is a dominating patriarch, and his mother is soft-spoken. Similarly, how has *this* family dynamic shaped Al's personality? Do Birdy and Al create a surrogate brotherhood based on their respective dysfunctional families?

In the following scene, Al and Birdy are walking through what looks like an industrial wasteland. A car is flipped over on a dirt mound and an abandoned railroad is seen in the distance. Philadelphia is nothing more than a machine-infested factory city—another reminder that, in many ways, this film may be critiquing the era of modernism.

Back to the present: A high-angle shot looks down on Birdy, who is lying on the floor to the left of his bed in a crucifixion position. Meanwhile, Al is outside in the gloomy rain, smoking a cigarette. There follows another shot of Birdy, who is now confined next to the toilet, a scene whose melancholy score is just as claustrophobic as the setting. From behind the cage, he is trapped: Al is now with him recalling a memory about the statue at city hall that makes Birdy smile (the first major breakthrough); Al says that it always reminded him of a guy with a "hard-on." A quick shot of the statue, most likely from Birdy's POV, comically captures the image of this phallic symbol.

At this point, Birdy's narration begins and the camera moves into a close-up. "If I'm going to learn, I'm going to have to watch them closely," he says thoughtfully. "Be there when they fly. I want them to be as free as possible. Nobody wants to be in a cage...." In another stunning shot, Birdy is captured under the sink, looking up into the window through which shines a "hopeful" heavenly white light—a light that suggests freedom. The image and piercing sounds of birds appear at the window, along with Gabriel's musical leitmotif. The larger-than-life shadows of the birds are projected onto the wall, revealing a surreal unique expressionistic utopia for Birdy (a motif that is used in a later part of the film to highlight Birdy's dreams). Thus, the first major act of the film comes to an end.

The second act continues the exploration of the past relationships between the two friends. In a flashback, Birdy and Al are speaking with the junkyard proprietor (Steve Lippe) concerning the purchase of their new Ford. The camera peers into the window where the three of them discuss business, but the dialogue is muted and replaced by the overpowering ambient sounds of running vehicles (more invasive machinery and technology). A money transaction is executed, Al and the proprietor shake hands and, by the end of the scene, the two friends have their car to work on so they can eventually sell it and make a profit. Aside from their overt personality differences, Al and Birdy appear to be the most "normal" with one another as business partners.

In the following scene Birdy and Al work proudly on the car as Al's father, Mr. Columbato (Sandy Baron), Parker's examination of the working class, steps out of the trash truck, wearing a dirty white "wife beater" tank top, tosses his cigarette on the ground and after seeing Birdy and his son working on the car, refers to the vehicle as "some piece of shit." He reminds them that the car needs to be registered, and, in an oddly compassionate tone, offers to take charge of this process. Al, who is constantly trying to please his unpleaseable father, speaks under his breath and calls him a "fucking garbage man"—a comment that is more of a personal attack on his character rather than a critique on his social class. Little do we know at this time that Mario has his own financial plans for the car. At the end of the scene, Al drives the convertible while Birdy stands up in the back, arms reaching above his head as he looks to the sky—he is flying! Al suggests they drive to the beach; Birdy has never been, and in the following abrupt shot the two of them are at the ocean. Birdy says that being in the water is like flying. He holds his breath for a long period and this makes Al very nervous. More of the duality is captured: Al remains a traditionalist, more of a grounded person, while Birdy's daredevil persona continues to define his own need to be free.

In the next sequence Birdy and Al are on a double date at an amusement park. Al is interested in having sex with his date, Shirley (Sandra Beall), while Birdy is clearly not interested in *his* date, Rosanne (Elizabeth Whitcraft). In the next shot, the four of them are riding the roller coaster, on which Birdy imagines himself to be flying. When the four of them stop to watch an underwater performer holding his breath for an extended period, Birdy watches in admiration. His date, however, is not impressed with this "freak" and rhetorically asks, "Think he's got a wife?" In other words, anyone (a reflection of Birdy) who acts like this will never "get the girl."

In a later scene, Birdy and his date sit on the sand while Al and his date make love. The scene ends disastrously when Rosanne tells her friend that she is leaving: "I ain't hanging around with that creep no more!" Both girls leave as Al looks at Birdy—the extreme high-angle shot on Al and the low-angle shot on Birdy indicates that Al has "lost" and Birdy has "prevailed."

In the following scene at the ocean (represented through a number of long- and medium-shots), Al, now very distressed, attempts to lecture his friend about the facts of life, mainly the wonders of the female body. Birdy, unimpressed, refers to female breasts as "overgrown mammary glands." Birdy's sociopathic behavior may be linked to recent studies of Asperger's Syndrome, yet the film isn't interested in overtly looking at any psychological disorder (PTSD included) as a main topic. In fact, Birdy exudes a certain omniscience that transcends the human condition—as if he knows something greater than the average person. Before his experience in the war, Birdy never second-guessed his individuality. What makes him so confident? Is he spiritually tapped into another realm of existence? Is the film looking at the hidden dimensions of psychotic behavior without labeling it as anything specific? In fact, Birdy (like the "psychotic" Elwood P. Dowd, who sees a giant rabbit in Mary Chase's *Harvey*) might even be the most "normal" person in the film.

The scene comes to an end when a police officer disrupts the boys' intimate discussion: "That your '53 Ford back there?" Then a jump cut: The boys are in jail. Birdy and Al eventually get bailed out by Al's parents. While they walk out to the car, Al's father backhands him. They have exited one jail and entered another, for the real imprisonment in the film is reflected through the lives of these dysfunctional families. (Perhaps this is the major theme of the story.)

Return to the present. Rinaldi lets Al back into the cell to see Birdy. The tone has changed; Al is already tired and frustrated. The angular composition helps to define this distorted perspective. Al sits to the left of the frame, and Birdy sits to the right. The camera slowly zooms into Al: "Come on, Birdy! Talk to me! You don't think I know what you're doing with all that squatting and sideways staring stuff? You're finally a bird. Big deal! If Weiss finds out he's going to put you in a display case and write papers about you forever." A close-up on Birdy. *Does he understand*? He turns to look out the window and from his POV we see a blue sky juxtaposed with rainfall—a dichotomy of hope and misery. In the next shot, Al is seen smoking in the rain. He has become an outsider, a common fate of the war veteran. His existential mode, including a loss of identity (physically and psychologically) is captured in this instance, which serves as a transition into another flashback. Birdy visits a woman, Mrs. Prevost (Nancy Fish), who sells birds out of her house; canaries fly everywhere. (The shot of a menacing cat looking at its prey foreshadows a later scene when Birdy's cat captures his canary in its jowls. Might the cat also be symbolic of Birdy's fate? After all, his "ability to fly" ends after he experiences war.) Birdy shows an immediate affinity toward a yellow canary, which he adopts and names Perta. The look of wonder on his face is followed by his voice-over narration: "The first day I saw Perta, I knew she was special. The way she took to the air. Like it was hers." The novel—and to a degree, the film—connects Birdy to Perta in a sexual manner (the novel goes into detail about Birdy's dreams, wherein he pictures himself as part of a canary family).

The next portion of the film continues to tell Birdy's and Al's backstory. While prancing about with his pair of homemade wings, Birdy insists that they confront Al's father, who sold their car to a mob-connected friend and demand that he return it to them. Al thinks this is a bad idea, saying that his father "will kill him." Fearless (emphasized by his flapping wings), Birdy says, "Sometimes Al, you're so full of shit." The line is significant in that it gives Al the courage to go along with Birdy's idea.

Cut to an image of Al's mother, Mrs. Columbato (Crystal Field), ironing. Offscreen, Birdy's angry voice is heard: "You have no right to sell the car, Mr. Columbato. It's worth more than the money you gave us. It belongs to Al and me." Mr. Columbato, now in view, informs him that the car is in his name, thus allowing him to sell it to whomever he chooses—and the argument intensifies. "Are you calling me a crook in my own house?" he asks threateningly. To which Birdy replies, "You sold something that wasn't yours." Al's father warns Birdy that if he antagonizes the man who now owns the car (a notorious mobster) he'll "end up at the bottom of a river." Furthermore, he insults Birdy, calling him a "skinny bucket of piss." Mrs. Columbato, acting as a mediator, finally intervenes and asks her husband to get the car back. The scene reinforces the relationship between the two friends. Al continues to live in fear of his father's imprisonment, and Birdy—in perhaps his most lively moment in the film—is metaphorically using those wings he was flapping in the previous scene. He darts by Al and upon his exit says, "It's *our* car, Al." The scene bridges to Al's voice-over: "I could never stand up to my old man like that."

Back in the cell, Birdy is on the left of the frame, posed as a bird; Al is on the right. This balanced composition provides a meaningful *mise-en-scène*: Al is facing his alter-ego, and says humbly, "I just want to make it through day by day like anyone else." As he exits, he is overcome with panic. "Let me out!" he yells. A shot of his legs fill the screen in a closed-form composition, his legs like prison bars providing confinement. This shot cuts to another shot of legs on the battlefield during combat. Al is experiencing a PTSD–related flashback; he feels helpless and trapped. Birdy responds through a grimace; he seems to understand what Al is feeling.

Al exits the cell and calls Birdy's name and as he does so, the film flashes back again to the combat scene. He yells Birdy's name one final time and the shot of the legs returns: a mine explodes—and Al wakes up, screaming. Renaldi, who is sleeping in the next bed, wakes up and comforts him. A role-reversal has occurred: Renaldi now becomes the "rap group" leader who consoles the vulnerable Al.

Al Columbato (Nicolas Cage, left), a Vietnam war veteran, tries to communicate with his nonverbal childhood friend, "Birdy" (Matthew Modine, right), also a war veteran, who has been institutionalized in an army hospital. *Birdy* **(1984), Tri-Star and A & M Films.**

In the next scene, Al is being questioned by Major Weiss's secretary, who has a chronic habit of spitting while he talks. He tells Al sardonically that he wants to know everything about him, and then asks if he has experienced any history of insanity or suicides. In the novel, this character is described in the following description from Al's point-of-view:

> Next morning I go to see Weiss. He's not in yet but there's a fat T-4 with a typewriter; Underwood, stand-up job. He says he just wants some information for the doctor ... he sits there grinning at me. He's got me pegged as a loon for sure.
> Great questions he asks, like, How many people in my family have done themselves in? ... What creepy questions.... He types it out, four finger hunt and peck, then he looks at it and spits! Spits right at my name on the paper....[17]

In the following scene, Al is in Dr. Weiss's office. In answer to Al's question, Weiss explains his secretary's penchant for spitting: "Ever since he was in combat, he's had a bad taste in his mouth." Weiss asks Al to talk about the time when he attacked the officer, which momentarily brings the focus on Al and not Birdy; this concerns Al, who is confused as to why he is suddenly being questioned. The doctor tells him that he is unsure of Birdy's progress and at this stage is ready to throw in the towel, so to speak (the authority figure can't see beyond the rules and regulations of the institution), but Al is convinced he can help his friend. Like many of the scenes in the film, there is a touch of hope that lingers throughout.

Despite this hope, however, Al, too, is a little dubious of his friend's recovery. He shows this in the next scene with Birdy when he says to him: "If you could see yourself ... you'd laugh yourself to death." When Al feeds his friend, Birdy looks at him in a way that anticipates a breakthrough. At this moment, something is definitely happening to Birdy...

Another flashback: Birdy is in his room playing with a remote-controlled bird, flapping its wings. Perta lands on him; he connects with her by blowing air at her and making bird noises. From the other room we hear his mother reprimanding his father about their son: "*You* tell him. *You're* his father." Moments later, Birdy's father reluctantly enters his son's bedroom and speaks with gentle compassion: "Come on, son, leave the bird alone." Birdy's father is somehow tuned into his son's passion yet he is unable to communicate it properly: he is not an intellectual man capable of expressing his true feelings, but he *does* love his son unconditionally.

This scene—in which Birdy is alone in his room experiencing a transformation while his family and society itself is outside judging him—reminds this viewer of Kafka's "The Metamorphosis" (1915). Birdy, the contemporary Gregor Samsa, has found himself "transformed" into a bird instead of a giant insect, yet the overall metaphor remains similar: both characters are existential society outcasts linked to a war (Gregor served in World War I; when re-examining the story, one may interpret *his* metamorphosis through the eyes of a disabled veteran).

At school, Birdy lectures his class about the dynamics of birds and how they fly and the model of the bird from the previous scene flies around the classroom to enhance his oral presentation. "It's a matter of confidence," he says, discussing specific details about how birds' feathers enhance their flight. Birdy exudes confidence as he eloquently teaches the class. The only time this young man is free is when he is involved with birds—again, a sort of explanation of his own need to be free from his surrounding culture and society. In this short segment, the viewer obtains a brief ornithology lesson about birds and their feathers. From a basic engineering standpoint, the chief characteristic of a bird's feather can be summed up thus: "It's the most complex growth of the skin known to be formed of any animal. It is one of the lightest and, at the same time, one of the strongest materials formed by any creature. It is durable, complex and flexible, a superb functional structure for both flight and heat retention ... of all forms of animal life on this earth, birds—and only birds—have feathers. All birds possess them ... it is easy to separate the barbs on a feather with the finger..." (as Birdy does in the film) "...and, of course, this happens in nature when a feather needs attention, the bird repairs the separation by drawing the feathers through its bill."[18] In short, birds are not only significant because they can fly but also because they are unique and possess individuality ... much like Birdy himself.

Birdy's lecture catches the eye of classmate Doris Robinson (Maud Winchester), a fact that Al observes; consequently, he attempts to prompt his friend to get to know the girl. Meanwhile, Birdy meets up with his father in the boiler room at the school (where he works as a janitor). The two of them connect in a discussion about their respective passions: Birdy wants to get another canary (a male for mating) and needs his approval so that he can convince his mother to allow him to have it; his father has a genuine interest in the well being of his son and explains to him that, in the past, he himself once had a real love for wicker, and if he were given the opportunity, he says proudly, he could make "the world's best wicker chair," but, he adds discouragingly, this interest (like Birdy's interest in birds) is simply not practical. The scene *does*, however, end with a touch of hope: he tells his son that, despite the odds, he *will* talk to his wife about the canary. This is one of the most poignant scenes in the film. Birdy and his father form another character duality; they are one and the same, individuals whose dreams have been lost and shattered because of a modern capitalistic society that favors capitalism over idealism.

The following sequence features Birdy and Al: they are together, doing their own exercises—Al lifts weights, and Birdy does arm lifts to increase his "flapping" power. It is a scene which exemplifies how the characters accept each other's idiosyncrasies: despite the fact that Al can't understand Birdy's perspective, and vice versa, they remain unconditional friends, sustaining a symbiotic relationship that continues to mirror Hermann Hesse's novels and Freud's psychoanalysis, respectively: the intellectual vs. the brute; the id vs. the superego.

In the next scene, Al peddles a bike while Birdy, attached to the handlebars, "flies" with the wings he has made. As the scene unfolds, Richie Valens's 1958 pop hit "La Bamba" plays, the lyrics of which reflect Birdy's flight, as Valens sings of needing a little grace to move up.

The mood shifts to the present. Al visits Birdy again; he refers to the details of the previous scene and asks him why he had a physical ailment every time he attempted to save him from a catastrophe. Birdy reacts with a smile! Moments later, in Dr. Weiss's office, Al explains that he got Birdy to respond to an inside joke regarding a phenomenon: every time Birdy got hurt, Al would get sick—yet another reminder that we are more than likely looking at two parts of the same soul. This is a detail so intimate between the two friends that it does not translate well to the doctor, who is ready to let this experiment go. In one final attempt to save Birdy, Al mentions the baseballs. He suggests that if Birdy's mother would locate and bring these balls in (Birdy always felt guilty that his mother kept the baseballs and never returned them to the kids; and, furthermore it was one of these baseballs that brought the two friends together), then he believes progress can be made. With trepidation, Weiss agrees and says, "I hope this works."

"Me, too," Al concurs.

Hope is all they have.

Al walks to a gymnasium: a paraplegic is moving his wheelchair around the floor while he shoots hoops. On the wall, a red, white, and blue banner reads: WELCOME HOME SOLDIERS, USA IS PROUD OF YOU. Al claps when the young man scores, a clap that honors and recognizes his fellow soldier's sacrifices. This is another critique on war, the irony of the returning veteran who has given his life away for his country, now incapable of adapting to civilian life. As Al works out with weights, the voice-over narration begins: "We didn't know what we were getting into with this John Wayne shit—did we?" The shot lingers on Al and, at this point, the viewer has temporarily entered his microcosm. In a series of POV edits, he observes Birdy (who is being bathed by Hannah, the nurse) through dim, low-key lighting. "Boy, were we dumb," he says out loud, facing the cell. "We were always dumb. Before the government it was some asshole on the street corner in Philly." He pauses and makes eye contact with Hannah, his angelic muse, who smiles at him. This sets the transition for the next flashback when Al and Birdy were dogcatchers, another one of their money-making ventures. "Remember the dogs, Birdy?" Al asks through voice-over narration.

Al and Birdy are riding in a truck with their employer Joe Sagessa (Robert L. Ryan), who explains to them about their role as dogcatchers: "The way I got it figured ... we're doing a good deed—and making a buck besides." Set to the lively "La Bamba," the three men attempt to capture a pack of dogs in a comedic montage that unfolds in a slapstick fashion. After they successfully capture the dogs, Al asks where they go once they have been caught. Sagessa cryptically says, "Hey—that's *my* department." En route, an irate man drives beside the men and informs the "sons of bitches" that they have his dog; he follows them to what is soon to be revealed as a slaughterhouse. Now Birdy and Al know where Joe takes the dogs once they have been caught; obviously, this revelation astounds them. It appears that whenever these men attempt to tap into the world of capitalism, they are set back, disillusioned by the reality and the inhumanity that is linked to the so-called American dream.

The next flashback, intercut with moments of Birdy and Al in the present day, begins with the image of a cat in stalking mode (the same cat that was seen earlier in the film) outside of Birdy's home. This image repeatedly cross-cuts to Birdy washing dishes in his kitchen. As usual, Birdy is trapped inside his own internal universe; he is merely going through the motions of housework while he daydreams. The juxtaposition builds and Birdy's voice-over begins: "I'm starting to worry I'll never fly, the way I've been going.... As scary as a bird's life must be, at least they have *that*—they can always fly away." A shot of his mother (possibly the film's biggest villain), who is seen sewing at a table, is followed by a pan to the cat moving up the stairway toward Birdy's room (the cat and the mother metaphorically become confining predators who threaten the well being of those who want to be free). His mother complains to her son that the bird feathers are giving her asthma. (Is this a wink toward Gregor Samsa's asthma-stricken mother in Kafka's "The Metamorphosis"?)

The scene builds with more suspense-filled cross-cutting: Birdy approaches his bedroom, unaware that the cat has entered his room where he keeps his birds. When he suddenly discovers Perta trapped in the cat's jowls, he runs and pries the bird out of the feline's mouth. Perta appears to be dead, but is miraculously still alive! Did Birdy somehow *save* the bird? The juxtaposition of the soft brassy musical score, bird sounds and pan flutes create a surreal moment that momentarily suggests a type of magical intervention. Birdy looks out the window into what appears to be another world...

This image *becomes* the next shot: present-day Birdy looking through the window in his cell. Al's words interrupt this prophetic moment: "All right, Birdy, it's time to start flapping your wings and peeping ... if you want to spend the rest of your life as a bird—at least be consistent. You don't hop like a bird. You don't really sit like one. And you sure as hell can't fly like one." (Al knows these words will get his friend to respond—and he is correct). Al continues; "If you don't like what I am saying, Birdy, why don't you just tell me to shut up?" During this volatile moment between the friends, Hannah enters which annoys Al; she has interrupted them. When she reminds him that attending to Birdy is part of her job, Al angrily retorts, "Yeah? Well, he's part of my goddammed life!"

Al exits and, in the next shot, he is seen leaning his head against a fence. Along with this image is a shadow of the cell door he just opened; the shadow represents the illusion of freedom within his ongoing existential nightmare. Hannah, the angelic muse, knows that Al needs healing and, consequently, she offers herself to him. She is gentle and nurturing and allows him to touch her breast. Afterwards he apologizes, admitting that he hasn't touched a woman "in a long time." Hannah has given him a sense of meaning; she is a mythical presence who, like Susan in *Midnight Express* (and even Nurse Graves in *The Road to Wellville*), uses her delicate femininity to console his bruised masculinity, and to prove that there is still hope.

The following shot complements this hope. In another well-balanced *mise-en-scène*, Birdy is attached to the back part of the bed frame—the way he is crouching and the way his feet hold onto the bars creates an uncanny resemblance to a bird in a cage. The left of the frame is mostly black, while the protruding white light from the window on the right side of the frame casts rich shadows on the wall just above where Birdy sits. Parker's expressionism continues to yield hope. The high-contrast lighting and the extreme depth-of-field places emphasis on Birdy's alter-egos—he is just as much of a bird as he is a man. Typically, one may assume that a character in Birdy's predicament should return to his so-called "normal" state of existence, to attempt to heal his psychotic behavior in order to be a functioning human being. The visual design indicates that Birdy is trapped in limbo (the high-contrast lighting may be seen as the opposition of good versus evil, real and surreal, man and bird)—yet while trapped inside this limbo he is truly able to find his bliss.

The viewer sees Birdy in an extreme close-up behind a bird cage, whispering and flirting with Perta. "Give me a kiss," he says. An abrupt cut brings us to the façade of an oversized silhouette of a bird projected on a brick wall (similar to the oversized projections of bird shadows in an aforementioned scene). Birdy's voice-over: "In a dream I'm trying to decide what I am. When I sleep I'm giving myself strength.... Perta and I become one. I see through her eyes. Fly on her wings. I am no longer alone." Abruptly, he wakes from the dream, sweating, and then sits up in bed. In Wharton's novel, Birdy experiences a series of dreams that blur the line between reality and illusion.[19] (In fact, it may be safe to say that one of the themes of this story is the question of what constitutes reality.)

Through binoculars, Birdy watches birds hatching and this juxtaposition of the present and the past suggests that he has finally become a bird. Voice-over: "It occurs to me that all I did was put two birds in the aviary. Some food, water and nothing else and now there are four of them.... It's one of the things life is about. But to see it happen in my own bedroom.... I'm getting so I don't care what happens in the outside world."

Another transitional shot of current-day Birdy, crouching and curled up in his cell by the toilet—the camera zooms in, becoming a tightly framed shot. Is Birdy imagining himself hatching from an egg as he reflects on this memory? In a series of shots, the film moves into flashback mode again.

It is now the late 1950s. The unsubtle bird song "Rockin' Robin" plays at the prom where Birdy and Doris dance awkwardly with one another. Birdy is disengaged, staring around the dance hall in every direction except toward her. In the next instant, Birdy sees his father and approaches him. His father tells him that he didn't want to embarrass him in front of his date; he then hands over money for him and his "girl." Birdy confidently retorts: "You wouldn't embarrass me," and reminds his father that Doris is *not* his girl. In fact, Birdy is not interested in *any* girl. The moment serves as another examination of this peculiar, but poignant, father-son connection.

The next scene not only shows Birdy's awkward behavior in the presence of females; it also explores the complexities of adolescence and sexuality. Ritchie Valens's song "Donna" plays while Birdy and Doris are on their date, sitting in the car ("parking"), a common practice for teenagers of that era. Doris, Birdy's *anima*, serves as his female counterpart: she is perhaps as socially awkward as he. She humbly tells him that she knows he didn't want to take her to the dance, and she appreciates that he did. In "exchange" for his goodwill she lifts her shirt and exposes her breasts. Birdy looks at her "overgrown mammary glands" and, out of curiosity, he touches them. Doris admits to not being experienced and Birdy replies, "It doesn't matter." And in reality, it *doesn't*.

Flashback: Birdy is in his bedroom; a high-angle shot looks down on him. This "birds-eye" view typically reveals something vulnerable about a character, but in this case, it captures Birdy's true persona. His reflection in the mirror (to the right of the screen) shows his duality and his conflicting identity of man/bird. He is naked in a high-contrast light— and the shadows of his birds on the wall suggest that there is a transformation occurring. In voice-over narration, he explains that he doesn't know when one dream begins and one dream ends and he wishes that he could tell Al about what was happening to him, but realizes he can't. Would Al understand and accept this? "I wish I could die now and be born again as a bird," he continues. The camera zooms in close on him; the birds' shadows are captured in fine detail, a more pronounced form than before. Gabriel's rhythmic leitmotif begins and the camera begins to "fly." In this scene the camera takes on Birdy's POV as a bird (as stated in the production notes, this is a Steadicam in a golf cart on top of a moving bicycle, invented after the SkyCam malfunctioned).[20] This bird-like POV moves haphazardly through the junkyard to the baseball field where Al and Birdy met, then back into the sky—all of this being juxtaposed with the shots of present-day Birdy perched on the back of the bed frame, watching these events through the window as if the window itself were a portal into his past.

A brief transition leads to Al captured at an extreme low-angle shot, highlighting his gentle and compassionate nature. He apologizes to Birdy about his previous behavior. Birdy is now on the floor, hugging the bed frame. He grimaces; he is angry at Al, which, from the looks of it, appears to be a hopeful response. Al says, "You *got* to come back, Birdy." Then he exits.

An abrupt cut to the image and piercing ambient sounds of a helicopter: A flashback to Vietnam during combat. Revealed: Al and his platoon are frenzied, surrounded by mines. One of these mines explodes, and the shattering fragments pierce Al's face, causing him to scream. The viewer now knows how Al was injured. Return to present-day Al, who sits down and cries as he recalls these memories, and then another abrupt cut back to Vietnam, replete with an overpowering sound of wind that muffles the other sounds of helicopters, explosions and men screaming…

Al falls asleep and awakens to a new hope, a new "American dream." The baseballs have arrived! Al appears at Birdy's cell, hoping these baseballs will be the answer to his recovery. When Birdy does *not* respond, Al breaks down: he tells his friend that he needs him, admitting to him that he is currently more afraid *now* than he was in the war—that, in so many words, he is incomplete without this friendship. Before the drama moves to the next level, another flashback interrupts the scene: It is a continuation of the previous scene with Birdy in his bedroom.

Al enters Birdy's room and after seeing his naked friend, assumes that he and Doris had sex the previous night (or, at least, he makes himself believe this). But instead of indulging Al with a sex story that never happened and never will, Birdy tells his friend about his dream: "Last night I flew.... When I fly, Al, I am a bird." This information is too much for Al to handle; he tells Birdy that this is all getting to be "too weird," that he is tired of all this "bird nonsense." Al finally says, "I hope the dream (or whatever) goes away.... I think it's bullshit!"

The viewer is now in the midst of the climax: The two worlds—past and present—have merged and begin to mirror one another. An extreme high-angle over Al shows his vulnerable, defeated state of mind, as he attempts to get Birdy to respond to the baseballs. It appears that the mythical arrival of this "Pandora's Box" has worked in reverse—rendering an irreversible hopelessness. Dr. Weiss arrives and, just outside the door, he and Al discuss Birdy's case. (Incidentally, the sound is muted as we watch them talk; this motif may be a gimmick that is used throughout the film in other scenes, but it may also build suspense, not unlike an Alfred Hitchcock "MacGuffin" ... the audience knows less than the characters). Weiss is the most sympathetic he has been in the film, although this doesn't redeem him; it merely accounts for the fact that he has truly lost hope with his patient. (The baseballs did not work, so *now what?*)

The scene is interrupted by an instant flashback of Birdy looking out his bedroom window (note how windows are still being used as portals into Birdy's mind), watching Al walk down the street, dressed in uniform, heading off to war. As Birdy walks away, one of his canaries (symbolically) flies out the window. It has escaped, yet now there is an ironic twist: the bird flies back to the window, but, in doing so, ends up hitting a wall and is instantly killed. The bird signifies a loss of freedom, but also a new rite of passage for Birdy—a reality beyond his delusional states—the reality that both he and Al have been drafted to fight in Vietnam and the death of the bird also serves as a form of foreshadowing, indicating that this new life of theirs will change them forever.

An abrupt cut to Vietnam. This time Birdy is in combat. A rapid anxiety-filled montage tells the story of Birdy witnessing the deaths of his fellow soldiers. After a helicopter crashes, Birdy remains alone on the ground, among the violent ruins. Time stands still. The ambient chirping of birds takes the place of music or any other sounds. At this moment, an exotic orange bird appears. Is this bird symbolic of Birdy? Birdy screams repeatedly and the intensity of these screams portrays a real horror, a real hell on earth. This is the moment at which Birdy snaps—and, according to earlier exposition, he subsequently disappears before he is captured and rehabilitated. (This event exemplifies the archetypal "shell-shocked" victim of PTSD. In *Stalag 17* [1953, Billy Wilder], the character Joey [Robinson Stone] is non-responsive and when the German guard Schultz suggests that he is faking the "crazy act," the barrack chief says, "How would *you* like to see the guts of 200 pals spilled out all over *your* plane?")

In the next scene, Birdy is in the hospital bed, crying. The camera focuses on a close-up of walking legs, which are revealed to be Al's. Al kneels down and offers himself to his friend. Hannah arrives and informs him that Dr. Weiss wants him to leave, that she is there to "retrieve" him. Al cradles Birdy like a child and tells Hannah that he is not leaving. In this shot, the characters are composed in a semi-circle: We see Hannah on the left, Al in the center and Birdy on the right, in a tightly framed shot that signifies comfort and security. On either side of the characters there is open space, which, despite the odds, still suggests a hope for escape and freedom. "We haven't had anything to do with making our own lives," Al says, filled with angst, followed by a cathartic, "Fuck!" He continues in a self-loathing manner: "It doesn't matter how special you are at war. I feel like one of those dogs nobody wanted. Remember? When that shell went off in my face, I could smell burning flesh. And it was crazy ... the smell was so sweet and familiar ... then I realized it was my own skin that was frying..." (He cries) "I don't even know what I look like anymore. I just want to be Al under here. What's so great about this fucking world anyway?" He continues by telling Birdy that they should hide out and every once in a while "go crazy."

During this rant, Birdy is hearing every word. And then suddenly—and ever-so absurdly at that—Birdy speaks: "Al, sometimes you're so full of shit," the same line he had said to his friend years earlier when they were talking about Mr. Columbato's rage. Al replies, "Was that you? It *was* you. You *talked*. It's *really* you. I can't *believe* this. Say something else." He asks Birdy what made him decide to finally speak. Birdy replies in his typical nonchalant tone: "I didn't decide. It just happened." When Weiss enters, Al tries to get Birdy to speak, but it doesn't happen. Al takes out his frustration on the doctor, who soon leaves to find orderlies to restrain Al. Meanwhile, Al asks Birdy why he didn't talk. Again, in a pragmatic, strangely comedic tone, Birdy replies: "I didn't have anything to say."

The next beat leads to a fight with an orderly who attempts to remove Al from the cell. Peter Gabriel's "flight" music begins, suggesting a hopeful possibility for escape. Through the montage-driven chaos, Al and Birdy *do* escape; they run out of the institution as they are being chased by the hospital authorities. The two friends have now begun their new life.

During the chase sequence, which leads both of them to the roof, Birdy takes this opportunity to "fly" and consequently he jumps off the ledge. This image is captured in slow-motion, not unlike the scene earlier in the film when he jumped off the gas tank. Al sees this and panics (it appears that Birdy jumped off a high ledge) but in the next shot he and the viewer are surprised: Birdy hasn't fallen far at all—no more than a few feet. He is still on the roof and standing on a mound of dirt. "*What?*" he asks Al nonchalantly, in what is surely the most absurd moment in the film. This uncharacteristic comedic beat leads to the start of "La Bamba," which notes the end of the film.

What can be said about this ending beyond the fact that it *is*, in its own unique way, certainly a surprise? It *does* bring about some questions, to be sure. Was Birdy faking all along? Was this all a ruse? Does the "group therapy" approach actually work—and, in this case anyway, can it bring on a "sudden" recovery? What about the final jump that ended up being only a short fall? Does this mean that Birdy *can* indeed fly—or is he cured of his delusions?

In a January 2011 article entitled, "Can We Facilitate Post-Traumatic Growth in Combat Veterans" from *American Psychologist*, University of North Carolina's Richard G. Tedeschi and Harvard University's Richard J. McNally wrote about new studies in post-traumatic growth in the aftermath of combat. In some of their interviews with former POWs, "They reported that imprisonment had produced favorable changes in their [the soldiers'] personalities, increasing their self-confidence and teaching them to value the truly most important things in life."[21] Bringing in this study, which was not available during the Vietnam era, may not explain the enigmatic ending of *Birdy*, but it might offer curious individuals some additional context regarding the symptoms associated with PTSD.

8

Angel Heart (1987)

March 6; 113 minutes/Color
Production Company: Carolco International N.V.
Distributor: TriStar Pictures
Director: Alan Parker
Screenwriter: Alan Parker (Based on the novel by William Hjortsberg)
Producers: Alan Marshall, Elliott Kastner
Production Designer: Brian Morris
Cinematography: Michael Seresin
Editor: Gerry Hambling
Original Music: Trevor Jones
Cast: Mickey Rourke (Harry Angel); Robert De Niro (Louis Cyphre); Lisa Bonet (Epiphany Proudfoot); Charlotte Rampling (Margaret Krusemark); Stocker Fontelieu (Ethan Krusemark); Brownie McGhee (Toots Sweet); Michael Higgins (Dr. Albert Fowler); Eliott Keener (Det. Sterne); Charles Gordone (Spider Simpson); Dann Florek (Herman Winesap)

> You know what they say: it's always the bad ass who makes a girl's heart beat faster.—Epiphany Proudfoot to Harry Angel, in *Angel Heart*

> The original attraction was the fusion of two genres—the detective film and the supernatural.—Alan Parker, Audio Commentary, *Angel Heart* Special Edition DVD

Notes on the Production

Sometime early in 1985, after having finished *Birdy*, Parker was paid a visit by veteran producer Elliot Kastner, who dropped a book on Parker's table at Pinewood Studios. The book was *Falling Angel* by William Hjortsberg, and Parker recalled reading it soon after its publication in 1978.[1] It tells the story of Harry Angel, a private eye, who is enlisted by a mysterious benefactor to track down a missing person. As Angel jumps down the rabbit hole in an attempt to unravel the mystery, he soon realizes that nothing is as it seems, and there may be a force of pure evil at work. The story is an interesting blend of the film noir and horror film conventions—particularly those of the Faustian tale—and Parker, who proved with *Bugsy Malone* that the idea of cross-breeding genre conventions appealed to him, told Kastner that he'd like to have a go at writing a script. Parker states, "The original attraction was the fusion of the two genres—the detective film and the supernatural."[2] The rights to the story had apparently moved around from person to person (one of whom was allegedly Robert Redford) but the book remained un-filmed, so Kastner supported Parker's decision and the director moved his family to upstate New York to begin writing.

The biggest change that Parker made to Hjortsberg's story is that he moved the bulk of the story from New York City to New Orleans. Parker made this fundamental change because he felt that the story, with its perpetual allusions to voodoo and the occult, naturally gravitated towards New Orleans. He also knew he wasn't a "New York" filmmaker, and after the less-than-perfect experience of shooting *Fame* in the city, Parker was looking for any excuse not to have to shoot there again.³ Feeling anxious about changing the story in such a drastic way, Parker met with Hjortsberg. It so happened that not only was he okay with Parker's placing the "voodoo" portion of the story in New Orleans, but he had actually considered doing it himself, only to relent at the last minute.⁴

Another alteration Parker made was to set the story in 1955, whereas in the book, the events take place in 1959. Although scaling the story back by a mere four years may seem inconsequential, Parker felt that this chronological regression would give the film an entirely different sociocultural subtext. He states:

> [The logic behind scaling the story back to 1955] was that 1959 was on the cusp of the '60s and considerable change; 1955 still belonged to the '40s. It was to try and make it a more period film, really. I was deliberately trying not to do a hip, Doris Day, '50s kind of thing. I wanted it to be monotone; I wanted it to be grittier. I suppose I wanted to make a noir film. [I] wanted to make a black-and-white film, but in color.⁵

Director Alan Parker (wearing a tee-shirt that advertises the performance high school in his 1980 film, *Fame*) with actress Lisa Bonet and young Jarrett Narcisse who plays her child. *Angel Heart* (1986), Carolco International N.V.; Distributed by Tri-Star.

So, Parker began work on the screenplay, writing most of it in New York. He changed the title to *Angel Heart*, feeling that *Falling Angel* was not unique enough—he wanted to "give the film an identity of its own."[6] When it was finished, Parker set about procuring the financing. He met with producers Andy Vajna and Mario Kassar (who had previously produced the *Rambo* films) in Rome, and they ultimately agreed to finance the project.

Parker assembled his usual crew in New York in January 1986 to begin casting, which, to him, seemed endless.[7] Initially, Parker had intended for Robert De Niro to play the part of Harry Angel, but De Niro expressed more interest in playing the part of Louis Cyphre (the Devil). However, De Niro proved to be more noncommittal than Parker had intended and although De Niro said he "had a mind to play the part," it took extensive convincing for him to actually commit to the role. Mickey Rourke was also one of the actors that Parker had in mind to play the lead, so the two of them met in New York and Rourke was emphatically interested in playing the part, asking Parker to "stop talking to the other guys."[8] Of all the actresses who read for the part of Epiphany Proudfoot, Lisa Bonet was Parker's favorite from the outset. Although she was extremely young, Parker felt that she had "an innate intelligence beyond her years." Being British, Parker was unaware of *The Cosby Show* and particularly of the squeaky-clean image that Bonet's character possessed on the show. This perhaps explains Parker's temerity in placing her in such a sexualized role.[9]

For the role of Margaret Krusemark, however, Parker had a bit more trouble finding his lady. Although it was a relatively minor role, her character is ubiquitous in the dialogue, and Parker felt that the actress for this part had to have the right balance of class and eccentricity.[10] Mickey Rourke had suggested Charlotte Rampling, so Parker phoned her in France, and she said yes.

Filming began in New York on March 31, 1986, and Parker faced the challenge of transforming 1986 New York into 1955 New York. He states:

> We had snow machines; wind machines; fire trucks wetting the roads; 250 period-costumed extras; loud speakers belting out the gospel music on playback; stuntmen and a giant crane on loan from another production. It's not unusual to be a week behind after the first week, but we were lucky and the juggernaut trundled onwards.[11]

After three weeks of filming in New York, the crew moved to Louisiana, to the town of Thibodaux. Parker and crew were lucky enough to find an entire plantation workers' village and, with some assiduous work by production designer Brian Morris, this location became Epiphany Proudfoot's world. The crew then ventured farther into the bayou of Cajun country to film the racetrack scene in which Harry first meets Ethan Krusemark. For this location, the crew carved the racetrack out of an unfarmed Louisiana field. They then moved to New Orleans, where they encountered some difficulty. During the scene in which Harry is chased through the stables, the crew had to deal with shying horses, trained dogs, gunshots, two hundred chickens, and a horse specially trained to fall on top of Mickey Rourke's stuntman.[12]

On Magazine Street, the crew built their very own 1950s version of New Orleans, and they modified every storefront in order to maintain temporal authenticity. Making New Orleans look authentic on film, according to Parker, proved to be a bit difficult. He states, "New Orleans is a stubborn city and if you're not careful, like an aging movie star, it will always offer up the side of its face that it wants people to see."[13]

With filming completed, Parker and crew returned to Europe with one hundred boxes containing 400,000 feet of film and 1,100 different shots. Four months later, they had the first cut of the film. The MPAA initially gave the film an X-rating in the U.S., which would substantially lower the number of theaters to which the film could be released. According to them, there was "something offensive lurking in reel three."[14] It turned out to be the shot of Mickey Rourke's bare behind thrusting up and down during the lovemaking scene. Parker decided to excise the "offensive" footage to obtain the more acceptable R-rating. Parker had initially been opposed to cutting the footage, but, as he states, "I figured that a few feet of Mickey's backside was no great loss to the history of cinema."[15]

Summary

As the opening credits appear on a black screen, Trevor Jones's viscerally haunting music invites us into a world of unsettling, nightmarish uncertainty. It is an eerie, thrumming synth score which is actually reminiscent of Giorgio Moroder's score from *Midnight Express*. To further augment the mood and atmosphere of menace, someone is faintly whispering the word "Johnny," suggesting that someone (or some*thing*) is speaking from the beyond.

The black then fades into the monochromatic, de-saturated opening shot, which is redolent of menace and dread. It is a low-angle shot that seems to peer up at the dark, haunting buildings of an isolated New York City street. The buildings seem to loom over the dark street like the Sword of Damocles, and it appears as though Parker is channeling the German expressionistic practice of utilizing haunting, abstract architecture to mirror the characters' (and perhaps the viewer's) sense of disorientation and dread.

Into the shot walks a lone figure, who, according to Parker, was supposed to be Louis Cyphre, although the figure was not Robert De Niro.[16] Parker then implements two devices that parlay to the audience that we are in a film which inhabits two worlds—the real and the supernatural. The first is the presence of multiple clouds of steam, which are swirling up out of the grates on the street. The clouds seem to have a sort of spectral quality as they swirl and dance out of the grates, suggesting an apparitional or ghostly presence. By placing these spectral clouds of steam on a gritty, realistic New York City street, Parker is suggesting that an otherworldly presence is infiltrating reality. The second device which bolsters the idea of two worlds colliding—of two diametrically opposed worlds clashing together—comes when Parker cuts to shots of a dog and a cat, respectively. The cat is in an elevated position, peering down from a fire escape at the dog, which is perusing the garbage on the street. The dog stumbles upon a dead body, the apparent victim of a murder as the victim's throat is smeared with blood. The cat then watches from its perched position as the dog walks away. Not only does the presence of a dog and a cat represent the idea of binary opposition (of two opposing realities), but the blocking and positioning of each animal is of particular significance. The cat seems to have a godlike power over the dog as it watches the dog wade in the decadence and decay of the city street. The cat seems to be insouciantly using the dog as a piece of catnip, remaining indifferent to the fact that the dog has been confronted with the horror of a mutilated body. This visually suggests that we are about to enter a world in which a powerless, unsuspecting being is about to be toyed with by a malicious being from another plane of existence. In his essay *The Devil You Know: Satanism in Angel Heart*, Carrol Fry succinctly summarizes the effectiveness of the opening scene:

> Steam rolls up from manholes, suggesting Hell below. A cat yowls (everyone remembers stories or films with cats as familiars).... The camera then tracks to a pile of garbage, where we see the corpse of a man lying in a pool of blood. And throughout the sequence, a cacophony of sound contributes to a Dante-esque illusion of damned souls in Hell.[17]

As the dog stumbles upon the dead body, a cool, sultry saxophone plays on the soundtrack. This is jazz saxophonist Courtney Pine playing "Girl of My Dreams," a 1920s-style song which ultimately serves as Johnny Favorite's theme. This serves as a musical motif a number of times throughout the film.

We then cut to a shot of a New York City street, which informs us that this is, indeed, a period film. A 1950s car drives through the frame, followed by a title card at the bottom of the screen, which reads: "New York, 1955." Into the frame enters Harry Angel (played by Mickey Rourke). Although the audience is not yet aware of Harry's occupation, his appearance (coupled with Rourke's mannerisms) immediately suggests that he is a private eye. First off, he is wearing a long trench coat, which is the garb of choice for movie private eyes from Humphrey Bogart in *The Big Sleep* to Ralph Meeker in *Kiss Me Deadly*—the only thing missing is the fedora. He is also smoking a cigarette, an accessory which perpetually hung from the mouths of Bogart, Garfield, Meeker, et al. Also, as played by Rourke, Harry immediately conveys to us a sense of *ennui*—of world-weary apathy, which, again, is reminiscent of the private eyes from the noirs of the '40s and '50s. He walks down the street (towards the camera) with a distracted indifference—the smoky, seedy streets of New York no longer faze him; he punctuates this nonchalance by vapidly blowing a bubble with the gum he is chewing.

We then cut to Harry's office, from which the shrill ring of a telephone is emanating. He sits down, answers the phone, and, in a very revealing shot, he opens his desk drawer to retrieve a pen and paper to take notes. The drawer is cluttered and messy (a familiar cliché of the cop genre—all bachelor cops are disorganized and messy), and we also see a gun in the drawer.

The man on the phone (as revealed by Harry's reiteration) is named Winesap, someone who apparently has a proposition for Harry, although the details divulged over the phone are vague and cryptic. This is yet another generic staple of the noir genre—the unsuspecting private eye is almost always offered a nebulous proposition at the beginning of the film by some mysterious stranger.

This scene also perpetuates yet another fixture of the noir genre. Although we can't hear what he is saying, Winesap evidently asks Harry if he knows what an attorney is, to which Harry replies, "Sure, I know what an attorney is. It's like a lawyer but the bills are bigger." It is obvious that he's wise to the fact that the world is corrupt and rife with greedy, unscrupulous people. This cynicism strongly mirrors the overall atmosphere which permeated the noirs of the '40s and '50s. These films were produced in the post World War II American landscape, a time in which the United States' national identity seemed to be under siege (or, at least, ambiguous). American forces dropped the bomb on Japan, and Americans were confronted with uncertainty, fear, and dread. This anxiety was channeled through the cynical mouthpieces of the private eyes who populated film noirs. Philip Marlowe (et al.) was acutely aware that the world could be a harsh place, and this awareness of corruption and greed was something that all private eyes in these films seemed to possess.

Harry agrees to meet with Winesap in Harlem to hear his proposition in more detail. We then cut to Harry exiting a car and walking into the building. He walks past a tableau which serves as a portent of death. Outside of the building, there is gathered a group of African Americans who have ostensibly just come from a funeral. They are all dressed in black, and one woman in particular seems acutely grief-stricken, frantically crying out, falling over herself, only to be helped to her feet by those surrounding her. Parker seems to be inviting us into a world where death, grief, and human suffering are omnipresent.

The next shot is from the top of the staircase of the building Harry enters, looking down on him. It is a stark, haunting shot as Harry appears to be walking into a trap or cage of sorts. On screen left we see the rungs of the bannister which, as lighted by cinematographer Michael Seresin, appear to be bars of a prison cell. On screen right is a metal gate with a lattice pattern which, again, suggests confinement. On the soundtrack, we hear what is ostensibly a preacher, fervently shouting "Hallelujah!" and preaching to a congregation of alacritous churchgoers. Harry walks into the proceedings and peers down at the ceremony from the balcony. He sees Pastor John (played by Gerald Orange), emphatically urging the congregation to profess their love to God. (This character was not in the book; Parker simply included him to reflect an accurate depiction of the religious practices of Harlem residents of the 1950s, as he had done extensive research in this area.)[18] If this scene accomplishes anything outside of infusing the film with authenticity, it is that it invites us into a world of theological fervor, which will later be mirrored by the voodoo ritual in Louisiana.

As he watches the proceedings, Harry is approached by Herman Winesap (played by Dann Florek). As Winesap escorts Harry away from the sermon, Harry stops as he notices a tiny room in which a woman dressed in black is crouched on her hands and knees, scrubbing blood off the wall. Winesap informs Harry that a member of Pastor John's flock unfortunately took a gun to his head. This ominous, creepy moment serves to further inform the viewer that, although religion will play a part in this film, it will not be depicted as a hopeful sanctuary or a place where salvation and comfort can be achieved. Rather, we are entering a dark world, where the theological powers from beyond are harbingers of death and suffering.

Winesap and Harry then enter a room. Parker cuts to a close-up of the hand of a man who is ostensibly sitting in the room that the two men have just entered. The man's fingernails are long and somewhat sharp. He is wearing a ring, and he is slowly twirling a cane from left to right in his fingers. This shot marks the introduction of Louis Cyphre (played with relish by Robert De Niro). Both the ring on Cyphre's finger and the cane he is twirling seem to have strange markings on them, as if they are symbols of some obscure religion. By introducing us to Cyphre in this discorporate manner (i.e., showing us a close-up of his hand and his accessories before showing us his face), Parker is subtly informing us that there is something metaphysical about Cyphre. The calculated way in which he is twirling his cane also harkens back to the shot of the cat from the opening scene. He is playing with the cane so as to suggest an almost playful torment, the way a cat would claw at a dying mouse.

We are then introduced to Cyphre himself. He sits, perched in a chair, which is atop an elevated platform. He appears monolithic, as if he is presiding over some kind of official proceedings. After Harry is introduced to Cyphre, Parker cuts to a close-shot of two circular, oscillating fans suspended from the ceiling, placed side by side. The fan on the left remains stationary, not oscillating, and the blade is circling quite sluggishly. It appears as though it may actually be broken. The fan to the right, however, is oscillating, and the blade is cutting through the air at a rapid rate. This fan appears to be working just fine. Once again, as with the opposition between the cat and the dog, Parker is implementing a visual device to convey the idea of a Manichaean binary—of two worlds colliding: dark and light, left and right, good and evil, etc. This shot is also the introduction of a leitmotif which permeates the entire film: the fan as a portent of death. In her review of the film, Pauline Kael seemed puzzled by this motif and found it glaringly arbitrary. She writes, "Why are ceiling fans always used as portents of death? Why not licorice drops or mayflies?"[19] Carrol Fry, however, offers a justification of Parker's choice. He asserts that most books on the occult tradition mention ceremonies that use five-pointed and six-pointed stars—pentagrams and hexagrams. These five- or six-pointed stars and various cross patterns can be made to have a striking similarity to fan blades, so Parker's choice of visual motif, according to Fry, is not arbitrary at all, but, rather, a perpetuation of the presence of the iconography of the occult which permeates the film.[20]

After getting acquainted, Mr. Cyphre informs Harry that he wishes to track down a man named Johnny Favorite (who's real name is Liebling), who was a somewhat famous crooner before World War II. Apparently, Mr. Cyphre helped Johnny at the beginning of his career, and he has an outstanding debt which Cyphre would like to collect. Johnny was in the war, which left him disfigured and with a case of both shell shock and amnesia. According to Cyphre and Winesap, Johnny is allegedly still alive and a patient at a hospital in Poughkeepsie, but when they tried to visit, they were given the runaround. Cyphre wants Harry (who was also in the war) to find out if Johnny is indeed among the living, and if he is, to escort him to Mr. Cyphre so that he may collect the debt that Johnny owes him.

This scene is mostly exposition, and Parker admits that it was challenging to shoot. In a scene which is composed mostly of people talking, states Parker, it is difficult to keep it visually interesting.[21] Narratively, however, this scene is pure noir. It features an unsus-

Louis Cyphre (Robert DeNiro, left) hires hard-boiled private investigator Harry Angel (Mickey Rourke, right) in the noir/horror film *Angel Heart* (1986). Carolco International N.V.; Distributed by Tri-Star.

pecting detective who is being roped into a murky, unclear scenario with which he is not entirely comfortable. Since audiences are educated in the conventions of film noir, we know that this assignment will not be as simple as it seems. We know that it will most likely not be as simple as Harry driving to Poughkeepsie, finding Johnny Favorite, and bringing him back to Cyphre. Not only would that scenario not be sufficient to round out the film's running time, but, since we are now aware that we are being invited into the archetypal noir scenario, we can surmise that Harry is about to jump down the rabbit hole, which will be fraught with intrigue, double-crosses, red herrings, wrong turns, and danger. The one interesting twist, however, is that, in the traditional film noir, the one who ropes the gumshoe into what ultimately becomes his demise is a woman—the femme fatale. Jane Greer in *Out of the Past*, Faye Dunaway in *Chinatown*, and Kathleen Turner in *Body Heat* are all examples of the sexy, sultry, feline woman with an ulterior motive, employing a combination of sexuality and helplessness to coerce the main character to do what she wants. In this case, however, it appears as though the femme fatale (if there even is one) is not the catalyst for the gumshoe's demise, but a mysterious man. This represents an interesting subversion of the sexual politics of the traditional film noir, in which the salaciousness of the femme fatale was intended to metonymically represent the American male's nationwide anxiety about how to reincorporate women into the patriarchal structure after having given them jobs during World War II. *Angel Heart* seems to be eschewing this particular social commentary by making the catalyst of the intrigue a man as opposed to a woman. This is most likely due to the fact that the film is a postmodern, revisionist *neo*-noir as opposed to a film which is totally a product of its time. Although it could certainly be argued that male identity in America is still fraught with uncertainty and anxiety, *Angel Heart* was not released at a time in which both second and third wave feminism were still yet to come. In other words, in 1987, when *Angel Heart* was released, the issue of women in the work place had already been addressed (although not completely resolved), so the anxiety the American male felt in the '40s and '50s had, if not disappeared, at least mutated.

As Harry is driving to Poughkeepsie, "Girl of My Dreams" again plays over the soundtrack. Harry also replays some of the dialogue spoken by Louis Cyphre at the meeting in his head, as we hear Robert De Niro's voice on the soundtrack. We then cut to a wide shot of Harry's car driving through the country from frame right to frame left. The framing and cinematography of this scene are quite remarkable. The colors are all heavily de-saturated, giving the frame a bleak, monochrome atmosphere. The bleak, gray sky appears huge as it envelops the entire background. The sheer eeriness of the expansively ominous sky has, in and of itself, an ethereal, metaphysical feel, as if Harry is driving through some sort of netherworld.

When Harry arrives at the hospital, he pretends to be a Harry Conroy from the National Institute of Health in order to gain access to Johnny Favorite's (Liebling's) medical records. This deceptive, disingenuous aspect of the Harry Angel character was added by Parker—it is not in the book, and this alteration complicates the viewer's identification with and sense of sympathy for the character of Harry Angel. As put by Carrol Fry, "Mickey Rourke plays Harry Angel as a less sympathetic character than the novel's characterization.... Parker never allows the audience to like Johnny Angel, so the viewer feels little remorse for his situation."[22] Further complicating our identification with the Angel character is how he leers at and objectifies the attractive nurse at the window. As she walks away to retrieve Liebling's records, Parker cuts to an eye-line match, aligning the camera's gaze with that of Angel's. It is a close-up of the nurse's backside, with Angel shamelessly staring at it. This, arguably, pushes Angel's character further into the unlikable category; a few more examples will crop up throughout the course of the film.

Harry is plunged further down the rabbit hole when he sees Liebling's record, which says that he was transferred to another hospital back in 1943. Using his detective skills, however, Harry is able to ascertain that the transfer order was signed with a ballpoint pen, which were nonexistent in 1943. In true noir fashion, Harry's seemingly simple task is already becoming increasingly complicated. He sees that the order was signed by a Dr. Albert Fowler, whom he then decides to pursue.

We cut to a shot of Harry inside a phone booth, then to a close-up of a page in a directory. As Harry underlines Albert Fowler's name, a spooky sound effect plays on the soundtrack. It sounds like a clarion call from Hell, and it can only be described as sounding like a porpoise or dolphin uttering a shrill cry of pain. It is a remarkably haunting aural effect, fraught with the sense of impending doom, and Parker effectively uses the sound to transition to the next shot, that of Harry breaking into Dr. Fowler's abode. As Harry walks through Dr. Fowler's basement in what is almost complete darkness, the stark, shadowy lighting enhances the sense of walking through a living nightmare (Parker himself comments on how proud he is of the lighting in this scene, and goes on to say that David Fincher copied the lighting style for the Gluttony murder crime scene in *Seven*).[23] As Harry arrives at the base of the staircase that ostensibly leads to the main floor of the house, we cut to another eye-line match, revealing what Harry sees. It is a static shot of the top of the staircase, the door leading to the house on screen left, and a series of jackets hung on hooks on screen right. In any other film (i.e., in the hands of any other director) this shot would be mundane and unremarkable. However, Parker's framing (coupled with Michael Seresin's eerie use of lighting and shadow) transform this otherwise banal shot into a creepy harbinger of terror lurking around the corner. One of the jackets appears to be a guard or gatekeeper of sorts, imposingly looming down the staircase, seeming as though it is staring at Harry admonishingly, warning him not to come up the stairs. Parker's ability to transform a simple staircase and some jackets into menacing heralds of doom is testament to his ability to use lighting and framing to convey atmosphere.

Harry then proceeds to snoop around Fowler's apartment, finding everything from an unloaded gun in his bedside table drawer, to hypodermic needles, to a seemingly endless supply of morphine sulphate in the refrigerator. Trevor Jones continues to keep the tension and anxiety at a fever pitch, peppering the soundtrack with sporadic, low-register, thrumming sounds, which holds the viewer in the vise grip of nail-biting anticipation as they wait for someone (or something) to jump out at Harry from behind a dark corner.

Fowler (played by Michael Higgins) finally returns home; and Harry, waiting patiently for him at the kitchen table, surprises him. The ensuing scene (much like the scene in which Harry first meets Cyphre) is essentially all exposition, and Parker was, again, reduced to filming the scene in a traditional shot/reverse-shot fashion. Fowler informs Harry that one night, many years ago, a man named Edward Kelley and a mysterious woman drove off with Liebling, and Fowler never saw him again. Kelley said that they were taking Liebling back home, which, to Fowler's recollection, was somewhere down south. Fowler was paid $25,000 to maintain the pretense that Liebling was still a patient at his hospital. Harry wants to know what Liebling looks like, and Fowler professes that he honestly does not know, due to Liebling's extensive facial scarring. Fowler says that's all he can remember.

To extract this information from Fowler, Harry bullies him, grabbing him violently by the necktie. When Fowler says he can't remember anymore, Harry says he's going to lock Fowler in his room for a couple hours, which is essentially a form of torture, as Harry is aware of Fowler's morphine addiction. Harry says, "Maybe a few hours cold turkey will refresh your memory." This callous behavior is further pushing Harry into the unlikable category, substantiating Carrol Fry's claim that Parker never allows us to like Harry. At this point in the movie, Harry is 100 percent the Dashiell Hammett, hard-boiled, seen-it-all, tough-as-nails detective without a shred of the decency with which Bogart or Mitchum infused their private eye characters.

As Harry carries a now-comatose Fowler into his own bedroom, we cut again to a shot of a fan, this time to Fowler's window fan, the blades of which slowly begin to turn as the two men enter the room. Notwithstanding the grievances of Pauline Kael, it is an effective shot, as the blades of the fan seem to have a life of their own; they also seem to have been supernaturally awakened from some deep slumber, slowly churning to life to inflict their dirty deed. After cutting to a brief shot of Harry laying Fowler down on the bed, Parker cuts back to the fan. This time, the slowly turning blades stop dead in their tracks, hold still for a moment, and then begin spinning in the opposite direction. This further augments Parker's motif of the fan as a portent of death as, again, the blades seem almost to be sentient (or at least being supernaturally guided by something sentient).

After Harry locks Fowler in his bedroom and leaves the house, Parker cuts back to another fan shot, but this time, it is only the shadow of the blades that fills the frame. There is a shoe on the ground and the giant, domineering blade shadows seem to be slicing at it. Whether or not Pauline Kael is correct in her assertion that the fan-as-portent-of-death motif is arbitrary and insignificant, Parker's use of lighting and the visual effect of implementing the shadow of a blade to appear to be slicing at a shoe both create the desired effect: the viewer is left with an eerie sense of impending doom. Could Parker have used a licorice drop or mayfly instead? Perhaps. But he didn't. The point is: even if the motif is indeed arbitrary, Parker still displays his aptitude for implementing the technical properties of film to create mood and atmosphere.

In the next sequence, Harry is walking down a snowy street, ostensibly biding his time while Fowler goes mad enough to give him the information he wants. Harkening back to *Midnight Express*, Parker implements a heartbeat on the soundtrack to heighten the sense of dread and anxiety. Then, recalling the eerie whispering that played over the title sequence, a disembodied voice from a place unknown whispers, "Johnny," and "Harry." Harry then looks screen left, and we cut again to his eye-line match: a shot of two very young African American nuns dressed in white, sitting on a bench in the foyer of a church. A strong wind is blowing the door to the church back and forth as well as making the nuns' habits dance and flow in the wind. The nuns have their heads down and are ostensibly reading Bibles. Harry approaches the swinging door to the church and peers in. It is almost completely shrouded in darkness. The two nuns innocently look up at him. We then cut to a close-up of a bowl on the floor, which is filled to the brim with what looks like a mixture of blood and water. We then cut to a shot of a metal gate (which appears to be the door to an old-fashioned elevator—an image which Parker revisits frequently, later in the film) with a lattice pattern, which is down the hall a bit from the bowl of blood water. The gate autonomously (and violently) slides open, and the stark, shadowy lighting seems to suggest that the supernaturally motivated gate is inviting Harry to walk into his doom.

This scene feels like a dream sequence, as it is rife with surrealistic, ethereal imagery. This moment's undeniable power lies in Parker's and Seresin's respective abilities to visually convey mood and atmosphere. Using spare set pieces, a minimal number of actors, and simply lighting and angling, Parker and Seresin have fashioned a surrealistic nightmare sequence which conjures up images of Luis Buñuel (particularly the haunting dream sequence from *Los Olvidados*) and, perhaps more specifically, the nightmare sequence from Clive Barker's *Hellraiser* (which he openly admitted was his tribute to the visual style of Dario Argento), in which Ashley Laurence's character witnesses a white-sheeted gurney become soaked with blood. At the same time she is being showered with what look like chicken feathers as we hear a baby crying in the background. In these aforementioned moments, narrative logic and plot are temporarily jettisoned in favor of disjointed, hallucinatory imagery to conjure up mood and an atmosphere of dread, which Parker and Seresin pull off magnificently.

We then cut to Harry, who is despondently eyeing a cup of coffee as he sits alone at a diner counter. The "Girl of My Dreams" theme is again heard on the soundtrack, only this time, it has been reduced to a spare, elegiac piano number. The somber tone of the music, coupled with the fact that Harry is sitting all alone, infuses the scene with a sense of isolation and loneliness, which perhaps Parker employed to make Harry more sympathetic—he is a lonely man searching for his sense of purpose and identity.

Harry then returns to Fowler's house to see if his cold-turkey torture has jogged Fowler's memory. When he opens the door, however, he sees that Fowler is lying dead on his bed, having been shot through the right eyeball in what was apparently a suicide (since the door was locked from the outside and Harry had possession of the key the entire time). As Fowler's gun was empty when Harry stumbled on it, he is confused as to how Fowler committed this act. He then sees the Bible that Fowler is clutching in his hands, inside the hollowed-out pages of which Fowler had hidden the bullets. Fowler's hiding place for his bullets augments the film's theme of the hidden dangers of religion and theological practices. The Holy Bible, in and of itself, ostensibly represents comfort, hope, and salvation. Buried within those pages, however, are instruments of death, which mirrors Harry's journey into the mouth of madness, in which the surface of things is merely a veil, concealing destruction and doom.

Harry then meets his client, Louis Cyphre, at a diner to inform him of his progress. He tells Cyphre how Johnny ostensibly disappeared from the hospital with a man named Edward Kelley. He also tells Cyphre about Fowler's death and how he is now a murder suspect and how he wants off the case. Cyphre offers Harry five thousand dollars to remain on the case; Harry tentatively accepts. This, again, seems to reinforce Fry's claim that Harry is an unlikable character, accepting large sums of money like a mercenary, callously dismissing the fact that a man is now dead.

Throughout this scene, as Cyphre and Harry converse, Cyphre is methodically peeling a hard-boiled egg, which he ultimately consumes. He tells Harry that in some cultures the egg is the symbol of the soul. He then, in an extreme close-up, and with a chilling display of malice, bites into the egg, overtly directing the bite *at* Harry. Although this symbolism is almost rudimentarily obvious, the moment works, mostly due to Parker's framing and De Niro's chilling performance.

Harry then returns to Cyphre's office in Harlem to snoop around. As he opens the door to one of Cyphre's closets, there is a medium-shot of some ritualistic, seemingly occult symbols and paraphernalia. There are mysterious beads, dolls, and candles. In the middle of the frame is a mummified, stuffed monkey. In an expertly crafted conflation of sound and editing, Parker cuts to a close-up of the monkey's terrifying visage, mouth agape, while at the same time, presenting an audio cut, abruptly cutting in the audio of the ensuing scene (which is Pastor John's congregation conduction a parade down the streets of Harlem, replete with a big band playing over fervent singing). The juxtaposition of the blaring audio with the abrupt cut to the close-up of the monkey's nightmarish face creates a remarkably startling effect.

We then cut to Harry walking towards a lone figure, dressed in black, seated in a chair in Pastor John's congregation room. The heartbeat plays again on the soundtrack as Harry slowly walks toward the figure (whose gender and identity remain ambiguous as he/she has his/her back to the camera and his/her head is shrouded in a black hood), and Parker again creates an effective mood of nightmarish unreality. Just as Harry places his hand on the shoulder of the figure in black, two men assault him. Harry fights the two men off, flailing chairs and punches at them, and a chase sequence ensues as the two men pursue Harry on foot through the streets of Harlem. We are never quite sure who the two men are or why they attacked Harry—it seems as though Parker simply felt that an action sequence was in order. Perhaps Parker also felt that the audience needed a real sense of danger—that Harry is plunging deeper still down the rabbit hole and everyone and everything around him is trying to obstruct his achieving his goal (a tried-and-true film noir trope).

Harry then meets with Connie (played by Elizabeth Whitcraft, who also had a small part in *Birdy*), an inside source who works for the *New York Times*. She hands Harry an envelope and says that she has some information for him. The two then go back to Harry's place and she tells him that Johnny Favorite used to play in a band called the Spider Simpson Orchestra, and that Spider is in an old people's home on 138th street. Connie also saw a photograph of Johnny with a guitar player called Toots Sweet, whom no one has heard from in years. She also tells Harry that Johnny used to be engaged to a rich woman named Margaret Krusemark, whose father, Ethan, owned half of Louisiana. Apparently, Krusemark was known as a bit of a crackpot, casting spells at high society events and such, which earned her the moniker "The Witch of Wellesley."

This scene, much like the one in which Harry is first introduced to Cyphre, is highly expository, and, therefore, runs the risk of being tedious and boring. To counteract this, Connie delivers all of the expository dialogue as Harry is undressing her as they prepare to make love. Parker explains:

What she [Connie] is doing is giving you a whole bunch of boring exposition. [Undressing her] was the craftiest way to get away with all this chatter, because I don't think most people were even listening anymore at this point.[24]

The price for this choice, of course, is that Harry is sinking ever more deeply into the unlikable category. He lies, swindles, cheats, and now, engages unemotionally in sexual intercourse.

Parker then introduces an atmospheric montage—another nightmarish dream sequence. There's a quick shot sifting through a crowd of sailors apparently just returning home from the war. We then cut to a haunting shot of a stone spiral staircase encompassing the entire top portion of the frame (which, in effect, looks like a haunting rendition of an Escher painting). On bottom screen right, a stone wall is smattered with the shadow of a grate which is forcefully slid downwards, apparently by no one at all. We then cut to the ominous, perennial figure in black who demurely sits on a bench and stares straight ahead. Again, with this scene, Parker is achieving effectiveness not through plot, narrative, or dialogue, but through his use of imagery to create atmosphere.

We then cut to Coney Island. Harry has discovered (ostensibly by examining the documents Connie had given him) that not only did Johnny have a secret love named Evangeline Proudfoot, who ran a "spooky store" in Harlem, but that he also frequented a palm reader in Coney Island named Madame Zora. So Harry meets with a man named Izzy (played by George Buck, who also played Birdy's father in *Birdy*) right on the beach. Izzy offers Harry a nose guard to protect him from the harmful rays of the sun. Although this may seem like an inconsequential exchange, Stephen Cooper, in his essay *Sex/Knowledge/Power in the Detective Genre* states:

> Interestingly, *Angel Heart* carries over the suggestion of psychosexual damage done the detective's nose in *Chinatown* by outfitting his protagonist with a grotesque sun-guard from Coney Island: if ever there was one, a displaced prophylactic![25]

The psychosexual damage done to Harry will, of course, not crop up until his affair with Epiphany Proudfoot, but this is, indeed, an interesting interpretation of what would otherwise be dismissed as nothing more than a garish, silly-looking prop.

The composition of this scene is also of note, as Harry, Izzy, and Izzy's wife (who is nonchalantly wading in the water) are the only three human beings seen on the entire beach. They are dwarfed by the expansive sky and sand, which engulf the entire frame. This augments Parker's visual motif of giving Harry an almost solipsistic control over his environment. The story is about his descent into the heart of darkness, and it is his identity (and the arduous quest for it) that this film explores. By dwarfing Harry in surroundings which seem to swallow him, Parker is perpetuating the notion that Harry is in complete isolation—he searches for his man (and himself) alone.

After finding out from Izzy's wife that Madame Zora and Margaret Krusemark are one and the same person, Harry decides to head down to Louisiana. The next shot is of his train arriving there (although it was actually filmed in Hoboken, New Jersey). We then cut to Harry walking the streets of New Orleans, which have a very drab, commonplace feel to them. Parker states that this is because he wanted to veer away from "the clichéd French Quarter, ironwork look; I wanted to keep it as period as possible and to be as true to New Orleans as possible, but to give it a different look—not the tourist postcard look."[26]

We then cut to Harry looking at a flyer posted in the window of a local shop, advertising the palm readings of Margaret Krusemark. He then jumps aboard a trolley in pursuit of an exotic, red-haired woman, whom we assume is Margaret Krusemark (played by the lovely and charming Charlotte Rampling). Harry sits in a seat a few rows back from Margaret, leaning on the seat in front of him, which has a very prominent sign reading "For Colored Patrons Only." This not only reflects the time period, in which segregation was still prevalent, but it almost seems to foreshadow Parker's next film *Mississippi Burning*, which deals extensively with racism and segregation.

Having made an appointment to have his palm read, Harry walks up to Margaret's apartment and rings her buzzer. She lets him in and, not long into the proceedings, Harry reveals who he really is—a guy snooping around, trying to find Johnny Favorite. Margaret is unhappy with this turn of events and asks him to leave. Harry, further perpetuating his unlikable, unsympathetic image, lecherously hits on her, and tells her that it's too bad he didn't get to have his palm read because he would have liked to have held Margaret's hand longer. Margaret looks at his hand and says, "I don't think you'd like what I see." This is a subtle moment, but it certainly foreshadows Harry's ultimate demise.

We then cut to Harry running across a street in the pouring rain. He enters Mammy Carter's Herb Store, and asks the cashier if she knows Evangeline Proudfoot, Johnny's secret lover who ran a shop in Harlem. She says that she did indeed know her, but that she had since passed away. We then cut to Harry driving through a rundown, seemingly impoverished part of town, replete with ramshackle houses and shanties and a dirt road spitting up dust from under the wheels of Harry's car. Parker intersperses shots of Harry's car driving by with those of the locals—close-ups of children playing by the mailboxes, dogs barking, and an elderly woman sitting in a rocking chair, watching dejectedly as Harry drives by. This series of inserts is indicative of Parker's willingness, for the sake of authenticity, to cut away from the main action to spend time, albeit a very brief amount, with the characters who comprise the very real world which the main character inhabits. In the brief shot of the elderly woman in the rocking chair, we have a sense of this place—the atmosphere, the general mood, etc., and a lesser director would have simply kept the camera on Harry and denied the viewer even the slightest visual access to the lives of the people in Harry's new environment.

Harry then visits the grave of Evangeline Proudfoot. There are religious symbols and objects strewn around her grave, and Parker cuts to a series of close-ups of each of them (including a statue of Jesus). It is not so much the actual meaning or purpose of the objects that is of importance, but Parker's ominous framing and use of the objects to create a sense of impending doom.

A young, attractive African American woman walks by, trying to console a crying baby. This is Epiphany Proudfoot (Lisa Bonet). He then follows her as she escorts the baby through the backyard of her shack, which is scattered with thick crabgrass and rotted wooden planks. Harry then watches her from a distance as she places her head under an outdoor basin to wash her hair. Before he approaches her, he is sure to put his glasses with the nose guard back on, reapplying his "misplaced prophylactic" as if he is aware that this woman is going to lead him down a path of sexual intrigue.

He approaches Epiphany, who is still washing her hair, and introduces himself. There are chickens scattered about her dusty driveway, and they startle Harry, to which he says, "I got a thing about chickens," the same line he gave to Louis Cyphre when Cyphre offered him an egg in the diner. This is a running motif and aspect of Harry's character which is never really expounded upon. Stephen Cooper states, "What is Harry Angel's *thing* about chickens, reiterated often enough to be downright annoying?"[27] However, as Cooper also points out, the film noir genre has a reputation for introducing unimportant or unresolved plot elements (he goes on to say that even Howard Hawks could not keep track of all the goings-on in *The Big Sleep*). Even Parker himself is wont for a resolute explanation for this aspect of Harry's character. He states, "I'm not really sure why we brought them [the chickens] into the story. I don't really like chickens very much. I'm probably scared of them."[28]

Harry asks Epiphany if she remembers her mother, Evangeline, ever mentioning Johnny Favorite, and Epiphany denies any knowledge of him. Harry then asks her if she's familiar with Toots Sweet, the guitar player with whom Johnny allegedly associated, which she also tacitly denies. Throughout this entire line of questioning, Parker keeps the framing close on Epiphany, accentuating her seemingly ritualistic act of cleansing her hair underneath the water pipe. Lisa Bonet's performance infuses Epiphany with an innocent yet mature sensuality, and as she plays with her now-wet hair, she gazes at Harry with wonderment, lust, and a feline sense of domination.

Harry gives Epiphany his card and tells her to contact him if she can think of anything that will help him find Johnny. We then cut to a smoky, dimly lit lounge, in which a blues ensemble led by Toots Sweet (played by Brownie McGee) is performing a soulful number. Parker, again, seems interested in probing this microcosm within the overall narrative of the story. He does not just present the set piece in a master-shot, then move back to Harry—the camera seems to possess a desire to infiltrate and examine this world of the performers and the people experiencing the performance, giving each one of them their own close-up (again, another Parker hallmark). Robert Altman would later direct certain scenes from his film *Kansas City* in a similar fashion, not simply relegating these minor characters to spare (or even non-existent) screen-time, but showcasing their lifestyles and the jubilant dedication to their enjoyment of entertainment.

After finishing the blues number "On a Rainy Day" (which was actually an original song composed by Brownie McGee), Toots sits at the bar, and Harry approaches him. He begins questioning Toots about Johnny Favorite (whom Toots claims to vaguely remember) and he, again, lies about his identity. He claims that he is a journalist writing a piece on the Spider Simpson Orchestra. Toots says to watch the next number, then make up whatever he wants for his story, since that's what newspaper people do anyway. Harry then follows Toots into the restroom, which further agitates him. Toots claims not to know anything, but is stopped dead in his tracks at the sight of a chicken foot on top of the urinal. Harry picks it up and asks Toots what it means, only to be thrown out of the place by an irate bouncer. Harry then waits in his car outside the club and waits for Toots to exit. The stark, high-contrast lighting of this scene places us squarely back in the world of noir. The plot is becoming increasingly convoluted and the jagged shadows slicing across Harry's face suggest a dark, impending menace. Harry then follows Toots to a voodoo dancing ritual being held deep in the woods, making sure to remain undetected. He hides in the brush and watches the frenzied, high-intensity dance ritual, replete with throbbing, kinetic drumming and seemingly possessed dancers and chanters. At the center of the ritual is Epiphany, who, while dancing sensually, holds a chicken over her head and slices its throat with a razor, spilling its blood all over her face and chest (which she then proceeds to rub all over herself). She then falls to the ground and begins to writhe and gesticulate spasmodically, as if exorcising a demon from herself. Harry watches with astonishment.

This is perhaps the most notorious scene of the film (along with the steamy sex scene between Harry and Epiphany). To the viewer, the scene does possess a stark, uncompromising sense of power and energy and, to the outside viewer, a sense of authenticity. This is not the voodoo we are used to seeing in Hollywood. It is not simply an evil witch doctor grinning malevolently as he sticks a voodoo doll with pins, watching with delight as the doll's human counterpart screams and writhes in pain. The chanting, dancing, and animal sacrifice all seem to suggest that there was research done on the part of the filmmakers and that this is what an actual voodoo dance ritual entails. The Reverend Severina, a voodoo priestess, somewhat agrees. She states that, although there is some authenticity in the scene:

> It's hard to know what that scene really means. I mean, the drums are beautiful, they're wearing the white clothes; you're kind of being told, "Look, this is a voodoo ritual." But what happens in the ritual is not what would happen in a true voodoo ritual. You don't see an altar, you don't see offerings being made—who are the spirits?[29]

Although the presence of voodoo in the film was, according to Parker, a "tiny aspect of the film which just happens to be an aspect of Epiphany and her character," he wanted to portray voodoo and its practices as realistically as possible. He felt that voodoo as presented in other films was clichéd and overly stylized.[30]

Notwithstanding the scene's authenticity (or lack thereof), it certainly possesses a raw power, and it achieves its cinematic goal. This scene is meant to illustrate that Harry has entered a world of strange (and possibly terrifying) unfamiliarity. The fast-tempo, implacable drums juxtaposed with Parker's rapid-fire editing as Epiphany slices the throat of the chicken create a frenzied sense of anxiety and unease. Harry has stumbled upon something he does not understand (and is not sure he wants to) and Parker expertly conveys Harry's uncertainty and anxiety by implementing lighting, editing, and sound.

We then cut to another close-up of a metallic fan blade slowly spinning counterclockwise. The viewer is now conditioned to anticipate violence or death, as Parker has previously instituted the imagery of the fan as a portent of death. We then cut to Toots trudging up the steps of his apartment building. Again, Parker and Seresin employ their masterful manipulation of lighting and composition to create a striking, German expressionistic atmosphere. The rungs of the bannisters and the shadows of the steps themselves create a haunting atmosphere, which bolsters the image of the fan as suggesting impending doom. As he is about to unlock his door, Harry attacks Toots from behind. The two grapple, and Harry holds a straight razor to Toots's throat, demanding that he come clean. Toots tells Harry that Epiphany is a mambo priestess, as was her mother. Harry then asks what the chicken foot in the bathroom meant, which evidently means that Toots has a big mouth. Harry gives Toots his hotel number and tells him to contact him.

We then cut to another ominous, Buñuelesque nightmare sequence. This time, Harry is standing behind the perennial figure in black, who is sitting in a darkened parlor, alone on a bench. Harry's shirt is soaked in blood. He looks to his left and sees an elevator descending, the metal, lattice-patterned gate of which is casting haunting shadows on the wall. We then cut to a close-up of a bloodied straight razor on the ground. Harry picks it up, and his bandaged left hand commences gushing blood inexplicably. He, again, slowly approaches the elusive (and ominous) figure in black, only to be startled awake by two snooping policemen (played by Eliot Keener and Pruitt Taylor Vince), who are ransacking his hotel room. They inform Harry that Toots Sweet was found dead in his room, his genitals having been cut off and shoved down his throat, thereby suffocating him to death. In keeping with the film noir formula, the bodies keep piling up, and our main character is becoming further embroiled in an escalating situation in which he is in over his head. The detectives then tell Harry not to leave town in case they need further information from him.

We then cut to a very interesting sequence in which Parker uses the technical properties of cinema to both create atmosphere and foreshadow Harry's imminent fate. In this sequence, Harry enters a phone booth and dials the number of Margaret Krusemark. Before she answers, Harry gazes pensively into the mirror in the phone booth. Mickey Rourke's performance suggests that Harry is filled with a sort of frightened anticipation—as if he is not sure what he sees when he looks in the mirror, and he is scared to find out. The imagery of the mirror, of course, serves to perpetuate the idea of identity. By initiating the upcoming montage with a shot of Harry looking in the mirror is Parker's way of conveying that the ensuing visuals will somehow give us clues as to Harry's identity.

We then cut to the perennial image of the elevator descending, which, as Stephen Frears would later use in the final shots of his film *The Grifters*, serves to visually represent the concept of the descent into Hell. This time, however, Harry is actually inside the elevator, as opposed to simply watching an empty elevator descend, as in the previous scenes. Harry is now locked into his fate—he is going down with the elevator and there is no stopping it.

Parker intercuts the shots of Harry looking in the mirror and of Harry descending in the elevator with shots of a raucous New Year's Eve party in Times Square in 1943 (a callback to the brief shot that was introduced while Harry was talking with Connie), and a zoom-in on a tenement building, which is symmetrically adorned with a series of windows, each one emitting a golden-colored light, except for one window, which is emitting red light. Again, the imagery is fairly obvious—the camera is tracking towards the red window, signifying danger (or Hell). However, the stark, simple imagery, when coupled with the frenetic, anxiety-inducing editing, and Trevor Jones's atmospheric music, is extremely powerful and effective. The last shot of the montage is of a hand reaching out from behind the camera, and turning a soldier around towards the camera. Before the soldier is completely about-faced, however, Harry is startled back to reality by a saxophonist tugging on his shirt, asking him if he wants a tune. At this point, it is clear that the flashback sequence of soldiers partying in Times Square on New Year's Eve of 1943 is going to somehow involve Harry.

Harry then returns to Margaret Krusemark's apartment. As he is walking into the front door, Parker intercuts a close-shot of the feet of a child who is tap dancing in the street. The sound of the shoes clapping on the street is very prominent on the soundtrack, and it sounds almost like military machine-gun fire. The frenzied, obtrusive sound of the taps serves to heighten the sense of anxiety.

When Harry opens the door, he sees Margaret's corpse sprawled on the floor, covered in blood. Harry retches, then proceeds to search around her apartment (Parker continues intercutting the shot of the tap dancing feet to maintain the sense of eager anticipation, an audio Greek chorus, in effect). He searches through her jewelry, her address book, and eventually finds a decomposed, mummified hand in a box on her dresser. He then slowly walks towards another desk, and the sound of the heartbeat plays again on the soundtrack. The inserts of the tap dancing feet are now much more frequent and shorter in length, heightening the sense of nail-biting tension. We then cut to what Harry is looking at on the desk, which is Margaret Krusemark's heart. On the soundtrack, an ethereal woman screams to bolster the startling effect of such a gruesome visual. Parker cuts one last time to the tap dancing feet, which slowly come to a stop, as if the tap dancing purely existed to build the suspense of Harry's grotesque discovery.

We then cut to a despondent moment of Harry drinking by himself at a bar, while the somber piano reprise of "Girl of My Dreams" plays on the soundtrack. As Harry downs a shot, Parker frames him lower screen left while a metal fan blade looms over him, once again suggesting that Harry is inexorably careening towards an ominous fate. Parker also intercuts shots of a religious statue, ostensibly one of the patron saints of Catholicism, to maintain the motif of religious artifacts serving as portents of doom, a visual quilt which Parker effectively sews with the eerie shots of artifacts and paraphernalia throughout the film. As Carrol Fry states:

> The film is more important for its pattern of Satanic imagery—sometimes obvious and sometimes subtle that permeates the film from the opening credits to the final shot. Director Parker uses images drawn from the Satanic and occult tradition, including pentagrams, hexagrams, imagery drawn from the Black Mass ceremony, and a host of other visual symbols and allusions to create the most consistently disturbing screen ambience of recent years.[31]

In other words, what is of importance is not whether the audience is apprised of the actual etymological significance of the artifact, or whether Parker displays an understanding of the historical significance of it, but how he visually depicts the artifact, infusing it with a cryptic, ominous sense of foreboding.

The next moment is an almost grotesque parody of the voodoo dancing ritual. A heavyset woman is being baptized in a murky river by a horde of emphatic zealots, who are vociferously shouting "Hallelujahs." We then see Harry drive over a rickety bridge, past the baptism, which suggests that Harry is forfeiting his chance for redemption. In Catholic dogma, baptism is a cleansing ritual, which ostensibly washes away impurity and sin so as to make the subject cleaner, and therefore, closer to God and salvation. Harry nonchalantly drives past this cleansing ritual, paying it no mind, which visually serves to suggest that he has left any hope of redemption or salvation behind.

We then cut to the second of the three "action" sequences of the film. Harry looks in his rear-view mirror and notices a red truck following him. Harry gets out of his car and approaches a street vendor for some food. The two men who were following him get out of their truck with a feral, menacing dog on a leash. They unleash the dog and it attacks Harry. While Harry is fending off the dog, one of the two men hits him in the back with a stick. Harry collapses and the two men warn him that Margaret Krusemark's father wants him out of town. This scene places us squarely back in film noir territory. The previous half hour or so of the film has taken us into an atmospheric, nightmarish exploration of unseen horrors, exploring the deep dark recesses of ritualistic murders and surreal nightmare sequences which augment the film's tone of seething malevolence. This moment, however, is where Parker shifts back to remind us that not only is this an exercise in terror and atmospheric horror, it is still couched in the milieu of film noir conventions. The goons' admonishing attack on Harry is a permutation of the tried-and-true film noir moment in which the detective is violently warned that he is in over his head.

The next scene finds Harry waiting for Epiphany as she disembarks a bus. The two talk, and Harry informs her that Toots is dead, and that he witnessed the voodoo dancing ritual and the sacrifice of the chicken. He then says, "That's quite a cute religion you people got," to which Epiphany retorts, "Yeah, well, nailing a man to a cross ain't so cute, either." This moral stalemate is the justification for Parker's use of religious imagery throughout the film. In the *Angel Heart* universe, religion (whether it be voodoo or Catholicism) is depicted as a creepy, frightening, alienating institution, not a source of joy or salvation. This explains why the grotesque voodoo imagery of mummified hands and chicken feet are framed with the same eerie lighting and composition as the Catholic artifacts in the film. By equating the two religions, i.e., by suggesting that they are equally irrational and unsettling, Parker has created a visual world of existential despair, in which external forces cannot save the doomed main character.

Another layer of the onion of intrigue is peeled away when Epiphany informs Harry that Johnny Favorite was her father. Once again, we are jumping further down the rabbit hole of the convoluted, intricate film noir world of double and triple crosses, and no one can be trusted. Harry then lecherously hits on Epiphany and tells her to call him.

We then cut to a church, where a Mass is taking place. Again, Parker does not visually depict Catholicism as a source of hope, redemption, or joy. The church choir is singing a hymn, which, as it echoes through the church, has a creepy tonal quality. Harry sits in a pew and meets again with Louis Cyphre, who is interested in learning of Harry's progress. Harry informs Cyphre of the three murders (Fowler, Toots Sweet, and Margaret Krusemark), and he tells him that strange religious practices seem to be looming under every stone Harry overturns. Cyphre replies, "They say there's just enough religion in the world to make men hate one another, but not enough to make them love." Again, Parker is depicting religion as a cynical, pejorative institution which breeds mistrust and unrest, as opposed to an enlightening, uplifting possibility for salvation. This concept is further bolstered by Harry's constant cursing, to which Cyphre responds by telling Harry to watch his language in a church. Harry says churches give him the creeps and that he's an atheist. Once again, Harry has willingly forfeited any chance for spiritual salvation.

Harry then returns to his hotel in the rain, only to find Epiphany waiting outside his door. The two enter Harry's room and have a drink, over which they discuss Johnny Favorite. Epiphany says that her mother thought that Johnny was as close to true evil as she ever wanted to come and that he was a terrific lover. To account for the leaky ceiling, Harry strategically places bowls around the room to catch the dripping water. Epiphany then informs Harry of a voodoo practice called *chevalier*, which means "mounted by the Gods." She is, in effect, telling Harry that she was impregnated by the Gods, further pushing religion into the category of the grotesquely strange and alienating. She then asks Harry if he wants to dance, and thus initiates one of the film's most notorious sequences. The two start kissing on the bed, and Parker intercuts their lovemaking with close-shots of the water dripping from the leaky ceiling. As their lovemaking becomes more passionate and intense, the water begins to flow and cascade more liberally, which is a pretty overt visual metaphor for sexual arousal. What follows, however, is a true visual nightmare.

In a close-up of a pitcher catching water from the ceiling, we see a red droplet hit the rim, suggesting, of course, blood. We then cut to an aerial shot of Harry making love to Epiphany in the missionary position, and red droplets begin to fall on his back as well. In the ensuing shots, Parker systematically ratchets up the tension with both the imagery and the pace of the editing. The blood starts to flow profusely from the ceiling, smattering the walls, the now-full bowls and pitchers, and the two naked, writhing bodies on the bed. As the lovemaking becomes more intense and animated, the editing also becomes more kinetic and frenzied, conveying a sense of things spiraling out of control. There are rapid inserts of Epiphany's screaming face, although at this point, it is difficult to ascertain whether she is screaming with pleasure or terror. We then cut to a nightmarish, séance-like tableau of the perennial figure in black scrubbing blood off a wall in the dark, by candlelight. This shot recalls the moment earlier in the film when Harry first sees the figure in black at Cyphre's office. We are then shown a quick shot of the soldier turning towards the camera at the New Year's Eve Times Square celebration. Then we cut to the ubiquitous image of the shadowy elevator descending while a man screams on the soundtrack. The next shot, which is interspersed with shots of Harry and Epiphany undulating spasmodically, now smeared with blood, is of a Caligulaesque orgy by fire. It features dozens of writhing, naked bodies groping and fondling one another in ecstasy, and it is highly suggestive of some occultist celebration. This frenzied montage conveys that things have gotten completely out of control and that there is no turning back for Harry. The elevator is descending into Hell, and there is nothing Harry can do to stop it.

After the intense lovemaking climax, Harry stands up, looks in the mirror, and punches it, effectively cracking it. This, of course, suggests that Harry's identity is unraveling. We then cut to the two detectives knocking on Harry's door. They question him about Margaret Krusemark's death, of which Harry claims he has no knowledge. They also notice Epiphany, sitting naked on Harry's bed, after which they proceed to make a series of racial slurs, telling Harry that the white folks down in these parts do not get involved with the "jigaboos." Not only does this overt racism capture the authenticity of the sentiments of the South at the time, but it, again, foreshadows the subject matter for Parker's next film, *Mississippi Burning*.

Harry then returns to his room to hear Epiphany, who is taking a bath, singing "Girl of My Dreams." He enters the bathroom and asks her what tune she's singing. She says, "You don't know it? It's one by Johnny Favorite." Harry just stares at Epiphany with a drained, exhausted, frightened look on his face, as if her singing that particular song is yet another portent of his imminent doom. With simply a look, Rourke's performance in this moment, which is bereft of dialogue, is by turns frightening and heartbreaking. Harry now suspects that there is no turning back and that something cataclysmic is about to happen to him. This is further augmented in the next moment in which Harry walks over to the cracked mirror and gazes pensively into it. Again, although the image of a cracked mirror serving to represent the fractious nature of an identity is fairly rudimentary, it is utilized in this moment to great effect, mostly due to Rourke's powerful performance. As he gazes into the cracked mirror, we see a tough, resilient man, one who is not used to being afraid, brought to his knees, and he is experiencing true fear for the first time.

The next scene is the third and final "action" sequence of the film. Harry, walking to his car, notices the goons with the dog (the ones who warned him on behalf of Ethan Krusemark to leave town), sitting parked across the street from his car. Harry brazenly approaches their truck, head butts the driver and chases the passenger, who has fled from Harry's violent outburst, into a horse stable. The passenger, who has a gun, begins firing at Harry. A stray bullet hits one of the horses, which proceeds to fall on Harry, trapping him. The two goons unleash the ferocious dog on a now-trapped Harry, but the horse kicks it away, allowing Harry to escape. He opens a door to a chicken coop and has to run through a sea of chickens to escape. This recalls the seemingly useless character trait of Harry, who "has a thing about chickens," but even Parker himself acknowledges the gratuitous insertion of this attribute. When Harry stumbles upon the chicken coop in this scene, Parker states, "More chickens. No reason, really, other than the fact that I hate chickens."[32] Perhaps Harry's aversion to chickens, which he reiterates throughout the film *ad nauseam*, does not possess any sort of thematic or symbolic power, but at least Parker acknowledges the admittedly arbitrary nature of its inclusion in the script.

Harry then pays a visit to Ethan Krusemark (played by Stocker Fontelieu). They meet at a horse race, which is not held at an Aqueduct-type racetrack, but one that is more spare and rustic, consisting simply of two dirt tracks cordoned off by short wooden fences. As Harry talks to Krusemark, they are both leaning on the wooden fence on screen left. The fence they are leaning on, which is littered with spectators, stretches away from them, veering screen right. The fence on the opposite side of the dirt track starts in the foreground on screen right and diminishes into the horizon, veering towards screen left. The track, therefore, forms the vanishing point which stretches seemingly to eternity. It is a strikingly composed, geometrically framed image which also possesses thematic significance. The vanishing point of the track seems to flow into the vast expanse of the skyline, like a sort of metaphysical tributary. This visually suggests that Harry's journey will ultimately lead to an ethereal place without limits—where there is no time, no space, and no limit to the extent of experience and suffering. From the vanishing point, the horses slowly come into view, and are careening inexorably down the track, towards the camera. This also has portentous significance, as the implacable approach of the horses bolsters the concept of reckoning, i.e., the horses are like nightmarish Valkyries, coming to collect Harry and whisk him off to his ultimate fate.

Harry accuses Krusemark of being the one who, posing as Edward Kelley, paid Dr. Fowler the $25,000 to lie so that he and his daughter, Margaret, could abscond with Johnny Favorite. Krusemark, clearly distraught by this accusation, suggests that he and Harry talk in private so Harry can sample his gumbo. They walk towards a small house nearby and Parker then abruptly cuts to a simmering cauldron of gumbo. The startling cut, compounded with the sound of the liquid bubbling and churning, serves as yet another portent, warning us that something sinister is boiling beneath the surface. Krusemark then proceeds to tell Harry that he was, indeed, Edward Kelley and he did pay Fowler $25,000 for Johnny Favorite. He tells Harry that Johnny sold his soul to Satan for stardom, but that he tried to outwit the Prince of Darkness by swapping his soul with that of another unsuspecting boy about the same age. Apparently, Johnny had stumbled upon an obscure rite in an ancient manuscript, so he abducted a soldier from Times Square on New Year's Eve in 1943 (which explains the recurring inserts throughout the film of such), bound him naked on a rubber mat, uttered complicated incantations in Latin and Greek, then, ultimately, ate his heart while it was still beating. While hearing this, Harry begins to unravel, and he appears close to a nervous breakdown. He is sweating profusely, and he eventually runs to the toilet as if he is going to vomit. He repeatedly screams out, "Who was the boy?" wanting to know the identity of the soldier whom Johnny abducted in 1943. He then looks into the mirror and Parker implements yet another powerful, nightmarish, rapidly cut montage of haunting imagery. As Harry screams into the mirror with abject desperation and fear, we cut to the shot of the soldier turning towards the camera in Times Square, then to an aerial shot of the figure in black, walking up a spiral staircase. Then there's a quick shot of Harry meeting Louis Cyphre for the first time, followed by a rapid insert of a smattering of blood hitting the wall. We then cut back to the previously used shot of the figure in black, scrubbing blood off the wall by candlelight. Harry then screams, "Who was that boy?" again into the mirror and Parker ends the nightmarish montage with a close-shot of a door slamming shut, signifying the finality of Harry's situation—he is now trapped behind the hellish door of his own fate, which he is careening towards implacably.

Harry then runs out of the bathroom to find Ethan Krusemark's body floating in the cauldron of gumbo. As Harry pulls the body out to examine it, Trevor Jones implements a blood-curdling woman's scream over the soundtrack as the viewer is presented with the blistery, boiled face of Ethan Krusemark's corpse. The effect is quite creepy and startling, and the viewer is now on par with Harry's anxiety and sense of spiraling out of control.

Harry then runs out of Krusemark's place and we cut to his car pulling up to Margaret Krusemark's in the rain. Harry then frantically ransacks the apartment, looking for the dog tags of the soldier with whom Johnny allegedly swapped souls (which, according to Ethan Krusemark, Johnny sealed in a vase and left in Margaret's apartment). He eventually finds the vase and smashes it open, only to find dog tags with the name ANGEL, HAROLD stamped into them. Harry then breaks down, unable to contain his panic and terror, which is beautifully conveyed by Rourke in a powerhouse performance. As he desperately and irresolutely shouts, "I know who I am!" we cut to a close shot of Cyphre's right hand, clutching his cane. His fingernails have grown substantially since the first we saw them, which adds to the sense of metastasizing menace Cyphre represents. We then pan over to Cyphre's face, revealing that his long hair, which has heretofore been pulled up, has been let down for the first time. As Carrol Fry describes it:

> At the outset, Cyphre has the beard and mustache described in the novel at his first meeting with Angel. But in this final appearance, he has a full beard and long, flowing hair. Clearly, director Parker intends us to see the resemblance to Christ. But to the knowledgeable viewer, Cyphre stands revealed as the Antichrist.[33]

This dichotomy, that of Cyphre appearing Christ-like yet revealing himself as the Antichrist, solidifies the concept of binaries which has permeated the film—of two opposing worlds colliding. This concept was introduced in the opening scene, in which we see a cat ostensibly toying with the dog. In Harry's first horrific dream sequence, he sees two identical nuns sitting on a bench, looking at him. As we are about to discover, Harry is inhabited by two souls, that of Johnny Favorite *and* Harry Angel. This Manichaean imagery of good vs. evil, light vs. dark is at the very core of theological discourse, and Parker masterfully depicts this concept of diametrically opposed forces battling.

At this point, Harry finally pieces together what has been transpiring throughout the course of the narrative. He deduces that the name "Louis Cyphre" is a permutation of "Lucifer"—his client has been Satan himself all along. He accuses Cyphre of leaving the trail of dead bodies on his investigative trail, and he repeats the phrase, "I know who I am." However, Rourke's powerful performance suggests that he does not know who he is and he is trying to convince himself rather than Cyphre. His eyes begin to tear up, and his voice reaches a whiny, quivering pitch. He is truly losing his mind and is trying to convince himself that he is not.

Cyphre then tells Harry that he is, of course, the soldier on whom Johnny performed the Satanic ritual in 1943, and that he's been living for twelve years on borrowed time with another man's memories. Cyphre then says, "The flesh is weak, Johnny. Only the soul is immortal. And yours belongs to me." As he utters the last sentence, he points his long-nailed index finger at Harry, and his eyes are a creepy, pale yellow, signifying his demonic nature. This is the first time that Parker implemented such an overt signifier of a demonic presence, having heretofore accomplished such primarily through the use of atmosphere, lighting, editing, and music. Even Parker himself was unsure whether to employ the yellow eyes. He states, "I agonized over whether to do that with the eyes. It takes the film away from its realism and I'm not sure it was such a smart move to do it."[34] Thanks mostly to Robert De Niro's convincingly creepy delivery of the line, the moment still manages to send chills up viewers' spines. However, it is quite a departure from the gritty, hard-hitting realism that has permeated the film, and it appears out of place and a bit disjointed.

Rourke then continues his mad descent into a complete breakdown as he begins weeping while staring in the mirror, perpetually screeching, "I know who I am!" Rourke paints a convincing portrait of a man at the end of his rope, a man who has never felt out of control and is experiencing it for the first time. His clammy, sweaty appearance, his red puffy eyes, and his high-pitched, strident whine all contribute to the sense of a realistic descent into abject, debilitating terror and fear.

As Harry breaks down in front of the mirror, Cyphre plays the record of Johnny singing "Girl of My Dreams" as Parker employs a flashback montage sequence in which we see Harry/Johnny murdering all of the people who were killed throughout the course of the film: Fowler, Toots, Margaret, and Ethan. This is yet another departure from the source material. In the novel, Cyphre either kills all the victims himself, or at least frames Harry for the murders, allowing Harry to maintain likability, as he comes off as an innocent corrupted by the forces of evil. In the film, however, Parker chose to make Harry the actual murderer, further pushing him into the detestable category. Not only is he a lying, cheating, womanizing letch, he is also a murderer. Although Rourke delivers a powerhouse performance in shading the character of Harry, it is true that Parker does not give us much to like about him.

We then cut to Harry running out the door and Parker settles on an elevated crane shot as Harry runs away from the camera, frantically, in the rain. From a composition perspective, the shot is very reminiscent of the last shot of *Midnight Express*, in which Billy Hayes runs towards his freedom. This shot, however, serves as a sort of grotesque parody of that shot, as Harry is certainly not running towards freedom, but to his eternal spiritual doom.

Harry then returns to his hotel room. Seated on a bench just outside his door, is the perennial figure in black, whose face we are allowed to see for the first time. It is the face of Louis Cyphre inhabiting the cassock, and we find out at long last that the elusive figure in black, the harbinger of death and despair, has been Cyphre all along. Harry then enters his hotel room to find Epiphany, dead in a pool of blood on the bed, Detective Sterne hovering over her. Harry's dog tags are slung around her lifeless neck. Detective Sterne asks Harry who she was, to which he replies, "She's my daughter." As we recall, Epiphany stated that Johnny Favorite was her father and, since Harry and Johnny are one and the same, Harry is Epiphany's father, which makes the lovemaking scene all the more disturbing.

Detective Deimos then emerges from the bathroom, holding Epiphany's son in his hands. As the child stares at Harry, his eyes turn yellow, much like Cyphre's did in the previous scene, suggesting that he is also a minion of the Antichrist, or perhaps the Antichrist himself. As Carrol Fry puts it:

> One of the policemen brings her child into the room. It raises its hand in the manner often portrayed in paintings of the Christ Child, and its eyes glow red as it points to Harry. At this point, the viewer should be reminded of Epiphany's disclosure earlier that she was impregnated during a Voodoo ceremony, "mounted by the gods." The film suggests that the God who gave her, in her words, "the best fuck I ever had," was Satan. Jeffery Burton Russell, in *Lucifer: the Devil in the Middle Ages*, points out that there are two traditions of the Antichrist. One holds that Satan himself is the Antichrist, acting as Christ's opposite number. The other states that Satan will beget a child who will begin the final battle (the tradition played on in *The Omen*). Parker mixes these traditions, as he has done with occult imagery throughout. But one point remains clear. The child pointing to Harry is reclaiming his property. In *Angel Heart*, the Antichrist has won.[35]

In this regard, by suggesting that Epiphany's son is potentially a Damienesque second coming of the antichrist, the film is perpetuating a cinematic trend in horror films which was, for all intents and purposes, initiated in 1968 with *Rosemary's Baby*. In that film, the forces of evil essentially win. The Antichrist is born, and Rosemary cannot take it back or impede its plan of action. Similarly, in *The Omen*, the forces of evil triumph at the end, which is captured with the cheeky, creepily mischievous smile Damien shoots at the camera in the film's final shot. *Angel Heart* perpetuates the fairly recent horror film idea that a film is scarier if Satan wins—if, despite the most valiant efforts of the hero to vanquish the forces of evil, those forces prove to be too formidable to overcome. However, in this film, Parker does not cheat by merely inserting a deflating, apocalyptic ending into an otherwise hopeful story. He has visually prepared us for the film's final shot, which is Harry's descent into Hell, as he insouciantly stares ahead while the elevator escorts him, like a wrought-iron Valkyrie, into the bowels of eternal torment.

9

Mississippi Burning (1988)

December 9; 127 minutes/Color
Production Company: Orion Pictures
Director: Alan Parker
Screenwriter: Chris Gerolmo
Producers: Robert F. Colesberry, Frederick Zollo
Production Designers: Geoffrey Kirkland, Philip Harrison
Cinematography: Peter Biziou
Editor: Gerry Hambling
Original Music: Trevor Jones
Cast: Gene Hackman (Agent Rupert Anderson); Willem Dafoe (Agent Alan Ward); Frances McDormand (Mrs. Pell); Brad Dourif (Deputy Clinton Pell); R. Lee Ermey (Mayor Tilman); Gailard Sartain (Sheriff Ray Stuckey); Stephen Tobolowsky (Clayton Townley); Michael Rooker (Frank Bailey); Pruitt Taylor Vince (Lester Cowens); Kevin Dunn (Agent Bird); Frankie Faison (Eulogist)

> The mayor is guilty; maybe we all are.—Agent Ward to Agent Bird

> Making a film is a bizarre charade, an illusion: a thousand hours of make-believe with a hundred crew members juggling their pizza slices and coffee cups in the middle of the night, up to their knees in Mississippi mud, whilst faking death and pain.—Alan Parker, *The Making of* Mississippi Burning, pg. 112

Notes on the Production

Although it later went on to achieve a cult status through the circulation of video and DVD, *Angel Heart* barely made its money back at the box office, leaving Parker in a state of uncertainty as to what his next project would be. Sometime in mid–1987, producer Frederick Zollo sent Parker a screenplay written by Chris Gerolmo—a thriller which was based on the real-life murders of three civil rights activists in Mississippi in 1964. The screenplay had been procured by Orion Pictures, which, as they would later prove with their runaway hit *The Silence of the Lambs*, were, according to Parker:

> The last bastion of responsible filmmaking, run on a shoe string and the good taste of stubborn but benign elder statesmen, who for a couple of decades before the banks caught up with them, defied the system and managed to make some of the best films in Hollywood.[1]

Although the script was based upon an actual incident, it was substantially fictionalized by Gerolmo, which allegedly bolstered Orion's interest in doing the picture, as they did not want to make a documentary but a detective story that just *happened* to be set against the civil rights struggle. Gerolmo states of his own script:

Director Alan Parker (left) on the set of *Mississippi Burning* with actor Willem Dafoe (right). *Mississippi Burning* (1988), Orion Pictures.

What I had in mind was more iconic—if you imagine, say, Clint Eastwood and Bill Hurt in those roles and what they represent. The idea was a working-through of a Western-type conflict like *The Man Who Shot Liberty Valance*, where the rule of law needs the rule of force.[2]

Parker, who was always more interested in making powerful narrative films as opposed to polemical, "political" films, agreed to do the project. He assembled his usual crew, including composer Trevor Jones (who had done the score for *Angel Heart*) and editor Gerry Hambling. The only exception was that Parker enlisted cinematographer Peter Biziou instead of his usual partner, Michael Seresin. Interestingly enough, Biziou's cinematography would earn the film its only Oscar, although it was nominated for a total of six.

The film was to be shot on location, so in December of 1987, Parker traveled to Mississippi to scout out his locations. As he had done with the Louisiana segments of *Angel Heart*, Parker wanted to maintain fastidious dedication to authenticity with the locations, so he, again, did not attempt to glamorize or polish the look of Mississippi, but rather accurately depict its rustic, dusty atmosphere. A large portion of the film was shot in a town called Vaiden, Mississippi, which is where the interior shots of the sheriff's office, courtroom and stairs from the courtroom were filmed, in Vaiden's old Carroll County courthouse. The remainder of the film was shot in a number of authentic Mississippi towns, including Bovina, Jackson, Ross, Barnett Reservoir, and Vicksburg. After filming wrapped in Mississippi, Parker and crew traveled to Highway 431 in Alabama for the Town Square scenes.[3]

Parker recalls arriving in Mississippi in December of 1987 with his producer, the late Bob Colesberry, standing on the stretch of road on which Mickey Schwerner, Andrew Goodman, and James Chaney (the three civil rights activists upon whom the film was loosely based) were shot and killed, and being completely emotionally overwhelmed by the realization that he was standing in the very spot in which three men were unjustly killed because of their beliefs. He states, "Bob and I stood there in silence for a few minutes, realizing that true life and death are much more important than the movies."[4]

When it came time for casting, Orion suggested Gene Hackman for the role of Agent Rupert Anderson. Hackman was always a favorite of Parker's and he was interested, so the casting of the lead was an extremely facile process. As for the role of Anderson's younger, scrupulous, naïvely ambitious partner, Agent Alan Ward, Orion was less resolute in terms of who they wanted. Having recently finished filming Martin Scorsese's *The Last Temptation of Christ*, Willem Dafoe expressed interest in playing the part and was cast shortly thereafter. Parker was extraordinarily pleased with his two leads, stating:

> The two of them are hugely professional, incredibly easy for a director to work with. Very rarely do you have such an opportunity to work with two very nice people but also extraordinarily professional; so each scene becomes a pleasure, not a pain to shoot.[5]

Parker recalls that the filming of *Mississippi Burning* was particularly grueling in that there were many long days, as a good portion of the film's key scenes took place at night (e.g., the opening car chase, the lynching, the burning of the churches, etc.). He kept a journal during principal photography, one entry of which read, "Hard week of night work—burned three churches—car chase for four nights—lynched Vertis Williams." He then goes on to state,

> Making a film is a bizarre charade, an illusion: a thousand hours of make-believe with a hundred crew members juggling their pizza slices and coffee cups in the middle of the night, up to their knees in Mississippi mud, whilst faking death and pain.[6]

Despite the obstacles and hardship, principal photography was completed in three months, after filming sixty locations in three states. Perhaps because a title card at the end of the film asserts that the film was "inspired by actual events which took place in the South during the 1960s," the release of Parker's film incited an explosive backlash from both film critics and political activists who indignantly pointed out the film's lack of historical accuracy. Harvard Sitkoff writes:

> However brilliant the cinematography and the excellence of Gene Hackman's acting, *Mississippi Burning* is a dishonest distortion of the historical record. Rather than helping lessen this nation's woeful ignorance of its racial past, this film does such injustice to the events with which it deals that its ultimate lynching is of history itself.[7]

Even Martin Luther King's widow, Coretta, vociferously criticized the film, calling it a disgrace to the movement for which her husband gave his life. The film's detractors were especially irked that the African American civil rights activists are depicted in the film as helpless, incapable victims who needed the strong white men to come in and save the day. The film suggests that the perpetrators were brought to justice thanks to the brash, no-

nonsense diligence of the two intrepid white agents, when, in actuality, bribes and payoffs were the catalysts.

Parker (who faced similar accusations concerning his departures from fact in *Midnight Express*) was confounded by this fervent backlash, stating:

> Journalists have always had a problem with this form—the union of drama and historical fact—because the sacred rule of good journalism is the preservation of corroborated facts, which cannot and should not be messed with. Cinema and the dramatic arts work in a different way. Movies are an artistic expression, which communicates viscerally. Great cinema is as much about ideas and possibilities as it is about facts.[8]

In other words, Parker is defending the film on the grounds that it is not a documentary and was never intended to be. The film has an undeniable power in its brutal, incendiary depiction of an unfortunate and shameful period in America's history. As is the case with most Parker films, it is evocative in a raw, stark, uncompromisingly visceral way, and it demands that we confront the horrors of racism and bigotry. It does not glorify or glamorize racism in any way, shape, or form; on the contrary, its hard-hitting, raw power serves to remind us of its odious nature, and the film need not be a historically accurate documentary to accomplish this.

Summary

The film opens on a medium-shot of two drinking fountains which, although no more than two feet apart, appear to be cordoned off from each other, separated by a prominent metal pipe running vertically down the center of the frame. A sign over the fountain to the left reads "White," while the one over the right reads, "Colored." This shot visually sets the entire tone of the film, and its pure simplicity contains a primal, almost elemental power. Not only does the shot suggest opposing binaries (Good vs. Evil, Night vs. Day, Dark vs. Light, etc.), but Americans possess an intrinsic understanding of the caustic and violent struggle their country trudged through in order to achieve desegregation, and this shot succinctly visualizes this xenophobic struggle by paring it down to an almost rudimentary visualization of a battle—of one side versus the other. Rather than muddle the point with visual pretentiousness or a strident attempt at misguided profundity, the primal simplicity of this shot invokes the viewer's elemental understanding of the term "segregation."

As the opening credits roll, Parker cuts to another primal, viscerally powerful shot which, again, derives its effectiveness through its simplicity. It is a shot of a burning church, completely engulfed in rolling, wild flames, which appear to be devouring the building. Not only is Peter Biziou's impeccable, richly rendered cinematography visually mesmerizing, but the leitmotif of fire serves a number of narrative functions. It is a powerful visual metaphor not only for the inflammatory, incendiary battle that was the civil rights movement, but for the many fires that will burn throughout the course of the narrative (the fiery nature of hatred, the burning power of passion and ambition, etc.). Interestingly enough, Parker did not initially intend to present this powerful shot at the beginning of the film. It was initially intended to compose a montage sequence later in the film, but Parker ultimately decided that there were far too many shots of burning churches to squeeze into the middle and end portions of the film, so he simply excised one such shot from the end of the film and placed it over the title sequence.[9]

As if to counteract the sentiment of burning hatred which the shot of the church incites, Mahalia Jackson sings "Take My Hand, Precious Lord" over the soundtrack while we watch the church burn. It is a heartbreakingly somber gospel song, and it serves in stark contrast to the hypnotic image of the church burning. If the burning church can be seen as visually representing the point of view of the perpetrators of hate crimes (i.e., their burning, fiery hatred), then the song aurally represents the sorrow and loss that innumerable African American victims were forced to endure at the hands of lynchings, burnings, and a slew of other odious, heinous race crimes.

The next is a static shot of a lone car, driving on a desolate back road at night. It is an interestingly composed shot, the car ascending then descending a series of hills as it drives towards the camera, perhaps informing the audience of the tumultuous roller coaster on which the ensuing narrative will take them. We then cut to a series of quick shots from inside the automobile, revealing a white man driving, a white man sitting in the passenger seat, and a black passenger seated in the back. (Although they are never given names, these three characters are clearly the civil rights activists based upon James Chaney, Andrew Goodman, and Mickey Schwerner). We then cut back to the wide shot of the dark, hilly street, but this time, a caravan of cars is seen following the heretofore isolated car. Trevor Jones's thrumming, ominous score kicks in, signaling impending danger—the caravan most likely does not have benevolent intentions. The composition, lighting, and atmosphere are all testaments to Parker's ability to generate suspense and mood. As critic Thomas Doherty puts it, "It is a stark and spooky sequence, the crisp efficiency of the textbook film grammar—isolating long shots of the vehicular pursuit and involving close-ups of the three tense youths inside their car—suits the ruthless suddenness of the crime."[10] As he had done with *Midnight Express* and *Angel Heart*, Parker showcases his aptitude for creating an anxiety-laden, horrific sense of tension.

After abruptly swerving off-road in an attempt to evade his pursuers, the driver finally pulls over when it is revealed that the vehicle immediately behind him is a police car. The police officers approach the driver's side of the vehicle and immediately commence with their intimidation tactics, calling the driver a "nigger-loving Jew boy." The crass, racists remarks of the bigoted policemen further augments the tone that the opening shot introduced: that we are in a divisive world of tension, of one side versus the other, of black versus white. One of the policemen (whom we later discover is Frank Bailey, played by Michael Rooker) pulls out his revolver, places it against the driver's temple, and fires. Parker then abruptly cuts to a close-up of the white passenger, on whose face the blood from the wound splatters, a shot which lasts only about a half a second, after which Parker immediately cuts to black. The stridence of the gunshot coupled with the rapid, frenetic editing creates a startling effect, the abruptness of which catches the viewer off guard. The visceral, powerful immediacy of the violence has a raw impact, leaving the viewers frantically searching for emotional absorption of what they have just witnessed.

Over the black screen, a title card reads, "Mississippi, 1964." The rowdy, riotous policemen, who have just witnessed a murder, are raucously cheering, and one of them says, "Y'all done left me a nigger, but at least I shot me a nigger." We then cut to the interior of a car, on a close-up of a series of photos ostensibly being looked at by a white man, who is flipping through them. The photos are a series of civil rights tableaux, the likes of which can be found in history textbooks. They depict riots, policemen brutalizing African Americans, KKK ceremonies, etc. These photos give the film a sense of credibility and political, historical significance, which is contrasted with the highly stylized, purely cinematic opening chase sequence. We then cut to a two-shot, revealing the man who is looking at the photos in the passenger seat—an older white man wearing a tie—and a younger, bespectacled white man driving the car. These are Agents Rupert Anderson (played by Gene Hackman) and Alan Ward (played by Willem Dafoe), respectively. Agent Anderson pulls out a piece of sheet music from the folder which contains the pictures and begins jubilantly singing a very racist KKK song, the lyrics of which espouse segregation as well as asserting that "the Ku Klux Klan is here to stay." Anderson seems to be getting a kick out of the song, while the straight-laced, stone-faced Agent Ward is not amused, telling Anderson that he can "do without the cabaret." With this opening interaction, Parker not only introduces us to each respective character and their opposing personalities (which we can surmise will clash later on in the film), but he showcases each respective actor's unique style and approach to acting. According to Parker, Gene Hackman is a much more extemporaneous, instinctive actor, while Willem Dafoe is a more erudite, intellectual actor. He states:

> Gene is someone who is a very intuitive and instinctive actor. I don't think he's someone who looks at books and pages and pages of research. I think, probably, Willem is a much more intellectual actor than Gene. The brilliance of Gene Hackman is that he can look at a scene and he can cut through to what is necessary, and he does it with extraordinary economy—he's the quintessential movie actor; he's never showy *ever*, but he's always right on. I think Willem is an actor who thinks about it much more, so in regards to research and things, I think that's more Willem than Gene.[11]

As the audience will come to discover, each actor's distinctive acting style as delineated by Parker will further enhance both their performances (i.e., their shading in of each character) as well as the friction and tension that these conflicting personalities will engender—Hackman's character being more volatile and impetuous while Dafoe's character is a teetotaler, a by-the-books Kennedy-era liberal.

After the two agents exchange a bit of expository dialogue, which reveals that Ward is actually the superior officer (an interesting subversion of the traditional "buddy cop" convention) and that he will not tolerate any of Anderson's ageist condescension, we cut to a wide-shot of the agents' car traversing through the back streets of Mississippi. The shot reveals the rustic, run-down buildings and the dusty, unpaved roads, which is testament to Parker's unflinching dedication to locational authenticity, as opposed to employing polished, well-built sets. The two agents disembark their vehicle and walk into a ramshackle building which, as an insert of the inscription on a door reveals is the Jessup County Sheriff's Office. Agent Ward approaches the deputy, seated behind a desk, and tells him that he is from the FBI. The deputy, Clinton Pell (played with unctuous sleaze by Brad Dourif), snidely replies, "You mean the Federal Bureau of Integration?" Again, the film's dramatic conflict is made abundantly clear. Agent Ward then says he wants to see Sheriff Stuckey, to which Pell responds glibly, telling him that the sheriff's busy so he'll have to wait or come back some other time. In keeping with his by-the-books, cerebral character, Ward accepts the news graciously as he demurely steps aside and sits down, preparing to wait. Agent Anderson's more volatile, impetuous personality, however, precludes his being as composed as Agent Ward and he brashly sits on Pell's desk and says, "Listen to me, you backwoods shit-ass, you: you've got about two seconds to get the sheriff out here before I kick the goddamn door in." Whatever was implicitly suggested about each man's character in the car-ride scene is now explicitly laid bare: Ward is the bookworm, a cerebral, educated agent who possesses an idealistic devotion to due process, while Anderson is the hotheaded, do-what-you-need-to-get-things-done type. In this regard, Anderson's character mirrors that of Officer Malone (played by Sean Connery) in Brian De Palma's *The Untouchables*. In that film, Kevin Costner's Elliot Ness is akin to Dafoe's Agent Ward: the idealism, the staunch dedication to working within the bounds of the law, etc. Malone, however, is not quite so idealistic. He informs Ness that sometimes one must fight fire with fire and "do what is necessary" to get results. In De Palma's film, this particular character conflict (i.e., idealism vs. world-weariness) worked to great effect, and Gerolmo seems to be employing the same dynamic between Anderson and Ward in his screenplay.

After Anderson's crass admonition, Sheriff Stuckey (played by Gailard Sartain) emerges from his office. His appearance is that of the stereotypical, clichéd bigoted "good ole boy": he is sweaty, grimy, substantially overweight, and chomping loudly on tobacco, like a cow chewing its cud. Critics have denigrated this casting choice, claiming that Stuckey is a caricature, a two-dimensional, cartoonish rendering of what Northerners think all Southern racists are like. It is in keeping, however, with the clearly demarcated boundaries Parker set up with the opening shot. The diametrically opposed drinking fountains establish a powerful simplicity in regards to the civil rights struggle, i.e., one side versus the other. Cryptic, ambiguous subtlety seems to have been jettisoned in favor of stark, powerful overtness, so Stuckey's stereotypical rendering seems fitting, as does his intolerant, excessively bigoted mindset. He asks Agent Anderson if he has come to town to "help them solve their nigger problems." When Agent Anderson replies that he is in town to investigate a missing persons case, Stuckey's rejoinder is that he believes the whole thing is a publicity stunt cooked up by "that Martin Luther King fella." Again, Stuckey's appearance (as well as his world view) is not exactly subtle—he is the apotheosis of an ignorant, racist Southern hick, which, although this could be construed as subpar writing, seems to suit Parker's intention of keeping the distinctions and sides clearly demarcated, choosing to focus more heavily on the raw, incendiary power the topic of race relations intrinsically possesses.

Anderson and Ward then reconvene in their car, and as they watch Stuckey and Pell meander around town, Ward regales Anderson (as well as the viewer) with the troubling details of the missing persons case. He says that Deputy Pell pulled over the three missing civil rights activists at 3:00 p.m. then released them at 10:00 p.m. which is startlingly close to the actual facts of the Schwerner, Goodman, and Chaney case. Pell then claims to have followed them as far as the county line, and that he never saw them again. Ward finds the testimony suspect, due to the fact that the activists have been inculcated with training which dictates that they check in with their headquarters every hour, immediately upon arrest. He finds it odd that, once the three boys had been released, they did not phone the headquarters to check in. He accuses Stuckey of lying about having no knowledge of the boys' whereabouts. Anderson suggests that perhaps the activists' headquarters was lying about having called Stuckey, to which Ward replies, "Who would you believe?" Anderson then informs Ward (and the viewer) that he was once the sheriff of a small Mississippi town, and if a sheriff claims that events unfolded in a certain way, then *that's* what happened, like it or not. Again, we see the two personalities clashing: Ward's idealism and Anderson's glib insouciance. Anderson is not so much disagreeing with Ward as he is attempting to open Ward's eyes to the harsh reality of the situation: small, racist towns have their own brand of incestuous justice. Ward is maintaining his corrective, crusading attitude, while Anderson is espousing that of it-is-what-it-is-like-it-or-not.

After Ward suggests that they get something to eat, the two men walk into a diner. When they are told that the restaurant is full, and that they'll have to wait to be seated, Agent Ward spots a couple of empty seats, right next to two African American gentlemen. Anderson warns Ward not to sit there, as it is "Colored Only" seating, a warning not heeded by the headstrong, foolhardy Ward. As he walks towards the empty seat, the white patrons turn their heads and glower at this unexpected transgression. Ward asks the African American whom he has just sat next to if he can ask him some questions. The man replies, "I ain't got nothing to say to you, sir," as he nervously scans the restaurant almost apologetically, silently imploring the white patrons not to blame him for what is transpiring. Ward asks a second time, and the man delivers the exact same retort, only this time, he gets up and walks away from Ward. Once again, this moment is not rife with subtlety, coded language, double entendres, complex performances, or character interactions; it is simple, honest, and straightforward: the white folks are adamant about segregation and they don't take kindly to the whites mingling with the blacks. The moment works, again, because of the stark, built-in power that the issue of racism elicits. The witnessing of racial prejudice and discrimination incites immediate recognition and sympathy, and Parker knows it.

We then cut to a close-shot of feet walking over rubble and debris. When we pull back to the wide-shot, we see that it is Anderson walking through the remains of a burned church, ostensibly the one from the opening sequence. Ward informs us that this was the site where the civil rights activists had planned on setting up a voter registration clinic, only to have their planned location burned to the ground before the locals could vote on it. Ward then says that the three missing boys (whom the viewer knows to be dead) talked to some locals nearby, and that he and Anderson should start there. Anderson's obdurate, cynical attitude resurfaces as he says, "You can talk to them but they won't talk to you. They have to live here after we're packed and gone. They'd rather bite their tongue off than talk to you." Ward retorts, "Bureau procedure, Mr. Anderson." Once again, the methodical Ward clashes with the cynical, world-weary Anderson.

We then cut to a rather upsetting close-up of a wide-eyed African American, lying on a bed, his face seeming to be frozen in a paralyzing expression of shock and horror. The next shot is a close-up of a haggard-looking African American woman who is answering questions being asked by Agent Ward. We then pull back to reveal the woman's abode, which is abjectly poverty-stricken. The paint on the walls is peeling and drying laundry clutters the filthy, tiny living space (this, incidentally, was not a set, but rather an actual, impoverished household that Parker and crew found while scouting out locations). The woman's appearance (and her performance) is also redolent of authenticity as she was not an actress, but a town local. This entire scene is testament to Parker's unwavering dedication to depicting locations, environments, and people with accuracy and a palpable sense of authenticity. A lesser director would have dressed up a set to look impoverished and used a trained African American actress, perhaps Whoopi Goldberg or Alfre Woodard, and asked us to believe said actress was a withered, impoverished Mississippi local by dressing her in tattered clothing. Although Goldberg and Woodard are, undoubtedly, both fine actresses, on some subconscious level, the viewer would recognize that they were suspending their disbelief, as each actress has a sort of ubiquitous notoriety. By casting an actual impoverished local, and by using an actual, decrepit shanty as opposed to a set, Parker attenuates the artifice of the film and brings it closer to authenticity. As Parker himself puts it, "When you realize people actually live in these places, suddenly you're not dealing with illusion anymore. You're not creating a reality; this *is* the reality."[12]

After the woman tells Agent Ward that her husband was attacked by four white men immediately following the burning of the church (an incident she chose not to inform the police), we cut to a night shot of three white men, aggressively knocking on the door of a disheveled, run-down home. When a young black boy answers the door, they tell him to wake his brother, Hollis, as they would like to speak with him. When Hollis walks into frame we see that it is the man from the diner—the one whom Agent Ward attempted to question. Hollis immediately runs, and a chase sequence ensues. Hollis runs through a pigpen, evading his pursuers, and the sequence somewhat mirrors one of the chase sequences in *Angel Heart*, when Harry Angel runs through a chicken coop to avoid his assailants. Hollis's chase, however, is fraught with more suspense and has a more primal power to it. This is primarily due to the fact that there is more at stake in *Mississippi Burning*. Viewers (particularly white viewers) squirm and writhe with guilt, discomfort, and horror at the thought of an African American being physically brutalized by white people, whereas in *Angel Heart*, we are simply watching a relatively unlikable white character being chased by other white characters. In other words, the chase sequence in *Angel Heart* relies solely on the implementation of the technical properties of cinema to generate suspense (musical score, rapid, frenetic editing, etc.), whereas, in *Mississippi Burning*, the tension, suspense, and sense of unease is substantially amplified due to the intrinsic knowledge that these kinds of acts of violence are actual blemishes on history's record.

After the hard-to-watch moment in which Hollis is actually beaten by the white men (a beating which comes with an admonition about talking to the FBI), we cut to an exterior shot of a modest, inelegant motel. We then cut to a close-shot of three photos being tossed onto a bed, one at a time—photos of the three missing civil rights activists. In this scene, Parker attempts to infuse the narrative not only with character depth, but also with a sociopolitical examination of the cause of racism. While looking at a disturbing photograph of a lynching, Agent Ward asks aloud, "Where does it come from, all this hatred?" Anderson then relates a story about his father. He says that, when he was a child, there was a "negro farmer" named Munro, who lived down the road. Munro, it seems, procured a mule, an investment which eventually endowed him with economic prosperity, enabling him to rent another farm to plow. One day, Munro's mule turned up dead—someone had poisoned the water. Although his culpability was never verbalized, Anderson's father was the culprit, and both he and his son knew it. Anderson's father then said to him, "If you ain't better than a nigger, son, who are you better than?"

From a character perspective, this moment aids in giving Anderson depth and shading. Hackman delivers a subtle, nuanced performance, and he delivers the speech with a remorseful resignation, as if he recognizes the odious, dehumanizing effects of racism, but he is too jaded and tired to do anything about it. From a socio-political standpoint, this speech offers a couple of hypotheses in regards to the sources of racism. First, it examines the inculcation factor, which is to say that, for some, having been raised in close proximity to racial hatred, their fertile minds having been planted with the seeds of unsubstantiated malice, instills a stronghold on their consciousness. In other words, "My Daddy raised me to believe niggers are evil, so I'll always believe niggers are evil." Second, it examines prejudice as stemming from white socio-economic anxiety and insecurity. This xenophobic anxiety possessed by white men with means (i.e., the fear that "outsiders" will steal their jobs, their wealth, and ultimately, their way of life) would later be explored in Joel Schumacher's *Falling Down*. It reflects an insecurity, which galvanizes whites to impose their hegemonic tyranny over African Americans. In other words, it is a product of the conservative, reactionary mindset which dictates that the socio-economic paradigm is fine the way it is, so to introduce an alien presence into said paradigm incites fear, more specifically the fear of loss (loss of resources, loss of wealth, loss of identity, etc.). And fear eventually turns to anger and hatred. Anderson's father possessed this brand of hatred to the point that, according to Anderson, "He was so full of hate, he didn't realize that being poor was what was killing him."

This moment in the film works more on the character level (i.e., in shading in the character of Anderson) than it does on the political one. Thomas Doherty corroborates this sentiment when he says, "The relationship between racism, authority, and social order is worked through at a dramatic level, not an analytical one."[13] This is due to the fact that Parker, by his own admission, is not a "political" filmmaker; he is more interested in jarring the audience viscerally, with powerful, raw moments and imagery, than he is with espousing a political agenda. The aim of this exchange between Ward and Anderson, according to him, was "to answer the impossible, which is 'Where does racism come from?' I wanted to point out that it is economic, that what was invented was an underclass which happens to be black."[14]

After Anderson delivers this final line, a gunshot is fired through the motel room window, hitting the mirror, and bringing Anderson and Ward to their knees. When they finally look out the window, they see a burning cross. They walk outside to examine it, and Ward expresses his desire to bring in more agents. Anderson, of course, disagrees and says that that is "exactly the wrong thing to do." At this point in the story, Ward still possesses the wide-eyed idealism of Elliot Ness in *The Untouchables*; he still contends that working within the bounds of the law will lead to the resolution of this case. Anderson, mirroring the ever-conservative and realist sentiments of Jim Malone, persists with his belief that things work differently in the South, and one must use fire to quell fire.

We then cut to a shot of a slew of new FBI agents (Ward evidently did not heed Anderson's warning) unloading files and equipment from cars, as they will be ostensibly setting up shop in a local, abandoned building. Trevor Jones's throbbing, intense musical score plays on the soundtrack, which heightens the tension, raising the stakes of suspense—we fear that Anderson may have been right about not bringing in more agents, even though we hope he is not.

After a brief shot of Hollis cowering in fear inside an abandoned chicken coop, covered in feathers (a shot which amplifies the sense of helplessness felt by the African Americans), we cut to Ward and Anderson walking through town. A caravan of cars drives by them, and Anderson informs Ward that they are Klan members. Once again, the stakes have been raised due to the innate knowledge that the Klan is not a benevolent organization. Ward says he is going to check on the license plates, while Anderson walks into a barbershop. He finds Sheriff Stuckey sitting in one of the chairs, nonchalantly reading the paper, next to another man who is in the middle of being shaved by the barber. This is Mayor Tillman (played by R. Lee Ermey), who proceeds to attempt to mangle respectability into segregation, claiming that the African American community was happy until the interference of the pesky, meddling civil rights activists. He informs Anderson that there are two cultures in Mississippi: that of the whites, and that of the "colored." When Anderson says that the rest of the country sees things differently, Sheriff Stuckey intervenes, uncouthly proclaiming, "The rest of the country don't mean shit. You in Mississippi, now." This moment is strongly suggestive of a Western-type showdown, seeming to bring to fruition Gerolmo's goal of infusing the story with a "Western-type conflict." One almost expects Stuckey to say something to the effect of, "You'd best get your posse out of town by sundown." In this moment, Anderson inhabits the John Wayne persona, the lone man, fighting for the forces of good, who is outnumbered by the dastardly villains, à la *Rio Bravo*.

Before he leaves, Anderson tells the mayor that he likes baseball because "it's the only time a black man can wave a stick at a white man and not start a riot." The first part of the declaration is delivered by Hackman with breezy nonchalance, and it is captured in a

Agent Rupert Anderson (Gene Hackman, left) and partner Agent Alan Ward (Willem Dafoe, right) surrounded by a frenzy of racial unrest brought on by the Ku Klux Klan in 1964 Mississippi. *Mississippi Burning* **(1988), Orion Pictures.**

medium-wide shot. When he gets to the line, "and not start a riot," however, Parker cuts to a closer, over-the-shoulder shot, tight on Hackman's face as he delivers the line with stone-faced gravity. There is also a pugnacious quality to the line, as if he's challenging the mayor to a fight. After Tillman has absorbed Anderson's seriousness, Anderson again reverts to levity, laughing and winking at Tillman before he leaves.

The editing, coupled with Hackman's performance, makes this moment feel as though it is fraught with socio-political significance. In other words, the emotional impact of the scene segues into a sense that we have just heard something profound. However, upon reflection, it is revealed as dramatic intensity masquerading as profundity. According to film critic Gavin Smith:

> Parker's contribution to the modernist hyperrealism that has become Hollywood's dominant aesthetic has always been characterized by bold stylistic intervention and unconventional choices—as in *Birdy* and *Angel Heart*—although at times you find yourself asking, "But what does it *mean*?"[15]

Whether it is a flaw or a talent is open to interpretation, but Parker has the ability to implement the technical and performative properties of filmmaking to elicit a visceral, primal emotional response from his audience that supersedes any latent socio-political commentary. What exactly did Anderson's baseball analogy mean? Was he trying to create a metaphor? Was it a prescriptive call to action for African Americans to take up arms against their white oppressors? Was he simply trying to anger Mayor Tillman? It remains unclear, but the fact is that it packs an emotional wallop; it hits us and invites us to conjure up the unsettling imagery of racism so that, perhaps, we may examine it for ourselves.

Back at the FBI Mississippi field office, an agent informs Anderson that the license plates of the car he saw are registered to Clayton Townley (played by Stephen Tobolowsky), the Grand Wizard of the White Knights of the Ku Klux Klan. We then cut to Agent Anderson strolling down the dusty streets of the small Mississippi town. He notices a beautiful woman, they exchange an intimate glance, and Anderson follows her into a beauty parlor called Gilly's. Anderson discovers that the woman is Clinton Pell's wife (played by Frances McDormand). Anderson's flirtation with Mrs. Pell is almost immediately cut short as an African American man is thrown from a speeding car, onto the street. Both a slew of FBI agents and the local law enforcement gather around the injured man, and Sheriff Stuckey assertively tells the FBI that it is a local problem. This is the film's second source of tension, state jurisdiction versus that of the federal government (the first source of tension being the opposing viewpoints of the two lead characters). Agent Anderson identifies the man who was thrown from the car as the man that Agent Ward approached in the diner. For the first time, we are witnessing that, although it may be an unfortunate reality, Agent Anderson may be right—that due process may be fruitless in this particular matter.

Working off a tip that a local Choctaw fishmonger knows the whereabouts of the three missing persons' vehicle, Ward, Anderson, and a slew of other agents visit the fishmonger, who is gutting fish in a muddy, impoverished area just outside a ramshackle shanty. (Once again, Parker displays his affinity for authenticity by laying bare the economic strain of the more destitute regions of Mississippi as opposed to glossing over this fact with opulent Hollywood sets.) The fishmonger then leads the agents through a murky, muddy swamp and they stumble upon the vehicle, battered and half-submerged in the water. They pull the car out of the swamp, and Agent Ward tells Agent Bird (played by Kevin Dunn) to enlist one hundred more agents to assist in dragging every inch of the swamp. As is to be expected, Anderson vehemently disagrees with Ward's choice of action, saying that such measures will start a war. Ward then says, "It was a war long before we got here." As delivered by Willem Dafoe, this line reveals that Agent Ward is beginning to unravel and that his confidence in "Bureau procedure" may be waning. Dafoe delivers the line frantically and with overtones of frustration and anger, as if his seething emotions are beginning to boil over. The viewer suspects at this point that, like Elliot Ness in *The Untouchables*, Agent Ward may be on the cusp of acquiescing to Anderson's cynical brand of street justice out of sheer desperation.

We then cut to an intense, disturbingly violent montage of acts of racist terrorism. The first is an exterior shot of a small ranch with a sign reading "Freedom" out in front. The ranch suddenly explodes, taking the sign with it. Parker's imagery is, again, simple, honest, and powerful: freedom is under siege and in danger of being destroyed. The montage that follows is a series of shots of white men throwing Molotov cocktails into various buildings (churches, domiciles, etc.), kidnapping and brutalizing an African American man, and pouring gasoline over church pews. Parker intercuts this violent imagery with shots of busloads of soldiers entering Mississippi. These are ostensibly the recruits that Ward has enlisted to help drag the swamps.

Back at the FBI field office, Agent Bird tells Agent Ward that Sheriff Stuckey's alibi on the night the boys disappeared checks out—he was playing poker. Smith then tells Ward that the owner of the motel at which the agents have been staying is going to evict them as their presence is bad for business. Ward forcefully tells Smith to buy the motel, telling him to spend "whatever it takes." Once again, Ward's level of stress and frustration seems to be veering him towards doing just that—whatever it takes.

Parker then implements another montage. It begins with a shot of a newscaster who is covering the FBI's search for the missing boys. The news reports are played over a series of shots of the frenzied, high-intensity search (which is made even more so with Trevor Jones's powerful score) through the swamps as scores of Naval reserves, FBI agents, and search dogs are combing every inch of the swamp. Parker intercuts the shots of the search with shots of town locals being interviewed by the newscaster. The interviews are shot in a quasi-documentary fashion, with the locals speaking directly to the camera. One of the local men who is interviewed says, "If they are in that there swamp, then they asked for it." Even the footage of the men scouring the swamp has a sort of quasi-newsreel footage quality to it. According to Parker, he implemented this "as a device to get you back to reality ... bring things a little closer to the truth."[16] Parker wisely uses this technique to remind us that, although we are not watching a documentary per se, this admittedly fictitious film is dealing with a very real sociological ailment.

In the next scene, Sheriff Stuckey is bombarded with questions by a slew of reporters, to which he reiterates his belief that the missing persons fiasco is nothing more than a publicity stunt. He then says that the NAACP stands for "Niggers Alligators Apes Coons and Possums." He then says that the SECC and COFO are B-U-L-L-S-H-I-T. This outburst further augments the assertion that the character of Stuckey is stereotypical and clichéd, as he possesses a cartoonish degree of overt bigotry, and seethes with hissable malevolence. As film critic Harvard Sitkoff puts it, "Parker gives us caricatures of the 1960s that are easy to accept in the 1980s. The racists are all loutish, pimply-faced rednecks. One could not visualize these ignorant tobacco-chewing 'crackers' in Howard Beach."[17]

We then cut to a shot of the local African American community, who have congregated at the charred remains of the burned-down church. A very young boy, no older than thirteen, is delivering an oration to the crowd, assuring them that "one day, there will come a time when the sheriff won't even be a white man." The boy's delivery, however, is not the fiery, emphatic, galvanizing speech that is part and parcel of the civil rights newsreel footage. The boy utters the words demurely, in an almost defeatist fashion. Although this moment was most likely intended to bestow the African American characters with agency, it ultimately validates the assertions of countless critics that the black people in this film are unjustly (and inaccurately) depicted as helpless. As Thomas Doherty puts it, "Oh, the blacks. They're background. Noble victims, holy sufferers, rocks of ages, and very uncolorful 'coloreds.'"[18] Parker defends this alleged infraction, however, by stating, "[The film is] not the definitive story of the civil rights movement or of the FBI's involvement in it. It's one story, our story, and very obviously fiction."[19]

The congregation disperses once they see Agents Ward and Anderson arriving in their car. Only two stay behind, Aaron (played by Darius McCrary), the young boy who was delivering the oration, and an older gentleman standing next to him, presumably his father. Ward asks if he can ask them some questions and Aaron declines, stating that people aren't talking to them because they're afraid it will get back to the law. When Ward says that he is a law enforcer, Aaron states, "Not around here, you ain't." Before he and his father walk away, however, Aaron advises the agents not to be talking to colored folks if they want information—he says they should start with the sheriff's office. The viewer gets the sense that Aaron knows more than he is letting on.

The next shot is of the loutish Clinton Pell eating his dinner in front of the television, while his silent, clearly frustrated wife sits embroidering. It is obviously a loveless marriage and although McDormand's sensitive portrayal elicits sympathy for the character, we question why this woman would be married to such a brute. As Doherty puts it:

> If this is the kind of town where a girl marries the first guy that makes her smile, it's hard to imagine Dourif as a high school cut-up—or why this sensitive, intelligent woman has stuck so long to a man so brutal and bigoted.[20]

The doorbell rings, and we overhear that Agents Ward and Anderson are at the door. Parker stays on a close-up of Clinton, who is stricken with anxiety and fear when he hears the identities of his visitors. At this point, we are convinced that, while he may not have been the triggerman, Pell was involved in the murders on some level. The agents enter, make themselves at home, and Ward interrogates Pell as to his whereabouts on the night of the murders. Anderson, as well as director Parker, leaves the living room and enters the kitchen to find Mrs. Pell doing the dishes. The two flirt heavily and there is an extremely telling shot/reverse-shot revealing that these two are drawn to each other. The viewer now assumes that Mrs. Pell will most likely have some kind of agency in the story, even if it is simply resigning herself to Anderson's unrequited love interest.

The agents leave and Anderson tells Ward that Pell is in the KKK, a fact he learned after seeing a photograph of Pell in which he is hinging his thumb on his belt in a particular way, prominently displaying three fingers. Once again, Agent Ward's studying and training are no match for Anderson's street smarts. We then cut to Anderson, sitting in his car like a beat cop on a stakeout, monitoring Clinton Pell's activity. It is another night shot and, once again, Peter Biziou's Oscar-winning cinematography is breathtaking. The lights and shadows create a moody, noirish, and effectively eerie atmosphere as the film, at this particular moment, veers resolutely back into cop genre territory.

Knowing that Pell is out on duty, Anderson then revisits his house to question his wife at the behest of Agent Ward, who says that a large portion of Pell's alibi hinges on her. He brings her flowers, furthering the unspoken, junior high school crush the two seem to have on each other. They chitchat, and Anderson tells her that he was once married, but his wife left, lacking the tolerance for an absentee husband. This is yet another cop film convention implemented by Parker: the cop "married to his police work," to the point where all of his relationships suffer. Al Pacino's character in *Heat*, Clint Eastwood's in *Tightrope*, and countless other cop film characters have lost wives due to their unhealthy devotion to their police work.

Anderson then asks her if she was, in fact, with her husband on the night of the murders, and she tentatively says "yes." Anderson, as well as the viewer, is skeptical, but he lets it slide for the moment, still intoxicated by his attraction to her, which is really what this scene is about. Before he leaves, Anderson gazes adoringly at Mrs. Pell in a close-up, and there is an awkward silence. We are convinced (hoping?) that they are going to kiss, but Anderson gallantly walks out the door.

We then cut to a ramshackle church inside which the African American community is in the midst of a spirited, rendition of the gospel hymn "When We All Get to Heaven." Parker intercuts the congregation with shots of a group of white men getting out of their cars, wielding weapons, placing hoods over their heads, which is a tableau we recognize and we can surmise what is about to happen. The men wait for the congregation to exit the church, and what ensues is a disturbingly effective marriage of image and sound. The congregation spot the hooded men, and immediately flee for their lives, screaming with terror. As the violent bigots chase down their prey and commence brutalizing them, hitting them with sticks, punching them, kicking them, etc., the beautifully melancholic, elegiac reprise of "When We All Get to Heaven," sung with somber repose by Lannie Spann McBride, plays on the soundtrack. The sequence is mesmerizing as Parker synthesizes the brutal, savage violence with the soulful grace of the gospel hymn, creating an indelible moment—a moment which is pure cinema, the impact of which is unforgettable (especially the climax of the beating, in which one of the hooded Klansmen kicks Aaron in the face as he is kneeling down in prayer—it is a very hard-to-watch moment of shocking brutality).

Parker then presents us with another sequence of the Naval reserves scouring the swamp interspersed with the quasi-documentary footage of the locals being interviewed. He cuts directly from the image of Aaron, having just been kicked in the face, squirming on the ground in pain, to a shot of a woman being interviewed. After having been asked, "How do you think the negroes have been treated here in Mississippi?" the woman replies, "I think they've been treated about fair." By presenting this shot immediately following the savage beating of the church congregation, Parker gives us a moment of interesting complexity. On the one hand, it is perversely (and disturbingly) humorous. Although it may be unsettling, cutting from a young African American boy getting kicked in the face to a woman claiming that African Americans are treated fairly is funny, albeit in a sick way. Perhaps more importantly, however, this moment is significant in that it subtly posits another possibility for the source of racism: abject gullibility. The viewer gets the sense that this woman is speaking not from firsthand experience, but from what she has been told. This is further substantiated by the next local who is interviewed, a man who says that he "heard" that Martin Luther King, Jr., is a communist. Again, we can surmise that, at least for this man, his fear and mistrust of blacks may not be socio-economic or religious, but was born from propagandist fearmongering and misinformation that, unless one ventures out and gathers one's own empirical data, is bound to be believed by people of the frightened, territorial mindset.

We then cut to an exchange that is, once again, testament to Parker's aptitude with implementing the technical properties of cinema to achieve maximum effect. Mrs. Pell is sitting in her backyard, holding an African American baby in her arms. Watching her is an African American woman, presumably the Pells' maid/cleaning woman. The two women are laughing, having a good time, until Clinton comes outside. The laughter stops, and Mrs. Pell returns the child to her mother forthwith. Parker cuts to a medium close-up of the maid's face, revealing fear and anxiety, clearly wanting to flee with her child, lest Clinton do something inappropriate or volatile. (Parker conveys this information without a word of dialogue, depicting the transition from joy to fear with editing and by coaxing good performances from his actors. The ability to convey such things without words is something exclusive to cinema, and Parker relishes in the show-me-don't-tell-me properties of the medium.)

Clinton watches the maid walk away, and says, "Funny, they're cute when they're young." With this moment, we once again revert to a stereotypical, clichéd portrait of racism, with Pell insinuating that all African American adults are grotesque, and he is also not-too-subtly suggesting that black people are not even human, delivering the line with a detached condescension. This cartoonishly over-the-top depiction of racism is furthered in the next scene, in which local high-profile businessman Clayton Townley is being interviewed by reporters. He states, "We do not accept Jews because they reject Christ; we do not accept Papists because they bow to a Roman dictator; we do not accept Turks, Mongols, Orientals, nor Negroes because we're here to protect Anglo-Saxon democracy." Not only is Townley espousing detestable, horrendously racist philosophies, but he is doing so on camera, in front of potentially countless viewers. His honesty and foolhardy temerity does not quite ring true—a respectable businessman with a reputation to uphold who moonlights for the Ku Klux Klan would most likely not be quite so vociferous about his extra-curricular activities.

The next scene pushes the film squarely back into reactionary, conservative, to-hell-with-due-process cop film territory, or as Harvard Sitkoff puts it, "[*Mississippi Burning*] rehashes Clint Eastwood's less-than-subtle investigatory techniques, Charles Bronson's approach to cleaning up another western town, and the formula for countless white cop buddy movies."[21] The scene follows Agent Anderson as he walks up a flight of stairs, into an exclusive, "Rednecks Only" club. The rogue's gallery of local racists is there, one of whom is in the middle of telling a racist joke (one gets the sense that these bigoted louts do nothing but sit around and conjure up racist thoughts, actions, and jokes, which substantiates Sitkoff's claim that the racists are all caricatures). The joke ceases the minute

Anderson walks into the room, like the new gunslinger in town who just walked into the saloon. Anderson has a beer and Frank Bailey (played by Michael Rooker), one of the local hot-headed racists, tells Anderson that "they ain't never gonna find those civil rightsers down here." He then tells Anderson to finish his beer and get out of their club, to which Anderson responds quite violently, grabbing and squeezing Bailey's testicles. Anderson tells him that the FBI is not leaving until the case is finished, i.e., until they find the bodies of the boys. Anderson then reveals his firearm to Deputy Pell and says, "Is that gun just for show, or do you get to shoot people?" Hackman embodies the ethos of John Wayne as he, with the utmost authority and virility, warns the villains that he's "gonna clean up this town and no one's gonna stop him." He also, however, is mirroring the behaviors of "Dirty" Harry Callahan and Jim Malone from *the Untouchables*—due process is thrown by the wayside in favor of brutal, "fight-fire-with-fire" street justice.

The next shot is of actual newsreel footage of a Ku Klux Klan rally, which is, by turns, startling, ugly, and unsettling. It showcases a young child, no older than five, dressed up in KKK garb, being led to the racist rally by his mother, who is also dressed in KKK garb. Parker had initially intended to re-stage and re-shoot the KKK rally footage, but, after seeing the original footage, decided that it was ugly and powerful enough.[22] We then cut to a civil rights march down the streets of Mississippi, a procession which is inciting the ire of the local racists, who are shouting obscenities from the sidewalk as the African Americans march stoically down the street, carrying American flags. It is a hauntingly beautiful scene, augmented by the soulful, elegiac gospel song playing over the soundtrack. It is a scene which takes the film out of *Dirty Harry* territory for a moment and places it back in reality. Parker claims that he replicated the footage from actual documentary footage he had seen, right down to the moment in which a police officer forcefully snatches an American flag out of a black boy's hands.

The next moment is also interesting from a dramatic standpoint. Agent Anderson walks into the beauty parlor where Mrs. Pell works, and the two have a conversation. However, the actual substance of the conversation is kept from the audience, as we watch through the window, seeing that information is being exchanged, but we do not know exactly what is being said. We can surmise that perhaps Mrs. Pell has reached her boiling point, and is finally ratting on her husband.

We are then placed squarely back in cop film territory as we cut to Agents Ward and Anderson, sitting in their car on a night watch, staking out the county jail (although we are not explicitly told, we can deduce that Mrs. Pell gave Agent Anderson some useful information). Sheriff Stuckey and Deputy Pell emerge from the building with a young black man, whom they let go and watch as he walks away. Then, a truck peels out and chases down the man, and a cop-thriller, suspenseful chase sequence ensues. Parker implements Trevor Jones's exciting music and cuts rapidly between the truck, Stuckey and Pell, and Ward and Anderson, who are arguing about whether or not they should pursue the truck immediately, or wait until Stuckey and Pell go back in the building. They end up doing the latter, and a car chase sequence follows, culminating in the discovery of the African American boy, beaten and brutalized, lying in the woods. We then cut to Agent Ward asking the boy's mother if she would persuade her son to press charges, to which she, of course, answers negatively. Again, the African American community is depicted as helpless victims. The next scene is of Agent Ward interrogating Deputy Pell in the back room of the FBI field office. He asks Pell if he is a member of the Ku Klux Klan, only to be met with obdurate denials across the board. Mayor Tillman then accosts Ward and Anderson, saying he is fed up with their harassment of the police department. Both Ward and Anderson have volatile rejoinders, assuring Tillman that they will not stop the harassment until the case is solved. Tillman then leaves, and Ward says to Anderson, "For a moment there, Mr. Anderson, it sounded like we were both on the same side." While this is somewhat of a clichéd buddy cop moment (the at-first-bickering partners becoming friends), it effectively illustrates that Ward's transformation is almost complete—he is inching ever more closely to the reactionary, fight-fire-with-fire side of the line.

After a brief shot of Anderson watching from his car as Mrs. Pell enters her house (a moment which further supports the idea that there is a mutual attraction between the two), we cut to another disturbing act of violence. A truck full of sweaty white bigots pulls up to a ramshackle shanty, and one of the men throws a smoking shoebox on the rotted porch. The shoebox explodes, igniting the building. A young African American man runs out of the house and looks back, watching his house burn. Once again, the stark, raw power and simplicity make for an effectively unsettling moment in which we sympathize with this beleaguered community.

We then cut to Agent Ward scouring the charred remains of the house for clues. Agent Bird tells him that none of the locals are willing to talk, to which Ward replies, "If they won't talk, Mr. Bird, shake it out of them." Ward's metamorphosis is almost complete. Like Elliot Ness in *The Untouchables* he is inexorably drawing closer to the conclusion that extreme, drastic measures are sometimes necessary. This is further substantiated in the next moment, in which Anderson tells Ward that his dedication to "Bureau procedure" is a waste of time. Ward then asks Anderson, "What would you do?" We then cut to Aaron, the young orator at the burned-down church, telling a young African American boy (who witnessed the shoebox bomb incident) to tell Ward and Anderson what he saw. Agents Ward, Anderson, and Bird then drive the young witness around the streets of Mississippi in the hopes that he can identify the perpetrators. To prevent any violent reprisals, they have placed a cardboard box with eyeholes over the boy's head.

We then cut to the sentence hearing of the men who bombed the house, having been presumably identified by the young boy. Although they pled guilty, the judge suspends their five-year-imprisonment sentences and lets them off without so much as a reprimand. As Parker describes this scene:

> It echoes the true story of the local court being too lenient on the guilty, the revelation being that they're never going to bring these guys to justice if you're going to rely on the local courts because the judge is just as bigoted as anyone else.[23]

We then cut to a shot of yet another house being burned, continuing the perennial image of rolling flames. In this scene the conflict between the local and federal jurisdictions, respectively, is again addressed. Agents Ward and Anderson try to pass through the local law enforcement barricade, only to be thwarted by Stuckey and Pell, who claim that "this is a local problem."

The next scene is one of brutal, disturbing power. After his house is besieged and set aflame by the whites, Vertis Williams (played by Lou Walker) wakes up his son Aaron, tells him to leave the house with his mother and grandmother, and grabs his shotgun. He marches outside, proclaiming, "I ain't taking this shit no more." The men strike Vertis over the head, wrap a noose around his neck, and string him up from a tree. All of this happens with the golden-hued tongues of fire rolling in the background and another elegiac gospel song being soulfully sung on the soundtrack. It is an indelible image, and Biziou's cinematography captures the dark, fiery essence of this horrific act of violence.

We then cut to another disturbing image—that of the charred remains of cows and horses, animals that belonged to Vertis. Ward and Anderson have another disagreement about their respective views on procedure (Ward's metamorphosis is not quite complete), and we then cut to a rally at which Clayton Townley is speaking to a horde of white people. He states, "I love Mississippi," to which the horde boisterously cheers. FBI agents are gathering license plate information from the various cars parked outside the rally, and Pell tells them they have no right to be there as it is a "political meeting" (which is clearly a thinly veiled euphemism for "Klan meeting").

Anderson then visits the salon at which Mrs. Pell works to meet with her. In this scene, Parker again attempts to infuse the narrative with a socio-political insight into racism. Mrs. Pell says, "Hatred isn't something you're born with, it gets taught. In school, they said segregation's what it said in the Bible." Mirroring the sentiments of the town local who claimed that Martin Luther King, Jr., was a communist, Mrs. Pell is bolstering the idea that gullibility and inculcation are substantial sources of racism. Mrs. Pell then tells Anderson where the bodies of the three boys are buried (at the Roberts farm, in an earthen dam), which is one of the sources of criticism the film has garnered. In reality, bribes and payoffs are what led the Justice Department to the bodies, not the testimony of a mousy housewife. However, Parker defends this dramatization of events, stating:

> In the real story, they did find the bodies in an earthen dam. No one knows where that information came from. We fictionalized it by giving the information to Mrs. Pell to impart. That's our fiction only because nobody knows who actually did tell where the bodies were buried.[24]

As the bodies are being rolled into the morgue on gurneys, Sheriff Stuckey says to Pell, "You got some problems at home you need to tend to." Stuckey knows it was Mrs. Pell who informed on them. Clinton then walks into his home with his cronies and proceeds to savagely beat his wife. It is an extremely hard-to-watch scene that further vilifies these already despicable men.

Ward and Anderson then visit the unconscious Mrs. Pell in the hospital, and the film again reverts to buddy cop, action thriller territory. Anderson is reduced to the Charles Bronson, *Death Wish* camp of the vengeance-seeking man who wants restitution because "it's personal." Rather than aggressively hunting down the perpetrators because of a social conscience or mission, Anderson wants to lock the men up because they brutalized the woman he loves. It is at this moment that Ward's metamorphosis is complete. After he and Anderson come to blows, he states that he's willing to do whatever it takes to bring the men to justice, even if it means doing it Anderson's way (which, as the audience knows, means that due process will be thrown out the window and brutal, vigilante justice will reign).

After a powerful, rousing eulogy delivered at the funeral of the three boys, Ward and Anderson drive off in a car with mysterious men, ostensibly the "hired guns" Anderson has enlisted to help him bring the men to justice. We then cut to Mayor Tillman getting into his car, only to be abducted by someone who was waiting for him in the back seat. We then cut to a dimly lit shack, in which Tillman is tied up with tape covering his mouth. Tillman's abductor, a large African American man sitting across from him, relates a bloody, gruesome story about a black man named Homer who had his scrotum cut off by racists. The man then pulls out a razor and shows it to Tillman, obviously insinuating that he is going to do the same to him unless he talks, which he ultimately does. Ward and Anderson have now gone past the point of no return. They are embroiling themselves in illegal, illicit coercion tactics. This spills over into the next scene, in which Anderson and one of his hired guns (played by Tobin Bell) coerce Lester Cowens (played by Pruitt Taylor Vince) to talk by lying to him, telling him that his partners already ratted him out. Once again, Anderson is engaging in illegal behavior as the film is now firmly in cop thriller territory. This pattern is continued in the next scene. Anderson walks into the barbershop where Clinton Pell is in the middle of being shaved. Anderson usurps the straight razor from the barber and continues shaving Pell, cutting his face on purpose. He then proceeds to beat Pell, throwing him around the room. Again we are steeped in the cop thriller cliché of the policeman who resorts to vigilante violence after the villains make it personal, attacking someone he happens to personally care about. We then cut to Lester Cowens's home, where a shotgun blast shatters his window. He looks outside and sees a burning cross. Lester attempts to flee and another tense chase sequence ensues. The cohorts on whom he has informed chase him down, tie a noose around his neck, and attempt to lynch him, only to be saved at the last minute by the arrival of Ward and Anderson, who chase down and capture his would-be assailants. These turn out to be Anderson's hired guns with hoods on— it has all been an elaborate ruse.

    This scene is followed by a montage of each of the perpetrators of the murders walking out of the courthouse after having already been sentenced. Parker again infuses this montage with a quasi-documentary feel to give the scene a sense of reality. As each perpetrator is escorted through the doors in handcuffs, Parker captures the moment in a black-and-white freeze-frame, and a title card with the man's name and his sentence superimposed over the image. This gives the scene a sense of gravitas and we are again reminded that this film was inspired by real events. Interestingly, Sheriff Stuckey is acquitted, suggesting that perhaps he was too shrewd about his involvement to leave behind any tangible evidence.

    The FBI agents then descend into a darkened basement (again showcasing Peter Biziou's impeccable cinematography, which accentuates the shadows, giving the scene the proper amount of noirish intensity). There, they find the corpse of Mayor Tillman, who has apparently hung himself. They delicately take his body down from the noose, and Agent Bird asks Agent Ward, "Why did he do it? He wasn't even in on it; wasn't even Klan." Agent Ward responds by saying that, in a way, he was as guilty as the triggermen. According to him, anyone who tolerates racist behavior without doing anything about it is just as guilty as the racists themselves. He then says, "He was guilty all right ... maybe we all are." This statement is conceivably supposed to exonerate the illicit investigative tactics that Ward and company resorted to, asserting that we live in an imperfect world, and that we are all imperfect. According to Parker, "Willem [Dafoe] originally had a longer speech at the end that I trimmed down because I thought it was too preachy. Now he just says, 'The mayor [who commits suicide] is guilty, maybe we all are.'"[25] The trimming down of Agent Ward's speech, while it maintains ambiguity and an invitation for interpretation, leaves the viewer with a sense of wanting a bit more of an elaboration, although its terseness does still possess a certain power.

The film's denouement finds Anderson driving up to the Pell residence to pay Mrs. Pell one last visit. The house has been completely destroyed by vandals. He walks into the house to find the interior just as demolished as the exterior, and he finds Mrs. Pell standing pensively in the kitchen. He apologizes, and she says that she's not going anywhere—she's staying in Mississippi because "if I wanted to leave I would have done it a long time ago. There's enough people here who know that what I did was right. And there's enough ladies who like the way I fix their hair." Frances McDormand's portrait of Mrs. Pell is one of decency and magnanimity. She has long suffered at the hands of her bigoted, abusive husband and is leading a completely unfulfilling life. She maintains, however, a dignified repose, accepting her suffering with quiet dignity.

The film's final scene is an integrated congregation gathered at a black-only cemetery, all singing a gospel hymn. In a way, the scene could be viewed as a sort of parody of the ending of *Bugsy Malone*, in which the heretofore antagonistic adversaries come together in the end to sing a song in harmony. The last shot is of the African American civil rights activist's desecrated gravestone, which reads, "Not Forgotten." As Gavin Smith describes this final moment, "It's a nice thought, if only because the film may reach an audience too young to know what was going on then."[26]

10

Come See the Paradise (1990)

December 23; 138 minutes/Color
Production Company: 20th Century–Fox
Director: Alan Parker
Screenwriter: Alan Parker
Producers: Robert F. Colesberry; Nellie Nugiel
Production Designer: Geoffrey Kirkland
Cinematography: Michael Seresin
Editor: Gerry Hambling
Original Music: Randy Edelman
Cast: Dennis Quaid (Jack McGurn); Tamlyn Tomita (Lily Yuriko Kawamura/McGann); Sab Shimono (Hiroshi Kawamura); Shizuko Hoshi (Mrs. Kawamura); Stan Egi (Charlie Kawamura); Ronald Yamamoto (Harry Kawamura); Akemi Nishino (Dulcie Kawamura); Naomi Nakano (Joyce Kawamura); Brady Tsurutani (Frankie Kawamura); Elizabeth Gilliam (Younger Mini McGann); Shyree Mezick (Middle Mini McGann); Caroline Junko King (Older Mini McGann); Colm Meaney (Gerry McGurn)

> We stopped being Americans the minute they put up that barbed wire.—Harry Kawamura in *Come See the Paradise*

> I felt as if I still had "unfinished business" in terms of the race issue in the United States.—Alan Parker, *The Making of* Come See the Paradise, pg. 118

Notes on the Production

After his polarizing, controversial film *Mississippi Burning*, Alan Parker felt that he still had "unfinished business" in terms of the race issue in the United States, and sought to rectify this with his next film. The inception of *Come See the Paradise* stemmed from a disturbing photograph that Parker had pinned to his wall for many years, which depicted an elderly Japanese man, sitting with his two grandchildren in San Francisco, 1941, awaiting deportation and internment.[1] Somewhere between 110,000 and 120,000 Japanese Americans (about two-thirds of whom were U.S. Citizens) were completely uprooted, forced to leave their homes and sent to internment camps in 1942, and this photograph inspired Parker to begin writing a love story set against that backdrop. For the title of this story, Parker very much wanted to use a line from a poem by Russian poet Anna Ahkmatova, which he had scribbled a snippet of into a notebook years before. The last line of the poem, in particular, stood out to Parker: Come See the Paradise.

Director Alan Parker (center) on the set with actor Dennis Quaid. *Come See the Paradise* **(1990), 20th Century-Fox.**

Parker immersed himself in his research materials, which consisted of over fifty books, numerous videotapes, newspaper and magazine articles, and began work on his script, a first draft of which was completed by the end of January 1989.[2] Parker had initially intended to enlist Japanese American playwright Philip Gotanda to help him write the script, but Gotanda, after hearing that the story was to center around a white male, and ultimately, a bi-racial relationship (as opposed to casting a Japanese male in the lead), was not interested. He met with Parker anyway, and asked him why he was making the main character a white male as opposed to a Japanese male. Parker replied, "That's simply the story I want to tell," which was, evidently, not a good enough answer for Gotanda, who resolutely turned the offer down, leaving Parker to be the sole writer of the project.[3]

Then came the task of finding financing (a tedious step in the process that Parker has bemoaned profusely), but this time around, it was not the arduous, thankless journey to which Parker was accustomed; Parker met Barry Diller, who was, at that time, the chairman of 20th Century–Fox, at a party at the Los Angeles Museum of Contemporary Art, and Diller effusively praised Parker's script, claiming that it had made him cry. So, an agreement was reached, and Fox agreed to put $15 million dollars behind the film, with Parker in the director's chair.[4]

Next came the business of casting. After writing the character of Jack, Parker thought that Dennis Quaid was the closest he could come to casting the character as he had envisioned him. Quaid is of Irish descent (as is Jack's character), and he possessed, according to Parker, an "openness and ingenuous honesty that I wanted in the character."[5] Parker met with Quaid, who was enthusiastic and agreed to do the project (somewhat ironically, at that meeting, Quaid reminded Parker that he had done a screen test for him for the lead role in *Midnight Express* twelve years earlier[6]).

Parker knew, however, that at the heart of the story was the Japanese American family, the Kawamuras, so he lent the casting of said family an assiduous diligence, a process which ended up lasting six months. He held open calls wherever he could find large Asian American populations, places such as San Francisco, Portland, Seattle, New York, Los Angeles and Hawaii. By the time the roles had all been cast, Parker had auditioned more than two thousand possibilities, eventually finding the main cast in Los Angeles and New York. Apparently, casting the main character, Lily Kawamura, was the most challenging, and Parker whittled it down to three actresses, all of whom tested with Dennis Quaid. In the end, Parker felt that Quaid had the most chemistry with Tamlyn Tomita, and she was subsequently cast.

Wishing to maintain his staunch dedication to locational authenticity (as opposed to relying on studios and sets), Parker began scouting out locations. His search took him to many of the same places he went for casting: Portland, Seattle, and San Francisco. In Portland, Parker was particularly taken with a downtown area, which was once the old "J" town, or "Japantown" (which is now, evidently, a cultural mixture of New York's Bowery and Chinatown). The biggest locational challenge that Parker and crew would face was finding a suitable location to build the internment camp. Parker knew that it was impossible to cover the square mile of the original 864 buildings of Manzanar (the site of one of ten internment camps), but the art department found a site in the Mojave Desert, near Palmdale, that was suitable, and they ended up clearing thirty-five acres of land to build their camp.[7]

Shooting began on August 19, 1989, in flower fields in Oregon. They then moved to Portland to film the footage of the "Little Tokyo" street, which was one of the production's bigger sets. Sign painters, including two elderly Japanese calligraphers, replaced over one hundred different signs to contribute to Parker's signature authenticity.[8] The most expansive day of filming was at the Portland railway station, as this scene called for five hundred extras and an enormous engine with eight carriages that had taken two weeks to bring down from Vancouver.

At the end of September, the crew moved to Astoria, Oregon, to film the Terminal Island scenes. Once those were completed, they moved to Cathlamet, a fishing town on the Washington coast to film the cannery scenes. They then moved to Southern California to film the internment camp set.

By the time the crew arrived on October 10, the internment camp set was ready for filming. Twenty-five 84-foot huts had been built, along with seven "production huts" (for electricians, makeup, hair, etc.), a camouflage factory, guard towers and water towers. They erected forty-six 40-foot power poles strung with twelve miles of rope to simulate cable and twenty miles of barbed wire stretched across 3,000 feet of fence. They dug 950 cement-filled holes to hold everything down, as the fierce desert dust storms posed a problem. Filming on this location proved to be quite difficult for Parker and crew, as the harsh sunlight in the desert makes it next to impossible to get a decent shot. Thusly, each exterior shot had to be worked out to the compass to calculate the best time of day to film.

Despite the obstacles, the film was shot in sixty-three days, the crew having worked eighteen-hour days to adhere to the impossible schedule (a feat that was not lost on Parker, who surmises that they should have taken ninety days to film.[9]) Interestingly, although the egregious issue of the Japanese internment was tangentially touched upon in the 1955 film *Bad Day at Black Rock*, Parker's film was the first to overtly examine and depict this unfortunate (and detestable) period in America's history. Although numerous critics (including Traise Yamamoto, in her essay "Masking Selves, Making Subject: Japanese American Women, Identity, and the Body") have criticized the film for irresponsibly eliding the racial ramifications of the internment by centering the story around a white main character, thereby depicting the minorities as weak, ineffectual characters with no agency (a cultural crime which Parker also allegedly committed previously with *Mississippi Burning*), it is noteworthy that Parker was the first director to overtly deal with this controversial subject.

Summary

After the 20th Century–Fox logo fades to black, the film's opening credits appear. On the soundtrack, the scratch and hiss of an old-fashioned record player is heard (signifying that this is a period film), and the Japanese tango-style song "Flower That Blooms In the Rain," performed by Mariko Seki, begins to play. It is a haunting song, sung with sultry (yet vulnerable) sexuality by Seki, and the song evokes both a nostalgic feeling as well as a sense of beleaguered love; i.e., the song is indicative of genuine, true love that has undergone strain and duress, which, as we will discover, mirrors the centrality of the film's dramatic conflict.

Parker then fades into the film's opening shot, which is a wide-shot of a young Japanese woman walking alongside a young Japanese girl. This is Lily McGann (played by Tamlyn Tomita) and her daughter, Mini McGann (played by Caroline Junko King). It is a wonderfully photographed, picturesque shot, as the two ladies stroll down a dirt road, towards the camera, flanked on either side by a plush field of yellow wildflowers. It is a nostalgic shot, in which Michael Seresin's sumptuous cinematography captures the essence of the golden-hued, autumnal tones, from which the most indelible memories are forged. Parker clearly wants the audience to bask in the splendor of this beautifully nostalgic shot, as he does not cut to a close-shot of the two ladies for some time. As they walk, they are discussing the imminent return of Jack (played by Dennis Quaid), Mini's father (also Lily's husband), and Mini is apprehensive, worried that he will not recognize her. Lily reassures her and peremptorily urges Mini, who is now resting on a dilapidated wooden fence, to continue walking. Mini asks Lily why she is in such a hurry, as they have plenty of time until Jack arrives. Lily does not respond to the question, but continues walking, which is a subtle, nuanced technique employed by Parker to inform us of just how much Lily loves Jack—she is brimming with excitement and eager anticipation, and cannot wait to see him.

Mini then asks Lily to "talk about Papa," and Lily smiles and consents, thus beginning the film's narrative thrust, which comprises extended flashback sequences interspersed with shots of Lily recounting her memories to Mini. Prof. Kent A. Ono, writes of this narrative device:

Mini is primarily a function within the film, not interesting in her own right but rather useful in advancing claims about social issues. Mini is the passive onlooker of events that happen around her and the receptacle for a subjective historical account of Japanese American incarceration.[10]

Ono, here, is identifying a narrative, thematic thread that will permeate the entire film. First, he is illustrating that Mini is, essentially, a device. Her purpose in the narrative is that of a proxy for the audience; i.e., Mini is being "educated" about the internment the same way an unaware viewer would. He also states:

Additionally, as the product of miscegenation automatically loved by her parents and grandparents, she serves as the salve that helps heal the wounding divide between Japanese America and white society.[11]

With this insight, it would appear as if Ono is attempting to rationalize Parker's choice to center the narrative around a white central character. Perhaps responding to his detractors' grievances in regards to his racial negligence in *Mississippi Burning*, Parker chose to incorporate miscegenation to propose the possibility of harmony or, at least, mutual racial understanding. As we discover later on in the film, Mini's character, while not "interesting in her own right," serves to bridge the gap between the two cultures and assuage the animosity between them.

We then cut to the first portion of Lily's account. The setting is a smoky movie theater, filled with moviegoers, and a subtitle reading, "Brooklyn, New York, 1936." The movie that is playing is *Under Two Flags*, a 1936 adventure film starring Claudette Colbert, Victor McLaglen, and Rosalind Russell. It was very popular at the time, and incorporates adventure (set against the historical backdrop of the French Foreign Legion) and melodrama. Not only is it a perennial Parker hallmark to depict his characters watching films within his films, this is perhaps Parker's wry wink at the cinephiles, informing them of the tone and approach his own film will be implementing.

Into the theater walk two men, Jack McGurn (Quaid) and Augie Farrell (played by Pruitt Taylor Vince, who previously appeared in Parker's films *Angel Heart* and *Mississippi Burning*). There is something fishy about the two men, as they both nervously scan the audience. Two other equally suspicious men walk down the aisle past Jack and Augie— something is clearly about to happen, which Parker conveys through fast-paced editing, cutting back and forth between both sets of men. Jack then takes a package out of his coat, places it on the floor, and lights it on fire. Jack and Augie then leave the theater, as the smoke bomb has incited chaos among the other moviegoers. Meanwhile, the two other mysterious men have set fire to the tapestry on the theater stage, which quickly spreads. Amid the mayhem, Jack heroically attempts to put out the fire, burning his hands severely in the process. This sets up Jack's character, introducing him as "the 'public man' of masculine agency."[12] This elicits a complicated emotional response to Jack—on the one hand, we saw him light one of the smoke bombs; he is clearly in cahoots with the men who set the building on fire. However, he seems to have scruples and dignity beneath his criminal exterior.

We then cut to a men's bathroom, in which Augie is bandaging Jack's burned hands. Jack is arguing with an older man, who is urinating behind him. This is Brennan (played by John Finnegan), and Jack is expressing his discontent to Brennan, claiming that a firebomb was never agreed upon at the committee. Brennan callously replies, "Smoke bomb, firebomb, what's the fucking difference?" to which Jack heatedly states, "A bunch of people could've gotten killed, *that's* the fucking difference!" This, again, illustrates two components of Jack's character: one, he does, indeed, have scruples—he is willing to stage a demonstration (the smoke bomb was a ploy to coerce the theater's owner to hire union people, as Jack is a union movie projectionist), but he knows where the line is, which the audience respects. Two, his heated, angry response to Brennan signifies that he is a strong-willed, fiery individual who does not quietly accept defeat.

Augie and Jack then enter Brennan's office to find him sitting behind a desk, counting money. Brennan offers Jack three hundred dollars to disappear, which further infuriates Jack. Augie explains that it is because of his principles that he does not fit in with the rest of the "demonstrators." This, again, sets up the nobility of Jack's character, which allows viewers to more easily align themselves with him.

We then cut to a theater full of Japanese American patrons applauding a live stage performance, which has just concluded. The actors, who have evidently performed one of Shakespeare's plays, as they are all wearing Elizabethan costumes, are taking their bows. A subtitle reads, "Little Tokyo, Los Angeles, 1936." Parker cleverly links this scene with the previous scene in the movie theater in Brooklyn (they both depict an audience enjoying a performance); however, he also contrasts the two scenes, showcasing the cultural divide between the Americans and the Japanese Americans (the Americans were watching a movie, while the Japanese Americans were watching a play). It is unclear whether Parker intended to qualify each respective scenario (is he insinuating that Japanese Americans are more refined and educated by enjoying theater as opposed to movies?), but the disparity is clear—this film will focus on the fusion of two differing cultures.

Following the performance, Parker focuses the camera on one Japanese man in particular, whom many men and women approach to congratulate. This is Hiroshi Kawamura (played by Sab Shimono), the owner of the theater. We then cut to Lily, whom we discover is Hiroshi's daughter, being propositioned in the hallway by one of the actors. Speaking Japanese, he asks another young Japanese woman why Lily speaks English instead of Japanese. Already, Lily's Japanese American status is identified—she is a Nisei, a second-generation Japanese citizen born in the new world, as opposed to an Issei, a first-generation Japanese citizen who immigrated to the States. The actor's advances prove fruitless, as Lily denies him, telling him it is bad luck to make a pass on the stairs. To promote cultural authenticity, Parker introduces an angry Japanese man, apparently the actor's father, who sternly shouts and gesticulates at him. Honor and gentility are of extreme importance in Japanese culture, and the boy is being berated for behaving shamefully.

Mr. Kawamura then introduces his entire family to one particularly interested patron. Again we see the cultural fusion—Japanese culture synthesizing with that of America. Kawamura's son Harry is an actor who dreams of making it big in Hollywood (a very American goal); his son Charlie is only interested in baseball (the quintessential American sport); and his son Frankie cannot even speak Japanese. The cultural divide is made abundantly clear when Mr. Kawamura agrees to play cards with his friend. Lily complains, reminding her father that he promised he wouldn't play cards, to which he replies, "If I want to play cards, I play cards." Although this is not a uniquely Japanese stance to take (the old "because I said so" is a classic excuse of the American father), Kawamura's Japanese-ness shines through in the indignant embarrassment he feels. He does not want to "lose face" in front of other Japanese men, so he privately scolds Lily for openly calling his behavior into question.

Next is a brief scene in which all the girls spy on Mrs. Ogata (played by Shinko Isobe), who is married to Mr. Ogata (played by Dale Ishimoto), Mr. Kuwamara's projectionist as well as the town drunk, as she is kissing another man in a back room. We then cut to Harry Kawamura being called on stage to sing the old Sammy Cahn standard "Until the Real Thing Comes Along," in English. According to film critic Farrah Anwar, this moment is significant in that it is the apotheosis of the younger Kawamuras' "apple-pie aspirations,"[13] and that it "contrasts strongly with the austere environment of Jack's blue-collar brother committed firmly to the American dream and uneasily coming to terms with the divisions between the traditionally taciturn Issei Japanese born Kawamuras and their more exuberant Nisei second-generation."[14]

Parker augments this contrast by cutting to Jack arriving at his brother's house in Los Angeles, interrupting Harry's singing to do so. Parker then cross-cuts between Jack and his brother, Gerry (played by Colm Meaney), and the Kawamura gathering at the theater. Harry is still crooning onstage, while Mr. Ogata, obviously having found out about his wife's infidelity, is shouting at her in front of everyone. She defends herself by saying she doesn't want to spend her life married to a drunk. We then cut back to the McGurn household to find Jack and his brother in the middle of a heated socio-economic debate. Jack is clearly taking the liberal stance, claiming that it is not fair for "some guy in a suit" to take money from the working man, while Gerry is the conservative, calling Jack a communist, telling him that anyone should feel lucky just to have a job in America. Jack's character is shaded in a bit more when Gerry, in a fit of rage, says to him, "No wonder your fucking wife left you." Gerry storms out, and Jack confesses to Gerry's wife, Marge (played by Becky Ann Baker), that his wife left him because she missed Ireland, but his delivery is diffident and unconvincing. Marge says that she left because Jack ruined it for her. The exchange is vague and ambiguous, but we sense that perhaps Jack failed somehow as a husband by placing his ideals before his marriage. Jack then walks outside and rejoins Gerry, who tells Jack, "Trouble sticks to you like shit to a blanket," which paints Jack as the flawed hero— the man who is basically decent but is betrayed by some character flaw (in this case, it appears to be either Jack's temper, or his provincial dedication to the causes he champions).

We then cut to a smoky back room, in which Mr. Kawamura is sitting with Mr. Fujioka (played by Takamuro Ikeguchi), who has just agreed to absorb Kawamura's debts (to whom he owes money and why are left unexplored). There is a catch, however: Mr. Fujioka would like Kawamura's daughter Lily to marry him. Once again, we see the cultural (and generational) divide. Arranged marriages, while they may be quite commonplace for Issei men, have no place in the American landscape.

Kawamura's son Charlie then bursts in to tell him that Mr. Ogata, the alcoholic projectionist, has killed himself, after having been shamed by his wife. Again, the audience is informed of the importance of honor and stature in Japanese culture—Ogata "lost face" and was so ashamed that he did not want to live anymore. We then cut to the Kawamura household, in which all of the children busily mill about, preparing for dinner. Here, Parker nicely balances the respective components of the Issei generation with that of the Nisei. As the children excitedly discuss the suicide (in a moment that could easily have been taken out of an American sitcom), Charlie interjects that Ogata killed himself instead of his wife because of honor. This is an interesting example of an Americanized tableau fused with a Japanese cultural component. Lily also expresses her discontent with the fact that her father is forcing her to meet with Fujioka, whom she absolutely does not want to marry. Kawamura sternly informs her that she will meet with him whether she wants to or not.

We then cut to the meeting between Fujioka and Lily, at an awkwardly tense dinner table at which Fujioka's mother is present, speaking to Lily in Japanese. Fujioka asks Lily if she would prefer speaking in English, as his mother does not speak it. Once again, the cultural divide is apparent. The scene, which is mostly played for laughs, finds Fujioka, smiling wide, revealing his unsightly yellow teeth, as he tells Lily that he will give her plenty of babies.

The next shot is testament to Parker's devotion to locational (as well as period) authenticity. It is a wide-shot of the Little Tokyo street, and, as the period automobiles drive by, we see the worn, faded signs on the businesses. We then cut to the inside of Kawamura's movie theater, in which Charlie is showing Jack around the projection room—Jack apparently has taken over for the late Mr. Ogata. Charlie says that the projectors are extremely old, and therefore need to be treated like a woman. Jack asks, "With love?" to which Charlie replies, "With patience." This, again, illustrates not only the cultural divide between the Japanese and the Americans, but it invites us to align ourselves with and sympathize with Jack a bit more, as he seems to be a hopeless romantic.

While screening the Japanese film *Oshidori Utagassen* (directed by Masahiro Makino), Jack is jubilantly switching out the reels in the projector, jovially singing along with the film in Japanese, which reaffirms Jack's openness of character—he is neither xenophobic nor racist, as he longs to learn all he can about Japanese culture. His song-and-dance number continues into the lobby, where he performs a Japanese number in the style of Fred Astaire or Gene Kelly, once again augmenting the film's theme of miscegenation and the fusion of two cultures.

As Jack and Charlie walk to lunch, they pass Lily in the sewing shop—Jack is immediately smitten and asks her to join them. After sitting down at the restaurant, Charlie realizes that he did not lock the door to the theater, which he tends to immediately, leaving Jack and Lily alone. The two of them chat, and Lily informs Jack (and the viewer) of California state law at that time, which prohibited Japanese-born people from obtaining citizenship in the United States.

The two continue to flirt, and there is a genuine, credible connection between them, as the conversation is breezy and effortless—we see a romance budding. With the utmost temerity, Jack then asks Lily if he can kiss her, which, of course, he does. Jack's devotion to learning about Japanese culture is again highlighted when he raises his glass and says to Lily, "Kanpai," which is the Japanese word for "cheers."

The next shot is of Lily and her sister applying makeup in front of the mirror as Lily's sister teases her about having kissed Jack. Lily's sister warns her not to let their parents find out (especially her father), and with this scene, Parker plants the seed of the dramatic tension that will arise between Jack and Mr. Kawamura. We then cut to Lily and Jack on a date, dancing cheek to cheek as a woman sings the Louis Armstrong song "If We Never Meet Again." The two kiss again, and Jack then takes Lily back to the projection room (where Jack is now staying, as he has nowhere else to go). He pours a glass of sake for each of them, and he tells Lily about his background as a champion for the unions. His explanation as to his downfall is cryptic: "We lost sight of what we were fighting for." Lily then asks Jack about his wife, and he informs her that they simply got married too young. Jack's character is shaded in a bit more, however, when he tells Lily that his wife was pregnant but lost the baby in an accident at the shoe store at which she worked. He then adds dolefully, "I wasn't there; I was at a meeting." With this line we are given a window into Jack's failures as a husband—he is too devoted to his causes. Lily then tenderly kisses him, and we hear Mini's voice cut through the soundtrack, asking Lily (in the present) if she really kissed Jack in the chop suey restaurant.

Lily and Mini talk about Jack for a bit, and Mini then asks her mother how Mr. Kawamura reacted when he found out about Jack and Lily's romance. Parker then cuts back to "the past," to a shot of the entire Kawamura family seated at the dinner table. Mr. Kawamura explodes in a fit of rage, slamming his fists down on the table, making it abundantly clear that he does not approve of this romance. Lily looks to her mother for consolation, but the older woman avoids eye contact. Cut to a close-up of Lily, revealing her disappointment and desperation. With this exchange, which is bereft of dialogue, Parker visually amplifies the sense of helplessness that Japanese women feel at the hands of the patriarchal family institution. Lily's mother wants to intercede, but cannot.

We then cut to Kawamura's theater, in which Jack and Charlie are attempting to escort an inebriated patron out the door. Mr. Kawamura comes storming in, pointing and screaming at Jack in Japanese. Charlie informs Jack that Kawamura has just fired him and has forbidden him from ever seeing Lily again. Jack storms out, looking for Lily, who is pensively overlooking the water. Once again, Parker is able to evoke, purely visually, the quiet, dignified suffering of oppressed women as Lily's mother peeks out from behind the door, and the two of them share a pained look.

A determined Jack muscles his way into Kawamura's smoky back room. He physically wrestles with one of the guards to be granted access, furthering his depiction as a headstrong, no-nonsense man who

Left to right: Dennis Quaid (Jack McGurn/"McGann"), Elizabeth Gilliam (young Mini McGann) and Tamlyn Tomita (Lily Yuriko Kawamura/McGann). *Come See The Paradise* (1990), 20th Century–Fox.

will fight for what he wants. He then sits down with Kawamura and pleads with him to allow Lily to go out with him. Kawamura refuses Jack's requests and walks out. We then cut to Jack packing his things as Lily enters the room. The two talk for a moment, and Jack tells Lily he wants to marry her, which segues into a passionate lovemaking scene.

We then cut back to "the present" as Lily and Mini are still walking to the train station. Mini asks if she had a big wedding, and Lily informs her that it was against the law in California for a white person to marry an Asian, so they were forced to get married in Seattle. (Once again, Mini is serving not so much as a character unto herself, but the tabula rasa on which Lily's historical facts are being written.)

Lily then recounts her wedding day to Mini, and we flash back to a montage of Jack and Lily (kissing, running through puddles, drinking champagne, etc.), set to Randy Edelman's sweeping musical score. In the next scene, Jack and Lily crash a wedding reception and proceed to dance with the numerous guests. Although they are ethnically conspicuous, the couple is welcomed with open arms, which (according to Anwar) "charmingly confounds the expectations of those viewers who might have foreseen the director underlining his message with an ugly, redneck brawl."[15] In other words, this moment serves to create a balanced backdrop against which the melodrama unfolds—Parker is not content with caricatures or two-dimensional figures.

In the interest of narrative expediency, Parker offers another montage to inform us of the next year or so of Jack and Lily's marriage. After a few shots of the newlyweds kissing, Lily tells Mini that she was born on Christmas Day 1937, as Parker cuts to a shot of Jack picking up Younger Mini (played by Elizabeth Gilliam). We are then shown a series of shots of fish on assembly-line conveyor belts, informing us that Jack has procured a job at a fish cannery. His Marxist, left-wing idealism again shines through as he tells one of his co-workers that the only way to oversee a revolution is to scare the shit out of the guys in the suits, who would not care if an employee was severely injured on the job. Jack's co-worker asks him, "If you're so smart, why don't you do something about it?" Jack replies that he cannot because he promised his wife that he would abandon his reckless devotion to his ideals. Here we see the seed for possible dramatic tension being planted, as Jack is clearly still passionate in his beliefs.

A fracas then ensues, as what is ostensibly a fisherman's union is sitting in a dinghy, holding a sign that reads "Working Men Unite." The factory owners are berating the men in the boat, throwing fish at them, and a riot of sorts ensues. Jack informs the owners that the men are legally entitled to picket if they so choose. As he carries one of the wounded picketers, he screams at the owners, telling them they have no right to quell the demonstration. Again, we see that it will not be so easy for Jack to abandon his principles, as his temper is brought to the forefront.

Parker then shows us Jack and Lily's first fight. As Lily is preparing dinner in the kitchen, the two of them are shouting at each other and Lily tells Jack that she vehemently disapproves of his getting involved in any more labor organizing demonstrations. Jack defends himself, saying, "I agreed to hand out a bundle of leaflets on a street corner and you act as if I'm going out to kill someone." According to Prof. Ono, this moment in the film speaks volumes. He states:

> We learn from this that Jack sees himself as willing to stand up against oppression in a way in which Lily cannot, that his sense of being American that requires standing up boldly against

oppression differs from hers, and thus that he is in a better position to challenge the incarceration of Japanese Americans.[16]

Lily's reservations about Jack's getting involved with labor activities are justified with the next scene, which depicts a violent, chaotic demonstration, replete with screaming picketers and policemen on horseback. Jack thrusts himself into the fray and is kicked by a horse, then hauled off by two police officers. Parker then cross-cuts between Jack, now with a cast on his broken right hand, and Lily, sitting somberly at the dinner table by herself, to signify the growing distance between them. We then cut to a shot of Lily holding Mini at a bus station, and on the soundtrack, we hear Lily telling Mini (in the "present") that she is still unsure why she left Jack—she just knew she had to see her parents again. At this point, the viewer is now preparing for the potentially tumultuous reunion of the Kawamuras and their prodigal daughter.

Next is a scene in which Jack is being interrogated by a police officer in regards to his past as a labor organizer, which he denies. The police officer then informs Jack that the Japanese have just bombed Pearl Harbor and that the U.S. is now at war. Parker then settles on a close-up of Jack as he absorbs this information. (Dennis Quaid's performance is a nuanced portrait of abject fear—Jack does not know what this information means in terms of his country or his marriage.)

We then cut to Lily and Mini arriving at her parents' house. She is greeted warmly by her brothers and sisters, but is unsettled by the sight of two strange men walking around the house. Harry tells her that they are FBI agents who arrested their father as a "possibly dangerous alien." Lily then walks into her mother's room, where she is sitting completely still in front of a lit candle. The scene also has a sort of "calm-before-the-storm" feel to it— the Kawamuras' suffering has only just begun.

Next a tearful, heart-wrenching exchange, in which Lily tells her mother that she loves her and she knows why she did not respond to any of her letters. Although Lily becomes more and more insistent, her mother remains stoic and silent, until Mini walks into the room. Lily's mother sees Mini, and immediately her obdurate exterior melts into loving affection. This moment augments Ono's assertion that Mini does not have any agency, and is merely a function in the film. He states, "It is not because of anything Mini does, says, or thinks, in particular, but because of Mini's presence alone, her very existence, that generational wounds heal."[17]

We then cut to the docks at Terminal Island, where Harry and Charlie reunite with Lily after having seen their father. Evidently, Mr. Kawamura is to be detained on Terminal Island for a day or two, and then shipped off to North Dakota. He is under suspicion because of his ties with the theater companies from Japan, and he is therefore considered a security threat. The gravity of the situation becomes apparent when Charlie tells Lily that the entire family will eventually be shipped off to an internment camp.

Back at the sewing shop in which Jack and Lily first met, she is sitting alone; suddenly, she hears the door open. Before she can inform the intruder that they are closed, she sees that it is Jack: he has come back for her. He asks her where Mr. Matsui is, and Lily tells him that he was arrested. When Jack asks why, Lily replies, "Because he's Japanese." This blunt, succinct statement brings to the forefront the blatant racism and xenophobia which surrounded the Japanese internment. Jack apologizes to Lily, and the two share a romantic kiss. We then cut to the two of them engaging in pillow talk after having made love, and Jack confesses his undying love for her, pledging that nothing will ever separate them again.

We then cut to a scene at a department store where Jack is standing in line with Mini, waiting for her to sit on Santa's lap. When it is finally Mini's turn, the bigoted Santa tells Jack that he does not want a Jap on his lap. Jack's volatility is highlighted when he threatens Santa, telling him that if he does not let Mini sit on his lap, he's going to "shove that fucking beard down your fucking throat."

On the one hand, this scene serves to showcase the xenophobia which swept the nation following the attack on Pearl Harbor, with a seemingly benign figure like Santa Claus representing the reactionary, racist nationalists. Ultimately, however, this scene, according to Ono, uses Mini as the device to shade in Jack's character. He states:

> While initially we might have understood the scene to be about Mini, eventually we come to understand that Mini is simply the reason for the confrontation. She helps us learn more about Jack's politics, his persistent and everyday struggles against oppression.[18]

After Jack and Mini are escorted out of the store, we cut to a Norman Rockwellesque tableau, featuring the Kawamuras, along with Jack and Mini, seated at the dining table, enjoying the Christmas festivities. After singing "Until The Real Thing Comes Along" yet again, Harry urges Jack to sing. Jack then launches into a somber song, which he sings in Japanese, and the entire mood changes. Whereas the tone of the scene was heretofore one of merriment and laughter, Jack's singing in Japanese almost serves as a portent, reminding these Japanese American citizens of their plight, and everyone absorbs the song pensively.

Over a montage of street violence (men breaking storefront windows, vandalizing businesses, knocking over merchandise, etc.), Lily tells Mini that those were particularly hard times for the Japanese, saying that people looked at them differently: they were no longer Americans—they were the enemy. Lily then tells Mini about Executive Order 9066, the Roosevelt-sanctioned order which authorized the internment camps. (Yet again, Mini is the proxy for the viewer.)

Next is a particularly effective scene, in which Japanese children are singing "Twinkle, Twinkle, Little Star" with their teacher in a classroom. The parents of the children silently enter the room, and the music stops. Mini turns around and looks at Lily gravely. The moment is infused with a raw power, insinuating that the gravity of the internment camps can no longer be escaped. The sense of the inexorable march of the internment is highlighted in the next shot, which is a close-up of a sign reading "Evacuation Sale"—their deportation is now a reality. A horde of white people are then seen rummaging through the Kawamuras' belongings, and inside the house, Harry says that they can only take with them what they can carry. The scene depicting the Kawamuras packing up their things is morose, somber. It is quietly haunting, not sentimentalized by dramatic music or histrionics—it is an elegiac, funereal scene which captures the sense of loss and upheaval.

The heart-wrenching impact of the Kawamuras' loss culminates in a scene in which Lily tells her brothers and sisters to break all of their records, since no one in America will want Japanese records. The family then cathartically smashes all of their records, highlighting the fact that there is anger boiling beneath the Kawamuras' quiet suffering.

Next is the disturbing sequence which depicts the actual deportation. Parker shows us shots of a slew of uprooted Japanese American citizens, walking down staircases, marching to the train station to be exiled. It is an emotionally powerful scene, as Jack kisses his family goodbye. The melodrama is heightened when Lily says that she has no idea where they are being taken, to which Jack replies, "I'll find you." This line augments the undying love that exists between the two—*nothing* is going to keep them apart. As the train pulls away from the station, Michael Seresin's smoky, de-saturated cinematography is highlighted, which gives the scene a historical, quasi-documentary feel.

After the train pulls away, we cut to Jack, walking through the empty Kawamura house, absorbing the sense of loss and abandonment. He is disrupted by a commotion coming from the backyard, and he finds that it is a band of hooligans, trashing the Kawamura's property. Again, the sense of vitriolic xenophobia and racial hatred is illustrated.

We then cut to the Kawamuras arriving at the internment camp. We are shown the dehumanizing check-in process, as they are all corralled like cattle into lines. Charlie is told by one of the guards that he is not allowed to take his camera with him. Parker then delves, with brutal honesty, into the squalid living conditions at the racetrack, which is where the Kawamuras are forced to stay temporarily. We see the dirty, cramped living space that the entire family is forced to inhabit, and the unsanitary nature of their surroundings. Lily (in voice-over) tells Older Mini that they were only quarantined at the racetrack for a brief time, before being shipped off into the middle of the desert.

Parker then displays his penchant for depicting angry, oppressed people rising up against their captors by presenting a riotous demonstration. A group of the Japanese internees are marching at night, waving the Japanese flag, and uniformed American soldiers are keeping them in line. In this regard, Parker is endowing the Japanese Americans with more agency than he granted the African American community in *Mississippi Burning*. He at least depicts the Japanese as having the fortitude to protest.

During this protest, a truck pulls into the camp, with Jack, wearing an army uniform, in tow. He disembarks the truck, and we are to believe that he is on his way to see his family. Lily's voice-over informs Older Mini that, after two days, the camp was opened, which allowed Jack to visit them for the first time in seven months. In the heartwarming scene that follows, Jack kisses Lily and lovingly scoops up Mini in his arms.

While the couple is sharing an intimate moment alone, Lily tells Jack that her father's health is failing. Apparently, Mr. Kawamura has been accused of giving out information to the FBI (the McCarthy-era equivalent of "naming names") and Charlie, his son, believes the allegations, leaving the two men in a standoff; Charlie is seated in the hospital next to his father, neither one of them talking. Once again, we are given a window into Japanese culture. Mr. Kawamura has been shamed ("lost face") and cannot face his son.

Lily then tells Jack that she has a job in the camps, making camouflage nets. She says that she either makes five nets a day, or works eight hours, all for fourteen dollars a month. In the interest of historical accuracy (and of presenting a balanced narrative), Parker does not depict the internment camps as savage, brutal, villainous places, fraught with torture and mistreatment. Unlike *Midnight Express*, *Come See the Paradise* is a melodramatic romance, and the separation of Jack from his true love is at the dramatic core of the narrative, which allows Parker to focus on the heart-wrenching nature of the separation itself. He is not, however, exonerating the perpetrators of the internment. It is still an odious, despicable blemish on America's record.

Jack must say goodbye to his family yet again, as he hops back on a truck and leaves the camp. In a wide-shot, we see Lily and Mini walk away from Jack. As the gates close, we see barbed wire stretching across the frame, separating us from Lily and Mini, which visually reaffirms the concept of oppression and containment.

Parker then gives us an accelerated montage to depict the passage of time (as well as Mr. Kawamura's descent into the deep, dark recesses of depression). With the camera in a fixed position, we see Mr. Kawamura working diligently, building a chair for himself. Lily's voice-over informs us that he slowly devolved into a resigned depression, so disappointed was he with America. He so yearned to make a fortune in the States and return to Japan a rich man, but his current situation has caused him to lose faith in the "land of the free."

We then cut to Lily and her sisters at work. Again, Parker visually reaffirms the sense of containment and isolation by placing them behind a netted fence. Lily is reading a decree aloud which asks the Japanese internees to volunteer for the armed forces. A man then approaches them and tells Lily that her mother is not allowed to work as she is a Japanese national—it's the law. Lily angrily responds that the law is flawed if it allows innocent citizens to be interned without having been convicted of a crime. We see that Jack's temperament may be rubbing off on her as she screams at the man, "Camp! You call this a camp!? This is a goddamn outdoor jail!" The anger that perennially crops up in Parker's work shines through in this scene, and we see that the internment is taking its toll on the Japanese. They are no longer going to stoically, silently accept their imprisonment. They (unlike the African American community in *Mississippi Burning*) have the agency and the anger to fight back and express their discontent.

The next scene finds the Kawamura family deliberating over a waiver they are essentially being forced to sign which will forever pledge their allegiance to the United States, thereby forswearing the Japanese emperor. They are caught in a conundrum—it is illegal for Issei to become American citizens, anyway, so if they say "yes," they will be *personae non grata*. If they say "no," they will most likely be in the internment camps forever. Charlie drives home the gravity of the internment when he says, "We stopped being Americans the minute they put up the barbed wire." He staunchly refuses to sign the waiver, while Harry agrees to, effectively agreeing to join the army and fight in the war.

Parker cuts yet again to a shot of the camp seen through the obstruction of barbed wire piercing horizontally across the frame. We then cut to Jack, once again visiting his family in the camp. He does not even recognize his own daughter, which suggests that it has been quite some time since he has seen them. After hearing that Mr. Kawamura has taken ill, the family visits him in the hospital. The Kawamuras leave Jack alone with Mr. Kawamura, and Jack tells him that he is not on leave. Rather, he ran away from the army. Apparently, his hubris allowed him to think that he could somehow help, that he could somehow free his family from their shackles. He confesses, however, that he now realizes his powerlessness. Kawamura tells him, "Just love Lily. That's enough." Once again, the melodrama and love story supersede the socio-political ramifications of the internment camps.

Jack kisses his family goodbye yet again, and we cut to him meeting with one of his superior officers, who is questioning his loyalties. The zeitgeist of the time is made clear when the officer tells Jack that he is either pro-Japanese or pro-American—there is no in-between. The officer then asks Jack if he thinks the camps are wrong, and Jack emphatically responds that he does. Although Jack's agency has waned a bit in the story's second half, this scene illustrates that he has by no means reneged on his ideals; he still feels passionately about oppression and tyranny. Perhaps to give the narrative a more balanced perspective, Parker strays from the common trope of depicting the superior officer as a blind reactionary who encompasses "the ultimate military mindset." The officer says that he, too, thinks the camps are wrong, likening them to "burning down Chicago to get rid of the gangsters." Another man then enters and asks Jack (who is now spelling his last name "McGann") if he ever spelled his name "McGurn." The man recognizes Jack, and knows that he is the same troublemaker he remembered from Brooklyn.

To depict the death of Mr. Kawamura, Parker implements a haunting, dreamlike sequence. On the soundtrack, we hear Mr. Kawamura unintelligibly humming; the visual is a sumptuous, golden-hued shot of him walking alone out in the open expanse of the camp, entering the abyss of death. Parker cross-cuts the shots of Kawamura walking with those of his family, gathered around what is ostensibly his grave, in a dusty, arid cemetery outside the camp. The shots of the cemetery are again obscured by looming barbed wire. The sequence is an interesting, hallucinatory depiction of a lonely man's journey into death, a journey he takes willingly and with dignity, reaffirming the Japanese devotion to honor.

We then cut to a somber scene in which the Kawamura women are commiserating, grieving over the loss of Mr. Kawamura as Mrs. Kawamura sorts through a box of his things. Mrs. Kawamura then succinctly states Kawamura's rationale for wanting to die when she says, "Sometimes, it's better to die than to give up on life."

The next shot is of Lily saying goodbye to her sister Dulcie (played by Akemi Nishino), who is being taken to Idaho. We then cut to Charlie playing stickball, as Lily's voice-over informs us that he is being taken away to another camp with all the other people who refused to sign their allegiance over to the United States. Parker again showcases his aptitude with raw, powerful emotion in the touching moment in which Charlie says goodbye to his little brother Frankie. As they hug, and Charlie walks away, Parker stays on Frankie, and we see a tear run down his cheek. Parker is again able to drive home the anguish and turmoil of the internment camps without the use of dialogue.

In the next sequence, Parker proves that, although this film is steeped in extremely grave subject matter, he still possesses an eye for humor. We first cut to Dulcie, throwing up in the girls' room. Lily's voice-over says that Dulcie is pregnant, much to the chagrin of their mother. The next shot, which is played for laughs, follows Mrs. Kawamura as she chases Dulcie through the camp with a broom. After witnessing the abject suffering of the Kawamuras, this moment of levity is extremely welcome.

We then cut to the Kawamuras rejoicing with their entire camp as they have just been informed that the internment camps have been declared unconstitutional, and they can all go home. Tragedy still looms over the family, however, as we cut to an elegiac scene in which they are informed that Harry, who volunteered for the army, has been killed. The family commemorates him by singing "Until the Real Thing Comes Along," while Mini eats her birthday cake. Lily then walks away with tears in her eyes, as she recounts the fate of Charlie, who has decided to repatriate to Japan. She is extremely worried for him, as he has never been to Japan and does not even speak Japanese. Parker cross-cuts Lily's pained face with a close-up of Charlie, facing the challenge that awaits him with fortitude and temerity. The strength of this entire family could almost be summed up in this one powerful shot.

Harry's rendition of "Until the Real Thing Comes Along" plays on the soundtrack as the Kawamuras pack their things and leave the internment camp. Parker is sure to linger on one haunting shot of Mr. Kawamura's chair, empty and covered in snow.

Lily informs us, via voice-over, that the Kawamuras did not have a house to return to after the internment camp, so they stayed with their mother's cousin on a strawberry farm. After a brief shot of the women hanging laundry on a clothesline, Parker cuts to a shot which possesses a striking austerity. It is a shot of all the Kawamura women, Mini included, sitting around the kitchen table, all of them sitting in complete silence, as if they are absorbing something with intense gravity. Parker then cuts back to Lily and Older Mini, and Lily, now crying, tells Mini that a big bomb (an atomic bomb) was dropped on Hiroshima. Tamlyn Tomita's performance in this scene is breathtaking, as she whispers to Mini, "In nine tiny seconds, 200,000 people were killed." Not only is the audience reminded of the gravity and historical significance of the Hiroshima bombing, but we suspect that, due to Lily's level of duress, perhaps Jack was killed in the bombing. We soon realize, however, that this is not the case, that Lily is simply carrying the weight of the war on her shoulders, and, for a moment, we carry it with her. Lily's monologue subtly and quietly punches the audience with the harsh ramifications of not only World War II, but with the Americans' questionable behavior during the war.

The train pulls into the station, and Lily and Mini excitedly run out to greet it. After frantically scanning the passengers, Lily finally finds her husband, and as Randy Edelman's operatic score kicks in, the McGann family is united once again, walking off into the sunset together.

11

The Commitments (1991)

August 14; 118 minutes/Color
Production Company: 20th Century–Fox
Director: Alan Parker
Screenwriters: Dick Clement, Ian La Frenais, Roddy Doyle (based on his novel)
Producers: Lynda Myles, Roger Randall-Cutler
Production Designer: Brian Morris
Cinematography: Gale Tattersall
Editor: Gerry Hambling
Original Music: Wilson Pickett
Cast: Robert Arkins (Jimmy Rabbitte); Michael Aherne (Steven Clifford); Angeline Ball (Imelda Quirke); Maria Doyle (Natalie Murphy); Dave Finnegan (Mickah Wallace); Bronagh Gallagher (Bernie McGloughlin); Félim Gormley (Dean Fay); Glen Hansard (Outspan Foster); Dick Massey (Billy Mooney); Johnny Murphy (Joey "The Lips" Fagan); Ken McCluskey (Derek Scully); Andrew Strong (Deco Cuffe); Colm Meaney (Jimmy Rabbitte, Sr.)

> The Irish are the blacks of Europe, and Dubliners are the blacks of Ireland. And the northside Dubliners are the blacks of Dublin. Say it lads: "I'm black and I'm proud."—Jimmy Rabbitte to his band in *The Commitments*

> I have not had a more enjoyable time making a film, and I couldn't wait to wake up in the mornings to go to work.—Alan Parker, *The Making of* The Commitments, pg. 132

Notes on the Production

Sometime in 1989, Dick Clement and Ian La Frenais were commissioned to write a screenplay version of Roddy Doyle's novella *The Commitments*, which told the story of working-class Irish blokes who sought to start a soul band. According to producer Lynda Myles, Doyle staunchly sought to adapt the screenplay himself, as he did not want to simply sign away the rights. Not being a seasoned screenwriter himself, however, Doyle's initial script needed some "beefing up," which La Frenais and Clement provided. Doyle was not at all threatened about the prospect of professional screenwriters fortifying his screenplay. He states, "I'm not precious about my material. I recognize the difference between something that works on paper and something that works on screen. As long as the spirit of the piece is retained, that's all right with me."[1]

After having been introduced to the novella by Clement and La Frenais, Parker immediately showed interest in the project, stating, "Roddy Doyle wrote this tiny little novel.

Every single page I laughed out loud."² Although he clearly found the read humorous, Parker had more personal reasons for wanting to make the film:

> I wanted to do this film because I identified with these kids, I suppose. They come from the north of Dublin—a very working class area. And I come from the North of London—also a very working class area ... in the end, it's about young kids who use music to get out of the world that they're in, in order to give them something else—a hope, a dream, and that's pretty relevant wherever you are in the world, I think.³

By June of 1990, Parker arrived in Dublin to begin preparations for the film, and he thrust himself right into the auditions process in an attempt to cast musicians who could also act. The casting directors, Ros and John Hubbard, scoured the Dublin clubs looking for likely candidates, and Parker ceaselessly listened to sixty-four bands, playing everything from heavy metal to hip hop. He states, "They say there are twelve hundred bands playing in Dublin at any one time, so I tried to see them all. I must have seen and read with over a hundred bands, just to make sure no stone was left unturned."⁴ In order to expand the process a bit, Parker and crew organized an open casting call at the Dublin Mansion House (town hall), where anyone and everyone who wanted to be a part of the film was invited.

Left to right: Lead actor Robert Arkins (as band manager Jimmy Rabbitte) watches director Alan Parker working with actors Ken McCluskey and Glen Hansard on the set of *The Commitments* (1991), 20th Century–Fox.

Parker, in keeping with his ethos, wanted to maintain an authenticity and a "gritty truth" to the story, so he did not want to cheat any of the instruments or singing in an attempt to do the music live.[5] Parker recalls when Andrew Strong (who would be cast as Deco Cuffe) came in to audition. He says that Strong's voice "was exactly as Roddy had described it in the book: 'a real deep growl that scraped against the tongue and throat on the way out.'"[6]

After sorting through the thirty hours of casting tapes, Parker whittled his one hundred possible "Commitments" down to the twelve final "Commitments," ten of whom were musicians and two of whom had previous acting experience. The casting of Dave Finnegan, who would go on to play the belligerent, hot-tempered drummer Mickah Wallace, was, according to Parker, quite interesting. Parker called Finnegan into the room, asked him to sit down, and the two of them talked civilly and humanely for a moment. Seemingly inexplicably, the exchange grew more and more heated, and before long, Parker and Finnegan were violently and heatedly hurling profane, excoriating insults at each other, threatening each other with increasingly graphic and disturbing acts of violence. Parker cast Finnegan immediately, claiming that he simply wanted to test the limits of Finnegan's aggression and pugnaciousness, as he wanted the truculence of the character to be convincing.[7]

Initially, for the role of Joey the Lips, the world-weary, seasoned veteran character, Parker, along with La Frenais, thought the part might be best given to an actual rock 'n' roll veteran musician. Parker then set up a meeting with Van Morrison and recalls giving him an inordinate number of sandwiches. The meeting did not go well, and, according to Clement and La Frenais, Morrison contentiously asked Parker, "Why don't you want to use my music?"[8]

Needless to say, Van Morrison was not cast as Joey the Lips, the honor going instead to Johnny Murphy, who seemed to grasp the essence of not only the entire film, but of the character. Of the latter, he states, "He's in a time warp and he doesn't want to leave. He loves the '60s. He's like a Peter Pan."[9]

For five weeks, Parker held dramatic rehearsals in the mornings and music rehearsals in the afternoons to hone everyone's chops. He claims that, by the time they were ready to film, the cast could perform all the songs and they could run through the whole script, from beginning to end, in one stretch.[10]

Filming began on August 27. Roddy Doyle had set his story in the fictional "Barrytown," which, as was obvious to Parker, was based on Kilbarrack, the working-class estate on the northside of Dublin, where Doyle had worked as a school teacher. To capture Dublin authentically, Parker and production designer Brian Morris gradually put together a patchwork of streets and buildings in and around Dublin, as they could not find one monolithic location with everything they were looking for.

The shoot took fifty-three days to complete in forty-four different locations around Dublin. According to Parker, "I have not had a more enjoyable time making a film and couldn't wait to wake up in the mornings to go to work."[11] It is perhaps for this reason, that the film shoot went so smoothly, that Parker did not keep an extensive journal while filming, claiming, simply, that all fifty-three days went swimmingly well and all was a success.

The film went on to win BAFTAs for best film, script, and director. All the cast members have gone on to varying degrees of success, including Andrea Corr (who plays Jimmy's sister, Sharon), who went on to form the Corrs, with her brother and two sisters. Also,

Glen Hansard (who played Outspan) went on to form the band the Frames, starring in (and writing the Academy-Award–winning best song for) the film *Once*.

Summary

While the opening credits appear over a black screen, the up-tempo Roy Head soul song "Treat Her Right" plays on the soundtrack. It is an energetic, jubilant song which immediately signals the audience, inviting them to anticipate the joyfully raucous, high-energy tone of the film. After Alan Parker's credit is displayed, the film fades from black into its opening shot, which depicts a crowded, working-class Dublin street during some kind of open-air market, replete with players performing traditional Irish music, vendors selling produce, and traders prying open horses' mouths to examine their teeth. Right in the opening shot, Parker features two horses, which, according to film critic Don Kunz, goes on to become a visual motif throughout the film. Kunz states:

> Throughout his film adaptation, Parker has developed a horse metaphor to express the hopelessness of the Irish rising above the myriad of forces arrayed against them. Horses, which are so much a part of Irish life, are often included in the mise en scène.[12]

Into the bustling open-air market walks Jimmy Rabbitte (played by Robert Arkins). As Jimmy (unsuccessfully) approaches some of the street vendors with T-shirts and other musical paraphernalia which he is ostensibly attempting to solicit, a narrator's voice comes in on the soundtrack, saying, "Tell us about the early days, Jimmy. How did it all begin?" Jimmy's voice-over replies, "Well, Terry, I was always in the music business, but I was more on the sales side in those days." This disembodied interview/conversation appears as if from nowhere, and the audience is unsure whether Jimmy is conducting a phony interview in his head, which most anyone who has ever entertained visions of fame and stardom has done. As he is turned down by vendor after vendor, Parker's devotion to locational authenticity permeates the *mise-en-scène*, and the fair has a strong working-class feel to it. Showcasing once again his affinity for performers, Parker takes time to give us a shot of a street performer doing an acoustic version of the Everly Brothers' "Cathy's Clown." Although the performer (and the song itself) will not have much narrative agency, Parker is setting up his universe of impassioned performers basking in their affinity for music.

Parker cuts from the street market to a wedding reception, at which a ridiculous wedding band is performing the song "Dearest Darling," taking themselves far too seriously as everyone dances. This moment is mostly played for laughs, as the audience cannot help but mock the band, especially the keyboard player, who is gyrating and undulating in an absurdly sexual way. With this scene, Parker makes it clear that this film will not be bereft of humor.

We cut away from the wedding reception to show Jimmy boarding a train as "Destination Anywhere" plays on the soundtrack. Jimmy is approached by numerous people on the train, all of whom want to buy something from him, which establishes Jimmy as a low-rate dealer of street goods (in a wry wink to the audience, one of the items which Jimmy gives to one of his patrons is a tape of *Mississippi Burning*). Parker intersperses the shots of Jimmy and his patrons with exterior shots of the working-class section of Dublin as the train passes by, once again showcasing Parker's affinity for locational authenticity.

We then cut back to the wedding as Jimmy enters. As he walks into the reception hall, Parker implements a subtle moment which is funny, but which also reaffirms Jimmy's lower-class status. As he enters the room, he sees a glass of half-drunk beer sitting on the shelf, ostensibly someone else's unfinished beer, which Jimmy proceeds to drink. Jimmy then notices the overwrought performance style of the wedding band, and joins in with the audience in mocking them. The singer/keyboard player informs the crowd that they will be taking a short break, but to "stay in the groove," a ridiculous comment at which Jimmy comically snickers. He then approaches a beautiful blonde woman, Imelda Quirke (played by Angeline Ball). Jimmy jokes that it will be Imelda who will get married next, and Imelda replies, "Why me? I'm not bleedin' pregnant." Again, although this line is funny, it reaffirms the socio-economic status of this particular section of Dublin.

Before panning over to the table at which Jimmy and the wedding band are singing, Parker fills the frame with a priest who voraciously grabs a pint of Guinness and walks away with it. This image elicits a chuckle, but it also sets up another of Parker's motifs, which Kunz, again, articulates. He states, "Organized religion is a presence in the Irish life depicted in this film, but not one whose moral authority is taken very seriously."[13] In this film, the utilization of music to transcend sectarian strife supplants the importance of organized religion.

At the table, Jimmy is talking with the wedding band, sans the singer/keyboard player Ray. Jimmy is thinking of managing the band, but he sees numerous changes that would have to be made first. When he asks what the name of the band is, one of the men replies, "And And And," claiming that Ray wants to put an exclamation point after the second "And." Jimmy is enraptured by a drunken man, singing boisterously onstage. This is our introduction to the erratic, boorish character of Deco Cuffe (played by Andrew Strong). Although the man eventually falls off the stage, and no interaction takes place, the audience knows that something will come of this "meeting."

Jimmy and the two band mates, Outspan Foster (played by Glen Hansard) and Derek Scully (played by Ken McCluskey) then watch Imelda from a distance as she argues with her boyfriend. They all gaze at her lustfully, wondering what she sees in her boyfriend, whom they refer to as a prick. Jimmy replies, "He's a prick with a job." Once again, the plight of working-class Dubliners is addressed, and Parker does not allow the comedy element to overshadow the reality of their working-class struggles.

We then cut to Jimmy, Outspan, and Derek walking down a dark alley at night, discussing different avenues for their band. Parker's use of *mise-en-scène* highlights the darkness of the city streets, and as they walk, a chain-link fence looms over them on screen right, which, according to Kunz, is another visual motif Parker implements throughout the film. He states, "Chain link and wooden fences are often foregrounded to suggest how trapped the Irish are by unemployment, poverty, and ill-temper."[14]

By the end of their conversation, Jimmy convinces the boys that they need to sing about where they are from and incorporate sex into the lyrics. When the boys ask what kind of music allows for such a synthesis, Jimmy replies, "Soul. We're gonna play Dublin soul."

Parker then cuts to a shot which introduces yet another visual motif as identified by Don Kunz, which is a shot of a dog standing atop a dumpster, ferociously barking and growling. According to Kunz:

Parker's camera shows dogs everywhere—on leashes, muzzled, behind fences, even pacing on top of tin-roofed sheds and abandoned automobiles. Dogs growling, snarling, and barking become a visual and aural motif conveying the Irish struggle for territory and prerogative, degenerated into inarticulate brutality.[15]

While a soulful rendition of "I Can't Stand the Rain" plays on the soundtrack, Parker's camera takes us through the squalid, dreary streets of working-class Dublin, and Gale Tattersall's bleak cinematography augments the dreariness as children boisterously ride through tattered, filthy streets. We then cut to another humorous exchange, this one between a young boy responding to the ad that Jimmy placed in the paper. When he knocks on the door, Jimmy Sr. (played by Colm Meaney) answers the door and is confounded by the boy's intentions, culminating in Jimmy Sr., telling the boy to fuck off. He then walks back into his house, and Jimmy informs his family that he's starting a soul band. Jimmy's father, whose appearance strongly suggests that he idolizes Elvis, with the greaser hairdo and long sideburns, asks if he needs a singer, and proceeds to sing the Elvis Presley song "Fools Rush In." When Jimmy says that Elvis was not soul, Jimmy Sr., replies, "Elvis was God," again implementing the motif of religion being used mockingly.

Next is a comedic montage of Jimmy slamming the door in the faces of the numerous applicants who are all interested in joining his band. He asks each of the applicants who their influences are, and he hears a number of hilarious replies, from Barry Manilow to Wings, and one applicant does not need to verbalize who his influence is, as he is garishly dressed like Boy George from "Culture Club." We then cut to Jimmy actually witnessing applicants auditioning for him in his house, playing everything from violin, to Dylanesque folk, to hard rock, and the scene almost becomes a parody of the audition segment from *Fame*, culminating in a humorous shot in which Jimmy Sr., cannot even walk through his own house, as it is crowded with would-be performers. The comedy is delivered at a rapid-fire pace as one lad comes to the door, and when Jimmy asks him what instrument he plays, he confesses that he does not play one—he came to the door because he saw everyone else lined up and assumed Jimmy was selling drugs.

Parker then cuts back to a dreary, drab exterior shot, replete with dirty laundry airing in the wind. Against this background Jimmy introduces Outspan and Derek to a saxophone player, Dean Fay (played by Fèlim Gormley). Jimmy Sr., walks by and Outspan mocks him by asking if he is still wearing his blue suede shoes (an overt reference to an Elvis song). Once again, although organized religion is an extremely prevalent component of Irish culture, in Parker's universe, religious icons have been replaced by musicians.

We then cut to Jimmy giving himself a phony interview in the bathtub, using the showerhead as a microphone. His sister knocks on the door and tells him that another applicant is waiting outside to audition. Jimmy, still in his shower cap, goes to the window, and yells down to the applicant, a young boy with a skateboard, and asks him to sing. The boy asks if he can come inside to sing, and Jimmy denies his request, leaving the boy to skate away, dejected. This moment is indicative of one of Parker's perennial themes in his films which deal with performance; it is also a way in which, according to film critic Dervila Layden, Parker's film pushes the boundaries of the conventional Hollywood product. Layden states, "Viewing *The Commitments* as a musical allows us to consider the ways in which it pushes the Hollywood boundaries—dispensing with the central couple, emphasizing the hard work required, foregrounding the distinct lack of talent evident in some of the band members, and even allowing the band to fail."[16] Show business is not all champagne, contracts, and parties, and Parker is devoted to the idea of showcasing the arduous journey performers must go through.

We then cut to a bar, in which Jimmy and his new band mates (Outspan, Derek, and Dean) are interviewing a drummer, Billy Mooney (played by Dick Massey). In walks Imelda, and all the men ogle her lustfully. We then cut to a strikingly photographed shot of Jimmy walking alone down a dark, mysterious street at night. Tattersall's noirish lighting highlights the shot's atmospheric quality, and this shot incorporates yet another visual motif pointed out by Kunz. He states, "[Parker's] *mise-en-scène* is dominated by the dark ends of streets which become a visual metaphor for terrorism."[17] As previously stated, Kunz views the entire film as an allegory for the Irish working class using music to transcend their oppression, another perennial Parker theme, and in this shot, we see "Jimmy emerging from the darkness of the street into lighted space as if he were the featured soloist making a grand stage entrance."[18] Jimmy then approaches Bernie McGloughlin (played by Bronagh Gallagher), a late-night food vendor, and he asks her if she'll consider singing in his band. He says he remembers her voice from the school choir, once again amplifying the theme of music supplanting actual, organized religion. He asks her to ask Imelda Quirke if she would be interested as well.

We then cut to another striking, dismal shot of Jimmy walking alone, this time into a car wash. He finds Deco Cuffe eating alone and tells him that he wants him to sing in his band, after hearing him sing at the Quirke wedding. Deco claims that he was drunk, and in a hilarious exchange, after Jimmy tells Deco that he indeed sang at the wedding, Deco responds, "Nobody told me."

In the next shot, Parker reintroduces the image of dogs to represent the angry, working-class desire to break free from the shackles of poverty as a woman walks her rambunctious dogs past a music store, in which the drummer they had previously interviewed at the bar plays a drum kit in the store, much to the chagrin of the annoyed store owner.

We then cut to the band watching footage of James Brown performing, and Jimmy says that it is not so much what Brown sings, but how he sings it—the showmanship. In a humorous display of ignorance, Dean thinks that James Brown injured himself with one of his stage moves, because his cohorts had to help escort him off the stage (which, of course, was James Brown's signature exit—walking offstage after having been cloaked in a cape). Jimmy then succinctly sums up the entire ethos of the band and that which their soul band is to represent. When Dean says they might be "too white" to play soul, Jimmy says, "The Irish are the blacks of Europe, and Dubliners are the blacks of Ireland. And the northside Dubliners are the blacks of Dublin." With this one admittedly funny summation, Jimmy is encapsulating all of the working-class struggle against oppression with which Parker infuses the film. Parker is drawing a parallel between working-class Irish youths with the forebears of rock 'n' roll and soul, depicting them both as oppressed, struggling minorities who need to rise up and break free of their socio-economic shackles.

In the book, Jimmy's comparing the Irish to the "blacks of Europe" is much more incendiary. The line in the book is "The Irish are the niggers of Europe." Roddy Doyle, wanting to preserve and translate as much of the spirit of his novel to the screen as possible, at first insisted that Parker keep the line in the film as it is in the book. However, Parker said to Doyle: "It's 1990; you'll never get away with a white character saying that word."

Doyle eventually agreed that the line would simply be too caustic and controversial, and acquiesced to Parker's request to change the line.[19]

In the next shot, Jimmy is at home, ironing his clothes, and Parker deliberately fills the frame with two paintings—one of the Pope and the other of Elvis, again reaffirming the transition of power within the film from organized religion to music. Jimmy then walks outside and meets a trumpet player named Joey "The Lips" Fagan (played by Johnny Murphy). Jimmy is intrigued when Joey, an older man, about the same age as his father, claims to have played with all of Jimmy's soul idols: Otis Redding, Sam Cooke, BB King, et al. According to Kunz, "Parker works hard to make Joey 'The Lips' Fagan an unlikely prophet who has returned from America to preach the good news of soul music to the Irish."[20] Much like Jake and Elwood from *The Blues Brothers*, who claim to be "on a mission from God," Joey claims that the Lord sent him to Jimmy. We then cut to Joey playing trumpet for the rest of the band. They are all impressed, save for the boorish Deco, who claims he did not join the band "to be playing 'Moon Fucking River.'" The seeds of internal dissent within the band have been planted, and we can see that the dynamic of the fellas is rife with opportunity for bickering. When Joey tells the lads that the Lord sent him to them, he makes clear the allegory Parker is implementing, linking musical unity with the unrequited unity of the fractious state of Ireland. He says that a reverend told him that "the Irish brothers wouldn't be shooting the arses off each other if they had soul." With this one statement, Parker makes clear his intention of using the band to synecdochically represent Ireland—their struggles are Ireland's struggles, their desire to cease fighting and unite reflects Ireland's desire to do so, etc.

We then cut to Jimmy and Outspan in the kitchen, having a debate over "the direction of the band." We then cut to a sexy shot of the legs of Imelda, Bernie, and Natalie Murphy (played by Maria Doyle) who are meeting with the band. Parker's camera lingers on the shot of Imelda scoping out her leg, but not in a lecherous way; as Layden puts it, "[*The Commitments*] pushed at the boundaries of Irish film in depicting working class Dublin and showing women as sexually liberated."[21] Imelda, Bernie, and Natalie are independent, sexually free women, and Parker subtly presents this with both the actresses' performances (they are all comfortable in their own skin), and with his camera placement, which asks us to bask in the fact that these women's legs (and therefore, their sexual identities) are free from restraints.

Evidently, the depiction of the women as liberated and strong was no accident, as Parker himself confirms Layden's assertions:

> I've been asked: "Alan, don't you think we're [Ireland] a kind of chauvinistic, Catholic country dominated by men?" Well, no. It's exactly the opposite ... in these three girls, I didn't want wimpy, bimbo-type backup singers. They had to be as strong as the boys. In fact, these girls are so gutsy, they come off as even stronger than the boys at times.[22]

After Imelda, Bernie, and Natalie (the Commitmentettes) join the boys at practice, we cut to another bar, in which the new lineup is sitting around, drinking. Parker then implements a montage of the band hanging out at various locations, becoming acquainted, which culminates in the group, sitting on a train together, as Jimmy delivers a rousing speech to get everyone excited about soul. The song "Destination Anywhere," which previously played on the soundtrack when Jimmy first boarded the train to go to the Quirke wedding, is playing on the soundtrack again, and Dean starts singing the song, breaking the fourth aural wall, so to speak. The entire band joins in, singing a song, the lyrics of which "voice both the Irish youths' desperation to escape debilitating circumstances by banding together and the heady prospect that there is no telling how far they might go if they take a chance."[23]

Parker visually reaffirms the theme of angry, working-class youths and their desperation to transcend their subjugation in the next shot, in which Jimmy and Billy are walking through a back alley. Behind them, a horde of young boys are angrily throwing rocks and debris at a dilapidated, rundown building. They then walk into a drab, gray warehouse and approach Duffy (played by Liam Carney) to commission him for some amplifiers and other electronic gear. Duffy has a Rottweiler in a muzzle, and again, the image of the dog representing socio-economic oppression is reinforced. Parker then implements another montage as the Motown song "Nowhere to Run" plays on the soundtrack. There are shots of the Commitmentettes dancing with one another, Dean practicing on his saxophone, and the drummer using various objects as drums in the welding shop in which he works. In another extremely funny scene, Jimmy finally tracks down a practice space for the band, a cramped abandoned loft. When he asks the apparent proprietor of the space how long his boss will be away for, the proprietor responds, "Only two months. Unless he gets time off for good behavior."

We then cut to the band's first official practice, with the full lineup and actual musical gear (amplifiers, equipment, etc.). They perform "Mustang Sally," which is a bit shaky, and Joey has to stop the band until they get it right. Of this scene, Kunz states, "To illustrate how difficult it is for the quarrelsome Irish to take to soul music as a means of salvation, Jimmy instructs the Commitmentettes that the chorus to 'Mustang Sally' is 'Ride, Sally, Ride,' not 'Riot, Sally, Riot.'"[24]

After the practice, the band convenes at a pool hall, and in another of the film's innumerable, hilarious bits of dialogue, Jimmy tells the piano player, Steven Clifford (played by Michael Aherne) that he looks better without his glasses. Steven replies that he is blind without his glasses, to which Jimmy responds, "So was Ray Charles." Deco is further established as the "prick" of the group when he salaciously tells the Commitmentettes that they are not infusing their singing with enough sexuality, a point he makes by crassly grabbing his crotch. We then cut to another humorous exchange, this one between Joey and Dean. Joey is tutoring Dean, attempting to coax his best saxophone playing out of him. He tells Dean to think of the reed as a woman's nipple, and when he tells Dean to set his sights high and "pick any nipple he wants," Dean informs him that he is going to imagine Kim Basinger's nipple, and his playing suddenly improves.

After the band finishes rehearsal, Jimmy tells Joey that the band performed "like shite." Joey agrees but says, "It's a start, and I believe in starts. Once you have the start, the rest is inevitable." This statement reaffirms the lyrics to "Destination Anywhere," suggesting that, if the band sticks with it and maintains conviction, there is no end to where they can go.

Next is a brief scene, which is comical, but which also underscores the film's theme of the struggling working class. Jimmy is in line at the welfare office, collecting his unemployment check. He sees Dean in line, and the two chat, culminating with Dean saying that it feels much better to be an unemployed musician than it does being an unemployed pipe fitter. Again, this comment is funny as it perpetuates the stereotype of the "poor musician," but Parker infuses the comedy with reality by showcasing that these lads are struggling to make ends meet.

Parker then cuts to a scene in Joey's house, as the boys are listening to one of his records with Joey's mother (played by Maura O'Malley), whose character is completely absurd and played mostly for laughs. She is an odd amalgamation of Norma Desmond and Baby Jane Hudson from *What Ever Happened to Baby Jane?*, an old, reclusive woman with questionable sanity who wears far too much makeup. The boys are all doubting Joey's grandiose claims of having played with musical legends, but his mother assures them that his assertions are truthful. She then tells them that she will disclose something to them that no one else knows about Joey Fagan. As the boys perk up their ears, on the edge of their seats, preparing to hear something profound, Joey's mother tells them that he always sent her a postcard, leaving the boys to sit, hilariously disappointed in the banality of Joey's mother's comment.

Jimmy then shows up at Bernie's building to see her, and, at the elevator to her building, is confronted with a boy and a horse (again perpetuating the horse motif). When Jimmy asks if the boy will be taking the horse on the lift, he replies, "I have to. The stairs will kill him." The anguish of the poverty-stricken lower class is showcased when Jimmy tells Bernie that it is unacceptable that she has been missing rehearsals. Bernie, right in the middle of feeding a baby, ostensibly hers, tells Jimmy that her mother cannot work and her father is in the hospital, leaving her as the only one bringing money into the household. Once again, Parker displays his affinity for juggling disparate subject matters—outlandish comedy with hard-hitting drama. Bernie assures Jimmy that she will try harder, as she "needs something to look forward to." Again, music is depicted as being a means to salvation, which Parker accentuates by immediately cutting from Bernie's last line to an interior shot of a church, replete with lit candles and a crucifix. We hear an organ playing in the background, and Jimmy walks up to discover that it is Steven playing Procol Harum's "Whiter Shade of Pale." Organized religion has again been replaced with pop music, which is augmented when the priest agrees with the two boys over the peculiarity of one of the lyrics in the song.

After ostensibly procuring a gig with the priest for the 28th, we cut to another jubilant rehearsal sequence, in which the Commitmentettes are performing the Marvelettes song "Too Many Fish In the Sea." Deco expresses his discontent with the Commitmentettes singing the lead on this particular song, and again, the pressure cooker continues to simmer, and we suspect a possibly violent confrontation between Deco and another member of the band is nigh.

Dean then goes out to smoke a cigarette, and catches Natalie kissing Joey. According to Kunz, this is the first example of "the girls fomenting their own sexual revolution for fun."[25] Joey is the experienced musician, and Natalie, in true groupie fashion, seems to want to take advantage of that, whatever her intentions may be.

After Jimmy tells the rest of the band about the gig at the community center on the 28th, Dean comes rushing in, telling everyone about Natalie and Joey kissing. Bernie dismisses the comment, saying that whatever happened is between Natalie and Joey, furthering the film's boundary-breaching depiction of these Irish women as sexually autonomous. Bernie's intractable defense of her and her band mates' sexual freedom culminates when she pushes Deco off the top of the piano after he makes a snide comment.

We then cut to the St. Bridget's Community Center, where the band is setting up for their gig. They are ostensibly playing for Father Molloy's anti-heroin campaign, and when two young boys show the band the banner for the benefit, they see that the word "heroin" has been misspelled (they added an "e" at the end of the word), and Dean says that no one around these parts can read anyway. The band then finds out that Jimmy has hired Mickah Wallace to do security, and they are all outraged, claiming that Mickah is a savage who will steal their money. The band then gets dressed for the gig, and much to the chagrin of the men, they all must wear tuxedoes. The crowd files in, and the band prepares to perform. They burst out into the Otis Redding song, "They Call Me Mr. Pitiful," and although it is a bit rocky at first (the Commitmentettes clearly feel awkward and diffident), it turns out to be a raucous, galvanizing rendition, and the crowd responds enthusiastically. Deco, however, incites the ire of the rest of the band by saying to the crowd, "I hope you enjoy me group." By staking a claim over the group, claiming that it is *his* band, we can see how the egos and internal dissentions within the band may lead to their downfall. Deco causes further chaos when he bumps into one of the Commitmentettes, nearly knocking all of them to the floor. Joey admonishes him, telling him that he will apologize, and Outspan screams at Deco, saying, "We're not your fucking group!" Deco then looks on with derision as

An Irish soul band perform onstage, led by troubled front man and singer, Declan "Deco" Cuffe (Andrew Strong). Left to right: Bronagh Gallagher, Angeline Ball, Félim Gormley, Maria Doyle, Johnny Murphy, Strong, Dick Massey, Ken McCluskey and Glen Hansard. *The Commitments* **(1991), 20th Century–Fox.**

Natalie sings lead on "Bye Bye Baby." However, as the crowd is responding favorably to the song, Deco, despite himself, joins in on tambourine as the song ends.

The concert, as a whole, is a roller coaster ride. There are good moments, bad moments, ups, downs, and, ultimately, it feels like watching the Beatles' film *Let It Be*. In that uneven documentary, underneath the squabbling and bickering (i.e., the trying moments in which it is simply not working), there is a talented band that clearly knows how to have fun together.

Jimmy's father walks into the concert to catch the band performing Joe Tex's "Show Me." Jimmy Sr., along with the rest of the crowd, is thoroughly enjoying the song, as it is really gelling—all the bugs seem to have been worked out. Deco, however, inadvertently hits Derek with his microphone stand, causing an electrical explosion onstage, which leads to a power outage. Although this is an admittedly disastrous end to a show, the crowd can be heard chanting, "We want more!" All in all, it would appear as though the show was a success.

As they wait in the hospital for Derek to recover, Dean comments on how, if Derek died, they would become instantly famous. In a hilarious rumination scene, the band then tries to remember as many instances as they can in which a famous musician died by choking on his own vomit. We then cut to another stark, nightmarish shot of a dark alley (which is, according to Kunz, a metaphor for terrorism) as Jimmy, Outspan, and Derek disembark from a truck. Outspan and Derek are both feeling a bit dejected, prompting Jimmy to deliver another rousing speech. He reminds them that the reason they are in a band is not for the money or the chicks; it is to be different and to scream from a mountaintop that you are different and you are not "a tosser." Once again, Parker wrests the success aspect of rock 'n' roll from the glitzy excess of "sex, drugs, and rock 'n' roll" and gives it a proletariat, class-warrior component.

We then cut to Jimmy giving another phony interview in his bed, which culminates in a moment of vulgar comedy, as his brother pops his head up to see who Jimmy is talking to. Jimmy hits him in the head with a magazine and says, "Fuck off, I'm giving an interview." We then see Joey, leaning over his bed, talking sexily to an, at first, undisclosed woman. We finally see that it is Bernie—Joey seems to be working his way through all of the Commitmentettes, supporting Kunz's claim that the girls have a sexual revolution of their own in mind.

Next is a brief scene which finds Imelda and Natalie walking together down a Dublin street. They discuss the men in the band (which ones they find attractive, etc.) and they are sporadically interrupted by a fan who wants either their autograph, or to know when they are playing next. Imelda says she feels like Madonna, which, according to Kunz, represents the band's desire for transformation through music—a transformation from poverty-stricken working-class people to successful people.[26]

At another band gathering at the practice space, Deco, again, showcases his boorishness by stridently banging away at Billy's drums, which makes Bernie's baby cry. Jimmy and Imelda then have an argument when Imelda says she will not be able to make their show on the 15th. Jimmy is outraged, and the cracks in the eggshell are starting to show.

After the band rehearses Otis Redding's "Hard to Handle," with Bernie's baby crying the entire time, we cut to Joey regaling Jimmy Sr., with a story about Elvis. Jimmy Sr., then asks Joey if he ever saw Elvis doing drugs, and when Joey replies in the negative, Jimmy

Sr., is relieved. It is almost as if he has been absolved by a priest, which, again, reasserts the theme of music supplanting religion. Jimmy Sr., is, as Kunz puts it, "overjoyed by the resurrection of his pop culture savior."[27]

We then cut to Imelda, who is clearly disgruntled about going on vacation with her family, which is the reason she told Jimmy she would miss the show. At the last minute, however, she tells them that she will not be joining them—her passion for the transformative power of music has taken her over. She then rushes into the venue, hair wet, and Jimmy and the band are delighted to see her. We then cut to the performance, which starts with a rousing rendition of the Al Green song "Take Me To the River." The band nails the song, and the crowd is thoroughly enjoying it, but the internal dissension within the band rears its ugly head again, when Billy accidentally knocks over his hi-hat cymbals at the end of the song, leading to a heated argument between him and Deco. The next song is "The Dark End of the Street," which speaks to secret, sinful meetings.

The lyrics, according to Kunz, are particularly significant in that they "articulate the fear and guilt over Irish sectarian strife."[28] Again, we are given a window into the collective psyche of a group of people trapped in a pit of despair who long to break free from their shackles.

We then cut to the band, sitting around the dinner table, discussing the gig. The discussion quickly devolves into a heated argument, however, as everyone is bickering about who wants to sleep with whom. Jimmy then chimes in and says, "Sex ruins everything," to which Imelda replies, "You told us soul was sex." Herein lies a possible explanation for the inability for the band to remain unified (and, if we are to lend any credence to Kunz's claims, this translates to Ireland's inability to remain unified): there seems to be an inherent, irreconcilable ideological disparity, and no one, including Jimmy, seems to be able to unequivocally articulate the "mission statement" of the band. When Jimmy goes outside to catch a cab home, Natalie follows him, and we, for the first time, see a desperation in her character. She professes that she wants Jimmy to take her home, and he refuses. Whereas, when she was sexually involved with Joey, it was presented as a focused plan, we now get the sense that Natalie suffers from low self-esteem, and is desperate for a man to validate her.

In the next scene, we see the band posing for photos on top of a trash heap. This symbolically represents the Commitments' bold attempt to rise above their poverty-stricken background. Billy, however, gets in his van and refuses to pose for the photos, claiming that he is leaving the band. Jimmy erupts in a fit of rage and tells Billy to fuck off, and the audience is slowly witnessing the degeneration of Jimmy's idyllic plan for musical transcendence.

We then cut to Steven confessing his sins to a priest in a confessional. For a moment, it would appear that Parker is attempting to grant organized religion actual narrative agency, trumping the idea that music is "the new religion." In a hilarious turn of events, however, when Steven confesses that he has been humming "When a Man Loves a Woman" by Marvin Gaye, the priest immediately corrects him, saying that Percy Sledge sings "When a Man Loves a Woman." As Kunz puts it, "Apparently, it is a greater sin not to know the proper soul artist than to have exchanged secular music for Christian hymns."[29]

With Billy out of the band, it would appear as if Mickah, the volatile savage, will be filling in for him, of which Parker informs us with a startlingly brief shot of Mickah wailing away at the drum kit in a whirlwind of activity, like Animal from "The Muppets." We then cut to Jimmy being muscled by Duffy, who wants his money for the gear that he provided the band. Again, the slow erosion of the band seems to be underway.

Next is a scene in which the band, to procure transportation to their next gig, steals Bernie's food vendor truck, which, again, drives home just how impoverished they are. On the drive, they again sing "Destination Anywhere," but at this point in the film, the lyrics are less hopeful and more foreboding, as we have seen the possible ingredients of their undoing. Parker keeps the comedy coming, however, when, after Deco contaminates the truck with his flatulence, the band opens the window to let in some fresh air. Thinking this means that the food truck is open for business, an older couple approaches them and orders some food, to which the band replies, "Sorry, we only have soul."

The internal combustion of the band is further suggested at their next performance. During another rendition of "Hard to Handle," Joey becomes annoyed with Dean, as he brazenly and selfishly solos over the entire song, and we can see that egos are starting to play a part in the band's unraveling. In the restroom, both Joey and Jimmy tell Dean that he was essentially masturbating with his solo. When Jimmy is seen counting the money from the gig, he is approached by a journalist, who asks him about the band. Jimmy reaffirms the band's proletariat, class-warrior ethos, and says that they are on a guerrilla mission to bring soul to Dublin. He then reminds the journalist that guerrilla is spelled with a "u" not an "o." While this punctuation is funny, it is significant, according to Kunz, as he states, "Their effort to achieve peace and dignity by appropriating it from another oppressed culture is inevitably self-destructive."[30]

As the Commitmentettes sing a soulful rendition of "Chain of Fools," Parker cuts to Duffy walking angrily into the venue, and the viewer prepares for a possibly violent uproar. From Mickah's point of view behind the drums, we see one of Duffy's henchmen grab Jimmy, forcing him to give Duffy the money. The tempo starts to falter as Mickah is fixated on the proceedings. When Duffy slaps Jimmy, Mickah jumps out from behind the drums, runs up to Duffy and head butts him, breaking his nose. Joey, the consummate professional, espouses the "show must go on" stance, and tells the girls to keep singing. After a full-on brawl breaks out, Duffy is escorted out, vowing revenge, and Jimmy remounts the stage and introduces the band, which elicits boisterous cheers from the audience. Once again, Parker effortlessly weaves together complete and utter self-destruction with moments of cohesiveness, clarity, and effectiveness. The band is dangerously straddling the line between implosion and success.

We then cut to Jimmy reading a positive review in the newspaper to Joey (once again, Parker makes a wry wink at the audience, as one of the reviews lauds Deco's voice, claiming that it is a voice that Bob Geldof would kill for—Bob Geldof, of course, being the singer for the Boomtown Rats and the lead in Parker's film *Pink Floyd—The Wall*). As Joey tells Jimmy to wait outside while he tries to contact Wilson Pickett, Parker cuts to a shot of two dead horses, perpetuating the visual motif of horses representing the hopelessness of the Irish rising above the myriad of forces arrayed against them. The journalist who is covering this crime scene is apparently the same journalist who wrote the glowing review of the Commitments, so Jimmy invites him to their next show.

The next shot is of the band backstage, and Deco asks Steven for career advice. Apparently, Deco has been offered to sing in another band, which incites the ire and insecurity of the rest of the band mates, all of whom feel slighted by Deco's apparent betrayal. A fight ensues, and Parker is digging us deeper and deeper into corrosive territory—we see the foundation beginning to crumble beneath the weight of disorganization and egos. Jimmy, to mollify the animosity, tells the band that Wilson Pickett has agreed to come in and play with them, based on Joey's word. The viewer, at this point, has become extremely skeptical about Joey, and we are now seriously questioning the validity of his outrageous claims.

We then cut to the performance, which starts off with a rousing rendition of "Mustang Sally." Parker lingers on the performance for quite awhile, and he implements his aptitude for building suspense and tension as we wait in anxious anticipation for something to go horribly wrong. Nothing does, however, and we cut to Jimmy in the bathroom giving another fake interview in which he expresses doubts as to whether Wilson Pickett is going to actually show up. We then cut back to Natalie singing a sultry version of Aretha Franklin's "I Never Loved a Man the Way I Love You," as Deco mingles with the crowd.

After a brief shot of another music journalist asking Jimmy if Wilson Pickett is going to show up, the band breaks into "Try a Little Tenderness." Parker, again, lingers on this performance, not wanting to rush through it, as if he, himself, is enjoying watching it. We then cut to Jimmy greeting another music journalist outside as he arrives in a cab. The journalist asks a now-nervous Jimmy if Wilson Pickett has arrived yet, and Jimmy, unfortunately, informs him that he has not.

After the show, Jimmy confronts Joey angrily and asks him where Wilson Pickett is. Joey says that he did his best, and that he is sorry if Jimmy doubts him. Back in the dressing room, the egos continue to flare, and Deco proclaims that, when he comes offstage, he wants a proper towel, not a tea towel. The internal dissent then spirals out of control, and soon, everyone is yelling at everyone. After an incessant cacophony of bickering, the band agrees to go out and do an encore. In honor of Wilson Pickett not showing up, which Deco angrily blames on Jimmy, they do a version of "In the Midnight Hour." During the performance, a representative from a record label approaches Jimmy and tells him that he is very interested in representing the band. We catch glimpses of their conversation, in which the rep tells Jimmy that they are small, and there would be no money up front, but that they would provide an engineer.

After the encore, we retreat back to the dressing room, and Parker demonstrates, once again, his deft ability to juxtapose inaction with action, relief with tension. At first the mood has lightened and everyone is celebrating. At the blink of an eye, however, everyone is arguing again. As he displayed with the entire suspense motif of *Midnight Express*, Parker is a master of letting the audience off the hook, but only temporarily, before he delves right back into hell again. As Jimmy is talking with the record label rep, Mickah and Deco unload the gear in a dark back alley. When Deco is swarmed with fans wanting autographs, Mickah's jealousy consumes him, and he attacks Deco, beating him to a pulp, and leaving him in a pile of trash. Jimmy attempts to break it up, but Natalie yells out the window that the rest of the band is murdering each other in the dressing room. Jimmy, in a fit of frustration, gives up and storms out. Parker then cuts to another image of a dark, depressing street with Jimmy walking alone. Joey pulls up beside him on his bike and re-instills a sense of worth and value into Jimmy. Jimmy proclaims that he accomplished nothing, but Joey, fulfilling the role of prophet (and perhaps, in this moment, of Greek chorus) tells him that his accomplishment was that he gave the members of the band a sense of purpose and the hope that their lives can change.

Jimmy then walks away, alone again, and a limousine pulls up and asks Jimmy if he knows of a pub called Gallagher's. When Jimmy tells the driver that it is closed, the driver says, "You want to just go back to the hotel, then, Mr. Pickett?" Joey was right—Wilson Pickett was going to show up. Jimmy is then left alone and dejected.

Using Jimmy's phony interviews as a narrative device, Parker informs us of all the disparate directions the band members went in after the Commitments disbanded. A montage reveals that two of them are singing on street corners for change, one has a country western band, another has a punk rock band, one is a successful pop recording artist, and one has become a doctor. According to Kunz, "Each has abandoned the uniform dignity of the Commitments' borrowed formal black dress or tuxedo for some shabby costume appropriate to individual aspiration against hopeless circumstances,"[31] which, also according to Kunz, serves as an allegory for Ireland's inability to unify.

12

The Road to Wellville (1994)

October 28; 118 minutes/Color
Production Companies: Beacon Communications; Columbia Pictures Corporation; Dirty Hands Productions; Per-Fo Pictures
Director: Alan Parker
Screenwriter: Alan Parker, based on the novel by T. Coraghessan Boyle
Producers: Tom Rosenberg (Executive Producer); Marc Abraham; Alan Parker, Armyan Bernstein, Robert F. Colesberry, Lisa Moran
Production Designer: Brian Morris
Cinematographer: Peter Biziou
Editor: Gerry Hambling
Cast: Anthony Hopkins (Dr. John Harvey Kellogg); Bridget Fonda (Eleanor Lightbody); Matthew Broderick (William Lightbody); John Cusack (Charles Ossining); Dana Carvey (George Kellogg); Michael Lerner (Goodloe Bender); Traci Lind (Nurse Irene Graves); Lara Flynn Boyle (Ida Muntz)

> Corn is the gift of the Injun to the New World. The corn flake is my gift to the entire world.—Dr. John Harvey Kellogg, responding to questions from reporters

> I was first sent the manuscript of T. Coraghessan Boyle's novel, *The Road to Wellville*, in July of 1992. I was drawn to the three interwoven stories and the outrageous, eccentric world that Tom Boyle had parachuted us into with all of his usual anarchic and irreverent wickedness.[1]—Alan Parker

Notes on the Production

In August of 1992, just a month or so after Alan Parker received T. Coraghessan Boyle's manuscript *The Road to Wellville* (the outlandish and surprisingly accurate historical account of eccentric health enthusiast and inventor, Dr. John Harvey Kellogg) he began the first stages of pre-production. He visited Battle Creek, in the southeast corner of Michigan, where the doctor's famous sanitarium operated during the early 1900s. According to Parker, the subsequent visits to Battle Creek "yielded a mountain of material—the Doctor's penchant for documenting everything gave us over two-thousand photographs and technical drawings to work from."[2] This project reflected Parker's penchant for U.S. history and was also an ambitious writing endeavor: He needed to successfully adapt Boyle's nearly five-hundred-page novel (one that echoed the literary styles of Charles Dickens and his contemporary John Irving) into a succinct two-hour film—and in just a little over a year (November 1993), the film was ready to be shot.[3]

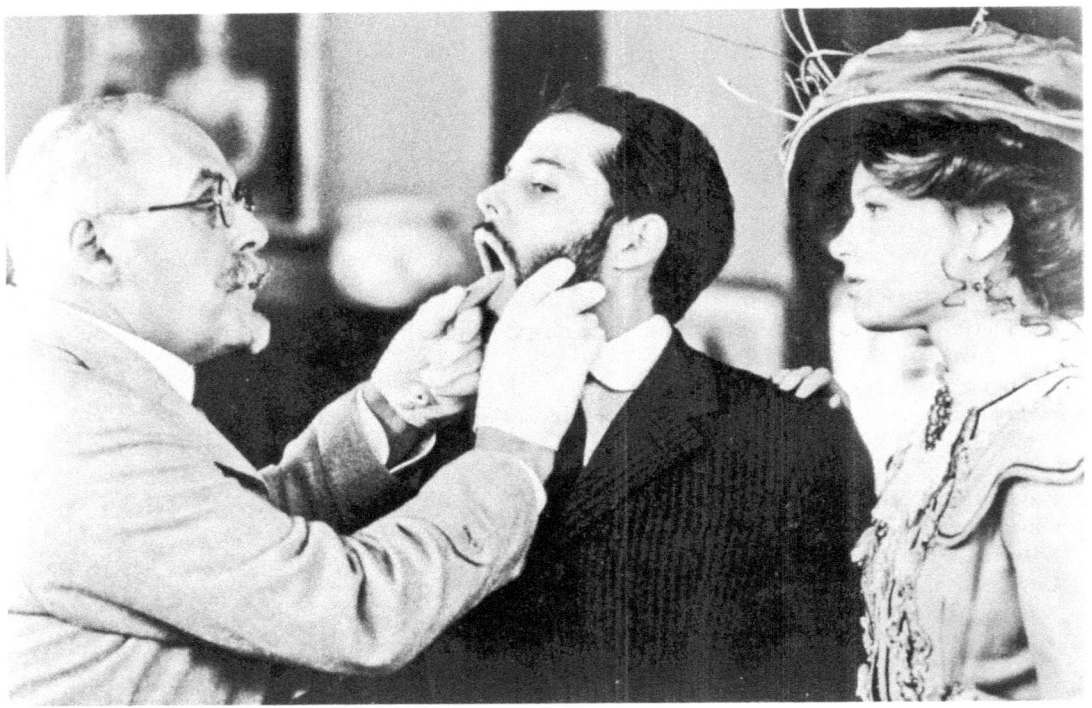

Left to right: Health enthusiast Dr. John Harvey Kellogg (Anthony Hopkins) gives a check-up to sickly William Lightbody (Matthew Broderick) at the behest of his wife, Eleanor (Bridget Fonda). *The Road to Wellville* (1994), Beacon Communications; Columbia Pictures; Dirty Hands Productions; Per-Fo Pictures.

Since *The Road to Wellville* is a period piece—the film takes place in 1907—scouting out locations, naturally, became a priority for Parker and his crew. After exploring institutions from Kenkakee, Illinois, to French Lick, Indiana, to prisons in Montana to Catholic seminaries in Baltimore—they eventually decided on the Quaker-owned Mohawk Mountain House, which was ninety miles north of NYC—and the town of Battle Creek was built at the film studios in Wilmington, North Carolina.[4]

Anthony Hopkins was Parker's first choice for the role of Dr. Kellogg; after a number of months, the actor finally agreed to take the part. Parker said, "Tony Hopkins has the ability to rehearse a scene, and then, on take five, suddenly, like a champion javelin thrower, take it to a place you never imagined it could go."[5] Apparently the well-trained actor always had a "rosy demeanor"[6] and an uncanny talent for impersonation. Once in an Italian restaurant, Hopkins mimicked Parker "crying" while begging the actor to take the role.[7] In addition to the fifty-six speaking parts and hundreds of hand-picked extras[8] the director worked with Bridget Fonda (Eleanor Lightbody), Matthew Broderick (Will Lightbody), John Cusack (Charles Ossining) and Dana Carvey (George Kellogg), who, according to Parker, were "all models of professionalism, making my life very easy as a director."[9]

The Road to Wellville was co-produced by Robert Colesberry (who worked with Parker on *Mississippi Burning* [1988] and *Come See the Paradise* [1990]), who died in 2004; this was the last film they worked on together. Parker once called him "a great and total filmmaker."[10] The film was shot in sixty-two days—from November 1993 to February 1994 and released on October 28, 1994, in the United States. The film was also released internationally in places like Argentina, Germany, France the U.K., Turkey, Hungary, Spain and Australia and the estimated budget was $25,000,000, but it only grossed $6,507,514 in the United States.[11]

Summary

Like the opening sounds of machine guns in *Midnight Express* and the chirping of birds in *Birdy*, *The Road to Wellville* also begins with sounds over a black screen: intense rhythmic breathing that fades into a close-up of a middle-aged woman, dressed in white, leading a group of women in synchronized breathing and movement exercises while engaging in Dr. Kellogg's "laugh therapy" technique. The women are among a chorus of other "laughers" while a woman, dressed in red, leads the procession by yelling through a megaphone, and another woman plays a simple eight-note piano scale that accompanies the ritual. Immediately, the viewer has become immersed in Dr. John Harvey Kellogg's microcosm—the Battle Creek Sanitarium. We are in the Temple of Health in 1907 Michigan.

The opening credits are juxtaposed along with this visual fugue of sorts. Following the names of the production companies (Columbia and Beacon, along with Parker's own Dirty Hands Productions) and lastly, Alan Parker's name as director, an offscreen voice is heard: "Sir, how often *should* one exonerate the bowels?" The image fades in to a close-up of our protagonist, Dr. John Harvey Kellogg, who is exercising on a machine he invented, surrounded by reporters. This brief interview of the acclaimed doctor provides the viewer with historical background and biographical context. In this minute or so, a number of Dr. Kellogg's philosophies are imparted. On *sex*, he says, "Sex is the sewer drain of a healthy body." This sentiment of the doctor's is actually historically accurate, as he was known to refer to *sexual urges* as "the sewer drain of the body" and *masturbation* "the silent killer of the night," two quotes that are in the novel and film (apparently when he went on his "honeymoon" with his wife, Ella Eaton, he used this time not as a romantic getaway but as a sabbatical to write a book).

On *eating meat* he informs the men that sausage (and all meat) is filled with tuberculosis—"Eat it and die!" When asked to comment on his Cornflakes invention (which was only one of his seventy-five inventions, along with peanut butter and the electric blanket), he said, "Corn is the gift of the Injuns to the New World. The corn flake is my gift to the entire world." Finally, a question is raised concerning his younger brother, Will Keith Kellogg, who is credited by many as being the official Corn Flakes inventor. Dr. Kellogg asserts with his typical egocentricity: "The world only knows me." Although the film does not directly address the sibling partnership and notorious rivalry, it is important to note that Will Kellogg was a very effective businessman. In 1884, when Dr. Kellogg employed his younger brother as a bookkeeper at the San, the Corn Flakes industry began. Despite the fact that Dr. Kellogg is credited as inventing the "corn flake," it was Will who placed his official "signature" on the cereal box, which was supposed to indicate the product's true authenticity. In 1906, he defied his brother's health vision and added sugar to Corn Flakes and the cereal was marketed into a new product, replete with his "W.K. Kellogg" signature.[12]

In 1956, Prentice Hall published a book by Horace B. Powell called *The Original Has This Signature* with *W.K. Kellogg* "signed" in a cursive writing font—a nearly exhaustive study of a man whom the author said lived three lives.[13] John Harvey despised commercialization and this is mainly where the sibling rivalry surfaced: Will was a capitalist at heart; conversely, John claimed to favor his health inventions over financial gain, despite the empire he created with the San.

After this initial introduction to the eccentric doctor (played to the hilt by Hopkins just three years after he won the Oscar as Hannibal Lecter in *The Silence of the Lambs* [1991]), a series of shots continue to show a number of people at the Battle Creek sanitarium doing a variety of things: jogging, riding bikes, and singing while doing the melodic laugh therapy number that musically sounds like a distorted version of "Jingle Bells." A quick cut, replete with the sound of a moving train (undoubtedly showing a dichotomy between Dr. Kellogg's natural holistic health world versus the outside world of industry and machines, a theme also portrayed in *Midnight Express* and *Birdy*) shows Eleanor Lightbody (Bridget Fonda) looking out the window daydreaming: her husband, Will (Matthew Broderick), enters and she implicitly asks him if he has had a bowel movement. He says he hasn't, then tries to kiss her, and she demurs. She is already showing signs that she is a student of the abstinent Dr. Kellogg.

In the following scene, we are introduced to Charles Ossining (John Cusack), who introduces his breakfast food company, PER-FO (note that PER-FO is listed as one of the film's production companies).[14] He is dressed professionally and eats oysters. He offers one to Will and Eleanor, and, in unison, they respond with an emphatic, "No!" Eleanor orders a digestive-friendly cucumber salad and informs the CEO that oysters are nothing more than urine ("slimy piss"), not to mention the fact that oysters are known to boost one's libido. Will scolds his wife, "Eleanor, will you never shut up?!" Will leaves the table and proceeds to vomit on a woman seated nearby. Charlie comically retorts: "Terrible thing, indigestion." The married couple, as it turns out, is en route to the Battle Creek sanitarium so Will can cure his dyspepsia and insomnia (he hasn't slept in three weeks). He also suffers from what Dr. Kellogg calls *autointoxication*. Once again Parker weaves historical accuracy into the farcical proceedings (the blending of fiction into stories based on fact is something Parker was pretty used to by now), as *autointoxication* and its treatment is something Kellogg actually studied. When he was twenty, in the early 1870s during Reconstruction and the rise of industrial modernism, he attended seminars at the Water Cure Institution in New Jersey.

A pull-back dolly shot reveals the old town of Battle Creek, Michigan, populated by groups of pedestrians and horse drawn buggies. Charlie is drawn to a sign that reads: CEREAL BOWL OF THE WORLD. All three characters have now arrived at their destination. Another transition into the sanitarium: we see a trickster character drinking liquor from a bottle; this is Dab (Roy Brocksmith), Dr. Kellogg's secretary. Boyle describes him the following way, which is an accurate portrayal of how he was cast: a "short large man with an unfortunate waddle."[15]

Cut to a red sign with white letters over the door in an assembly room where Dr. Kellogg lectures. The sign reads: THE BOWELS ARE OUR PASSAGE TO HEALTH. Dab enters with two baggies and whispers to the doctor, "He's here," meaning that his son George has arrived. An audience of admirers has gathered to witness the demonstration of an experiment led by Dr. Kellogg which aims to prove that horse manure and a fine cut of Porter House steak contain the same bacterial elements, thus asserting that people should not eat meat. Throughout this experiment, the camera frequently cuts to a pale-faced woman sitting in the audience, a character who eventually assists Dr. Kellogg with this experiment. This is Miss Ida Muntz (Lara Flynn Boyle). T. Coraghessan Boyle describes her the following way: "She was pretty, yes, and she gave them something to look at, green sickness and all, but he should have thought to choose someone with a little less leg bone."[16] Throughout the film, this overtly sexual being who suffers from *chlorosis*, a form of anemia, becomes a temptress for Will who has a difficult time controlling his sexual urges. While she serves as Dr. Kellogg's lab assistant, helping him prove that horse dung and a steak have the same microbe activity, the Lightbodys' make their entrance into the institution (this is not Eleanor's first visit), and are greeted by a concierge dressed in red (the color of the uniforms worn by Kellogg's staff members; probably because red symbolizes the color of healthy blood). An optimistic Eleanor says to her husband that they are both going to get well: Will is dressed in black, and Eleanor in white (are they meant to represent good and evil?). Dr. Kellogg, always dressed in white clothing, is a proponent of heat therapy and believes that wearing white supposedly aids a person in absorbing the rays of the sun.[17] Thus, Eleanor is (temporarily anyway) a true student in Dr. Kellogg's "school of health," and Will, a victim of darkness, plagued with autointoxication and an overactive libido, is the antithesis of this white purity.

This scene is cross-cut with Dr. Kellogg making the rounds to meet his guests. Eleanor spots the doctor and says, "There's the great man himself." She is a rather ironic entity especially since, later in the film, her impressionability leads her to succumb to a world of sexual debauchery. She reaches the doctor, but is almost immediately interrupted by a repulsive, rotten-toothed figure dressed in rags. This is Dr. Kellogg's "black sheep" adopted son, George (played by *Saturday Night Live*'s Dana Carvey). This moment in the film represents the last sentences of the first chapter called "Of Steak and Sin," which is a visual description of George Kellogg:

> But the figure moved and spoke and cut him off. The words seemed to come from deep inside him even as the sparkling audience flowed through the doors of the Grand Parlor and made their way in a knot toward them; the words spat themselves out like a curse, twisted by the unshaven lips, forced from the stinking rags and the feverish eyes: "Hello, Father. Aren't you going to introduce me?"[18]

George, who has arrived unexpectedly (and unwelcomed) at the San, is there to get money from his father. He looks at Will and says, "You look like you are on your last legs"— a most ironic statement from someone who looks like a disgruntled street urchin from a Charles Dickens story. When he exits, Dr. Kellogg, who doesn't acknowledge that George is his son, refers to him as "a poor ratchet charity patient." In the next beat, Will is separated from Eleanor and taken away in a wheel chair to begin his long line of treatments in an attempt to cure his autointoxication and insomnia. Eleanor walks over to Dr. Frank Linniman (Michael Goodman), whom she knows from her previous visit, and their amiable rapport suggests that they have gotten to know each other quite well. As Will is being wheeled away he yells foolishly, "I want my wife!" not realizing what Dr. Kellogg has in store for him.

The following scene shows Charlie's personal journey through the rain, which is viewed in high-contrast lighting, led by the sharp, painterly eye of cinematographer Michael Seresin, whose lighting in many Alan Parker's films is an aesthetically pleasing character unto itself. While Charlie sits in the rain, he is approached by a young boy who asks him if he is Charlie Ossining and thus informs him that he has been sent by Goodloe Bender, his business partner, to lead him to his appropriate destination. In the novel, the young boy is described in Boyle's typical Dickensian rhetoric:

> Charlie felt a tug at his sleeve and turned to find one of the superfluous boys gazing up at him expectantly from beneath the brim of a porkpie cap. The boy was about fourteen, sleepy-eyed and heavy-set, and he slouched in his overcoat like the old man he would one day become.[19]

The scene cross-cuts back to the Battle Creek sanitarium: Will is introduced to the young pretty Nurse Irene Graves (Traci Lind), who informs him that she will be his personal nurse during his stay at the San. In the novel, she is described the following way:

> Her voice was a tiny puff of breath, as if she were unused to speaking above a whisper ... and her uniform: It was an unbroken file of white from the hem of her skirt to the cap perched atop the pinned-up mass of her hair, and it was perfectly—and naturally contoured to the shape of her body.[20]

Will creates a fantasy that plays itself out in vivid detail: Nurse Graves is naked—and then he catches a glimpse of Ida Muntz through the doorway of her room; she smiles at him; she is a sexual temptress, one who will soon be involved in his life.

In the following scene Nurse Graves orders Will to undress. While doing so, Will tells her she is beautiful; she responds that he shouldn't be saying such things. By the end of this quick scene she kneels down in front of him in a pose that suggests (to Will and the viewer) that she is about to perform fellatio. The temptation is broken when she suddenly exits the room, informing Will that she will return later to give him his bath. Meanwhile, a quick cut to Charlie and the boy walking through the streets of Battle Creek, then back to Will and Nurse Graves. Will conjures up another sexual fantasy: He pictures the nurse dressed in lingerie. Back to reality—she warns him that "sexual stimulation could be fatal," followed by her administering a colonic wash. "Clean thoughts make for clean bowels, Mr. Lightbody," she tells him. Despite the nature of what is occurring here, Will is still sexually aroused and informs her that he has an erection. Nurse Graves ends the scene by saying, "Try to think of me as one of nature's nurses here in the Temple of Health." Incidentally, in reality, Dr. Kellogg didn't pay his staff of nurses; he gave them free room and board and believed that the experience of working and learning from him merited its own form of payment.[21]

The film makes a comical transition from Nurse Graves squeezing the apparatus that begins the colonic wash process to a bartender pouring ale from a tap in the notorious pub called the Little Red Onion that serves alcohol, meat and what Dr. Kellogg would refer to as other taboo foods. When Charlie enters the pub, the waltz-like leitmotif plays, a peculiar combination of brass instruments and the kazoo—music that confirms that we are in a modern business world of jesters and tricksters, led by the nefarious, pompous cigar-smoking hypocrite, Goodloe Bender (played by the ubiquitous character actor Michael Lerner in an entertaining, melodramatic performance who is, along with Dana Carvey's George, the most outlandish character in the film). The novel carries on for pages describing Charlie's search for his frequently (and purposely) absent partner. In the chapter called

"PER-FO," Boyle builds the character in a series of typically over-indulgent stylistically driven descriptions which are just as outlandish as the characters he creates. The following two excerpts describe Charlie's didactic partner:

> Bender hissed, and he was in command again, his face serene, unperturbed, sunk back into the mask he customarily wore.

> And without waiting for a reply he turned portentously in his seat and hailed the waiter, in the fruity rich commanding voice he used on the public like some old Shakespearian faker. When he turned back round he drew a cigar from his breast pocket, clipped the end, and leaned forward to light it off the tallowy candle puddled in a dish in the center of table.[22]

Bender is perhaps a version of Charles W. Post—Kellogg's major arch-rival, replete with the black suit and cigar, who allegedly stole the Grape Nuts recipe from Kellogg's kitchen. In fact "Charles" and Bender may *both* be farcical interpretations of Post. In reality, when Kellogg accused Post of stealing the recipe, Post blew cigar smoke in his face and called him a "dog" to which Kellogg wittily responded: "Yes, and you know what *dogs* do to *posts*."[23]

In the next scene, Charlie and Bender discuss their business prospects and this exchange serves as essential narrative exposition. Bender had been given a sum of money from Charlie's well-to-do aunt, Mrs. Hookstraten (Carole Shelley), with the intention that the money would be used wisely toward the expenses of the PER-FO warehouse. Bender—attempting to distract Charlie from the reality of the financial situation (he has taken the money with no intention of using it for the factory)—directs his attention to Charlie's written copy on the cereal box, which he reads and facetiously calls "brilliant": "It perks up tired blood and exonerates the bowels." Bender is a man of walking colloquialisms—it is clear that he is interested in nothing but his own personal capital gain. The following quote adequately sums up this flat character's philosophy: "Health is the open sesame to the sucker's purse."

The scene cuts to a quick shot of Nurse Graves looking in on Will who is finally—after weeks of insomnia—sleeping soundly, the colonic wash apparatus humorously positioned by his bed. A follow-up scene shows Eleanor in a high-angle shot leisurely sitting in a warm bath pool, being pampered by two servants dressed in red-and-white uniforms. Above her, another prominent Battle Creek sanitarium sign reads: A BEACON OF GOOD HEALTH. Suddenly, a point-of-view shot voyeuristically scopes the contours of her body and legs. Revealed: George Kellogg. Eleanor is startled and embarrassed. George admits to her the two reasons why he as arrived—to receive his "allowance" from his father and to look at the nude ladies. Then he proceeds to undress. The purpose of this scene is to provide more backstory: Through his dialogue, we learn that George was one of Dr. Kellogg's thirty-nine adopted children, the son of a prostitute who was taken in by the doctor who wanted to provide a better life for unfortunate children—a mission of humanity that ultimately backfired for him when he realized that George could not be saved. When a nurse discovers the half-naked George, she screams and what ensues is a chase sequence that evokes the silent slapstick comedies of Max Linder, Mack Sennett and Charlie Chaplin.

During the pursuit, the camera tilts to a shot of Dr. Kellogg pensively looking out of the window. This leads to a flashback of years earlier: the doctor is reprimanded young

George for not hanging up his jacket on the coat rack. Consequently, he forces the defiant child to repeat a ritual until bedtime to "teach him a lesson" on how to behave: first, the boy must enter the house through the front door; then he must ascend to the top of the stairs to hang up his jacket on the coat rack. The young troubled boy, however, repeats the ritual for hours after his bedtime, refusing to stop. The segment is represented in a rapid montage fashion with dissolves showing the passage of time. Eventually, Dr. Kellogg yells, "George, stop this madness!" When the boy finally stops, he defiantly drops the jacket in front of the rack, rendering the entire punishment completely ineffective. This segment is described over the course of several pages in the first section of the novel in a chapter appropriately named: "Father to All, Father to None."[24]

The flashback ends with a dissolve back to Dr. Kellogg as he plaintively continues gazing out the window. It is, perhaps, the sole moment in the film illustrating true humanity. Although the movie is saturated with ludicrous farce and purposely flat characters, this father/son relationship proves to be slightly more layered and complex.

A slow pan begins the next shot, introducing the friendship between Eleanor and Virginia Cranehill (Camryn Manheim in a boisterous comedic role). The women are enjoying the purity of the clean outside air and green grounds, while Virginia (her name proves to be ironic; she is anything but virginal) talks about her sexual awakening through the joys of masturbation, making it perfectly clear to the more conservative Eleanor that she has "little use for her husband in the sexual gratification department." She adds confidentially that she enjoys riding bikes because, in short, she can reach an orgasm by the way she sits and peddles—a term she refers to as a "bicycle smile." Virginia comes to represent the archetypal sexually liberated woman attempting to escape the confinements of an unsatisfying patriarchal marriage, similar to the repressed, male-dominated women portrayed in the works of such 19th-century writers as Kate Chopin (*The Awakening* [1899]) and Charlotte Perkins Gilman ("The Yellow Wallpaper" [1892]).

The talk of sexual arousal is interpreted by an abrupt cut to the massive invasive presence of Nurse Bloethal (Marianne Muellerleile), who, to Will's dismay, will be giving him his next colonic wash. She is described by Boyle as having "arms like hams, hams like sacks of grain, with a squarish face and a smile full of crooked teeth."[25] Needless to say, she is the antithesis of Nurse Graves.

Meanwhile, another cross-cut (the dominating editing technique used to help interconnect these three vignettes) leads to a series of cross-cuts: Charlie vehemently enters the hotel, where Bender had been staying and demands to see his partner; he is consequently evicted and the circus-like brass-kazoo leitmotif returns, replete with the silent film–slapstick gags. A quick cut leads to a montage of Will, who succumbs to Dr. Kellogg's water therapy—then back to Charlie walking through the streets. In the next scene, Charlie arrives at the Red Onion and finally locates Bender.

In a scene of haughty proportions, Bender and Charlie discuss "business." Charlie, responding to his partner's overt effrontery, reminds him that they had an appointment to discuss where the PER-FO factory was going to be. Before anything else can be discussed, however, George Kellogg appears quite suddenly from under the table, surprising Charlie. Bender introduces him as Dr. Kellogg's son. Charlie, slightly enamored, calls Dr. Kellogg "a great man," to which George retorts: "He's a *fuck-pig*. I hate him!" The conversation that follows, in its absurd anarchic delivery, unfolds in a vaudevillian style, like something out of a Marx Brothers film or an Abbott and Costello "who's-on- first" type routine, a dialogue that makes no literal sense and ultimately ends with nothing accomplished. The routine begins when Will suggests that they use George to help them on their business venture. Bender—playing straight man to Will's trickster—says, "Charles, you need your steak. You're delirious." By the end of the conversation, when the dishonest entrepreneur realizes that Will (who has the *real* mind for business) is using dishonest tactics, he is now interested. He dramatically dictates that dishonesty is "the enterprise ... the *very life blood* that pumps through the veins"—words that continue to reflect his didactic and facetious persona. Following these lines, the men look offscreen to the next shot—an image of Wellville, their utopia. This brief, seemingly insignificant beat is, in fact, the essence of the title *The Road to Wellville*, a direct reference to Dr. Kellogg's rival—Grape Nuts entrepreneur Charles W. Post. In the novel, Will makes a *faux pas* in the presence of Dr. Kellogg when he innocently says, "Three months and I'll be on the *Road to Wellville*, eh? ... All at once it came to Will: *The Road to Wellville*. This wasn't one of the doctor's slogans, not at all—it was C.W. Post's." Kellogg responds irately, "We don't speak cant here, sir ... not in this institution. Cheap slogan-mongering, that's all it is.... We do not mention that name in this institution ... ever."[26] Will, still perplexed by Dr. Kellogg's anger, makes another (worse) *faux paux*: he says that he is merely quoting information from what he read in Post's booklet that was given to consumers inside the boxes of Grape Nuts. Post later established forty-two companies in Calhoun County that manufactured cereal and coffee substitutes; he also founded Sanitas Food Company, a venture that served as a catalyst for the Kellogg brothers' longtime feud. Over time, W.K. eventually bought out his brother and consequently became the number-one cereal manufacturer, making Battle Creek, Michigan, one of the most well-known cities in the United States.[27]

The following major sequence opens in a dining room, where Will is searching for Eleanor. Under the restrictions of his diet, he orders dry toast and water and meets an ensemble of San residents, including an English man named Endymion Hart-Jones (John Neville). Another member of this entourage is the chronically flatulent Professor Stepanovich (Alexander Slanksnis), whose nickname is "Mr. Unpronounceable," from the Academy of Astronomical Sciences in St. Petersburg, Russia. Author Boyle describes him as "a dwarfish man with a tiny pointed beard and bulbous head."[28] Also among the crowd is Mrs. Tindermarsh (Monica Parker), and the Cleveland industrialist Homer Praetz.

In this scene, the conversation turns to the topic of enemas. Endymion Hart-Jones tells Will (who is "suffering from a sore rectum" brought on by an average of five colonic washings a day) that he'll get used to these enemas; moreover, he'll "look forward to them like an old friend with a cold nose." This discussion then turns into a rather absurd musical number that appears to come out of nowhere: Ida Muntz informs Will about the significance of mastication and the group looks at a sign above the entrance that reads: FLETCHERIZE! The novel explains:

> Fletcher was the naturopathic genius who's revealed to the world the single most fundamental principle of good health, diet and digestion: mastication. Thorough mastication. Fletcher maintained (and Dr. Kellogg concurred with all his heart) the nearest thing to a panacea for gastric ills and nutritional disorders was the total digestion of food in the mouth.[29]

The group song which follows highlights this concept, with lyrics emphasizing that good food can only be good for you if you chew, chew chew.

Moments later, Will finally sees Eleanor with Dr. Linniman, then passes out. Eleanor explains to the others that it must be because of his all-toast diet. In the next major scene, Will tells Eleanor that he wants to go home. The camera captures her in a vulnerable high-angle shot and she replies, "But we both made a promise. We're not well. Neither of us. Don't you see we can never be happy until we're healthy again? Such small sacrifices for all the happy years ahead of us." An alternating POV low-angle shot captures Eleanor on the stairs (she has taken charge again). In this moment the viewer receives vital backstory. She reminds Will of their troubled past, which includes two major facts: he was an alcoholic—a "useless drunk"; and due to *his* neglect, their baby daughter died. Consequently, she leaves, followed by plaintive woodwind music that accurately matches her melancholy state. When she is gone, Will thoughtfully, even poignantly, speaks to the closed door in front of him: "I'm sorry—I'm truly sorry." What the viewer eventually discovers, however, is this reality: Will is ill *because* of his wife. As a result of trying to cure his alcoholism and philandering, Eleanor purchased something called *The Sears White Star Liquor Cure*, an antidote that was supposed to cure a husband's wanderlust. According to the instructions, she had put five drops of the medicine into his coffee, and this dosage assured that he would "roam no more."[30] Ironically, however, Will became addicted to the medicine! Boyle's third chapter—"Sears' White Star Liquor Cure"—provides the reader with most of Will and Eleanor's history, setting the foundation for their present plight.[31]

In the next scene, this aforementioned backstory is continued when Eleanor explains to Virginia (while they both soak in a steam bath) how she virtually "poisoned" her husband. This is the catalyst that leads to a discussion that questions the institution of marriage and the role of men. "Marrying is legalized prostitution," Virginia exclaims. Eleanor admits that, as a woman, she "wanted to be more than a hole in the mattress that answers to a name," to which Virginia replies, "Amen!" In the following scene, Eleanor finishes telling Virginia about her past, including the story of the Sears White Star Liquor Cure and her losing a child. These women continue to represent the "sexually awakened" Victorian-era female on the verge of breaking away from their respective patriarchal prisons.

A quick cut leads to a new transition, beginning in a pigsty. The following cut shows someone's legs rapidly walking and then an upward tilt reveals this human swine—Bartholomew Bookbinder (Marshall Efron), a rotund man with a thick dark mustache. Another upward tilt reveals Bender, who is explaining to Charles that Bookbinder is one of Kellogg's "top men." He, along with George and Charlie, walks through the pigsty (the metaphor is not subtle in that they are *all* pigs) into their meeting place where they drink to "new prospects ... to shining aspires of Wellville," replete with the framing of the PER-FO sign above them. Throughout the film, these types of signs help to frame the story; they are visual transitional devices.

Back to the San: Men draped in white sheets exercise while muttering the mantra: "No fish or fowl is a friend of the bowels." Will is among this group and, as he is getting undressed, an entourage of reporters watch Dr. Kellogg examine Will's stools. The doctor is outraged by the musty foul smell; according to him, the perfect stools should be like *his*: "gigantic, and with no more odor than a hot biscuit." He proceeds to photograph Will with a large-format camera: Will, moving cataclysmically on Dr. Kellogg's exercise machine, discusses his sexual urges. Again, Dr. Kellogg reprimands him and warns him about the dangers of sexual activity and the loss of vital bodily fluids. He further reports that Bulgarians live the longest lives because of the great amount of yogurt they consume. Will tells him that he simply can't eat the fifteen gallons of yogurt that the doctor has prescribed. Sadistically, Kellogg says, "Oh, it's not going in *that* end, Mr. Lightbody!"

A rapid cut leads to a montage of Will exercising on a type of treadmill, wearing a contraption that looks like a gas mask, while undergoing water therapy. This scene transitions to a follow-up scene where Will and other San patients are receiving electrotherapy between their legs (to cure sexual urges).

In the next scene—which takes place outside, among a group of hospital beds—Will and Ida Muntz are positioned in adjacent beds, and this eventually leads to their first sexual encounter. (Why is it that Dr. Kellogg's anti-sexual treatments make his guests desire sex even *more*?) Ida explains to Will that her pale complexion is a result of "green sickness"— she tells him that he has "kind eyes" and "a noble nose" and then proceeds to ask him for a "great favor." Without skipping a beat, Will gets under Ida's sheets and proceeds to have intercourse with her while a woman in the background leads an aerobic exercise with the humorously appropriate mantra of "in and out, in and out, in and out...."

In the following scene, Eleanor visits Will and tells him she wants to have another baby, but not until they are both well. They are both sexually charged (undoubtedly triggered by their involvement with other people), and engage in a kiss. Like a mythical conscience of sorts, Nurse Graves enters the room and breaks up this moment. Eleanor leaves rapidly and the jealous nurse tells Will that she is disappointed in him (which suggests that she likes him) and although she preaches Dr. Kellogg's law of abstinence, she, too, is sexually repressed and needs to be liberated. Will informs her that he has feelings. "I do, too," she says sensitively. A lingering shot on Will: He looks into Ida's room and sees her head covered (she is embarrassed), but her breasts are revealed, inviting him to enter the room. Unbeknown to the great doctor, his Temple of Health has become the Temple of Sex!

Cut to Ida's room: Ida vulnerably asks Will what color her face is. Non-judgmentally he tells her that it is more pale than green. She asks him to lie on top of her, and he happily obliges. A jump cut follows, humorously showing Will's clothes on the floor, leading to a dissolve into a high-angle shot of a group of patients doing exercises while snow falls from the sky (time has passed). A band with French horns and a group of carolers set the new time frame of the film—Christmas. In an exterior shot outside the San, Will and Nurse Graves are throwing snowballs at each other, suggesting that an unexpected romance may be budding.

While the festivities ensue (the first chapter of the second section of the novel is called "Tis the Season"),[32] a new character, Lionel Badger (Colm Meaney), steps out of his horse-drawn buggy and enters the San. This is followed by a low-angle shot on Eleanor and Virginia with the Battle Creek sanitarium sign framed above them; the shot reveals that these *women* have been empowered—psychologically and physically. According to the novel, Badger arrived at the San as a guest to give a lecture. The viewer learns about him through an exchange between Virginia and Eleanor:

Virginia: He wrote a fabulous book on the clitoris.
Eleanor: But I thought you said he was a veterinarian.
Virginia: It's all related, darling.

The novel describes Dr. Kellogg's perspective of Badger:

The Doctor pictured Badger's great swollen head fringed with a red fluff the consistency of pubic hair, the bulging eyes the grim set of the jaw. The last time he'd visited he'd had the temerity to take the Doctor to task for wearing shoes of animal hide—leather, that is—while he, Badger, wore rope sandals, winter and summer. Lionel Badger—he was a fanatic of the worst stripe, the nearest thing to a flagellant the Vegetarian Movement could lay claim to...[33]

The low-key lighting following this scene is reminiscent of the look and style of a Dutch Still life painting: Charles, Bender, George and Bookbinder are making and sampling batches of their own corn flakes. In a comedic montage, the entrepreneurs eat batch after batch and continuously spit out their burned, discolored, unsavory cereal. This sequence is cross-cut with Virginia and Eleanor, who are experiencing Badger's sexual therapy. Virginia tells Eleanor that—as would be expected—Dr. Kellogg *hates* Badger's therapy and further states, "The only thing hateful about sex, my dear, is when women don't get enough of it when they want it, or don't get to enjoy it when they do."

Cut to Will: he is walking peacefully down the lobby singing "O' Come All Ye' Faithful." Suddenly he is attacked by "projectiles." George has arrived and, according to Dr. Kellogg's secretary, Poultney Dab (Roy Brocksmith), he is "throwing boxes of shit at the guests." The film certainly immerses itself in scatological references, but the narrative isn't merely relying on bathroom humor for laughs; instead, the film is a parable that uses the scatological humor to make a point about the role of capitalism and greed. Similarly, the 1975 Pier Paolo Pasolini film *Salo*—a horrific and disturbing film about the dangers of Italian fascism—has a few scenes when the tortured "guests" are forced to consume a platter of feces. Upon closer examination, the scene critiques the role of aristocrats and their tendency toward autonomy as well as the role of consumerism, which (like *The Road to Wellville*) speaks to the "you are what you eat" adage. At the end of the scene Dr. Kellogg regresses and reprimands his son as if George were a little boy again: "You're a bad boy, George"—and this leads to a flashback in which "O' Come All Ye' Faithful" plays in a different context: Young George, the only one in a church choir, "farts," eliciting laughter from the other children. This outrages Dr. Kellogg, who (knowingly) asks who did this rude act.

The memory returns to the present: Dab is walking in the snow and suddenly drops dead of what is later revealed as a heart attack. When Kellogg stumbles upon his secretary's carcass, he calls him a good man but in the same breath scolds him, telling him that death is "unprofessional"—then he kicks him. The novel describes this scene thus:

> The little Doctor lifted his head from the secretary's chest, dropped the wrist he'd gathered between thumb and forefinger. Dab's features were locked in the vise-grip of death, mouth open, tongue prominent, eyes fixed in blind contemplation of the lowering sky. John Harvey Kellogg pushed himself up from the street, brusquely rubbing his palms together to remove any particulate matter that might have adhered to them.[34]

Most ironically, Dab dies as a product of poor health while he worked for Dr. Kellogg in The Temple of Health!

The following scene continues the film's foray into black comedy. Will is with Endymion Hart-Jones in the Electrical Department in a steam bath, where an electrical short causes the death of the Russian professor "Mr. Unpronounceable" and a bath attendant named Alfred Woodbine (Mark Jeffrey Miller). In the novel the attendant is described as an "impeccably dressed attendant, with [a] crisp bow tie, immaculate collar and pomaded hair."[35] Will panics and runs out of the room like a silent movie comedian as he searches for Nurse Graves. Instead of finding the lovely nurse, he runs into the grotesque Nurse Bloethal, who tactlessly informs him that Ida Muntz has died. Will yells, "Everyone's dying!

If this is the healthiest place on earth, why is everyone dying?" This sequence ends with a close-up of Dab's dead body and the outrageous expression on his face is, admittedly, funny—at least in a macabre way.

In an abrupt cut, Lionel Badger is preaching to a group of women about animal cruelty and, while doing so, he makes a suggestive tongue gesture toward Eleanor. He didactically speaks about animal rights as though he were hamming his way through a Shakespearean monologue, further accenting the film's penchant for esoteric poetic style: "Do we not hear the bleeding of the calves? The bellowing of the bull? The cackling of frightened geese?" One cannot help but wonder: Is this character a critique on the perceived hypocrisy associated with vegetarian activism?

As the conversation about slaughtered animals ends, the film cuts to the Red Onion, where men are savagely consuming meat and drinking alcohol. Will, disheartened by the services of the San, has arrived at the pub and orders a burger and asks for it to be not just rare, but "cold in the middle." (Incidentally, "Cold in the Middle" is also the name of chapter three in the third part of the novel.)[36]

Meanwhile, Lionel Badger is in a room talking to Eleanor about animal cruelty (he informs her that glue is made of animals' hooves, and "quack medicines" are obtained from their testicles) while attempting to seduce her. He touches her breast and tells her that "the bust is the fountain of life" and that "flat-chested women are a danger to themselves." A quick cut to the Red Onion shows Will and Charles discussing finances. Charles talks of his misfortunes in business, and Will reminds him that people "should never live in a world where dreams are rarer than money," then offers him a thousand-dollar check for his troubles. Like in the previous scene with Eleanor and Badger, a dominant character consoles a vulnerable character, using money as a vehicle to critique this "root of all evil."

The Christmas festivities continue back at the San. Dr. Kellogg is dressed as Santa Claus while promoting more vegetarian propaganda. A caged goose (symbolizing meat-eating consumerism and imprisonment) is wheeled into the assembly room. Facetiously, the Doctor says to his audience, "Here at the San, [your] goose is *not* cooked!" Unlike Badger, Dr. Kellogg, despite his egomaniacal shortcomings, supports humanitarianism first ... he believes wholeheartedly in his seventy-five inventions as means of helping to cure people. His shortcomings, ironically, may be seen as a result of his extreme idealism. For instance, the fact that he wanted to rescue George and the other orphans, or the idea that the notorious rivalry with his brother Will and Charles Post (note how these first names have been given to characters in this story) is partially a result of Dr. Kellogg's anti-capitalistic/pro-humanitarian life mission. Shouldn't a real humanitarian, ideally anyway, have a healthy relationship with his own son and brother? Shouldn't a humanitarian consider the sexual needs and pleasures of one's own wife (perhaps Eleanor and Virginia represent the sexually dissatisfied "everywoman")? Shouldn't a true humanitarian who claims not to be interested in consumerism and capital gain be running a very profitable business populated by the aristocracy? That said: Is Dr. Kellogg, in fact, a hypocrite à la Badger? Are both of these men using vegetarianism to feed their own egotistical needs—Kellogg's cerebral intellectualism versus Badger's id-driven libido?

Back at the Red Onion, Will and Charles are now drunk and they use scatological humor to critique Dr. Kellogg's enterprise.

Will: Charlie, with friends like you, who needs *enemas*?
Charlie (responds by toasting): To friendship.... To looking like shit.... To being full of shit.... To bad health.... To indigestion.... To *Shitsville*.

This talk of excrement shifts (through parallel edits) to bodily fluids as Badger talks to Eleanor about the importance of addressing one's sexual impulses. "Why pretend sex doesn't exist?' he asks her. Then he contradicts Dr. Kellogg's abstinence theory and says that keeping bodily fluids *inside* the body is detrimental to one's good health. Again, the film is using figurative means, like parable and allegory, as vehicles for understanding the central themes of the narrative—letting go of repression and understanding the hypocrisy of humanity.

In the following scene, a very drunk Will, now back at the San, is singing in a mud bath as Eleanor is led to him by an orderly. A low-angle POV shot shows Will looking up at his infuriated wife, who is all too aware of his condition. He informs her about the recent deaths, insisting that "Mr. Unpronounceable" and Woodbine were "murdered" in the "suicidal bath"—"fried like pork chops," he adds graphically. Defeated, she retorts: "You make it so difficult to love you." Dr. Kellogg arrives, still in his Santa costume, and Will vomits on his beard. Without reacting or skipping a beat, the Doctor catches a whiff of the remains and realizes that his guest had been eating pickles, relish and pork! Consequently, the Doctor schedules him for an emergency surgery; in the next scene, Will is being pushed around the institution in a wheelchair. This farce is cross-cut with Bender, Charles and George, the three hopeless jesters captured in their pseudo-business microcosm. Back to a quick beat of Will flirting with Nurse Graves, returning to a jump-cut of the three buffoons who, after many failed attempts at making their own cereal, resort to stealing Kellogg's Toasted Corn Flakes and putting the cereal in their ready-made PER-FO boxes. Perhaps these thieves all represent G.W. Post, who was accused of stealing the Grape Nuts recipe directly from Kellogg's kitchen!

Meanwhile, the frenzied cross-cutting continues, ending the sequence with Dr. Kellogg preparing for Will's surgery while (yet again) being observed by an audience of admiring nurses, who applaud him. After the surgery, Will asks Nurse Graves if he died and went to heaven and she replies, "Heaven on Earth.... You're at the San." Will's newfound feeling of peace is a result of Dr. Kellogg's successful operation; he cured Will of "the kink." The dialogue in the novel helps explain this further. Dr. Kellogg speaks:

> [Sir Arbuthnot Lane] happens to be one of the most eminent physicians in the world, attached now to the Royal College of Surgeons, London, and he has perfected a surgical technique to improve motility and correct the often fatal consequences of autointoxication. To amateurs, the operation—an abdominal section to remove a portion of the lower intestine where stasis routinely occurs—is known as the "Lane's Kink" surgery.... I've located my own "kink" as it were ... though no one has taken to calling it "Kellogg's Kink" yet, to my knowledge, but they will, they will ... and my technique has relieved scores of severely auto-intoxicated and even moribund patients from the symptoms that afflict you.[37]

As *The Road to Wellville* progresses, the film's main stories become more consciously linked while continuing to use the technique of cross-cutting to build suspense. The next phase of the film explores Eleanor's journey into sexual enlightenment. The scene begins with a claustrophobic closed-form *mise-en-scène* at a dinner table in the outdoors: Eleanor occupies the upper-left portion of the frame; another reluctant woman who refuses to do "anything German" (Is this comment a reference to German pornography, which is notorious for its use of scatological sex?) takes up the lower-left side; Badger and Virginia (the most sexually liberal characters of the four) balance them out on the right side of the frame. Badger becomes an exhibitionist and takes off his shirt, while reporting: "I'm not afraid of my body ... it's completely natural." During this exchange, there is a mention of Professor Kunts (the innovator of the German Nudist Movement, known as *Freikorper Kultur*, as described in Chapter 3 in the third part of the novel), who helps women become healthy by "manipulating their wombs."[38] At this time the film introduces another character: the renowned holistic healer Dr. Spitzvogel (Norbert Weisser), a local student of Kuntz and a specialist in "movement therapy," a branch of *Freikorper Kultur*.

During this exploration of bodily pleasures, Eleanor quite abruptly gets up, moves toward a woman at the next table, and consequently spills wine on her, then removes the fox collar she is wearing. The vegetarian advocate tells the perturbed woman that the spilled wine represents animal's blood, indicating that no animal should suffer to make *her* look beautiful. Badger and the others applaud. She has been converted.

The following sequence returns to the vaudevillian antics of Bender and Charles. Charles is the pedantic neurotic, concerned because he has received a letter from his aunt Amelia Hookstratten, who is planning to visit the San to calm her nerves; she also stipulates that she wants to see the PER-FO factory (completely unaware that no such place exists). Bender is the pompous straight man whose deceptive disposition surmounts that of his partner—instead of taking anything seriously, he continues to justify his actions by speaking didactically through cliché: "Behind every shining fortune lurks the shadow of a lie."

In the next scene, Endymion Hart-Jones leaves the San, and Will sees him off (the two of them have built an unlikely friendship). Like in a previous scene, in which Dr. Kellogg reflects upon his past, the film transcends all farce and black comedy and offers instead— even if just for a moment—a compassionate human exchange. The old man's thoughtful parting words of wisdom to his friend are the following: "What is life but a temporary victory over that which causes our inevitable death." He adds, "Follow your heart; it is the one organ that will surely let you down one day but don't waste it while you're living." Unlike the absurd hypocrisy of Bender's arcane verbiage, Endymion, although darkly comical in tone, speaks to a useful Buddhist theme—to live *in the moment*.

The final stretch of the film begins by juxtaposing Will and Eleanor's respective exposure to sexual pleasures: Eleanor through Dr. Spizvogel's "womb manipulation," and Will through a new toy given to him as a gift by Endymion—The Dusselberg Belt, a masturbation harness invented by Professor Kuntz. The husband and wife, once detached from one another, are now "together" (juxtaposed through parallel editing) receiving sexual pleasure via *Freikorper Kultur*.

Meanwhile, the sequence builds in a cataclysmically sexual rhythm, leading the viewer back to the San at Dr. Kellogg's luncheon, a festivity that will end with him exposing Charles Ossining's fraudulence. The Doctor experiences another flashback, this one involving young George sitting at the dinner table with the rest of the children, refusing to eat the vegetarian food set before him. The boy revolts, "*Food*? You call this *food*? We want *proper* food. Meat and potatoes!" Later on, a defeated Dr. Kellogg asks his hired nurse/nanny what he has been doing wrong; after all, he claims, he has given George everything he needs. She humbly replies by saying, "Maybe what you're giving him isn't what he *needs*." In the novel this story is told in a chapter called "Father to All, Father to None."³⁹

During this time, Charles is searching for Bender at the hotel where he has been staying, only to discover that his partner has disappeared (in the novel, Charles is perpetually looking for Bender). The concierge informs Charles about Bender's unpaid bill and consequently demands payment. Charles sprints out of the building, resulting in another slapstick comedy moment.

Back at the San: Dr. Kellogg informs Will that Eleanor has been carrying on with Dr. Spitzvogel, who has been "manipulating her womb," and accuses him of neglecting her. At this time, Kellogg reveals the confiscated Dusselberg Belt and reprimands Will: "Nurse Bloethal found this apparatus under your bed, sir." During this exchange the nurses (the doctor's ever-admiring audience) watch their mentor as he curses masturbation. "Build up your resolve ... not your genitals," he exclaims, bringing the scene to an end.

At Kellogg's luncheon, Mrs. Hookstratten has coerced her nephew Charles to attend the San with her so that, over lunch, he can update her on her investment. At this time, Virginia and Eleanor sneak off together, eventually meeting up with Badger and Dr. Spitzvogel (who, in this section of the novel, is referred to only as "the womb manipulator") for a session in *Freikorper Kultur*, fifteen miles from Battle Creek, in the woods of Kalamazoo.

Meanwhile, Nurse Graves asks Will to go for a walk to Goguac Lake, and he gladly accepts the offer. The two of them end up on a boat and their "innocent walk" turns into a brief, awkward romantic interlude during which they eventually kiss. After the kiss, however, Will realizes that he still loves his wife, and Nurse Graves, who realizes, too, that they had made a mistake, resigns to Dr. Kellogg's words: "Sex is the sewer drain of a healthy body, Will."

The scene continues to build through rapid cross-cutting as the stories intertwine more intricately. At the luncheon (referred to as "The Fatal Luncheon" in the novel) Dr. Kellogg—in yet another public spectacle—reveals to his guests that Charles Ossining is a fraud. "You took advantage of this

Cartoon by Alan Parker from his book, *Will Write and Direct for Food* (London: Southbank Publishing, 2005).

good woman for vulgar profit!" he exclaims, highlighting the doctor's disdain for capitalism. Charles retorts vehemently, first by informing the doctor and the audience that it was *Bender* who should be blamed, not he. Charles then prepares a scathing attack on his accuser. He calls Dr. Kellogg a fraud and a hypocrite who makes a profit by feeding his guests "sawdust and grain" so that he can perform his enemas. These words bring about Charles's fate and Kellogg orders constables to take him away and the now-familiar "Keystone Kops" chase sequence ensues, replete with the fast-paced brass and kazoo accompaniment.

More fraudulence: While walking through the woods, Will stumbles upon Eleanor, Virginia, Dr. Spitzvogel and Lionel Badger engaged in a very intimate act of *Freikorper Kultur*. This discovery results in another slapstick scene, this one involving Will confiscating the doctor's walking stick and using it as a weapon against the entire group. The novel describes this scene from Will's POV, providing a good description of the way the scene unfolds on film:

> He saw that there were two men there by the riverside and two women and that they were naked, all of them—completely, entirely, utterly naked, right down to their toes. The women were lolling on their backs, propped up on two legs at waist level and one of the men stood between them, the stark white bunch of his buttocks facing the spot where Will stood concealed. The man's arms were extended on each side of him, his hands working between the women's legs. The other man—it was Badger—stood just behind them, masturbating himself. And the women? One of them, the one on the right was Virginia Cranehill, her great tanned slippery dugs splayed out across her chest, her eyes closed and face transported in ecstasy. The other woman was Eleanor....[40]

Once the group disperses, Will and Eleanor come face to face. Despite the absurdity of her statements—that things were not what they appeared and that Will was overreacting—she *does* seem genuinely interested in Will's overall health. Quite suddenly the tone changes and they are a happily married couple again. Will admits, "I never felt better in my whole life." Eleanor, elated, announces that they have been cured and they can now go home. They kiss each other passionately. These figurative fireworks, so to speak, transition into real fireworks that explode in the sky over the San, while Charles is being escorted to prison.

The last stretch of the film—seen through a stylized montage—returns the viewer to the final father-and-son reunion. George, who has already started a fire at the San, warns his father that he is going to burn the building to the ground. The camera captures Dr. Kellogg in an extreme close-up as he yells, "You're mad and you're drunk!" More chaos results and, at this stage, all three vignettes have merged, reaching their narrative crescendo. In one of the doctor's labs, George throws "projectiles" (excrement) at his father and the two of them struggle until George falls into a large vat filled with some kind of hot liquid, which, in the novel, is described as "the rich rising effluvia of macadamia butter."[41] Dr. Kellogg rescues his son and, while dripping and oozing from the hot butter, George regresses and in a childish voice says, "Give us a cuddle, Daddy," which endears the doctor, and they embrace; the scene also mirrors the reunion of Will and Eleanor. The novel, however, takes a less romantic view:

> George was an experiment that hadn't worked.... George was weak. An aberration. He should have never been born.... [Dr. Kellogg] let him go, let him drift away, face down, a glow with precious oil. It was a hard thing to do, as hard a thing as he'd ever done in his life. But as he

stood there, bleeding quietly into the tatters of his clothes, even as George bobbed gently away from him, he knew he would draw strength from it. For he was no weakling, he was no George. He was John Harvey Kellogg and he would live forever.[42]

These aforementioned words end the novel, followed by a brief coda that in the film begins with Eleanor's narration: "The San burned for three nights and three days. The glow in the sky could be seen as far as Kalamazoo." This is ensued by a dissolve into an aristocratic milieu, replete with a white house surrounded by a green lawn. Will is seen holding a little girl in his lap. Eleanor continues with the narration: "Will and I lived very happily in Peterskill, where we had four daughters and I operated Westchere's first health store." She explains that, in the confusion of the fire at the San, the charges against Charles Ossining had been forgotten and over time he eventually became very rich when he founded Cola Kane, the first experiment in "taking sugar water and impregnating it with the leaf of the coca plant." In the novel, Grape Nuts founder C.W. Post and Charlie worked together to form the Perfect Tonic Company (PER-FO became PER-TO), which was a great success.[43]

Finally, Dr. Kellogg's epilogue: The old doctor, still a picture of good health, makes an announcement before making a big dive into a lake. He informs his press (always the exhibitionist surrounded by an audience of admirers) that he will live forever because his "bowels are immaculate." Kellogg takes his dive and while he is in mid-air, the image freezes. Eleanor narrates: "Alas, Dr. Kellogg dies mid-somersault, proving once and for all that even *he* was not right about everything." Although the novel does not mention this dive, the final words of the coda bring this story to a close:

> In the end, though he received and administrated more enemas than any man in history, though he ate more vegetables, smoked less, drank less, slept less and exercised more than practically any man of his time, even Dr. Kellogg couldn't live forever. On December 14, 1943, like his nemesis, C.W. Post, before him, John Harvey Kellogg passed on into eternity. He did die, yes. But could anyone ask for more?[44]

An ambitious undertaking in many regards, *The Road to Wellville* is certainly one of Alan Parker's most idiosyncratic endeavors and a film that moves him further away from the pigeonholing of the Auteur theory. What he has crafted is not just a stylized comedy but also an offbeat and oddly accurate biopic of one of America's most eccentric figures to emerge from the 20th century.

13

Evita (1996)

December 25; 134 minutes/Color
Production Company: Hollywood Pictures, Cinergi Pictures, Dirty Hands Productions
Distributor: Buena Vista Pictures (U.S.); Entertainment Films (UK)
Director: Alan Parker
Screenwriter: Alan Parker, Oliver Stone (Based on *Evita* by Andrew Lloyd Webber and Tim Rice)
Producers: Alan Parker, Robert Stigwood, Andrew G. Vajna
Production Designer: Brian Morris
Cinematography: Darius Khondji
Editor: Gerry Hambling
Original Music: Andrew Lloyd Webber (Lyrics by Tim Rice)
Cast: Madonna (Eva Perón); Antonio Banderas (Ché); Jonathan Pryce (Juan Perón); Jimmy Nail (Agustín Magaldi); Victoria Sus (Doña Juana); Julian Littman (Brother Juan); Olga Merediz (Blanca); Laura Pallas (Elisa); Julia Worsley (Erminda); María Luján Hidalgo (Young Eva); Servando Villamil (Cipriano Reyes); Andrea Corr (Perón's mistress); Peter Polycarpou (Domingo Mercante); Gary Brooker (Juan Bramuglia)

> While *Evita* is a story of people whose lives were in politics, it is not a political story.—*Evita* concept album liner notes

Notes on the Production

In November of 1976, Andrew Lloyd Webber and Tim Rice released their concept album *Evita*, which was a modern, sung-through opera on the life of Eva Perón. Alan Parker was intrigued by the album, and, soon after its release, he asked Webber and Rice's manager, David Land, if they had thought of making a film of the record, as Parker immediately recognized its cinematic potential.[1] He was told by Land that "the boys" wanted to make it a stage show first, so Parker bowed out for the time being. In 1979, however, Robert Stigwood invited Parker to the Broadway opening and asked him if he would be interested in making a film of *Evita*. Having just completed *Fame*, however, Parker informed Land that he did not want to make back-to-back musicals. Stigwood was extremely disappointed (according to Parker, he actually started hitting him with a tennis racket out of frustration), and so the film was ostensibly going to go to another director.[2]

For fifteen years, Parker waited in the wings as the film adaptation of *Evita* was *about* to be made, and Parker began to regret saying no to Stigwood, feeling that he had missed the boat, as he had heard that directors such as Francis Ford Coppola and Oliver Stone were being considered for the project. It seemed that fate was on his side, however, when

Director Alan Parker on the set of *Evita* with actress and singer Madonna (portraying First Lady of Argentina, Eva Perón). *Evita* (1996), Hollywood Pictures; Cinergi Pictures; Dirty Hands Productions.

at the end of 1994, everything came full circle as Robert Stigwood again approached Parker and asked him to make the film.[3]

The actress who was touted to play Evita was Michelle Pfeiffer, so Parker met with her in late 1994. The two of them both came to the realization that, with two small children to tend to, Pfeiffer was less than willing to embark on a journey to Argentina, a long way away from Hollywood sound studios. Around Christmas 1994, Parker received a letter from Madonna. The hand-written, four-page letter was an impassioned plea to play the part of Evita. As far as she was concerned, she was custom-made for the role, and no one else could play Evita as well as she could. Parker was taken by her enthusiasm and agreed to cast her in the part.[4]

For the pivotal role of Ché, the film's narrator and sort of moral barometer (the Greek Chorus, as it were), Antonio Banderas was the favorite. Parker viewed a tape of him singing in a cold audition he had done, and was immediately convinced. For Juan Perón, Parker decided on Jonathan Pryce, a classically trained British actor. After his scintillating performance as Lytton Strachey in *Carrington*, Pryce was intrigued by the script, but wanted to meet with Parker before committing. Parker flew to see him at Marseilles, where Pryce was vacationing. However, Pryce's New York agent neglected to tell Parker that the meeting had been canceled, so Parker was forced to wait around at the Marseilles airport to no avail, eventually surrendering and flying back to London. They eventually met in London, however, and Pryce agreed to play the part.[5]

Parker then commenced his assiduous research on Evita, as he wanted write a balanced story, or as balanced a story as could be written on such a controversial, polarizing figure. He wanted to maintain the heart of the original stage play. The following is an excerpt from the original liner notes of the album, which Parker no doubt read:

> While *Evita* is a story of people whose lives were in politics, it is not a political story. It is a Cinderella story about the astonishing life of a girl from the most mundane of backgrounds, who became the most powerful woman her country (and indeed Latin America) had ever seen, a woman never content to be a mere ornament at the side of her husband, the president.[6]

While he intended to keep this mission statement intact, however, he decided to ultimately ignore the execution of the stage play, as most of the directorial decisions bore little comparison to a cinematic interpretation. One major change that Parker made was to jettison the idea that the character of Ché be clearly identified as Ché Guevara, the iconic revolutionary, which the stage play had done. Parker felt that since Guevara almost certainly never met Eva Perón, it would suffice to simply call the character Ché, which is a common nickname in Argentina, like "buddy" or "pal" in the U.S.[7]

When his version of the script, which contained 146 changes to the original score and lyrics, was finished, Parker apprehensively sent it to Andrew Lloyd Webber and Tim Rice. Thankfully, they liked the script, and were not indignant about any of the changes Parker had made. Webber and Rice then had to collaborate to write a new song for Parker's film, and Webber was required to write entirely new scoring for some of the numbers.

On October 2, 1995, after intense rehearsals with the cast in London, Parker and crew decided to begin recording in London, at CTS Studios in Wembley. Things got off to a rocky start, however, as Madonna attempted to lay down a vocal track for "Don't Cry For Me, Argentina." She did so simultaneously with an eighty-four-piece orchestra, and Webber, who was attending the recording session, soon devolved into a vitriolic fit, proclaiming his intense unhappiness with the frenetic, unfocused performances of Madonna, the orchestra, and the conductor. After Madonna was brought nearly to tears, Parker knew he had to make things right. He and Webber met with Madonna at her hotel room, and the three of them reached a productive creative conclusion—they would recruit a new conductor, and assuage the strain on Madonna by allowing her to record only every other day, allowing her voice to rest.[8]

After dealing with this stressful diversion, Parker had to return to his primary duty, that of being a film director, so he traveled to Buenos Aires to meet with then–Argentine president Carlos Menem, seeking to gain his approval to film in his country. Menem did not meet Parker's requests with alacrity, claiming that he would face possibly violent reprisals at the hands of the Peronistas if he granted Parker the right to film in the Casa Rosada. His assiduous dedication to locational authenticity not to be deterred, Parker decided that he would at least have to shoot *some* of the film in Argentina. At the very least, he surmised that he could film the scenes of Eva's early life in Los Toldos, Junín, and Chivilcoy. He decided that he would start filming in Buenos Aires, and then move to Budapest, where he felt he could accurately replicate the European architecture of Buenos Aires in the 1930s and '40s. He planned on shooting in Buenos Aires for two weeks; however, the crew's stay there would be contingent upon the degree of backlash they received from the irate Peronistas.

Parker's reservations proved legitimate, as he, his cast, and crew were greeted less-than-graciously by the Argentinians. As they drove down the streets of Buenos Aires, they were faced with graffiti and signs reading, "Fuera Madonna (Go Home Madonna)," and, "Chau Alan Parker and your English task force." Although overcome by fear, Parker trudged on, casting the scores of locals for the smaller parts and finalizing his locations. The torment and harassment continued, with journalists and locals shouting threats and obscenities at Parker as he was filming. Parker was even accosted in the bathroom of his hotel by a headstrong journalist who proceeded to grill the director as he was urinating.[9]

Then came the issue of filming at the Casa Rosada. President Menem had already expressed his discontent at the idea to Parker, so Parker told production designer Brian Morris to begin constructing an exact replica at Shepperton Studios in England. Madonna, however, had somehow managed an unofficial meeting with Menem. A week later, she, Parker, Jonathan Pryce, and Antonio Banderas were sitting with Menem, eating pizza, when Madonna brashly stood up and said to Menem, "Let's cut to the chase here. Do we have the balcony or don't we?" Menem smiled and nodded, "You can have the balcony."[10] In a remarkable moment of life imitating art, imitating life, Madonna proved why she was cast in the eponymous role of the film.

As four thousand extras watched Madonna perform "Don't Cry For Me, Argentina" on the balcony of the Casa Rosada, a transition took place—the Argentinians had accepted the presence of the film crew, and they shot in Argentina for five fruitful weeks. They then moved to Hungary, as they transported all of their equipment to Budapest, which, according to Parker, was a decidedly bleak, unpleasant place, and they were plagued by everything from horrendous food to rashes on their private parts, due to the unsanitary toilet paper. To add insult to injury, Madonna informed Parker that she was pregnant, sending him into an anxiety-ridden tizzy, calculating the shooting days left, wondering if they were going to be able to pull it off. After five weeks of shooting, they left Budapest (not a moment too soon for anyone on the crew) and returned to London, to the comfort of Shepperton Studios, where the vibe was much more relaxed, as everyone was now sleeping in cozy beds and avoiding rashes on their private parts. Filming wrapped on May 30, after filming for eighty-four days in three different countries. The film went on to do quite well, grossing over $141 million, having cost only $55 million to make. It garnered five Academy Award nominations ("You Must Love Me" winning for Best Original Song), five Golden Globe nominations (winning three—Madonna for Best Actress, Best Original Song, and Best Motion Picture in the Musical or Comedy category), and eight BAFTA nominations. The success of the film engendered a 2006 West End revival of the stage play, as well as a recent 2012 Broadway revival in New York City. It also prompted the government of Argentina to release its own film biography of Perón, entitled *Eva Perón*, which attempted to set the record straight and remedy any misconceptions or inaccuracies they felt Parker's film espoused.

Summary

As the Cinergi Pictures logo fades and the opening credits appear over a black screen, the sound of horse hoofs galloping over a dusty, dirt surface plays on the soundtrack, which, at first, conjures up images of the Wild West, of outlaws on horseback, gallivanting around the open frontier, searching for gold and adventure. The horse then whinnies as gunshots ring out, and a fracas ensues—a crowd of people raucously clamoring and shouting. Adventure/Danger music then plays over the fracas, then fades away, until only the voice of a woman and a man are heard, exchanging words in Spanish as a church bell rings in the distance. Parker has, implementing exclusively the elements of music and sound, already visually created the landscape of the film in the viewer's mind. We envision not a world of modernity, but of rustic (and perhaps savage) simplicity. The stark, atmospheric, dust-ridden *Cangaçeiro* films of Brazilian director Glauber Rocha spring to mind as we envision banditos on horseback, terrorizing a small, arid, Catholic village somewhere in Latin America, as frightened, devout mothers dressed in black protect their children from the onslaught. Andrew Lloyd Webber's sweeping musical score then envelops the soundtrack, which informs the viewer that this film will be less brutal and savage than bandito films; it will be powerful, yes, but it will possess a more lyrical, elegiac quality.

The first shot reveals that the myriad sounds playing over the opening credits were part of a film within the film, as we see that the woman and the man who were speaking in Spanish are two characters in a black-and-white period melodrama being watched by a packed audience in a smoke-filled theater. A title card then appears over the film (Parker's film, not the film within a film) that reads "Buenos Aires 1952." Darius Khondji's beautifully stark cinematography is reminiscent of an early Tony Scott film: smoky, dark, claustrophobic, and redolent of a noirish underworld, as shadows and chiaroscuro lighting are featured prominently. When speaking about his approach to the cinematography in the film, Khondji states, "There was something really dark and moody about it; it was really beautiful. I have a tendency to prefer the dark side of things."[11]

The film projector then stops, the lights come on in the theater, and the moviegoers respond with a fervent, clamorous uproar. This moment actually accomplishes two primary goals. First, it establishes that the Argentinian people are emphatic people, prone to concerted acts of passionate expression. Secondly, and perhaps more playfully, Parker seems to be commenting on the power of cinema itself—it takes an emotional stranglehold over audiences, inciting a furor when it is not allowed to deliver.

The theater manager then addresses the audience, stating the Eva Perón has died, after which Parker cuts to a montage, a series of close-ups of the devastated moviegoers, most of whom are weeping with grief. This moment illustrates just how loved and respected this woman was to the Argentinian people. The camera then settles on one young man in particular, who sits stoically and accepts the news. This is Ché (played by Antonio Banderas), who, although he does not have any actual dialogue in this particular scene, will most likely have some kind of agency later in the story.

We then cut to a wide shot of what looks like a funeral procession, dragging through a rustic, dusty landscape—it is clearly not a funeral for an affluent, well-to-do member of society. Once again, Darius Khondji's sumptuous cinematography stands out as he captures both the aridity of a small Latin American village, but he infuses it with a rich, saturated quality, which is reminiscent of a David Lean film. Khondji states that painter George Bellows was a visual inspiration for how the film was going to look. He says:

[Bellows] was an American realist painter of the twenties and thirties. He was a realistic painter, but realistic in a way that was close to Impressionism. That style worked very well for the early scenes in *Evita*, which are more idealized; a lot of the film was shot through a glow of light and dust.[12]

A rusty old truck pulls over to the side of the dusty road, and a family, all dressed in black, disembarks. The family comprises a woman, ostensibly the mother, two older girls, probably in their teens, a teenage boy, and two younger girls, one of whom is holding her mother's hand. This is young Eva, played by María Luján Hidalgo. Parker then cuts to the interior of a modest, ramshackle church, in which a funeral, that of an older man, is underway. We then cut back to the mother of the family in black, who is arguing with a woman at the gate of the church, pleading for her children to be allowed into the ceremony, so they may pay their final respects to their dead father. The woman at the gate denies their access, saying that they are bastards, illegitimate children (which reflects the true story—Juan Duarte was never married to Juana Ibarguren, and to allow his illegitimate children into his funeral would be a social faux pas). Not to be deterred, however, the brash, headstrong Eva wrestles past the sentries and runs into the church to pay her respects. Andrew Lloyd Webber's operatic, grandiose musical score plays over a crying, hysterical Eva being dragged back out of the church. It is an intense, heart-wrenching moment that packs an emotional punch, and it dramatically sets up Eva's character: she is strong-willed and will stop at nothing to attain whatever goal she may have set for herself. However, it is not entirely true to the real-life events. In actuality, Juana met privately with Eva's godfather and an agreement was reached: Juana herself was forbidden from attending, but her children were allowed to witness their father's funeral.[13] So, once again, Parker alters historical events to heighten the dramatic and visceral intensity of the narrative, and to inform us of Eva, the film character's impassioned dedication.

Parker then starkly contrasts the meager, impoverished decorum of Duarte's funeral and accentuates the class tensions at the heart of the film by cutting to Eva's funeral, which is more opulent, and on a far grander scale. It is a lavish procession, replete with a garishly decorated casket, being led by decorated military officers on horseback, and a teeming horde of grieving onlookers, silently weeping, as a sign reading "Silencio" admonishes the crowd to honor the deceased's memory with a moment of silence and serenity. Once again, Webber's operatic musical score takes the moment to epic proportions, as Parker focuses on a close-up of a fiery torch burning, symbolizing the undying power this woman's legacy holds.

From an editing perspective, this contrast, that of cutting from Eva's impoverished background to the lavish, upscale life she left behind, is a fairly simple cinematic device. However, it is extremely effective in establishing Eva's character, that of a driven, headstrong woman. As film critic Peter N. Chumo puts it, "This hunger to break through boundaries (both physical and metaphorical) is repeated throughout the film, and the cut from the father's relatively poor country funeral to Eva's lavish state funeral sets up the beginning and end of Eva's social rise."[14]

The next scene reveals Ché to be the Brechtian Everyman narrator of the film. He is sitting alone at a bar, and upbeat, mariachi-style guitar music plays on the soundtrack. Ché then sings "Oh, What a Circus" as he walks through the funeral procession, his existence not acknowledged by any of the extras in the film as he sings directly to the camera, breaking the fourth wall. The song is not the effusive, reverential ode one would expect to hear at this point in the film, having just witnessed the magnitude of the dedication this nation felt for Perón, but rather a sardonic, embittered castigation. With the opening lines, which seem to mock the spectacle that Eva has become, it is immediately apparent that this song will most likely be reproachful as opposed to laudatory, as he disrespectfully refers to Perón as simply "an actress" and not "the First Lady of Argentina." The middle portion of the song is more speculative, calling into question Argentina's devotion to this woman. Ché then angrily approaches the camera and sings about how she did nothing for years.

Ché, at this particular moment anyway, is clearly espousing the anti–Peronista sentiments. Immediately after the last line is uttered, Parker cuts to the dedicated, loyal Peronistas at her funeral, singing "Salve Regina Mater" in unison. Again, through editing, Parker is presenting us with a contrast, a tension, a binary. On one side are the loyalists who revere and cherish the memory of Eva, and on the other are the ones who scorn her.

Ché then throws a rock at a picture of Eva, and the tempo of the song becomes even faster as Parker segues into a montage, which visually captures the polarizing, partisan nature of Eva's legacy. The montage is a visually exhilarating depiction of the passionate uproar Eva incited. There are shots of rioting, of buildings exploding, of soldiers beating rioters in the streets, of hordes of people clamoring in the streets. He intersperses shots of Eva (played by Madonna) speaking at rallies, being adored by her supporters, as Ché continues to sing his vitriolic rant, denigrating her. It is a viscerally rousing sequence and it illustrates that, while *Evita* is not a political film per se, it will not be shying away from the fact that this woman was a polarizing figure with rabid detractors as well as supporters.

We then cut back to Eva's funeral procession. At this point, her casket is on display in the center of a church, and her many supporters are lining up for the viewing. Over this tableau, Madonna sings "Don't Cry For Me, Argentina," the lyrics of which establish Eva as an ordinary, humble bleeding heart, dedicated to social and political egalitarianism.

We then cut back to a young Eva, crying as she watches her father's casket being driven away. Khondji's earth-toned cinematography captures the rustic, impoverished region in which Eva was raised, which is a hallmark of Parker's style. Khondji describes Parker's dedication to locational authenticity, which is a stylistic choice that permeates all of his films, giving them a gritty, realistic look:

> Alan told me he wanted *Evita* to be not only a glamorous musical, but also gritty and real. He wanted a lot of dust, and a feeling for the Pampas and the little Argentine towns in the twenties and thirties; Alan wanted the film to be "Parkerized."[15]

We then cut to a darkened alley at night, showcasing Khondji's aptitude with shadows and light. A title card reads "Junin 1936, " and we then cut to a shot of a man and a woman lying in bed inside a small, cramped bedroom. The man quickly gets dressed and rushes out, and we see that the woman with whom he has been sleeping is Eva. As the man descends the staircase, Ché, our singing narrator, informs us that this man, Agustín Magaldi (played by Jimmy Nail), is a tango singer and that he is the first man "to be of use to Eva Duarte," as she was born into poverty with no opportunities. Once again there is a sense of ideological tension, of sympathizing with Eva's plight on the one hand, while acknowledging Ché's scornful, reproachful assertion that Eva simply used Magaldi in a selfish, Machiavellian manner.

We then cut to Magaldi singing "On This Night of a Thousand Stars," a tango song. Eva appears to be smitten as she watches him perform, and when he is finished, Eva drapes herself over him, backstage, commencing her manipulation of him. She says she loves him, but she sings the lines "I want to be a part of B.A. Buenos Aires, Big Apple," far more emphatically, signifying that escaping her destitution is of more importance than love.

With the help of her townsfolk, who essentially call out Magaldi for being a chauvinistic pig by thinking he can have a one-night stand with no repercussions, Eva convinces Magaldi to take her with him to Buenos Aires, mostly through manipulation, claiming that she wants to be with him and she loves him. The manager of the hotel says to Magaldi that he might as well give in: "She's made up her mind, you've no choice." He is vocalizing one of the fundamental components of Eva's character—she is determined, ambitious, and unable to be deterred. Eva further elucidates her proletariat, class-warrior identity when she says, "Screw the middle classes! I will never accept them." Again we are invited to align ourselves with her underdog status—the champion of the poor.

Magaldi then sings "Eva, Beware of the City," the lyrics of which warn her about the degrading quality of Buenos Aires, that it usurps innocence, swallows people whole, and turns them bad. It is at this point that the film becomes a tragedy in the making, one of operatic proportions (which has already been established to a degree, considering that there is no spoken dialogue in the film, every line, no matter how mundane, being sung). In true operatic fashion, this scene foreshadows Eva's ultimate downfall at the hands of the savage city, and, akin to a Greek tragedy, the audience sees it coming before she does. Magaldi serves as the soothsayer, warning Eva that her ambition is dangerous, but she is, of course, unrelenting.

After kissing her friends and family goodbye, Eva boards a Buenos Aires–bound train with a very reluctant Magaldi. The up-tempo, salsa-style drums of the next song, "Buenos Aires" kick in as Eva watches her rustic impoverished upbringing fade from view. Parker implements a particularly effective shot to augment this idea—that Eva is leaving her modest life behind in pursuit of bigger and better things. It is a medium-wide shot of the train, heading screen left. A band of men on horseback enter the frame from screen left, heading screen right. By depicting the train and the horses moving in opposite directions, this shot effectively contrasts Eva's diametrically opposed habitats: machinery versus nature, modernity versus underdevelopment. As Chumo puts it, "Throughout the film, Eva is also aligned with technology, specifically technology that allows for greater mobility (whether it be physical or communicative) and thus modern."[16]

Eva then begins singing "Buenos Aires" as the train pulls into the bustling whirlwind of the city. The lyrics of the song are quite interesting as they elucidate Eva's myriad sentiments about her big move. First, there is her frenzied excitement; she is a small-town girl, visiting the grandeur of the big city for the first time, and her anxious anticipation is evident in both the lyrics, and in Madonna's exuberant delivery of them. Compounding the wide-eyed excitement of a debutante, however, is Eva's brash arrogance and self-assuredness, when she admonishes Buenos Aires to stand back and make way for her. Her cockiness and self-confidence seem excessive, as she has never been to the big city, and is completely unaware of what it has in store for her. This brashness borders on hubris, which serves to bolster the film's setup as a tragedy in the making. We feel for Eva, as she is struggling to break free from the male-dominated shackles of her small town, but her foolhardy entrance into the beast of Buenos Aires is reminiscent of a Shakespearean downfall, and once again, the audience is aware of it at this point, while Eva is not.

The lyrics to the song adumbrate yet another interesting aspect of Eva's character. She appears to be taunting the city, placing it in an adversarial position, daring it to foist its dirt upon her. This elucidates Eva's background a bit more, informing us that all she's ever known is struggle, fighting tooth and nail to be heard and to achieve the goals that her constrictive, misogynistic oppressors have heretofore disavowed. She acknowledges the city as a worthy adversary, but challenges it to "do its worst" because she is confident that she will vanquish it, which, again, heightens the emotional impact of the tragedy to come.

The song continues as Eva and Magaldi walk into a nightclub containing a live band and scores of dancing patrons. As Magaldi scowls at her, Eva proceeds to dance indiscriminately with numerous men, vivaciously flaunting her newfound enthusiasm. She and Magaldi then leave the nightclub, and walk down a dark, unpopulated street, away from the camera. We then cut to Magaldi's house, and Parker visually conveys that he and Eva's courtship is defunct. There is a shot of Eva standing at the base of a stairwell, watching Magaldi ring the doorbell to his house. Parker then cuts to a shot from the top of the stairs, ostensibly Magaldi's eye-line match, looking down on Eva as she gazes up at Magaldi longingly. In this strikingly composed shot, the bannister of the stairwell slices through the frame, visually augmenting the sense of severance, of detachment. There is then a close-up of Magaldi, peering down the steps at Eva. The door then opens, and a young child shouting "Papa" runs out and greets Magaldi, who scoops the child up in his arms and walks into the house, leaving Eva behind.

Implementing the visual properties of cinema in an exchange bereft of dialogue, Parker effectively conveys not only the severance of Eva and Magaldi's relationship, but suggests that it was Magaldi who did the severing. By framing him at the top of the staircase, above Eva, he bestows Magaldi with a domineering sense of power, as Eva is left helpless, watching her abandonment in progress. It is a genuinely moving sequence, and Eva then dejectedly walks back down the steps, suitcase in hand, and sings the somber lament "Another Suitcase in Another Hall," in which she sadly and anxiously professes her lack of a plan or direction, now that her benefactor has abandoned her. This beautifully melancholic song underwent a major transformation from the stage version to the screen version. In the stage version, it is Juan Perón's mistress who sings it, after having been thrown out of the house by Eva, who has replaced her as Perón's love interest. In the screen version, however, it is Eva who sings the beautifully downtrodden song about displacement and uncertainty, effectively altering the emotional attachment the audience has to Eva. As Chumo puts it:

> The change obviously softens the character of Eva by denying the young mistress her voice and by depicting Eva's struggle in the big city. This also gives Eva an added dimension since there is no hint of a struggle in the original material, in which she arrives with Magaldi in Buenos Aires and then quickly discards him for other men and great success. Thus, in the film, we see Eva's vulnerability before her ruthlessness.[17]

As Eva sings the song while sitting alone despondently in a bar, we see that Ché, the Brechtian narrator, is the bartender. As Eva sings the line, "Where am I going to go?" Ché sings a backing vocal: "You'll get by, you always have before." As they sing this exchange, Ché and Eva share an unspoken bond, Eva being the hurt, emotional *persona non grata*, seeking reassurance and approval, and Ché delicately coddles her, assuring her that everything is going to be all right. This marks a drastic shift in the sentiment of Ché's character who, in the song "Oh, What a Circus," proclaims a profound disdain for Eva who "did nothing for years." In this scene, he is acting as her good-natured confidante, which informs the audience that Ché is not so much an embodied character as he is the disembodied proxy for the audience, a tour guide of sorts walking us through the story of Eva Perón.

During the musical interlude of the song, over which a heart-wrenchingly despondent saxophone solo plays, Parker implements another montage, which depicts Eva begrudgingly engaging with a few male suitors, being picked up in bars, dancing perfunctorily in lounges, etc. Eva's acquiescence to this kind of behavior informs the audience that Eva, acknowledging that a destitute woman of her socio-economic status, like it or not, must sidle up to a man if she wants to fulfill her dreams of stardom.

The song ends as Eva walks out the door of what is, ostensibly, a casting director after a failed audition. She walks past the horde of other girls, all of whom are evidently auditioning for whatever it was that Eva was auditioning for as she sings the final verse, and we then cut to another unsavory tableau, in which Eva is reservedly getting undressed as a lecherous, sweaty man is essentially forcing himself upon her. This is Huevo (played by Marcelo Alejandro Auchelli). The next shot is of Eva, posing in a number of lavish, garish costumes for Huevo, who is revealed to be a photographer. We then cut to Eva, walking down the street, picking up a magazine and looking at photos of herself, smiling exuberantly with satisfaction.

The next shot is of Eva walking amorously, hand in hand with Emilio (played by Luis Alday), a more powerful man than Huevo, ostensibly his boss, as Huevo watches dejectedly. In this sequence, which is devoid of dialogue, Parker illustrates his deft ability to convey information visually by informing us that Eva, although essentially against her will, resorts to using her sexuality to attain her goal, again accentuating the idea that Eva is a warrior in an oppressive, male-dominated society. Eva seems to be emotionlessly bouncing from man to man with the sole purpose of furthering her own ambitions, which adds complexity to Eva's character—she is not simply a saintly, pious, morally rigid debutante, but a realist who recognizes that, although she may not be proud of it, she is manipulating the patriarchal hegemony around her to get what she wants.

Eva's rise to stardom is then charted in the musical number "Goodnight and Thank You," which is sung by both Eva and Ché (who appears as both a janitor consoling Huevo as Eva discards him, and a waiter, who consoles Emilio when Eva discards him). The lyrics to the song are surprisingly cynical, as they attempt to exonerate Eva for her excessive gallivanting. Together, they sing of how deception and opportunism permeate every relationship, and there is no such thing as absolute trust. Although they are clearly intended to exonerate Eva from her questionable behavior, the lyrics are not only cynical, but obtrusively presumptuous. They assume that everyone views love the same way, that is to say that it is simply an arena to foster selfish manipulation. In other words, a lover is simply a vehicle, a pawn one can manipulate to achieve one's own selfish needs. This is an interesting development of Eva's character, which, again, depicts her not as a nobly suffering Madonna (pardon the pun), but as a shrewd, morally questionable person. Parker chooses to jettison excessive sentimentality, which would have been the outcome had he painted Eva as a meek, mousy, always-does-the-right-thing victim, in favor of depicting her as a morally complex individual.

We then cut to Eva singing a jingle for Zaz soap in a sound booth, the jingle having the same melody as "Good Night and Thank You." Eva's rising status as a media darling is depicted in her descent down a staircase, dressed lavishly, as she walks past all the dejected men she has slighted, all holding gifts and flowers, unrequited gifts for Eva, and, in unison, the jilted men sing of how Eva has subverted the paradigm of Argentine men calling the sexual shots. The film has now resolutely depicted Eva as a revolutionary, paradigm-changing presence who will not simply be another Buenos Aires citizen—her ambition and drive seems to be paying off already.

Next we cut to another montage, which Parker implements to deliver expository information about the political backdrop of Argentina at the time Eva was living there. He cuts to shots of buildings exploding, of armed soldiers and tanks marching down the streets, quelling a crowd of fleeing rioters. In a voice-over, Ché begins singing "The Lady's Got Potential," the lyrics of which refer to the afternoon of June 4, 1943, the day on which the military (the *Grupos de Oficiales Unido*, or G.O.U.) marched into the city from Campo de Mayo, laid siege to the Casa Rosadas, and ousted President Castillo, the Fox. The coup was engineered by General Ramirez, a reactionary and anti-feminist known as the "Little Stick," who was Castillo's minister of war, who then went on to appoint himself as the new president.[18] Parker implements Ché's admittedly abridged history lesson, which skimps on the details, to illustrate that military coups and dictatorial corruption were extremely prevalent components of the Argentine government at this time, which, for the purposes of Parker's narrative, is sufficient. He effectively infuses this montage with powerful, brief shots of street violence, of citizens being clubbed and beaten by law enforcement, to visually illustrate the turmoil and dissent going on at this time, and he charts the ruthless rise to power of Juan Perón with myriad shots of military men seizing the Casa Rosada and placing a new president at the balcony. He also inserts into the montage shots of Eva performing a scene quite poorly, much to the chagrin of the flustered film director (played in a cameo by Alan Parker himself). Parker, through editing, makes a connection between Eva and Perón by cross-cutting his rise to power with her rise in the acting world.

This montage also illustrates a subtle, tongue-in-cheek piece of art imitating life. By Parker himself playing the frustrated director who is unhappy with Eva's performance, he is perhaps ironically calling attention to the fact that Madonna had heretofore been frequently criticized for her poor acting ability, so Parker (in real life) was facing the challenge of molding Madonna's performance in the film.

The end of the montage documents the San Juan earthquake in 1944, after which Perón organized a charity benefit for the victims ravaged by the destruction, the benefit at which Perón first met Eva. We then cut to the benefit to see Magaldi singing "On This Night of a Thousand Stars" again, this time to an auditorium full of people, including Perón. Magaldi finishes, walks backstage, and Eva, wearing an expensive fur coat and talking with a high-profile military figure, notices Magaldi and stops him. She says, "Your act hasn't changed much," to which Magaldi replies, "Neither has yours." This moment is a bit of a détente, in which each of them acknowledges the other's conniving, self-serving nature.

Colonel Perón then takes the stage and showers the audience with praise, bestowing them with power by telling them that the people are the most important thing in a society, not the government. It is a moving speech, but Ché, the realist who is perpetually keeping the audience informed of the truth, sings the brief interlude, "The Art of the Possible," in which he says that Perón tells the people what they want to hear and switches from left to right. Much like "Oh, What a Circus," this song serves to pierce through the fervent public opinion to get to the truth.

Perón and Eva then meet and they sing "I'd Be Surprisingly Good For You." They both exude an awkward, junior-high-school manifestation of puppy love. Perón says he did not come to the benefit with a date, and Eva says the same. The two then walk outside, stultified by their mutual, instant attraction to each other. This scene is most likely an oversimplification of the first meeting of Eva and the colonel. Eva displays a reluctant vulnerability, coyly and forthrightedly professing her feelings and asking Juan if he feels the same, when, in actuality, their courtship was most likely more intellectual and clinical than that. But, dramatically, it furthers the ethos of the film, which is an operatic, epic charter of the rise and fall of a tragic figure—the wide-eyed, foolhardy yet shrewd Eva Duarte.

The romantic song culminates with Juan and Eva slow dancing while a sultry saxophone solo plays on the soundtrack. Juan then reciprocates Eva's profession of attraction, and they both say that they want more than just a one-night stand—the seed of a lasting relationship has been planted.

Further perpetuating his penchant for dramatic realism, however (as well as an unwillingness to allow the film to keep its head in the naïvely unrealistic clouds of romance and saccharine love), Parker plays the reprise of "Good Night and Thank You" over shots of Perón and Eva courting each other, to remind the audience that, while Eva's (and Perón's) feelings may be genuine, these are two people who are calculating and, perhaps, manipulative—people who, while they are capable of feeling vulnerability, have their self-serving goals at heart. This is evident when Eva storms into Perón's bedroom and deposes his current mistress, forcing her out of bed and telling her that Perón no longer needs her, while she sings "Hello and Goodbye." She (Eva) is the new gun in town. Perón's discarded mistress then sings the lyrics that Eva had previously sung to Ché at the bar: she sings "What happens now?" to which Perón replies "You'll get by, you always have." This moment is actually quite moving and we feel for the rejected mistress. This, again, displays Parker's devotion to parlaying a balanced, dramatically interesting story which is not simply the one-sided canonization of Eva—Parker deftly conveys that Eva's actions had myriad consequences and affected numerous people in numerous ways.

We then cut to an affluent, high-society game of polo, which is being witnessed by the elite of Argentina, including innumerable military figures. Perón arrives with Eva and begins introducing her to everyone. Parker intercuts her introductions with shots of the disapproving, indignant socialites who are clearly disdainful of this peasant girl's intrusion on their wealthy microcosm. Once again, Ché is there to parlay, unbiased, the information to the audience as he sings "Perón's Latest Flame," which elucidates the derision of the high-society types about Eva's encroachment into their world. Ché is very well dressed in this scene, seamlessly blending in with the society types, which, again, reinforces Parker's decision to make Ché the Brechtian Everyman narrator, as opposed to the military figure of Ché Guevara, who, in the stage version, serves to represent the voice of opposition to the Perón regime. Chumo discusses the effect that this alteration had in the film version:

> He [Ché] appears as a patron in the movie theater when Eva's death is announced, a hotel clerk, a waiter, and a well-dressed mingler among the upper classes at the polo grounds. In this way, Ché is an icon of effortless mobility and becomes a mirror for Eva's social climbing—her conscience, really, more than a simple opposition figure.[19]

"Perón's Latest Flame" then transitions into another montage, which reflects the true story of Eva—that she was starkly at odds with Perón's military cohorts, the G.O.U., from the start. The montage depicts military men, chiding and degrading Eva in the shower, sitting at a bar, and marching in the streets. Parker then gives us a series of shots of Perón and Eva at a number of high-society social functions, people applauding Perón while Eva signs autographs. One again, Ché perpetuates Chumo's assertion that he is Eva's conscience when he, dressed as a newspaper man, asks Eva what her plans are—is she going to quit acting? What does she want? These are questions that Eva was no doubt asking herself, and her internal monologue is being parlayed to the audience through the voice of Ché.

The next musical number, "The Dice Are Rolling," finds Perón and Eva riding in the back seat of a car, both of them staring pensively out the window. Perón begins to sing the song, in which he verbalizes his awareness of the devious political machinations surrounding him, stating that there are men out there who would do anything "to see us six feet underground." This moment depicts Perón as a shrewd, calculating tactician, well aware of the complex, diabolical plots waiting in the wings. In this sense, Parker presents Perón as a Don (or Michael) Corleone–type figure—a beleaguered man hovering over his empire, keeping tabs on who wants to see him fall, in a very calculating, Machiavellian manner. It is hard to say whether this is an accurate depiction of Perón—whether he actually possessed this degree of intellectual and tactical fortitude. Mary Main would almost certainly disagree, as she writes, "He was hard-working and ambitious but not brilliant; he knew better how to make use of the knowledge of others than how to acquire knowledge for himself."[20] Whether it is accurate or not, however, Parker endows Perón with his shrewdness to augment the film's tone of an operatic tragedy in the making, giving Perón the paranoia and self-reflexive doubt of a Shakespearean king. This component of the film is bolstered by Eva's insistence that Perón disregard the potentially nefarious plans of the G.O.U., while Perón expresses pragmatism, stating, "Maybe we should quite while we're ahead." Eva persists, however, which grants her the attributes of Lady Macbeth: the headstrong, calculating wife of a powerful man who, jettisoning reason and insight, provincially urges him to continue with his politics, without examining the possible consequences.

In the next scene, Perón is placed under arrest and wrenched from Eva's loving grip as military figures escort him down the elevator. Eva hysterically cries after him as military men forcefully detain her, leaving her to helplessly watch as her lover is taken away from her. This incident is faithful to the actual story, in which, on the night of October 11, 1945, in response to rabid anti–Perón sentiment, the military arrested Perón and escorted him to the prison island of Martín García.[21] In this scene, Eva plays the part of the nobly suffering woman, which is reminiscent of the saintly women who populated Mexican melodramas, such as *Maria Candelaria*. For a moment, her ruthlessness and conniving nature are abandoned so that we may sympathize with her as she suffers, watching her lover being arrested.

We then cut to another montage, which documents the fervent uprising of the people, clamoring in the streets for Perón, whom they view as the representative who fights for the rights of the proletariat, to be released. Parker intercuts the shots of the workers' uprising with those of Eva addressing the nation via the airwaves, galvanizing the people into backing the release of Perón. Madonna's performance in this scene bolsters Eva's image as a powerful demagogue as she emphatically delivers her speech. Her aptitude with powerful oration is carried into the next shot, in which Eva is standing up before a crowd, vehemently proclaiming into the microphone that she was once indigent and underprivileged as well, and that Perón is the answer to the workers' plight. She then visits Perón at Martín García, and Perón, again, expresses uncertainty about his political ambitions, reasserting that, perhaps, they should "quit while they're ahead." Eva, again, persists, asserting that they stay the course and keep fighting. In this sense, Eva is now a conflation of two Shakespearean figures. On the one hand, she is Lady Macbeth, obdurately urging her man, almost against his will, to continue with his ambitions, which clearly possesses a potentially dangerous outcome. She is also Julius Caesar, a figure whose blind ambition clouds the fact that there are powerful forces conspiring to thwart her success. Either way, both of these similarities augment the film's overall tone—that of the tragic story of an ambitious figure's downfall.

In another rousing oration, Eva addressing a horde of Argentinians, proclaiming that Perón is resigning from the military, for the *descamisados* (the Argentinian word for "shirtless ones"; i.e., the lower and working classes[22]) are the ones he is fighting for and representing. We then cut to Eva, marching in the streets (right next to Ché) in a Marxist rally, clamoring for "A New Argentina" under Perón—an Argentina where the poor and the working class will be bestowed with a newfound voice. Eva's devoted, incessant rallying pays off as Perón is released and is greeted with cheerful adoration by the Argentinian people. We then cut to the wedding ceremony of Perón and Eva. Shot in a church, in a ceremony delivered in Latin by the priest, the lighting of the scene is highly suggestive. Khondji's cinematography is luscious and rich, but enshrouded in smoke, which seems to be filtering in through the windows. It is not darkly lit, nor does it implement harsh shadows, indicative of chiaroscuro, noirish lighting. The smoke, however, serves as a sort of portent, hanging over the marriage like the Sword of Damocles, again augmenting the film's operatically tragic tone.

Next, Parker presents us with another montage (which, at this point in the film, demonstrates his ability with narrative efficiency—he manages to deliver loads of exposition and background information succinctly), which displays the opposing sentiments surrounding Perón's campaign for the presidency. On the one hand, he shows us Perón's supporters, the workers who are fervently rallying behind he and Eva. On the other, he depicts the violent opposition, parlaying scenes of violence and rioting (there is one particularly effective shot of one of Perón's promotional posters being vandalized by a smattering of red paint). Parker then implements the cinematic trope of the spinning newspaper (again, in the interest of narrative efficiency) to document Perón's election to the presidency. On the balcony of the Casa Rosadas, Perón delivers a rousing speech to a teeming mass of supporters, claiming that "we are all workers now." He then introduces his wife, Eva Duarte de Perón, and she takes the stage, demands silence from the crowd, as she sings the film's signature musical number, "Don't Cry For Me, Argentina." Parker intercuts the performance with flashbacks to Eva's youth, including her departure to Buenos Aires and her time dancing in the tango bar, to reinstate how far she has come. Interestingly, the song is more than just a rousing, galvanizing profession of her devotion to the working class of Argentina; it becomes an apology of sorts. She sings honestly about how she had to change, lest she watch opportunity pass her by. Eva seems to be espousing a latent desire to renounce her success, as she appears to be overcome with guilt about her ascension to glory. The huge audience, however, does not spite her and allows her to revel in her newfound status of privilege. This is interesting in that Parker is, consciously or not, infusing the film, which is about Argentina, with a

First Lady of Argentina, Eva Perón (Madonna), waves to her public. *Evita* **(1996), Hollywood Pictures; Cinergi Pictures; Dirty Hands Productions.**

very American sentiment—as Chumo puts it, craving "fame and fortune and yet feeling compelled to make excuses for one's success when it is achieved."[23]

Parker then flashes back to Eva's train ride to Buenos Aires, which reminds us of both her inextricable link to technology as well as her implacable mobility. Eva, ostensibly finished with her oration, walks back into the Casa Rosada, where a cynical onlooker comments, "Statesmanship is more than entertaining peasants." This peripheral character actually usurps the role of Ché in this scene, as he serves as the Greek chorus.

Eva then reemerges on the balcony in an encore of sorts, and again addresses her *descamisados*, assuring them that she was once as they are now, and that Perón will fight for the rights of the lower class and the workers, which Parker augments with a brief montage depicting various members of the lower class (butchers, farmers, etc.) listening to Eva's speech on the radio.

Parker then cuts to a brief, but extremely effective, moment, which, without the use of dialogue, suggests the decomposition of Eva and Perón's affection for one another. Perón demurely approaches two closed doors. Next is a shot of Eva, brushing her hair in front of a mirror. Perón places his hand on the doorknob and begins turning it. Eva turns her head and watches the doorknob being turned. The look on her face is one of disappointment, as if she does not want Perón to enter. As if sensing this, Perón, defeated, walks away. This brief scene is reminiscent of one particular sequence in Orson Welles's *Citizen Kane*. In Welles's film, he visually conveys the degradation of a marriage with a montage, which starts with Kane's wife sitting on his lap as they eat, as the two are smitten with each other, blinded by their love for one another. Over the course of the ensuing montage, they sit increasingly farther and farther away from each other, a visual metaphor for the erosion of their intimacy and affection.

At a posh, high-society event, Ché, dressed in a tuxedo, begins singing "High Flying, Adored," as Eva dances elegantly, first with Perón, but ultimately, with many different well-groomed men, which again augments the distancing of Eva and Perón. Ché's portion of the song is almost a lament of Eva's success as he sings about how she has reached the highest echelon of admiration, with nowhere to go but down. He seems to be espousing one of the themes of Brian De Palma's *Scarface*: the depressing, deflating sense of emptiness one is faced with once they achieve material success. He warns her that her boredom will eventually lead to apathy, to the point where she will not care whether the workers love her or not.

Eva then sings the rejoinder in which she disagrees with Ché, once again supporting Chumo's claim that one of Ché's myriad functions is to serve as Eva's conscience. She once again sings of how she is ordinary and usual and not glamorous at all, and she seems to be having an internal conflict. In keeping with the *modus operandi* of tragic heroes, she dismisses what is most likely the truth in favor of a delusional, provincial version of reality.

Eva then bursts into her next number, "Rainbow High," which is a montage depicting Eva's insatiable appetite for material goods. Parker presents us with inserts, close-ups of Eva applying lipstick and eyeliner, and shopping for expensive clothing and jewelry, as she sings of the importance of looking garishly opulent. Once again, Parker displays his willingness to present a balanced story, as he depicts Evita as thoroughly enjoying being showered with expensive accessories. Rather than two-dimensionally lionizing Evita as a bleeding heart who fought for the masses, Parker also includes sequences like this one, which add complexity to her character.

In the interest of verisimilitude, Parker infuses this montage with quasi-documentary footage and still photos of Eva and Perón, ostensibly newspaper photos. This reminds the audience that, while they are watching an epic, operatic drama, it is based on historical fact.

At the end of the song, Eva reprises the melody of "Buenos Aires." Eva then boards a plane and departs, as Perón sings, "People of Europe, I send you the Rainbow of Argentina." This segment of the film is, again, making reference to actual events. In 1947, at the request of the foreign minister, Juan Atilio Bramuglia, Eva embarked on a tour of Europe which came to be known as the "Rainbow Tour," in which she visited Spain, Rome, France, and Switzerland. So as to preemptively mollify any political uproars (which proved fruitless), the tour was billed not as a political one, but as a non-political "goodwill" tour.[24]

Eva's "Rainbow Tour" is chronicled in *Evita* as a film within a film as Perón, his cohorts, and Ché watch black-and-white newsreel footage. This directorial choice, of depicting the "Rainbow Tour" as a film within a film, contains interesting implications, according to Chumo, who states, "By presenting this number in the form of a movie, Parker's *Evita* subtly suggests that the media that made Eva can ruin her just as easily; American show-biz success has a double-edge."[25]

In this sequence, Ché, once again, assumes the role of the realist narrator who drags Eva's highfalutin delusions of ubiquitous grandeur and adoration back to reality. Although the "Rainbow Tour" starts well, Ché takes over the vocals and reminds everyone that, in Italy, she was not welcome with open arms. Parker then cuts to shots of Eva's car being egged by irate onlookers. Ché again reminds us that while Eva and Perón were undoubtedly extremely popular, they also had many rabid detractors.

Ultimately, however, as the chorus of the song suggests, the "Rainbow Tour" was a success, despite the opposition that greeted her in Rome. Parker then cuts to Eva's next number "The Actress Hasn't Learned the Lines (You'd Like to Hear)," which is an indignant, angry song in which Eva scorns the judgmental, snotty high-society types who still refuse to accept her. After shaking hands with a few of these types whilst holding a parasol, she then sits alone and metaphorically points her finger at them, saying, "They'll all just disappear." Ché then usurps the spotlight as he sings "And the Money Kept Rolling In" from behind a wrought-iron gate, a song in which he is the mouthpiece representing the disgruntled workers who want the promises Eva made to be fulfilled—they are still poor, starving, and suffering and they demand that Eva assume responsibility for her shortcomings. In this song, Ché also points out the alleged corruption and financial irresponsibility behind the Eva Perón Foundation, which, according to Parker's brief montage of sweaty workers inexplicably handing over money to men in suits, allegedly engaged in unsavory activities such as embezzlement and fraud (which, again, to this day remain unproven allegations, although it was a widely circulated sentiment at the time). The montage that the song accompanies accurately (and succinctly) conveys the ambiguous nature of Eva's foundation, as, while Parker does give us shots of Eva opening hospitals, schools, and other social developments, he contrasts these shots of goodwill with inserts of expensive shoes and other fancy accessories that Eva allegedly (and selfishly) used the profits of her foundation to procure. Again, Parker gives us a balanced narrative, giving us a montage which amply exposes both sides of the still-unresolved story.

Eva then decides to run for vice president, much to the chagrin of the military, and even the citizens of Argentina. At a board meeting, Juan sings the number "She Is a Diamond," in which he denigrates the men for criticizing Eva's desire to be vice president, claiming that Eva is the only one who has been attempting to fulfill the promises his party made to the people. Parker then cuts to another montage while "Santa Evita," a tune sung to the melody of "Don't Cry For Me, Argentina," plays on the soundtrack. The montage reiterates the violent opposition Eva incited, and Parker again contrasts shots of Eva and Perón being adored by their supporters with those of violent uprisings, bombed-out buildings, riots, etc. A newspaper headline reads, "Railway Workers Strike," and Parker visually parlays the rabid anti–Peronista sentiment by presenting a shot of a painting of Eva being vandalized.

In the next sequence, Parker implements cross-cutting to link two diametrically opposed visuals, much like Francis Ford Coppola did in *The Godfather*. In that film, Coppola cross-cuts the baptism of Michael Corleone's child, a sacrament in the Church, with shots of shocking brutality, as Michael has ordered the eradication of his rivals. In this scene, the cross-cutting serves to link the act of baptism (a rite of passage which marks an entry into a life, so to speak) with that of extreme violence, suggesting that Michael's child is being born into a troubled world. In *Evita*, Parker achieves something similar. He cross-cuts Eva's receiving communion (again, a sacrament in the Church) with shots of rioting in the streets and the police and military subduing the rioters with violence. In this instance, the cross-cutting could be seen as a way to suggest that, since Eva has been canonized and adored by the public in much the same way they would a saint, being lauded in such a way has its price. Eva has been adored, but at what cost?

Eva then collapses in the church—there is something wrong with her health. She is taken to the hospital and, as the anesthesia is administered, Parker whisks us away to Eva's dream sequence, in which she is dancing with Ché in a grand ballroom to a song aptly titled "Waltz for Eva and Ché." It is a wonderful, sumptuously shot sequence, which has entirely different implications than that of the stage version. Chumo points out that, in the stage version, since Ché is explicitly made out to be Ché Guevara, when he and Eva dance, it is a confrontation between two opposing, political sides—the dictator and the revolutionary. In the film, however, since the dance takes place in Eva's mind, Ché is essentially a stand-in for Eva's conscience as she is confronting herself and the choices she has made.[26] In other words, when Che asks how she can claim to be a "savior, when those who oppose you are stepped on, or cut up, or simply disappear?" he is not so much representing the voice of the people as he is Eva's own conscience as she, again, is made to feel apologetic about her rise to fame.

Parker also makes this scene more cinematic by opening up the setting of the dance sequence. In the stage version, the entire dance takes place on one set—a grand ballroom. In the film, however, Parker has Ché and Eva dance through a series of different settings, reflecting Eva's rise from poverty (a shantytown, a slaughterhouse, etc.) to power.

We then cut to Perón, sitting by Eva's bedside in her hospital room. Her condition is worsening and it is clear that she is dying. It is a touching scene, made even more so when Eva again sings the reprise from "Another Suitcase in Another Hall." In this context, however, the lyrics take on an entirely different meaning. When Perón bluntly tells Eva that she is dying, she begins to tear up, looks at her husband with frightened eyes and sings, "So what happens now? Where am I going to go?" When she had previously sung these lyrics, it was a profession of anxiety and uncertainty about the future, about not having money and being unsure how she was going to survive. In this context, however, the lyrics take on a deeper, philosophical meaning, as Eva seems to be pondering the nature of mortality and the possibility of an afterlife.

This song segues into "You Must Love Me," a poignant song which plays while Perón carries the dying Eva up the stairs. As Eva sings, the film resolutely enters love story territory, as Parker flashes back to the many moments in which the two lovers shared tenderness with each other, and we are given a montage of hugs and smiles. In the lyrics, Eva asks Perón why he's still at her side, as she no longer has anything to offer him. It is a touching moment which reveals quite a bit about Eva's character. First, there is the apologetic, self-deprecating woman who feels undeserving of the success she has achieved, as well as the devotion her husband has given to her. Secondly, when she sings, "How can I be any use to you now?" we surmise that Eva has completely defined herself by her ambitions and drives and goals, not by marriage itself. She is the painter who has gone blind, the baseball pitcher whose arm is broken—she is no longer able to partake in that which has defined her existence.

The song ends with Perón sitting down contemplatively, with his head in his hands. A crowd of Eva's supporters then gathers outside the Casa Rosada, clamoring for "Evita! Evita!" She is escorted out to the balcony to sing "Eva's Final Broadcast," which is a reprise of "Don't Cry for Me, Argentina." She tells the crowd that, although she is resigning and renouncing all of her political ambitions, she will always be with her staunch supporters in spirit. Madonna shines in this scene, and her performance is one of controlled panic—she is a strong woman, fighting back tears as she says goodbye to her loyal supporters. Notwithstanding her questionable morals, behaviors and decisions, her supposed self-serving, conniving nature, we see Eva as simply a scared woman facing death.

While an eerie Latin chant plays on the soundtrack, Parker cuts to an aerial shot of a slew of black umbrellas in the rain. The camera pulls down to reveal a horde of people holding pictures of Eva in anticipation of her death. Next is a haunting, elegiac montage of various groups of people grieving serenely. Khondji substantially darkens the lighting to augment the mood, and the fiery orange glow of candles gives each shot an ominous quality.

In the scene in which Eva sings "Lament" on her deathbed, Madonna once again shines, as she is attempting to maintain control and repose in the face of her abject fear of dying. This time, however, her fear and sadness overwhelm her, and she breaks down.

After showing her grief-stricken supporters holding a candlelit vigil, Parker cuts to Eva's funeral, while operatic music hangs over the proceedings. Ché, who is at the funeral, then sings his contribution to "Lament": "She's no longer there to shine/To dazzle or betray."

This moment is steeped in existential despair, and Parker chooses to focus on the reality of mortality and death, as opposed to attempting to evaluate her political value. As Ché leans over and kisses Eva's coffin, the end credits roll, bringing Parker's balanced narrative to a close. The audience feels much like Argentina itself, torn between opinions, torn between the desire to laud and revere such a noble, hard-working, well-intentioned martyr, and the desire to chastise and castigate this conniving, manipulative, self-serving demagogue who used and stomped on people to get to the top.

14

Angela's Ashes (2000)

January 21; 145 minutes/Color
Production Companies: David Brown productions, Dirty Hands Productions, Scott Rudin Productions
Director: Alan Parker
Screenwriter: Laura Jones and Alan Parker, based on the memoir *Angela's Ashes* by Frank McCourt
Producers: David Brown; James Flyn; Kit Golden; Doochy Moult; Morgan O'Sullivan; Alan Parker; Scott Rudin; Adam Shroeder (Executive Producer); Eric Steele (Executive Producer); David Wimbury (Line Producer)
Production Designer: Geoffrey Kirkland
Camera Operator: Mike Roberts
Cinematography: Chris Connier; Michael Seresin
Editor: Gerry Hambling
Original Musical Score: John Williams
Cast: Andrew Bennett (Narrator); Emily Watson (Angela McCourt); Robert Carlyle (Malachy McCourt); Joe Breen (young Frank); Ciaran Owens (Middle Frank); Michael Legge (older adolescent Frank); Ronnie Masterson (Grandma Sheehan); Liam Carney (Uncle Pa Keating); Eanna MacLiam (Uncle Pat)

> When I look back on my childhood, I wonder how my brothers and I managed to survive at all. It was, of courses, a miserable childhood. The happy childhood is hardly worth telling. Worse than the ordinary miserable childhood is the miserable Irish childhood. And worse still is the miserable Irish Catholic childhood.
> —Opening narration by adult Frank McCourt

> *Angela's Ashes* was the last film I made with Mike Roberts, my camera operator who died in 2000. He was one of the world's great operators—some say the best.... I made eight films with him and he is sorely missed by me and by many other directors who worked so well with him.—Alan Parker[1]

Notes on the Production

Alan Parker read an early publisher's proof of Frank McCourt's childhood memoir about his life in New York City and Limerick, Ireland, prior to the book's great success: It went on to win the Pulitzer Prize, became a *New York Times* best seller for over a hundred weeks and was published in twenty-five languages, selling over six million copies in thirty countries. Although the book is not particularly long, it is an epic that spans about fifteen years of McCourt's early life and adolescence. The film is another ambitious undertaking for Parker in that he was faced with the challenge of compressing an over three-hundred-

14. Angela's Ashes, 2000

Frank McCourt's family: left to right (front): Young Malachy (Shane Murray-Corcoran); Young Frank (Joe Breen); Mother, Angela McCourt (Emily Watson) holding twin son Eugene (Ben or Sam O'Gorman) Left to right (Back): Grandma Sheehan (Ronnie Masterson), Father, Malachy (Robert Carlyle) holding twin son Oliver (Sam or Ben O'Gorman). *Angela's Ashes* (1999), David Brown Productions; Dirty Hands Productions, Scott Rudin Productions.

page novel into a nearly two-and-a-half-hour film. "If I filmed the whole book," Parker said, "people would have been sitting in the movie theater for eight hours."[2]

During their preparations, Parker and his faithful production designer Geoffrey Kirkland traveled around Ireland to find locations; this process proved to be difficult because *Angela's Ashes* spanned the mid–1930s to the late 1940s and much of the older architecture had since been replaced by modern structures. Eventually, they shot a majority of the film in Dublin (which is close to Ardmore, where they built the interiors of "Roden Lane" in Limerick), where a bulk of the story takes place.[3]

After the script was completed, Parker embarked upon the open-casting call process, which, like his previous films, were very involved and covered many locations. The casting of young Frank required three young actors—young Frank (aged five to eight), middle Frank (aged ten to thirteen), and the older adolescent Frank. The open calls occurred in Limerick, Ennis, Dingle, Tipperany and Dublin, to name a few places, and in a couple of months they had held fifteen thousand auditions. Among these child actors was the novice Joe Breen, a real natural, who would eventually be cast as young Frank.[4]

Parker's first choice for Angela, Frank's mother, was Emily Watson (*Breaking the Waves* [1996, Lars Von Trier]; *Punch-Drunk Love* [2002, P.T. Anderson]). The intensity of her role can be summed up by Watson herself: "You get to the end of the day and you order room service and hope that the work was good, but something's nagging in the back of your mind [that] something awful happened. And you think, 'Oh yeah, my baby died.'"[5]

The locations moved from Cork to Limerick; in Cork, the production crew received help from the local police to close down streets so they could create the alleyways and rain machines, which added greatly to the film's somber tone. According to Parker, "*Angela's Ashes* was the dampest film I ever made."[6] Furthermore, they located to Portrane and turned St. Ida's mental institution into a film studio to create the necessary architecture for the dilapidated Limerick lanes.[7]

Angela's Ashes took seventy-five days to shoot and wrapped on December 22, 1998. The acclaimed John Williams (*Jaws*, [1975, Steven Spielberg]; *Star Wars* [1977, George Lucas] and *Superman* [1978, Richard Donner]) completed the score at Sony Studios in Los Angeles. On the film maestro, Parker said, "Williams' wisdom, graciousness and total, effortless control of the task of scoring the film was awe-inspiring."[8]

Summary

The opening shots of *Angela's Ashes* reveal a mini-montage of the gloomy blue and grayish-green imagery of Ireland, replete with rain and fog, not unlike a number of other Parker films that meticulously blend sordid scenery with a richly-textured chromatic aesthetic. The narrator—an adult Frank McCourt recalling the memories of his childhood from age five to nineteen—speaks: "When I look back on my childhood, I wonder how my brothers and I managed to survive at all. It was, of course, a miserable childhood. The happy childhood is hardly worth telling. Worse than the ordinary miserable childhood is the miserable Irish childhood. And worse still is the miserable Irish Catholic childhood." Juxtaposed over these words are more shots of the Irish landscape, specifically a shot of the Shannon River with seagulls hovering over it, and in the industrial background (similar to the opening shots of Istanbul in *Midnight Express*), there is an icon of Mary and the Baby Jesus, setting up two of the film's major themes: industrial modernism and religion. The film's title follows, along with the opening credits. When author Frank McCourt first saw this opening, he admitted he was "in a state of shock"; to him, the imagery looked authentic; it was a true reminder of what life was like in Ireland when he was a child.[9]

The opening insert establishes the setting: Brooklyn, 1935. The camera pans through the prison-like bars of McCourt's home, capturing an elated Malachy (Robert Carlyle), who holds his "wee girl" baby daughter, the first girl in a family of four sons. The baby is described as having brown hair and blue eyes just like her mother, Angela (Emily Watson). Undoubtedly, this is Malachy's pride and joy, yet the tightly framed prison imagery seems to foreshadow this family's doom. A beat later, the audience hears an offscreen scream, followed by an extreme close-up of Angela covering her mouth (further accenting the stifling closed-form *mise-en-scène*). Malachy is on the left side of the frame, vulnerable behind the window, while Angela is positioned on the right, creating another stifling shot. Various shots capture the reactions of the young boys, Frank, Malachy and the twins, Oliver and Eugene (Joe Breen, Shane Murray Corcoran, Sam O'Gorman and Ben O'Gorman, respectively), eventually leading to a lingering shot on Frank, who has the major point-of-view of this entire story. A high-angle shot on Angela accents *her* vulnerability as Malachy discovers his dead daughter. Another shot of Frank, while the melancholy, elegiac narration continues: "Everyone liked little Margaret. Dad said there must have been a holiday in heaven the day this baby was made.... Poor Margaret, just a few days in this world and she was taken back by the same angels who brought her here." Throughout the film, the mentioning of angels is a motif used to help with Frank's understanding of these inexplicable acts of human tragedy. Within minutes, the audience begins to connect with this family's unfortunate fate—Malachy, the well-meaning and gentle-spirited patriarch who is overcome by drink, and Angela, the perpetual victim, constantly a prisoner of her poverty and her husband's irresponsible behavior and absence. Arguably, one could surmise that this event alone (and throughout the course of the film the McCourts lose two more children) begins the downward spiral of this Irish family who immigrated to America, searching for that so-called American dream, but their disappointments forced them back to their native land early in the story. McCourt's novel begins this way: "My father and mother should have stayed in New York where they met and married and where I was born. Instead they returned to Ireland when I was four, my brother, Malachy, three, the twins Oliver and Eugene, barely one and my sister, Margaret, dead and gone."[10] The remaining portion of the story chronicles the McCourts' hardships in Limerick—a nearly fifteen-year struggle for Frank who, throughout the narrative, constantly speaks of someday returning to America.

In a brief sequence, Angela's brutish cousins—Delia and Philomena MacNamara (Helen Norton and Eileen Colgan) serve as the savior muses who—outraged at seeing the sickly condition of Angela and the dirty, malnourished children—write a letter to Angela's mother, Grandma Sheehan, hoping that she can come to their rescue. The stock's brownish sepia-tone, coupled with the shot of a morose Frank, suggests a real loss of hope, and in an abrupt transition Frank and young Malachy are running to the ship moving out of New York City, away from the Statue of Liberty, and consequently away from the American dream. The narrator's voice explains: "We must have been the only Irish family in history to be saying goodbye to the Statue of Liberty. We were going back to Ireland where there was no work and people were dying of starvation and the damp." A high-angle shot looks down menacingly on the McCourt family, who will experience many more hardships. In the mid-1930s, the McCourts were traveling from one Great Depression to the next, yet despite the problems Ireland faced, it was under a promising new reform, which may have contributed to this decision.

The McCourts journey back to their native Ireland, where the third president Eamon de Valera (a major reformer responsible for the execution of the Constitution of the Free Irish State in 1922) was in the process of drafting a new constitution to overcome the autonomous British Empire; that became official by early 1937, about the time the McCourts returned home. The short sequence is represented through a montage showing the impressive Irish landscape, accented by John Williams's fully orchestrated score.

The first article of this new constitution stated the following: "The Irish nation herby affirms its inalienable, indefeasible, and sovereign right to choose from its own form of government, to determine its relations with other nations, and to develop its life, political, economic and cultural, in accordance with its own genius and traditions." Under Article 44, the state acknowledges that "the homage of Public worship is due to Almighty God. It shall hold His name in reverence, and shall respect and honor religion." In short, the constitution attempted to "give expression to two very different notions—the liberal and secular tradition of parliamentary democracy and the concept of a state grounded upon Catholic social teaching"—a dynamic that is ever-present in the book and film.[11]

Throughout the film, Malachy is a fierce critic of what he calls "the New Ireland." In an earlier scene he brings Frank to the unemployment office and reminds the cold-hearted officials that, years earlier, he had served Ireland, and he demands of them not only money but also respect. When he is only offered bus fare to go back home, he humbly asks if they can chip in more so he can get a pint in the pub instead. The outraged man dishonors him in front of his son and tells him that he is not there to support the Guinness family! When the defeated Malachy leaves belligerently, he curses this New Ireland: "Free, my arse!" he exclaims, then tells Frank to come along with him. An extreme long-shot of Malachy through the doorway, with four empty chairs on the right of the frame, symbolizes his loss of hope in this new world. Throughout the film, Malachy is viewed as a traditionalist and, despite his alcoholic binges, he values the classical roots of his heritage and history; this is the essence of his character. In this way, Malachy continues to be a victim—a well-meaning family man with a penchant for Irish nationalism and Catholicism, who is controlled by the fate of his tragic life. Under different circumstances, perhaps, he might have been a model family man and citizen.

When the McCourts arrive in Limerick (a scene that shows the modernization of Ireland through public transportation and the surrounding industrial background), they are greeted by the family matriarch Grandma Sheehan (Ronnie Masterson) and her daughter, Angela's sister Aunt Aggie (Pauline McLynn). Malachy is given the cold-shoulder by the women (because of his drinking and because he comes from the less respected "North" of Ireland), but Uncle Pat (Eanna MacLiam) accepts his handshake. For the time being, the McCourts plan is to stay on Windmill Street, in Limerick, near Aggie's and Pat's home, as Grandma Sheehan has no room in her own home to harbor the family. Angela is seen wearing a prosperous-looking red coat she obtained in New York City from her cousin, a coat that becomes more faded as the film progresses ... a symbol of her descending economic status and emotional state.

In their new residence: A close-up of a portrait of Jesus serves as a constant reminder that, despite these hardships in their lives, religion is ever present. Angela tells her children that the portrait is the Sacred Heart of Jesus. The children don't know this detail, prompting Grandma Sheehan (who, along with Malachy, is the most pious character in the film) comments on how ignorant and uninformed they are. Young Malachy innocently and humorously says, "Will you tell the Baby Jesus we're hungry?" The film periodically juxtaposes religion with their poverty—one such example comes in a later scene when Frank writes a composition called "Jesus and the Weather," a bittersweet and clever piece that explains why Jesus would never want to live in Limerick.

The sequence continues as a series of shots showing the family adjusting to their new living conditions. That night, they are awakened by an infestation of fleas in their bed. Frank humorously narrates: "St. Patrick drove the snakes out of Ireland and the English brought in the fleas and the damp." As they all pound the mattresses to free them of bugs, Malachy entertains his children by making up amusingly tall tales, one of the characteristics that endears Frank to his father.

The following sequence features the personalities of Malachy and Angela. Malachy walks through Limerick with his son Frank, and after he is denied his request of receiving a portion of coal from the charity organization the St. Vincent de Paul (where the McCourts received many of their necessities), he is overcome by pride, so much that when Frank picks up the "leftover" coal remnants on the ground he tells his son that (despite the circumstances) they are not beggars. Conversely, in the following scene, Angela (tightly framed and perpetually a prisoner of her home) is concerned that their baby needs to eat and she informs her husband that unlike him she is not "too proud" to pick up coal remnants if it means feeding the family (in later scene Frank shamefully watches his mother begging a group of priests for food scraps). Against Malachy's wishes (although she always seems to have the upper hand), she brings her children outside, and in a series of low-angle shots they are all captured in a saturated blue-hued, foggy street, desperately picking up as much coal as they can get.

The next beat features Aunt Aggie, Uncle Pat, Grandma Sheehan, Angela and her boys, first on the crowded streets of Limerick, then back in their home. In this scene the viewer learns about Aggie's and Pat's fate, especially as Catholics—that they don't have any children. This may, in fact, be a reason Aggie's disposition is the way it is—embittered and cynical (in a later scene with Frank, her maternal side emerges, indicating that she desperately wants to be a mother). Uncle Pat appears to have a paternal side, which is seen in the endearing way he holds little Eugene in his arms. Covered with the blackness from coal mining, he humorously says that Eugene likes him because he thinks he's Al Jolson, a reference to the famous song and dance man whose minstrel act was featured in *The Jazz Singer* (1927, Alan Crosland). Aunt Aggie, however, continues to condemn Malachy and his background. Malachy has experienced much prejudice from being from the north of Ireland (a detail that will be discussed more fully in this summary), which may be another reason he has turned to drink.

The death of young Oliver begins the next poignant series of scenes in the film, beginning with a shot of Frankie and his brother Malachy at the end of a bed watching their mother holding their dead baby brother, crying. Malachy, forever a victim like his wife, has his head lowered in sadness and remorse. More loss on both ends. Grandma Sheehan, in perhaps her most tender moment in the film, sits back helplessly (and for once without judgment) in a chair. Frank hugs his father (throughout the narrative Frank is perpetually trying to connect with his father) and young Malachy sobs. More shots of rain and fog: Malachy smokes a cigarette outside, while inside, Uncle Pat, forever the blissful optimist, is telling funny stories while Grandma Sheehan prays quietly before the Sacred Heart of Mary. Cut to a lingering shot on a tired Malachy, intense and heartbroken.

As the funeral procession passes by the streets of Limerick, the citizens drop buckets of water at the oncoming carriages. This was a ritual in Limerick; people would use this water to bathe the dead in their coffins.[12] A low-angle shot on Frank, followed by his narration: "I don't know why we can't keep Oliver; I don't know why they sent him away in a box with his sister … it's not right. I wish I could say something to someone."

An abrupt jump-cut to Malachy, exiting a pub and vomiting on the ground. The extremely low-key lighting makes it difficult to see the image clearly, which is the idea; it sets the somber tone for Malachy's downward spiral and perhaps foreshadows the fact that, eventually, he will be "out of the picture."

A rapid transition changes the tone of the film completely. In a tightly framed shot, school children are fighting with one another, followed by the arrival of a school master who reprimands Frank and young Malachy, blaming their poor behavior on their affiliation with living in America. (He facetiously calls them "Yankee Doodle Dandies.") During this time, the narrator provides exposition regarding the school masters. He explains three reasons these teachers will hit a student: first, if you can't ask for something in Irish; second, if you don't know that Eamon de Valera was the greatest man who ever lived; and third, if you didn't know that Irish leader Michael Collins was the greatest man who ever lived.

Another story bridge brings the viewer back into a state of tragedy and mourning: the death of Oliver's twin, Eugene. In a surprisingly disturbing moment, Frank lifts the covers from the bed and, to his dismay, discovers his dead, white-faced brother. This image is so horrific that Eugene looks like a Holocaust victim, a ghost of the past. Next, Frank and young Malachy sit with Malachy in front of the Sacred Heart of Mary while their father prays passionately: "Please God. Is this what you want, is it? And I'm not supposed to question this, am I? You took my son Oliver, you took his brother Eugene. You took his beautiful wee sister Margaret Mary.… Dear God above, why do want children to die?" When his father leaves, Frank prays, "Please God. Don't let Malachy and me and the rest of us be taken off in the box for the hole in the ground. Or even Aunt Aggie or Mr. Benson at the Limmney School. In the name of the Father, the Son and the holy Toast." Frank's replacement of the word "toast" for "ghost" provides the viewer with a poignant moment that serves as a reminder that, despite these "adult" horrors, he is still a child.

Eugene's funeral has passed and Frank finds Malachy in the pub drinking, and subsequently he reprimands his father for using Eugene's coffin as a table for his pint of ale! Instead of being irate with his son, Malachy, fully ashamed, he wipes the coffin dry with the back of his sleeve; he solemnly respects his son's demands, which continues to show him as an enigmatic complex, well-rounded character who exudes true human characteristics. As Alan Parker points out in the DVD commentary track, Malachy is not a clichéd "wife-beating drunk"; instead, he is his own worst nightmare, an anomaly, a man who appears to love his family but who is unable to handle the overwhelming circumstances that surround him.[13] According to Frank McCourt, when Malachy was sober he was "a very good father."[14]

Throughout the film, there are only a few moments where the audience sees Angela smiling or happy. Typically, Emily Watson acts entirely with her eyes, evoking the brooding intensity of her character, which is not unlike her equally brooding performance in the gut-wrenching Lars von Trier drama *Breaking the Waves* (1996). Incidentally, after Parker saw her in this film he was convinced she would make the perfect Angela.[15] This following scene shows a close-up of Angela as she pathetically stands in front of the St. Vincent de Paul board. A long-shot of the three "wise men judges" on the left side of the frame and an abnormally large icon of Jesus on the cross in the center of the shot creates irony—a dichotomy of good versus evil. Although these judges are members of a charity, they are harsh critics of the ones they supposedly support. They ask Angela where she got a name like McCourt, a direct attack against Malachy, whose name suggests that he is from Denoo in the undesirable north of Ireland. When she voices her concerns that the used furniture that she will be given to her may have been used by people who died of consumption, she is coldly told that "beggars can't be choosers."

Regarding the ongoing criticism of Northern Ireland, a bit of historical context is necessary to better understand all the verbal attacks on Malachy. According to Robert Kee in his book *Ireland: A History*: "It is undeniable that the government of Northern Ireland are to blame for the manner in which they conducted affairs of their state in the half century which followed the Anglo-Irish Treaty of 1921 and that they must bear the responsibility for the outbreak of the trouble of their own time."[16] In his chapter "Stormont," he explains the complicated reasons the Northern Ireland government behaved the way they did:

> As long ago as 1911 they had accepted that they must give up their opposition to Home Rule for the greater part of Ireland. That acceptance had immeasurably strengthened their resolve to defend Ulster [Northern Ireland] at all costs and under [Irish Unionist leader and barrister, Edward] Carson and the officers of the Ulster Volunteer Force they had organized themselves very effectively to do so.... There had followed two years of violent terrorism and counterterrorism in Ireland as a result of which British government had surrendered sovereignty over twenty-six of the thirty-two countries of Ireland.[17] Consequently, Northern Ireland had ongoing economic and social problems and, in the 1920s and '30s, unemployment averaged 25 percent of the insured population.[18]

In the next significant scene, the McCourts are settling into their new home in Limerick. Malachy honors a picture of Pope Leo XIII, whom he regards as "a friend of the working man." In a rare moment, Malachy and Angela are dancing together, and although their happiness is short-lived, they share a rare moment of bliss. This is disrupted almost immediately when they discover a man emptying a bucket of human waste outside of their door; they are told, to their dismay, that the entire lane, due to continuous rainfall, is being used as a public sewer. According to the real Frank McCourt, those who lived in the lanes were considered to be "branded."[19]

Time progresses, and the perpetual rains continue. Frank and young Malachy enter the ground floor of their home which has been flooded beyond livability. This forces the family to reside in the small upstairs quarters. In this scene, dominated by low-key lighting, Frank speaks one of the film's most memorable lines regarding his baby sibling: "He's fatter than the baby Jesus." Angela speaks of the children's need for new shoes to Malachy and angrily says, "You'd let them go barefoot before you got off your arse, you lazy fuck." Consequently, in the next scene, Malachy grudgingly proceeds to "repair" the shoes by using tire rubber for the souls. As he mends the shoes with a hammer he exudes pride and dignity, stating that, despite his unluckiness, he is not useless. The author has said that his father was no handyman and this is certainly proven when he "repairs" the shoes so poorly that when the boys wear them to school they are mocked by the other children.[20] At the McCourts' defense, however, is one of the hard-edged school masters, who reminds the class that Jesus died shoeless ("You don't see him on the cross sporting shoes," he says, making the class repeat the phrase for extra emphasis). These school scenes (in contrast to the depressing scenes in the lanes of Limerick) provide the film with a refreshing sense of humor and hope.

The following sequence focuses on the misfortunes of Malachy. Through narration, Frank explains: "Everyday me dad would look for a job, but somehow never seemed to get one. Mam said it was because of his northern accent.... Grandma said it was because of his folly nature." Eventually, Malachy *does* land a job in a cement factory and, in a short sequence suggesting yet another new hope, he is seen preparing for work with great pride—even sporting a tie. According to Malachy, "A man without a tie has no respect for himself." This is shown quickly through a montage set to Ella Fitzgerald's upbeat standard "Dipsy Doodle." The optimism, however, is short-lived because Malachy (once again) wastes his wages on alcohol, and when he finally returns home, he is drunk, and very loudly sings songs of Irish nationalism. As he ascends the staircase, he yells, "Those Red Branch Knights!" "Those Fenian men!" and "The glorious I.R.A.!" (The Red Branch Knights were a standing army who flourished during the first century. Cuchulain, who is referenced in the film but discussed in more detail in the novel, was the most renowned hero of the Red Branch Knights.)[21] When he sees his sons he offers them the "Friday penny," but disgusted with his drunken stupor they reject it and go back to their rooms. Malachy sleeps through the next day and, consequently, loses another job.

The next sequence shifts back to the goings-on at school, where Irish history continues to be taught. One master professes: "Irish is the language of patriots, and English of traitors and informers." Additionally, Hollywood is critiqued, yet it serves as an important part of the children's leisure, namely the films of James Cagney (who, incidentally, served as a symbol of Irish-American pride in such films as *The Irish in Us* [1935, Lloyd Bacon] and *The Fighting 69th* [1940, William Keighley]). These scenes are reminiscent of Parker's childhood when he used to watch movies at the local odeon.[22] In this sequence Frank learns about the birds and the bees through the local authority on sex, Mikey Molloy (Edward Murphy). Although he appears only briefly in the film, Malloy is a more significance character in the book. McCourt writes:

> It is very handy to have Mikey Malloy living around the corner from me, he's eleven, he has fits and behind his back we call him Molloy, the Fit. People in the lane say the fit is an affliction and now I know what affliction means. Mikey knows everything because he has visions in his fits and he reads books. He's an expert in the lane on Girls' Bodies and Dirty Things in General and he promises, "I'll tell you everything, Frankie, when you're eleven like me and you're not so thick and ignorant."[23]

The next two sequences capture two major Irish traditions of which Frank McCourt partook: his First Communion; and the culture of Irish dancing (which was originally omitted from the final cut of the film but after McCourt's insistence, Parker kept it in).[24] On the morning of his First Communion, the pious Grandma Sheehan holds the reigns. The following sequence is captured in a montage. Impatiently, Grandma Sheehan attempts to be proactive as she helps Frank to prepare for this once-in-a-lifetime milestone. In her typically harsh Irish matriarchal tone she curses her grandson and his father's northern heritage and says that with his hair sticking up in a cowlick he looks like a Presbyterian—an obvious attack on Protestantism. And after the memorable moment of accepting the Body of Christ, Frank chews the wafer loudly and is reprimanded by the curmudgeon priest, who tells him to "stop his clucking" and to get back to his seat.

Later on when Frank vomits on his First Communion dinner, an outraged Grandma Sheehan makes him go to Confession. Furthermore, she insists that he ask the priest if she should use ordinary water or holy water to clean the remnants of the vomit, and the priest, another religious curmudgeon, tells Frank to tell his grandmother not to bother him again (a rather humorous irony that puts the old matriarch in her place).

In the next transition, the narrator explains his introduction to Irish dancing, and begins by saying that it was "worse than joining the army police or becoming a nun in Africa." Moreover, he describes Irish dancing as "moving with steel rods up the ass." In the book, Frank makes a friend named Paddy and the boy's father, incidentally, knew Angela, who was considered to be a champion dancer in her day.[25] Dancing was a bruise on Frank's budding masculinity and the next transition shows the boy, along with a group of cheering kids at the Lyric Cinema, watching a "masculine" western. Again, Hollywood is portrayed as being part of the idealistic American utopia. During this time period the Hollywood studio system churned out an uncountable amount of genre films—from westerns to gangster films to musicals to war films to melodramas to screwball comedies—movies that mirrored a new kind of mythology, replete with heroes and villains that were most appealing to audiences who, during the Great Depression, came to rely on movies as a way to escape the harsh realities of everyday living.

Another return to the classroom where we learn more about Ireland's past: A passionate, boisterous master preaches about topics that are obviously beyond the students' interests or comprehension. He didactically speaks, "The *Messerschmitt* could never have taken to the sky and dart from cloud to cloud and bomb the bejesus out of the English who deserved it after what they did to the Irish for eight hundred years." This romantic view of the famous World War II German aircraft is a continued attack on the rule of the British Empire. The master also explains in a very esoteric manner how one must have a pure love for Euclid, the Father of Geometry. On the blackboard he had written the words: *Euclid, Geometry* and *Idiot.* Quite simply, those who don't love and understand Euclidian Geometry are idiots! This is the end of the act, which sets the stage for the transition into the "middle Frank" years.

Time has passed. Frank has gotten older and is now experiencing puberty. This rites-of-passage segment is reminiscent of a number of European films that chronicle the lives of young boys (e.g., *The 400 Blows* [1959, François Truffaut], *Closely Watched Trains* [1966, Jiří Menzel] and *Au Revoir les Enfants* [1987, Louis Malle]). In this scene, Mikey Malloy has persuaded his friends to go to Peter Dooley's house (Peter [Eamonn Owens] is nicknamed "Quasimodo" because, like the Victor Hugo character, he has a hunchback) to spy on his naked sisters through the window. Consequently, Quasimodo would charge each boy a shilling to peek in on the girls, thus profiting from this voyeurism.

The narrative returns to Frank and his family. Malachy proudly marches his son (who knows his Latin well and who has been told by a school master that he has the mind for entering the priesthood) to meet with the priests so he can finally become an altar boy. Once they arrive, however, another despicable priest shuts the door on them, again shattering any hopes and dreams of a promising future for this family. In some ways, it is evident why Malachy succumbs to the drink; he is well-meaning and filled with optimistic spirit, but his seemingly predestined world of malaise around him dictates otherwise.

In the next scene, the more pragmatic Angela, who never has a problem speaking the truth (like her husband, she is a victim of ill fate and, unlike her husband, she no longer carries a spirit of hope) explains to Malachy that Frank was turned away by the church because he was from the lane. She takes out her frustration on her husband, whom she calls useless. She exits the house and he follows her, leading to one of the film's most poignant moments captured through Frank's point-of-view. Malachy tenderly promises his wife that he will get a job and that he will finally change. A new hope surfaces (again) and the viewer *wants* this change to happen.

"God is good," he tells Angela.

Angela responds with a slight smile, "God has not been seen in the lanes of Limerick."

Malachy retorts comically, "You'll go to hell for saying that," and then he gently hugs her.

Part of the ongoing drama of this narration is the dichotomy of hope and despair, and how these people keep going around in the same existential circles as if they were characters in Samuel Beckett's *Waiting for Godot*. They want change, but, in the end, there is only disappointment. In other words, they constantly "wait for Godot," but Godot, like in Beckett's play, never appears.

The existential circle continues: A new baby (Alphie) arrives, but instead of wiping the slate clean so to speak, Malachy inexplicably returns to his drinking binge. Why? Maybe this is the only way he can handle sudden change. Angela is in the same predicament as always—she is caring for a baby, with no money to support him. The lighting is extremely low-key and the mood is somber. Angela tells Frank to go and find his father, and then he is to announce to everyone around him that he is drinking the family money away! Frank does as he is told and, in the next sequence, when he sees his troubled, alcoholic father talking to himself at the bar, the boy finds himself in an emotional predicament. All he can do at that moment is recall fond memories the two of them had in the past, especially the times when Malachy would tell him stories of the prominent heroic figures Cuchulain, Roosevelt and Dela Vera. Unable to approach his father, Frank leaves and sits on the sidewalk surrounded by a saturated blue hue, eating food that he somehow scrounged. Through voice-over narration, the truth is spoken: "A man who has drunk the money for a new baby has gone beyond the beyonds."

When the boy returns home, he tells his mother he couldn't find his father. Angela pauses and the viewer wonders if she believes him or not. Nevertheless, she tells him to go upstairs to wash for dinner.

The upcoming sequence chronicles Frank's descent into illness. The scene begins with a diabolical school master preaching religious fanaticism and the wonders of confirmation. In a monstrous tone and larger-than-life disposition he dictates, "With confirmation you will become true soldiers of the Church. That entitles you to die a martyr in the event we are invaded by Protestants or Muhammadans or any other class of Hedons. You will have the gifts of the Holy Ghost. Wisdom. Understanding."

In a follow-up scene, Frank passes out after attempting to answer a question from a priest; consequently, he ends up in a hospital room. Once again, the association with Catholicism brings about an ironic twist of fate. The priest had asked him to define the Fourth Commandment and Frank begins his answer—"Honor thy father and mother"— before losing consciousness. This exchange is curious because Frank recites the beginning of the *Fifth* Commandment, not the Fourth: "Honor thy father and thy mother; that thy days may be long upon the land which the LORD thy God giveth thee." The commandment promises a long life to those who honor their parents and older people in general, and those who *don't* honor it will die young.[26]

During Frank's recovery period, he is being examined by Doctor Campbell (Alan Parker, in a practically unrecognizable "walk-on" role), eventually leading to a tender moment between father and son: Malachy calls his son a "grand old soldier," then, after a beat, kisses Frank on the forehead before exiting. The boy smiles ear to ear and through voice-over he speaks, "That was the first time my dad ever kissed me. I felt so happy I could have floated."

It is also during this segment at the hospital where Frank discovers the charm of Shakespeare: "It was like having jewels in your mouth when you said the words." In a brief interlude, he recites a quote from *Hamlet*, Act III, Scene I, which is part of the now-famous "To be or not to be..." soliloquy before Hamlet and Ophelia's exchange. "To die, to sleep; To sleep: perchance to dream...."[27] In a follow-up scene, he sits in the bathtub and, in different voices, recites lines from Act II, Scene IV in *Henry VIII*. It's not so much that these particular tragedies have specific meaning to the themes of *Angela's Ashes*; rather, they show the genesis of a future writer who has a real penchant for classical language and storytelling.

In some ways, *Angela's Ashes* is an archetypal "Telemachus/Odysseus" story, replete with the search for the home and wandering father motifs. When Frank returns home, he finds that things have still not changed. He knows his father is out of work again, but he still loves him. The dynamics between father and son are captured through a brief montage where the two of them are walking together in a moment of bliss. Frank narrates: "He was the Holy Trinity was my dad, with three people in him: The storyteller in [the] morning; the one who tried to find work; and the one who came home at night with the smell of whiskey on him."

This elegiac sequence is interrupted by an abrupt cut, returning to the school. Because of his illness, Frank is forced to repeat the fifth class; this causes him great shame and humiliation, especially since he is now in the same grade as his younger brother, Malachy. Angela is there as his support and he looks up at the Statue of Liberty in the middle of Limerick and, at this moment, he finds a penny on the ground. This spiritual moment serves as another symbol of hope for Frank—the symbol of America is a type of visual foreshadowing that predicts his eventual arrival there (this iconic statue was not in the book; it was added specifically to the film to accent Frank's dreams).[28] This lucky moment also sets up the next beat of the film, the memorable "Jesus and the Weather" composition which serves two major purposes. First, it shows Frank's talent for creative thinking and writing; and second, the quality of this controversial piece coming from an adolescent who convinces the head master that he can indeed progress to the next class, where he will be back at grade level. The composition, which is taken from McCourt's words in the book, is also a smart ideological critique on religion and the tragic quality of Limerick at that time.

> This is my composition. I don't think Jesus Who is Our Lord would have liked the weather in Limerick because it's always raining and the Shannon keeps the whole city damp. My father says the Shannon is a killer river because it killed my two brothers. When you look at pictures of Jesus He's always wandering around ancient Israel in a sheet. It never rains there and you never hear of anyone coughing or getting consumption or anything like that and no one has a job there because all they do is stand around and eat manna and shake their fists and go to crucifixions. Anytime Jesus got hungry all He had to do was go up the road to a fig tree or an orange tree and have His fill. If He wanted a pint He could wave His hand over a big glass and there was the pint. Or He could visit Mary Magdalene and her sister, Martha, and they'd give Him His dinner no questions asked and He'd get his feet washed and dried with Mary Magdalene's hair while Martha washed the dishes, which I don't think is fair. Why should she have to wash the dishes while her sister sits out there chatting away with Our Lord? It's a good thing Jesus decided to be born Jewish in that warm place because if he was born in Limerick he'd catch the consumption and be dead in a month and there wouldn't be any Catholic Church and there wouldn't be any Communion or Confirmation and we wouldn't have to learn the catechism and write compositions about Him. *The End.*[29]

Back to the McCourts in the lane. Again, the mood changes from an upbeat, high-key lighting tone to somber low-key. Malachy curses the neighbor for announcing to the lane what they will be eating for dinner; she retorts by telling him to go get a job in England. "I wouldn't give England the steam off my piss," he tells her, yet ironically in a later scene he *does*, in fact, leave for England to search for work. Angela is captured in her typical state of despair, perpetually depressed and smoking cigarettes. She offers to work, but Malachy (exuding his pride) says that a factory is no place for a woman. At her breaking point, she says, "Sittin' on your arse is no place for a man." A shot of Malachy; his look of worry seems to say, *I wish things were different.*

Following this moment, Frank watches his parents in bed together. Malachy wants to make love, but Angela is adamant about not having any more children. Malachy reminds her that this attitude defies the role of a good Catholic woman, and he even warns her that abstaining from procreation will result in eternal damnation. Angela's bittersweet retort: "Eternal damnation is okay if there are no more children." The lighting in this scene is extremely low-key—hope has, once more, been severely dimmed.

Time has passed. The McCourts are now at the train station, seeing Malachy off; despite his hubris, he has decided to work in England, which is the only reasonable way the family can attain income. Malachy boards the train and, as the weeks pass, the same scenario ensues: The family waits for a telegram with Malachy's wages, but nothing arrives. Frank is forced to go to work for Mr. Hannon (Shay Gorman), shoveling coal. This sequence reprises Ella Fitzgerald's "The Dipsy Doodle" in another montage. For the first time in his life he feels like a man and is able to give his mother wages for the family. During this time, however, Frank succumbs to a bad case of conjunctivitis, which limits his working potential.

Back at the St. Vincent de Paul Society: Angela receives a rather unsavory-looking goose that becomes the McCourts' Christmas dinner. Malachy arrives on Christmas Eve (two days late), and the return is awkward on all ends. He gives his family a box of chocolates from the boat, but still no wages. He catches hell not just from his wife but from Frank and young Malachy, both of whom say, "You drank the money!" Angela informs him that she does not want him to go out and return home drunk, singing his "stupid songs." Soon after Christmas dinner, he escapes his prison again and returns to London. As he leaves, he tells his children to say their prayers and be good to their mother. Despite his own hypocrisy he still holds this mantra sacred.

In the last part of the act, Malachy walks away and Frank follows him, hiding himself behind buildings so as not to be discovered. In voice-over narration, Frank says, "If I were in America I could say 'I love you Dad' like they do in the films, but in Limerick they'd laugh at you. In Limerick you're only allowed to say you love God and babies—and horses that win. Anything else is softness in the head." Malachy, who knows his son is there, simply says, "Go home, Frankie." The subtext of this line carries several meanings. First, it is stoic, keeping the Limerick way of life; second, it is tragic: Malachy is saying goodbye to his son (this is the last time he is seen in the film); and third, it is a line that serves as a rites-of-passage transition. Frank is now the "man of the house" as he enters the next stage of his development. And so ends this era of "middle Frank," which makes the transition into the film's third (and final) act, the journey of "older Frank," the last stage of his adolescence before he arrives in America.

Although Frank is older, the living conditions in the lane are the same as he enters his dilapidated home; the downstairs portion of the house is completely flooded. In order to keep warm, Angela and her sons (who have moved upstairs) break down a wall and use this wood to feed a fire; this act ultimately leads to their eviction, yielding another series of hardships that continue to plague the McCourt family: Grandma Sheehan dies of pneumonia; Angela and her sons move in with her first cousin Laman Griffin, a formidable character who agrees to take the family in free of rent; and Frank gets a job delivering mail. During this time, the American dream becomes more attainable for young Frank McCourt. He stands in front of the "Statue of Liberty" in the center of Limerick, a scene that is set to the music of Billie Holiday. Frank's voice-over narration: "Oh Billie, I want to be with you in America where nobody has bad teeth and everyone has a lavatory."

Living at Laman Griffin's house, however, proves to be just as taxing (if not more so) as living in the lanes. Griffin is the ultimate glutton—excessive in his eating and drinking, he believes that Angela must attend to him, which is part of her "woman's work." Additionally, he is abusive (in one scene he attacks Frank); he even forces Angela to sleep with him, much to Frank's outrage and disgust.

On the kitchen wall there is a political poster in favor of the Cumann na n Gaedheal party. The 1932 election poster shows a large silhouette of an outlaw looking over a home with a gun and above him is the legend THE SHADOW OF THE GUNMAN. Enclosed in a triangle are the words: KEEP IT FROM YOUR HOME. Underneath these words—*Vote For Cumann na n Gaedheal.* The poster reminded prospective voters that the Fianna Fail party (represented as a dark gunman) had its roots in violence and bloodshed in the 1922 Irish Civil War and served to warn the voters not to allow the "return" of the gunman, while the pro–Anglo-Irish Treaty party Cumann na n Gaedheal (Society of the Gaels) which was in power in 1923 (and who retained its power in 1933 after the election), represented "law and order." A certain irony prevails here: the violent Laman Griffin was apparently a supporter of the peaceful Cumann na n Gaedheal.[30]

During this Laman Griffin sequence, the film cross-cuts to Frank's school experience. The introduction to school master Mr. O'Hollaran (Brendan Cauldwell, who also played the tavern keeper in *Far and Away* [1992, Ron Howard]) offers a refreshing alternative to the previous school masters. O'Halloran is not only kinder and more passionate than his colleagues, he also embraces American culture and has a vested interest in Frank; in class, he tells the boy that he has a mind for either the priesthood or for politics and encourages him to leave Ireland and move to America. Thus, the Statue of Liberty, the music of Billie Holliday, and Mr. O'Hollaran all become part of the triumvirate symbolizing Frank's hopeful future.

After Frank leaves Laman Griffin's house (in a poignant scene he tells his brother Malachy that he will kill Griffin if he stays), he ends up, unannounced, at his Uncle Pat and Aunt Aggie's home. In one of the film's funniest moments, Frank tells his naïve uncle that the bruises on his face from Laman's hands are actually the marks of famous boxer Joe Lewis, an absurd fact that his uncle (who is probably intoxicated) appears to accept as the truth. When his aunt finds him in bed dressed in her "dead mother's dress," she is naturally outraged. Frank informs her that his own clothes were in the wash. In the next beat, his uncle comes upstairs and "compliments" his nephew in another amusing moment: "You look gorgeous, Frankie!" he says, laughing.

Throughout this sequence Frank bonds with his aunt, whom he refers to as "a mystery." She takes him clothes shopping so he can be presentable for his new mail-delivery job. The otherwise disgruntled woman takes this time to be nurturing, which adds an endearing quality to her character; in a way, she is mothering the child she could never have—and Frank, in a touching moment, kisses her, and although she responds awkwardly by grimacing, one can tell she is still moved by the gesture.

During one of his deliveries, Frank falls off of his bicycle then appears at the doorstep of Theresa (Kerry Condon, in her first acting role),[31] the young daughter of one of his customers, who becomes his summer fling (and in his adolescent mind, his first true love). Despite the fact that she is dying of tuberculosis, he is enamored of her red hair and green eyes and, consequently, he makes love with her. In a voice-over narration, the audience realizes the impact of this relationship as the two have sex: "If this is a sin, I don't give a fiddler's fart." Even though her days are numbered, Theresa also symbolizes Frank's hope. After a session of lovemaking she asks him what he wants more than anything—and he tells her what we've known all along—to go to America. In a follow-up scene, he rides his bike and passionately prays out loud: "Please God, it wasn't Theresa's fault. I love her, God, just as St. Francis loved any bard or beast or fish. Please God, take the consumption away and I promise I'll never go near her again." Nevertheless, Theresa *does* pass away and Frank watches the funeral from afar. In a poignant voiceover he says: "But I knew that with all the people that died in my family and all the people that died in the lanes around me—I never had a pain like this in my heart and I hope I never will again." In this way, Theresa, the love of his life, is also a symbol of his rites-of-passage: her death confirms his manhood and his inevitable departure for America.

Throughout this sequence, Angela pays a surprise visit to her son. Here we find out that his brother Michael and Alphie are well, and "Mad Malachy" has joined the bugle corps in the army. Frank breaks down, cries and says he misses Malachy, and the two of them embrace. This sequence is additionally effective because, in a later scene, Uncle Pat takes him for his first pint at a pub and, when he returns home, he becomes a facsimile of his father—drunk and singing Irish songs ("It's your father you've become," Angela says to him shamefully). An altercation ensues. Frank responds to his mother unabashedly: "I'd rather be like my father than *your* Laman Griffin!" He then calls her a *slut* and then slaps her face, an act that he regrets for the remainder of the film (and perhaps the rest of his life). As disturbing as this moment was for mother and son it serves as yet another chapter in Frank's rites-of-passage story, another sign that he is ready to leave to home. Furthermore, slapping his mother and cursing Laman was an outlet for Frank trying to reach his own absent father, whom he loves as much as he resents.

In a follow-up scene, the guilt-ridden boy visits the church and lights many candles in front of a statue of St. Francis (incidentally it was on this street in Ireland where the actress Maureen O'Hara was born in on August 17, 1920).[32] He confesses to a priest the sin of hitting his mother and in a quick montage we see a number of shots from previous moments in the film that have greatly affected the boy: the deaths of Mary, Oliver and Eugene; comforting images of his father; Theresa; the memory of watching a girl and engaging in a group masturbation with other boys; the time when the Christian brothers closed the door on him when he inquired about becoming an altar boy; and the tears in his eyes when he slapped his mother. The priest says, "God loves you and forgives you." After Frank leaves, he thanks St. Francis.

A few notes on St. Francis before moving forward: Saint Francesco—Francesco di Pietro Bernardone—was born in Assisi in 1181 of humble beginnings (it can be argued that his life mirrored Frank's). Although his father was a wealthy cloth merchant, he had an ordinary childhood and was not much of a student. Over the years, the festive young man, an aficionado of music, parties and quiet prayer, claimed that Jesus spoke to him, telling him that he was chosen to repair the dilapidated church of San Damiano. Consequently, Saint Francesco became a martyr for the poor and, before long, had his own disciples. He related to the poor, even sharing their scraps of food. Francesco was identified with Jesus and apparently received the stigmata in 1244: He was marked by Jesus as his own (replete with his Passion), thus making him a living saint.[33]

In addition to his job as a mail carrier, Frank lands another odd job as a delivery boy for the old spinster Mrs. Finucane (Eileen Pollock)—a job that, incidentally, gives him the funds he needs to travel to America. When she discovers that her delivery boy has a penchant for reading and writing she hires him to compose threatening letters to the people who owe her money. Frank's love of the English language is eloquently expressed in the way he writes these scathing letters and, because they are so effective, she offers him a commission for every letter he writes, plus a bonus when someone pays off their debt.

Nearing the final stretch of the film, Frank runs to the house of Mrs. Finucane and discovers that the spinster has passed away. He takes her money and discards her book that holds the names of her debtors in the Shannon River: Now, no one owes her anything! In this way, Frank becomes a sort of martyr and friend for the working class, much like St. Francis. Consequently, he now has the money he needs to go to America. In the novel, this scene is expressed thus:

> The Friday night before my nineteenth birthday Mrs. Finucane sends me for the sherry. When I return she is dead in the chair, her eyes wide open, and her purse on the floor wide open. I can't look at her but I help myself to a roll of money. Seventeen pounds. I take the key to the

trunk upstairs. I take forty of the hundred pounds in the trunk and the ledger. I'll add this to what I have in the post office and I have enough to go to America. On my way out I take the sherry bottle to save it from being wasted.[34]

The next scene, another rites-of-passage moment in Frank's young adult life, takes place at a family gathering at the home of Aunt Aggie and Uncle Pat. Angela, along with Alphie and the others, are singing a song that references a mother's love. The song makes Frank cry; the look on his face shows that he not only feels guilty that he hit his mother, it also indicates his awareness that he may not see her for a long time. In the book the song is merely referred to as "[Angela's] sad song."[35]

The arrival of a lunar eclipse marks the new hope associated with Frank's future. Everyone stands in awe as the moon passes behind the earth, blocking the sun's rays on the moon. Aunt Aggie, the eternal pessimist, comments on how "the moon is practicing for the end of the world." Uncle Pat, on the other hand, sees things differently: "It is only the beginning for Frank McCourt," he says, and speaks of his nephew's potential prospects in America. When the group disperses from the lane, Frank remains alone. After a moment, he encounters the younger and middle versions of himself, a powerful scene made even more so by Williams's commanding fully orchestrated score. In the DVD commentary, Parker cites this as being his favorite moment in the film. He calls it "totally cinematic" and says, "Everything that has gone before is summed up in that one shot. It serves as a cinematic curtain call for the young actors."[36]

In the final stretch of the film, Frank is on the boat called *Irish Oak*. When he finally sees the actual Statue of Liberty, he smiles, and the accompanying music complements his internal satisfaction—he has made it! The last shot creates a meaningful *mise-en-scène*: a long-shot of the boat on the left of the frame balanced with the Statue of liberty in the center—and, to the right of that, the sun (a reminder of the eclipse?)—a triumvirate of images all in harmony with one another represented in a clear depth-of-field—as the image fades and the credits role.

The last few pages of McCourt's memoir include a few more details that were omitted in the film. Aboard the boat, Frank meets a priest, who serves as a paternal guide and a critic on American society. The priest warns him about the prostitutes; he calls them "bad women, occasion of sin." This doesn't stop the young man from meeting and eventually sleeping with one of these prostitutes, a woman named Frieda. At the very end of the novel Frank stands on the deck with a wireless officer who also spent the night with a prostitute and says to him, "My God, that was a lovely night, Frank. Isn't this a great country, altogether?"

Frank replies, "'Tis," which is the name of the sequel to *Angela's Ashes*.[37]

15

The Life of David Gale, 2003

February 21; 130 minutes/Color
Production Companies: Universal, Intermedia, Dirty Hands Productions, Mikona Productions GmbH & Co. KG, Saturn Films
Director: Alan Parker
Screenwriter: Charles Randolph
Producers: Mortiz Borman (Executive); Nicolas Cage; Guy East (Executive); Norman Golightly (as Norm Golightly—co-Executive Producer); Lisa Moran; Alan Parker; Nigel Sinclair (Executive); David Wimburg (Line Producer)
Cinematography: Michael Seresin, Director of photography
Editor: Gerry Hambling
Production Designer: Geoffrey Kirkland
Original Music: Alex Parker & Jake Parker
Cast: Kevin Spacey (David Gale); Kate Winslet (Bitsey Bloom); Laura Linney (Constance Harraway); Matt Crave (Dusty Wright); Gabriel Mann (Zack Stemmons)

> Although considered a polemical film, the studio made it because they saw it as a thriller and this is what sparked the controversy around the film.... I was accused of trivializing an important political issue by delivering a thriller. In the end, I was proud that it got made at all in a Hollywood climate where political films are no longer on the studio's agendas. No doubt, in [its] own small way the film fueled the debate, for and against the death penalty.[1]—Alan Parker

> You know you're in the Bible Belt when there are more churches than Starbucks.
> —Bitsey, to Zach, while driving to Death Row

Notes on the Production

The Life of David Gale was written by novice screenwriter Charles Randolph, a Texas-raised professor of Philosophy at Vienna University. He wrote the script back in 1998, but it was shelved at Warner Bros. until September of 2000, when Alan Parker became involved. The story was developed by Nicolas Cage's production company. Parker stated, "I read it in one sitting ... and was astonished that such a well-written, page turner of a script hadn't already been made.... Although the script—an original story, a fiction—most certainly had an important political issue at its core ... it was also a terrific thriller."[2] When Nicolas Cage (with whom Parker had worked in *Birdy*) was unable to be involved due to numerous other commitments, Parker stepped in, and, after speaking with Stacey Snider (the head of Universal), decided to commit to the project. Soon thereafter, Randolph met with Parker in London, where they both worked on revising the screenplay.

Parker and his crew spent a number of months scouting locations. According to the director, "You try to absorb the place, because the place becomes another character in the film."[3] A number of scenes were filmed in Austin, as well as neighboring Texas towns. They used the old Mueller Airport in Austin as a de facto film studio to build sets, which primarily became the interiors of the two prisons. The first part of the filming involved David and Constance's backstory, while the final six weeks focused primarily on Bitsey and Zack's present-day investigative narrative.[4]

After the filming in Austin was completed, the crew then proceeded to shoot the Huntsville and Ellis Prison scenes. Parker, with a crew of two-hundred (outfitted with fifty vehicles and two helicopters) jokingly said of this filmmaking circus, "I felt like Attila the Hun at the Gates of Rome." The fictionalized University of Austin scenes were filmed at another Austin college, but not at the university itself (this college preferred to remain anonymous).[5] Parker's production designer, Geoffrey Kirkland, recreated a strikingly authentic facsimile of Ellis (which had a Death Row section until 1999; it is currently a modernized, less "prison-looking" structure), by making the set out of the same high-security material of which the prison had been constructed, including bullet-proof glass.

The filming process was most impressive: Parker and his crew were on schedule and

Radical reporter Bitsey Bloom (Kate Winslet) with young intern partner Zack Stemmons (Gabriel Mann) facing the unseen death row inmate David Gale for the first time. *The Life of David Gale* (2003), Universal, Intermedia, Dirty Hands Productions, Mikona Productions GmbH & Co. KG, Saturn Films.

on budget after a sixty-one-day shoot. Parker's two sons, Alex and Jake, scored the film in a very organic manner—they composed the music as the film was being edited instead of after the final cut. The classically trained Jake was responsible for the idiosyncratic orchestrated pieces, while Alex provided the film with the more contemporary, percussion-based score.

Like any film, *The Life of David Gale* had its technical challenges, but, in this particular case, Mother Nature intervened: while filming a scene in a diner in Austin with Bitsey and Zack, a tornado struck. The entire cast and crew (including Kate Winslet and her newborn baby) had to be put into a storage room for their own safety. The scene needed to be reshot later at another diner.[6]

As far as casting was concerned, Brad Pitt and George Clooney originally showed interest in the part of David Gale. When Parker was serving as a judge of the Shanghai International Film Festival, Kevin Spacey (who had just recently won his Oscar for *American Beauty*) contacted him and agreed to do the film. Kate Winslet—the British actress who worked extensively on her American accent with a dialect coach (she pulled off the accent rather impressively in James Cameron's *Titanic* about five years earlier)—created the believable young radical reporter Bitsey Bloom. Laura Linney (*The Exorcism of Emily Rose*, *The Other Man*, *The Squid and the Whale*, *John Adams*) was also part of this talented ensemble, portraying poetry professor/death watch coordinator Constance Harraway.[7]

Although *The Life of David Gale* received its share of criticism (not unlike *Mississippi Burning* and *Midnight Express*), Parker once again produced a controversial ideologically driven drama that brought important social issues to the foreground. Regarding his own stance on the film's topics, Parker said, "I am very much against the death penalty personally, although I hope the film is balanced in the argument."[8]

Music in The Life of David Gale (by Alan Parker)[9]

When I first got to Austin, one block's walk away from my hotel I soon discovered Sixth Street, where for ten blocks on either side it was jam-packed with bars—all of them blaring out live music. The banners across the street proclaimed it to be "the live music capital of America," and although some other cities might make the same boast, you couldn't deny the quantity and diversity of music on offer. Catering as they do for the eclectic tastes of a student population of 50,000, I pored through the shelves of the local record stores to narrow down the source music relevant to The Life of David Gale.

At the same time, during the pre-production period, I began to experiment with the music that would become the score of our film.

Over the years, I had worked with my two sons, Alex and Jake, on the music for many of my films. Often they have helped me, without credit, with temp scores, and on Come See the Paradise *they provided the main theme. Both are very different in their musical backgrounds. Jake is classically trained, having earned his master's degree in composition at the New England Conservatory of Music in Boston. Alex, who trained in audio engineering, and who plays many instruments, has mainly been involved in contemporary music. However, my films over the last ten years have involved different musical situations—*

with The Commitments *(soul music)*; Evita *(Andrew Lloyd Webber)* and Angela's Ashes *(John Williams)* there had been little opportunity for us to work together since. During the preparation and shoot of The Life of David Gale *I asked Alex to experiment for me in areas where I thought the score might go. I wanted a modern, rhythm-driven score to serve the thriller aspect of the movie and I also wanted it to echo the themes within it. I sent Alex a pile of research materials to do with the political heart of the film and included some biblical quotations, which had been often used both for and against the death penalty. He sent me many demos in Austin, which were very promising.*

There came a point when the film required them to work together—something they hadn't done for some time. Alex's contemporary multi-tracks had to fuse with Jake's classical themes. The cues they had named from the script, so Jake's "Lacan" theme (named from the French philosopher in David's first lecture) suddenly became musically and nominally "Ominous Lacan" as Jake's cello pieces fused with Alex's less elegantly entitled cues, i.e., "Ominous House Vibe." The very titles themselves are a reflection of their different musical educations. The two of them worked through the night to work and rework their stuff [for the film]. When I had completed the shoot and returned to London to edit the film I showed Alex and Jake the scenes that we had already cut and the hours of footage that we were still working on.

The first thing that we completed musically was the song that Alex had been working on—"Another Bleeding Heart"—and which he then took into the studio. Jake wrote the string sections for the song and we were suddenly off on a musical experiment. I have to say now, that as proud as I am of my sons' accomplishments, I would always be far too selfish with regard to my film to mess it up with notions of nepotism. But, little by little, we started to nudge towards a score that I felt was fresh and original, and one that I couldn't possibly replicate with a more starry-named composer. Universal were very patient during this period: "Who's doing the score, Alan?" they asked weekly. "I'm experimenting," I would answer. "All will be clear when I show you the finished film." Alex and Jake would immediately work on each scene, as it was hot off the Moviola. Jake took the scenes that needed more traditional, orchestral pieces and Alex worked on the rhythmically driven "thriller" scenes. It was a completely organic process—the music was created at exactly the same time as we cut the scenes, something that I had never been able to do before on my films. They adapted their work as we cut: Alex, in his back room studio, layering dozens of complex tracks to affect the scenes, and Jake, working to picture on his Clavinova, adjusting his music bar by bar.

Jake's pieces for "Almost Martyrs" and "Huntsville Epitaph" and Alex's pieces for "Shack 2 Cell," "Dusty's Cabin" and "Media Frenzy." Family connection aside, I doubt that any director ever got so much work out of his composers, especially as they hadn't been paid a cent at this point. (We were still in the experimental zone, as far as Universal was concerned.) And, as closely entwined as we are as a family—and also, it has to be said, as opinionated as we usually all are with regard to our different musical tastes—miraculously we got through it without a single argument. Finally, Universal saw and approved the film with its (up to now, electronically recorded) score. We then had to finish the music. At Abbey Road in Studio 1, Jake—who had orchestrated his pieces for a 70-person orchestra— received a round of applause at the end of the sessions from the collected players (not usually known for their altruism). Alex worked away in Studio 3, laying down the dozens of tracks he had created himself in his backroom studio and augmenting them with live musicians.

Needless to say that, family connections aside, I am immensely proud of the score Alex and Jake did for my film.

Summary

The Life of David Gale—like a number of the aforementioned Alan Parker films—begins aurally off-screen: over black, the overlapping sounds of birds and traffic transition into the opening shot—a long-shot/low-angle shot (both extreme in their compositions), looking up onto a road from a banking covered in dirt. From this angle, a figure is seen running away from a parked car and this leads to a brief montage (set to Alex Parker's palpitating percussion score, which suggests the rhythm of a heartbeat) represented in many angles ... the juxtaposition of the images and the sound complements the frantic running. Within moments, a Ford pickup passes by the person (revealed as a young woman—reporter Bitsey Bloom, played by Kate Winslet). This scene is actually part of the film's climax, but before it moves forward any further, the image dissolves into the interior of an office building.

A rotund African American woman (Barbara Kreuster, played by Cleo King) sits in an office, munching on potato chips while watching the latest breaking news on the mock–CNN channel CTS: It concerns the life of David Gale (Kevin Spacey), seen in a series of news clips that provides the viewer with critical introductory exposition. Throughout this footage, the main backstory is revealed: the rape and murder of Constance Harraway (Laura Linney), Gale's colleague and fellow activist/abolitionist for the non-profit anti-death penalty organization Death Watch. In another clip, Gale is at a rally and says, "You understand how much money the tax payers pay to put one person to death?" Barbara—who turns out to be Bitsey's boss at a magazine—takes a call from Joe, the supervising editor who is discussing David Gale with her. Here the audience begins to piece together two major facts: First, Gale is going to be executed in four days; and second, because of Bitsey's former involvement with a kiddie-porn story that landed her in jail, she had been "chosen" by Gale's attorney in Austin to interview his client. Barbara tells Bitsey: "I think they liked the kiddie porn piece, and going to jail and stuff." In short, Bitsey, like Gale, is an activist who is willing to go to any extremes—including breaking the law—to support the integrity of her cause. When Bitsey asks her boss what the story will entail, Barbara says, "Rape, murder, Death Row...." Barbara implies that Gale may even be innocent, and Bitsey, who is first portrayed as a hard-as-nails cynic, retorts, "Yeah right"—an attitude that will gradually turn around over the course of the story.

In a continuous scene, Barbara and Bitsey meet chief editor Joe Mullarkey (Lee Ritchie) in his office. He voices his concerns about the possible reasons *she* has been singled out to be the one and only person allowed to interview Gale in his final days. Furthermore, he tells her that she will be working with a young intern named Zack (Gabriel Mann), a prospect that Bitsey does not relish. The first few minutes of the film rather succinctly present the story's setup. The film embraces a number of very familiar narrative devices, including the socially conscious drama, the detective "buddy" film (throughout the film, Zack and Bitsey are investigative journalists whose job essentially becomes to piece together Gale's enigmatic history) and the film noir/suspense thriller, replete with mystery and flashbacks.

The following scene—a number of interior and exterior shots of Bitsey and Zack in their car—reminds the viewer that the film is also an archetypal journey/road picture. While driving, they pass the sign for Huntsville as they look at photographs and discuss Gale en route to Ellis Prison, where death row inmates resided until 1999 (currently Death Row is at Polunski, a high-tech modernized institution).[10] Zack—who comes to idolize Gale, referring to him as an "academic stud"—discusses the former professor's accomplishments: he was tenured at twenty-seven; he graduated from Harvard; and he is a Rhodes Scholar. Furthermore, he attempts to impress her by informing that 73 percent of all serial killers vote Republican. "A person's politics has nothing to do with his propensity to commit a crime," she tells him, deflating his ego, and further reminding him—unabashedly—of their hierarchical status: she is the *reporter* and he is the *intern*. (Incidentally, in *Mississippi Burning*, Parker also explores a serious ideological topic through the eyes of a quirky detective/buddy duo.)

The next scene has the duo at the side of the road, checking the condition of the car that was (in a previous scene) experiencing engine problems. Undoubtedly, this motif functions as a form of foreshadowing, which sets us up for the climax when Bitsey abandons the car just moments shy of Gale's execution. While Bitsey stays with the car, Zack goes off to a nearby restroom, leaving her alone. From a number of aerial-shot angles, the camera captures the black Ford pickup, along with its shady-looking driver: a man with strong, angular features, wearing a cowboy hat. Bitsey calls for Zack and, together, they watch as this man menacingly approaches, picking up considerable speed as he zooms by. *Who is he? Is he following them?* As the film unfolds, this cowboy character will be a pivotal part of the narrative's intricate puzzle. But, for now, he remains enigmatic—perhaps even dangerous. The story of *The Life of David Gale* has been set into motion.

The image dissolves to a group of clouds, setting up the transition for DAY 1—the first of four days that the film spans, the last four days of David Gale's life. The camera pans, then tilts down from a motel sign, then to Bitsey walking in a diner called Vic's. Zack is already inside, reading David Gale's book *Dialogical Exhaustion*; he is continuously enamored of Gale's accomplishments, and informs Bitsey that Gale "is a genius." Although he manages to get a rare smile from her after he conveys a quick anecdote he heard from the waitress, she continues to give her apprentice a hard time, reminding him again that David Gale is *her* interview, *not* his. His retort is immature and misogynistic: "Your reputation as Mike Wallace with PMS does not do you justice." Instead of taking offense at this, she says, "My reputation got me here. I play by the rules even if my colleagues don't like it."

A new transition: Bitsey and Zack are back in their red Ford, en route to Ellis. Bitsey critiques the surroundings: "You know you're in the Bible Belt when there are more churches than Starbucks." As they arrive at the prison yard, they pass a chain gang working on the road. In the next few shots they pull up to the prison and a sign reads "Ellis Unit—Department of Corrections." In the background, the eerie Texas theme resonates—a moody Southern blues riff, replete with slide guitar. Inside the prison, a number of point-of-view shots capture Bitsey and Zack in an unfamiliar world: Zack sits fidgeting nervously and looks at the sign, reading, "NO HOSTAGES WILL EXIT." The background is surrounded by bars— the closed-form composition of the *mise-en-scène* accents this Sartre-like existential world.

Like in many prison films, the next significant scene occurs in the warden's office; this is the final stop before the first encounter with David Gale. Duke Grover (Jim Beaver), TDCJ Community Relations, serves as the guide as he conducts a tour through the prison, providing exposition along the way. During the tour, we learn that this prison is the home to all 442 death row inmates, their final "home" before being transported to Huntsville, where the actual executions occur. Additionally, we learn that the average death row wait is nine years. Grover reinforces the need for safety and further informs Bitsey of an inmate's foot fetish, telling her that open-toed shoes (which she luckily was not wearing) drive certain inmates crazy. Nevertheless, Bitsey still becomes an object to a group of voyeuristic prisoners who watch her walk by; the inmates—excited to see an attractive female on the inside—show their appreciation by touching their own nipples in a most suggestive way. This segment curiously mirrors the scene in *The Silence of the Lambs* (1991, Jonathan Demme), in which Clarice Starling—who, like Bitsey, is objectified by men—travels into the Dante-like depths of purgatory as she is led to the cell of serial killer Hannibal Lecter.

The short tour ends once Bitsey and Zack arrive at their destination: the visitation room where David Gale is first introduced. They are greeted by Gale's attorney, Braxton Belyeu (Leon Rippey)—a unique specimen with angular features, bad teeth, and a ponytail. This questionable character represents the shady legal system in Texas, and he turns out to be quite the shyster counselor (especially with his curious, ambiguous involvement with "cowboy" Dusty, which will be addressed later in the summary). On the DVD commentary track, Parker admits that Rippey does not have a typical actor look and, naturally, this is what contributes to his enigmatic persona. Moreover, Parker stated that the local actor was "easy to work with" and along with the professionalism of Kate Winslet, Kevin Spacey and Laura Linney, the film's performances remain rich and emotional. On Spacey, Parker noted, "Kevin has the ability to twist [the] imperfections and flaws in a character and take them by the scruff of the neck and throw them back so that the character can still be noble ... and still be sympathetic."[11]

When the camera first reveals Gale in his white DR (Death Row) uniform, he is immediately seen as a product of the institution, a caged animal that is judged by the guards around him, who practice—according to Gale—"cruel and unusual punishment." At this time, Gale breaks the ice and says hello in a rather composed manner. This tone, however, does not set Bitsey at ease; it will take some time before Gale will earn her trust and respect. Belyeu informs Zack that he can't stay—that the interview *must* be conducted by Bitsey alone. When Zack and the lawyer leave, Bitsey is left alone with Gale. Her disposition is cold, yet once the viewer becomes better acquainted with her, it is clear that this is really a cover for her compassion, vulnerability and naiveté. She jokingly asks Gale if the pen she is holding counts as a recording device (earlier on, she is informed that all recording devices are strictly forbidden in this interview). Gale, amused by her sense of humor, smiles, not in a calculated or cynical manner, but genuinely so; it appears that he trusts her immediately. In the next beat, she asks Gale the obvious question: what is *she* doing there? Gale, a consummate philosopher and orator, answers didactically: "No one who looks through that glass sees a person; they see a crime. I'm not David Gale; I'm a murderer and a rapist four days shy of his execution. You're here because I want to be remembered as much for how I led my life and the decisions I made as for how my life ended." Furthermore, he admits to her that he has chosen her because, in so many words, he sees her, perhaps, as a female version of himself—a person willing to fight for a cause until the very end. In Jungian terms, she comes to represent the *anima*, which is part of his *persona*. He is interviewing her as much as she is interviewing him. He continues, "Well I have a hard story for you to tell, Ms. Bloom," he says. "It's not going to be easy." During the scene the viewer is given the illusion that Winslet and Spacey are captured in a two-shot, but, in fact, throughout the exchange, Winslet is not even present. This is additionally impressive because she listens so attentively to Spacey that one would assume she was in the room with him.[12]

The first major flashback begins when Gale says, "I suppose I should tell you how I became the Head of Philosophy at the University of Austin...." Instead of resorting to traditional flashback techniques, Parker decides to use percussion instruments along with a camera moving chaotically in frenzied 360-degree spins, replete with flashes of key words that are all from Bitsey's future article (*Truth, Desire, Power, Life, Lust, Fantasy*—each word telling a piece of her forthcoming story). This technique is used frequently throughout the film to signal the transitions from act to act.

David Gale is teaching his philosophy class at the University of Austin, an engaging introductory lecture on Jacques Lacan, the French-born psychiatrist whose teachings manifested itself into a number of disciplines, namely literary analysis, film theory, psychoanalysis, philosophy, linguistics and mathematics. In philosophy alone, Lacan has done studies in the categories of Philosophical Anthropology (Oedipal Complex, Castration, Desire of the Other, etc.), Philosophy of Language (Language and Law) and Philosophy of Ethics (Lacan's Conception of Fantasy). In this particular lecture, Gale discusses Lacan's Conception of Fantasy. He asks the class what they fantasize about. He further explains, "It's not the *it* you want, it's the *fantasy of it*.... Living by your wants will never make you happy because in the end the only way we can measure the significance of our lives is by valuing the lives of others." The notes on the blackboard additionally accent Lacan's theory and include the phrases *Menial Causality* and the *Objet petit a fantasy* theory, the latter being a significant part of Lacan's Conception of Fantasy. According to the theory, the *objet petit*—an unattainable object of desire—is an anamorphic object that yields an idea known as the object-gaze, something "that can only operate its fascination upon individuals who bear a partial perspective upon it ... that object that represents the subject within the world of objects that it takes itself to be a wholly 'external' perspective upon. If a subject happens upon it too directly, it disappears." Thus, by simple definition, it is an object that has come into being in being lost.[13] Gale paraphrases these theories with lines like "be careful what you wish for" and "the hunt is sweeter than the kill"; he also includes a philosophy from Pascal, stating that we are only truly happy when daydreaming about future happiness. The emphasis on these Lacanian theories is twofold: first, it is used as a vehicle into further defining David Gale's academic milieu; and second, it mirrors the themes and ideologies of the narrative, especially with the aforementioned quotation: "The only way we can measure the significance of our lives is by valuing the lives of others."

When class ends, Gale's student Berlin (the woman who was the one seen coming to class late) approaches him. She uses her sexuality to try to save her failing grade in the class. She tells him she will do *anything* to pass the class—and she means *anything*. Gale plays her "fantasy" game, leans over as if giving into her seduction and softly says, "Okay, Berlin—I will give you a good grade.... I will give you a *very* good grade ... if you would just ... *study*." The humiliation and rejection shows on the girl's face in an extended reaction shot.

The complicated relationship between Gale and his colleague Constance Harraway

(Laura Linney), a professor of poetry, begins to unfold. The professors and fellow Death Watch activists discuss the role of their cause, specifically a quote from the governor regarding *his* view on death row convicts: "I say bring them in, strap them down and let's rock and roll." Gale, serving as a critic for such right-winged rhetoric, retorts: "It's nice to know that our governor is in touch with his inner frat boy." (Might this be an ideological critique against Texas governor Jeb Bush?) Meanwhile, they discuss an upcoming debate with the governor on a locally televised program. Constance, unable to appear on the show, turns it over to David, who will be there to represent Death Watch.

A brief but significant scene at Gale's home helps build the continued tension associated with the rest of the story. He tucks his young son Jamie (Noah Truesdale) into bed and before he leaves the bedroom his boy tells him what he'd like for breakfast in the morning: pancakes with syrup, chocolate shavings, strawberries and whipped cream. This seemingly insignificant fact proves to be a significant foreshadowing detail, as this will be the last meal Gale requests before his execution. He exits the house and says goodbye to the babysitter, whom we later discover is one of his students. Little does he know that when this evening is over, his life will change forever—and this includes losing the privilege to see his son.

Gale attends a university party where he encounters Berlin (Rhona Mitra), who, according to one of his colleagues, is "pretty livid" about her recent letter of expulsion. Nevertheless, she remains at the party, continuing to exude her seductive "femme fatale"

English professor and capital punishment activist Constance Harraway (Laura Linney) with colleague, friend and fellow activist, philosophy professor David Gale (Kevin Spacey) on the University of Texas campus. *The Life of David Gale* (2003), Universal, Intermedia, Dirty Hands Productions, Mikona Productions GmbH & Co. KG, Saturn Films.

charm while she drinks and flirts with her professor. As the party continues, and more alcohol is consumed, the group convenes around a pool to listen to intellectuals reciting rather sophomoric limericks (perhaps this is showing how professors wind down at the end of a scholarly day). When it's Gale's turn to recite, the drunk philosophy professor mutters the following, which in its own way serves as a metaphor for what eventually happens between Gale and Berlin: "There once was a lesbian from Cancun/Who took a young man up to her room/Where they argued all night/As to who had the right/And to do what and how much and to whom." The crowd cheers and by this time Berlin has moved herself onto Gale, hanging onto him as if they were a couple. When Gale leaves to find a bathroom, the camera focuses on Berlin, who watches him with the eyes of sexually charged black widow ready to prey on its victim.

Inside the bathroom: Gale is surprised to discover Berlin has made her way inside, closing the door behind her. The femme fatale moves slowly toward her teacher, reciting her own limerick: "There once was a girl named Berlin/Who wanted it now and again/Not 'now and again'/But now!/And again and again and again." She moves closer and whispers to him that she was never really after the grade. Gale steps back, indicating to her that—although one can tell he is very aroused by her—it's not a good idea for them to take this any further. She disagrees and says, "We can talk, analyze, contemplate—or you can put your mouth on my body.... Don't reject me.... Please." She is an alluring muse—playing not only to his libido but his intellect. Clearly, she enjoys intricate game-playing, to which Gale succumbs. When they begin to have sex, she demands that he bite her; he complies, while digging his nails into her back. (These two physical acts that will be used against him later.) The scene cross-cuts back and forth from the party to bathroom sex, and this juxtaposition complements the rhythm of their lovemaking. David has committed adultery (yet earlier in the scene, the viewer learns through broken discussion that his wife was currently in Spain—and that his marriage is a troubled one).

Return to Constance and David: The camera pans, and in an extreme low-angle shot (as extreme as the one in the opening, where Bitsey is seen running) looks up at both of them sitting at a table in the university cafeteria. This movement of the camera creates tension in that it looms about the setting like a voyeuristic entity, watching and judging Gale. A subdued, nervous and distracted David bites his nails while Constance is discussing the preparation for the upcoming debate with the governor. She accuses him of "actively listening" and he eventually confesses to her what happened between him and Berlin.

The scene switches to an intimate two-shot: Constance, outraged, calls him weak; David retorts by saying she's not his wife and she replies, "Fuck you." This subtext has two meanings: first, she is disappointed with him; and secondly, judging by the expression on her face, she just might be jealous. The beat quickly shifts to a new tone: Gale asks her if she is okay; she abruptly says *yes* and motions to leave. (Constance's inner feelings are captured very effectively through Linney's subtle acting choices that transcend any need for expository dialogue.)

In the following scene, Gale is on the debate program *Batter's Box*, with Governor Hardin (Michael Crabtree). This exchange is nothing more than a battle of wits (an extreme left-winged versus right-winged discussion)—so much so, in fact, that the issue of capital punishment isn't really being discussed objectively. The professor begins to exercise his acumen through a series of historical quotations. At the start of the debate, the governor refers to the words of the Bible, specifically addressing the "eye for an eye" proverb as a means of justifying capital punishment. Gale retorts by quoting from the pacifist Indian prophet, Gandhi: "The old law for an eye for an eye leaves us all blind." In fact, this quote could serve as the motto for the mission of Death Watch. Gale, now on a roll, mentions another quotation: "A healthy society must stop at nothing to cleanse itself of evil." The governor pauses and pompously asks if this was a phrase that *he* once said, and Gale (ever so graciously) says, "Oh no—that was *Hitler*," highlighting the nationalistic attitude often associated with right-winged conservatives—at least from a liberal perspective. The "cleansing" is obviously referring to ethnic cleansing and, in this way, makes a point that capital punishment is, similarly, a form of genocide. The debate now gets heated and admittedly out of hand, and by the end, Gale actually loses the debate when he can't respond to the governor, who asks him to name just one time when an innocent man *was*, in fact, executed. If there is evidence of a person's innocence, he adds, he promises to call a moratorium (which would satisfy the needs of Death Watch). Gale has no answer, however, which admittedly is peculiar: Why is such a clever man, actively engaged in this cause, unable to recall even *one* instance that would support this critical argument? Aside from the fact that this might be an inconsistency with the writing, maybe it actually reflects Gale's current volatile state of mind, resulting from the recent goings-on with Berlin. Nevertheless, he is defeated. A cross-cut to Constance shows her disappointment—and, in the next scene, she reprimands him. Although Gale claims to be a death penalty advocate, in the debate he lost track of the issue at hand and got caught up in his own intellectual dogma. In this way, the film critiques the function of ideology. After all, capital punishment was merely used as a vehicle for the professor's and the governor's personal esoteric rhetoric (religion vs. academia). Furthermore, this public humiliation is taken to a more extreme level in the next scene when police officers approach Gale (who is walking with Constance) and take him into custody on alleged rape charges. Gale's plight has begun.

Abruptly, a new transition is made with the panning camera, replete with the quick-flashing subliminal words: *Rape, Bruises, Denial,* and *Punishment*. Back to Bitsey and Gale. She asks him why Berlin did this to him. (Is she starting to believe him yet?) He doesn't know; the only answer he can muster up is that perhaps she wanted to challenge authority. That said, he tells her that he recently received a postcard from "the student who would do anything," who wrote, "I'm sorrier than you'll ever know." What does this note mean? Does Berlin feel that she overstepped her bounds with the false accusations?

Next, Zack and Bitsey sit in Sam's Bar-B-Que (an actual restaurant in Texas) to discuss the investigation.[14] Zack believes that Gale is innocent, although he doesn't use any real evidence to reach such a conclusion; again, Zack is in love with the *myth* of David Gale. Bitsey—not yet convinced (or at least not apparently so)—appears more close-minded and merely says that the courts found him guilty and "that's good enough for [her]." Are we, the viewers, led to believe that Zack, the young apprentice, has some insight into Gale's situation, and that Bitsey, the more experienced advocate, is not in the least bit convinced? Both characters appear to exude naiveté, but is it really that simple? Are these questions all part of the film's unreliable narration, especially since the movie is as much of a whodunit as it is a treatise on the ideologies surrounding capital punishment?

Before the next act begins (Day Two), the camera pans slowly to the phantom cowboy in his truck; opera music blasts from the stereo.

Day Two. The film switches to an investigative procedural mode. Although Gale hasn't been lying about his innocence, he also hasn't been truthful about his disclosure of the facts, and this brings up a necessary question of this unreliable narrator: Why does he use this four-day interview process as an investigation? Also curious is the fact that Gale never seems interested in reprieves or moratoriums. *Why*? It's as if he knows he is meant to die. He tells Bitsey earlier on that the main purpose for this interview is to have a documented story so that, after he is gone, his son—and the rest of the world—will know the *real* story and, ultimately, what David Gale stood for in his short, controversial life.

Bitsey and Zack travel, in a torrential downpour, to Constance's house, where the new owner, "Goth Girl" Nico (Melissa McCarthy) has turned the residence into a commercially profitable amusement park, charging her visitors admission to see the crime scene where Constance was murdered. The scene—in addition to critiquing the absurdity of capitalistic enterprises—serves as exposition: When Constance was "raped and killed" she was blindfolded and handcuffed with a plastic bag over her head and the key to the handcuffs was found in her stomach. This fact soon becomes one of the most significant details of the story.

Another scene, one in which Bitsey and Zack converse over food, reveals the cowboy in the Ford pickup. He is definitely a key player in this story—but *how*? The film has now become a full-fledged detective movie, a jigsaw puzzle that has begun to build the film's backstory.

Back at the prison: Gale begins putting some of these pieces together by explaining the details of Constance's death via the *Securitas Method*, wherein the victim is forced to swallow the keys to the handcuffs while their mouth is taped and their head and face covered with a cloth hood or bag. Gale further explains that the Securitas (secret communist Romanian police) did this to Romanians when they didn't confess something. (Interestingly enough, Gale once wrote an article about the Securitas yet, mysteriously, the D.A. never mentioned this in court.) Consequently, Bitsey asks him if he was framed. Gale replies, "Oh, it was more than that." It becomes clear in this scene that Gale is relying on Bitsey to prove his innocence: "You know I'm innocent," he tells her, to which she replies, "No.... I don't." And this leads to a new act break—the rotating camera reveals the words, some of which include the following: *Anger, Energy, Nothing...* Another flashback. Another piece of the puzzle...

Gale's miserable marriage is the focus of the next sequence: David's wife, Sharon (Elizabeth Gast), is in the driveway, packed and ready to leave her husband; David is perturbed and helpless as she and their son, Jamie (Noah Truesdale), proceed to enter the car. When David insists that they discuss the situation, she says, "I sent you an email.... Just read it." Jake Parker's plaintive violin score accents the melancholy tone. Jamie hugs his father in a way that shows that he understands that he will never see him again (he won't) and gives him his prized stuffed animal, Club Dog, a prop that appears later in the film as David's "security blanket," of sorts.

Time passes. The camera captures a long shot of the university, leading to Gale's office, where he sits in front of his computer, drunk, reading Sharon's email: The camera focuses on the phrases "I want a divorce" and "custody" which rather succinctly sum up the circumstances. To add insult to injury, Constance arrives with more bad news: the tenure committee has voted him out. She admits to him that even though the committee decided to let him go, she still voted for him, despite that fact that this decision went against her personal politics. The last scene of the sequence shows a desperate David in front of his home (with a hopeless "For Sale" sign on the lawn), attempting to call Sharon from his cell phone; he is unsuccessful and therefore frustrated. In the background, a group of children are playing in a deserted pool, covered in mud. Parker was intrigued by the desolate look of this "eccentric and bizarre" location[15]—and although this juxtaposition appears offbeat, it can be seen, perhaps, as a reflection of Gale's own permanent loss of innocence and a reminder that he has lost his son. (Additionally, in many of his films, Parker successfully represents the innocence of childhood, which may, in fact, be an homage to his own childhood when he and his friends played around dilapidated war-torn London.) Thus, David Gale has entered an existential purgatory from which he never exits.

A new downward spiral begins with a scene in a restaurant where a fellow academic—most likely a dean who holds the professor in high regard—tells David that although he sees him as "brilliant," he admits that it would be a bad idea for him to hire a "rapist." Additionally, he comments on Gale's well-known drinking problem, which is played out in a bittersweet follow-up scene, filled with tragedy, humor and catharsis. Gale is seen walking through the streets of Austin (this is Sixth Street in Austin; the scene is shot with a Steadicam that helps to capture his drunken tirade and serpentine maneuvering)[16] and gives a "lecture" to random passersby about ancient Greek philosopher Socrates. He comments on how ugly the old philosopher was and how Aristotle was a "prissy dresser," further discussing the unjust Athenian democracy that eventually sentenced Socrates to death: "More judges voted to kill him than voted him guilty," he asserts. "It doesn't make sense." The inclusion of this tirade (which was so convincing that people on the sidewalk didn't see the camera operator and really thought Kevin Spacey was drunk!)[17] is twofold: first, it reflects in an obvious way how Gale's situation, à la Socrates's own execution "doesn't make sense"; second, and perhaps even more tragically, it serves as Gale's humiliating final lecture. The once-respected scholar and popular professor has now been reduced to a farcical jester. He mocks not only his profession but the field of philosophy itself—he's no longer enlightening young minds in the theories of Lacan; instead, he pontificates about the trivial "tabloid" facts associated with the most recognized philosophers in history.

David Gale has succumbed to alcoholism. In a brief yet effective moment he is captured inside his home, lazily sitting, drunk and, this time, a genuinely hopeless case. The low-key lighting, complementing the melancholy mood of the rainy day, serves as a segue into the following scene, wherein he and his lawyer, Braxton Belyeu, convene in a bar, the latter discussing the fate of his client. When an inebriated David suggests that he try to get custody of his son, Jamie, by abducting him from his wife in Spain (while talking, he spins his wedding band on the table as if it were a top). Belyeu (in his most serious moment in the film) impatiently responds to David's childish behavior and tells him that if he ever wants to see his son again he needs to get his life together—*pronto*!

Jump-cut to David at an Alcoholics Anonymous meeting, which is shot in Taylor, Texas; this leads to an immediate transition into a scene with David interviewing for a managerial position at Radio Shed.[18] The hiring manager (played by local Texas actor Chris Drewy) asks the former academic to name three things that would make him a competent manager. Before the viewer is able to hear his reply another jump-cut brings us to Constance's house, where David appears—is it funny or tragic?—in his new Radio Shed uniform, a sight that takes Constance aback; in nervous embarrassment, she laughs at him, then immediately resorts to a sort of sympathetic recoil when she realizes that her former colleague has been dehumanized. She hugs him in a nurturing manner. After this embrace, David notices a bruise on her back and asks where she got it, a fact that is trivialized but a detail that has significant bearing on the rest of the story. The two continue their involvement with a Death Watch case—Death Row inmate Betty Sue Anderson (a seventeen-year-old who murdered a police officer) whose execution has been rescheduled for the 8th of the month. Meanwhile, the mysterious cowboy, named Dusty, who is still a mystery to Bitsey and Zack, is working in Constance's garden; David callously calls him "her cowboy," and when he kisses her before leaving, there is a shot of Dusty looking over at them. Although his expression appears to be neutral, one may still surmise that he is jealous of this exchange (later in the film, Belyeu tells Bitsey that Dusty was indeed enamored of Constance).

In a continuous shot, Gale walks onto the street and sees Jo Edna (Larissa Wolcott), his former student/babysitter in her car, driving; she reluctantly says hello then rolls up her window to escape him. Immediately following this humiliating moment, another such moment occurs. David is sitting in the office at Death Watch with Constance and overhears the phone conversation of fellow advocate John, who tells her: "David's relationship with Death Watch is over. The last thing we need is this rape thing ... ban him from the premises!" David has kept his cool to this point, but hearing this line of prejudice outrages him. He storms out of the room, and Constance, now very concerned, follows him. Further complicating his own scenario, the volatile David Gale attempts to call Sharon in Spain so he can speak with Jamie. He either gets cut off or Sharon hangs up on him, but either way, his volatility culminates in a necessary cathartic eruption, one that has been brewing for a while. He kicks and punches the phone booth, which was such an intense acting moment for "Method" actor Spacey that he actually cut his hand.[19] The blending of Alex and Jake Parker's classical/contemporary score reflects David Gale's conflicting state of mind, and, as the scene ends, it builds to a loud, piercing crescendo.

Next, David arrives at Constance's house, drunk, depressed and completely defeated, clenching his son's stuffed sheep dog as a security blanket. (One of the film's most important [and understated] themes is the loss of his son. On one level, the film could be viewed from this perspective alone; the capital punishment story may be viewed as a vehicle for Gale's failures as a family man.) Gale is in such an altered state—pontificating about how Judas "ratted out" Jesus—that he doesn't realize that Constance has disappeared. It takes him seeing her mail being blown around the room by the wind before he realizes that she has collapsed. In a panic, he takes her to the hospital and when he insists on following her into the emergency room, he experiences more prejudice: An orderly who recognizes him, coyly says, "You want to get arrested again?" Moments later, the physician informs him, to his own surprise, that Constance has leukemia. Abruptly, the transition leads to Bitsey's words flashing cataclysmically before us: *Pain, Honor, Self-Sacrifice, Deranged*—words that undeniably reflect not only Gale's and Constance's adversities but symbols of things to come. The film moves into a new perception shift, a new act break, where Gale's ever-changing, unpredictable story begins to take shape.

Back to Bitsey and David: Bitsey is curious as to why Constance didn't tell David about her illness. David says he doesn't know the answer but suggests that since "death was chasing *her,"* maybe she wanted to help others, and in this way she kept the illness to herself. He then cries and says, "She left this world a better place than she found it." This "two-shot" switches to an extra-long take on Bitsey's reaction, a disturbing grimace. She is perturbed and, for the first time in the film, she begins to show a genuine concern and humanity toward Gale. *Does she believe him?*

The next shot captures a group of (real) prisoners playing handball in the prison yard.[20] Zack is in front of the fence, smoking a cigarette (throughout the film, Bitsey puts down Zack's smoking, almost as if the film is deliberately addressing another controversial issue). In this scene, a brief expository-driven dialogue ensues that adds another critical—if still purposely ambiguous—piece to the puzzle. Zack refers to Gale's lawyer as "a joke." Apparently, Belyeu "seriously fucked up the penalty phase," meaning that the defendant could have been sentenced to life in prison instead of death. Due to mitigating factors, not to mention "a major *pro bono* offer from some of the top lawyers in the country," Gale stayed with Belyeu all the way through the appeals process, which, as Zack adds, "Belyeu *continued to screw up.*" *Why?* Naturally, this newfound knowledge intensifies the mystery; Bitsey and Zack are no longer just reporters; they are also amateur sleuths who, as we later discover, are still being manipulated by Gale's unreliable storytelling.

The tone of the film now shifts into a true suspense-thriller, replete with the rain and nighttime location shots, and although it does not utilize traditional stylized expressionism, it *does*, at times, suggest a sort of *film noir* milieu, yet unlike many of Parker's other expressionistic-influenced endeavors (*Midnight Express, Angel Heart*) the style doesn't cross the line into the realms of the subconscious; it stays somewhat realistic and straightforward. The plot thickens further when Bitsey and Zack first discover that the door to the Randolph Motel (note that Randolph is the screenwriter's last name) leading to her room has inexplicably been pried open. Like two characters entering a haunted house in a horror film, they move cautiously into the hotel room (suspense is built through Geoffrey Kirkland's well-paced continuity editing and Michael Seresin's semi-expressionistic cinematography, showing broken silhouetted images of rain through the blinds), only to discover a video tape hanging from the ceiling. A low-angle shot captures Bitsey looking up at this object as if the tape itself might be dangerous. And alas, Bitsey's name is on it! In the next scene they watch the video and soon discover they both get more than they bargained for—Constance is on the tape ... she is handcuffed, her head covered with a plastic bag, and she is struggling on the floor as she fights for oxygen. The TV switches to a snowy picture and, in the next shot, Bitsey is standing vulnerably against the wall in a state of shock. Her character is evolving rapidly—not only does she seem taken in by Gale's narrative of Constance, she has finally witnessed the victim prior to her demise. Zack—not used to this emotional side of Bitsey—embraces her as she sobs.

Next, Bitsey and Zack convene in a diner while continuing to piece this puzzle together. Bitsey supposes that Constance's murder could be a way to get at Gale—not only to get rid of him, as she suggests, but also to make all abolitionists "look crazy." Furthermore, she mentions some other possible connections regarding the meaning of the tape, each speculation intending to destroy the memory of Gale. Zack responds by saying, "That's a lot of hate." Then he asks, "Why release the tape at all?" Bitsey replies, "Hate's no fun if you keep it to yourself." And the next scene shows Dusty continuing to follow them…

In Belyeu's office: The pompous lawyer informs the amateurs that this tape "could have been made by anyone with twenty dollars and a tolerance for vulgarity," further insisting that the mere existence of this tape will, in no way, yield a reprieve as moratorium; in fact, he guffaws at such an absurd prospect. His shifty nature doesn't rule him out as being directly involved in this foul play. The veteran counselor, alluding to the young woman's naiveté, says, "This ain't my first rodeo, Miss Bloom." When he leaves, he further states, "Let's not throw a pity party and sit around reading Kafka." (This reference to Kafka is undoubtedly referencing the author's 1925 novel *The Trial*, the existential journey of a mild-mannered banker Josef K., who woke up one morning only to discover that he had been arrested for a crime that is never revealed to him, even up to the final moment of his execution.)

The suspense intensifies in the next scene, when Bitsey reaches the lobby of Belyeu's office. After realizing she has forgotten her jacket, she proceeds to go back to retrieve it and, in doing so, sees Dusty heading toward the elevator (to Belyeu's office?). Immediately, she rushes outside to Zack and explains the situation to him, then she demands that he wait in the car until Dusty exits the building so he can write down the license plate number of the Ford truck. Meanwhile, she plans to take a taxi to the prison to see Gale—and, in the next scene, David tells her who the mysterious cowboy character is.

The rhythm of the "two-shot" method of editing (again, Spacey and Winslet were not in the same room together) creates a state of paranoia and claustrophobia as the two characters continue with the interview. David informs Bitsey that "Dusty Wright" was the local Death Watch director before Constance was. Gale calls him "a zealot who thinks a good demonstration has to end with riots and arrests." Apparently his liberal antics led to violence and, consequently, he was fired from the position, but Constance, who always believed in him, somehow allowed him to remain in the organization. Furthermore, Dusty has always been in love with Constance and, after her murder, he testifies against David, citing his problematic drinking (alcohol is a mitigating factor). "Dusty is a man easily blinded by hatred," he adds. "I guess he really believes I killed her. " Not only does this information create a new twist with more complicated details, the viewer and Bitsey are still not being fed the truth. Note that Gale's unreliable narration, ironically, is soon revealed to be a pack of lies intended to reveal the truth (the real truth, however, is not known until the final seconds of the film's ending)—so, for the remainder of the film, anything goes, and the twists keep coming. The viewer thinks the mystery is about deciphering all these aforementioned "clues"—yet the puzzle itself is much more intricate. When Bitsey suggests that Dusty was upset that Gale was seeing Constance, David says, "It's more complicated than that"—and, with this line, another flashback occurs, replete with the spinning camera and the following words in a bleeding red font: *Abolish, Barbaric, Collapse, Suffocate…*

We have entered a flashback of a Death Watch rally, where the abolitionists attempt to save the aforementioned seventeen-year-old Death Row inmate Betty Sue Anderson who had murdered a police officer. Constance appears before the crowd, giving a speech about how executions only create more hatred: "He who seeks revenge," she says, "digs two graves." A jump-cut to the next scene: Constance loses control after she finds out that regardless of their protests, Anderson had been executed. She places a giant red "X" on her photograph, the one that hangs in her office with a series of other inmates she and other death watch activists are supporting. Out of frustration, she refers to the photographs on the wall, calling all these people names like *losers, ghetto hustlers* and *rednecks*. In a state of hopeless frenzy, she states an existential truth: Death Watch is nothing but an endless cycle that "goes on and on and on...."

In perhaps the most poignant moment in the film, Constance and David discuss the significance of life and death. Alan Parker names this as his favorite scene in the film. "I shot it simply because I wanted to do it justice," he says.[21] Constance admits to David that she is most likely in the "denial" stage of the dying process. She further tells him that one of her main regrets in life is not having enough sex—and, furthermore, she admits she wanted to have a child. The irony of this epiphany, Constance asserts, is that throughout her entire life she worked hard not to be seen as a sex object and then, quite darkly, she adds that "before long you're not seen at all." When David offers to sleep with her she tells him she does not want a "pity lay." He assures her that this would not be the case, and in the next scene they are in bed together.

This follow-up "sex" scene is exceptionally moving and creates its own verisimilitude. During the act of intercourse, Constance exposes herself in a gamut of raw emotions—she is vulnerable, scared and admits to being tired, one of the chronic symptoms of a cancer patient. Despite her illness, she lets herself go in favor of sexual pleasure. David is kind and gentle with her. The two of them possess a symbiotic union: he is helping her cope with her fear of dying; and she is serving as his lover after losing his family. They are both in great pain, physically and emotionally, and by making love (which transcends the cliché Hollywood sex scene, replete with stylized close-ups and soft-blue lighting) they keep their friendship at bay. In addition to Spacey and Linney's realistic performances, Parker credits his cinematographer Michael Seresin for the scene's success; in fact, he goes so far as to say that this is Seresin "at his best."[22] The juxtaposition of the images—replete with a series of elegiac shots, including high- and low-angle shots and a number of intimate hand-held shots that adds to the scene's intimacy—is more or less the antithesis of the cross-cutting sex scene with David and Berlin at the faculty party. Through his two distinctly different editing techniques, Gerry Hambling successfully distinguishes between the acts of "meaningless sex" (reflecting the ideals of Lacan's fantasy theory) versus the tenderness of two friends "making love."

The next couple of scenes concentrate on David's plight: he sits on the swing of his former home and contemplates his past until he is driven away by the current owner, who simply sees him as a trespasser. Next, a police officer—amidst the expressionistic blue lighting and moody, dreamlike fog—discovers David drunk, sleeping in his car. Before the scene advances any further, another transition follows, one shot with a gyrating camera and a new set of words flashing on the screen: *Almost, Guilty, Cruel, Condemned, Mental...*

Back to the prison: Bitsey mentions the possibility that Dusty may have committed the murder. Of course, she is incorrect. Yet Gale, still the unreliable narrator, controls the story (note that, unlike many detective stories, Bitsey, even up to the film's final moments, never truly discovers the real truth). David says that if he knew that Dusty was, in fact, the murderer, then they wouldn't be having this conversation. "That's what I need you for," he says. "That's why I chose you." At this moment, Gale says that all he wants is to have her help unveil the real truth so that his son will have a favorable memory of him in years to come. The prominent grid bars that frame him remind the viewer that Gale is both physically and psychologically imprisoned. David raises the stakes in this game as he continues to play with her: "Bitsey, we spend our whole lives trying to stop death. Eating. Inventing.

Loving. Praying. Fighting. Killing. But what do we really know about death? Just that nobody comes back. But there comes a point in life—a moment—when your mind outlives its desires.... Maybe death is a gift. You wonder. All I know is that by this time tomorrow I'll be dead. I know when, I just can't say why. You have twenty-four hours to find out. Goodbye, Bitsey." A guard takes Gale back to his cell and, in the next shot, Bitsey is now framed with the bars behind *her*. She turns around and cries as the film score prevails: a combination of Jake Parker's classical sound bridged over Alex Parker's contemporary percussion score suggests a sense of duality, including the dichotomy of life versus death. This concludes the first ninety minutes of the film—the end of the second act which sets the stage for Act Three—the fourth and final day.

The final stretch: Bitsey, Zack and Belyeu are outside the Randolph Motel. The lawyer advises them to stay close to the motel and as he proceeds to enter his vehicle he points at them in a rather condescending way and jokingly says, "Watch yourselves." Although this may appear to be harmless in its seemingly playful tone, it *does* create a rather sinister, even macabre, quality. What does he mean by this bizarre statement? *Why* should they watch themselves? Set to the backdrop of a somber scene, accented by the high-contrast lighting and chiaroscuro, Belyeu is continually represented as an enigmatic, diabolical figure of the law. Bitsey asks him if Constance and Dusty were close. Belyeu says that they were "thick as thieves," setting up another potentially significant piece of data in this outlandish case.

Day Four. A white van pulls up to the prison yard (this was actually shot on the premises of the prison), and Gale exits the vehicle in handcuffs and is escorted inside.[23] The scene's intensity plays out in a traditional melodramatic flare replete with Alex's and Jake's piercing, almost overwhelming, musical score.

Cut to Bitsey in the Randolph Motel: She wakes up rather abruptly, heads to the bathroom to brush her teeth and, while contemplating her reflection in the mirror, receives an epiphany. She then wakes her partner, who is asleep on the floor. In the next scene, they steal the motel room's television and drive to Constance's house.

Next, they are greeted by Niko, the Goth girl. Bitsey asks her if she wants to make a hundred dollars and explains to her that she and Zack want to revisit Constance's death scene. Niko agrees and, before long, the young woman is positioned on the floor precisely where Constance had lain. Meanwhile, Bitsey and Zack watch the footage of Constance on the television and discover that while she was tied up with the bag over her head, she moves her foot in a way that brings attention to itself; it's as if this movement was deliberate, a signal of some sort. Before the scene ends, Bitsey decides to partake in the ultimate role-playing experiment: Under Zack and Niko's reluctant supervision, she puts herself in Constance's position so she can better understand the struggle. During this segment the film cross-cuts to the prison, where the viewer learns that the Supreme Court desk clerk gave the "go-ahead" to follow through with Gale's execution. Back to Bitsey who, after a few moments of experiencing air loss, discovers that Constance must have done this to herself, proving her original theory to be fact. The juxtaposition of this scene with Gale in his cell (Spacey does a convincing job showing Gale's underplayed anxiety) continues to build tension.

In a follow-up scene, Zack asks Bitsey why Constance wanted to make this look like a murder. She answers, "To prove that the system convicts innocents." She recognizes the fact that Constance lived for her cause—she would also die for it.

Cut to Dusty in his home listening to the opera *Turandot* (which appeared earlier in the film and is significant to the film's climax). The three-act opera by Giacomo Puccini, based on a Persian fable set in China, is about a beautiful princess who is *so* desirable that she has thousands of suitors who court her. Any of these suitors who wish her hand in marriage must answer three vexing riddles; if they answer incorrectly, they are beheaded.[24] At the end of the opera, the princess commits suicide (at the end of the film, Dusty is in a theater watching the suicide scene, crying, obviously relating this moment to Constance's "suicide"). Perhaps the opera itself can be seen as an updating of this classical fable.

Meanwhile, Bitsey and Zack stand outside the hermit's shack, realizing now that Dusty is definitely linked to this case, and in the next scene the "detectives" continue to piece the story together. Bitsey is convinced that Dusty (who allegedly has the video tape) plans to release the tape only after Gale is executed; in this way there *is* no real plan to save Gale— after all, as Bitsey states, "This would only prove that the system works ... *almost* martyrs don't count."

The suspense thickens when Zack gives Dusty an anonymous call, telling him he wants to "talk about the tape." The stakes are now raised; the cross-cutting back and forth from Dusty to Bitsey to Zack and Gale creates more anxiety and disorientation as the clock continues to tick: Cut to a close-up of the clock which reads 5:05, and a news team reports that Gale's last meal will be pancakes with maple syrup, strawberries, chocolate shavings and whipped cream—the meal he never got to make for his son. Cross-cut to Bitsey watching Dusty from afar as he peels out in his Ford, en route to a meeting with Zack. Slowly, she enters this shack, complemented by a score of slide guitar, percussion and piano—all capturing the essence of this brooding Texas milieu.

Inside Dusty's home, Bitsey frantically searches for the tape. In this montage, she learns more about his involvement with death penalty ideologies, namely through a number of photographs of previous executions as well as a print media history of the electric chair. Moreover, Dusty is a compulsive hoarder; it's as if he has been driven mad with his obsessions. Cross-cut to Zack on Highway 71, anxiously waiting for Dusty in front of a food mart/gas station. A truck approaches—but it's not him. Another cross-cut to Bitsey, rummaging through Dusty's VHS tapes. What she discovers is that the eccentric hermit is a TV junkie who has taped shows like *Mr. Ed* and *The Tonight Show Starring Johnny Carson*. Eventually, she locates a tape labeled "CONSTANCE." On it, Constance looks into the camera from her kitchen sink and exaggerates the action of swallowing a pill. The classical music score reflects Bitsey's state—a combination of horror and melancholy. She fast-forwards the tape, revealing Dusty, who is seen locking the handcuffs on Constance's wrists; he then looks menacingly into the camera—his expression is aimed toward his future viewers! In this way, a majority of the story itself is revealed through the filmmaking process— in one way or the other it has all been—from Constance's death to Gale's interview—a performance. (Winslet's own performance is additionally genuine and effective because she—like her character—is experiencing the events for the first time. According to Parker, Winslet did not want to see the tape until filming began.[25]) This is perhaps Bitsey's most fragile moment in the film. Zack arrives suddenly, startles her and urges her to come with him. Both exit the shack and, as they do so, Dusty is seen watching them from afar. He grins, which reveals to the viewer that he does indeed know what is happening. We, however, still do not know the details. Dusty could be a killer, for all we know.

In the next shot, Gale looks at his last meal and he grins as if to say, *I love you, Jamie.* A quick shot to Bitsey, who tells Zack she wants him to call the governor, the Supreme Court—*anyone* who can help buy them more time. At this moment she thinks she knows that Gale is "innocent," and that it's time for her to save him even though that is not the convict's intent or hope; his hope, again, is to salvage his memory for his son, whom he will never see again. She gets into the car and peels out. The race is on!

Cut to Gale in the shower, then back to Bitsey speeding in her red Ford. The "check engine" light comes on again; the engine smokes. "Not *fucking now!*" she curses, then darts out of the car and in the final countdown, she runs toward Huntsville, which, by this time, is a media circus surrounded by reporters, helicopters and abolitionist groups, including Death Watch. Rapid overlapping sound bridges complement the rapidly edited visual frenzy. Many activists hold signs bearing such legends as *Murder Does Not Stop Murder*; *Death Watch R.I.P*; *No More Execution*, etc. Throughout this cataclysmic montage, the following words are finally heard: "The state of Texas has executed David Gale." Bitsey arrives on the scene just as these words are spoken. Gale was pronounced dead at 6:12 p.m. Although the sequence builds like an endless number of "ticking-clock" suspense films, the climatic results are, to say the least, anything but traditional. After all, the protagonist has failed to "save the day." Bitsey collapses, horrified and defeated, while captured in slow-motion over an array of muted sounds, reinforcing Gale's demise.

An abrupt cut to Gale's image on the wall of photographs in the Death Watch office: It gets the fated red X, indicating another failed attempt to save an individual from capital punishment. The system has prevailed again. Another abrupt cut shows Dusty leaving his home. When he exits he grabs his hat, and then slams its down angrily. His emotional state seems to be mixed: He is perturbed, yet relieved. What does this all mean? We have begun the film's final plot point, leading to the dénouement. Where is he going? Does the slamming down of the hat suggest the end of an old chapter in his life? The following sequence begins to answer these questions.

The airport: amidst a montage of the news reporters covering Constance's death, Dusty, carrying a briefcase (which serves as a temporary MacGuffin: the contents of the suitcase, at least for the time being, remain a mystery to the audience), meets Gale's lawyer, Belyeu, in the bathroom. The lawyer looks at Dusty through the mirror as if in a bizarre way the character is an apparition or even an enigmatic reflection of himself: the suspense continues. A series of rather choppy, purposefully confusing edits, including a cross-cutting segment of the police who appear to be on Dusty's trail (the tape revealed that he had been involved in the murder, so at this time, he must be a prime suspect). Dusty assures Belyeu that the contents of the suitcase (money) are "all there." The lawyer asks if the passport and tickets are also there. This exchange of money adds another complication to the plot. Apparently (and the last part of the film confirms this), Dusty has been in on these theatrics—a key player in this video drama. At this point, it's still not quite clear what has been occurring, only that Belyeu and Dusty have succeeded in uncovering the truth (or what is currently perceived to be the truth).

An abrupt cut to Governor Harding's rhetoric: "We're still behind the death penalty," he asserts victoriously in the aftermath of Gale's execution. "The system cannot be to blame for the deranged acts of one individual." This leads to a shot of past news footage, with Gale among the protesters. In the background, a series of sound bridges overlap and one reporter's voice can be heard: "Gale may have accomplished in death what he couldn't in life...."

Dusty, playing the part of messenger, arrives at the door of David's ex-wife's residence in Spain and leaves the briefcase of money along with a palm tree–decorated bag, stating Miami as a "duty free" city. Cross-cut to Bitsey at her office desk looking at a Federal Express box that was mailed to her; the attached note on the box reads: *David wanted you to have this. He said it would be the key to your freedom. Regards, Braxton Belyeu.* When she opens it, she unveils the stuffed animal, Club Dog, that Gale obtained from his son, the personification of the little boy he has lost.

Another cross-cut to Spain: Gale's ex-wife opens the door and brings the bag inside. She reads a postcard addressed to David at Ellis Unit—*I'm sorrier than you'll ever know. Berlin—The student who would do anything.* She seems to be confused, but we all know that soon enough she will discover this meaning. Cut back to Bitsey, who finally discovers a VHS in the stomach of the stuffed animal (à la the Romanian Securitas method)—leading to last scene of the film, the dénouement.

Bitsey slips the tape into the VCR and watches what will be the final act of the David Gale/Constance Harraway drama. On video: the camera focuses on Constance's dead body and, offscreen, a voice announces, "It's over." This cues Gale, who walks slowly over to Constance. He leans down and lovingly touches her head. He then rises and walks almost in slow motion, peering into the eye of the lens as if to say, *Now you know the entire story—what* really *happened.* Gale—with the help of Dusty (the one whose voice we just heard)—assisted in Constance's suicide. This look of disgust is aimed toward everyone involved with his persecution, not to mention the governor and all others who support the death penalty. He reaches up to turn the camera off. FADE TO BLACK.

One may have expected a final shot of Bitsey's reaction to this new evidence, but, instead, the film ends with the video (which ultimately reveals the real story) and this is followed by Alex Parker's riveting percussive piece "Another Bleeding Heart" playing over the final credits. Alan Parker stated that he is very proud of *The Life of David Gale*, a film that—like other controversial films including *Midnight Express* and *Mississippi Burning*—will be, if anything else, a vehicle that provokes the ongoing debate regarding the death penalty.[26]

Conclusion

Our goal for the conclusion of this book was twofold: first, to give honorable mention to Parker's other artistic talents—his writing (including a book on the making of *Evita* in addition to his novels *Bugsy Malone, Puddles in the Lane* and his 2003 novel *The Sucker's Kiss*, an engaging first-person historical fiction narrative about the journey of American pickpocket Tommy Moran, which spans his life, beginning with the 1906 earthquake and ending with the Great Depression), and his intelligent satiric cartoons, most of them scathing critiques on Hollywood and the film industry; and second, to bring Parker's career up to date to see what projects he has been working on since *The Life of David Gale* (2003). I contacted Mr. Parker, for the fourth time, with a few questions. As you will see below, he took a good deal of time to compose the answers via email exchanges, which I have included verbatim. In this way, we conclude this book, with the words of Alan Parker, who has been very cooperative and supportive of this book. We are forever honored and grateful that we have been given the opportunity to meet such an artist—and with his help—write such a comprehensive study of his impressive, ambitious canon.

I began the interview by asking him if he would comment on *The Sucker's Kiss* and his book of cartoons *Will Write and Direct for Food* (examples of these cartoons are featured throughout). He directed us to the Camerimage book (*Alan Parker*) he sent us (the one on which we relied heavily for the primary research in this book). He told us that the quotations in both of these books "say[s] it all."

The Sucker's Kiss: "I wrote my novel *The Sucker's Kiss* while waiting for *The Life of David Gale* to happen. Writing a novel is a liberating experience—you do it on your own, not with a hundred people, and you don't have the budgetary constraints that you have when writing and directing a film. My novel starts with a recounting of the 1906 San Francisco earthquake and then covers twenty different American states during a thirty-year time span and the Great Depression. I hate to think of the cost of that as a movie!"

Will Write and Direct for Food: "Over the years I've scribbled my cartoons—mostly instead of sending rude letters to studio executives, journalists and friends. I've published three collections of these observations on the filmmaking process, mostly reflecting on the ever-present insanity, hypocrisy, sadism, masochism, pretension, deceit, hubris and greed—oh, and the rare moments of jubilation."

The next set of questions pertained to two films in which he was involved prior to the all-child cast Hollywood musical gangster parody *Bugsy Malone* (1976): *Melody* (1971), written by Parker and directed by Waris Hussein, and *The Evacuees* (1975), written by well-known dramatist Jack Rosenthal and directed by Parker. All three films, incidentally, although very different in subject matter, are stories told from the points-of-view of chil-

Cartoon by Alan Parker from his book, *Will Write and Direct for Food* (London: Southbank Publishing, 2005).

dren. *Melody* is an endearing film about the romance between pre-adolescents who tell their parents and friends that they have decided to get married; *The Evacuees* is a BBC drama about two young Jewish boys evacuated from Manchester to Blackpool during the Blitz. These films set the stage, so to speak, for Parker's mainstream film career. Parker mailed us personal copies of *Melody* and *The Evacuees*, which (at this time) are available only in the "region two" DVD format, making it a bit more difficult for American audiences to see these films (American DVDs are in the *region one* format and *region two* typically includes DVDs in most of Europe and other regions including the Middle East and Egypt to name a couple. Note: Very recently I discovered that *Melody* was available to "watch now" on Netflix). Although this book studies twenty-seven years of Parker's films, from *Bugsy Malone* to *The Life of David Gale*, we wanted to provide a more personal approach to these earlier films, so instead of including production notes and complete, annotated summaries like we did with the other feature films, we chose to ask Mr. Parker specific questions about the films. Again, these essay-length answers are included at the end of Chapter 1.

My next question involved getting a statement on the music in *The Life of David Gale*. Parker once again provided a most generous several-page reply, which is included in the chapter on that film after the "Notes on the Production" section.

Additionally, he emailed us more useful information, including a biographical sketch, an article he wrote on *Mississippi Burning* for the *London Times* and some website links to *Angel Heart* and *Fame*. Excerpts from these sources are referenced throughout the specific chapters on these films.

We then asked him to comment on his writings and drawings, and finally asked him the obvious but necessary question: What have you been doing since *The Life of David Gale*? The following brief interview with Alan Parker was conducted over several email exchanges that followed an initial phone conversation on October 8, 2009.

Would you make a statement on your novel writing and cartoons?

Re cartoons: in addition to Will Write and Direct for Food *I also did a small book of cartoons* Hares in the Gate *(1982) and a book the BFI published,* Making Movies *(1998) (which contained some drawings also in* Will Write and Direct*).*

I wrote the novel of Bugsy Malone *(1976) which Harper Collins have recently re-published in their Essential Modern Classics library (November 2011). The book was originally published at the time of the film. I wrote it before, during and after the film. I also did a graphic novel, comic book version—which was my favourite—and which they hopefully will re-publish next year. I also wrote a simplified, theatrical version for schools. (It's the most performed "school play" here in England. I recently gave permission for it to be performed by a school in Ho Chi Minh City!)*

I was asked to write another children's book, published in 1977, entitled Puddles in the Lane. *(The story of four children evacuated to the countryside in 1940 after their home in London's East End had been bombed.) I had originally written this story as part of a trilogy called* Stories of the Blitz*—the first film of which I made (*No Hard Feelings*) which we (my producer, Alan Marshall and I) financed ourselves from our commercials business. (The third story was a script I wrote called* The Blackmarket Man.*) We expanded it to six stories but I had a hard job setting it up with the BBC, however they did buy* No Hard Feelings *and offer me Jack Rosenthal's script,* The Evacuees. *[Jack was a doyen of British television writing]. This film was quite successful winning a BAFTA for best TV drama and also the International Emmy. Consequently it rendered my own story on wartime evacuees rather redundant, so I decided to write it as a novel instead—hence the book of* Puddles in the Lane.

I also did a book on The Making of Evita.

I have recently done a whole batch of cartoons, drawn directly on the iPad, for a new book I hope to do, INT. ROOM. NIGHT.

[Author note: Parker made photocopies and sent these to us—examples of these cartoons are seen at the end of this chapter.]

In addition to *The Sucker's Kiss*, have you been working on any projects since *The Life of David Gale*?

I'm always working on something, although it might not look that way!

Firstly I have to say I was the first chairman of The UK Film Council (the previous

Labour government's umbrella body for film and film funding) for five years, which rather disrupted my own filmmaking, somewhat, but it (the organization I helped found and shape) did result in some good films—culminating with King's Speech last year and Shame this year. The UK Film Council lasted for a decade but the Conservative government, in their infinite wisdom and for crass political reasons, abolished it when they came to power in 2010.

Here are the projects I have been working on since Life of David Gale:

1. For some time I worked on a script called Yuri with my friend Lee Hall who wrote Billy Elliot. This was ostensibly a story of Yuri Gagarin and the successful Soviet space program, but more than that, it was an allegory of the Soviet Union and the demise of communism. It was hard to set up with American studios (Soviet Russians are still seen as the bad guys after all). We had offers of Russian money and I even went to Moscow to meet with an oligarch who served us caviar and vodka with real gold flakes floating in it. Alas, the film never happened, and I moved on.

2. I worked on a script called Ice at the Bottom of the World (a story of an eccentric, dysfunctional family on Chesapeake Bay) originally written by Marc Richard, which I rewrote (2005/2006). This was to star Charlize Theron who was also producing the film. She was a very good producer and we got almost to the starting blocks, but it was derailed when New Line and its subsidiaries started to implode and my impatience got the better of me.

3. I wrote a script of Blood Brothers with Willy Russell. Our script was based on Willy's successful stage musical which has been playing in the West End here in London for over twenty years. I must say we wrote a very good script, but again, the powers that be in Los Angeles didn't see it as a film, despite its considerable pedigree. They didn't respond to a dark/funny period English musical set in Liverpool. They made that crappy Hairspray instead! This disappointed me greatly as it was some of my best work and Willy is a great talent. The upside is that I had a great year working with Willy and it was creatively very satisfying in that we wrote an extremely thorough and detailed script which was a bit like making the film, only without the camera.

4. I then wrote a script called Coram Boy, which was based on the novel by Jamila Gavin and the successful National Theatre stage play. It's a story set "in the dark heart of the 18th century"—a Dickensian story not written by Dickens: of orphans, fathers, sons, poverty, wealth and infanticide—set against the wonderful creation and beauty of Handel's Messiah. It was going to be produced by an English producer (Alison Owen) and the great U.S. producer, Scott Rudin (who I made Angela's Ashes with). When I was halfway through writing the script, the play opened on Broadway and was not successful and—considering it had an enormous cast—it closed. I think from that moment, Scott was not convinced American audiences would respond to a film about 18th century England, infanticide and Handel's Messiah! I finished the script—it was one of the best I ever wrote, I thought—much superior to the play. But to recreate 18th century London would be expensive and Scott decided that it wasn't do-able. The last I heard the BBC were working on multiple part BBC-type production. But not with my screenplay.

5. I next rewrote an old script of mine called Beautiful Love based on a 1923 novel by Vernon Bartlett called Calf Love. It was set in 1913 and was a coming of age story

concerning a young English boy and his love affair with the two daughters of a German family in Prussia—with whom he spends the summer, a year before the outbreak of World War I. I originally wrote a draft twenty years ago and had found it whilst moving offices. On re-reading it, I was so appalled at the younger me's efforts that I totally re-wrote every word of it! It is a delicate story and will probably be made one day. Or maybe not.

6. I then worked for over a year on a film called "The Scottish Screenplay" (it never had a title). It was originally written by a Scottish writer called John Milarky and I considerably re-worked and re-wrote it. It was a contemporary, black comedy set among working class Glaswegians in a run down housing estate (project). I described it as The Commitments—*without the music. I got close to making it but fell out with the financier who is the biggest independent distributor here.*

I then got disillusioned about it—and having done as much as I have over the years—I am very intolerant of film politics and not good at kissing ... er ... feet—a necessary attribute if you want someone to part with many millions of dollars. My old friend, the producer David Puttnam, says that if I can find a reason not *to make a film than I'll find it. Whether he's right or not, I'm not sure, but I must admit that as I get older the romantic notion of filming at 3 a.m., whilst up to my knees in Mississippi pigs' shite, has less of an attraction to me than it once did.*

7. I also had a project I wanted to be available for this year called Failan Project *which I have been waiting on for some time. It's based on a Japanese novella, that was made into a Korean movie, that a Puerto Rican American playwright, Jose Rivera, adapted with a screenplay set among the Russian American immigrants in Brighton Beach. It's this weird pedigree that has resulted in a beautiful, highly original love story. The producers, Beacon, are the same company that I made* The Commitments *with. It is a small story that a very big American actor has said he very much likes and basically we have been waiting a while on him to actually commit and say yay or nay. Whether the film will be made or not depends on this. I'm not holding my breath.*

Chapter Notes

Introduction

1. Jonathan Hacker and David Price, *Take Ten: Contemporary British Film Directors* (New York: Oxford, 1991), 334.
2. Alan Parker, *Alan Parker* (Poland: Plus Camerimage, 2008), 36.
3. Ibid., 112–13.
4. Hacker and Price, *Take Ten*, 313.
5. Ibid., 334.
6. Parker, *Alan Parker*, 59.
7. Leonard Maltin, *Video Guide, 2010 Edition* (New York: New American Library, 2009), 427.
8. Parker, *Alan Parker*, 190.
9. Peter Bondanella, *Italian Cinema: From Neorealism to the Present* (New York: Continuum International, 1983), 116.
10. Peter Wollen, *Signs and Meaning in the Cinema* (Bloomington: Indiana University Press, 1973), 74–78.
11. Hacker and Price, *Take Ten*, 332.
12. Jim Hillier, ed., *Cahiers du Cinéma, The 1950s: Neorealism, Hollywood, New Wave* (Cambridge: Harvard University Press, 1985), 5.
13. Parker, *Alan Parker*, 192.
14. Ibid., 192.
15. John Desmond and Peter Hawkes, *Adaptations: Studying Film and Literature* (New York: McGraw-Hill, 2005), 34.
16. Parker, *Alan Parker*, 192.
17. Ibid., 192.

Chapter 1

1. Parker, *Alan Parker*, 8.
2. Ibid., 192.
3. Ibid.
4. Hacker and Price, *Take Ten*, 333.
5. Ibid.
6. Ibid., 321.
7. Parker, *Alan Parker*, 8.
8. Ibid., 8–9.
9. Parker, *Alan Parker*, 9.
10. Ibid., 14.
11. Ibid., 10.
12. Andrew Horton, "Britain's Angry Young Man in Hollywood," *Cineaste* (December 1986): 31.
13. Parker, *Alan Parker*, 11.
14. Hacker and Price, *Take Ten*, 314.
15. Parker, *Alan Parker*, 14–16.
16. Hacker and Price, *Take Ten*, 316.
17. Ibid.
18. Parker, *Alan Parker*, 19.
19. Hacker and Price, *Take Ten*, 317–18.
20. "Dialogue on Film: Alan Parker," *American Film* 13.4 (January/February 1988), 12, 14–15.
21. Parker, *Alan Parker*, 24.
22. Alan Parker email message to author, May 19, 2012. These pages include Sir Alan Parker's own words regarding his early films *Melody* (1971), *The Evacuees* (1975), and his commercial work. When we asked him to comment on those early works, he responded with these very generous essays, which we've included verbatim, with only slight editing for style.

Chapter 2

1. Ibid., 24.
2. Ibid., 26.
3. Ibid.
4. Ibid., 28.
5. Ibid., 26.
6. *Bugsy Malone* Special Edition DVD, Alan Parker Interview.
7. Robert Warshow, "The Gangster as Tragic Hero," in *The Immediate Experience: Movies, Comics, Theatre, and Other Aspects of Popular Culture* (Cambridge: Harvard University Press, 2001), 131.
8. Paul Williams, "Paul Williams's Reflections," Paul Williams *Bugsy Malone* Page, David Chamberlayne, ed., last modified Mar 13, 2007, http://www.paulwilliamscouk.plus.com/pwnbugsyh.html.
9. Ibid.
10. Todd Berliner and Philip Furia, "The Sounds of Silence: Songs in Hollywood Films Since the 1960s," *Style* 36.1 (Spring 2002): 32.
11. Warshow, "Gangster as Tragic Hero," 131.

Chapter 3

1. Alan Parker, "Anatomy of a Film: The Making of *Midnight Express*," Personal Essay/memoir, included as DVD insert for the Thirty-Year Anniversary Edition of *Midnight Express* (1978).
2. Parker, *Alan Parker*, 32.
3. Ibid., 37–38.
4. Parker, "Anatomy of a Film: The Making of *Midnight Express*," n. p.
5. Ibid.
6. Charles L. P. Silet, *Oliver Stone Interviews* (Jackson: University Press of Mississippi, 2001), 11.
7. Susan Bluestein Davis, *After Midnight: The Life and Death of Brad Davis* (New York: Simon & Schuster, 1997), 56.
8. Ibid., 61.
9. Parker, "Anatomy of a Film: The Making of *Midnight Express*," n. p.
10. Ibid.
11. Ibid.
12. Parker, *Alan Parker*, 39.
13. *Midnight Express*, Special Thirty-Year edition DVD, Alan Parker/Director's Commentary.
14. Ibid.
15. Davis, *After Midnight*, 68.
16. Billy Hayes and William Hoffer, *Midnight Express* (New York: CBS Publications, 1977), 11.
17. Hayes and Hoffer, *Midnight Express*, 21.
18. Tim Welles and William Triplet, *Drug Wars: An Oral History from the Trenches* (New York: William Morrow, 1992), 11.
19. Silet, *Oliver Stone Interviews*, 11.
20. Hacker and Price, *Take Ten*, 315.
21. Ibid.
22. Parker, "Anatomy of a Film: The Making of *Midnight Express*," n. p.
23. *Locked-Up Abroad: The Real Midnight Express* (Season 4, Episode 1), National Geographic Channel, September 16, 2010.
24. Parker, "Anatomy of a Film: The Making of *Midnight Express*," n. p.
25. Hayes and Hoffer, *Midnight Express*, 80.
26. Douglas A. Howard, *The History of Turkey* (Westport, CT: Greenwood Press, 2001), 145.
27. Ibid.
28. Ibid., 146.
29. Parker, *Alan Parker*, 36.
30. Silet, *Oliver Stone Interviews*, 23.
31. Ibid., 25.
32. Hayes and Hoffer, *Midnight Express*, 240.
33. Ibid., 25.
34. David Gonthier, *Seventy Years of the American Prison Movie: From* The Big House *to* The Shawshank Redemption (New York: Edwin Mellen Press, 2006), 7.
35. Parker, *Alan Parker*, 43.
36. Hayes and Hoffer, *Midnight Express*, 205.
37. Ibid., 208.
38. Parker, "Anatomy of a Film: The Making of *Midnight Express*," n. p.
39. Hayes and Hoffer, *Midnight Express*, 265.
40. *Midnight Express*, Special Thirty-Year edition DVD, Alan Parker/Director's Commentary.
41. Hayes and Hoffer, *Midnight Express*, 129–30.
42. Gonthier, *Prison Movie*, 52.
43. Stuart Voytilla, *Myth and the Movies: Discovering the Mythic Structure of 50 Unforgettable Films* (Studio City, CA: Michael Wiese Productions, 1999), 6.
44. *Locked Up Abroad: The Real Midnight Express* (Season 4, Episode 1), National Geographic Channel, September 16, 2010.
45. *Midnight Express*, Special Thirty-Year edition DVD, Alan Parker/Director's Commentary.

Chapter 4

1. Bobbi Leigh Zito, "Alan Parker Interview," *Focus on Film* 35 (1980): 5.
2. Ibid.
3. Parker, *Alan Parker*, 45.
4. Zito, "Alan Parker Interview," 5.
5. "How It All Began: The Making of *Fame*," *International Cinematographers Guild Magazine* 80.9 (2009): 39.
6. Zito, "Alan Parker Interview," 5.
7. Parker, *Alan Parker*, 49.
8. Ibid., 45.
9. "How It All Began," 39.
10. Parker, *Alan Parker*, 46.
11. "How It All Began," 39.
12. Ibid.
13. Parker, *Alan Parker*, 54.
14. Hacker and Price, *Take Ten*, 321.
15. Zito, "Alan Parker Interview," 5.
16. Ibid.
17. Al Auster, "*Fame* Review," *Cineaste* (April 4, 1980): 35.
18. Stanley Kauffmann, "Singing the Body Electric: *Fame* Review," *The New Republic* 23 (1980): 22.
19. "Movie Reviews: *Fame*," *Variety Magazine* 1 (1980): 38.
20. Hacker and Price, *Take Ten*, 324–25.
21. Ibid., 320.
22. Ibid., 324.
23. Auster, "*Fame* Review," 35.
24. Ibid.
25. Hacker and Price, *Take Ten*, 325.
26. Ibid.
27. Auster, "*Fame* Review," 35.

Chapter 5

1. Cast/Crew Data, Internet Movie Database (IMDb), www.imdb.com.
2. Parker, *Alan Parker*, 58–59.
3. Ibid., 58.
4. Ibid., 59.
5. Horton, "Britain's Angry Young Man," 32.
6. Parker, *Alan Parker*, 59–60.

7. Ibid., 60.
8. Ibid., 68.
9. Ibid., 61.
10. Scott Coltrane, "Families and Gender Equity," in *Selected Readings in Marriage and Family*, ed. Lorene H. Stone (Farming Hills, MI: Greenhaven Press, 1998), 60.
11. Ibid.
12. Horton, "Britain's Angry Young Man," 33.
13. Susan DeWitt, "Parents, Children, and Gender Roles," in *Selected Readings in Marriage and Family*, ed. Lorene H. Stone (Farming Hills, MI: Greenhaven Press, 1998), 253–58.
14. Graham Nichol Forst, "Northrop Frye and Homo Ludens," *Mosaic* 36.3 (September 2003): 73. (Electronically retrieved from Infotrac-college.com.)
15. *Shoot the Moon*, DVD Commentary Track from Screenwriter Bo Goldman.
16. John Perry, *Jack London: An American Myth* (Chicago: Nelson-Hall, 1981), 264–65.
17. Alex Kershaw, *Jack London: A Life* (New York: St. Martin's Press, 1997), 246–47.
18. *Shoot the Moon*, DVD Audio Commentary Track with Alan Parker.

Chapter 6

1. Parker, *Alan Parker*, 69.
2. Alan Parker, "*Pink Floyd—The Wall*: The Making of the Film," *American Cinematographer* (October 1982): 1025.
3. Parker, *Alan Parker*, 69.
4. Parker, "Pink Floyd," 1061.
5. *Pink Floyd—The Wall* Special Edition DVD, *The Other Side* (documentary).
6. Parker, *Alan Parker*, 70.
7. Parker, "Pink Floyd," 1062.
8. Ibid.
9. Parker, *Alan Parker*, 78.
10. Hacker and Price, *Take Ten*, 320–21.
11. Parker, *Alan Parker*, 73.
12. Ibid., 78.
13. Ibid., 79.
14. Jorge Sacido Romero and Luis Miguel Varela Cabo, "Roger Waters's Poetry of the Absent Father: British Identity in Pink Floyd's 'The Wall,'" *Atlantis* 28.2 (December 2006): 46.
15. Parker, "Pink Floyd," 1063.
16. Romero and Varela Cabo, "Absent Father," 50.
17. Ibid., 48.
18. Parker, "Pink Floyd," 1062.
19. Ibid., 1064.
20. Ibid., 1063.
21. Ibid., 1062.
22. Romero and Varela Cabo, "Absent Father," 53.
23. Parker, "Pink Floyd," 1062.
24. Romero and Varela Cabo, "Absent Father," 55.
25. Parker, "Pink Floyd," 1065.
26. Ibid.
27. Ibid.
28. Ibid., 1063.
29. Ibid., 1068.
30. Romero and Valera Cabo, "Absent Father," 54.

Chapter 7

1. Parker, *Alan Parker*, 81, 90.
2. Ibid., 81.
3. William Wharton, *Birdy* (New York: Vintage Books/Div. of Random House, 1978). (Information taken from *Kansas City Star* from the book review blurbs preceding the novel.)
4. Ibid. (Information taken from *Philadelphia Enquirer* from the book review blurbs preceding the novel.)
5. Ibid. (Information taken from "Author Biography" blurb following the novel.)
6. Parker, *Alan Parker*, 81.
7. Ibid., 82.
8. Ibid., 84.
9. Ibid., 88.
10. Ibid., 85.
11. Ibid., 86.
12. Ibid., 90–92.
13. Ibid., 92.
14. Ghislaine Boulanger, PhD, "Post-Traumatic Stress Disorder: An Old Problem with a New Name," in Stephen M. Sonnenberg, MD, Arthur S. Blank, Jr. MD, et al., *The Trauma of War: Stress and Recovery in Vietnam Veterans*. (Washington, D.C.: American Psychiatric Press, 1985), 20.
15. Ibid., 168–69.
16. Ibid., 169.
17. Ibid., 53–54.
18. Allan D. Cruickshank and Helen G. Cruickshank, *1001 Questions Answered About Birds* (New York: Dover Publications, 1976), 80–83.
19. Wharton, *Birdy*, 3–4.
20. Parker, *Alan Parker*, 87–88.
21. Richard G. Tedeschi and Richard J. McNally, "Can We Facilitate the Post Traumatic Growth in Combat Veterans?" *American Psychologist* 66.1 (January 2011), 19–24. (The authors received the article from Senior Airman Jason Esposito after his experience with PTSD, in hopes that we could use it for our studies.)

Chapter 8

1. Parker, *Alan Parker*, 94.
2. *Angel Heart* Special Edition DVD, Alan Parker interview.
3. Parker, *Alan Parker*, 94.
4. Ibid.
5. *Angel Heart* Special Edition DVD, Alan Parker interview.
6. Parker, *Alan Parker*, 97.
7. Ibid., 99.
8. Ibid., 98.
9. Ibid., 100.
10. Ibid.

11. Ibid.
12. Ibid., 103.
13. Ibid.
14. Ibid., 106.
15. Ibid.
16. *Angel Heart* Special Edition DVD, Alan Parker Audio Commentary.
17. Carrol L. Fry, "The Devil You Know: Satanism in *Angel Heart*," *Literature Film Quarterly* 19.3 (1991): 3.
18. *Angel Heart* Special Edition DVD, Alan Parker Audio Commentary.
19. Pauline Kael, "The Current Cinema," *The New Yorker*, April 6, 1987, 85–86.
20. Fry, "The Devil You Know," 5.
21. *Angel Heart* Special Edition DVD, Alan Parker Audio Commentary.
22. Fry, "The Devil You Know," 5.
23. *Angel Heart* Special Edition DVD, Alan Parker Audio Commentary.
24. Ibid.
25. Stephen Cooper, "Sex/Knowledge/Power in the Detective Genre," *Film Quarterly* 42.3 (1989): 29.
26. *Angel Heart* Special Edition DVD, Alan Parker Audio Commentary
27. Cooper, "Sex/Knowledge/Power in the Detective Genre," 29.
28. *Angel Heart* Special Edition DVD, Alan Parker Audio Commentary.
29. *Angel Heart* Special Edition DVD, *Voodoo ... the Truth* (documentary).
30. *Angel Heart* Special Edition DVD, Alan Parker interview.
31. Fry, "The Devil You Know," 5.
32. *Angel Heart* Special Edition DVD, Alan Parker Audio Commentary.
33. Fry, "The Devil You Know," 5.
34. *Angel Heart* Special Edition DVD, Alan Parker Audio Commentary.
35. Fry, "The Devil You Know," 5.

Chapter 9

1. Parker, *Alan Parker*, 109.
2. Gavin Smith, "'Mississippi Gambler': Alan Parker Rides Again," *Film Comment*, November 24, 1988, 28.
3. Sandy Nelson, "On Location: *Mississippi Burning* Filming Locations," 1999, http://www.fast-rewind.com/locations_mississippiburning.html.
4. Parker, *Alan Parker*, 108.
5. *Mississippi Burning* Special Edition DVD, Alan Parker Audio Commentary.
6. Parker, *Alan Parker*, 112.
7. Harvard Sitkoff, "*Mississippi Burning* Film Review," *The Journal of American History* (December 1989): 1019.
8. Parker, *Alan Parker*, 112.
9. *Mississippi Burning* Special Edition DVD, Alan Parker Audio Commentary.
10. Thomas Doherty, "*Mississippi Burning* Film Review," *Cineaste* (1989): 48.
11. *Mississippi Burning* Special Edition DVD, Alan Parker Audio Commentary.
12. Ibid.
13. Smith, "Mississippi Gambler," 28.
14. Ibid., 30.
15. Ibid., 27.
16. Ibid., 29.
17. Sitkoff, "*Mississippi Burning*," 1019.
18. Doherty, "*Mississippi Burning*," 48.
19. Smith, "Mississippi Gambler," 30.
20. Doherty, "*Mississippi Burning*," 49.
21. Sitkoff, "*Mississippi Burning*," 1019.
22. *Mississippi Burning* Special Edition DVD, Alan Parker Audio Commentary.
23. Ibid.
24. Ibid.
25. Smith, "Mississippi Gambler," 30.
26. Ibid., 29.

Chapter 10

1. Parker, *Alan Parker*, 118.
2. Ibid.
3. David Mura, *Where the Body Meets Memory: An Odyssey of Race, Sexuality, and Desire* (New York: Anchor, 1996), 241.
4. Parker, *Alan Parker*, 118.
5. Ibid.
6. Ibid.
7. Ibid.
8. Ibid.
9. Ibid., 123.
10. Kent A. Ono, "The Biracial Subject as Passive Receptacle for Japanese American Memory in *Come See the Paradise*," ed. Beltrán, Mary and Camilla Fojas (New York: New York University Press, 2008), 137.
11. Ibid.
12. Ibid., 143.
13. Farrah Anwar, "*Come See the Paradise*," *Monthly Film Bulletin* (December 1990): 350.
14. Ibid.
15. Ibid.
16. Ono, "Biracial Subject," 143.
17. Ibid., 145.
18. Ibid., 141.

Chapter 11

1. *The Commitments* Special Edition DVD, "Making-Of" documentary.
2. Ibid.
3. Ibid.
4. Ibid.
5. Parker, *Alan Parker*, 131.
6. Ibid., 132.
7. *The Commitments* Special Edition DVD, "Making-Of" documentary.
8. Ibid.
9. Ibid.
10. Parker, *Alan Parker*, 132.

11. Ibid.
12. Don Kunz, "Alan Parker's Adaptation of Roddy Doyle's *The Commitments*," *Literature/Film Quarterly* (January 29, 2001): 56.
13. Ibid., 55.
14. Ibid.
15. Ibid.
16. Dervila Layden, "Generic Migrations: The Productive Relationship Between Ireland and Hollywood," *Film Ireland* (March/April 2008): 25.
17. Kunz, "Parker's Adaptation," 54.
18. Ibid.
19. *The Commitments* Special Edition DVD, "Making-Of" documentary.
20. Kunz, "Parker's Adaptation," 56.
21. Layden, "Generic Migrations," 25.
22. *The Commitments* Special Edition DVD; "Making-Of" documentary.
23. Kunz, "Parker's Adaptation," 54.
24. Ibid., 55.
25. Ibid., 54.
26. Ibid., 56.
27. Ibid.
28. Ibid., 54.
29. Ibid., 56.
30. Ibid., 55.
31. Ibid., 56.

Chapter 12

1. Parker, *Alan Parker*, 139.
2. Ibid.
3. Ibid., 148.
4. Ibid., 141.
5. Ibid., 145.
6. Ibid.
7. Ibid., 141.
8. Ibid., 141–42.
9. Ibid., 145.
10. Ibid., 148.
11. Cast/Crew Data, Internet Movie Database (IMDb), www.Imdb.com.
12. "The Kellogg Brothers: Cornflakes Kings," A&E *Biography* episode, original airdate: November 27, 1995.
13. Horace B. Powell, *The Original Has This Signature* (Upper Saddle River, NJ: Prentice-Hall, 1956), ix.
14. Cast/Crew Data, Internet Movie Database (IMDb), www.Imdb.com.
15. T.C. Boyle, *The Road to Wellville* (New York: Viking Press, 1993), 15.
16. Ibid., 10.
17. "The Kellogg Brothers: Cornflakes Kings."
18. Boyle, *The Road to Wellville*, 15.
19. Ibid., 74–75.
20. Ibid., 57.
21. "The Kellogg Brothers: Cornflakes Kings."
22. Boyle, *The Road to Wellville*, 140.
23. "The Kellogg Brothers: Cornflakes Kings."
24. Boyle, *The Road to Wellville*, 43–50.
25. Ibid., 62.
26. Ibid., 118.
27. Benjamin Kline Hunnicutt, *Kellogg's Six-Hour Day* (Philadelphia: Temple University Press, 1996), 42.
28. Boyle, *The Road to Wellville*, 66.
29. Ibid., 70.
30. Ibid., 28.
31. Ibid., 26–34.
32. Ibid., 167–184.
33. Ibid., 281.
34. Ibid., 275.
35. Ibid., 215.
36. Ibid., 198–219.
37. Ibid., 253.
38. Ibid., 26–52.
39. Ibid., 35–52.
40. Ibid., 432.
41. Ibid., 461.
42. Ibid., 463.
43. Ibid., 469.
44. Ibid., 475–76.

Chapter 13

1. Parker, *Alan Parker*, 149.
2. Alan Parker, *The Making of Evita* (New York: Collins Publishers, 1996), 3.
3. Ibid.
4. Ibid.
5. Ibid.
6. Peter N. Chumo, "'The Greatest Social Climber since Cinderella': Evita and the American Success Story," *Literature/Film Quarterly* (January 29, 2001): 32.
7. Ibid., 16.
8. Ibid.
9. Ibid., 18.
10. Ibid., 22.
11. Stephen Pizzello, "An Iconic Evita," *American Cinematographer* (January 1997): 40.
12. Ibid., 41.
13. Mary Main, *The Woman with the Whip* (London: Corgi Books, 1977), 17.
14. Chumo, "Social Climber," 33.
15. Pizzello, "Iconic Evita," 41.
16. Chumo, "Social Climber," 33.
17. Ibid., 34.
18. Main, *The Woman with the Whip*, 52.
19. Chumo, "Social Climber," 35.
20. Main, *The Woman with the Whip*, 46.
21. Ibid., 75.
22. Ibid., 79.
23. Chumo, "Social Climber," 35.
24. Main, *The Woman with the Whip*, 109.
25. Chumo, "Social Climber," 34.
26. Ibid., 35.

Chapter 14

1. Parker, *Alan Parker*, 173.
2. Ibid., 163.

3. Ibid.
4. Ibid., 63.
5. Ibid., 170.
6. Ibid., 163.
7. Ibid.
8. Ibid., 173.
9. *Angela's Ashes* DVD Special Features: Frank McCourt Audio Commentary.
10. John McCourt, *Angela's Ashes: A Memoir* (New York: Scribner, 1996), 11.
11. John A. Murphy, *Ireland in the Twentieth Century* (Dublin: Gill & MacMillan, 1975), 88–90.
12. *Angela's Ashes* DVD Special Features: Alan Parker Audio Commentary.
13. Ibid.
14. Ibid., Frank McCourt Audio Commentary.
15. Ibid., Alan Parker Audio Commentary.
16. Kee, *Ireland*, 225–29.
17. Ibid., 225–26.
18. Ibid., 228.
19. *Angela's Ashes* DVD Special Features: Frank McCourt Audio Commentary.
20. Ibid.
21. Patrick Weston Joyce, "A Concise History of Ireland," circa 1910. (Retrieved from libraryireland.com.)
22. *Angela's Ashes* DVD Special Features: Alan Parker Audio Commentary.
23. McCourt, *Angela's Ashes: A Memoir*, 114.
24. *Angela's Ashes* DVD Special Features: Alan Parker Audio Commentary.
25. McCourt, *Angela's Ashes: A Memoir*, 164.
26. Retrieved from www.chabad.org, a webpage dedicated to the Ten Commandments.
27. William Shakespeare, *Hamlet* (New York: Oxford University Press, 1987), 239–42.
28. *Angela's Ashes* DVD Special Features: Alan Parker Audio Commentary.
29. McCourt, *Angela's Ashes: A Memoir*, 206.
30. Murphy, *Twentieth Century*, 59–77.
31. *Angela's Ashes* DVD Special Features: Alan Parker Audio Commentary.
32. Ibid.
33. Valerie Martin, *Salvation: Scenes from the Life of St. Francis* (New York: Random House, 2001), 53.
34. McCourt, *Angela's Ashes: A Memoir*, 354–55.
35. Ibid., 357.
36. *Angela's Ashes* DVD Special Features: Alan Parker Audio Commentary.
37. McCourt, *Angela's Ashes: A Memoir*, 359–63.

Chapter 15

1. Parker, *Alan Parker*, 3.
2. Ibid., 174.
3. *The Life of David Gale* DVD Special Features: Alan Parker Audio Commentary.
4. Parker, *Alan Parker*, 180.
5. *The Life of David Gale* DVD Special Features: Alan Parker Audio Commentary.
6. Ibid.
7. Parker, *Alan Parker*, 179.
8. *The Life of David Gale* DVD Special Features: *Death in Texas* (documentary).
9. This entire section (before "Summary") was written by Alan Parker in an email message to the author, January 20, 2012. It has been edited for style only.
10. *The Life of David Gale* DVD Special Features: Alan Parker Audio Commentary
11. Ibid.
12. Ibid.
13. Charles Sheperdson, "Lacan and Philosophy," in *Cambridge Companion to Lacan*, ed. Jean-Michel Rabaté (Cambridge: Cambridge University Press, 2003), 116–47.
14. *The Life of David Gale* DVD Special Features: Alan Parker Audio Commentary.
15. Ibid.
16. Ibid.
17. Ibid.
18. Ibid.
19. Ibid.
20. Ibid.
21. Ibid.
22. Ibid.
23. Ibid.
24. Alexander Bauer, "Puccini: *Turandot*." *Opera News* 63.27 (January 1999): 70. (Retrieved electronically from infotrac-college.com.)
25. *The Life of David Gale* DVD Special Features: Alan Parker Audio Commentary.
26. Ibid.

Bibliography

Anwar, Farrah. "Come See the Paradise." *Monthly Film Bulletin* (December 1990): 350.

Auster, Al. "*Fame* Review." *Cineaste* (April 4, 1980): 35.

Bauer, Alexander. "Puccini: *Turandot.*" *Opera News* 36.27 (1999): 70.

Berliner, Todd, and Philip Furia. "The Sounds of Silence: Songs in Hollywood Films since the 1960s." *Style* 36.1 (Spring 2002): 32.

Bondanella, Peter. *Italian Cinema: From Neorealism to the Present.* New York: Continuum International, 1983.

Boulanger, Ghislaine. "Post-Traumatic Stress Disorder: An Old Problem with a New Name." In *The Trauma of War: Stress and Recovery in Vietnam Veterans*, edited by Stephen M. Sonnenberg, MD, Arthur S. Blank, Jr., MD, et al. Washington, D.C.: American Psychiatric Press, 1985.

Boyle, T.C. *The Road to Wellville.* New York: Viking Press, 1993.

Chumo, Peter N. "The Greatest Social Climber since Cinderella: Evita and the American Success Story." *Literature/Film Quarterly* (January 29, 2001): 32.

Coltrane, Scott. "Families and Gender Equity." In *Selected Readings in Marriage and Family*, edited by Lorene H. Stone. Farmington Hills, MI: Greenhaven Press, 1998.

Cooper, Stephen. "Sex/Knowledge/Power in the Detective Genre." *Film Quarterly* 42.3 (1989): 29.

Cruickshank, Allan D., and Helen G. Cruickshank. *1001 Questions Answered About Birds.* New York: Dover Publications, 1976.

Davis, Susan Bluestein. *After Midnight: The Life and Death of Brad Davis.* New York: Simon & Schuster, 1997.

Desmond, John, and Peter Hawkes. *Adaptations: Studying Film and Literature.* New York: McGraw-Hill, 2005.

DeWitt, Susan. "Parents, Children, and Gender Roles." In *Selected Readings in Marriage and Family*, edited by Lorene H. Stone. Farmington Hills, MI: Greenhaven Press, 1998.

Doherty, Thomas. "*Mississippi Burning* Film Review." *Cineaste* (1989): 48.

Forst, Graham Nichol. "Northrop Frye and Homo Ludens." Infotrac College Edition, 2003.

Fry, Carol L. "The Devil You Know: Satanism in *Angel Heart.*" *Literature Film Quarterly* 19.3 (1991): 3.

Gonthier, David. *Seventy Years of the American Prison Movie: From* The Big House *to* The Shawshank Redemption. New York: Edwin Mellen Press, 2006.

Hacker, Jonathan, and David Price. *Take Ten: Contemporary British Film Directors.* New York: Oxford University Press, 1991.

Hayes, Billy, and William Hoffer. *Midnight Express.* New York: CBS Publications, 1977.

Hillier, Jim, ed. *Cashiers du Cinéma, The 1950s: Neorealism, Hollywood, New Wave.* Cambridge: Harvard University Press, 1985.

Horton, Andrew. "Britain's Angry Young Man in Hollywood." *Cineaste* (December 1986): 31.

"How It All Began: The Making of *Fame.*" *International Cinematographers Guild* 80.9 (2009): 39.

Howard, Douglas A. *The History of Turkey.* Westport, CT: Greenwood Press, 2001.

Hunnicutt, Benjamin Kline. *Kellogg's Six-Hour Day.* Philadelphia: Temple University Press, 1996.

Joyce, Patrick Weston. "A Concise History of Ireland." http://www.libraryireland.com.

Kael, Pauline. "The Current Cinema." *The New Yorker*, April 6, 1987.

Kauffmann, Stanley. "Singing the Body Electric: *Fame* Review." *The New Republic* 23 (1980): 22.

Kershaw, Alex. *Jack London: A Life.* New York: St. Martin's Press, 1997.

Kunz, Don. "Alan Parker's Adaptation of Roddy Doyle's *The Commitments.*" *Literature/Film Quarterly* (January 29, 2001): 56.

Layden, Dervila. "Generic Migrations: The Productive Relationship Between Ireland and Hollywood." *Film Ireland* (March/April 2008): 25.

Main, Mary. *The Woman with the Whip.* London: Corgi Books, 1977.

Maltin, Leonard, ed. *Video Guide, 2010 Edition.* New York: New American Library, 2009.

Martin, Valerie. *Salvation: Scenes from the Life of St. Francis.* New York: Random House, 2001.

McCourt, Frank. *Angela's Ashes: A Memoir.* New York: Scribner, 1996.

"Movie Reviews: *Fame.*" *Variety Magazine* 1 (1980): 38.

Mura, David. *Where the Body Meets Memory: An Odyssey of Race, Sexuality, and Desire.* New York: Anchor, 1996.

Murphy, John A. *Ireland in the Twentieth Century.* Dublin: Gill & MacMillan, 1975.

Nelson, Sandy. "On Location: *Mississippi Burning* Filming Locations." *Fast Rewind,* edited by Nick Alaway, 1999. http://www.fast-rewind.com/locations_mississippiburning.html.

Ono, Kent A. *The Biracial Subject as Passive Receptacle for Japanese American Memory in* Come See the Paradise. New York: New York University Press, 2008.

Parker, Alan. *Alan Parker.* Poland: Plus Camerimage, 2008.

———. "Dialogue on Film: Alan Parker." *American Film* 13.4 (1988): 12, 14–15.

———. *The Making of* Evita. New York: Collins Publishers, 1996.

———. "*Pink Floyd—The Wall*: The Making of the Film." *American Cinematographer* (October 1982): 1025.

"Paul Williams's Reflections." http://www.paulwilliamscouk.plus.com/pwnbugsyh.html.

Perry, John. *Jack London: An American Myth.* Chicago: Nelson-Hall, 1981.

Pizzello, Stephen. "An Iconic Evita." *American Cinematographer* (January 1997): 40.

Powell, Horace B. *The Original Has This Signature.* Upper Saddle River, NJ: Prentice-Hall, 1956.

Romero, Jorge Sacido, Varela Cabo, and Luis Miguel. "Roger Waters's Poetry of the Absent Father: British Identity in Pink Floyd's *The Wall.*" *Atlantis,* December 2006.

Shakespeare, William. *Hamlet.* New York: Oxford University Press, 1987.

Sheperdson, Charles. "Lacan and Philosophy." In *Cambridge Companion to Lacan,* edited by Jean-Michel Rabate. Cambridge: Cambridge University Press, 2003.

Silet, Charles L.P. *Oliver Stone Interviews.* Jackson: University Press of Mississippi, 2001.

Sitkoff, Harvard. "*Mississippi Burning* Film Review." *The Journal of American History* (December 1989): 1019.

Smith, Gavin. "Mississippi Gambler: Alan Parker Rides Again." *Film Comment,* November 24, 1988.

Tedeschi, Richard G., and Richard J. McNally. "Can We Facilitate the Post Traumatic Growth in Combat Veterans?" *American Psychologist* 66.1 (January 2011): 19–24.

Voytilla, Stuart. *Myth and the Movies: Discovering the Myth Structure of 50 Unforgettable Films.* Studio City, CA: Michael Wiese Productions, 1999.

Warshow, Robert. "The Gangster as Tragic Hero." In *The Immediate Experience: Movies, Comics, Theatre, and Other Aspects of Popular Culture.* Cambridge: Harvard University Press, 2001.

Welles, Tim, and William Triplet. *Drug Wars: An Oral History from the Trenches.* New York: William Morrow, 1992.

Wharton, William. *Birdy.* New York: Vintage Books, 1978.

Wollen, Peter. *Signs and Meanings in the Cinema.* Bloomington: Indiana University Press, 1973.

Zito, Bobbi Leigh. "Alan Parker Interview." *Focus on Film* 35 (1980): 5.

Index

Numbers in **_bold italics_** indicate pages with illustrations

A & M Films 121, **_130_**
Abbey Road Studios 272
Abbott and Costello 26, 223
Academy Awards *see* Oscar Winners
Adana (Red Cross) 51
aerial shot 110
Aerosmith (band) 113
After Midnight: The Life and Death of Brad Davis (Book: Susan Davis) 42
Agnew Mental Hospital 121–2
Aherne, Michael 207
Ahkmatova, Anna 183
Ahmet (Negdir) 58
AIDS (Brad Davis) 42
Alabama 164
Alan Parker (Camerimage Book) 9, 290
Alan Parker Film Company 14
Alday, Luis 242
Aldrich, Robert 54
Alice in Wonderland (C. S. Lewis) 93
Alien (1979) 11
All Quiet on the Western Front (1930) 126
Allah 53, 59
Allen, Karen 84, 92
Allen, Woody 2, 84
"Almost Martyrs" (Music: *The Life of David Gale*) 272
Altman, Robert 31, 73, 86, 152
ambient sound 47
American Beauty (1999) 271
American Film (magazine) 9, 15
American History X (1998) 61
Analyze This (1999) 27
Anderson, Betty Sue 282, 284
Anderson, Lindsay 9
Anderson, Paul Thomas 254
Anderson, Wes 18
Angel, Harry 31, 138
Angel Heart (1987) 2, 3, 6, 8, 9, 47, 73, 77, 78, 138–161, 163, 166, 170, 173, 187, 283, 292
Angela's Ashes (1999) 3, 6, 8, 9, 11, 12, 47, 252–268, 272, 293
Angela's Ashes (novel) 3
Anglo-Irish Treaty (1921) 259

Angry Young Man Movement 11, 15
anima 135, 276
animation (Pink Floyd—*The Wall*) *see* Gerald Scarfe
Anna Christie (1930) 30
Annie Hall (1977) 84
"Another Bleeding Heart" (Music: *The Life of David Gale*) 272, 289
"Another Brick in the Wall, Part I" (Music: *Pink Floyd—The Wall*) 108
"Another Brick in the Wall, Part II" (Music: *Pink Floyd—The Wall*) 109
"Another Brick in the Wall, Part III" (Music: *Pink Floyd—The Wall*) 114
"Another Suitcase in Another Hall" (Music: *Pink Floyd—The Wall*) 250
Antichrist 161
Antonioni, Michelangelo 2, 96, 121
Anwar, Farrah 189, 192
Anzio 106, 107, 114, 116
Ardmore (Ireland) 254
Argentina 217, 246–7, 251; *see also* Menem, Carlos
Argento, Dario 148
Aristotle 281
Arkins, Robert **_200_**, 202
Armstrong, Louis 190
Army Specialized Training Program 120
"The Art of the Possible" (Music: *Evita*) 243
Asperger's Syndrome 128
Astaire, Fred 22
Atlantic Monthly (magazine) 120
Attenborough, Sir Richard 9
Au Revoir les Enfants (1987) 261
Auchelli, Marcelo Alejandro 242
Auster, Al 67, 77, 79
Australia 217
Auteur Theory 4, 5, 6, 7, 82, 232
autointoxication (*The Road to Wellville*) 218
Avery, Tex 36

The Awakening (novel) 222
ayip (Turkish for "dirty") 53

Baby Face (Fletcher) 38
Bacall, Lauren 28, 29
Bacon, Lloyd 260
Bad Day at Black Rock (1955) 186
"Bad Guys" (Music: *Bugsy Malone*) 32, 33, 38
"bad machines" (*Midnight Express*) 59
Baio, Scott 23, 26, **_30_**
Ball, Angeline 203, **_209_**
Baltimore, Maryland 216
Banderas, Antonio 234, 236, 237
The Bank Dick (1940) 36
Barber, Jeremy 8
Barker, Clive 148
Barnstable (Burnham Beaches) 105
Baron, Sandy 127
Barrytown 210; *see also* Ireland
Bartlett, Vernon 293
Batter's Box (*The Life of David Gale*) 278
Battle Creek Sanitarium 217, 218; *see also* Michigan
bazaar (*Midnight Express*) 44, 46, 47
Beacon Communications **_216_**, 217, 294
Beall, Sandra 128
The Beatles 16, 66, 92, 102
Beautiful Love 293; *see also* Parker, Alan (Unproduced Scripts)
Beaver, Jim 275
Beckett, Samuel 262
The Bee Gees 16, 17
Begelman, David 83, 85, 105
Behr, Jack 121
Bell, Tobin 181
Belzer, Richard 81
Ben-Hur (1959) 14
Bensons & Hedges 14; *see also* Parker, Alan (Commercials)
Bergman, Ingmar 46
Berliner, Todd 27
Bermondsey (South London), 105, 108

303

Bertolucci, Bernardo 2
Besterman, Paul 19
The Big House (1930) 49; see also prison films
The Big Sleep (1946) 4, 142, 152
Billy Elliot (2000) 20, 293
Bingham, David 105, 108
Birdman of Alcatraz (1962) 44; see also Prison films
Birdy (1984) 2, 3, 6, 8, 47, 73, 120–137, 138, 149, 150, 173, 217, 218, 269
Birdy (novel) 120
Biziou, Peter (cinematographer) 110, 112, 114, 116, 117, 163, 165, 176, 181
Black Mass 155
The Blackmarket Man 292; see also Parker, Alan (Unproduced Scripts)
Blackpool (England) 14, 19, 291
Blade Runner (1981) 11
Blood Brothers 293; see also Parker, Alan (Unproduced Scripts)
Blousey Brown 28
Blow-up (1966) 2
Blue Hall (Movie Theater) 12
The Blues Brothers (1980) 206
Bodner, Rennee **64**
Body Heat (1981) 145
Bogart, Humphrey 24, 25, 28, 29, 142, 147
Bogart, Neil 42
Bonet, Lisa 3, **139**, 140, 151
Bonicelli, Paolo 48
Boomtown Rats (Rock band with Bob Geldoff) 105, ***111***, 212
Bottin, Rob 112
Boulanger, Ghislaine 123
Boyle, Lara Flynn 219
Boyle, T. Coraghessen 3, 215
Brando, Marlon 22, 74, 78
The Breakfast Club (1985) 78
breakfast foods: Corn Flakes 217, 228; Grape Nuts 221, 223, 232; Perfect Food Company (PERFO) 218, 222, 229, 232; Sanitas Food Company 223
Breaking the Waves (1996) 254, 259
Breathless (1959) 4
Breen, Joe 253, ***259***
Brighton Beach 294
"Bring the Boys Back Home" (Music: *Pink Floyd—The Wall*) 116
Bringing Up Baby (1938) 4
British Academy of Film and Television Arts (BAFTA) 14, 236, 292
British Broadcasting Corporation (BBC) 14, 18, 19, 291, 293
British Film Institute (BFI) 292
Brocksmith, Roy 28, 226
Broderick, Matthew 216, 218
Bronfman, Edgar 16
Bronfman, Edgar, Jr. 16
Bronson, Charles 177, 180

Brooklyn, New York 187, 255
Brooks, Mel 34
Brooks, Richard 42
Brown, Garret 122
Brown, James 205
bu (Turkish for "this") 52
Buck, George 124, 150
Buenos Aires 235, 243, 247
"Buenos Aires" (Music: *Evita*) 240, 248
"Bugsy Malone" (Music: *Bugsy Malone*) 37
Bugsy Malone (1976) 2, 3, 6, 8, 11, 12, 13, 18, 20, 22–38, 40, 41, 82, 138, 182, 290, 291
Bugsy Malone (novel) 290, 292
Buñuel, Luis 148, 153
Burns, Walter 28
Bush, Jeb 277
Butch Cassidy and the Sundance Kid (1969) 37
"Bye Bye Baby" (Music: *The Commitments*) 210

The Cabinet of D. Caligari (1919) 24
Cabo, Luis Miguel Varela 107, 109, 11, 114, 118
Cage, Nicolas 122–23, ***130***, 269
Cagney, James 26, 36, 69, 260
Cahiers du Cinéma (French film journal) 4
Calf Love (novel) 293
Call of the Wild (Jack London novel) 93
Camerimage (Poland) 290
Cameron, James 271
Campo de Mayo 243
"Can We Facilitate Post-Traumatic Stress Disorder in Combat Veterans?" (*American Psychologist* magazine) 137
Cannes Film Festival 18, 43, 122
capital punishment 279
Cara, Irene (Coco) 69, 71, 79
Carlito's Way (1993) 35
Carlyle, Robert ***253***, 255
Carney, Liam 207
Carolco International N.V. ***139***, ***144***
Carpenter, John 112
Carrington (1995) 234
cartoons (book images by Alan Parker): **5**, **13**, **119**, **230**, **291**
Carvey, Dana 219, 220
Casa Rosada 235, 236, 243, 247, 250
Casablanca Filmworks **41**, 42, **50**
Cassevetes, John 86
Cassisi, Johnny (Fat Sam) 23, 25, **30**
Castillo, Ramón (President of Argentina) 243
"Catch a Rising Star" (Music: *Fame*, 1980) 81
Catch-22 (1970) 126
Catholicism 156
Cathy Come Home (1966) 14

"Cathy's Clown" (Everly Brothers song) 202
Cauldwell, Brendan 266
"Chain of Fools" (Music: *The Commitments*) 212
Chaney, James 164, 166; see also Goodman, Andrew; Schwerner, Mickey
Chaplin, Charles 221
"The Chase" (Music: *Midnight Express*) 47
Ché see Ché Guevara
Chesapeake Bay 293
chevalier 156; see also voodoo
chiaroscuro 48, 91, 237
children (sociological study of) 90, 290–1; see also *Angela's Ashes*; *Bugsy Malone*; *The Evacuees*, *Melody*, *Shoot the Moon*
Chinatown (1974) 145, 150
Chivilcoy (Buenos Aires, Argentina) 235
chlorosis 219
Chopin, Kate 222
A Chorus Line (1985) 67
Chumo, Peter N. 238, 241, 244
Cimino, Michael 63
Cineaste (film journal) 9, 84, 87
Cinematography see Biziou, Peter; Connier, Chris; high-angle shots; Khondji, Darius; lighting; low-angle shots; Seresin, Michael; Tattersall, Gale
Cinergi Pictures **234**, 236, **247**
Citizen Kane (1941) 31, 247
City of God (2002) 25
Civil Rights 1, 9
Claire's Knee (1970) 4
Clapham Baths (London) 108
Clark, Bob 74
Clarke, Alan 19
Clarke, May 30
Clifford, Linda 69
Clift, Montgomery 74, 78
Clooney, George 271
Close Encounters of the Third Kind (1977) 43
Closely Watched Trains (1966) 261
Cola-Kane 232
Colbert, Claudette 187
Colesberry, Robert **64**, 164, 216
Colgan, Eileen 255
Collet, Dickenson & Pearce (CDP) 13, 15, 17
Collins, Michael 258
Coltrane, Scott 87
Columbia Pictures **41**, 42, **50**, **216**, 217
Come See the Paradise (1990) 3, 6, 8, 11, 183–198, **184**, 216, 271
"Come See the Paradise" (poem) 183
"Comfortably Numb" (Music: *Pink Floyd—The Wall*) 112, 117
commercials: Benson & Hedges 14; Collet, Dickenson & Pearce (CDP) 13, 15, 17; Hamlet Cigars 14; Heineken 14; Hugh Hudson

42; *Oliver Twist* 14; YouTube 15
The Commitments (1991) 3, 6, 8, 9, 11, 12, 31, 88, 199–214
composition (framing) 92, 96, 97, 98, 126, 129, 136, 145, 150, 153, 156, 160, 166
Condon, Kerry 266
Coney Island 150
Connery, Sean 168
Constitution of the Free Irish State (1922) 256
Contempt (1962) 2
Cooke, Sam 206
Cool Hand Luke (1967) 54
Cooper, Stephen 150, 151
Coppola, Francis Ford 11, 29, 31, 233
Coppola, Roman 18
Coppola, Sophia 18
Coram Boy 293; *see also* Parker, Alan (Unproduced Scripts)
Corcoran, Shane Murray **253**, 255
Corn Flakes *see* breakfast cereals
Corr, Andrea 201
The Cosby Show (TV series) 140
Costner, Kevin 168
The Court Game 88–9, 93
Crabtree, Michael 278
"La Creation doit être l'ouvrage d'un seul" *see* "Creation Must Be the Work of One Person"
"Creation Must Be the Work of One Person" 5
Cries and Whispers (1973) 6
Crosland, Alan 257
cross-cutting editing 86, 90, 96, 101, 107, 111, 133, 189, 193, 222, 226, 228, 249–50, 266, 279, 285, 287, 288, 289
Cuchulain 260, 262
Culture Club *see* Boy George
Cumann na n Gaedheal 265
Curreri, Lee 69
Cusack, John 216
"Cyphre Louis" 140

Dafoe, Willem **163**, 164, 167, **172**, 181
The Dam Busters (1955) 113
Dandy Dan 31
Dante 46
Darabont, Frank 4, 9, 54
"The Dark End of the Street" (Music: *The Commitments*) 211
David, Eleanor 112
David Brown Productions **253**
Davis, Brad **41**, 42, **50**
Davis, Susan 42
Davis, Viveka 86
The Day of the Locust (1975) 109
Days of Heaven (1978) 42
Dead Poet's Society (1989) 68
Dean, James 74, 78
"Dearest Darling" (Music: *The Commitments*) 202
Death Row 270, 274, 275, 282
Death Watch 273, 277, 279, 282, 288

Death Wish (1974) 180
The Deer Hunter (1978) 63
Demme, Jonathan 275
De Niro, Robert 8, 74, 140, 141, 143, 144, **145**, 160
De Palma, Brian 11, 24, 168
descamisados 246, 247
De Sica, Vittorio 10, 14
Desmond, John 6; *see also* Hawkes, Peter
"Destination Anywhere" (Music: *The Commitments*) 201, 206, 207, 212
detective films *see Angel Heart* (1986); *The Life of David Gale* (2003); *Mississippi Burning* (1988)
De Valera, Éamon 253, 258
"The Devil You Know: Satanism in *Angel Heart*" (article) 142; *see also* Fry, Carrol
Dialogical Exhaustion (David Gale's book) 274
DiCaprio, Leonardo 8
"The Dice Are Rolling" (Music: *Evita*) 245
Dickens, Charles 14, 215, 219, 293
Diller, Barry 184
Diogene, Franco 51
"Dipsy Doodle" (Ella Fitzgerald song) 260, 264
Director's Guild of America 8
Dirty Hands Productions 8, **216**, 217, **234, 253, 270, 277**
Dirty Harry (1971) 178
The Divine Comedy (Dante) 46
divorce films *see Shoot the Moon* (1982)
Doherty, Thomas 166, 171, 175
"Donna" (Richie Valens song: *Birdy*) 134
Donner, Richard 254
"Don't Blame Me" (Music: *Shoot the Moon*) 85, 89, 90, 91, 95, 101, 102
"Don't Cry For Me Argentina" (Music: *Evita*) 235, 236, 239, 246; *see also* "Eva's Final Broadcast" (Reprise)
"Don't Leave Me Now" (Music: *Pink Floyd—The Wall*) 113
Dourif, Brad 167
"Down and Out" (Music: *Bugsy Malone*) 38
Doyle, Maria 206, **209**
Doyle, Roddy 201
Drewy, Chris 281
Duarte, Juan 238
Dublin, Ireland 210
Dugger, Florrie (Blousey) 28
Dunaway, Faye 145
Dunn, Kevin 174
"Dusty's Cabin" (Music: *The Life of David Gale*) 272
dystopia 59

earthquake *see* San Juan Earthquake
East Molesy (London) 105

Eastwood, Clint 176, 177
Eclipse (1962) 96
Edelman, Randy 192, 198
editing *see* cross-cutting editing; montage; two-shot editing method (*The Life of David Gale*)
editors *see* Hambling, Gerry
egg (as symbol in *Angel Heart*) 148, 151
8 1/2 (1963) 2
"Eine Kleine Nachtmusik" (Mozart) 75
Eisenstein, Sergei 4
"Eleanor Rigby" (Beatles song) 16
Elixir 61
Ellis Prison 270, 274
"Empty Spaces" (Music: *Pink Floyd—The Wall*) 112
enemas 223
Ensign, Michael 51
Epiphany *see* Proudfoot, Epiphany
Epsom, Downs (Great Britain) 105, 107
Eraserhead (1978) 121
Ermey, R. Lee 172
Escape from Alcatraz (1979) 44
Euclid 261
"Eva, Beware of the City" (Music: *Evita*) 240
Eva Perón (biography) 236
The Evacuees (1975) 7, 9, 11, 14, 15, 18–20, 290, 291, 292
"Eva's Final Broadcast" (Music in *Evita*: Reprise of "Don't Cry for me Argentina") 250–1
Everly Brothers 202
Evita (1996) 3, 6, 8, 47, 67, 69, 78, 88, 233–251, 272
Executive Order 9066 194
existentialism 6, 53, 59, 131, 156, 251, 262, 274, 285
The Exorcism of Emily Rose (2005) 271
Expressionism 43, 45, 47, 56, 85, 99, 102, 123, 127, 134, 141, 283, 285

Fabian, Harry 37; *see also* Widmark, Richard
Fahrenheit 451 (Ray Bradbury novel) 60
Failan Project 294
Falling Angel (William Hjortsberg novel) 138, 140
Falling Down (1993) 171
Fame (1980) 2, 6, 8, 11, 12, 31, 47, 63–82, 83, 88, 92, 103, 120, 139, 204, 292
Family Ties (television show) 84
Fanny and Alexander (1983) 6
Far and Away (1992) 266
Fat Sam 23, 24, 26; *see also* Cassisi, Johnny
"Fat Sam's Grand Slam" (musical number) 27, 28
Faust (1926) 24
Faust (tale of) 138

Fellini, Federico 2, 4, 6, 12
feminism 87
femme fatale 34, 145
Fianna Fail Party 265
Field, Crystal 129
Fields, W.C. 36
The Fighting 69th (1940) 260
Film Adaptation (Desmond/Hawkes book) 6
film criticism 7
Film Culture (magazine) 4
film noir 3, 12, 25, 28, 73, 78, 123, 138, 142, 144, 145, 146, 149, 152, 155, 176, 205, 283
film theory 4
The Final Cut (Roger Waters album) 106
Fincher, David 146
Finnegan, Dave 201
Finnegan, John 187
Finney, Albert 3, 84
"First of May" (Bee Gees song) 16
Fish, Nancy 129
Fitzgerald, Ella 260, 264
"Fizzy" (Jenkins) 30
Flashdance (1983) 11, 75
Fletcher, Dexter (Baby Face) 38
Fletcher, Louise 71
Florek, Dann 143
"Flower That Blooms in the Rain" (Japanese Song) 186
Fonda, Bridget **216**, 218
Fontelieu, Stocker 158
"Fools Rush In" (Elvis Presley song) 204
Footloose (1984) 75
Footsteps (1973) 14; see also Parker, Alan (Early Films)
Ford, John 4, 63
Forman, Milos 125
Foster, Jodie 23, 28, **30**
The 400 Blows (1959) 4, 116, 261
Fourth Commandment (Holy Bible) 263
Fox-Rank Pictures (*Bugsy Malone*) **23, 30**
The Frames (Irish band) see Hansard, Glen
France 217
Franceschi, Antonia 74
Frankenheimer, John 44
Franklin, Aretha 213
Frears, Stephen 9, 154
Freikorper Kultur 229, 231
La Frenais 199, 201
French Lick (Indiana) 216
French New Wave Cinema 4; see also Goddard, Jean-Luc; Rohmer, Eric; Truffaut, François
Freud, Sigmund see psychoanalysis
Fry, Carrol 142, 144, 145, 155, 159, 161
Frye, Northrop 93
"Fuera, Madonna!" (*Evita*) 235
Furia, Philip 27

Gabriel, Peter 122, 125–6, 127, 135, 137
Gagarin, Yuri 293
Gaines, Boyd 74
Gallagher, Bronagh **209**
The Game (Jack London novel) 93
Gance, Abel 108
Gandhi, Mahatma 279
gangster genre 2, 26
Garbo, Greta 30
Garrett, Tony 14
Gast, Elizabeth 280
Gavin, Jamila 293
Gaye, Marvin 211
Geldoff, Bob 105, 107, 108, **111**, 113, 116, 212
George, Boy 204
Gere, Richard 42
German Expressionism see Expressionism
German Nudist Movement see *Freikorper Kultur*
Germanic Eagle of War (animated version in *Pink Floyd—The Wall*) 109–10
Germany 217
Gerolmo, Chris 162
Gibson, Guy 113
Gilda (1946) 35
Gilliam, Elizabeth **191**, 192
Gilman, Charlotte Perkins 222
"Girl of My Dreams" (Song in *Angel Heart*) 142, 145, 148, 155, 157, 160
Gladiator (2000) 11
Glaswegians 294
"Go home, Madonna!" see "Fuera, Madonna!"
Godard, Jean-Luc 2, 4
The Godfather (1972) 29, 31, 33, 35, 249–50
Gold, Jack 19
Gold, Tracey 84, 85
Goldberg, Whoopi 169–70
Goldman, Bo 83, 93
"Goodbye Cruel World" (Music: *Pink Floyd—The Wall*) 109, 114
Goodfellas (1990) 25
Goodman, Andrew 164, 166; see also Chaney, James; Schwerner, Mickey
Goodman, Michael 219
"Goodnight and Thank You" (Music: *Evita*) 242, 243, 244
Gorman, Shay 264
Gormley, Felim **204**
Gosford Park (2003) 31, 73
Gotanda, Philip 184
Grand Slam Speakeasy 26
Grant, Cary 28, 69
Grape Nuts see breakfast cereals
The Grapes of Wrath (1940, John Ford) 63
Great Depression 38, 261, 290
The Great Escape (1963) 54
Great Expectations (Charles Dickens novel) 14

Great Expectations (1946, David Lean) 4, 12, 17
Green, Al 211
Greer, Jane 34, 145
The Grifters (1990) 154
Growing Pains (TV series) 84
Grupos de Oficiales Unido (G.O.U.) 243
Guber, Peter 40, 41
Guevara, Ché 235, 250

Haaren High School (New York City) 65
Hacker, Jonathan 2, 9, 47, 48, 73, 81; see also Price, David
Hackman, Gene 2, 164, 167, **172**
Hague, Albert 69
Hairspray (2007) 293
Hall, Lee 293
Hambling, Gerry 6, 8, 19, 67, 1212, 125, 163, 285
Hamid (*Midnight Express*: novel) 48
Hamidou (Paul Smith: *Midnight Express*) 48
Hamlet (Shakespeare) 263
Hamlet Cigars see Parker, Alan (Commercials)
Hammersmith (Great Britain) 105
Hammett, Dashiell 147
Handel's *Messiah* 293
"Hangover Plaza" (David Gonthier song) 301
Hansard, Glen **200**, 202, 203, **209**
"Hard to Handle" (Otis Redding song) 210, 212
Hares in the Gate 292; see also Parker, Alan (Books); Parker, Alan (Cartoons)
Hargreaves, Christine 108
Harlem 149, 150
Harlow, Jean 29
Harper Collins Publishing 292
Harkins, John 125
Harum, Procol 208
Harvey (Mary Chase play) 128
Hawaii 185
Hawkes, Peter 6
Hawks, Howard 4, 28, 29, 99, 151–2
Hayes, William (Billy) 1, 9, 40, 41, 48, 61; see also Hoffer, William
Hayworth, Rita 35, 69
Hazeldine, James 112
Head, Roy 202
Hearts (Card game: *Shoot the Moon*) 91, 101
Heat (1995) 176
Heckerling, Amy 84
Heineken (commercial) 14; see also Alan Parker (Commercials)
"Hello and Goodbye" (Music: *Evita*) 244
Hellraiser (1987) 148
Henry VIII (Shakespeare) 263
Herald Tribune 44
Herrmann, Bernard 6
Hesse, Hermann 132

Hidalgo, Maria Lujàn 238
high-angle shot 5, 9, 86, 90, 98, 102, 125, 127, 135, 143, 221, 224, 225, 256, 285
"High Flying, Adored" (Music: *Evita*) 248
Hill, Dana 84, 86
Hill, George 49
Hill, Henry 25
Hiroshima 198
His Girl Friday (1940) 28
Hitchcock, Alfred 4, 6, 8, 136
Hitler, Adolf 279
Hjortsberg, William 138
Hoboken, New Jersey 150
Hoffer, William 1, 40; *see also* Hayes, William (Billy)
Holiday, Billie 265, 266
Hollywood Pictures **234**, **247**
Homer's *The Odyssey* 51
homo ludens 93
homosexuality 55, 75, 76
Hopkins, Anthony **216**
Hopkins, Bo 46
horror films 138
Hoskins, Bob 117
Hot Lunch (*Fame* script) 64
"Hot Lunch" (Music: *Fame*) 71
Howard, Ron 2, 66
Hudson, Hugh 42; *see also* Parker, Alan (Commercials)
Hugo, Victor 261
Hung Fu Shin Laundromat 33
Hungary 217, 236
Huntsville (prison) 270, 288
"Huntsville Epitaph" (Music: *The Life of David Gale*) 272
Hurt, John 42, 49
Husbands (1970) 86
Hussein, Waris 16, 17, 290
Huxley, Aldous 59
Hyde, Tracey 17

"I Can't Stand the Rain"(song) 204
"I Don't Like Mondays" (Boomtown Rats song) 105
"I Never Loved a Man the Way I Love You" (Aretha Franklin song) 213
"I Sing the Body Electric" (Music: *Fame*) 82
Ibarguren, Juana 238
Ice at the Bottom of the World (Unproduced Alan Parker Script) 293
"If I Fell" (Beatles song) 92, 102
"If We Never Meet Again" (Louis Armstrong song) 190
Ikeguchi, Takamuro 189
"I'll Be Surprisingly Good for You" (Music: *Evita*) 244
"I'm Feeling Fine" (Music: *Bugsy Malone*) 34
"In the Flesh" (Music: *Pink Floyd—The Wall*) 107, 108, 117
"In the Midnight Hour" (Music: *The Commitments*) 213
industrial modernism 11–2, 114, 116, 124, 127, 218, 240, 254, 255, 256
Inferno (Dante) 49
Inönü (Prime Minister of Turkey) 51
INT. ROOM.NIGHT **119**, 292; *see also* Parker, Alan (Books); Parker, Alan (Cartoons)
Intermedia Productions **270**, **277**
International Drug Trade Wars 45, 51, 60
internment camps *see* Japanese internment camps
Inwood, Steve 81
Ireland 201, 214, 254, 255; Ardmore 254; Ennis 254 Cork, 254; Denoo (Northern Ireland) 259; Dingle 254; Dublin 210, 254; Limerick 252, 254, 256, 258, 259, 263, 265; Shannon River 254, 267; Stormont 259; Tipperary 254
Ireland: A History 259
Irish Civil War 265
The Irish in Us (1935) 260
Irish Oak (boat) 268
Irving, John 215
"Is There Anybody Out There?" (Music: *Pink Floyd—The Wall*) 114
Ishimoto, Dale 189
Islington (North London) 11, 16
Isobe, Shinko 189
Issei 189, 196
"Istanbul Blues" (Song: *Midnight Express*) 56
Istanbul, Turkey 1, 43, 255

Jackson, Mahalia 166
Jackson, Michael 27
Jacob's Ladder (1990) 11
Jagger, Mick 95
Japan 17
Japanese internment camps 3, 183, 195
Japanese words *see* "Kanpai"
Japantown (Portland, Oregon) 185; *see also* Nihonmachi
Jaws (1975) 43, 254
The Jazz Singer (1927) 257
Jenkins,"Humpty" Albin 30; *see also* "Fizzy"
"Jesus and the Weather" (Frank McCourt's Composition: *Angela's Ashes*) 257, 264
John Adams (2008, TV miniseries) 271
Johnson, Betty Sue 282
Johnson, Hildy 28
Johnson, Lyndon B. 51
Jolson, Al 253
Jones, Trevor 141, 154, 163, 166, 178
Joplin, Janice 45
Josef K. (from Kafka's *The Trial*) 50
Jung, Carl 276
Junin 235

Kael, Pauline 85, 144, 147
Kafka, Franz 50, 131, 133, 284
Kalamazoo (Michigan) 230
"Kanpai ("Cheers" in Japanese) 190
Kansas City (1996) 31, 73, 152
Kansas City Star 120
Kassar, Mario 140
Kastner, Elliot 138
Kauffmann, Stanley 68
Kawamura, Lily 185
Kazan, Elia 29
Keaton, Diane 3, **84**, 86, 93, **95**
Kee, Robert 259; *see also Ireland: A History*
Keene State College (New Hampshire) 8
Keener, Eliot 153
Keighley, William 260
Keller, Franklin J. 64
Kellin, Mike 50
Kellogg, Dr. John 3, 9, 215, 217, 232
Kellogg, Will (W.K.) 217
Kelly, Gene 22
Kenakee, Illinois 216
Khondji, Darius 237, 246
King, Caroline Junko 186
King, Cleo 273
King, Coretta 1, 164
King, Martin Luther 177
The King's Speech (2010) 293
Kirby, Bruno 126
Kirkland, Geoffrey 254, 270
Kiss Me Deadly (1955) 142
Kiss of Death (1947) 35
"Kitchen Sink" Realism 11, 15
kogus (*Midnight Express*) 49, 53, 54, 60
Kowalski, Stanley 65
Kracauer, Siegfried 4; *see also* film theory
Kroopf, Sandy 121
Krusemark, Margaret 140, 149
Ku Klux Klan 167, 173, 175, 178
Kubrick, Stanley 93, 126
Kunz, Don 202, 203–4, 207, 210, 211, 214
Kurosawa, Akira 121

"La Bamba" (Richie Valens song: *Birdy*) 132
Lacan, Jacques 276; *Menial Causality* 276; *Objet petit a fantasy* 276, 285
"The Lady's Got Potential" (Music: *Evita*) 243
"Lament" (Music: *Evita*) 251
Land, David 233
The Last Supper (Leonardo da Vinci) 6
The Last Temptation of Christ (1988) 122, 164
Laugh Therapy (*The Road to Wellville*) 217
Layden, Dervila 204
Lean, David 4, 12, 14, 237
leitmotif 46, 61, 85, 101, 127, 135, 144, 165, 220, 222
Lennon, John 114
Leo XIII, Pope 259
Leonardo da Vinci 6

Lerner, Michael 220
Lester, Mark 17
The Life of David Gale (2003) 3, 6, 8, 30, 269–289, 290, 291, 292, 293
lighting 65, 73, 74, 78, 79–80, 85, 99, 102, 108, 110, 112, 114, 116, 117, 134, 135, 143, 146, 147, 148, 152, 153, 156, 166, 176, 220, 226, 258, 262, 264, 281, 285; *see also* low-key lighting
Limerick *see* Ireland
Lind, Traci 220
Linder, Max 221
Linney, Laura 271, 273, 275, **277**, 285
Lipman, Maureen 19
Lippe, Steve 127
"The Little Boy That Santa Claus Forgot" (Vera Lynn song: *Pink Floyd—The Wall*) 106
Little Caesar (1930) 26
"Little Stick" *see* General Ramirez
Little Tokyo (Los Angeles, CA) 188, 190
"Live Aid" **111**
Liverpool 66, 293
Loach, Ken 4, 9, 14, 19
Locked Up Abroad: The Real Midnight Express (TV series) 41
Lolita (1996) 11
London, Jack 92, 93–4, 99
London Blitz 9, 14, 18
London Times (newspaper) 15, 292
The Longest Yard (1974) 54; *see also* Prison films
Looking for Mr. Goodbar (1977) 42
"Looney Bergonzi" (*Bugsy Malone* character) 35
Los Angeles, California 84, 96, 104, 121, 185; Little Tokyo 188; 293
Los Angeles Times (newspaper) 120
Lotz, Poland 8
Louisiana *see* New Orleans; Thibodaux
Loussier, Jacques 14
low-angle shot 48, 51, 58, 60, 85, 90, 102, 125, 135, 141, 224, 225, 228, 258, 273, 277, 283, 285
low-key lighting 46, 57, 89, 100, 123
Lucas, George 11, 254
Lucifer: The Devil in the Middle Ages (article) 161; *see also* Russell, Jeffery Burton
Lumet, Sidney 40
Lynch, David 121
Lyne, Adriane 11
Lynn, Vera 106, 116; *see also* "Vera" (Music: *Pink Floyd—The Wall*)
Lytham, St. Annes (England) 19

MacGuffin 136, 288
MacLiam, Eanna 256
Madam Zora 150
Madonna **234**, 236, 239, **247**
Magazine Street (Thibodaux, Louisiana) 140
Main, Mary 245
Making Movies (1998) 292; *see also* Parker, Alan (Books)
The Making of Evita 292; *see also* Parker, Alan (Books)
Makino, Masahiro 190
Malick, Terence 42
Malle, Louis 261
Malta 42, 43
Mamur (Character in *Midnight Express* book) 48
Manchester, England 14, 19, 291
Manheim, Camryn 222
Mann, Gabriel **270**, 273
Maria Candelaria (1944) 245
Marlowe, Philip 143
Marseilles 234
Marshall, Alan 8, 14, 18, 19, 23, 65, 83, 122, 292
The Marvelettes (musical group) 208
Marx Brothers 223
Marxism 113, 192, 246
*M*A*S*H* (1970) 86
"Masking Selves, Making Subject: Japanese American Women, Identity and the Body" (article) *see* Yamamoto, Traise
Massenburg, Carol 67
Massey, Dick 205, **209**
Masterson, Ronnie **253**, 256
McAvoy, Alex **104**, 109
McBride, Lannie Spann 176
McCarthy, Melissa 280
McCarthyism 195
McCluskey, Ken **200**, 203, **209**
McCourt, Frank 3, 252, 259
McCrafy, Darius 175
McCrane, Paul 66
McDormand, Frances 173, 182
McGee, Brownie 152
McKeon, Kevin 105, 108
McLynn, Pauline 256
McNally, Richard J. 137; *see also* "Can We Facilitate Post-Traumatic Stress Disorder in Combat Veterans?" (*American Psychologist*)
Meany, Colm 204, 225
Meara, Anne 71, 72
"Media Frenzy" (Music: *The Life of David Gale*) 272
Meeker, Ralph 142
Meirelles, Fernando 25
melodrama 3
Melody (1971) 7, 9, 11, 14, 15–18, 290, 291; *see also* Parker, Alan (Early Films); *To Love Somebody* (U.S. Title)
"Melody Fair" (Bee Gees song) 16
Melvin and Howard (1980) 83
Menem, Carlos 235, 236
Menzel, Jiri 261
Mercer, Bob 103
Merlin, Joanna 74
Messerschmitt 261
Messiah *see* Handel's *Messiah*

"The Metamorphosis" (Franz Kafka story) 131, 133
Method Acting 74, 78, 122, 282
Metro-Goldwyn-Mayer (MGM) 83, **84**, 91, **95, 104**, 105, 106, **111**
Metzman, Irving 98
Michigan: Battle Creek 215, 220, 223; Battle Creek Sanitarium 217, 218; Kalamazoo 230
Mickey Mouse watch (*Pink Floyd—The Wall*) 107
Midnight Express (Billy Hayes/William Hoffer novel) 1
"Midnight Express" (meaning of title) 50
Midnight Express (1978) 1, 2, 3, 6, 8, 9, 12, 25, 29, 30, 40–62, 63, 64, 65, 77, 115, 123, 125, 126, 134, 147, 160, 165, 166, 185, 195, 213, 217, 218, 255, 271, 283, 289
"Midnight Special" (song) 50
Mikona Productions GmbH & Co.KG **270, 277**
Milestone, Lewis 126
Miller, Barry 68, **70**
Miller, Mark Jeffrey 226
Millward, Colin 17
Miracle, Irene 44
mise-en-scène 46, 58, 76, 79–80, 96, 97, 100, 123, 126, 129, 134, 202, 203, 205, 228, 255, 268, 274
Mississippi: Barnett Reservoir 163; Bovina 163; Carroll County 163; Jackson 163; Vaiden 163; Vicksburg 163
Mississippi Burning (1988) 1, 2, 6, 8, 77, 151, 157, 162–182, 183, 186, 187, 196, 202, 203, 205, 228, 271, 274, 289, 292
Mr. Ed (TV series) 287
Mitchum, Robert 25, 147
Mitra, Rhona 277
Modine, Matthew **121**, 122, **130**
Mojave Desert 155
"Money" (Pink Floyd song) 110
montage editing 43, 47, 67, 71, 102, 110, 113, 114, 119, 123, 124, 150, 153, 154, 157, 159, 160, 165, 174, 192, 196, 207, 214, 222, 225, 226, 231, 243, 245, 246, 247–8, 249, 251, 254, 256, 260, 263, 264, 267, 273, 288
Montana (prison location scouting) 216
Moody, Jim 71
Moonrise Kingdom (2012) 18
Morodor, Giorgio 42, 3, 45, 46, 47, 53, 57, 60, 61, 141
Morris, Brian 201 236
Morrison, Van 201
"Mother" (John Lennon song) 114
"Mother" (Music: *Pink Floyd—The Wall*) 111
Motion Picture Association of America (MPAA) 141
Motown 207
Mozart *see* "Eine Kleine Nachtmusik"

Mueller Airport (Austin, Texas) 270
Muellerleile, Marianne 222
Muni, Paul 26
Murphy, John 201, **209**
Murphy, Paul 23, 37
Music & Art (Harlem school) 65
"Music in *The Life of David Gale*" (Essay by Alan Parker) 271-3
musicals *see Bugsy Malone* (1976); *The Commitments* (1991); *Evita* (1996); *Fame* (1980); *Pink Floyd The Wall* (1982)
musical score: *Angel Heart* (Trevor Jones) 141, 154, 163, 166, 178; *Angela's Ashes* (John Williams) 43, 254; *Birdy* (Peter Gabriel) 122, 125-6, 127, 135, 137; *The Life of David Gale* (Alex Parker and Jake Parker) 271, 271-3, 286; *Midnight Express* (Giorgio Morodor) 42, 3, 45, 6, 47, 53, 57, 60, 61, 141
"Mustang Sally" (Music: *The Commitments*) 207, 213
"My Name Is Tallulah" (Music: *Bugsy Malone*) 35
My So-Called Life (1994, TV series) 76
Myth and the Movies (book) 61; *see also* Voytilla, Stuart

Nail, Jimmy (Character in *The Commitments*) 239
Narcisse, Jarett 139
National Lampoon's European Vacation (1985) 84
Ne Oldu (Turkish for "What happened?") 57
Ness, Elliot (*The Untouchables*) 171, 174, 179
Neville, John 223
New England Conservatory of Music (Boston, MA) 271
New Jersey (Water Cure Institution) 218
New Line Cinema 293
New Orleans, Los Angeles 139, 143, 150
New York Board of Education 65
New York City 84, 139, 140, 141, 142, 185, 255
New York City School for the Performing Arts (*Fame*, 1980) 64
New York Post 120
New York University (Tisch School of the Arts) 8
Newman, Paul 37
Nichols, Mike 126
Nicholson, Jack 71
Night and the City (1950) 37
Nihonmachi 185; *see also* Japantown (Portland, Oregon)
1984 (George Orwell novel) 60
Nisei 189
Nishino, Akemi 197
Nixon, Richard 44, 51
No Hard Feelings (1974) 14, 18, 19, 292; *see also* Parker, Alan (Early Films); *Stories of the Blitz*
"Nobody Home" (Music: *Pink Floyd—The Wall*) 115
Normandy (World War II battle) 107
North Carolina *see* Wilmington, NC
Norton, Helen 255
"Nowhere to Run" 207
nuclear family 87
Nuremberg (Bavaria) 117
Nykvist, Sven 6

O'Brien, Timothy 48
"O Come All Ye Faithful" (Christmas Carol) 226
The Odyssey (Homer) 51, 60, 91
Oedipal Complex 111, 114
oeuvre 4
Of Mice and Men (John Steinbeck novel) 27
O'Gorman, Ben, and Sam (twins in *Angela's Ashes*) **253, 255**
"Oh, Billy!" (Susan in *Midnight Express*) 59
"Oh, What a Circus" (Music: *Evita*) 238, 242, 244
O'Hara, Maureen 267
"An Old Fashioned Love Song" (Music: *Bugsy Malone*) 24
Oliver Twist (Alan Parker commercial) 14; *see also* Parker, Alan (Commercials)
Oliver Twist (Charles Dickens novel) 14
Olivier, Laurence 66
Los *Olvidados* (1950) 148
O'Malley, Maura 208
The Omen (1976) 161
"On a Rainy Day" (Brownie McGee Blues song: *Angel Heart*) 152
On the Waterfront (1954) 29, 36
"On This Night of a Thousand Stars" (Music: *Evita*) 240, 243
Once (2006) *see* Hansard, Glen
One Flew Over the Cuckoo's Nest (1975) 71, 83, 125
"One of My Turns" (Music: *Pink Floyd—The Wall*) 113
Only Angels Have Wings (1939) 69
Ono, Kent. A. 186, 192-3
opera (in *The Life of David Gale*) *see* Turandot
Operation Shingle (World War II) 106
Orange, Gerald 143
"Ordinary Fool" (Music: *Bugsy Malone*) 37
Oregon: Astoria 185; Japantown 185; Portland 185
The Original Has This Signature: W.K. Kellogg 208; *see also* Powell, Horace B.
Orion Pictures 162, **163**, 164
ornithology 131
O'Rourke, Steve 104
Orwell, George 59

Oscar winners: *Evita* (Best Song) 236, 250; *Fame* (Best Music) 2, 6, 8, 11, 12, 31, 47, 63-82, 83, 88, 92, 103, 120, 139, 204, 292; *Midnight Express* (Best Adapted Screenplay) 3, 40, 41, 42, 43, 45, 51, 52, 233; *Mississippi Burning* (Best Cinematography) 110, 112, 114, 116, 117, 163, 165, 176, 181
Oshidori, Utagassen 190
Othello (1965) 66
Our Cissy (1973) 14; *see also* Parker, Alan (Early Films)
"Out Here on My Own" (Music: *Fame*, 1980) 79
Out of the Past (1947) 25, 34, 145
Owen, Alison 293
Owens, Eamonn 261

Pacino, Al 176
Palance, Jack 13
Papathanassiou, Vangelis 42
parallel editing *see* cross-cutting editing
Paramount Pictures **23, 30**
Parker, Alan:
  Books: *Alan Parker* (Lotz, Poland) 9, 290; *Bugsy Malone* 290, 292; *Hares in the Gate* 292; *INT. ROOM.NIGHT* **119**, 292; *Making Movies* 292; *Making of Evita* 292; *Will Write and Direct for Food* 7, 9, 290, 292
  Cameos: *Angela's Ashes* 263; *The Commitments* 243; *Midnight Express* 43
  Cartoons: **5, 13, 119, 230, 291**; *Hares in the Gate* 292; *INT. ROOM.NIGHT* **119**, 292; *Will Write and Direct for Food* 7, 9, 290, 292
  Commercials: Benson & Hedges 14; Hamlet Cigars 14; Heineken 14; Hugh Hudson 42; *Oliver Twist* 14; YouTube 15
  Dirty Hands Productions: 8, **216**, 217, **234, 253, 270, 277**
  Early Films: *The Evacuees* (1975) 7, 9, 11, 14, 15, 18-20, 290, 291, 292; *Footsteps* (1973) 14; *Melody* (1971) 7, 9, 11, 14, 15-18, 290, 291; *No Hard Feelings* (1974) 14, 18, 19, 292; *Our Cissy* (1973) 14; *Stories of the Blitz* 14
  Photographs (Still Frames): **64, 84, 104, 139, 163, 184, 200, 234**
  Political Activism Films: *Come See the Paradise* (1990) 3, 6, 8, 11, 183-198, 216, 271; *Evita* (1996) 3, 6, 8, 47, 67, 69, 78, 88, 233-251, 272; *The Life of David Gale* (2003) 3, 6, 8, 30, 269-289, 290, 291, 292, 293; *Mississippi Burning* (1988) 1, 2, 6, 8, 77, 151, 157, 162-182, 183,

186, 187, 196, 202, 203, 205, 228, 271, 274, 289, 292
Unproduced Scripts: *Beautiful Love* 293–4; *Blackmarket Man* 292; *Blood Brothers* 293; *Coram Boy* 293; *Failan Project* 294; *Ice at the Bottom of the World* 293; "Scottish Screenplay" 294; *Yuri* 293
Parker, Alex 271, 271–3, 286
Parker, Jake 271, 271–3, 286
Parker, Leslie (Alan Parker's mother) 12
Parker, Monica 223
Parker, William (Alan Parker's father) 12
Partner (1968) 2
Pasolini, Paolo Pier 48, 226
Paths of Glory (1957) 126
Pearce, John 13, 14
Pearl Harbor 193, 194
Pell, Clinton 167
People Magazine 120
Perfect Food Company (PER-FO) 210, 222, 229, 232
Perfect Tonic Company (PER-TO) 232
Per-Fo Pictures **216**
Peron, Juan 243
Peron, Maria (Eva/Evita) 3, 9, 233
Peronistas 235
Perry, Penny 42
persona (psychoanalysis) 276
Pfeiffer, Michelle 234
Phantom of the Paradise (1974) 24
Philadelphia 120, 121, 127
Philadelphia Enquirer 120
Pinchel, Irving 5
Pine, Courtney 142
Pinewood Studios (London, England) 23, 24
Pink Floyd (Rock Band) 2, 73, 103, 105, 107, 110
Pink Floyd—The Wall (1979 Album) 103, 105, 106
Pink Floyd—The Wall (1982, Alan Parker) 1, 2, 3, 6, 8, 47, 50, 73, 85, 103–119, 120, 126, 212
Pinky and the Brain 27
Piro, Sal **64**
Pitt, Brad 271
Platoon (1986) 42
"Play with Fire" (Rolling Stones song) 95
Polanski, Roman 54
political activism films: *Come See the Paradise* (1990) 3, 6, 8, 11, 183–198, 216, 271; *Evita* (1996) 3, 6, 8, 47, 67, 69, 78, 88, 233–251, 272; *The Life of David Gale* (2003) 3, 6, 8, 30, 269–289, 290, 291, 292, 293; *Mississippi Burning* (1988) 1, 2, 6, 8, 77, 151, 157, 162–182, 183, 186, 187, 196, 202, 203, 205, 228, 271, 274, 289, 292
La Politique des auteurs 4
Pollock, Eileen 267
Polunski (Death Row) 274

Poor Cow (1967) 4
Porky's (1982) 74
Porter, Cole 26
Post, Charles W. 221, 232
Post-Traumatic Stress Disorder (PTSD) 123, 125, 129, 136, 137
"Post-Traumatic Stress Disorder: An Old Problem with a New Name" (article) 123; see also Boulanger, Ghislaine
Powell, Horace 218
Presley, Elvis 204, 206
Price, David 2, 9, 47, 48; see also Hacker, Jonathan
Prinze, Freddie 76–7, 82
prison films: *The Big House* (1930) 49; *Cool Hand Luke* (1967) 54; *Escape from Alcatraz* (1979) 44; *The Life of David Gale* (2003) 3, 6, 8, 30, 269–289, 290, 12, 291, 292, 293; *The Longest Yard* (1974) 54; *Midnight Express* (1978) 1, 2, 3, 6, 8, 9, 25, 29, 30, 40–62, 63, 64, 65, 77, 115, 123, 125, 126, 134, 147, 160, 165, 166, 185, 195, 213, 217, 218, 255, 271, 283, 289; *Pink Floyd—The Wall* (1982) 1, 2, 3, 6, 8, 47, 50, 73, 85, 103–119, 120, 126, 212; *The Shawshank Redemption* (1994) 49, 54, 60
prisons see Ellis; Huntsville
producers see Marshal, Alan; Puttnam, David
production designer see Kirkland, Geoffrey; Morris, Brian
Prohibition 26
Proudfoot, Epiphany 3, 140
Proudfoot, Evangeline 151
Prussia 294
Pryce, Jonathan 234, 236
Psycho (1960) 24
psychoanalysis 132
The Public Enemy (1931) 26, 30, 34
Puccini, Giacomo 287; see also *Turandot*
Puddles in the Lane 15, 290, 292; see also Parker, Alan (Books); Parker, Alan (Cartoons)
Pulitzer Prize (*Angela's Ashes*) 252; see also McCourt, Frank
Punch-Drunk Love (2002) 254
"Put the Blame on Me" 35; see also *Gilda* (1946)
Puttnam, David 8, 14, 15, 16, 17, 18, 23, 41, 294
Puttnam, Maurice 16

Quaid, Dennis **184**, 185, 186, **191**
Quaid, Randy 48

racism 1, 2, 65
Raft, George 22
Raiders of the Lost Ark (1981) 84
"Rainbow High" (Music: *Evita*) 248
"Rainbow Tour" (Music: *Evita*) 248–9

Raindrops Keep Falling on My Head" (song) 37
Rambo producer see Mario Kassar
Ramírez (General) 243
Ramis, Harold 27
Rampling, Charlotte 140, 150
Randolph Motel 286
Rashomon (1950) 121
Ray, Gene Anthony 68
Razamataz 27; see also Jackson, Michael
Reagan, Ronald 116
The Real World (MTV series) 76
Reality Bites (1994) 76
Red Branch Knights 260
Red Cross (Adana) 51
Red Desert (1964) 121
"Red Light" (Music: *Fame*) 69
Red River (1948) 4
Redding, Otis 206, 209, 210
Redford, Robert 17, 138
Reed, Carol 4, 11
religion 204, 254
religious imagery (in *Fame*, 1980) 78
Reservoir Dogs (1992) 115
revisionist genre 3, 36, 37, 145
Revue du Cinéma (film journal) 5
Rice, Tim 3, 233, 235; see also Webber, Andrew Lloyd
Rififi (1955) 35
Rifki (*Midnight Express* character) 48
Ringwald, Molly 78
Rio Bravo (1959) 172
Rippey, Leon 275
Ritchie, Lee 273
Rivera, Jose 294
The Road to Wellville (Boyle, T. Coraghessen novel) 3, 215
The Road to Wellville (1994) 3, 6, 8, 9, 69, 134, 215–232; meaning of the title 223
Robinson, Edward G. 26
Robinson, Roxy 25, 26
Robocop (1987) 84
Rocha, Glauber 237
"Rockin' Robin" (song in *Birdy*) 134
The Rocky Horror Picture Show (1975) **70**, 80
Roeg, Nicholas 9
"Roger Waters's Poetry of the Absent Father: British Identity in Pink Floyd's *The Wall*" (article) 107
Rohmer, Eric 4
Rolling Stones (band) 95, 113
Romanian Securitas Method see Securitas Method
Romeo and Juliet (Shakespeare's play) 70
Romero, Jorge Sacido see Louis Cabo
Rooker, Michael 166, 178
Roosevelt, Theodore see Execution Order 9066
Roots (1977) 42

Rosemary's Baby (1968) 161
Rosenberg, Stuart 54
Rosenthal, Jack 14, 19, 290, 292
Ross, Katharine 37
Rourke, Mickey 140-1, 142, **144**
Rudin Productions *see* Scott Rudin Productions
"Run Like Hell" (Music: *Pink Floyd—The Wall*) 117
Russell, Jeffery Burton 161
Russell, Rosiland 28, 187
Russell, Willy 293
Ryan, Robert L. 132

Saatchi, Charles 15-16
Sage, Delores 124
Sagmalicar Prison (Istanbul, Turkey: *Midnight Express*) 47, 48, **50**, 53
St. Bridget Community Center 209
Saint Francesco (Francesco di Pietro Bernardone) 267
St. George's Cross 109
St. Paul's Church 16
St. Vincent de Paul Society 264
Salford (England) 19
Salo (1975) 48, 226
"Salve Regina Mater" (Music: *Evita*) 239
Samsa, Gregor (Kafka's "The Metamorphosis") 131, 133
San Damiano 267
San Francisco 83, 84, 85, 88, 93, 96, 104, 185
San Juan earthquake 243
Sanitas Food Company 223; *see also* breakfast foods
"Santa Evita" (Music: *Evita*) 249
Santini, James 124
Sarris, Andrew 4
Sartain, Gailard 168
Sartre, Jean-Paul 6, 53, 274
Saturday Night and Sunday Morning (1960) 84
Scarface (1932) 4, 26
Scarface (1983) 248
Scarfe, Gerald 104-5, 108, 109, 118
Schlesinger, John 9
School for the Performing Arts (New York City) 64
Schumacher, Joel 171
Schwerner, Mickey 164, 166; *see also* Chaney, James; Goodman, Andrew
Scorsese, Martin 2, 6, 8, 11, 25, 115, 122, 164
Scott, Ridley 11
Scott Rudin Productions **253**
"The Scottish Screenplay" 294; *see also* Parker, Alan (Unfinished Scripts)
Screwball Comedy (genre) 99
The Sea Wolf (Jack London novel) 93
Sears White Star Liquor Cure (*The Road to Wellville*) 224
Seattle, Washington 185
Securitas Method 280, 289

Segar, Bob 101
Seki, Mariko 186
Sennett, Mack 221
Seresin, Michael 6, 8, 65, 66, 72, 73, 76, 78, 85, 104, 105, 143, 146, 148, 186, 220, 283, 285
Sergeant Pepper's Lonely Hearts Club Band (Beatles Album) 66
Se7en (1995) 146
Seventy Years of the American Prison Film (1930-1994) 54
Severina, Reverend (voodoo priestess) 153
"Sex/Knowledge/Power in the Detective Genre" (article) 150; *see also* Cooper, Stephen
"Shack 2 Cell" (Music: *The Life of David Gale*) 272
Shakespeare, William 188, 245, 263
Shame (2011) 293
Shane (1953) 4
Shanghai International Film Festival 271
Shannon River 254, 267; *see also* Ireland
The Shawshank Redemption (1994) 49, 54, 60; *see also* prison films
Shelley, Carole 221
Shepperton Studios (England) 236
Shimono, Sab 188
The Shining (1980) 93
Shivas, Mark 19
"shoot the moon" (game of Hearts) 101
Shoot the Moon (1982) 2, 8, 11, 12, 30, 83-102, 104, 120, 121-2
shot-reverse shot (*The Life of David Gale*) 146
"Show Me" (Joe Tex song) 210
Siegel, Donald 44
Sign of the Pagan (1954) 13
Signs and Meaning in the Cinema 4; *see also* Wollen, Peter
The Silence of the Lambs (1991) 162, 218, 275
Simpson, O.J. 68
Simpson, Spider *see* Spider Simpson Orchestra
"Singin' in the Rain" (song) 77
Sitkoff, Harvard 164, 174-5, 177
SkyCam (*Birdy*) 122, 135
Slanksnis, Alexander 223
Sledge, Percy 211
Smith, Gavin 173, 182
Smith, John Russell, MA 124
Smith Leroy (character in *Fame*, 1980) 23; *see also* Murphy, Paul
Smith, Paul (*Midnight Express*) 44
Snider, Stacey 269-70
"So You Want to Be a Boxer" (Music: *Bugsy Malone*) 37
Socrates 281
Sonoma Valley (California) 93
"Sophie Breams" *see* "Eleanor Rigby (Beatles song)"
Sorry! (board game) 91

"Sounds of Silence: Songs in Hollywood Films Since the 1960s" (article) 27; *see also* Berliner, Todd; Furia, Philip
Southern California 185
Spacey, Kevin 271, 273, 275, **277**, 281, 282, 285
Spain 217
Spider Simpson Orchestra 152
Spielberg, Steven 84, 254
The Squid and the Whale (2005) 271
"Stabat Mater" (Rossini) 72
Stalag 17 (1953) 4, 6, 54, 60, 126, 136
Stanier, John 65
Stanislavsky, Constantin 74
Star (publisher of *Puddles in the Lane*) 15
Star Wars (1977) 254
Statue of Liberty (in *Angela's Ashes*) 255, 263, 265, 266, 268
Steadicam 281
Steinbeck, John 27
Stevens, George 4
Stewart, James 8
Stigwood, Robert 233, 234
"Still the Same" (Bob Segar song: *Shoot the Moon*) 101
Stone, Oliver 3, 40, 41, 42, 43, 45, 51, 52, 233; *see also* Oscar Winners (*Midnight Express*)
Stone, Robinson 136
Stories of the Blitz 14, 18, 292; *see also No Hard Feelings* (1974)
"Stormont" 259; *see also* Kee, Robert (*Ireland: A History*)
Strasberg, Lee 74
Streisand, Barbra 17
Strong, Andrew 201, 203, **209**
Sturges, John 54
The Sucker's Kiss (Alan Parker novel) 290
Sula bula (Turkish: "Like this, like that") 53, 55
Summer, Donna 42
Sunset Blvd. (1950) 25
Superman (1978) 254
"Swanee River" (song) 68
"Switching" (working title for *Shoot the Moon*) 83
Sword of Damocles 25
Sybil (1976) 42

"Take Me to the River" (Music: *The Commitments*) 211; *see also* Green, Al
"Take My Hand, Precious Lord" 166; *see also* Jackson, Mahalia
Take Ten: Contemporary British Film Directors (book) 2, 9, 47; *see also* Hacker, Jonathan; Price, David
The Talk of the Town (1942) 4
Tallulah (Jodie Foster in *Bugsy Malone*) 28
Tarantino, Quentin 115
Tattersall, Gale 204, 205
Taxi Driver (1976) 6, 115

Tedeschi, Richard 137; see also "Can We Facilitate Post-Traumatic Stress Disorder in Combat Veterans" (*American Psychologist* magazine)
Teefy, Maureen 68, **70**, 74
Temple of Health (Michigan) 217
Terminal Island 185, 193
"Tex" (Bo Hopkins in *Midnight Express*) 46
Tex, Joe 210
Texas 3, 275, 287; Austin 270, 281
Theron, Charlize 293
"They Call Me Mr. Pitiful" (Music: *The Commitments*) 209
Thibodaux, Louisiana 140
"Thin Ice" (Music: *Pink Floyd—The Wall*) 108
The Thing (1982) 112
The Third Man (1949) 4, 12
"The Three Little Pigs" (fairy tale) 93
Three Stooges 26, 28, 46
Tightrope (1984) 176
Time magazine 120
"Time Warp" (Music: *Rocky Horror Picture Show*) 80
'Tis (Frank McCourt novel: Sequel to *Angela's Ashes*) 2, 68
Tisch school of the Arts (Cinema Studies Program) 8; see also O'Brien, Timothy; *Titanic* (1997)
"To Build a Fire" (Jack London short story) 93
To Have and Have Not (1944) 28
To Love Somebody (U.S title for *Melody*) 17
Tobolowsky, Stephen 173
Los Toldos 235
Tom Jones (1963) 84
Tomita, Tamlyn 186, **191**
"Tomorrow" (Music: *Bugsy Malone*) 30, 31
The Tonight Show (Johnny Carson) 287
"Too Many Fish in the Sea" (Marvelettes song) 208
Tourneur, Jacques 25
The Towering Inferno (1974) 68
tracking shot 32
Trainspotting (1996) 20
"The Trial" (Animated musical sequence: *Pink Floyd—The Wall*) 118
The Trial (Franz Kafka novel) 50, 284
Tri-Star Films **121, 130, 139, 144**
true stories: *Angela's Ashes* (1999) 3, 6, 8, 9, 11, 12, 47, 252–268, 272, 293; *Evita* (1996) 3, 6, 8, 47, 67, 69, 78, 88, 233–251, 272; *Midnight Express* (1978) 1, 2, 3, 6, 8, 9, 12, 25, 29, 30, 40–62, 63, 64, 65, 77, 115, 123, 125, 126, 134, 147, 160, 165, 166, 185, 195, 213, 217, 218, 255, 271, 283, 289; *Mississippi Burning* (1988) 1, 2, 6, 8, 77, 151, 157, 162–182, 183, 186, 187, 196, 202, 203, 205, 228, 271, 274, 289, 292; *The Road to Wellville*, (1994) 3, 6, 8, 9, 69, 134, 215–232
Truesdale, Noah 277
Truffaut, François 4, 5, 261
"Try a Little Tenderness" (Music: *The Commitments*) 213
Tufano, Brian 19, 20
Turandot (the opera as portrayed in *The Life of David Gale*) 257; see also Giacomo, Puccini
Turkey (government of) 21; see also Istanbul, Turkey
"Turkish Revenge" (*Midnight Express*) 53
Turner, Kathleen 145
TV Guide 81
20th Century-Fox 83, **184**, 186, **191, 200, 209**
two-shot editing method (*The Life of David Gale*) 284

Umberto D. (1952) 14
Under Two Flags (1935) 187
United Artists **64, 70**
United Kingdom 217
United Kingdom Film Council (U.K. Film Council) 292
United States Information Agency 51
Universal Studios **270, 277**
University of Akron 90
"Until the Real Thing Comes Along" (Sammy Cahn song: *Come See The Paradise*) 189, 194, 197, 198
The Untouchables (1987) 168, 171, 174, 1778, 179

Vajna, Andy 140
Valens, Richie 132, 134
Valentine's Day 11
Valley of the Moon (Jack London novel) 93
Variety 72
"Vera" (Music: *Pink Floyd—The Wall*) 116; see also Lynn, Vera
Verhoeven, Paul 84
Vienna University 269
Vince, Pruitt Taylor 153, 181, 187
Virgil 46
Vonnegut, Kurt, Jr. 59
von Trier, Lars 254, 259
Voodoo (as portrayed in *Angel Heart*) 139, 143, 153, 155, 156
Voytilla, Stuart 54

Waiting for Godot (Samuel Beckett play) 262
"Waiting for the Worms" (Music: *Pink Floyd—The Wall*) 118
Walker, Lou 179
The Wall see *Pink Floyd—The Wall* (Album); *Pink Floyd—The Wall* (1982, Alan Parker)
Wallace, Mickah 201
"Waltz for Eva and Ché" (Music: *Evita*) 250

Warshow, Robert 26, 33
Washington Post 120
Water Cure Institution (New Jersey: *Road to Wellville*) 218
Waters, Roger 103, 106
Watson, Emily **253**, 254, 255, 259
"The Way We Were" (song) 68
Wayne, John 172, 178
Webber, Andrew Lloyd 3, 233, 235, 237, 238; see also Rice, Tim
Weir, Peter 68
Weisser, Norbert 48
"Welcome to the Machine" (Pink Floyd song) 73
Weller, Peter 84, 92
Welles, Orson 5, 22, 247
West, Mae 29
West Side Story (1961) 32, 33
"We've Only Just begun" (Music: *Bugsy Malone*) 24
Wharton, William 120, 122, 134
What Ever Happened to Baby Jane? (1962) 208
"When a Man Loves a Woman" (song) 211; see also Gaye, Marvin; Sledge, Percy
"When the Tigers Broke Free" (Music: *Pink Floyd—The Wall*) 106
"When the Tigers Broke Free, Part II" (Music: *Pink Floyd—The Wall*) 109
"When We All Get to Heaven" (song) 176; see also McBride, Lannie Spann
Whitcraft, Elizabeth 128, 149
White Heat (1949) 69
"Whiter Shade of Pale" (Music: *The Commitments*) 208; see also Harum, Procol
Widmark, Richard 37
The Wild Bunch (1969) 38
Wilder, Billy 4, 25, 46, 54, 126, 136
Will Write and Direct for Food 7, 9, 290, 292; see also Parker, Alan (Books); Parker, Alan (Cartoons)
William Morris Agency 8
Williams, John 43, 254
Williams, Paul 24, 26, 27, 32
Williams, Vertis 164, 179
Wilmington, North Carolina (film studio for *The Road to Wellville*) 216
Winchester, Maud 131
Windmill Street 256; see also Ireland (Limerick)
Winslet, Kate **270**, 271, 273, 275
Wise, Robert 29
Wish You Were Here (Pink Floyd album) 73
"Witch of Wellesley" 149; see also Krusemark, Margaret
Witt, Susan D. 90
The Wiz (1978) 40
The Wizard of Oz (1939) 91–92
Wolcott, Larissa 282
Wolf House (Jack London home) 93

Wollen, Peter 4; *see also Signs and Meaning in the Cinema*
A Woman Under the Influence (1974) 86
Woodard, Alfre 169–70
working class films: *Angela's Ashes* (1999) 3, 6, 8, 9, 11, 12, 47, 252; *Commitments* (1991) 3, 6, 8, 9, 11, 12, 31, 88, 199–214; *Evita* (1996) 3, 6, 8, 47, 67, 69, 78, 88, 233–251, 272; *Fame* (1980) 2, 6, 8, 11, 12, 31, 47, 63–82, 83, 88, 92, 103, 120, 139, 204, 292
World War I 294

World War II 3, 14, 261
Wright, Jenny 113

xenophobia 44, 59, 123, 165, 171, 193-195

Yamamoto, Traise 186
"The Yellow Wallpaper" (Short story) 222
Yesil (*Midnight Express* character) 51, 54; *see also* Diogene, Franco
Yesilkoy International Airport 43
Yothers, Tina 84, 86

"You Give a Little Love" (Music: *Bugsy Malone*) 38
"You Must Love Me" (Musical Number) 236, 250; *see also* Oscar winners
"Young Lust" (Music: *Pink Floyd—The Wall*) 113
YouTube commercials 20–1
Yukon 94
Yuri 293; *see also* Parker, Alan (Unproduced Screenplays)

Zap soap (Music: *Evita*) 242
Zollo, Frederick 162

www.ingramcontent.com/pod-product-compliance
Lightning Source LLC
Chambersburg PA
CBHW081539300426
44116CB00015B/2686